History of
Medieaval Hindu India

History of Medieaval Hindu India

Downfall of Hindu India

By

C.V. VAIDYA

Vol. III

GYAN

Published by

GYAN

Gyan Publishing House
5, Ansari Road
Daryaganj, New Delhi-110002
Phone: 011-47034999, 9811692060
E-mail: books@gyanbooks.com

Distribution Network
gyanbooks.com
India, USA, Canada, UK, Australia, France

ISBN : 978-81-212-0006-6 (Set)
978-81-212-0050-9 (HB)
First Published, 1926

2nd Impression 2022

Printed at: Gyan Press, Delhi.

History of Medieaval Hindu India:
Downfall of Hindu India (Vol. III)
Author: C.V. VAIDYA

PREFACE

By the grace of God this third volume of the History of Mediæval Hindu India as I had projected it several years back is ready and I place it before the indulgent reader under the second name of 'The Downfall of Hindu India.' Indeed the idea of writing this history was originally suggested to me by Gibbon's Decline and Fall of the Roman Empire, as Mediæval Hindu empire in its decline and fall struck me as greatly resembling the Roman empire. It fell before the Turks* like the other and its fall closed with the taking of Kanauj on the Ganges as the latter's did with the storming of Constantinople on the Bosphorus. The Grecian capital became, moreover, the seat of the Turkish Mahomedan empire in Europe as Delhi became the seat of Turco-Afghan Mahomedan empire in India. The Greeks or Eastern Romans had declined in martial virtues and the same may be said of the Hindus generally, though the Rajputs, unlike the Greeks, even then maintained their high reputation for valour and love of independence and still maintain their semi-independence in the sands and hills of Rajputana. Prithviraj and Jaichand strike us, unlike the last Grecian emperors, as redoubtable warriors who have immortalised their names in Indian history by their tragic but heroic end on the battlefield. Yet for various reasons, the generality of the people in Hindu India had become meek and accepted dependence without a tough national resistance.

This volume thus brings down the history of India to about 1200 A. D., when the whole of Northern India practically fell before the Mahomedans. The fall of Hindu India began in the very beginning of the sub-period treated of in this volume, as Kabul and the Panjab fell before Mahmud from about 1000 to 1009 A. D. In the first book (VI) in this volume is given the history of Mahmud's invasions of India, a history which has been reconstructed, so to speak, from original authorities, Mahomedan and Hindu. The common supposition that Jaipal of Lahore was a different king from the king of the same name

---

* Although Shihabuddin was an Afghan, his army contained more Turks than Afghans; and the Rajputs always called their enemies by the name of Turukdā or the bad Turk

of Kabul has been found, on a careful consideration of the available evidence, to be mistaken and, as has been shown, the Hindu kingdom of the Shahis of Kabul extending from the Paropamisus to the Sutlej, fell before Mahmud. I have tried to explain at the end of this book why the sturdy Hindus of the Panjab fell before the Mahomedan Turks of Ghazni. Thus in the beginning of this sub-period, the Panjab was lost to Hindu India in addition to Sind, which was lost in 712 A. D.

For two centuries more, Hindu kingdoms flourished in the rest of India under Rajput kings and in these kingdoms powerful kings ruled from time to time like Bhoja of Malwa, Jayasinha of Gujarat, Govindachandra of Kanauj and Vikrama of Kalyan. Yet Northern India fell before Shihabuddin Ghori about 1200 A.D., even though there were such warrior kings as Prithviraj and Jaichand to defend the independence of Hindu kingdoms. The causes of this catastrophe, different as they are from those which led to the downfall of the Panjab, have been discussed at the end of Book VII and they will be found at least interesting and suggestive.

But most interesting will be found Book VIII in this volume in which is taken a general survey of the whole condition of India in this sub-period, which practically led to the demoralization and weakness of the Hindus as a people. It will be seen how caste became infinitely subdivided in this sub-period, how religious schism increased by the rise of new sects, how the doctrine of Ahiṁsā again became predominant and led to the adoption of vegetarianism by most people and how bigotry increased and manifested itself in the rise of Āgamas, Upasmṛitis and Upapurāṇas. This is the most interesting portion of this volume and the views which I have expressed therein may at least be carefully considered by my Hindu readers.

The history of Hindu kingdoms in this sub-period given in Book VII is based chiefly on inscriptions which have been published upto this time by the labours of able researchers, both European and Indian, to whom I am wholly indebted for being able to synthetically put the facts recorded therein into consistent coherent history. Although I have, now and then, differed from these scholars on certain points and have criticised their views, I must record here my extreme gratefulness to them and duly recognise their services to the cause of pre-Mahomedan history of India. The authorities relied on have been quoted in the body of the book, instead of being given in foot-notes as the usual pratice is, in order that the reader may have the authority before him at once and in large type. The history of some kingdoms has already been formulated by Bhandarkar, Fleet and other scholars and that part of this history is taken mainly from them. But the history of other kingdoms, notably that of the Imperial Gāhadavālas of Kanauj has been for the first time I think, put together in this volume and certain difficult problems, such as the identity of the Gāhadavālas with the Rathods, have been solved in it.

This volume closes this work, though Hindu kingdom lived on for a hundred years more in Southern India. But they were ready to fall, for causes recorded in this volume, at the slightest push, as we actually find that they toppled down at once at the onslaught of Allauddin and his general Malik Kafur about 1300 A. D. Mahārāshtra (Deogiri), Telingaṇa (Warangal) and Karnāṭaka (Dvāra-Samudra) fell successively in one expedition which Malik-Kafur led upto Cape Comorin. South India rallied once more under Vijayanagar and it fell finally in 1565 A. D. at the battle of Talikot before the combined Mahomedan kings of the Deccan. In one sense Hindu India fell finally at this date and Vijayanagar may be looked upon as the Constantinople of India, though while Constantinople still lives, Vijayanagar has been blotted out of existence. This later history of Hindu India, commencing from the downfall ol Deogiri and ending with the catastrophe which overtook Vijayanagar, requires a separate volume, no doubt, written with the view-point taken in this history ; but this is a work which I may leave to other hands.

A Political map of India of circa 1100 A. D. has been added and will be found interesting. But more interesting will be found the three sketches of the battle-field of Chhachha where finally was lost the independence of the Panjab, of Kot-Kangra and of the old Delhi of Prithviraj, which I have prepared after personally visiting these places.

An Index has been affixed as usual and a chronological table has been added.

As the first edition is out of print and there is a demand for this volume, this new impression has been issued Dussera, October 28, 1933.

January 25th 1926 C. V. VAIDYA
POONA CITY

BIBLIOGRAPHY

It would be advisable to give here the Bibliography for this volume and indeed for this whole history. It is based principally on inscriptions published in (1) Indian Antiquary, (2) Epigraphia Indica, (3) Journals of the B. B. R. A. S. and (4) Journals A. S. J. Bengal and (5) the volumes of Corp. Ins. Ind. In consulting these one is assisted by Keilhorn's lists of Northern and Southern Inscriptions published in E. I. Vols. V and VIII. These lists are arranged in chronological order in groups according to the different kingly families to which they belong, and give references to the books where they are published. (6) The District Gazetteers of the several provinces contain valuable information under 'history' and 'people'. (7) For Mahomedan accounts, Elliot Vols. I and II and translations of Al-Beruni's India, Yamini and Tabakat-i-Nasiri were consulted. (8) Harshacharita, Skanda Purāna, Hiuen Tsang's Travels and Prithvirāj Rāsā supplied useful information.

CONTENTS.

BOOK VI.

INVASIONS OF MAHAMUD.

BOOK VII.

THE THIRD SET OF HINDU KINGDOMS.

BOOK VIII.

GENERAL SURVEY.

BOOK VI.

INVASIONS OF MAHMUD

CHAPTER I.

POLITICAL GEOGRAPHY OF INDIA, (ABOUT 1030 A. D.)

from Al-Beruni.

We have a detailed and authentic account of India in the 'India' of this famous writer which is invaluable for the history of the sub-period (1000–1200) treated of in this volume. It is as important for this period as that of Hiuen Tsang was for the first sub-period (600–800). For both Al-Beruni and Hiuen Tsang are foreigners and both had studied Sanskrit, the language of the wise men of India. Both had a critical acumen worthy of a historian. And Al-Beruni is in one respect the better of the two, as he shows an unbiassed mind. Mahomedan though he was, he did not look down with contempt upon the Indians, their religion and their philosophy, their science and their art. Like Hiuen Tsang he obtained knowledge about India and its science and philosophy on the spot, studying them under Indian Pandits at Multan and Peshawar, and collected and carefully sifted information obtainable from Hindu and Moslem travellers. He was a native of Khwarism and when Mahmud of Ghazni conquered that country, he brought him to Ghazni among the prisoners of that kingdom. Beruni was a learned man already, being a mathematician especially. He had studied astronomy including astrology as it was known to the Arabs from Greek sources, and he particularly studied Hindu astronomy and astrology which were equally advanced, if not more, at that time. We will chiefly rely upon his work 'India' in taking a general survey of the condition of India in this volume. But we here begin with describing India as it was divided politically at this time, from the chapter on the geography of India in that work (chap. 18, Vol. I p. 196 and following-Sachau). Al-Beruni had probably Indian works of geography also before him, perhaps among them a work of Rājaśekhara, court poet at Kanauj, for guidance which we will notice in a note. Al-Beruni gives distances also as ascertained from travellers; but these distances, though often correct, cannot be relied upon as they are given in 'farsakhs,' a measure (which is said to be nearly four English miles) not altogether free from doubt. With these introductory remarks we proceed to give the information recorded by Al-Beruni in the chapter above noted. Al-Beruni wrote about 1030 A. D. when Mahmud was just dead.

India to the Arab writers was always divided into Sind and Hind. Sind already conquered and turned into a Mahomedan kingdom was separate from Hind. The chief part of Hind was the middle land (Madhyadeśa as the Hindus called it), the country round Kanauj, which was not only the centre of Hind, geographically but politically also. "It was the capital and city of residence of the greatest king of India." We have shown in Vol. I that the Pratihāra imperial family still ruled in Kanauj at the beginning of the eleventh century. Kanauj was the imperial capital of India from the days of Harsha and naturally became the centre of Hindu civilization, learning and art. Nearly four centuries of imperial importance had made Kanauj the centre of attraction for wealth, wisdom and valour. Naturally the geography of India is given by Al-Beruni by taking Kanauj as the centre. Rājaśekhara in his Kāvya-Mīmānsā indeed states that distances should be measured and directions given with reference to Kanauj, a remark borne out by Al-Beruni's description. Antarvedi or the land between the Ganges and the Jumna was the central land of India and the natural starting point of description with the Āchāryas or ancient writers. But Kanauj was in the middle of Antarvedi and being the capital of the central empire and the place where Rājasékhara resided, he gives the opinion:—"The territory between the Ganges and the Jumna to the east of Vinaśana and west of Prayāga is Antarvedi and with reference to it the directions should be given according to the Āchāryas. But Yāyāvara thinks that even in Antarvedi they should be given with reference to the city of Mahodaya."*

Al-Beruni begins by remarking that if you have to go to Sind you march from Sijistan, but in going to Hind you go via Kabul. In the mountains on the frontier of India "there are tribes of Hindus, or people akin to them, which are rebellious and savage races." It seems clear that they had not yet been

* गंगायमुनयोर्विनशनप्रयागयोरंतरमंतर्वेदी । तदपेक्षया दिशो विभजेतेत्याचार्याः । तत्रापि महोदयमवधीकृत्येति यायावरीयः ।

converted to Mahomedanism. Coming to Hind and its capital Kanauj he says that it was situated on the west of the Ganges But the town is now deserted (owing to Mahmud's invasion) and Bari is the present capital east of the Ganges, distant about 4 days' journey (50 miles)". This town has not yet been identified. Starting from Kanauj and going south, you come to Jajjamau and other places and lastly to the Prayāga tree at the confluence of the Ganges and the Jumna. This (Pīpala) tree of Prayāga from which devout Hindus wishing to end their lives threw themselves into the river was still famous, still doing its duty (at present we have a stem of the tree shown in the fort of Allabadad). From Prayāga, Al-Beruni takes us southwards to the sea-coast and at once mentions the Jaur (Chola) king who was then in possession of Daraur (Dravida), Kanji (Kānchi), Malaya and Kunk which is the last of Jaur's possessions in that direction. The power of the Cholas was undoubtedly supreme at the time, in the territory comprised at present in the Madras presidency and represented then by three or four countries.

Then Al-Beruni mentions cities eastwards of Bari, viz:— Ayodhyā and Benares, Pātaliputra and Mungiri (Mudgagiri or Monghyr, capital of the Pālas of Bengal who were still supreme), Janpa (Champā), Dugampur (?) and Gāngāsāgara where the Ganges falls into the ocean.

Going east via Bari (North east) you come to Bihat and Tilwat (where people are black and flat-nosed like the Turks) and to Kamrup (Assam), and in the opposite direction (West) Nepal, beyond Bhūteśvara and the highest mountain.

Going south-west from Kanauj you come to Jajāhūti, capital of which is Khajuraha and which has the two hill forts Kalanjar and Gwalior. This is a correct description of the kingdom of Bundelkhand ruled by Chandella kings. Then southwards Dahàla (southern part of Bundelkhand) capital Tiauri (Tewari or Tripur) "of which Gāngeya is king now". This is also a correct description of the Chedi kingdom of the Haihayas and it seems that their great king Gāngeya was still alive. Al-Beruni mentions only two great kings of middle India, viz. Gāngeya and Bhoja.

Again south (-west) from Kanauj "Asi, Sahanya, Jandrā, Ràjauri and Bazan the capital of Gujarat". The last town defies identification though Gujarat is recognised, from inscriptions, to be the country round modern Jaipur. It was certainly part of what is modern Marwad, and Bazan, according to our view may be Bhinmāl which was once capital of Gujarat or Kuchalo of Hiuen Tsang. For Al-Beruni states that the town was in ruins and the people had gone to another place called Jadura. "Moslems called the town Naraina" which also may be explained by the fact that there was a temple of the sun (Nārāyaṇa) at Bhinmāl. Bhinmāl and Srīmāla are one and Srimali Brahmins and Banias are still well-known sub-castes. Al-Beruni adds that Mathura was as distant from Bazan as Kanauj was from Mathura. Probably he refers here to the Sambhar kingdom of the Chauhans. Al-Beruni does not mention Ajmer which was not yet founded nor made capital by the Chauhans.

From Mathura, Al-Beruni takes us southward to Ujjain via two or three towns not recognisable. But Bhâilsân (Bhailla-svámin), or modern Bhelsa is mentioned and the important statement made that Bhaillasvámin was the name of the idol there and the town was named after the idol. Bhailla-svāmin is mentioned in inscriptions (vide Vol. II p. 127) and this statement of Al-Beruni gives us for the first time the reason of the name of the town. Then again the word Svāmin shows that it was an idol of Vishṇu and we further remember that there was a famous temple near Bhelsa of Vishṇu on whose Garudastambha an inscription of a Yavana Buddhist king, as old as the first century B. C. has been found. In Sanskrit literature the name of the town, however, is Vidiśā.

From Bazan southwards you come to Mewad the capital of which is Jattaraur (Chitod). From thence you go to Dhar the capital of Malwa. Ujjain is 7 farsakhs east of Dhar, and Bhaillasvāmin is 10 farsakhs east of Ujjain. This is a correct description of Malwa with its important towns.

From Dhar, south (–east), are given certain towns upto Mandagir on the Godavari as also Nemāvar on the Nerbudda, and south, "Marāthadeśa and Kunkan the capital of which is Thana on the sea-coast." The name Marāthadeśa had come into use by this time even with foreigners and in Konkan was the northern Śilāhāra kingdom at this time, its capital being Thana. Its fame had reached even Kashmir as we shall see later on.

From Bazan southwest was Anhilvāra with Somnath on the sea-coast and south of Anhilvāra, Lārdeśa capital Bihruj and Rihanjur on the sea-coast. From Bazan west was Multan and

Bhāti and southwest, Aror fifteen farsakhs from Bhāti, a town between two arms of the Sindh river, Bahmanwah, Al-Mansura and Loharani at the mouth of the Indus. These were towns in Sind which was under the Arabs.

Al-Beruni reverts to Kanauj and says N. N. W. of it are Shirsharaha and Pinjaur on the mountains, and opposite in the plain, the city of Thanesar, Dahamāla, capital of Jālandhar at the foot of the mountain, Ballāwar, westward Ladda, fortress Rājagiri, thence marching northward, Kashmir.

Again west (N. W.) Diyāmau, Kuti, Ānār, Meerut, Panipat, "between the two the Jumna flows," Kawital and Sunnām. Then going northwest we come to Adittahaur, Jajjanir, Mandahukur, capital of Lauhawar on the Ravi, Chandraha, the Bias and Jailam. Wahind, capital of Kandhar west of the river Indus, Purshawar, Dunpur, Kabul and Ghazni.

Al-Beruni further describes Kashmir and says that there are no horses or elephants in Kashmir; people ride in palanquins. No one is admitted to Kashmir now except Jews. Even formerly accredited persons alone were admitted. He mentions Baramula on the Jhelum which, he says, rises in the same place as the Ganges where snow never melts. The Jhelum comes into Kashmir, the capital being on both sides of it, then gets into a swamp and through it into the gorge which is guarded.

The Sindh rises in the Kulārjak mountain where you reach through Gilgit where live the Bhatta Turks. Their king is called Bhatta Shah. (This shows that these Turks were Hindus still and gilgit according to Sir Grierson still shows traces of Vedic civilization and language). Lahur and Rājagiri are south of it (Kashmir). "These are the strongest places I have seen. This is the northern boundary of India. On the western frontier live the Afgan tribes."

"The southern boundary of India is the ocean. After Munha small and great (mouths of the Indus) on the seacoast, come Cutch noted for Bawarij (pirates) and Somnath. The cities on the coast are Tawalleshar, Loharani, Kachha, Bàroi, Somnāth, Kambayat, Asawil, Bihroj, Sandan Sopara, Tana, thence to Lārān, city of which is Jimur, then to Vallabha, Kanji, Darvad and then Sarandib (Ceylon). Al-Beruni finally mentions Rameshwar on the junction of the western and eastern oceans with its ridge. He also mentions the Div islands "which appear and disappear (a phenomenon doubted by many)."

Al-Beruni states that there is no rain at Multan but near the mountains the rains last four months from Āshādha. In the mountains the rainy season extends over two and a half months from Śrāvana. Beyond the mountains there is again no rain. In Kashmir snow falls in Māgha and there are some showers in Chaitra. Al-Beruni gives Hindu months which are immoveable through the seasons and not the Mahomedan months naturally enough and he is thoroughly conversant with Hindu astronomy.

Unfortunately Al-Beruni mentions no Kingdoms nor kings. nor does he make any reference to the political events of which he has personal knowledge certainly. He does not mention any of Mahmud's expeditions. He does not tell us that Kanauj was abandoned owing to its being captured and plundered, nor does he say when he mentions Somnath that the place had recently been carried and the temple and the idol of Somnath broken by Mahmud. One would have thought that such statements could not have been avoided by any writer who is almost an eye-witness of the events. However, certain it is that he does not mention any political events. This silence may be of set purpose and therefore cannot be construted either for or against the truth of these events. We, however, think that his description affords us a complete and a good picture of the political condition of the country. There was the big Kanauj empire of the Pratihāras still in existence; east of it was the Pāla kingdom of Monghyr. Nepal and Kamarupa, Bhutan and Tirhut are also mentioned. In the south Cholas are alone mentioned and they were undoubtedly supreme in the Madras presidency at this time. The Chandella kingdom of Kalanjar and the Chedi kingdom of Tripura are mentioned, as also Chitor and Dhar, capitals of Mewad and Malva. Naharwala, Lāta and Konkan kingdoms are well alluded to. Kachha and Sind are there. Bazan is, according to our view, a town of the Chauhan kingdom of Sambhar or Marwad. North of Kanauj and north-west are mentioned Meerut and Panipat, Thaneshwar and Kabithal. Properly enough, there is no mention here of Delhi. Delhi was an insignificant place in 1030 A. D. and the Tomaras there were petty kings. Lahore on the Ravi was the capital of a kingdom or a province and Jalandhar and Rajauri were separate kingdoms. Kashmir was of course a powerful kingdom at this time and is well described. Then we have Wahind, capital of Khandhar, on the west of the Indus and finally Kabul and Ghazni. This is a correct description of the political divisions of

India obtatning at this time. We miss the country of Mahārāshtra and Karnāṭa, but they are, we think, alluded to by the words Marāthadeśa to the south of the Nerbudda and Vallabha occurring later on.

NOTE

GEOGRAPHY OF INDIA AS GIVEN BY RĀJASEKHARA.

Rājaśekhara the well-known poet-laureate and also Guru of Mahīpāla (910-940 A. D.) of the Imperial Pratihāras of Kanauj has given in his Kāvya-Mīmānsā a detailed geography of India and it is very probable that this work or the work Bhuvanakośa of the same author, to which it refers, was before Al-Beruni when he wrote his India a hundred years later. One may wonder why geography of India is introduced in a work on poetics. But the occasion is taken to give this information in warning poets not to make geographical mistakes as they offend the sense of the hearer or reader; for instance he should not describe Kānchi as situate in the east of India or even give a wrong complexion to the various peoples inhabiting this country. (It is allowable, we suppose, to make historical mistakes and to mention Krishṇa, as Kalidāsa does in Raghu VIII. in a speech of the companion of Indumatī who married at a Svayamvara Aja, ancestor of Rāma, for ordinary people are not expected to be so conversant with ancient history). Whatever the propriety, this geographical chapter in Kāvyamīmānsā is important for the history of this period, as the Skanda Purāṇa geographical chapter was important for the history of the last period (Vol. II p. 41) or the Varāha Mihira geography was important for the first period (Vol. I p. 143). Of course we must note that Indian authors are not as scrupulous as Al-Beruni, as they introduce names of countries which are not traditional though these countries may not exist in their time. With these remarks we give below the geography of India sketched by Rājaśekhara in his work Kāvya-Mimānsā chapter 17.

" He who conquers Bharata Khanda from the Himalayas to the southern sea is called a Samrāṭ while he who conquers the country from Kumārīpura to Bindusara (lake) is called Chakravartin.

There are seven mountain ranges, Malaya and others. The country between the eastern and western seas and the Himalaya and Vinddhya mountains is called Āryāvarta (this difinition extends the usual limit and includes Bengal); from here good conduct (religiously considered) proceeds.

In this the country to the east of Benares is called the eastern country. The peoples therein are Anga, Kalinga, Kośala, Tosala, Utkala, Magadha, Mudgara, Videha, Nepāla, Paundra, Prāgjyotisha, Tāmralipta, Malada, Malla, Vartaka, Sumha, Brahmottara &c. The big rivers (Nada) are Śoṇa, and Lauhitya and lesser rivers (Nadis) are Gayā, Karatoyā, Kapiṣā &c. The products are lavali, Granthaparṇika, Agura, Drāksha, Kastūri and others.

To the south of Māhishmati is the Dakshiṇāpatha (or southern path). The people are Mahārashtra, Māhishaka, Aśmaka, Vidarbha, Kuntala, Krathakaiśika, Śūrpāraka, Kāñchī, Kerala, Kāvera, Murala, Vanavāsaka, Sinhala, Choda, Dandaka, Pāndya,, Pallava, Ganga, Nāsikya, Konkaṇa, Kollagiri, Vallara &c. The rivers are Narmadā, Tapī, Payoshṇī, Godavari, Kaverī, Bhaimarathi, Vaṇā, Vanjarā, Tungabhadrā. Tāmraparṇī, Utpalāvatī, Rāvaṇa-gangā and others. Products are Chandana and pearls.

"To the west of the Devasabhā river is the western country. The people are Devasabha, Surāshtra, Dāseraka, Travaṇa Bhrigukachha,

Kachcha, Ānarta, Arbuda, Brahmaratha, and Yavana. Sarasvati, Prabhāvatī, Vārtaghnī, Mahī, Hundirā and others are the rivers. The products are Karīra, Pīlu, Guggula, Kharjūra, and Karabha (camels).

"Beyond Prithūdaka is the Uttarāpatha or the northern path, where the peoples Saka, Kekaya, Vokkara, Hūṇa, Vaṇāyuja, Kāmboja, Bāhika, Palhava, Limpāka, Kulūta, Kīra, Tangaṇa, Tushāra, Turushka, Hūrahuṇa, Hūhūka, Sahuda, Hansamārga, Ramatha, Karakantha and others live. The rivers are Gangā, Sindhu, Sarasvatī, Satadru, Chandrabhāgā, Yamunā, Airāvati, Vitastā, Vipāsā Kuhu and Devikā &c. The products are Sarala Devadāru, Rudrāksha, Kunkuma (saffron), Chamara, Ajina, Sauvira, Śrotonjana, Saindhava and horses.

"Within these four countries is the middle country". Strangely enough Rājaśekhara gives no information about this part, remarking that the peoples, the rivers and mountains and products of the middle country are well-known. Thus the most valuable information is withheld from future ages.

"The country between the Ganges and the Jumna and from Vinaśana to Prayāga is called Antarvedi. The ancient authors declare that the directions should be given in reference to this land. But I, Yāyāvarīya, opine that directions should be given measured from Mahodaya (Kanauj)."

"The complexions of the people are dark in the eastern country, black in the southern, whitish (Pāndu) in the western and white in the northern. In poetical descriptions there is not much difference between the dark and the black complexions and the fair and the white. But the speciality is that in the eastern country the complexion of Rājput women and others may be fair or white; so also in the southern."

These remarks about the complexion of the people are very interesting. They show clearly that the predominant people in the east and south were Dravidians of black complexion while those on the west and north were Aryans of fair complexion. But even in the east and the south, the higher classes, Rajputs and Brahmins, may be described as of a fair or even white complexion.

It is curious that in the north Kashmir and Kabul, the two most important Aryan peoples, are not mentioned. Almost all those mentioned being Mlechchha people of mixed Aryan and Turanian races. The Yavanas are mentioned in the west and they are the Arabs of Sind. Kabul had not yet been conquered by the Turks in the beginning of the 10th century when Rājaśekhara wrote and Kabul probably had not yet extended its sway over the Panjab. But one expects that Kashmir should be mentioned as also Trigarta and Jālandhara. All the Panjab rivers even the Kubhā are mentioned and among the products saffron and salt peculiar to Kashmir and the Panjab are mentioned.

CHAPTER II.

(A) THE SAMANIDES OF BOKHARA.

In order that one may understand correctly the power and the civilization of the Turkish kingdom of Ghazni, one must go back to the Samanide empire at Bokhara under which the kings of Ghazni rose and grew. Combining the history given by Utbi and others, a writer has given a short account of this empire in J. R. A. S. Bengal XV Part I from which we take the leading facts in the following summary. The founder was a converted Persian Zoroastrain king of Bokhara whose name was Asad (825 A. D.) His son Ahmad acquired the sovereignty of Samarcand, Bokhara and Ferghana. His son was Nasr whose son Ismail was the first great king of the Samanides and came to the throne in 903 A. D. He encouraged science and literature and raised Bokhara to eminence. The kings were called Amirs a title which was taken up by aspiring noblemen later on like Sabuktagin and from them it came to India in the form of Hammir. Historians have given each Amir from Ismail a distinctive epithet and this first illustrious king is called Amir Māzi. His son was Ahmad who is called Amir Shahid as he was killed in a religious war and his son was Nasr II who is styled Amir sa'id (August). It was in the time of this king that a brave and ambitious brazier by name Yakubi-lais collected turbulent spirits and made raids on India, first taking Herat in 301 H. (912 A. D.). India, it must be remembered, then included almost the whole of modern Afghanistan which was then divided into Zabulistan and Kabulistan or Zabul and Kabul. Kabul in the north was governed by the Brahmin dynasty founded by Lalliya or Kallar (Vol. I p. 201) and Zabul in the south was governed by Rajput or Kshatriya kings probably Bhattis. Yakub-i-lais not only took Zabul but also Kabul and it appears that the citadel of Kabul from that day remained in the possession of Mahomedans.

The Brahmin kings of Kabul regained possession of the town. But it seems that they from this time removed their capital to Wahind on the west bank of the Indus. Of this we shall speak again later on. Yakub-i-lais is said to have laid the foundations of the city of Ghazni by building a fort there. He conquered Zabulistan and drove away the Rajputs and these appear to have crossed the Indus and settled in the Panjab.

This part of modern Afghan territory is known by the name of the land of Rahbuts, which is a misreading for Rajputs in Persian, in the Mahomedan histories of that period (see Raverty's Afghanistan). Yakub-i-lais was not able to supplant the Samanide power nor to found a kingly line but appeared and disappeared like a comet.

Nasr II was succeeded by Nuh who is called Amir-i-Hamid (laudable) in 334 H. (942 A. D.). In his reign Turkish slaves began to acquire power in the kingdom. These Turkish slaves were kept as guards by the Samanide kings. Turks from beyond the frontier (Jaxartes) were entertained in the army also. They were often bought as slaves when young and being bold and courageous were often given military commands. The employment of foreigners as guards has throughout eastern history led to the destruction of the power of the employer. The Turks thus supplanted the Persians at Bokhara and founded a kingdom at Ghazni. Ghazni in its turn was supplanted by the Afghans, the Afghans by the Moguls, the Moguls by the Marathas and the Marathas at Poona by the English. A nation or a kingly dynasty which entrusts the protection of its country to an army of foreigners, however small, must naturally enough be overtaken by this fate.

It would interest the reader to recount here how a just but strict minister of Nuh met his death at the hands of disaffected noblemen. Indeed ministers under Mahomedan governments usually ended their lives in strange fashions. There were two cedar trees at the palace gate and they were forcibly bent down and tied to the two legs of this obnoxious servant of the state and then were let go, hoisting up the unfortunate man and tearing him into two pieces. The historian remarks pithily "The fame of being too just was as dangerous at Bokhara as at Athens".

Nuh was succeeded by Abdul Malik styled Amir-i-Rashid (orthodox) in 343 H. and he was followed by Mansur called Amir Sadid (steadfast) in 350 H. Powerful Turkish officers began to form independent principalities and Alptagin who was first Hajib or doorkeeper to the king Abdul Malik established such an independent principality at Ghazni. His slave was Sabuktagin who was also in the beginning Hajib or doorkeeper to the Samanide king at Bokhara.

Mansur was succeeded by Nuh II who reigned from 986 to 1008 A. D. The daring and intrepid Sabuktagin, known for his justice also, was already elected king at Ghazni by Turkish officers there, after the death of Alptagin, in place of his incapable son. The power of Sabuktagin was acknowledged by Nuh who sought his aid when Ilekkhan the Turkish ruler of Kashgar invaded Bokhara and Sabuktagin went in person to relieve his master with a large army and 300 elephants obtained from Indian kings as we shall presently relate. In the battle fought, Mahmud son of Sabuktagin was present and received his first lesson in fighting. The battle was won and Sabuktagin was awarded the title of Nasir-ud-doula or supporter of the realm and Mahmud was given the title Saif-ud-doula or sword of the realm.

But the days of the Samanide empire were numbered. Turks who were in service and Turks who were invaders brought the kingdom soon to an end. The final stages of the catastrophe are interesting. Nuh was succeeded by Mansur who was blinbed by his own officers, who raised Abdul Malik, an infant, to the throne of Bokhara. But Ilekkhan the Turk invaded Bokhara and capturing it imprisoned every Samanide claimant. One claimant Muntasir, however, escaped from custody in the dress of a female. He made gallant efforts to regain power; but being unfortunate like Dara Shikoh was opposed by the officers of even Mahmud. He had to fly from place to place till at last he took refuge in an Arab camp. The chief of the Arab camp fell upon him at night and killed him. Mahmud of Ghazni had so much respect for his once superior lord that he seized the perpetrator and put him to a cruel death.

The civilization of the Samanides and their empire was inherited by the Turkish kingdom at Ghazni. The empire was extensive and included Khorassan and Mawar-ul-nahar and other territories such as Sistan, Karman, Jurjan, Ray, and Tabaristan. The duration of its rule from Ismail was one hundred and two years and sixteen days as given by Utbi in Tarikh-i Yamini (Utbi gives the names of the kings and their periods of rule by days even), i. e. from 903 to 1005 A. D. Mahmud conquered and annexed many of their provinces especially Khorassan and Khwarism which were the centres of the civilization of this modern Persian empire. The Persian language was cultivated by the learned of these provinces which were to Persia what the provinces of Antarvedi and Kashmir in Mediaeval and Deccan in modern history, were to India and learned men from these two provinces always came to the court of the kings of

Ghazni and even to that of the Mahomedan kings at Delhi. Persian was the ordinary language of official business at Ghazni and Delhi and Arabic was used for religious and select state records. The form of administration and names of offices were naturally borrowed from Bokhara. Curiously enough this presents an aspect much like Mediaeval Hindu India where Sanskrit was the language of state documents, Prakrit the language of the learned and a mixed jargon the language of the common people. We find in Ghazni also three languages being used, Arabic for religion, Persian for literary discourse and Turki for slaves and the army. Even Mahmud speaks in Turki to his servants (see Baihaki) whenever he has something private to say.

(B) FOUNDING OF THE KINGDOM OF GHAZNI.

The Turkish kingdom at Ghazni, which later under Mahmud became so powerful as to engulf not only Khorasan and Khwarism in the west but the whole of the Panjab in the east, was first founded, as stated above, by Alptagin, a Turkish general under Mansur king of Bokhara. The history of Mahmud resembles so completely the history of Shivaji that the similarity extends back even to the history of his father and grandfather. Like Maloji, the acquirer of the original Jaghir, the centre of Bhosla power, Alptagin was the founder of the small principality of Ghazni. He was first the Hajib of Amir Abdul Malik, father of Mansur and subsequently governor of Khorasan. Having opposed the accession of Mansur, he had to leave the kingdom and he went towards India and seized Ghazni and established his rule there. His slave was Sabuktagin who filled the same position as his master at Bokhara and he gave him his daughter in marriage. Sabuktagin naturally acknowledged the sovereignty of Mansur though Ghazni was his separate acquisition in the same way as Shahaji acknowledged the suzerainty of the Bijapur Darbar though his Jaghir of Poona and Supa was his own acquisition from the Nizamshahi now no more. Sabuktagin acquired great power and influence in the court of Bokhara in consequence of his efficient army composed of Turks, Afghans and others which he maintained in the same way as Shahaji whose army was always a valuable asset of the Bijapur Darbar. And Sabuktagin fought the battles of the Samanides against their enemies as Shahaji did those of Bijapur. Extensive additional territories were assigned to

Sabuktagin as to Shahaji. Indeed they were both almost kings though nominally sardars of the suzerain power at Bokhara or Bijapur. Both laid the foundations and evolved the necessary ingredients of an independent kingdom, though they never aspired to independence in their own life and left that glory to their sons Mahmud and Shivaji.

The ordinary title of Sabuktagin was Amir and he was invested with the further title of Nasiruddoula for his services in repelling the Turkish invasion by Nuh. Utbi, the historian of Mahmud, usually calls him Nasiruddin and gives instances of his great justice and strict discipline. Seeing some poultry in the hands of a Turkish soldier, he enquired how he had got it and when told that he had purchased it he called the alleged seller, a villager, who replid " A Turk never pays ". The enraged king ordered the soldier's ears to be bored and the birds to be suspended from them and the soldier was paraded through the army, the birds flapping violently against the head of the guilty Turk. By such strict discipline Sabuktagin kept the turbulent Turks in control and advanced the prosperity of the country he ruled.

It is natural that popular belief should invest such a man and father of Mahmud with illustrious pedigree. It was believed that though a slave of Alptagin, he belonged to a Turkish family of chieftains who were descended from a daughter of Yezdgird, the last emperor of the Persians. High pedigree is also assigned to Shahaji whose descent from the Udaipur Sisodia Rajput family was believed in even in his days. The story of Sabuktagin being descended from Yezdgird is said to have been told by Mahmud himself (Tabakat-i-Nasiri). It is not necessary that great men must have illustrious lineage, but popular sentiment is not satisfied unless an illustrious origin whether real or imaginary is assigned to the great men of the nation. Whatever the truth of the story, we may note the similarity of Shahaji and Sabuktagin in this respect also.

Popular belief also assigns divine greatness to the birth of Mahmud as to the birth of Shivaji, Mahmud being as great a favourite, religiously considered, with the Mahomedans, as Shivaji is with the Hindus. It is related that Sabuktagin once while hunting seized a buck and taking it up on horseback turned homewards. Seeing the mothar of the buck following him to a great distance, he was moved with compassion for the affliction of the mother and set down the buck to the delight of the female deer. Mahomet appeared to him in a dream and applauded his act of kindness and promised him a kingdom. It is also stated that when Mahmud was born, Sabuktagin had a dream, presaging the birth of the great king, in which he saw a tremendous tree grow suddenly from the fireplace in his house. As he was telling his dream, news came of Mahmud's birth which fell on the same day as the day of the birth of the great prophet and Sabuktagin said "I name the child Mahmud". Such stories about heroes naturally arise after they have achieved their greatness. A third story relates that, on the day Mahmud was born, the idol temple at Wahind fell in the same way, as at the birth of the great prophet, the fire temple in the palace of the Persian kings was destroyed by an earthquake. This presaged the relentless war which Mahmud was to wage against the idolatry of the Hindus. Mahmud was born on the 10th of Mohurrum in 361 H. corresponding to 2nd October 971 (Tabakat-i-Nasiri and Elliot p. 69) but Firishta has given the 9th of Mohurrum 357 H. (note ditto). This makes a difference of nearly four years. Sabuktagin ruled from 977 to 997 A. D. He extended his dominions in the south by conquering Kandahar and Bust, the capital of Zabulistan and he tried to extend the same towards the east where the kingdoms of India lay. His immediate neighbour on that side was Jaipal described variously as king of Hindustan, of Kabul and of Lahore. We must, determine who this king was, as even so late as Sir Vincent Smith, different views have been entertained on this subject.

CHAPTER III.

JAIPAL KING OF HINDUSTAN.

Who was Jaipal king of Hindustan? He is evidently the king of Kabul belonging to the Brahmin dynasty founded by Lalliya and described in the previous volumes (Vol. II. p. 157 and Vol. I. p. 201). But this obvious identification has not been accepted by the now almost authoritative Early History of India which states even in the third edition (1914) as follows, "In those days a large kingdom comprising the upper valley of the Indus and most of the Panjab to the north of Sind extending westward to the mountain and eastward to the Hakra river was governed by a king named Jaipal whose capital was Bathinda (Bhatinda) situated s. s. w. of Lahore and westward from Patiala". This, though not expressly, clearly distinguishes this Jaipal from the Brahmin Jaipal king of Kabul. In the foot-note here (p. 382) Smith remarks that this summary statement has been given by him from Raverty, "differing as it does from current accounts". He gives greater details in his article on the Chandellas in I. A. XXXVII (1908) where he refers for Bathinda to a note in Raverty's translation of Tabakat-i-Nasiri and further observes in a note there that Miss Duff in her 'chronology' is wrong when she identifies this Jaipal with the Jaipal of Wahind. He further states in a note on p. 383 E. H. I. that "Elliot mixes up the dynasty of Bathinda commonly called the Shahis of Ohind with that of Kabul and so renders the whole story unintelligible". But after giving due consideration to the arguments advanced by Raverty in the aforementioned note and the whole evidence on this subject, it appears to us that Sir Vincent Smith is mistaken in setting up a distinct kingdom for this Jaipal and that the earlier view of Miss Duff and Elliot is correct. We proceed to examine this question at length.

In the first place the reason why Raverty was led to suggest this new theory appears to be that Wamand was read in Nasiri for Wahind, where the statement is made that "On the day Mahmud was born, an idol-temple in Wamand in Pershaur on the Indus fell." Raverty supposed that this temple was to the east of the Indus and he made an attempt to read the name Wamand in several ways. It may be noted that in Persian and probably even in Arabic writing, the absence of dots defeats the correct pronunciation of Indian names; as b, p, t, n as also v, and d, and h, ch and j are often not to be distinguished. And Col. Raverty finally fixed upon Bathinda as the proper pronunciation of the name and took hint for this from a Persian history of the Rajas of Jammu written by a Hindu author, wherein was found the statement that Jaipal's capital and place of residence was Bathinda. Now no reference is given to this history, nor is its date mentioned and it is possible that even here Bathinda is a misreading, or miswriting in the Persian copy, of an original Wahind. Nay, more, since the Jammu chronicler appears to be a modern writer and not a contemporary of Mahmud, he must have taken this statement from some previous Persian history and himself read Bathinda wrongly for Ohind or Wahind. It is to be wondered how Col. Raverty was misled by this Jammu chronicle and it is still more to be wondered how Sir Vincent Smith was misled by this note of Col. Raverty. We proceed to give in detail the arguments which arise against this view.

In the first place Al-Beruni, a contemporary of Mahmud and a well-informed writer, does not mention in his geography of India this capital of Jaipal. We have specially given this geographical chapter from Al-Beruni's 'India' in order that the reader may have a correct idea of the political divisions of India, existing at the time of Mahmud. Al-Beruni mentions distinctly Wahind as the capital of Kandhar which is equivalent to Gāndhāra and places it on the west of the Indus and then gives Peshawar, Kabul, and Ghazni. He mentions Mandahukur as capital of Lohawar east of the Ravi. This town has not been identified but it can not be equated with Bathinda as it is not on the Ravi and on the east of it. (Perhaps this is a wrong translation for Lohawar capital of Mandahukur). It seems probable that the Brahmin kings of Kabul were at this time masters of the whole of the Panjab. The extent of the kingdom of Jaipal as given by Smith from Mahomedan historians is of course correct. From the mountains to the west of the Indus it extended over the Panjab to the river Ghaggar or Hakra of the Mahomedans. But the kingdom of Wahind and Kabul cannot be separated from this kingdom; for these were one and the same kingdom.

Al-Idrisi again writing some years after Al-Beruni distinctly states that Atrasa on the Ganges was a frontier fortress of the Kanauj kingdom the limits of which extend *as far as Kabul and Lohawar.* He distinctly makes Kabul and Lohawar one kingdom conterminous with the kingdom of Kanauj. The state of political divisions in India in the beginning of the eleventh century clearly shows that there was no separate kingdom of the Panjab. The same thing appears from the statements of Al-Masudi who wrote about 953 A. D. that the Indus comes from the uplands of Sind, Kanauj, Kashmir, Kandhar and Tafan. Only four kingdoms are here mentioned; Kandhar being the kingdom of Gāndhāra of which Pershawar (Peshawar formerly Purushapur) was the ancient capital. Lastly even in the Tabakat-i-Nasiri the idol temple is said to be in Wamand or Wahind *in Pershaur* which plainly means "In the province of Peshawar."

Historical considerations as well as geographical point to the same conclusion. First the names of the three kings mentioned are identical and come in the same order. Jaipal was succeeded by Ānandapāla and he by Trilochanpāla both in the kingdom of Kabul and in this supposed kingdom of Bathinda. In his article in I. A. XXXVII Smith gives the name of the last king as Brāhmaṇapāla but this is again a misreading for Trilochanapāla, 't' being mistaken for 'b' and 'ch' being mistaken for 'h'. Any person conversant with Persian orthography can see how Brāhmaṇapāla may be read for an original Trilochanapāla. The name is in fact read by some as Tirojanpal. Brahmaṇapāla is not a name which can be taken to be a Hindu name and is certainly a misreading for Trilochanapāla which was long ago suggested as the proper reading even by noted European scholars. The identity of the three names and their identical order would go far in favour of the two kingdoms being one.

Further, these 'kings of Hindustan' are everywhere described as Brahmin kings and we know that the kings of Kabul were Brahmins. We find Brahmin kings at this time in Kabul only and this also shows that the two kingdoms must be the same. Again the great glory of the Shahi kings of Wahind or Udabhānda described and deplored by Kalhana in the Rājataranginī can only be explained by holding that their kingdom extended over nearly the whole of the Panjab. It could not have been confined to Kabul and Wahind only. Lastly when it is stated that Mahmud, after conquering Jaipal in the battle fought near Peshwar, went and attacked the capital of Jaipal, we are nearly certain that this capital was Wahind in the vicinity of Peshawar on the west of the Indus and could not have been Bhatinda so very distant as to require Mahmud to cross all the rivers of the Panjab and come as far as Patiala on the south of the Sutlej. It is, therefore, almost certain that the capital of Jaipal king of Hindustan was Wahind.

It would be interesting to explain how Jaipal is called king of Hindustan as also of Kabul and often of Lahore. It is clear that before the 10th century the whole country east of the Helmand was Hindustan. Even Ghazni when it was first taken by Yakub-i-lais was in India and so was Kabul (See Vol. I p. 191) and Kandahar which was in the country of Rajputs (Al-Masudi, 953 A. D.). When the Ghazni kingdom was founded, it was bounded east, south and north and even west by Hindustan and Sabuktagin conquered the adjacent parts of India gradually and included them in the kingdom of Ghazni. Jaipal was king to the east and north of Ghazni; this country was still properly called Hindustan, the people being still Hindus. The Brahmin dynasty founded by Lalliya ruled originally in Kabul. When Yakub-i-lais conquered Kabul and the citadel was taken and retained by the Mahomedans, it appears probable that the Brahmin kings removed their capital to Wahind though they still retained possession of the town of Kabul. The surrounding country was also in their possession. That they did not dislodge the Mahomedans from the citadel of Kabul seems strange; but the fact of its being in the hands of the Mahomedans seems certain from its being clearly mentioned in Mahomedan writings. Possibly the Brahmin dynasty for a time acknowledged the supremacy of the Mahomedans (See Vol. I p. 193). One Kabul Shah even offered to assist his suzerain Mahomedan king of Ghazni against the invading Turks (See ditto). Whatever the reason, a Mahomedan garrison remained in the citadel of Kabul and the Brahmin kings of Kabul must have found it convenient to shift to Wahind or Udabhānda on the west bank of the Indus.

But they retained possession of the town of Kabul and always respected it as their original capital. Writers have stated that every king of this family had to be crowned in Kabul; "otherwise the people would not acknowledge him king" (Vol. I p. 201). The Brahmin kings though they resided in Wahind went to Kabul for their coronation. Such action can well be conceived when we remember that in modern history the Peshwas residing in Poona had to go to Satara and be invested with the robe of Peshwa or minister at the hands of the titular king. The Brahmin kings of Kabul were similarly originally commanders-in-chief (or Sphalapati) of the Kshatriya kings of Kabul and people would insist on their assuming their dignity in Kabul. The above remark of the Mahomedan writers becomes easily understandable when we remember that Kabul was the original capital and Wahind the new capital of these Brahmin Shahi kings.

The kings of Kabul and Wahind appear to have extended their dominion to the Panjab some time in the 10th century and not before. We know that Lalliya the founder was conquered by a Kashmirian king and Kabul itself was held in subjection for a time by Kashmir. In the Punjab then ruled some Tekka king and Kashmir kings and even the kings of Kanauj and Multan held territories in the Panjab adjacent to their kingdoms. But in the 10th century the evidence of Al-Masudi * and Al-Idrisi show that the Kabul or Gāndhāra kings held the Panjab as far as Lahore so that their territory was conterminous with that of Kanauj. Lahore was their capital in the Panjab. Who founded this city does not appear. It was called Lohapura and popular tradition says it was founded by Lava son of Rāma, (Lahore Gazetteer); but historically speaking, as Hiuen Tsang does not mention it, we may safely hold that the city was founded or at least it came to importance in the days of these Brahmin kings who are thus described variously as kings of Hindustan, of Kabul, of Wahind and of Lahore. Lahore is written usually in early Mahomedan writings as Lohāwur, or even Lohur which in Sanskrit would be Lohapura.

Rao Bahadur Dayaram Sahani has noted in the annual report for 1917 (p. 20) three inscriptions belonging to these kings described by him properly enough as kings of Kabul and the Panjab, now lying in the Lahore museum. The first belongs to Bhīma described in the inscription as king of kings, Bhīmadeva with the mace son of Kalaka (ma) lavarman. The other two short inscriptions belong to Jayapāladeva who is described as son of Bhīmadeva. Rao Bahadur Sahani thinks that the title varman given to Kamala makes it certain that he was a Kshatriya and not a Brahmin "as Al-Beruni and those that follow him believe". But it is impossible to ignore the statement of such a critical and contemporaneous writer as Al-Beruni. There is no reason why he should wrongly describe these kings as Brahmins. The name-ending suffix whether varman, gupta or dāsa is again not conclusive as to caste as we find all these three originally applica-

---

* Translation by Aloys Sprenger Vol. I, has the following sentence 'the Hindu nation extends from the mountain of Khorasan to that of Tibet.'

ble to Kshatriyas, Vaiśyas and Śudras * respectively, taken by Brahmins. But further the dynasty of Kamala was for all practical purposes Kshatriya and it is no wonder if Kamala who was actually a king is called Kamalavarman. It may, therefore we think, still be believed that these kings were Brahmins by caste though their marriage relations were made with Kshatriya ruling families. Chandanadāsa Vaiśya, Nārayaṇadas Brahmin and Bhagwāndas Rajput are other instances.

---

* It may be mentioned that Mahīdāsa Aitareya the author of the Aitrareya Rigveda Brahmaṇa is treated in legend a son of a Brahmin from a Śudra woman but even then according to caste rules then obtaining he would be a Brahmin like Vyāsa. Sudāsa similarly of the Vedas is wrongly treated from name ending by some as a Śudra king. But Sudāsa is a Kshatriya name in both the solar and lunar genealogies. Vishṇugupta author of the Panchatantra was a Brahmin.

NOTE—MOHYAL BRAHMINS.

The Mohyals who are a subsect of the Sārasvata Brahmins and who are found all over the Panjab, the North-Western Frontier Province and even Afghanistan claim with justice and propriety that Jaipal and Ānandapāla were Mohyal Brahmins. The Mohyal Brahmins throughout Mahomedan, Sikh and British times have undoubtedly distinguished themselves as great generals and soldiers. Indeed these Brahmins hold that begging or trading is prohibited to them. They believe that they are descended from Aśvatthāmā and other Brahmin heroes of the Mahābhārata. Whatever this may be, it is probable that this Brahmin sub-caste became Kshatriya or military caste and attained to fame in the days of the Shahi Brahmin kings of Kabul. Indeed their case, is similar to the case, in later times, of the Chitpawan Brahmins. From the days of Balaji Vishwanath, first Peshwa, the Chitpawans became a military caste and in the time of the Peshwas they were employed both as military and civil officers. Under the British they are employed only in civil services naturally enough.

The Mohyals are divided into seven exogamous families; Datta, Vaid, Bāli, Chhibbar, Mohan, Bamwal and Lawa. Jaipal is said by Mohyals to be a Datta with Bhāradvāja gotra. It may be mentioned that Rambhuj Datta Chowdhari of Amritsar was a Mohyal Datta and the revenue minister to the late Amir of Afghanistan, Dewan Narayandas of Bhera now aged 90, is a Mohyal Chhibbar. It is not necessary here to mention the noted Mohyal commanders who distinguished themselves in Mahomedan, Sikh and British times.

CHAPTER IV

SABUKTAGIN AND JAIPAL.

The history of the conflicts of Turks and Hindus and especially of the invasions of India by Mahmud has been written in detail by Mahomedan historians from Al-Utbi a contemporary of Mahmud to Firishta who lived about 1500 A. D. in the Deccan and by European writers from gifted Gibbon down to Elliot, Elphinstone &c. and Lane-Poole and Smith, as also by noted German and French writers. Dr. Vincent Smith further has brought to bear upon this history his extensive knowledge of Indian epigraphic and numismatic evidence. Yet the history requires to be sifted and reconsidered from the Indian point of view and in the light of modern Indian research. It requires to be examined in the crucible of historical probabilities and tested by the fire of historical criticism. It is no doubt impossible to add many new facts but it is possible to reject some absurd stories and ideas. We shall try to do this in the succeeding chapters, as far as can be done by bringing to bear upon this. history the light derived from modern Indian research and by looking at it from the view-point of the Hindus. It may be pointed out that even contemporary historians like Utbi who are more to be relied upon than any later writers have to be subjected to the usual criticism; much more so later writers like Firishta.

Sabuktagin having established himself in the principality of Ghazni naturally tried to extend his dominon. This small principality was like a drop of oil on the surface of the expanse of Hindu waters. But the oil expanded on all sides till it spread, in the days of his son, over the whole expanse of Afghanistan and the Panjab. Sabuktagin first conquered Kandahar and Bust, capital of the Rajput country, as stated before. He also conquered and annexed Al-Rukhaj or Arachosia of the Greeks which was called "White India" by the Parthians (Vol. I. p. 191). Conquering Kasdār the capital and its king he made him a tributary using the coin and name of Sabuktagin (Utbi p. 33). Having thus secured his rear, Sabuktagin aspired to conquer east and north and naturally came into conflict with Jaipal king of Kabul and Wahind.

It is needless to enquire who was the aggressor, for the law among kings and even nations or peoples not only in ancient times but even in the twentieth century was and is the law of the brute, viz. that the strong should despoil and even destroy the weak. Utbi simply says, "Having completed the conquest of Kasdār, Sabuktagin directed his thoughts towards the conquest of the infidels". "To the desire of conquest was added the zeal of the true believer". "With sincere fervour and pure design of pleasing God he undertook the hardship of that sacred war and possessed himself of many castles and strongholds of those far lands". "By these fortified places and territories he augmented the boundaries of his kingdom". "But when Jaipal king of Hindustan marked these things and saw the line of his frontier continually diminishing and the losses caused every moment in his states, that grievance rendered him inconsolable" (Utbi. p. 34). He, therefore, attempted to muster his full force to oppose Sabuktagin. Utbi relates that a strong force composed of many allies entered into the territory of Sabuktagin who advanced from Ghazni to meet it. There was a terrible conflict lasting for many days. "Eventually Mahmud suggested to his father that in the region where the encampment of the accursed lay, the water of a spring was clean and bright, but whenever any impure thing was thrown into it, furious winds arose and a bitter cold succeeded. Nasiruddin, therefore, commanded that they should cast some wine flasks into the fountain. Immediately a grey mist spread over the land, extreme cold came and the soldiers of Jaipal could not endure their sufferings. He therefore sued for peace and on his threatening that all the Rajputs would die the death of despair on their swords, peace was granted on condition that a large sum of money was given and a number of elephahts, as also certain fortesses in the country of Jaipal were handed over to the Moslems. Thereupon Jaipal retired but eventually when in his country he refused to hand over the fortresses and imprisoned the men who had come to take possession. Sabuktagin who had marched back to Ghazni again set out with his army and plundered Jaipal's territory, massacred the inhabitants and carried away the children and cattle as booty" (Utbi. p. 39). He made the territory of Lamghan entirely stript and bare and destroying the temples built mosques in their place.

"When Jaipal witnessed the destruction of his kingdom and the consequences of his treacherous infraction of the treaty he found himself powerless to do anything. He, therefore, despatched letters to the various princes of India imploring aid". "An innumerable army assembled and advanced. The Amir, whose forces were comparatively few, ordered that successive attacks by cohorts of his horsemen should be made and in this way they forced their onward march and terrified the infidels. Then they made one simultaneous charge and made some prisoners while the rest fled throwing away their weapons and incumbrances". "The judgment of God is upon those who stray away from Him and this judgment cannot be evaded". "The Hindus did not invade again and this territory was entirely annexed to the land of Islam and the inhabitants brought beneath the wings of his prosperous care". "And whenever he needed, a thousand horsemen attended his stirrup".

Such is the account given by Utbi of the conflicts between the Amir Sabuktagin and Jaipal. They were two in number and until the end of his reign Sabuktagin does not appear to have had any further conflicts with Jaipal worth mentioning, his attention being engaged towards the west in succouring his overlord Mansur bin Nuh, the Samani king, in increasing his influence at his court and in acquiring provinces, so to speak in Jaghir. Mahmud is said to have assisted his father in both these conflicts as also in his activities in the west in the Samani empire.

Subsequent Mahomedan historians have added to this account many more details which may be neglected; but this account itself requires to be subjected to the test of probability and historical criticism. Utbi has not given the dates of these events and Utbi's dates are often faulty (Elliot II). Sabuktagin ruled from 977 to 997 A. D. and these events may be taken to have happened about 980 to 985 A. D. If the date of Mahmud's birth be taken as October 971, he would be too young to take part in these wars but if it be taken four years earlier, he would be then from 14 to 17 years of age and a young prince of this age in the east is considered fit, and is allowed, to take part in actual fighting. But he can not be taken to be able to give counsel to his father or to insist on continuing hostilities to the bitter end, as later Mahomedan historians represent. Then again, the supernatural element in the account has to be given up and we may believe that the intense cold and mist or snowfaul which came to discomfit the Hindus in the first battle was a natural phenomenon and was not caused by any supernatural agency. The story of the water of the fountain in the Hindu camp being defiled may, however, be believed in as the Rajputs of those days, at least the reigning kings, abstained from wine, as even Arab writers testify (See Vol. II p. 185). Especially Jaipal being a Brahmin must certainly have abstained from wine. The spoiling again of the water from which the enemy drinks is a measure which is often resorted to in war. It is advocated even in the Mahābhārata. It was practised in ancient western fights and was resorted to even in the last European War. Handicapped for want of pure water to drink and harassed by the intense cold of the inclement adventitious weather to which the soldiers of the plains of Northern India were not accustomed, this confederacy of Indian princes failed to achieve its object. But it was not defeated and the Rajputs were ready to sell their lives dearly if necessary. It seems probable that the negotiations for peace at this first battle must have ended in honourable terms of peace, viz: the payment of an indemnity and the present of a number of elephants. And the allies must have returned home.

This view is further supported by Indian epigraphic evidence (as already stated in Vol. II p. 127) which shows that the Chandella king Dhanga who appears to have taken part in this confederacy of Indian princes is declared to be "the equal of Hammīra". This battle was most probably a drawn one and the Indian allies returned in consequence of inclement weather. The battle may be taken to have been fought in 980 A. D. Dhanga began his reign about 950 and ruled long till about 1000 A. D. and died when he was above a hundred years old.

When Firishta and other later historians write that kings of Delhi, Ajmer, Kanauj and Kalanjar took part in this war, they certainly exaggerate and bring kings of later renown into the affair. We know and have seen that Delhi was insignificant in 980 A. D.; it is not even mentioned by Al-Beruni in his geographical chapter on India. And Ajmer had not even been founded; and the Chauhan kings of Sambhar were not so strong as to send a contingent. Bhoja of Malwa came later still, i. e. in 1010 A. D. to the throne. Al-Utbi has not given the names of the countries in India whose kings took part in this general endeavour. And Indian epigraphic evidence speaks of Dhanga only. Kanauj or the imperial Hindu kingdom of Northern India might have taken part in the confederacy. From the Chamba Gazetteer we find that its king Sāhilavarman took part in this religious war.

Utbi's account of the second battle seems to be of more doubtful credibility. In the first place the first defeat of the Hindus was only nominal and the delivery of fortresses in Jaipal's territory was a condition too exacting. Secondly, if it had been agreed upon, Jaipal was not the man treacherously to break it as soon as he was safe within his own country. The Brahmin kings of Kabul, like in fact the Rajput kings of the whole of India at this time, were men of honour. Even Al-Beruni praises this high character; Mahomedan though he was, he was a truthful observer of the Hindus and their character and he gives a very flattering description of the probity and goodness of these kings of Kabul. "In all their grandeur" he remarks (Vol. II Sachau p. 10) "they never slackened their ardent desire for doing what was good and right; they are men of noble sentiment and noble bearing." Thirdly, it is not possible that kings of different countries in India would again combine so soon after their first attempt had failed. Lastly, if the combined army was so vast as to number about one lakh of men and included several hundreds of elephants, the tactics of Sabuktagin in attacking them incessantly with bodies of 500 horsemen could not have succeeded and the Hindus could not have been so signally defeated. Sir Vincent Smith mentions here the fact that Alexander had adopted the same tactics in his battle with Porus. But Alexander's cavalry was disciplined and Sabuktagin's cavalry could not have been a disciplined force in the sense that Alexander's cavalry was. The Rajputs too were not less known for their cavalry and it is impossible to believe that in such a vast force there was no cavalry with the Hindus. The Pratihāras of Kanauj were, even according to Arab writers, known for their numerous and efficient cavalry. And the Kanauj monarch, the foremost king and emperor in Middle India contiguous to the kingdom of Jaipal, must have been one of the allies assembled to assist Jaipal and he is actually mentioned as taking part. The probability is that this account of the second battle is an exaggerated one containing a repetition of the story of the assembling of allies with a vast force. It seems that Sabuktagin must again have invaded the territory of Jaipal afters ome time on one pretext or another or on no pretext whatever for reasons stated in the beginning. And Jaipal must have opposed him with such force as he could muster from his own kingdom and he was signally defeated. He lost much of his territory upto the Indus but not the whole of Gāndhāra. He may have lost the southern part of it including Bannu, for he still appears to be ruling in Parshawar and Wahind as we shall presently see.

Sabuktagin appears to have thoroughly incorporated the conquered territory with his own kingdom, by forcible conversion of the people to Mahomedanism. Elliot thinks that both the battles may have been fought in the valley of Lamghan or Jalalabad (II. p. 436). And Lamghan south and north of Kabul river must have been lost to Jaipal. The story of the conversion of the Aspahdad of Kabul, incidently related by Al-Beruni, must have belonged to this period and not to the time of Alptagin as is supposed by some (Elliot II p. 420), as it appears that Jaipal was long called king of Kabul also.

After this affair, according to Utbi, Sabuktagin's attention was absorbed by his affairs in the Samani empire, and this was feasible as his eastern frontier up to the moutain range to the west of the Indus was now safe. Mansur died about this time and he was succeeded by his son Nuh who called upon his services in crushing certain rebellions in his provinces and Sabuktagin gladly and loyally gave this assistance and quelled the rebellions. He was rewarded with the governorship of Khorasan and Sabuktagin appointed Mahmud to that post. Mahmud was here attacked by a rebel, Abu Ali, and in the fierce battle fought with him Mahmud distinguished himself by his personal bravery. In this battle Hindu soldiers and elephants were used by Mahmud. As we shall have to explatn elsewhere, Hindu soldiers had no objection to fight for any one who paid them. But the chief thing to be pointed out here is that Mahmud could use elephants with great advantage and the cavalry of the enemy could not do any thing against them. "The war elephants seized the horsemen with their trunks and broke their backs beneath their feet until innumerable people perished on that battle-field." (Utbi p. 162).

Eventually Sabuktagin became so powerful in the Samani empire by means of his powerful and disciplined army that he could make and unmake viziers at Bokhara, the capital of the Samani kings, as Shahaji could make and unmake kings in Nizamshahi and even kept the Samani emperor Nuh in fear of himself as Shahaji was feared at Bijapur. Sabuktagin usually resided at Balk and not at Ghazni latterly and eventually died there. He intended to return to Ghazni but that was not to be. He left the Ghazni kingdom to his son Ismail by will, probably thinking that Mahmud would be satisfied with his governorship of Khorasan at the capital of which, viz. Nishapur, he resided. This was again something like what happened to Shivaji.

Shahaji left his own acquisitions at Bangalore to his other son and left Shivaji to remain content with the Poona Jaghir. Apparently Mahmud and Shivaji, though more capable, were less favourite with their fathers than their brothers. However in both cases the more capable son asserted himself and eventually became the master of the whole estate. It is needless to relate at length how Mahmud laid claim to Ghazni and the treasure amassed there and being opposed, advanced on Ghazni, fought a battle with Ismail before its walls, defeated him and eventually took him prisoner. In this battle "black masses of elephants fought on the side of Ismail but to no avail." • Elephants were useful within certain limits and Sabuktagin like other Mahomedan kings kept elephants and used them in fighting. Naturally these were at this time in the hands of Ismail whose incapacity, however, prevented him from using them with effect. By this battle Mahmud became the master of the Ghaznavide kingdom in 997 A. D.

CHAPTER V.

MAHMUD AND JAIPAL.

After coming to the throne, Mahmud's attention was for a time directed towards the west. From the Samani emperor Nuh, he requested investiture with his father's dignities and Nuh confirmed him in the government of Balkh, Herat, Bost and Sarmadh. As to the governorship of Nishapur (Khorasan) and the generalship of the army the new emperor Mansur, Nuh's son, thought they might remain with Bektuzun a loyal and capable servant of the state who had meanwhile been entrusted with them. But Mahmud would not tolerate this and moved with his army against Bektuzun; but when Mansur himself advanced against him, he was loyal enough not to attack his master and retired to a safe distance. But the Samani kingdom was now nearing its end and certain unscrupulous officers seized the young emperior Mansur and put out the eyes of that young and handsome prince. Mahmud in rage moved against these rebellious officers who fled with the new king whom they had raised to the throne in place of Mansur. Mahmud refused allegiance to this puppet and declared himself independent king of Khorasan and Ghazni. The Khalif Kadir Billa of Baghadad acknowledged him as sovereign ruler and sent him a robe of investiture and conferred upon him the title Yaminuddaulat-va-Aminulmillat (right hand of the empire and guardian of religion). Mahmud received the messenger with great honour and the title assumed by him as independent king was not Amir which he and his father used already but Sultan a title never used before him by any Mahomedan king. This title after him became general and Amir came down to signify a subordinate Sardar. Utbi records that Mahmud ruled justly and wisely in Khorasan and secured happiness to the people. As to the Samani capital Bokhara, as already stated, it was subsequently seized by Ilekkhan, the Turkish king of Kashgar who imprisoned and eventually probably put to death all the representatives of the Samani dynasty which thus came to an end in the beginning of the reign of Mahmud. This was just like what happened at Bijapur. Shivaji proclaimed himself king by his Rajyābhisheka or religious ceremony of coronation at the hands of Gāgābhatta who gave him the new title of Chhatrapati, as the Mahomedan religious head at Baghdad gave the necessary religious sanction to the assumption of independence by Mahmud and gave him the new title of Sultan. And Shivaji's overlord, the Bijapur Sultan, was soon overthrown after this by Aurangjeb, the Ilekkhan of India, who removed the last claimant of Bijapur to Delhi and annexed the remaining territory of Bijapur to the Mogul empire. The actions of destiny working through human nature which is the same every where must necessarily be usually similar.

These events happened between 997 and 1000 A. D. (the Samani kingdom ending five years later in 1005 A. D.) and Mahmud became the master of a large portion of the Samani kingdom including Khorasan. He was engaged in conquering Sistan, another province of the Samani kingdom when news reached him that Jaipal was arming himself; probably Mahmud's generals had attacked Jaipal's dominions and he was preparing for a conflict. With the suddenness of resolve and celerity of movement which distinguished this great vanquisher as also Shivaji, Mahmud moved from the west and entered the territory of Jaipal at the head of 15,000 cavalry. For such sudden movements, cavalry is best suited and we find both Mahmud and Shivaji using cavalry on such occasions. " Pershawar (Peshawar) was in the midst of the land of Hindustan " (Utbi p. 280) which means that Jaipal was still master of this part west of the Indus, with his capital at Wahind. It appears that Jaipal's preparations were not complete. He delayed the commencement of the battle in order that those men of his army who were coming up should arrive (Utbi p. 81). But the Sultān saw his opportunity and at once attacked Jaipal. The battle was bloody and by mid-day 5000 of the infidels were cut in half by the sword. And Jaipal with all his family and children and several officers was taken prisoner. "The booty in ornaments was incalculable. So many necklaces were found on the necks of the princely prisoners and of the wounded and the slain, set with rubies and pearls and diamonds, that the army of Islam obtained unlimited riches." The rage of Hindu kings and nobles for ornaments has been marked even by Arab travellers (See Vol. II, p. 187); but it is strange that Jaipal and his Sardars and even soldiers should have gone to the battle-field, bedecked as if for a marriage procession. It seems probable that they were not prepared for battle and were attacked when encamped. "Thousands of children and young people and girls were obtained from that country and all those provinces of India which were on the side of Khorasan (i. e. on the west of the Indus) submitted to the Sultan." This victory took place on the 8th of Mohorrum in the year 392 H. (1001 A. D.) and "the news of it spread to the most distant horizon." (Utbi p. 283).

Such was the memorable battle fought on the plains of Peshawar in 1001 A. D. which put an end to the dominion of the Hindus to the west of the Indus and even their future existence there. For the Sultan finished his victory by pushing on to Wahind, the capital of Jaipal and conquered and captured that place. This place could not be Bhatinda as is supposed by some as the latter would be too distant from Peshawar, being on the south of the Sutlej. Mahmud could not have traversed the whole of the Panjab with his limited force as stated already and as pointed out long ago by Elliot (II p. 438). The whole country to the west of the Indus, or on the side of Khorasan in the words of Utbi, was annexed and not only brought under Mahomedan rule but entirely "purified from filthy ungodliness" by the forcible conversion of the people. "The soldiers of India in the hills and castles of these frontiers who stirred up violence and wickedness were made the food of swords and the subject of justice." The frontier tribes gave trouble to Mahmud as they do now and he punished them severely. Their conversion and the conversion of the people to the west of the Indus generally belongs to this period. Mahmud thus not only knew how to annex provinces but also knew how to cement his annexations by forcible conversion, a subject on which we shall have to speak at length later on.

With regard to Jaipal and his family, Mahmud is said to have ordered their detention in a fortress in Khorasan. Whether Jaipal was taken to such a distant place or not, it appears that Mahmud soon released him, taking from him 50 elephants as ransom and his son as hostage and dismissed him to his kingdom which now lay to the east of the Indus. Instead of returning to it, Jaipal, feeling deeply the ignominy of his capture and imprisonment and being perhaps very old, thought himself unfit to rule and burnt himself on a pyre as many Hindus, even kings, in those days did. Utbi says that a letter was received by his son who was a hostage with Mahmud announcing this self-immolation and this son who was Ānandapāla himself, the successor of Jaipal, Mahmud set at liberty and allowed peacefully to go and rule his kingdom. The tragic end of Jaipal and his long life, unfortunate throughout its length, cannot but raise our pity and admiration for his dignified death.

Mahmud after this event consolidated his power in the west by entering into a formal alliance with Ilekkhan the Turk who had taken Bokhara by this time. Mahmud obtained the southern provinces of the Samani kingdom, Khorasan and others, while Ilekkhan retained Mawarun-nahar the province to the north of the Oxus, with Bokhara the principal city of the Samani kingdom. Mahmud appears to have strengthened this peace with Ilekkhan by marrying his daughter to his son. Thus secure in the west of his kingdom, Mahmud was free to devote his attention to Hindustan the riches and idols of which tempted his desire and offended his religious zeal. It need not be supposed, however, that India was the sole or chief subject of thought with Mahmud henceforward. For his activities and his energies required, and found scope in, watching the west as well as the east and are described with equal detail by Utbi. We will, however, properly enough confine our attention now to Mahmud's doings in reference to India. It is somtimes represented that Mahmud made a vow to make every year a religious expedition to India. This is, however, not only not correct in fact but it is also an afterthought of Mahmud's later chroniclers and Utbi mentions no such vow.

CHAPTER VI.

EXPEDITION TO BHATIA.

Later Mahomedan historians have counted these expeditions as twelve and this number has become traditional even with European historians. That they were more than twelve cannot be doubted and Elliot enumerates seventeen expeditions in a detailed note in an appendix to his second volume. It is not necessary to discuss here the question of the number of these expeditions which is more academic than important and we will describe these expeditions in detail without numbering them. The next expedition which Mahmud undertook was against Bhatia. Unfortunately the exact position of Bhatia cannot yet be fixed as historians differ most materially on this subject and as we find no arguments strong enough to decide in favour of any particular place. We will first give the description of this expedition as per Utbi (p. 322-24). "When the Sultan concluded the settlement of the affairs of Sistan, he determined on executing his design for the conquest of Bhatia. He passed over the Sihun (Indus) and the province of Multan and encamped before Bhatia. The city had walls which could be reached only by eagles and the watchman on it, if he liked, might give kisses on the lips of the planet Venus (!!!). It had a moat like the girdling sea with a deep and wide abyss. The king relying on his migthy heroes came out of the city and gave engagement. For three days the Sultan fought and on the fourth when the sun arrived in the middle of the ocean of the sky, the cry of 'God is great' rose to the heavens and she Moslems made a charge which wiped out the blackness of those infidels. Most of the enemy fled into the fortress, but the champions of religion seized upon the passage to the fort. Young men of the army filled up the moat and widened the passage. Bijairai escaped by a rope from the fortress into a fissure of the mountain and sought refuge in a wood, where he was pursued; but he drew his khanjar and killed himself with it. As for his army the greater part passed through the sword. A hundred and sixty elephants were captured. The Sultan made that place a station in order that the country might be cleansed from the odiousness of idolatry. And he drew the people under the bond of Islam, arranged the construction of mosques and appointed Imams. During his return many misfortunes befell the army, men and baggage were destroyed, many suffered from disgrace and fear; but the precious life of the Sultan was saved. Abul-Fath Bosti, Mahmud's confidante, gave him excellent counsel and refused his consent to such aims and enterprizes but the Sultan did not accept his advice."

We have given this long description from the pen of Utbi both to show his poetical manner of description and the difficulties which consequently arise. Utbi was not an eye-witness of these events and he, a secretary of Mahmud, wrote from information. It is first difficult to understand why this expedition to such a distant place was resolved upon. Utbi assigns no reason. Subsequent historians have stated that Bijairai was a subordinate of Jaipal and did not pay his quota of the tribute to be paid to Mahmud. But that was no reason for Mahmud to attack Bijairai. Moreover it does not appear that any tribute was promised to be paid by Jaipal when he was released by Mahmud. Nor was Ānandapāla allowed to depart on condition of payment of tribute. In fact Mahmud had despoiled a large portion of Jaipal's territory and that was sufficient compensation. The cause of this war was, therefore, some thing else than this and Utbi gives no clue. The Bhatia king was perhaps a powerful indepenent king to the south-west of Multan who laid claim to territory on the western side of the Indus and incited the people there. The Bhattis were originally masters of Zabulistan as we have already seen. The surmise that Jaipal, Ānandapāla and others were not Brahmins but were Bhattis is not correct according to our view. Though the name-ending changed here from deva to pāla in the Brahmin Shahi line, it does not indicate a change of dynasty for deva is as much taken by Kshatriya kings as pāla and the Shahi kings though Brahmins were practically Kshatriyas, marrying Kshatriya princesses and giving daughters to Kshatriya princes. In fine, it does not appear that Mahmud determined to march against Bhatia because the king of the place was an offending relation of Jaipal.

Whatever the reason which induced Mahmud to undertake this difficult and distant expedition, he executed it with his usual vigour and completeness. Bijairai (Vijayarāja) also appears to have fought bravely and refused to become a prisoner and killed himself before the same disgrace as befell Jaipal could overtake him. The fighting inhabitants of Bhatia probably mostly died on the battle-field and the others accepted Islam. No mention is made of persons taken into captivity, or of any plunder. This expedition, therefore, does not appear to have been undertaken for the sake of plunder or the destruction of any famous idol. The place and the people were in dangerous proximity to the territory of Ghazni on the west bank of the Indus and hence probably its complete subjugation and conversion.

Where was this place? That it was an important place there is no doubt; for Al-Beruni mentions Bhatia in his geography as a place further than Multan which was to the west of Bazan. Now Multan itself is not to the west of Bazan exactly, but a little to the north-west and Bhatia may be to the south-west of Multan and not to the north-west of it. Thus it cannot be Bahawalpur which has further no mountain near it. But it may be mentioned that the description of the fort or city of Bhatia shows that it was not in the immediate vicinity of a mountain. For a mountain fort cannot have a deep moat round it, though it may have a wall reaching the heavens. Plainly Utbi writes poetically and without personal knowledge, Mahmud is said to have passed the territory of Multan and therefore he must have come to the south-west of Multan. He is described as crossing the Indus only and not any other river; so that this town may have been to the south-west of Multan between the Indus and the Sutlej which agrees with its situation given by Al-Beruni. Firishta, when stating that Bijairai took shelter in the wood on the bank of the Indus, may be right, if we take this Bhatia as situated between the Sutlej and the Indus.

Elliot, however, is for correcting the reading and instead of Bhatia would read Bhera and place it in the north-west (?) of Multan, somewhere under the Salt Range on the left bank of the Jhelum (p. 440). He would took upon the Pālas of Wahind, Jaipāl and Ānandapāla as Bhattis and relations of Bijairai. But this guess is not correct as stated above and is also not necessary. Elliot, no doubt, rightly observes that for this expedition Mahmud came via Bannu through Kurram valley, crossed the Indus and came to Bhatia by the border of Multan without entering it. As we shall presently see, Mahmud did not like to create difficulties by entering foreign and also hostile territory viz. that of Ānandapāla or of Multan and he took the most circuitous road. But this does not fix the position of Bhatia to the north-west of Multan, for in that case Mahmud would not have had to even go along the border of Multan territory. The difficulty created by Utbi's statement that Bijairai took refuge in a mountain-wood would be removed by looking upon it as an hyperbolical description and by holding that there were only hills in the neighbourhood of Bhatia. In any case no modern town can be fixed upon as representing this Bhatia and we must leave it unidentified, simply stating that it was a town well-known in the days of Al-Beruni south-west of Multan and between the Indus and the Sutlej.

NOTE.—BHATIA.

(1) The Bahawalpur Gazetteer looks upon Bhatinda as Bhatia (p. 32) and states "In 1004 A. D. Mahmud was engaged in the reduction of Bhatinda whose governor Raja Bijai Rai had revolted against the suzerain Ānandapāla and had molested Mahmud's deputies." "In the next campaign Mahmud advanced on Multan by way of Bhatinda." Both these statements do not seem to be probable from what Utbi has stated about the march of Mahmud. (2) The Imperial Gazetteer under Bhatnair (Hanumāngarh) Bikaner States states that it is believed that that was the place Mahmud attacked in 1004 A. D. but adds that this is doubtful. (3) The Bikaner Gazetteer makes the same remark and adds that the fort was taken by Timur from a Bhati chief named Raja Dulchand and was described as an extremely strong and fortified place "renowned throughout Hindustan" (p. 397). (4) The Jaisalmer Gazetteer gives the ancient tradition of the Bhatis as follows :—" They were descended from Jadu and after the dispersion of the Yādavas from Mathurā they went beyond the Indus and a king named Gaj founded the city of Gazni. They were subsequently defeated by a Khorasan chief and they recrossed the Indus and settled in the Panjab. They regained Ghazni but in the time of Baland, they were driven out of Ghazni. Baland's son Bhati conquered many of the neighbouring chiefs. He was succeeded by his son Mangalrao, whose fortune was not equal to that of his father; and who on being attacked by the king of Ghazni abandoned his kingdom and fled across the Sutlej and found refuge in the Indian desert which has been ever since the home of his descendants." This tradition supports to some extent the existence of a town of Bhatis somewhere between the Indus and the Sutlej which was destroyed by the Turks and the Bhatis then crossed the Sutlej and entering the desert settled in Jaisalmere.

CHAPTER VII.

EXPEDITION AGAINST MULTAN.

Knowing that Mahmud was engaged in a distant war, Ilekkhan's army invaded Mahmud's territory in the west and he himself taking the aid of Kadir Khan of Chin crossed the Jihun (Oxus). Mahmud getting information returned like lightning to Ghazni and proceeded to Balkh. A terrible battle was fought with Ilekkhan who was signally defeated and he fled beyond the Oxus. In this battle, Utbi records, Mahmud's army was composed of Turks, Khiljis, Afghans and Hindus and there were five hundred elephants which Mahmud posted in the centre and Mahmud himself rode a furious elephant, attacked the personal guard of Ilekkhan of five hundred select Turks and killed many of them by his own elephant. This shows that materials which, with incapable leaders, were of little avail could be used with effect by a capable commander. The same Hindu soldiers and elephants who could not secure victory to Jaipal were used by Mahmud with conspicuous efficiency against his own Turks.

Mahmud returning to Ghazni resolved upon capturing Multan and driving away the heretic Mahomedan governor there. Multan was at this time an independent state, Mahomedan Sind being divided into two kingdoms, Multan in the north and Mansura in the south. The king of Multan was a Mahomedan but he belonged to the Karmatian sect. This sect was founded by one Abdulla bin Maimun, a Persian. He preached that the seventh Imam was the last Imam. He denied resurrection and believed in incarnation. This sect was driven out of Persia and coming to India found many adherents here. (Indeed these two doctrines were perhaps taken from Hindu philosophy). There were esoteric doctrines also such as the sacredness of the numbers 7 and 12, stages of initiation, mystical interpretations and so on which are always catching with religious simple minds, especially in India. The governor and many people in Multan were Karmatians and Mahmud who was a staunch Mahomedan properly resolved to wipe out this heresy from India. Indeed it appears that the father of the Governor of Multan had been driven out of Khorasan by Sabuktagin.

Mahmud knew the difficulties and dangers of the direct route to Multan. While returning from Bhatia, as stated before, his army was harassed, his baggage was lost and even his life was in danger, how and where the discreet Utbi does not even mention much less describe. He was a court historian; he poetically describes at length Mahmud's victories but is very succinct in describing his reverses. Possibly the people in the country of Bhatia, exasperated at the tragic fate of their king and their capital, rose against Mahmud and harassed him as he returned. More probably still, the troublesome tribesmen who inhabited the valleys and mountain gorges on the frontier of the present N. W. Frontier Province, attacked Mahmud. Whatever the exact nature of the difficulties, Mahmud this time preferred a less troublesome though circuitous route to Multan and requested permission from Ānandapāla the king of the Panjab to pass through his territory. This proves that Ānandapāla was king in the Panjab at least and was an independent king. But he refused permission as the governor of Multan was his ally. It is said that the governor had even assisted Jaipal in his great battle with Sabuktagin. Mahmud, however, would not have a refusal and resolved first to attack Ānandapāla and then Multan. Ānandapāla was defeated and pursued till he fled into Kashmir. The place where this battle was faught is described as situate in the province of Peshawar by Elliot but Peshawar was already in the possession of Mahmud. It must have been some place in the Panjab on the east of the Indus. Utbi does not give the place at all. He simply says "So the king commanded his army to plunder and destroy and burn the villages and cities." "And they cast Ānandapāla from one strait into another until they expelled him into the province of Kashmir." "When Abdul Futah saw the fate of Ānandapāla he packed up his treasures and sent them on backs of camels to Serendib (Ceylon) and fled."

Mahmud entered Multan and finding the citizens involved in heresy fined them a heavy sum. "The account of this stand for religion passed to all cities and even went to Egypt and the main source of infidelity and heresy in these parts was cut off." (Utbi p. 328–329). It appears that along with Karmatian heresy, there was also the schism about the Khilafat. While some followed the Khalifa of Baghdad as the true Khalifa, others followed the Khalifa of Egypt whose name was read in the Khutba. Mahmud was of course the champion of the Khalifas of Baghdad and had even declined to accept a robe of honour sent by the Khalifa of Egypt.

By what route Mahmud went and returned from Multan is not clearly stated by Utbi. But it seems possible that he did not go via Bhatinda as stated by some later historians; and Elliot properly holds that he must have gone by the road of Bhera *i. e.* from the north (Elliot II. p. 432). In what year this expedition was undertaken is also not clear. Some historians place it after the defeat of Ilekkhan while others place it before that event. Elliot inclines to the latter view, following Utbi. But Utbi's dates are not always consecutive and he does not give the year of this event. We have, however, given it before this expedition to Multan in order to fit in the very important account of Ānandapāla's letter given by Al-Beruni (Vol. II p. 10), already quoted in Vol. I of our history (p. 199.) "I learn the Turks have rebelled against you. If you wish, I shall come myself or send my son with a force of 500 horse, 1000 soldiers and 100 elephants. I have been conquered by you and wish that another man should not conquer you." This chivalrous offer could not have been made by Ānandapāla after he had been causelessly attacked and defeated by Mahmud when the latter proceeded through his country to attack Multan. Internationally speaking, Ānandapāla's refusal to allow Mahmud to pass through his territory to attack a friendly state like Multan or even a neutral one was proper and just, as indeed his conduct had generally been even according to Al-Beruni. But strong powers disregard such obstacles; as Germany did when Belgium refused her permission in the recent European War to pass through her territory to attack France and drew the attack of Germany on herself first. And Mahmud acted like Germany and first dealt with and punished Ānandapāla. After this plainly unfair conduct of Mahmud, Ānandapāla could not have written the above letter. He, in fact, became a stern enemy of Mahmud as Al-Beruni himself tells us; but the cause he assigns is different. "The same prince Ānandapāla cherished opposite feelings when his son was a prisoner; but this Trilochanapāla was the opposite of his father." i. e. was on friendly terms with the Mahomedans and had love and respect for them. When Trilochanapāla was made a prisoner cannot be determined. He might have fallen into Mahmud's hands even in this expedition against Multan; and subsequently released with honour which may have made him of a different frame of mind. No doubt Al-Beruni, when giving the above substance of Ānandapāla's letter, adds the remark 'that their relations were strained' when the letter was written. But this expression cannot cover an actual attack by Mahmud on Ānandapāla and his pursuit from place to place till he fled into Kashmir, and may refer to previous ordinary relations which were never friendly.

Mahmud while returning from Multan does not appear to have seized any territory of Ānandapāla though, as stated before, he had plundered and devastated it. When Mohmud retired beyond the Indus, Ānandapāla must have returned to his territory feeling his defeat bitterly and, as we shall presently relate, resolved to make a desperate effort to crush the power of the Ghaznavide ruler.

———

CHAPTER VIII.

(A) FINAL FIGHT OF THE COMBINED HINDUS.

Ānandapāla called to his aid the several kings of India and Firishta gives a very exaggerated account of this final effort of combined Hindus to crush the growing danger to their religion and independence. But Utbi does not give any such general aspect to this effort. As usual, the truth lies between the two. Marathi Bakhars, we know well, exaggerate incidents as time rolls on, each later Bakhar adding to the marvellous. Indeed this is also true of even the ancient history of India, each later edition of the Rāmāyaṇa or the Mahābhārata adding to the marvellous element in the story. Mahomedan historians are not an exception and cannot resist the natural temptation to add to the marvellous. Thus Firishta states (Elliot II p. 446):—

"In the year 399 H (1008 A. D.), Mahmud having collected his forces determined to invade Hindustan and punish Ānandapāla who had shown much insolence during the late invasion of Multan. Ānandapāla invited the aid of other Hindu kings who now considered the expulsion of the Mahomedans from India as a sacred duty. Accordingly, Rajas of Ujjain, Gwalior, Kalanjar, Kanauj, Delhi and Ajmer entered into a confederacy and collected an army greater than ever had marched against Sabuktagin. Ānandapāla himself took command and advanced against Mahmud. The two armies met on the plains of Peshawar and encamped facing each other. They remained so for 40 days, neither side showing any eagerness to come to action. The troops of the idolators daily increased. The infidel Gakkhars also joined them in great strength. The Hindu females sold their jewels and sent the proceeds from distant parts to supply their husbands with necessaries. Those who were poor contributed from their earnings by *spinning cotton and other labour*".

This is certainly an exaggerated account when we compare it with what the contemporary Utbi states about this fight. "When the Sultan arrived on the bank of the Wamand Wabal-bin-Abdbal came to confront him with a numerous army. And from morning to evening the fire of battle burnt. And it had nearly happened that the army of the Sultan was worsted and the infidels had obtained the high hand. However, the promise respecting victory to the word of Islam was fulfilled and the Sultan with his own guards made a charge under which the feet of the rebels were unable to stand (Utbi p. 340—41).

The statement of Firishta that ladies contributed to the expenses of the soldiers by selling their ornaments and by receipts from spinning and other labour is simply an exaggeration. The kings of India were rich enough to support their soldiers and contributions from merchants and from rich temples could have been taken if necessary. The coming together again of contingents from several Hindu kingdoms may be believed in, though not mentioned by Utbi, as the force gathered was evidently so large as to make the result of the fight tremble in the balance for a time. Moreover, Indian epigraphic evidence is in support of some kings coming to assist Ānandapāla. But, as before, the names of the states given by Firishta are mentioned from imagination working on the basis of later history. Ujjain does not appear to have taken part though Bhoja was then ruling Malwa and was strong enough to send a contingent. As will be stated in Paramāra history, Bhoja is said in an inscription to have fought with the Turks but is said to have conquered them. Kalanjar certainly took part in this conflict, the king being Ganda, following the example of his father Dhanga who had taken part in the previous combined effort against Sabuktagin. Kanauj of course must have sent a contingent as it was the Imperial power of Northern India. Gwalior was subordinate to Kalanjar and there was a feudatory powerful king belonging to the Kachhapaghāta (modern Kachhwaha) clan and a contingent from Gwalior might have taken part though inscriptions yet found do not mention the fact. Delhi and Ajmer were either not yet founded or were not able to take any part in the conflict. Many Panjab chiefs, however, subordinate to Ānandapāla may have joined him. Firishta does not mention Kashmir and the Rājataranginī also does not allude to any contingent being sent to assist Ānandapāla on this occasion. However, it seems undoubted that a formidable force was collected by Ānandpāla for this heroic effort to protect Hindustan from the new power at Ghazni which threatened to destroy its independence and its religion.

Firishta places this decisive battle in the plain of Peshawar, but Elliot does not think this probable. Utbi has not mentioned the site of the engagement. But as Wahind and the territory to the west of the Indus was already under Mahmud, he might have taken steps to meet the enemy in his own land, like a consummate commander. Utbi mentions the bank of the Wamand (p. 340) but what river it is cannot be determined He also does not mention whether the river was crossed and if so by whom. The Gazetteer of the Attock District places this battle in the plain of Chhachh lying in that district between Attock and Hazro, and the Rawalpindi Gazetteer reiterates the statement. Both opine that the battle was fought between Mahmud and Ānandapāla Shahi Kabul king who was also master of the Panjab. The king's name as read in Utbi is Wabal-bin-Abdbal, but this is certainly a misreading; the last name is no doubt Ānandapāla; Wabel may have been the name of one of his sons.

The manner and course of the fight described by Firishta so completely resembles the course of the fight between the Hindus and the Mahomedans in 1761 at the battle of Panipat that one might have been tempted to suggest that the description of Firishta was copied from the description of the fight between Sadashiv Bhau and Ahmadshah Abdali. But Firishta wrote more than two hundred years before the latter battle was fought. We are, therefore, simply reminded here of the maxim history repeats itself. On the plain of Chhachh, in 1008 A. D., the Hindu and Moslem armies lay in front of each other in entrenched camps for forty days, being equally balanced, each watching for an opportunity to gain advantage over the other, like two powerful wrestlers in touch with each other yet motionless for a time. The Gakkhars whose number 30,000 seems to be exaggerated, wild, bareheaded, half-civilized men who had come to the assistance of the Hindus, however, began the fight by rushing the entrenched Ghazni camp and slaying a few thousand Mahomedan soldiers in a few minutes. The two armies now became grappled in conflict and until midday the advantage was with the Hindus as even Utbi admits. The tide, however, turned, by what accident Utbi does not relate, but Firishta states " that the Sultan seeing the fury of the Gakkhars* withdrew himself from the thick of fight that he might stop the battle for that day. But it so happened that the elephant which Ānandapāla rode became unruly from the effects of naptha-balls and arrows hurled at him, turned and fled. And the Hindus

* The Gakkhars are now Mahomedans and inhabit chiefly the Rāwalpindi District Raja Jahāndād Khan a Gakkhar chief states that Firishta wrongly gives the name of Gakkhars for Khokkars who really attacked Mahmud. Khokkars are a different wild tribe which is also Mahomedan now.

believing that this was a signal for flight on the part of their general all gave way and fled. Abdulla Tai pursued them and 8000 Hindus were cut to pieces." This account is not given by Utbi but he states another fact which is more important viz. that the Sultan with his own guards made a charge "under which the feet of the infidels could not stand." All this was exactly like what happened in the battle of Panipat between the Marathas and the Afghans. Till noon the tide was in favour of the Marathas, under the execution of the guns of the battalions of Ibrahimkhan and the charge of the Huzurat horse. Suddenly a ball struck Vishvasrao dead on his elephant and the news spreading that the general was dead, the army gave way. At this advantageous moment, Ahmadshah Abdali like Mahmud made a furious attack with a force of Afghans which he had kept in reserve and the Maratha army broke and fled. Probably Ānandapāla like the brave but unfortunate Bhaoosaheb rushed into the thick of the fight on foot and embraced death on the battle-field. For we do not know what became of both after the battle nor do we hear that they were found dead or alive. Such was the momentous battle fought in 1008 A. D. between the Hindus and the Mahomedans, a precursor of the struggle seven and a half centuries later. The Hindus after this battle no doubt continued in strength in Panjab for a time as after Panipat, but the blow was severe. Indeed both battles put an end to the dream of the Hindus to drive the Mahomedans out of India.

We must pause here a little before proceeding with our narrative and consider the causes of the defeat of the Hindus As at Panipat, so at Chhachh they were not handicapped for want of sufficient numbers. If at all, they had the advantage of number on their side. They were again not less brave than the Moslems. Here as at Panipat the Hindus fought bravely and even desperately. Thirdly there was no superiority of arms on the side of the Mahomedans in either battle. At Panipat both had artillery and if at all the artillery on the side of the Hindus was more efficient. In the battle near Hazro neither side had any fire arms. They were not known then. Both used the same weapons viz. swords and lances. And Hindu swords and lances were as sharp and strong, if not sharper and stronger, as those of the Mahomedans. For one thing it may be said fate favoured the Mahomedans at Hazro as at Panipat. Those who deny fate as one of the factors leading to success properly maintain that fate is the cause overspreading every event in this human world. But when fate is said to be favourable or unfavourable, the word is usually used in the sense that certain accidents which are outside the control of man occur to help the winning side and to discomfit the losing one. In the previous fight of the Hindus beyond the Indus with Sabuktagin, we saw that a sudden snow-storm arose to harass the Hindus who being residents of the plains of India were unaccustomed to such cold weather. At this battle the elephant of Ānandapāla under arrows and naptha-balls became unruly and turned and fled. But we must remember that war elephants were always trained to encounter such missiles. Arrows and naptha-balls were not new or strange weapons, for the first time used in this battle. This accident was exactly like the accident which happened at Panipat by which Vishvasrao was killed. At this distance of time we, not at all conversant with the modes of elephant fighting, are tempted to observe that it is indeed strange that in such fights commanders, especially when kings in person assume the command, should ride elephants and become easy targets for naptha-balls, arrows and especially gun bullets. But when we find that Mahmud himself rode an elephant when he fought with Ilekkhan near Balkh, we cannot suppose that Ānandapāla committed a blunder in riding an elephant, though we may hold that Vishvasrao's riding an elephant and exposing himself to bullets was a serious blunder at Panipat. There were no guns in the days of Ānandapāla and the only missiles that could be thrown against him were arrows and naptha-balls against which his armour and that of the elephant were a sufficient protection.

But the historian cannot but observe that Hindus have always failed to exhibit that grip, that resourcefulness which brave and strong men are expected to exhibit when an adverse accident befalls them. We have already noted this defect in Vol. II (p. 246) and have tried to explain the strange behaviour of Indian armies which, often unbeaten, fly when an accident happens to the commanding king, by the fact that Indian soldiers in consequence of the absence of all feeling of nationality have no sense of patriotic self-interest in the success of the fighting. All the same, we may note this defect in Indian character (Hindu and perhaps even Mahomedan) viz. that Indians do not possess that doggedness of fight under adverse circumstances which distinguishes the western and notably the British soldier. There is no doubt that Mahmud possessed this quality so necessary in a commander. Like Shivaji he never was despondent when fortune seemed unfavourable and fought on stubbornly. Moreover, Mahmud clearly was a great general. Like Ahmadshah Abdali he had a reserve force of resolute and brave body-guards which the Ghaznavide kings and Mahmud particularly, maintained at a high level of efficiency and at great cost. Mahmud himself with this guard led the final attack at the proper moment like Ahmadshah Abdali and gained eventual success in this memorable battle which practically sealed the fate of the Panjab, if not of the whole of India.

NOTE:—THE SITE OF THE CONFEDERATE BATTLE.

As stated above, Firishta places this battle near Peshawar and some native writers even state that it was fought between Peshawar and Jamrud where is a plain extensive enough for a fight between armies numbering at least a lakh on either side. The Attock and Rawalpindi Gazetteers, however, place it in the plain of Chhachh on the east side of the Indus near Hazro. Indeed the geography primer for Attck District now taught in Vernacular schools therein states distinctly that the battle was fought near Hazro. We personally saw this plain and the town of Hazro and we think that this surmise of the Gazetteers may be accepted. On what authority this statement is based cannot be ascertained. Utbi mentions a river Wamand at which the Sultan arrived. As there is no river of this name in Peshawar district, we may read here river (Indus) *near* Wahind. The similarity between this battle and the battle of Panipat in 1761 A. D. which has been already noticed suggests that Mahmud crossed the river Indus himself as Abdali did the Jumna lower down while Bhausaheb was thinking of crossing the Jumna higher up and meeting Abdali in Antarbed. Probably Ānandpāla advanced from the south as far as Hazro and wished to cross the Indus himself at Wahind. The sketch map, given here, of the position will explain the movements of

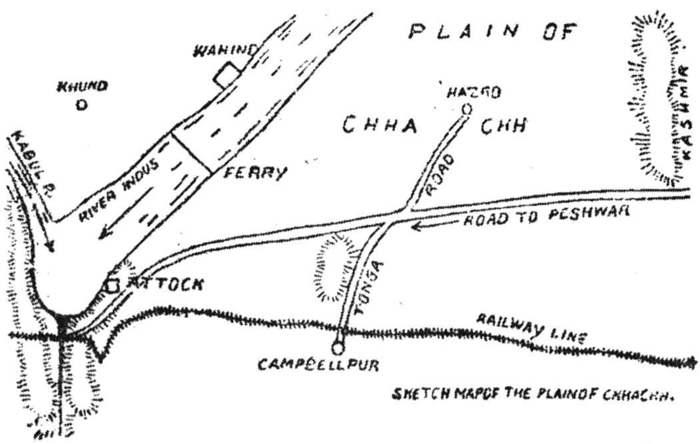

SKETCH MAP OF THE PLAIN OF CHHACHH.

the armies. Mahmud entrenched himself seeing the superior force or position of the enemy. Why Ānandapāla did not oppose Mahmud's crossing the river may be explained on the supposition that Ānandapāla did not think that Mahmud would cross the Indus; or that he wished to fight with him on the east of the Indus; or that he did not get information in time. As Chacha is known to have opposed Kasim when the latter crossed the Indus in Sind, we have no mention of Ānandapāla opposing Mahmud when he crossed the Indus. Perhaps Mahmud was already to the east of the Indus when Ānandapāla advanced against and met him. In this case Hazro must have been in the possession of Mahmud. The plain to the south of Hazro is wide enough for such a big battle and there is plenty of water to be found at a depth of 10 to 15 ft. in this plain and there are no

holes or drops in the ground so that the plain is like the plain of Panipat suitable for movements of cavalry. Even now it seems that the plain is used for military manœuvres by the British army.

The plain is flanked by the hills of Kashmir and Ānanadapāla is said by some writers to have fled into Kashmir after his defeat. The Gakkhars inhabit these valleys and we can see easily how Gakkhars in great number joined Ānandapāla's army in this fight. The shock of the defeat must have been felt throughout the Panjab, as the shock of the defeat at Panipat was felt so far south as the Nerbudda and it was thus easy for Mahmud to march on to Kot Kangra and plunder that place.

It may be added that if we suppose that the battle was fought near Peshawar in Mahmud's territory as it then was, with the Indus before the fugitives, it would have been difficult for Ānandapāla or much of his force to pass beyond the Indus. It is recorded by Utbi and others that only a small number of persons (8000) was slain in the pursuit. The number would have been far greater had the Indus confronted the fugitives.

(B) THE RAID ON NAGARKOT.

Having routed the Hindu confederate army and put it to flight, Mahmud took advantage of this favourable moment to make a sudden raid on Nagarkot which was famed then for its great idol as well as for its immense riches. This was the first expedition undertaken by Mahmud with the set purpose of obtaining immense plunder. Whether Mahmud can be blamed for attacking Hindu temples and cities for mere plunder we will discuss later on. Here it will suffice to remark that like Shivaji, Mahmud must have maintained an efficient intelligence department and obtained accurate information as to where plunder might be obtained, through emissaries who travelled openly or in cognito in the Hindu kingdoms of Northern India. Nagarkot was a stronghold in the kingdom of Kangra. There was a famous idol there of what Hindu deity is not stated anywhere; for the Jvālāmukhī temple which is sometimes confounded with this temple was different; (Jvālāmukhī is fifteen miles distant from Nagarkot and there some jets of gas issue from the top of a hill which priests ignite when worshippers come.) People from distant parts came to worship the Nagarkot idol as well as Jvālāmukhī and made rich presents. There being a strong fort there, the Kings of India, as Mahomedan historians relate, kept their treasures there. Nagarkot is the modern name but the ancient name was Bhīmagar; the town was said to be founded by Bhīma supposed to be the Mahābhārata hero, but probably by Bhīmadeva of the Brahmin Shahi dynasty of Kabul. Utbi gives the name "Fort of Bahim" which would be read easily for Bhim. The account which he gives of this raid is as follows: "And *then* he (Mahmud) arrived at the base of the fort of Bahim Bagra (Bhimnagar). This is a castle in the midst of water high as a mountain.........And the people of India made it a treasury for their great idols, and load upon load of precious goods and jewels had been transported there, for the purpose of obtaining salvation..........The Sultan closely surrounded this fortress and they began to fight in defence of the castle with resolute fierceness;......(eventually)........they capitulated and consented to serve under the banners of the Sultan ....The Sultan found such an amount of jewels and precious stones and rare treasures that fingers could not count and account-books were not equal to catalogue them. The gold and silver was given into the charge of his two chamberlains Altontash and Istargin, while he himself took charge of the jewels and transported the whole on the backs of men and camels. And as far as could be computed, the treasure consisted of 1070 packets of royal dirhams and 700800 mans of gold and silver. And as for robes of silk and cloth, they were so many that the clerks of the state could not arrange them and acknowledged that they had never beheld such beauty of workmanship and delicate excellence. And they found a large house of silver, sixty cubits long and fifty wide, with broad flooring so arranged and so contrived with ropes that the whole could be thrown together or could be separated into divisions, that it could be folded or expanded; with curtains of Grecian brocade and two golden statues and two silver statues. The Sultan then left trustworthy officers to protect the fortress and returned to Ghazni, where he exhibited the jewels, pearls, jacinths, emeralds and other precious stones on a carpet in a serai and chiefs of countries and deputies of provinces and envoys of the king of Turks put the finger of astonishment into their mouths." We have given this description of the spoils as a specimen in order that the reader may realize the enormous quantity of plunder which Mahmud obtained in his raids and in order that such descriptions may not be repeated. It may also be pointed out that Mahmud like Shivaji kept a detailed account of all the treasures he obtained by plunder and that the same was duly appraised and certain rules must have been observed by which the share of the state was reserved and the rest distributed among the soldiers. We know that Arab expeditions in the beginning of the spread of the new religion were conducted under strict rules of divison of plunder between the state or Khalifa and the commander with the soldiers. In short as under Shivaji the plundering was systematic as also the division of the spoil.

"The impassable waters which surrounded Nagarkot" were according to Elliot, "the Bānagangā and the Biyāhī rivers. The town of Bhīma was on the spot now called Bhawani (goddess) about a mile from the fort" (Elliot Vol. II p. 445). This raid of Nagarkot must have immediately followed the defeat of the confederate Hindu forces near Hazro as Utbi clearly seems to convey by the introductory words '*And then*'; but some historians place it in the following year viz. 1009 A. D.

NOTE—KANGṚA, ITS FORT AND TEMPLES.

Kangṛa is a most fertile plateau in the Himalayas with a snow-clad range at its back and with perennial streams running through it into three or four khuds or rivers. It must have come under Aryan civilization in most ancient times and we have seen that lunar race Rajput kings now called Katoch ruled there from the days of the Mahābhārata. The fort of Kangṛa which had usually been their strong place for retirement is also an ancient fort and was indeed impregnable in those days when cannon was not known. The fort stands on an eminence at the confluence of two deep khuds or rivers named the Bāṇagangā and the Manūnī, only a narrow strip of land dividing the two deep basins. The steep sides of the fort along the rivers are almost perpendicular rising about 300 feet. In the neck of the narrow strip between the rivers a deep moat has been dug and the entrance to the fort is beyond this artificial chasm. The fort can easily be defended on this narrow neck by a small garrison. There was a famous temple in this fort according to Mahomedan historians which was destroyed by Mahmud. What temple it was we will now try to determine from local information as well as from the Arch. S. R. for 1905 wherein we find much information about Kangṛa temples which existed before the earthquake of 1905.

The history of the fort is thus given in this report (P. 11): "The fort was taken by the irresistible Mahmud in 1009. In 1337 it was again taken by Muhammad Tughlaq and also in 1351 by his successor Firozshah. It permanently fell into the hands of the Mahomedans when conquered by Jahangir in 1621. When Mogul power declined it was taken back by Raja Samsārchand II in 1786 (or by his father Ghamandchand according to Col. Janakchand member of Council, Jammu and Kashmir, and himself a Katoch). It was handed over, however, to Ranjitsing in 1809. The Sikhs handed it over to the British in 1846 and it was garrisoned by British troops till 1900." At present of course it is in ruins.

"The most important monuments in the fort were the temples of Lakshmī-Nārāyana and Śītalā; both of them have fallen in the last catastrophe. 'We may safely assume that they were posterior to the sack of the fort by Mahmud."

"The temple of Ambikā still used for worship is a plain structure and has not been damaged by the earthquake. The features of the construction of the temple indicate that it happened during the Mahomedan occupation."

"To the south of the Ambikā temple there are two Jain statues, one a pedestal and the other a seated statue of Adinātha with a partly obliterated inscription dated according to Cunningham St. 1523 i. e. 1466 A. D. in the reign of Samsārchand I" (p. 15.)

"Plate III shows the temple of Indresvara in Kangṛa town. It is ascribed to Rājā Indrachandra and is a Siva temple. If he is identified with Indrachandra mentioned by Kalhaṇa as a contemporary of Anantadeva (A. D. 1028-63) it shows that this temple dates from the 11th century. There are two Jain images on both sides of the temple on one of which is the date 30 of Lokakāla. It was supposed to be contemporaneous with the praśasti on the Baijanāth temple and hence as old as 854 A. D. But as the date of the Baijanāth inscription has been recently read as 1204 St. the image may be 1154 A. D. old. The four pillared pavilion has been levelled to the ground in the earthquake, but the rest of the building is safe with the two Jain images" (p. 16).

"But the most celebrated sanctuary of Kangṛa District was the temple of Vajreśvarī in Bhavan, a suburb of Kangṛa town. From a remote age the spot was sacred but the temple which fell down in the earthquake was not an old one. An inscription preserved in the porch says it was built in the time of Śri Mahammad (identified by Cunnigham with Mahammad Sayyad who ruled at Delhi from 1533 to 1546). At the time of its foundation Raja Samsārchand was the king of Kangṛa." This temple has now been built again by the Hindu community.

The above information will show to us that neither the Lakshmīnārāyaṇa and Śītalā temples in the fort nor the Indreśvara temple in the town could be the temple thrown down by Mahmud, as they are all later constructions. The only temples that remain are the Ambikā temple in the fort and the Vajreśvarī temple in Bhavan. Now the Hindu community in rebuilding this Vajreśvarī temple in Bhavan, in their printed prospectus, state that this temple was destroyed by Mahmud in 1009 and was rebuilt by a Kangṛa king in 1043. It was again destroyed by Muhammad Tughlaq in 1337, again rebuilt by the Hindus and again thrown down in 1360 by Feroz. It was rebuilt by Samsārchand I in 1440. It was thrown down again by Khawas Khan, general of Sher Shah, in 1540 and rebuilt by Raja Dharamchand in Akbar's days. The present Maharaja of Guler who is indeed a very learned and well informed person and of urbane manners told us that in his opinion the temple thrown down by Mahmud was the Vajreśvarī temple in Bhavan and that there was once a wall round Bhavan. This opinion is also entertained by many persons. But it seems to us that the Vajreśvarī temple was first built in the days of Samsārchand I. We will give our reasons for this view. In all descriptions of Mahomedan writers, Mahmud is said to have taken the fort of Kangṛa and destroyed a temple there. The Vajreśvarī temple is not in the fort but is in Bhavan a suburb at a distance of about two miles from Kot Kangṛa or town Nagar Kot. In order that the reader may understand the situation

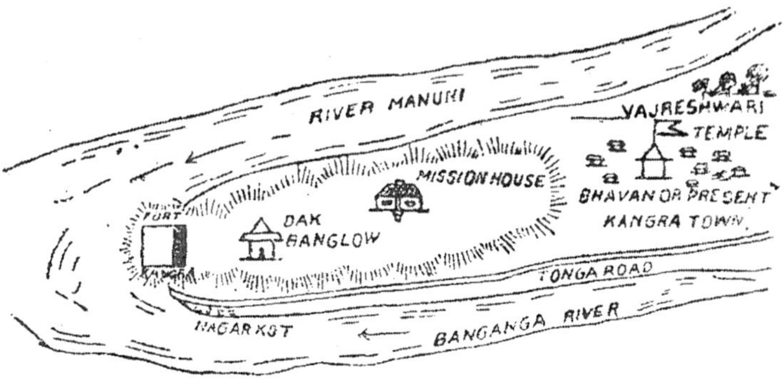

SKETCH MAP OF KOT KANGRA

we give here a sketch of the position of Kot Kangṛa, Nagaṛa Kot and Bhavan. If there was a wall around Bhavan, it could not have been a strong one and it could not have been as difficult to take it as Kot Kangra. Then again the temple with idol thrown down by Tughlaq appears also to have been in the fort which he took. The Katoch kings retook the fort and rebuilt the temple in the fort which was again taken by Firoj Tughlaq. It appears that after these repeated disasters, the Hindus moved down the temple to Bhavan in the days of Samsārchand I.

It must be mentioned further, that the idol in the Vajreśvarī temple is not fashioned by the hand but is a svayambhū idol viz, a natural stone coming out of the earth, having some appearance of a head, at least eyes. This is the only svayambhū idol of Devī which we have seen. The legend is that the deity was discovered by a cultivator who, while ploughing his field, accidently struck the deity with the iron-head of the plough and brought out blood. This is, of course, the usual story of the discovery of a swayambhū deity. It seems probable that as at Benares or at Ujjain (Mahākāla) the Mahomedans even under Mahomedan rule allowed the Hindus to have a temple of the same god in the vicinity of the old temple thrown down, so in Kangṛa the fort remaining in the possession of Māhomedans, the Hindus were allowed to have a temple of the same deity in Bhavan. Samsārachanda the first erected the Vajreśvarī temple in 1440, and the iconoclastic Shershah again threw it down a hundred years later. The tolerant Akbar allowed the temple to be rebuilt by king Dharamchand.

This interesting history, however, shows the strong Hindu spirit of the Katoch Rajas of Kangṛa and the temple of Dharamchand built about 1600 was standing till it was destroyed by the earthquake of 1905. Strong Hindu sentiment has again caused the temple to be built, the dome of which is being now adorned with gold.

It is necessary, however, to add that the Ambikā temple in the fort is still the place where Katoch Rajputs go to worship. In fact we were told that every Katoch sends his hair cut in the godāna ceremony to be placed before the Ambikādevī in the fort. This fact along with the legend of the discovery of the Vajreśvarī idol, leads us to believe that the famous temple in Kangrā which was thrown down by Mahmud was the Ambikā temple in the fort * or it may have been the original Vajresvarī temple in the fort. The idol in the present Ambika temple is also an unfashioned one or swayambhū. In all such cases there are movable idols in the temple also and Utbi actually states that the people of India made the temple a treasury for their great idols.

When Utbi relates that "he (Mahmud) came to the fort of Bahim Bagra "a castle in the midst of water high as a mountain and an inaccessible pit" (p. 341) he refers to this very fort at the confluence of the two rivers. Of course Bahim Bagra has to be read as Bhim Nagar and it is believed that Bhīmashah of Kabul founded the town Bhavan. The further description by Utbi cannot apply to Bhavan and Bhimnagar must be taken to mean the whole place including Nagarkot, Bhavan and Kot Kangra.

---

* The present building of the temple is according to the A. S. Report later than Mahmud.

CHAPTER IX.

SUBJUGATION OF THE PANJAB.

The Sultan's attention, as stated before, was constantly divided between the east and the west and his farreaching and unceasing activities extended in both directions with equal vigilance. Having settled some disputes and troubles in Kirman and Kohistan in the west and the north, Mahmud again directed his attention to the settlement of the question of the Panjab. He had humbled the king of the Panjab and taken one of the strongholds of that kingdom, Kangrakot. He determined to capture Nardin another strong place on which probably the king relied. And he arrived in the provinces of India, and "began to devastate the land, to punish the infidels, to overturn the idols and to make an example of high and low. And as to the prince of those accursed ones, he sent him prostrate to hell. And when the king of Hind saw these wounds in the nearest and distant parts of his kingdom, he sent his kindred to offer submission" (Utbi p. 361). Such is the succinct account which Utbi gives of this expedition. Although he mentions Nardin as stormed in the heading of this chapter, he does not describe it. From later historians-Elliot thinks that there were two expeditions and not one, as some suggest, and that by Nārdin Utbi means to refer to Naharwala the capital of Gujrat. The second expedition was against the fort of Nandan, as will be stated in the next chapter, and is described by Firishta and others. It indeed appears plain, even according to Utbi, that there were two expeditions and the second he describes later on. It is, however, difficult to identify Nardin with Naharwala as Mahmud could not have gone so far south, leaving the Panjab yet unsubjugated. We, therefore, take it that Nardin was some place in the Panjab itself and that Mahmud carried a devastating campaign which compelled the king of India to proffer submission. Who this king was is not mentioned; no doubt one chief is said to have been killed, and it is probable that Ānandapāla himself was killed in one of these combats. His son Trilochanapāla must have offered submission. We have already seen that Al-Beruni has recorded that Ānandapāla had latterly become a deadly enemy of Mahmud but that Trilochanapāla his son was better disposed. We, therefore, take it that Ānandapāla, instead of being killed in the battle of the confederate Hindus, was killed at this time (1009 or 1010) and

Trilochanapāla offered terms of submission. Mahmud granted the terms and by these Panjab practically became a subordinate province of the Ghaznavide empire. The terms were as follows :— "The king bound himself to tribute and fidelity and appointed sixty yokes (?) of elephants and a payment to be mutually fixed and sent by the nobles of the province and the people to the treasury. And by way of acting as viceroy the king was to keep two thousand men at his court and acknowledge fealty every day and month and year, and the succeeding rulers were to obey and follow the same law. The Sultan was content with these conditions !!! and this secured tax became a fixed source of revenue in the book of the finance court of the Empire. Thus the road for caravans and merchants between the districts of Khorasan and Hind became open" (p. 362).

Such is the normal course of the successive steps in the fall of kingdoms. We are here reminded of the fall of the Maratha kingdom eight centuries later. There was a stubborn struggle in the beginning by the combined Marathas against the English in 1803. The Maratha confederacy was defeated in the battle of Assaye by the greatest general of the English, Wellesley, much as the great Hindu confederacy was defeated by the masterly tactics of Mahmud in 1008 near Hazro. Bajirao like Trilochanapāla, submitted and consented to maintain a subsidiary force at Poona, of British regiments. This was the opposite of what was stipulated by Ānandapāla's son. He, as the usual fashion then was with subordinate kings, promised to maintain at Ghazni a force of two thousand soldiers for the service of the Ghazni empire at his cost. The British method of compelling subordinate kingdoms to maintain a British force at their capital was more effective and efficient for accomplishing extinction and was tantamount to the imposition of a heavy tribute for the time being. That final extinction overtook Trilochanapāla soon enough (after about 4 years) as we shall presently see ; but in the parallel case of Bajirao, it overtook him after the lapse of 15 years.

This subjugation of the Panjab was necessary in order that Mahmud should securely direct his attention towards the troubles which often arose in the west. And one of these we will specially mention as it has an interest for the Indian reader. In the immediate vicinity of Ghazni towards the west was the small province of Ghor, a mountainous valley inhabited by an unruly tribe which constantly gave trouble to caravans and merchants under the very nose of Mahmud. "The infidelity and the insolance of these inhabitants of Ghor who levied heavy imposts on caravans and travellers on the strength of their appalling cliffs required to be corrected. And the Sultan ordered his army to attack them in their fastness and himself went with his body-guard and cutting his way through the passes, arrived before the stronghold-nest of the king of Ghor. After stubborn fighting, the Sultan ordered his men to turn their backs and to show as if they were yielding. These doomed ones were deluded and the *Hindu* no longer remained firm but fascinated by the desire to plunder came into the open plain. Upon this the Sultan wheeled round and laid them all on the couch of sweet sleep. He took the son of the chief as prisoner and carried away as booty, wealth and arms which chief after chief and infidel after infidel had acculumated" (Utbi p. 364–65). The inhabitants of the valley of Ghor were originally infidels and even Hindus. They were forcibly converted by Mahmud and in the course of about two hundred years, themselves becoming zealous Mahomedans they conquered the Hindus of India. Secondly, we find here Mahmud employing the same tactics in fighting as were employed by Shivaji and the Marathas (called in Marathi Bakhars the *ganīmī kāvā* or enemy deception). Thirdly, like a great ruler Mahmud always bestowed attention upon the safety of roads for the encouragement of commerce. He wished to see that caravans between Khorasan and Hind should safely travel. Mountain tribes in those days as in later times levied heavy imposts on them whenever the central government was weak. And Mahmud exhibited the same vigilance and power as is exhibited by the British Empire at the present day in this respect.

CHAPTER X

BATTLE OF NAZIN AND THE ANNEXATION OF THE PANJAB.

For four years Panjab remained unmolested. Probably Trilochanapāla quietly paid the stipulated tribute without demur, and Mahmud also appears to have been engaged in the west. A terrible famine is described by Utbi as raging in Khorasan and its capital Nishapur. He also mentions troubles with Ilekkhan the Turk who must have taken advantage of these difficulties. Utbi also describes the conquest of Garjistan (Georgia) which had belonged to the Samani empire and the Shar of which ("the king of Georgia was called Shar, as the king among Hindus was called Rai, among Turks Khan and among Greeks Cæsar"—Utbī p. 377) defied Mahmud, and Mahmud with his usual swiftness and completeness reduced him to subjection. Mahmud then found time to turn his attention to Hindustan. Human feelings would tempt Mahmud to finally annex the Panjab which had been only subjugated and the same would impel even Trilochanapāla to rebel and throw off the yoke imposed upon nim. It is, therefore, probable that some pretext must have been found by one party or the other to begin the conflict again, as in the parallel case noted before viz: the Maratha war of 1818 wherein after the defeat of Bapu Gokhale Bajirao II finally lost his kingdom.

Utbi describes this conflict thus (p. 389-392):—"The Sultan having in 400 H. (1009) reduced Hindustan and built mosques &c. wished to take possession of the remainder of the land of the infidels. Therefore, he summoned his victorious armies and covered them with great honour. When he arrived at those territories, much snow had fallen and hence he returned to Ghaznī but returned again in spring. The king of India sat down under the protection of the mountain and took refuge in a pass and posted elephants in its narrowness. He summoned the cavalry and infantry of his kingdom. And a great army of infidels from Hindustan, Sind and all quarters raged like hornets in heat and heads were cast upon the battle-field like balls. And wherever the elephants came into the engagement, the Moslem army with swords and spears cut their throats and trunks. When the Sultan saw him (his lieutenant Abdulla Tai) in destress, he sent some stars from his special guard and the flame of battle blazed in this way until it was quenched by the water of victory. And at one blast of the good fortue of Mahmud all their affairs were scattered like dust. And they made prizes of their property and elephants. Thus this territory became exalted amongst the extent of Islam and this victory was entered in the register of expeditions."

From this description it may be inferred that Trilochanapāla made a third attempt to collect the forces of many Hindu States for his final fight with Mahmud; and a stubborn and terrible battle was fought which was gained by the Mahomedans through Mahmud's good fortune and the bravery of his bodyguard. This battle was fought in 404 H. or 1014 according to Elliot who quotes Utbi himself for this date though, as above stated, in some copies the year 400 H. is given, and other historians also give the same date. The place where this battle was fought is also in dispute. Utbi mentions, in the heading of his chapter, Nardin; others call the place Ninduna. It is suggested by some that the battle was fought near the mountains of Jud and the hill of Bālnāth overhanging the Jhelum. Elliot, however, thinks that the pass referred to by Utbi is the Margalla pass (Elliot II p. 451). Elliot gives the following further account of the battle from a fuller description of it by Nizamuddin Ahmad:—

"In 404 H. the Sultan marched his army against the fort of Ninduna, situated in the mountain of Bālnāth. Puru-Jaipal left veteran troops for its protection while he himself passed into one of the valleys of Kashmir. Having taken the fort by mining and other operations, the Sultan went against Puru-Jaipal but he fled further. The Sultan obtained great spoil and many slaves. Having converted many infidels and spread Islam, the Sultan returned to Ghazni." Elliot thinks that the chief who fought at Ninduna was Bhima, son of Jaipal. In fact he refers to Utbi for this name given as Nidar Bhim We do not find that name in the translation we have used of Utbi. Possibly there are variations in the available copies of Utbi. But strangely enongh Elliot does not go on to explain who Puru Jaipal was. We plainly see here a misreading of the name Trilochanapāla who was the king at this time and that name may easily be read in Persian or Arabic as Puru Jaipal. Jaipal and even Ānandapāla were already dead and Trilochanapāla was on the throne of the Shahis in the Panjab. His son was Bhima and it is probable that Trilochanapāla retired into

Kashmir leaving his fearless son (Nidar Bhim) to fight this battle. The battle was lost and the further account of Utbi may be construed as showing that the Panjab or at least its largest part was annexed to the kingdom of Ghazni. As Al-Beruni has stated that Trilochanapāla died after this date, having lived upto 1021, the other account may also be accepted and it may be believed that he and even Bhima escaped into Kashmir and for about seven years more reigned in the hilly submontane districts of the Panjab at the base of the Himalayas.

But Stein the editor of the Rājatarangini thinks that the important battle fought between Trilochanapāla and Mahmud on the Tausi river which falls into the Jhelum from the west in the Hazara District which is conterminous with Kashmir and so vividly described by Kalhana in that history of Kashmir was fought at this time (404 H. or 1013). In this battle Trilochanapāla was assisted by a strong contingent from Kashmir under Tunga. Trilochanapāla advised him to fight a cautious battle with the wily Turks by taking the support of the hills. But Mahmud used his usual stratagem, and sent a contingent beyond the Tausi river which being attacked and defeated by Tunga fled back across the river. Tunga was emboldened and came into the open and joined battle with Mahmud* (Raj. VII 47). The battle was hotly contested, many Kashmir officers fell in battle and Trilochanapāla himself performed deeds of valour. The cause of the Hindus was, however, destined to be lost and Mahmud was victorious. Trilochanapāla escaped into Kashmir never to return. And Kalhna utters a painful lamentation here over the final destruction of the Shahi kingdom of Kabul which we have already quoted in our first volume. If we reconcile this account with the statement of Al-Beruni that Trilochanapāla ruled till 1021 and Bhima ruled for five years after him, we have either to postpone this battle to 1021 A.D. or to believe that Trilochanapāla lived and ruled till 1021 some other insignificant portion of the hilly submontane part of the Panjab or went to Kanauj and there again fought with Mahmud.

Lastly, it would be interesting to note that the Jhelum Gazetteer identifies Ninduna with Nandana a hill fort in the Salt

---

* तुरुष्कसमरे यावन्न यूयं कृतबुद्धयः । आलस्यविवशास्तावत्तिष्ठतास्मिन्गिरेस्तटे ॥
हम्मीरेण तदा सैन्यं जिज्ञासार्थं विसर्जितम् । तौषीपारे ततस्तीर्त्वा मितप्रायैर्वधिद्धलैः ॥
ततस्तेनाहितोत्सेकमपि शाहिः पुनः पुनः । जगादाहवतत्त्वज्ञः पूर्वां तामेव संविदम् ॥
सर्वाभिसारेणागच्छच्छलाहवविशारदः । प्रातस्ततः स्वयं कोपात्तुरुष्कानीकनायकः ॥

Range where there are some remains of ancient buildings belonging to Kashmir rule. At page 62 it states that the district was once in the possession of Kashmir and then went under the Shahis of Kabul, "Ānandapāla and Jaipal described by Mahomedan historians as kings of Lahore being really Shahi kings of Kabul." But when the Gazetteer quotes Firishta as placing the capture of Nandana in 1008, it may be noted that this is very probably a mistake, the year 400 being a misprint for 404 H. The conversion of the Rajputs of the Salt Range dates according to the Gazetteer from the days of Shihabuddin Ghori. "Though it may be that Rajputs and Jats and others were forcibly converted by Mahmud, yet they must have returned to Hinduism as soon as his back was turned." But we have to remember that this district remained in the possession of Mahmud and his successors at Ghazni ever since this conquest. The Mahomedan Rajputs of the Salt Range, the Janjuas, are believed to be the most ancient inhabitants of the Panjab being descended from Anu the fifth son of Yayāti and it is even thought that Jaipal of Lahore was himself a Janjua (Jhelum Gazetteer).

Utbi relates that a stone was brought out of the temple the writing on which declared that the building was forty thousand years old. "What a folly" the Sultan observed "when the learned of the world have agreed that the world is itself not more than seven thousand years old!!!" To us in the twentieth century, both the statement on the stone and its criticism appear equally absurd. Probably this was a very ancient inscription dating from the time of Aśoka and the people in the neighbourhood not knowing its exact date assigned it to a fabulous age. Nandana in the Salt Range is undoubtedly an ancient place as its remains indicate.

NOTE 1—THE FORT OF NANDANA.

The Jhelum Gazetteer thus describes this fort (pp. 46-47) "Fourteen miles due east of Choa Saidan Shah, between the villages of Baganwala below and Ara above, the outer Salt Range makes a remarkable dip. There is a steep rocky hill which has absolute command of the route across the range. There are extensive remains here of a temple, a fort and a large village. The temple is in ruins. It is like other temples in the range in the Kashmirian style; but the platform on which it stands is of very great age and older than the temple. In later times a mosque was added close to the temple and is also now in a ruinous state. In its court-yard is a fragment of an inscription of the same period which is now too far gone to be legible. This fort was attacked by Mahmud of Ghazni, a fact which has strangely enough hitherto escaped notice."

It may be added that Bhera which is about twelve miles distant from Nandana might have served as a third capital to Ānandapāla when Wahind was lost. The present town of Bhera is on the east bank of the Jhelum, but we know * that the old town was on the west bank where mounds still show the ancient site and where ancient coins are still found. Bhera even now is, like Poona, a centre of learning, trade and art and the elite of the Panjab lawyers, engineers &c. come from Bhera. They are usually Kshatriyas by caste who have taken to civil professions. Bhera was also a centre of learned Brahmins as also of skilled artizans in wood, metal and cotton. In short Bhera exhibits all the marks of being a capital city, and lying as it does, midway between Lahore and Wahind may have served as a third capital to the Shahi kings.

---

* The Imperial Gazetteer under Bhera states that the old town was on the west bank of the Jhelum and was plundered by Mahmud as also later by an army of Janghiz. The new town was founded in 1549 A. D. round a mosque which still exists and is now a terminal Railway Station.

NOTE 2—THE SHAHI KINGS WITH REVISED DATES AND THEIR COINS.

We gave the probable dates of Shahi kings in Vol. I (p. 201) and Vol. II (p. 157) estimated on the usual average of 20 years per reign, going back from 1021 A. D. given by Al-Beruni as the last date of Trilochanapāla's reign, as given here in the margin. It is necessary to reivse these dates from the detailed information available now in the writings of Utbi and other chroniclers. It is certain that Jaipāl ruled till 1001 A. D. He may be taken to have ruled from 960 i. e. for forty years. We know that he burnt himself on a pyre both on account of his dishonour as of extreme old age. Wahind was taken possession of by Mahmud; and Ānandapāla must have resided at Bhera the next city in the kingdom which was on the trade route from Wahind viz. Hazro and the Margalla pass and caravans took the fruit of Kabul to Peshawar and Lahore and Multan via Bhera and took back Indian goods, cotton &c. to Kabul. Ānandpāla was killed in the battle of Nardin in 1009 or 1010 A. D. and Trilochanapāla made his submission and accepted terms and ruled without molestation till 1014 A. D. In that year Mahmud again invaded India and was confronted by Trilochanapala in the Margalla pass. He was defeated and he escaped into Kashmir. His son Nidar Bhim defended Nandana fort and the access to Bhera. He too fled and retired into Kashmir. Bhera was taken by Mahmud and plundered. Trilochanapāla ruled in some hilly part of the Panjab near Kashmir till 1021. He was immediately pursued in 1014 and was defeated in the battle of the Tauśī fought in that year or in 1021. He then again escaped into Kashmir and thence to Kanauj. As stated in a subsequent chapter we, however, do not believe that Trilochanapāla went to Kanauj, his mention there by later historians being a misreading for Rājyapāla. He died as stated by Al-Beruni in 1021 probably in the battle on the Tauśī and Bhima died five years later. Perhaps he went to Kanauj and died in the battle of the Rahīb described in a subsequent chapter. The emended dates with the name of Bhīma in addition would be as given in the margin. One prince of the family is spoken of as taking refuge with Bhoja of Mālwa (Sachau).

Jaipāl 960–980
Ānandapāla 980–1000
Trilochanapāla 1000–1021.

Jaipāl 960–1001.
Ānandapāla 1001–1009.
Trilochanapāla 1009–1021.
Bhimapāla last king of the Shahis 1021–1026.

That these kings ruled from Kabul to Lahore is conceded by almost all historians. Sachau the translator of Al-Beruni writes in his preface to the latter's India "When Al-Beruni wrote, the Pāla dynasty which ruled Kabulistan and the Punjab had disappeared from the theatre of history and their dominions were in the firm grasp of Mahmud and his slave officers." This is incontestably proved by the fact that coins of these kings are found all over the Panjab. Thus in the Gazetteer of the Ludhiana District we read that coins of Sāmantadeva who was king of Kabul and the Punjab are found in the mound of the dilapidated town of Sunet; no coins of Delhi kings or of Mahomedan kings are found, though coins of ancient kings, Kushan and others, are also found which shows that Sunet was destroyed by Mahmud of Ghazni."

Of the Shahi kings, Sāmanta was a great king whose accession is placed by Thomas in 935 (but this is not certain, Elliot II p. 425) and he appears to have conquered the Panjab as his coins are plentifully found there. Coins of Bhīma are also found though rarely in the Punjab, but they are plentifully found in Kabulistan. We have seen that he founded Bhimanagar below Kot Kangra. He was grandfather of Diddā the notorious queen oppressor of Kashmir. No coins of Jaipal have been, strangely enough, yet found; but coins of Ānandapāla are found in plenty in the Panjab and even in the northern parts of the Gangetic Duab: (ditto). No coins have been found of Trilochanapāla or Bhīmapāla who probably did not rule over any part of the Panjab.

These rulers appear to have been Saivites from their coins which contain a figure of Nandi (Śivas' bule) but Bhīma I seems to have been a Vaishṇava as he is said in the Taranginī to have built a temple of Keshava in Kashmir as already noticed in Vol. I (p. 194). Vaishṇavism appears to have been prevalent at this time in the Panjab as also in Kabulistan.

Elliot mentions that the last king Bhīma wrote a letter to Chandrarai (of Bundelkhand) advising him not to fight with Mahmud; and quotes Utbi as his authority (p. 427) extract from whose work is given at page 48 (Elliot II). As already stated, different copies of the Yamini read differently at certain places especially in giving names. The translation which we have used of the Yamini does not contain this name; and we have taken the advice given to Chandrarai to retire as coming from Rājyapala of Kanauj which is more probable as Bhīma could not have come so far south. But if he did, as his father Trilochanapāla is also represented to have done, he must have then been an ally of Mahmud whose subordinate he had become. The mention of his uncle being converted to Mahomedanism which we have in one copy also, seems to refer to one Sevakapāla (nabira nuptra-Jaipal i. e. a daughter's son of Jaipal) who had accepted Islām and who had been appointed by Mahmud governor of Peshawar. Subsequently he revolted and Mahmued attacked him and he was eventually killed.

CHAPTER XI.

THE EXPEDITION TO THANESAR.

We may pause here a little and see how the small kingdom of Ghazni had become an extensive empire by this time. It is sometimes urged that Mahmud merely undertook plundering expeditions without the object of annexing territories and solidifying a powerful state. This appears to be wrong from what we have seen of the expansion of Mahmud's kingdom upto this time. He achieved a conscious expansion of his territory and solidified his state by forcible conversion. In this he was actuated by religious zeal as well as by a correct appreciation of the essentials of a strong state. He first secured Khorasan and other provinces immediately to the west of his kingdom over which even in the days of Samani supremacy Sabuktagin had ruled. He next turned his attention to the East. The provinces of Jalalabad and Kabul (Lamghanat) were already annexed and forcibly converted to Mahomedanism. Mahmud first secured the Bannu district of the present N. W. Frontier province which was an ancient tract of the Hindus and was clearly in possession of the Shahis of Kabul. There are extensive mounds near Bannu which show that this district said to be settled first by Bharata, brother of Rāma (vide Rāmāyana Uttarakanda), was in the possession of the Kabul Shahis. "In these mounds coins are found plentifully not only of Azij and Vāsudeva of Indo-Bactrian period but also of the last Brahmin kingly line of Kabul"; but they contain no coins of any Mahomedan kings showing that the city was destroyed by Mahmud. The old road to Hindustan from Ghazni was via modern Bannu and the Kurrum and it fell into disuse when the Khyber pass was opened (Bannu Gazetteer). This district was, it seems, seized by Mahmud first and the people forcibly converted in order to enable him to pass over to India easily. Mahmud annexed the Peshawar District next, capturing Wahind after the signal defeat of Jaipal in the plain of Peshawar. Wahind was the capital of the Kabul kingdom and was also on the then second route to India, being a little above the junction of the Kabul river with the Indus. The basins of the two rivers Kramu and Kubhā (Kurrum and Kabul) well-known even in the Rigveda and situate in the first home of the Vedic Aryans, were thus in the hands of Mahmud and were now Mahomedan lands. Mahmud hereafter extended his kingdom westward by reducing the more distant provinces of the Samani empire and also eastward by first acquiring Multan which was already a Mahomedan State as also by annexing the kingdom of Bhatia which, as shown before, lay to the Southwest of Multan and between the Indus and the Jhelum. Finally he annexed the Panjab, the remaining province of the Kabul Shahis. He did not, for reasons which we will explain later on, apply to this province the process of forcible conversion though probably even here he appears to have converted many people. Thus the extension of the empire upto this point was by the gradual absorption of *neighbouring* provinces just in the same manner as the British empire gradually extended from Calcutta, Bombay and Madras by the gradual absorption of *neighbouring* provinces. We see Bengal first acquired by the British, then Bihar, then the U. P. and finally the Panjab by defeating the Sikhs. The process was here as with Mahmud the same, viz. first subjection with retention of previous powers as payers of tribute and then total absorption. Having thus extended his rule over the Panjab, Mahmud next turned his attention to the conquest and the plundering of the provinces further east. And the first kingdom which naturally he would attack was the kingdom of Thanesar which was immediately to the southeast of the Panjab.

That there was a kingdom at Thanesar is probable, as Al-Beruni mentions Thanesar in his geographical chapter. (Strangely enough he mentions Thanesar once between the Jumna and the Ganges and again in the place where it should properly come; probably the first name has to be corrected). There was also a famous deity at Thanesar and there is one even now. Mahomedan later writers name it Jagsom, a word which cannot be reduced to its Sanskrit equivalent. Here was the ancient kingdom of Pratāpavardhana, father of Harsha the last Buddhist emperor of Northern India. Mahmud is said to have undertaken this expedition against Thanesar to take possession of some celebrated elephants which Utbi calls by the name of Silmān, while later writers call them Moslem, as they bent down, in prayer as it were, like Mahomedans, in jenuflexion. Probably all the motives for Mahmud's expeditions were present viz: desire of obtaining plunder, of breaking a famous idol and of subjugating an adjacent kingdom. Utbi describes this expedition as follows (p. 394-5): "Accordingly the Sultan marched towards Thanesar with an army educated in the chamber of the sacred war and passed a desert so dreadful that a bird would not fly over its atmosphere. But providence granted aid and they came to that place. Before them they fouud a running stream full of water, lofty mountains and ground full of impracticable stones. The enemy retired into the mountains. The Sultan crossed the river by two fords and attack the enemy and (by evening) scattered them among the rocks. And as for the stamping elephants which constituted their confidence they left them on the spot. The Sultan's elephants went after them and brought them to the Sultan's halting place. The army shed so much blood that the water of the river became undrinkable."

The above account is simple and indicates that there was a stubborn fight with some chief not mentioned and that the elephants for which Mahmud principally came were secured There is no mention of an idol being broken, but Utbi in the beginning mentions idol-breaking as one of the objects of Mahmud. The identification of Thanesar becomes doubtful owing to the difficulty of arriving at a stream after marching through a desert which does not fit in with the actual position of Thanesar (Elliot Vol. II, 452). But we must remember that Uthi does not write from personal knowledge and is always hyperbolical in his descriptions. There is the river Sarasvati near Thanesar and the Karnal District Gazetteer, in describing its physical aspects, states that there are hilly tracts to the north of Thanesar from which torrential rivers come such as the Sarasvatī (p. 1). The battle may not have been fought in the immediate vicinity of Thanesar but at some distance. The battle is rightly placed in 1014 A. D., as the Gazetteer also does, a year after the annexation of the Panjab and Mahmud may have come upon Thanesar suddenly through the desert via Multan. The whole of the Panjab was now under him and he could take any route he liked. He had visited Multan ere this a second time and punished the Mahomedans there for again relapsing into the Karmatian heresy.

The account given by Firishta of this expendition is, we think, wholly imaginary. Firishta places this event in 402 H. (1011 A. D.) and relates that Ānandapāla on learning Mahmud's intention to attack Thanesar and desecrate the famous idol there named Jagsom, although he was subordinate to Mahmud, submitted a respectful protest. But Mahmud refused saying that the followers of the religion of Mahomet exerted themselves in the subversion of idolatry to obtain reward in heaven. The Raja of

Delhi thereupon called upon the Hindus of the whole of India to come together to defend the idol of Thanesar. But Mahmud attacked Thanesar before the Hindus could assemble. After capturing Thanesar, Mahmud wished to march on Delhi; his nobles told him that he could not safely do it till he had conquered and annexed the Panjab behind him. All this is pure imagination as Delhi was not then in such a leading position as to appeal to the Hindus of the whole of India. It was, if it had come into existence, an insignificant subordinate kingdom. The expedition again according to Utbi took place after the reduction of the Panjab to the position of an annexed province at the battle of Nazin (Nandana) and when Ānandapāla was already dead. Firishta by ante-dating this event has given this imaginary glowing account. Even Elliot rightly says here, though he restricts his remark to Delhi only, "There is nothing in the Yamini to warrant the reference to Delhi; the existence of which is nowhere alluded to by contemporary writers." (Al-Beruni, as already stated, does not even mention Delhi in his geographical chapter). "The frequent mention by Firishta of Delhi and its Raja in connection with the Ghazni kings does not rest on solid foundation." (p. 454). The fact is that writers coming four or five centuries later cannot divest themselves of their surroundings and must bring in Delhi which was so famous in their days!

CHAPTER XII.

THE SACK OF MATHURA.

The last expedition convinced Mahmud that it was possible to extend his raids into Mid-India where the city of Mathura famed for its temples and their riches was situate. He had also a cause of quarrel with the Pratihāra Emperor of Northern India, Rājyapāla, as he had twice assisted the kings of the Panjab in their fights with him. But he took time before he undertook this distant expedition and made due preparations. He wished to secure his rear and there were troubles in his western provinces. Utbi has related them in his history with fullness. He mentions also a change of viziers at Ghazni. The government at Ghazni was an ordered one and Mahmud exercised strict control over the governors of provinces. Khorasan was the centre of learning in those days and learned men from there were appointed to high offices. The language of the learned was Persian, but the new vizier who was himself a poet and a man of learning ordered all documents to be drawn up in Arabic. Ilekkhan king of Turks died about this time and he was succeeded by his brother. While Mahmud was attacking and subduing idolators in Hindustan, the idolators of Chin and Mongolia came down upon the Mahomedan Turks of Kashgar with a force of one hundred thousand men. This was a precursor of those dreadful inroads of the Moguls under Changiskhan which devastated Asia two centuries later. Togankhan, brother of Ilekkhan, sent for succour from all Mahomedan states to oppose this formidable invasion and probably Mahmud sent a contingent. A fierce battle was fought and the idolators of Chin like the idolators of Hind were defeated and almost annihilated. Mahmud continued his previous friendly relations with the Turks under Togankhan and cemented them further by marrying a daughter of Ilekkhan to his son Masa'ud, whom he appointed governor of Balkh.

Uthi also describes how Mahmud by his zeal for religion had become renowned and "by his intelligence had even come to be considered a guide in expounding the law" and "watched that the ordained statutes should be kept pure from the dust of innovation." The sultan commissioned spies to discover heretics and their places of meetings. They were brought from different places and cities to the court and impaled on trees or stoned. And the venerable Abu Bakar, a religious nobleman, coincided in opinion with the Sultan. Utbi further relates how a certain Tahirti who claimed to be a Sayyad and an emissary from the king and Khalifa of Egypt with letters and robes was proceeding to Ghazni but was stopped by order of Mahmud at Herat and conveyed back to Nishapur, capital of Khorasan and there tried for heresy and finally executed with the consent of Kadir Billah the Khalifa of Baghdad, Mahmud sternly suppressed heresy as well as the schism of Khilafat throughout his extensive dominions and thus acquired fame throughout the Mahomedan world (p. 444). It is no wonder that zealous soldiers collected at Ghazni to take part in his religious wars against infidels which by the destruction of idols and acquisition of plunder secured advantage in the next as well as in this world.

Having conquered Khawarism which had meantime rebelled and having annexed that land to his other kingdoms, "the Sultan thought he would undertake a third sacred conquest and he arrived at Bost and examined the accounts of collectors. The conquest of Hindu territories so as to become the territory of Islam were overflowing and "the veil of infidelity remained nowhere except in Kashmir." "Nearly twenty thousand men had come from the plains of Mawarannahar (beyond the Oxus) through zeal for Islam. They excited the purpose of the Sultan and he desired to proceed with those troops to Kanauj. This was a country quite unknown to foreign kingdoms."

Utbi thus describes the march to Kanauj and the fight near Mathura. "From the rivers Jihun (Sind) and Jhelum and Chand he went straight to Tibet. And wherever he came, envoys came to meet him, offering submission and allegiance. And when he arrived near Kashmir, Habali son of Shasin, general of the army of Kashmir joined his service. As he was told that there was no room for any one who had not accepted Islam, he took his position with robbers (skirmishers) and went before the troops. The army passed valley after valley and every night before the crowing of the cock the sound of fife and drum arose (vide description of the march of Harsha by Bāṇa Vol. I p. 143). On the 29th of Rajab in 409 H. (1018) they left the Jumna behind and came to the castle of Barm (Baran) in the country of Harun; the king was the greatest of the sovereigns of India but when he saw the army sea, he came down with about 10,000 men and accepted Islam. From hence they came to the fortress of Kaljand who had immense riches, strong cavalry and grand army. He arranged his army, his cavalry and his elephants and waited for the approach of the Sultan in a wood into whose intricacies a ray of the sun could not penetrate and from whose leaves and branches a needle would not reach the ground. The Sultan commanded his advanced guard to force themselves into the midst of the forest. They found a road from the upper castle and when the green sea struck out "Āllah Akbar" they stood firm for a time and made charges from their position. At length it became known that all events are in the grasp of destiny and the well-formed scimitar, though its force may be extreme and its edge sharp, is but a vassal to the decree of fate, if it penetrate to the Moslem blood. The despicable ones threw themselves into the river in order that the current might be the means of their preservation, but some came to the sword and some were drowned. Five thousand perished and Kaljand drew his dagger, killed his wife and ripping himself up went to hell. Of their wealth 185 heads of elephants and other plunder came to the Sultan. In the city there was a place of worship of the Indian people, and when he came to that place he saw a city of wonderful fabric and conception, so that one might say this is a building of paradise."

4. From this poetical but concise account of the secretary of Mahmud who was probably in Ghazni, we can determine the course of the expedition by the help of other information. Mahmud marched with an army of about one lakh of men of whom 20,000 were irregular amateur Turkish soldiers from beyond the Oxus. But he kept strict discipline on the march, as a great commander does, rising in the early morning and marching throughout the day. For he had to surprize the enemy by the celerity of his movement. He marched along the foot of the Himalayas in order probably to avoid crossing big rivers lower down. And on the way, every castle must have submitted to, or been conquered by, such a formidable force. He did not allow Hindus, in the name of submission, to join his army and create a discordant treacherous element and he asked the Kashmir contingent to march ahead. (It is difficult to imagine that Kashmir could have really sent one and we will speak about this later on). Having crossed the Jumna, on the 20th of Rajjab or in December 1018 he marched southwards without crossing the Ganges, through Antarbed, as Kanauj was on the west bank of the river and as he did not wish to place that river before him as an obstacle in attacking Kanauj. Naturally he was opposed

here and there by feudatory Rajput chiefs, but generally they submitted as the king of Baran did. Baran is undoubtedly the modern Bulandshahar; it is an ancient town sometimes identified with the Vāranāvata of the Mahābhārata and ancient coins of the second century B. C. of Śaka satraps and Kushans have been found there as also a copper-plate belonging to the Gupta period. There was a feudatory king probably belonging to the Dor Rajput clan and his name was Haradatta (which was read as Harun in Persian). A copper-plate belonging to this line of kings dated 1096 A. D. has been found here, giving the genealogy of this line and in it Haradatta is the 7th king and he submitted to Mahmud (Bulandshahar Gazetteer). Probably his conversion with ten thousand of his followers is an hyperbole of Utbi. Marching southwards, Mahmud was opposed near Mathura by one Kaljand with a considerable force and this Kulachandra fearlessly and stubbornly fought with the vast army of Mahmud. He was most probably a general of, and a feudatory chieftain under, the Pratihāra emperor Rājyapāla of Kanauj.

Mathura the most sacred city of the Hindus, especially the Vaishnavas, was in the heart of the empire of Kanauj and the Pratihāra emperors were often devotees of Vishuu. Mathura had been founded by Śatrughna, a brother of Rāma and it was the birth-place of Śrikṛishṇa. Mathura was sacred to the Buddhists also and during the Hindu period its importance still more increased. The superb temples built there and the immense treasures accumulated therein could not be given up to the idol-breaker and plunderer without a struggle and Rājyapāla though unwilling to sacrifice himself must have sent a strong force to oppose Mahmud. The battle is said to have been fought in a wood; and the place has been identified with the village of Mahāban on the maps. And there must have been then a great forest surrounding the place; for this is the place where Nanda lived and reared Śrikrishna in a forest, which long remained uncut down to recent times. The place is about six miles from Mathura and Shahajahan is recorded to have killed tigers in the jungle (Mathura Gazetteer). There is a small hill and a fort there and Kulachandra may even have been the hereditary protector of this Mahaban which is also a sacred place. He fought stubbornly with his infantry, cavalry and elephants and Utbi as usual attributes the success of Mahmud to the dictates of fate. Mahmud had no doubt come with an irresistible force, but it may be related to the credit of the Hindus that they did not deliver their sacred city to plunder and devastation without making a frantic effort to save it. Kulachandra in the usual Rajput fashion when unable to avert his fate killed his wife first and himself thereafter. The almost superhuman grandeur of the city of Mathura and the immense booty which Mahmud undoubtedly got in its sack are thus described by Utbi.

"They had built one thousand castles which they had made idol-temples and in the midst of the city they had built a temple higher than all, to delineate the beauty and decoration of which the pens of all writers and the pencils of all painters would be powerless. In the memoir which the Sultan wrote of this journey he thus declares that if any one should undertake to build a fabric like that, he would expend thereon one hundred thousand packets of a thousand dinars and would not complete it in two hundred years with the assistance of the most ingenious masters. And among the mass of idols there were five idols made of pure gold of the height of five cubits; and one had a jacinth arranged on it which the Sultan would have bought in the bazar gladly for fifty thousand dinars; and another had a sapphire of azure water of one solid piece weighing four hundred *miskāls*. From the feet of that idol they got 400 miskals weight of gold. Of silver the idols were so many that they who estimated their weights took a long time in weighing them. They devastated all that city and the Sultan passed therefrom towards Kanauj, leaving the greater part of his army there."

Such is the account, painful to a Hindu, of the sack of Mathura by Mahmud in the declining days of the Imperial Pratihāra kings of Kanauj. Wealth always has passed from the weak to the strong and one is reminded here of the sack of Rome by Alaric in the declining days of the Roman Empire so graphically described by Gibbon " Eleven hundred and sixty years after the foundation of the Imperial city which had subdued and civilized a considerable part of mankind, it was delivered to the licentious fury of the tribes of Germany and Scythia. The recently converted Goth spared the Vatican and many Christians found asylum there; but a cruel slaughter was made of the Romans; gold and jewels were removed and the palaces of Rome were stripped of their splendid furniture. Many a statue was melted for its precious material and many a vase was shivered into fragments by the stroke of a battle-axe. It is not easy to compute the multitude who from a honourable position and prosperous fortune were suddenly reduced to the miserable position of captives. Fugitives from Rome filled the provinces and this awful catastrophe of Rome filled the astonished empire with grief and terror."

CHAPTER XIII

THE FALL OF KANAUJ.

Grief and terror must have seized the Emperor of Northern India and Râjyapâla, like Honorarius the emperor of Rome, fled and was neither in Mathura nor in Kanauj but was already in Bari beyond the Ganges, a place not yet identified. Mahmud must have heard all this through his informers. He, however, took care to take an augury on the Koran and pursued Râjyapâla beyond the Ganges with a small force that he may be tempted to come to a fight. Utbi rightly describes him as the chief of the kings of India and says that all kings bent their necks to him and acknowledged his power and dignity. The name of this king, we now know, was Râjyapâla a word which might be read in Persian as Raja Jaipal or Haipal and Elliot in the absence of the epigraphic evidence we now possess, it is no wonder, identified him with Jaipal, king of Lahore who was already dead and who perhaps, he thought, was acknowledged king even in Mid-India. Later Mahomedan historians call him by various other names which are all absurd guesses and some have called him Kunvarpâla i. e. heir apparent of Jaipal. On the 8th of Shaban (January 1019, Elliot II p. 457) "Mahmud reached Kanauj where a mountain rose before him and his army passed the Ganges to pursue the fugitive emperor. As the Sultan did not probably come at him, he (returned and) reduced the seven fortresses of Kanauj placed on the margin of the water of the Ganges" (Utbi p. 457). "Nearly 10,000 temples were built in these castles and the lying iodlators declared that the fabrics were two or three hundred thousand years old." Kanauj is an ancient town supposed to be ruled by the Vedic king Kuśika father of Viśvâmitra and its sacredness was as great as that of Mathura. It was a flourishing city at this time and its grandeur had begun in the days of Harsha four hundred years before. It was already a vast city in his days as recorded by Hiuen Tsang whose description of it we have quoted in Vol. I (p. 28). The greater number of the people had left the place and the Sultan took the forts in one day and plundered them. Kanauj appears, however, to have been not as grand as Mathura. The glowing description given by Mahmud is sometimes wrongly transferred to Kanauj but from Utbi it is clear that it belongs in reality to Mathura. Mahmud is not clearly stated to have destroyed the temples here as at Mathura.

"The Sultan thence turned to Manj a fortified place of the Brahmins" and they for a time resisted him but finding resistance unavailable "they threw themselves down from the castle while some killed themselves with darts and the edge of swords." What place this was has again not been ascertained. It must have been a place lower down on the Ganges and said to be in the present Etawa District. From hence the Sultan came to the fortress of 'Aster' held by Jandbal the Violent. "This fortress was situated in the midst of a forest upon an eminence and deep moats were drawn around it." This place is identified with Asni now a village on the western bank of the Ganges in the Fatehpur district where there is even now a strong fort on the Ganges. Its chief was probably subordinate to Kanauj and likely to give trouble. Having subdued this chief, Mahmud directed his course towards Chandrarâi who was the owner of a very strong fortress." This was of course the Chandel king, the owner of the almost impregnable fort of Kalanjar, who was an independent king, as even Utbi relates that "he had never owned submission to any one and knew nothing but boasting and pride." (p. 450).

Utbi mentions here a quarrel between Jandbal the Violent (perhaps a chief belonging to the ancient Gautama clan which even now inhabits the Fatehpur District–Fatehpur Gazetteer—or a Sengâr chief whose descendants are now on the south of the Jumna and known as the Maharajas of Jagmanpur in the Jalaun District) and Chandrarai, which cannot be well understood and in the midst of this quarrel Mahmud came upon Chandrarai who "depending upon the repelling power of his forts and his numerous army determined to oppose the Sultan. But Haibal advised him not to fight and he retired with his army and treasures into a mountain." Utbi attributes this advice of Haibal to the treacherous motive of taking possession of the fort (probably Kalpi) of Chandrarai himself when the Sultan had defeated him; but "the Sultan without stopping to reduce the fort pursued Chandrarai into his place of retirement for three successive days and killed many men and seized their arms and accoutrements. They took some elephants by force and others came willingly whom they gave the name of Khudādād or God-given. They obtained from the treasure of Chandrarai three thousand packets of gold, silver and jewels and saphires and so great an abundance of slaves that the price of each did not exceed ten dirhams. The Sultan returned to Ghazni and the renown of his prosperity extended from the east to the west."

This certainly was the most extended, the most fruitful and the most energetic expedition undertaken by Mahmud in which he came as far south as modern Cawnpore and Kalpi. Later Mahomedan historians and Firishta especially have made many incongruous statements and additions in consequence of their ignorance of the real history of the period and even of the geography of Antarbed. And European historians have been at pains to explain the movements of Mahmud by relying chiefly on Firishta. But as Elliot has pointed out all this arose from following Firishta too implicitly without referring to more original and authentic sources (p. 408). That principal source is the Yamini of Utbi and we have given the above account from it. The real probable course of Mahmud after entering the Antarbed appears to be this:—he moved via Meerut and Baran south as far as Mahāban, then crossed the Jumna and plundered Mathura. He then repassed the Jumna, arrived at Kanauj, crossed the Ganges to frighten Rājyapāla and returning took Kanauj. Going south through Antarbed he defeated a powerful chief and crossing the Jumna again at Kalpi pursued Chandrarai into the mountains but not as far as Kalanjar. He recrossed the Jumna at Kalpi and returned as he had come through the Antarbed. The same course is described in the history of Nizamuddin Ahmad, an extract from which is given by Elliot (Vol. II, p. 460–1) in which Nizamuddin makes only a few alterations in what Utbi has stated.

The real difficulty is in determining the names and actions of Hindu chiefs and we have already stated on the basis of epigraphic evidence now available which was not before Elliot that the king of Kanauj was the Pratihāra emperor Rājyapāla and the Chandrarai was the Chandel king Ganda both of whom had assisted Ānandapâla in his fight with Mahmud. Mahmud would certainly have not returned without giving a lesson to both. The advice which Haibal (Rājyapāla) gave to Chandrarai appears to us to be a friendly advice and both escaped without being reduced to subjection. This must have troubled Mahmud and this is, in our view, the reason why he returned again next year as described by Utbi, Nizamuddin Ahmad and even Firishta.

The year is not given by Utbi and Nizamuddin gives 400 H while Firishta gives it as 412 which Elliot considers most probable. Nizamuddin states that when Mahmud heard that Raja Ganda had killed the Raja of Kanauj for having recognised and submitted to the Sultan, he resolved to invade his territory. But this event must have happened later and Nizamuddin is wrong in assigning this cause for this expedition. For then there was no reason for attacking Kanauj and its chief Haibal and defeating him at tho battle of the Rahib as Utbi and Nizamuddin both describe. Further we are not yet told by Utbi that Jaipal (Rājyapāl) had submitted to the Sultan. He had fled to Bari and had not come to any fight with Mahmud. To completely subjugate him the next expedition was undertaken by Mahmud. And it appears that like Shivaji or any astute general, Mahmud did not inform even his army that he was proceeding against Rājyapāla. Utbi says that Mahmud set out with the avowed intention of punishing the Afghan robbers who from their mountain fastnesses troubled caravans. Having done this Mahmud suddenly turned towards Hindustan "passed the desert and left behind fords and passages of rivers, ravaged the country as he passed and arrived at the river Rahib (not identified) whose whirlpools could carry away horsemen. Here in a fitting place Jaipal (Rājyapāla) had halted and would not permit any one to pass the water. The Sultan ordered hides to be inflated and eight men at night threw themselves into water. And Rājyapāla sent five elephants and a body of men to oppose them but they held on and pierced those elephants through and through with arrows and bore the men to the ground. And the Sultan encouraged every one to swim saying "we ought to endure the toil of a day for the rest of a whole life." And men holding horses' manes swam over. We are reminded here of a similar feat accomplished by Govind III, when he attacked Kanauj itself, described in Volume II (p. 166). And they killed many men and brought seventy elephants to the Sultan's yoke by compulsion. The infidels fled leaving their treasures as booty. The Sultan had taken augury from the Koran and the promise was fulfilled and "the Sultan was raised on the effectual settlement of the seat of justice and felt assured of extended prosperity and empire." Here ends Utbi's account of this expedition and even here Utbi does not mention that Rājyapāla submitted and even that Mahmud returned to Ghazni. It, however, seems that Mahmud did not retire without obtaining a formal submission from Rājyapâla who, as we shall have to state later on, must have promised to pay a yearly tribute to the Sultan. Thus fell the empire of Kanauj, though the Pratihāra line of its kings for a time continued to rule, as stated elsewhere, till it was supplanted by the Gāhadavālas under Chandra. Other historians bring in here Puru Jaipal. Nizamuddin mentions him and states that he opposed the crossing of the Jumna by Mahmud. Firishta mentions him as the grandson of Jaipal, Raja of the Panjab. Jumna is of course wrongly substituted for the Rahib which may have been the Ghaggar or some other river in Oudh in which province Bari is placed by Al-Beruni. We know that Oudh was directly under Kanauj and it may be possible, as Elliot has surmised, that Trilochanapāla after his defeat on the confines of Kashmir at the battle of the Tauśi may have taken refuge with Rājyapāla king of Kanauj. Al-Beruni states that Trilochanapāl died in 1021 A. D. (412 H.) and this battle on the Rahib may have been fought in that year and Trilochanapāla must have fought bravely in this battle and ended his life on the battle-field on the east bank of the Rahib.

CHAPTER XIV.

EXPEDITION AGAINST KALANJAR

From here onwards we lose the guidance of the account written by Utbi, a contemporary and secretary of Mahmud and have to rely on later historians or Bakharkars who wrote two or three hundred years later. Why Utbi finishes his account here is inexplicable. There is not the smallest doubt that he lived upto the year 420 H and later for he mentions that in that year Kadhi Abdulla Said went on pilgrimage to Mecca and he also relates the controversies which raged between him and Abu Baker on his return. The translator of Utbi remarks in a foot-note here that if this year be correct Utbi must be taken to have lived longer than he is supposed to do (p. 474). Again Utbi states that Mahmud passed a long life and the translator again remarks in a foot-note that this expression would imply that Utbi lived during a greater part of Mahmud's life than is usually supposed (p. 483). It is, therefore, a puzzle why Utbi does not carry on his narrative down to the year 420 H or 1019 A. D. Probably he finishes his account with the climax attained at this time (1020 A. D.) by Mahmud's good fortune. His empire at this moment was so extensive that it reached on the north-west to the Caspian sea, including as it did Khwarism and even Georgia, while on the south-east, it touched the Sarsuti including the Panjab and Thanesar. He had further humbled and subjected to a yearly tribute the emperor of Northern India, at the battle on the Rahib and perhaps he had defeated and entered into friendly relations with the king of the Turks beyond the Oxus. He had finally obtained incalculable wealth from the raid on Mathura and Kanauj and human nature impelled him to expend it on a magnificent mosque at Ghazni, being incited thereto, perhaps, by the sight of the magnificent temple at Mathura "which the best architects" he said "could not have built in two hundred years." He, therefore, at this time designed and reared a splendid mosque at Ghazni, the old mosque there being built for a smaller number of people and at a time when Ghazni had but a small territory. Utbi describes the building of the grand Juma Masjid of Ghazni on which "slaves from Hind and Khorasan worked day and night and superintendents richly paid supervised from morning to evening. Trees were brought from Hind and Sind and used on the said works; mighty stones of marble, square and hexagonal, were brought from distant places. And they drew out the domed porticoes so perfectly spherical that the arch of the sky was but a myth in comparison." They spared not the purest gold in their paintings and gilding, and crushed the body like idols and fastened them in the doors and walls. The Sultan commanded a closet to be constructed for his own use. "He commanded the fabric to be square with expanding porches and interlacing curvatures." The pavement was made of white marble and on the sides of every court they delineated golden paintings shaded with lapis-lazuli. "Every one who saw this fabric took the finger of wonder into his mouth and said 'Oh thou who hast beheld the mosque of Damascus and are maddened thereby and profess that no building like that is possible' come and see the mosque of Ghazni." "In front there was an immense nave for great festivals and congregations in which six thousand servants might fulfil their duties." "And he built near the precincts a college and supplied it with valuable books and rare volumes of theology and to these pure walls of instruction professors and Imams and students directed their course; and from the endowments of the college they received daily maintenance and necessaries and a salary monthly or yearly was paid to them. And during the reign of the Sultan the extend of Ghazni exceeded all cities in spacious buildings and solid edifices. And amongst other fabrics there were a thousand walled enclosures for elephants with their grooms, the suppliers of food etc. It was God who was the promoter of all this prosperity of the land." (p. 468–469). Utbi probably finishes his narrative with a further description of the Sultan's just rule and the rule of his younger brother in Khorasan where he was appointed by Mahmud but unfortunately where he died young. It is probably at this climax that Utbi ends his account which does not seem to have an abrupt end. But we at this time are unfortunately deprived of a reliable account of the subsequent doings of this great sovereign. Elliot mentions the battle of the Rahib as the thirteenth expedition and enumerates four more expeditions thereafter on the authority of Nizamuddin and Firishta. These do not mention their own authorities, yet it is probable that they had some reliable sources of information for their narrative, though we find that owing to distance of time and ignorance of localities they make many wrong statements. Utbi mentions state documents such as a register of expeditions and even memoirs written by Mahmud himself and it is probable that other contemporary writers such as Baihaki whose works are not available to us, supplied them with information. It is not, therefore, possible that these later writers give us imaginary stories though we must accept their accounts with caution and try to tally them with information available from Indian epigraphic evidence. Thus the statement of Nizamuddin that the Raja of Kanauj was killed by a Raia named Nanda for having submitted to the Sultan (Elliot II p. 63), a statement made by him from some contemporary Mahomedan writer, is borne out and supported by Chadella and Kachhapaghāta inscriptions. As will be related in Chandella history later on, a Chandella inscription states that Vidyādhara son of Ganda destroyed the king of Kānyakubja (E. I. I. p. 222) and that in this he was assisted by Bhoja and the Kalachuri king. This combined force was led by a Kachhapaghāta king of Gwalior who was a feudatory of the Chandella king and another Kachhapaghāta chieftain of Dubhkund (in Gwalior territory) by name Arjuna is said in an inscription to have actually, when engaged in the service of king Vidyādhara, by his arrows in a great battle cut through the neck of Rājyapāla. This speaks volumes of the spirit of the Rajput kings of this time who did not like the action of Rājyayāla in submitting to a foreign king the breaker of the idols of Mothura, and a combined army of Chandella, Paramāra Kalachūri and Kachhapaghāta kings attacked Rājyapāla in Kanauj and killed him. Probably they returned without doing more and Trilochanapāla son of Rājyapāla succeeded him in due course at Kanauj.

Though thus the account of Rājyapāla being killed is true, it seems to us that Nizamuddin is wrong in placing this event before the expedition of Mahmud against Rai Jaipal (Rājyapāla) and the battle of the Rahib described above and in misstating that the eight men who crossed the deep stream of the Rahib crossed the Jumna where further Puru Jaipal opposed Mahmud. Again, Nizamuddin states that the eight men advanced on Bari which is mentioned by no other writer (Elliot II p. 464). The advance and capture of Bari must be correct as we know from Al-Beruni that Rājyapāla had made it his residence. It must have been after the battle on the Rahib that Rājyapāla must have submitted and consented to the payment of a tribute. It was after this that Rājyapāla must have been attacked by the Hindu confederacy led by the Chandella king and Mahmud on hearing of this must have thought it necessary to chastise both the Chandella and the Gwalior kings. Lastly Nizamuddin twice leads Mahmud against the Chandella king once after the capture of Bari and again in what Elliot calls the fifteenth expedition viz. that against Gwalior and Kalanjar on the authority of the same author. Utbi does not mention that Mahmud went against Chandrarai after the battle of the Rahib, for at that time Rājyapāla had not yet been killed. It seems probable that Chandrarai was only once attacked and not twice.

Mahmud led in 1022 an expedition against Kirat, Nur, Lohkot and Lahore (reckoned as fourteenth by Elliot); the first two are identified with Swat and Bajaur where Hinduism still lingered and the people were worshippers of the lion which Elliot thinks means Sākya Sinha or Buddha. But though this district was a staunch Buddhist district in the days of Hiuen Tsang yet, we think, Buddhism was dead in the tenth and eleventh centuries throughout these territories. The lion refers to the man-lion Avatāra of Vishnu and we have shown in Volume I, that the worship of Narasinha was prevalent in the Panjab, Multan, being known as Prahlādapura or the city of Prahlāda, devotee of Narasinha. Mahmud conquered this territory and converted the people to Mahomedanism. He then went to Lohkot the impregnable fortress of Kashmir and returned without effecting an entrance into that inaccessible country, after paying a visit to Lahore* which was now the capital of one of his Indian provinces. He must have learnt here of the events at Kanauj and determined to lead an expedition against Gwalior and Kalanjar next autumn.

In 404 H (1023 A. D.) he led this expedition and he must not have crossed the Jumna at all as he had first to chastise the king of Gwalior. This king submitted without fighting and as he was merely a feudatory of Kalanjar, Mahmud did not wait here long but proceeded against Ganda, called Nanda wrongly by Mahomedan writers. Some European writers doubt the truth of this expedition and Elliot could not explain the inclusion of Gwalior in it (Elliot II. p. 467); but when we know from inscriptions that both Gwalior and Kalanjar had together attacked Rājyapāla, we may not only grant the necessity and truth of this expedition but see why Gwalior was first attacked and

* Elliot II p. 466; this contradicts the statement in the Lahore Gazetteer that Mahmud did not visit Lahore at all which seems incredible.

humbled. Nizamuddin detaining this expedition says that Mahmud again attacked Kalanjar which as we have seen is a repetition. In reality this was the first expedition against Chandrarai of Kalanjar (perhaps the second if we take into account the first invasions of Kalpi after Kanauj and Mathura were taken in 1018 A. D.). Ganda at this time retired to Kalanjar which Mahmud invested. Nizamuddin writes that "this fort was unparalleled in the whole of Hindustan for strength. Nanda presented three hundred elephants and sued for peace." "He also sent a few Hindi verses in praise of the Sultan which were shown to learned men of the country and court-poets who bestowed high praise upon them; the Sultan was pleased and sending some presents bestowed upon Nanda fifteen fortresses." It seems that Mahmud was prudent enough not to waste his power upon the reduction of such fortresses as Kalanjar and Gwalior, and contented himself with accepting their submission, and their non-interference with the king of Kanauj paying him a tribute. It is natural that Trilochanapāla who had succeeded Rājyapāla must have consented to pay a yearly tribute as covenanted by his father.

NOTE:—It seems to us that Sir Vincent Smith implicitly following Nizamuddin has given a different and probably mistaken account of these events in his article on the Chandellas in Indian Antiquary XXXVII (p. 142). He observes "In the course of the 12th expedition in Jan. 1019 Rājyapāla submitted and promised an indemnity of one million dirhams and thirty elephants. For this submission Rājyapāla was killed by Ganda's son in May 1019. Mahmud invaded again and an ally of Ganda whose identity is obscured by the imperfection of the Persian alphabet but who was almost certainly Trilochanapāla, son of Rājyapāla, opposed Mahmud's passage of the Jumna but failed. Mahmud crossed the river and captured and sacked the town of Bari and then marched southwards to chastise Ganda in his own territory. He collected a force in accordance with the usual Hindu custom comprising 36,000 horse, 115000 foot and 640 elephants. The Sultan felt uneasy and reconnoitred the army from an eminence. In the night Ganda fled. The Sultan carefully attacked the deserted camp lest there might be a ruse and got immense booty. The cowardice and the immense plunder again induced the Sultan to invade his territory via Gwalior in 1023 A. D. Mahmud invested Kalanjar. Ganda gave him 300 elephants and immense presents and accepted back Kalanjar and 15 forts from Mahmud. Notwithstanding the success gained so easily by Mahmud, the Chandel kingdom was not again attacked by Mahomedans until 180 years had elapsed and Ganda's successors were left free to manage their own affairs." This account is full of apparent incongruities owing to Smith's following Nizamuddin implicity as stated above. Nizamuddin gives two expeditions against Kalanjar instead of one and places both after the defeat and death of Rājyapāla at the hands of the Chandellas. In this case the second expedition becomes an unnecessary expedition as undertaken merely for plunder and via Gwalior for no reason. Secondly, Ganda's running away at night when he had such an overwhelming force is on the face of it unbelievable. Utbi never describes such scenes; but later Mahomedan writers are tempted to imagine such encounters wherein overwhelming forces are assigned to the Hindu king and he is shown to have run away without fighting. Even Utbi has described Ganda as an independent king full of pride and courage. This is a plainly imaginary scene invented by Nizamuddin. For even on his own showing, if this expedition had been undertaken by Mahmud to punish Kalanjar for killing Rājyapāla, there was no necessity to cross the Jumna and go against Kanauj. It does not seem likely that Trilochanapāla would oppose Mahmud to whom his father had submitted. Lastly Utbi does not relate that Mahmud went against Nanda after the battle of the Rahib where the eight men crossed the turbulent river in face of opposition as stated by Nizamuddin himself. The proper explanation is that Nizamuddin is wrong in describing the march against Nanda at this time and also placing the event of the Raja of Kanauj being attacked and killed by Nanda before the battle of the Rahib. The course of events according to our view was this. In the 12th expedition against Kanauj (1019) Rājyapāla did not submit but fled to Bari. In the 13th expedition Mahmud led an army against Rājyapāla and Bari and conquering him in the battle of the Rahib accepted his submission on condition of payment of tribute (1021 March). In May Rājyapāla was attacked and killed by Nanda assisted by Gwalior which Mahmud learnt at Lahore in 1022 March and he led an expedition in 1022 December against Gwalior and Kalanjar and exacted submission from both in Jan. 1023. In this view Ganda does not appear to be craven-hearted a he is made to appear.

CHAPTER XV

EXPEDITION TO SOMNATH

We now come to the crowning event in the idol-breaking and plundering career of Mahmud, the expedition to Somnath. Somnath was famous then as a great Siva shrine described in detail in the Skanda Purāṇa of the 9th century A. D. and also mentioned by Al-Beruni both as a sacred place and a resort of pirates. Mahmud certainly would think of attacking Somnath and plundering it of its fabulous riches. Unfortunately we have no mention of this expedition, the highest achievement of Mahmud, in the work of Utbi though he lived up to 420 H (1029 A. D.) as stated before, i. e. four years after this event. Nor does Rashiduddin who wrote more than two centuries later mention the Somnath expedition, or Hamidulla Mustafi who followed him twenty years later (E. II p. 430–431). The first description is found in Ibn Asir and later writers have only embellished his account (ditto p. 468). And there is no mention whatever of this great calamity which overtook Gujarat in the palmy days of the Solankhi rulers whose account is fully given by many Gujarat Jain and Hindu chroniclers from the time of the founder Mūlarāja who came to the throne of Anhilwad, as will be shown later on, in 961, sixteen years before Sabuktagin. We do not also find the slightest hint about this calamity in any inscription found upto this time. Under these circumstances one is disposed to doubt whether this expedition was actually undertaken by Mahmud in distant Gujarat where he must have arrived after traversing a wide desert. Yet considering that Hindu writers would be loth to mention this disaster to one of their greastest gods and kings and that writers though writing centuries after the event had certain Moslem accounts before them and are not likely to invent a wholly imaginary story, we give the account given by Ibn Asir from the extract from his work given in Elliot II (p. 469).

We may at the outset state that this account, exaggerated as it must be, still more increased in the marvellous element in later writers who added imaginary stories to it, chiefly from a desire to heighten the religious greatness of Mahmud. The story, for instance,—a story told by even Gibbon—that immense treasure was concealed within the idol of Somnath, that Brahmins offered as ransom several crores of rupees to Mahmud which his generals advised him to accept and that Mahmud refused saying that he would like to be known on the judgment day as an idol-breaker and not as an idol-seller is a fabrication of some one, if not of Firishta himself. Wilson, as quoted by Elliot (II p. 476) commenting on this embellishment of the story of Somnath, observed "The earlier Mahomedan writers say nothing of the mutilation of the features of the idol, for in fact it had none; nor of treasure it contained which as it was solid, could not have been within it. Firishta invents the hidden treasure of rubies and pearls with quite as little warrant". This story is plainly absurd, as the linga of Somnath must have been a solid block of stone. Similarly the story that Mahmud was led into a waterless desert by a treacherous Hindu guide and that Mahmud eventually by prayer was able to find water, as also the story that Mahmud wished to ramain in Gujarat as it was a fertile country possessing gold mines but was induced to give up this idea on the representation of ministers that Khorasan was the country inherited from his father and the best for him to live in, are incredible. The story of Dabshilim, a recluse and a relative of the fugitive king, being entrusted with the government of the country when Mahmud retired from it is strange and unbelievable, though it has been suggested that he was an uncle of Bhīma the reigning monarch of Gujarat at this time, who had indeed retired and who lived on the bank of the Sarasvatī as a recluse.

Elliot has given extracts from many historians relating to this expedition which the curious reader may refer to, if necessary, but we do not think it necessary to summarise their accounts as they are mere embellishments of the story first given by Ibn Asir which is itself an exaggerated account. We, however, give this account in short. "The idol of Somnath was the greastet in India to which people came, especially on lunar eclipse nights. Souls of men went to this place, it was believed, when separated from the body. The temple was endowed with 10,000 villages (?). Water from the distant Ganges was daily brought with which the idol was washed. One thousand Brahmins performed the worship of the idol and introduced the visitors. Three hundred persons were engaged in shaving the heads and beards of the pilgrims. Three hundred women sang and danced at the gate of the temple. (Female singers and dancers, in ancient times, danced before Śiva idols as described by Kalidāsa in Meghadūta, a custom still prevailing in Śiva temples in the south, such as the Mangeśa temple in Goa territory). It was believed that Somnath was displeased with the idols of Hind for not opposing Mahmud who, when he heard this, resolved upon breaking the Somnath idol and proving to the Hindus that their gods were false and that they might embrace the true faith.

So he left Ghazni with 30,000 horse, on the 10th of Shaban 414 H (1023), besides volunteers and reached Multan in the middle of Ramjan. Taking water and corn on 30,000 camels he started for Anhilwad through the desert. The chief of that town Bhīma fled for safety to a fort (named Kandana by later writers and probably Kanthad in Cutch). Mahmud passed on to Somnath (it is not described anywhere that Anhilwad was captured and plundered) through a desert. He came to Dabalwārh, a place ten days journey from Somnath. The people stayed there believing that Somnath would destory Mahmud. But Mahmud took the place, plundered it and slaying the people marched on to Somnath.

He arrived at Somnath on a Thursday in the middle of Zilkad, and beheld a strong fortress on the sea-shore washed by the waves. The people of the fort were on the walls laughing at the Moslems and telling them that their deity would destory them all. On Friday the Moslems advanced to the assault and the Hindus fled. The Moslems scaling the walls with ladders entered and a fearful slaughter ensued. A body of Hindus entered the temple, cast themselves on the ground before the idol and implored him to grant them victory.

Next morning the battle was renewed and the Mahomedans drove the Hindus to the temple. A dreadful slaughter took place at the gate of the temple. Bands of Hindus would enter the temple and weeping and clasping their hands would entreat the idol, then issuing forth would fight until they were slain. Some took to the sea in boats but they were attacked there and were either killed or drowned.

The temple of Somnath was built upon fifty-six pillars of wood covered with lead. The idol itself was in a chamber and was five cubits in height and three in girth and must have been two cubits hidden in the basement. It had no appearance of having been sculptured. Mahmud seized the idol, part of it he burnt and part sent to Ghazni, where it was made a step at the entrance of the Jami Masjid. The shrine of the idol was dark but it was lighted by most exquisitely jewelled chandeliers. Near the idol was a chain of gold to which bells were attached which were rung every watch hour to rouse Brahmins to worship. The treasury was near and in it were many idols of gold and silver, and veils set with jewels of immense value. The worth of the whole plunder exceeded two million dinars and the number of the slain exceeded fifty thousand, (E. II p. 469-471).

This is an account simple and credible enough. The Brahmins or perhaps Rajputs made a frantic resistance at the temple itself only to be slain. But the ruler of Gujarat Bhīma could have made a stubborn resistance before Somnath. He could have brought into the field a greater army even, consisting of cavalry, than that of Mahmud if he had been but true to his name and the Rajput character. But it must be remembered that Mahmud's prestige by this time as a conqueror, had by his constant success, risen to its highest pitch like that of Napoleon who himself was latterly looked upon as equal to one lakh of men. But even Napoleon was stubbornly opposed by the Germans and the English at the battle of Waterloo. The Hindu character, as stated already, lacks in stubbornness under unfavourable circumstances and it is no wonder that Bhīma took refuge in a fort in Cutch. After taking Somnath, Mahmud is said to have attacked him there, though he was impeded by the water of the Runn of Cutch and passing it was dangerous in consequence of the possible rise of water at tide time. Bhīma, when he saw the conqueror coming, fled even from there. Mahmud returned to Ghazni via Sind through the desert by a more westerly course where he knew water was available and where he could not have been deceived by treacherous Hindu guides. He was troubled extremely by the pirates of the Indus who are supposed to have belonged to the Jud country.* By a subsequent expedition against these Jats, Mahmud gave them condign punishment.

Mahmud is said to have come to Somnath via Multan through the desert by an easterly course taking Ajmer and Anhilwad on the way and returned via Cutch, Sind and Multan conquering Mansura on the way, as he feared that "Paramāra-

---

* Mahmud in 1024 while returning from Somnath is said to have been harassed by the Jats of the Salt range but these Jats must have belonged to the Lower Indus (Jhelum Gazetteer page 83).

deva of Malwa (Bhoja) who was preparing to attack him would intercept him as he returned." Probably he was afraid of losing the great plunder he had obtained, in a possible conflict with the Hindus.

NOTE—SOMNATH.

Somnath Patan or town of Somnath is situated on the west coast of Kathiawar and is at present under Junagadh. The place was visited in 1843 by a traveller and described in J. R. A. S. VIII p. 173. " The old temple is in ruins and a new temple has been built by Ahilyābai near the site of the old. But the extreme grandeur of the old temple is visible even in the ruins now remaining". This old temple according to our view was the one built by Siddharāja Jayasinha and Kumārapāla and the temple which was destroyed by Mahmud was probably the one built by Bhoja Paramāra of Malwa as stated in one of their inscriptions to be noted in Paramāra history. The building of Bhoja was probably of wood as stated by Mahomedan historians. This building must probably have been erected before 1026 A. D. The building of a new stone temple was undertaken by Jayasinha of Anhilwad and completed by Kumārapāla as is evident not only from Gujarat croniclers but from an inscription in a temple in somnath Patan which will be noticed in the history of Anhilwad. This Bhadrakāli temple Praśasti dated 1169 A. D. is very interesting and begins with the description of a Brahmin from Benares who appears to have undertaken the rehabilitation of temples (probably destroyed by Mahmund) fallen into ruin and he travelled on this meritorious mission throughout India and came to Somnath after visiting Ujjain. This mention of the sage Brahmin's efforts corroborates in our view to some extent the story told by later Mahomedan writers about Mahmud's expedition to Somnath and the description of the temple by them. It is expressly stated that the temple was now built of stones. This temple was destroyed by the Mahomedan kings of Gujarat in the fourteenth century. The story that Mahmud removed the sandle gates of the temple of Somnath to Ghazni has not been credited by modern scholars and the gates which were brought by the English in 1843 after their conquest of Afghanistan are lying unnoticed in the fort at Agra. (Sardesai).

We may mention that there is a reference to Somnath in the Bostan of Sadi and he relates a queer story which is probably a concoction of his own. Sadi in his extensive travels came to Somnath and saw there an ivory idol surmounted with precious jewels beautifully arranged, seated on a golden chair set on a throne of teakwood. The Brahmin pujari had a contrivance by which the idol would raise its hand. Sadi discovered the contrivance by accident when the Brahmin fled pursued by the deceived indignant Sadi who even killed him. Sadi fearing vengeance of the Brahmins fled the country. This story is clearly an invention, for Sadi would not have been allowed even to approach the idol, much less to go behind it. Moreover it is not probably allowed that idols should be made of ivory. To the historian, however this refercnce by Sadi to Somdath is remarkable as it makes no mention of Mahmud's invasion of Somnath and the breaking of the famous idol of śiva there. One would naturally expect some illusion to that event. This omission strengthens the doubt which is entertained sometimes about the truth of Mahmud's expedition to Somnath. Sadi who was born in 1175 A. D. must have visited India when about 40 years old i. e. about 1215, and he wrote his Bostan when 80 years of age i. e. about 1255 A. D. Delhi was already on both dates under the Mahomedans, though Gujarat was not. And the first writer to describe the expedition to Somnath is Ibn Asir who wrote about 1270 A. D. at the earliest. But after all, omission to mention a fact unless that mention is unavoidable or imperatively necessary is doubtful evidence and we cannot rely upon it and hold that Mahmud's expedition to Somanath is not imaginary.

CHAPTER XVI.

IDOLATRY OF THE HINDUS.

We may pause here a little and reflect upon the superstitious debasement of idolatry into which the Hindus had drifted at this time. It indeed seems to us that the iconoclastic inroads of Mahmud had come upon the Hindus as an eye-opener and as a chastisement. Unfortunately the Hindus did not then take the lesson which these disasters taught them nor have they learnt it even now. This is not a place to enter into the question whether idol-worship is countenanced by the Vedas or whether it is reasonable. There is not the smallest doubt, however, that idol-worship is accepted by Hinduism and perhaps properly accepted as leading to concentration of the mind on the deity. But idol-worship almost always leads the human mind into some superstitious beliefs, especially to the belief that the idol itself possesses the powers of the deity it represents. Belief in the miraculous powers of idols prevailed in ancient times throughout all countries and prevails to this day wherever idol-worship is practised. Buddhism began with almost the denial of the Deity and drifted later into rampant idolatry viz: the worship of the Buddha himself and however learned and philosophic Hiuen Tsang may be, he believed in the miraculous powers of Buddha's relics and Buddha's idols as described in Volume I (p. 103). Hindus too amongst whom idolatry was already prevalent to a certain extent and who became still more idolatrous through the example of Buddhism which they supplanted believed to such an extent in the miraculous powers and sanctity of certain idols that the Pratihāra emperors of Kanauj, though powerful enough to capture Multan, were always held back by the threat of the Mahomedan possessors of Multan that if the Hindus advanced they would break the famous sun-idol of Multan (see Vol, II p. 166). Even in the west the Romans and the Greeks who were in advance of other peoples in philosophy believed in the miraculous powers of certain idols. And Christianity in the beginning preached the formless God and often progressed among the pagans by actually proving to the world that no such miraculous powers existed. The frantic but unavailing prayers of the worshippers of Somnath to destroy the sacrilegious conqueror remind us of a similar spectacle at

Alexandria about six hundred years before at the demolishing of the idol of Serapis by the order of the emperor Theodosius (389 A. D.), so graphically described by Gibbon. "Alexandria which claimed his peculiar protection gloried in the name of the city of Serapis. His temple which rivalled the pride and magnificence of the capital was erected on the spacious summit of an artificial mound raised one hundred feet above the level of the city. The sacrifices of the pagans prohibited by Theodosius were still tolerated in the city and temple of Serapis owing to the superstitious terrors of the Christians themselves as they feared to abolish these rites which alone could secure the inundation of the Nile, the harvests of Egypt and the subsistence of Constantinople. But at length an explicit order from Theodosius arrived to demolish the temple and the idol. A great number of plates of different metals artificially joined together composed the majestic figure of the deity which touched on either side the walls of the sanctuary. He held in the right hand an emblematic monster the head and body of a serpent branching into three tails terminated by the heads of a dog, a lion and a wolf. It was confidently affirmed that if an impious hand should move to offend the majesty of the god, the heavens and the earth would instantly return to their original chaos. An intrepid soldier armed with a battle-axe ascended a ladder and even the Christian multitude expected with anxiety the result of the combat. He aimed a vigorous blow against the cheek of Serapis and the cheek fell to the ground; but the heavens and the earth continued to preserve their accustomed order and tranquillity. The victorious soldier repeated his blows and the limbs of Serapis broken into pieces were ignominiously dragged through the streets of Alexandria. The Nile, though late, with its usual flood fertilized the plains of Egypt and falsified the prediction of false prophets. Many attributed their conversion to this impotence of the tutelary deity of Alexandria".

Gibbon moralises here upon the inadvisibility of staking the truth of a religion on the miraculous powers of idols which are but pieces of stone, metal or wood. And yet Christianity itself, like Buddhism, later drifted into the same superstitious idolatry which it had exposed, in the worship of idols of Jesus and Mary and Mahomedanism arose almost as a natural consequence to correct this error. The iconoclastic expeditions of Mahmud were similarly an eye-opener to the Hindus to correct their erroneous belief in the miraculous power of idols. But they also came to correct another error viz. the natural but absurd impulse to dedicate riches to temples and to decorate idols with gold and jewels. This added to the religious zeal of idol-breaking Mahomedans the further motive of greed for the gold and the jewels. Wherein is the merit of making idols of entire gold or of decorating them with priceless jewels? Does an idol of five cubits height of pure gold contribute more powerfully to the concentration of the mind on the deity than a stone idol? The old teachers of the Hindu religion prescribed small unworked stones in their natural shape as the proper *Pratikās* or idols of the four gods Śiva, Vishṇu, Gaṇeśa and the Sun while Vedic Rishis were content with concentrating their mind on the sun itself and the wind. But the human mind cannot but descend into the superstitious desire first of having finished idols and then of having idols of gold and silver or of decorating them with precious jewels. Śiva worship indeed in selecting the linga as an idol selected natural blocks of stone. And yet prosperous kings who were worshippers of these Swayambhū or natural lingas adorned them with crowns of gold covered with diamonds and rubies, thus tempting robbers and even avaricious kings or conquerors and even priests and thereby themselves causing the desecration of temples and the sacrilege of idols. Indian history is full of the mention of the building of new temples or of new rich endowments of temples by prosperous kings in every kingly line and specially holy places such as Mathura, Kot-Kangra, Somnath or Ujjain were overflowing with rich donations of hundreds of pious kings and thousands of rich merchants. All these riches might have been differently employed, the historian and politician will observe, in the maintenance of strong armies by kings and the amelioration of the people by rich merchants. Both were apparently neglected and temples were enriched and idols sumptuously decorated doubly accelerating the fall of the country by whetting the appetite, and strengthening the resources, of the foreign conqueror on the one side and weakening the power of resistance of our own kings and people on the other. But the Hindus did not learn these obvious lessons from these iconoclastic and plundering expeditions of Mahmud and they continued to build temples and accummulate riches in them. It may finally be observed that Hindus are not still alive to the two errors into which idol-worship when it degenerates into superstition descends viz. the belief of the miraculous powers of particular idols and the belief in the merit of donating riches to temples and idols leading to the demoralization of Mahants and pujaris.

It is curious to observe that human nature usually leads men to the same actions. Mahmud, the breaker of idols and the plunderer of temples expended his acquisitions on the Juma mosque of Ghazni and used the gold, the rubies and the diamonds obtained from Hindu idols, in decorating its walls, by the same impulse of the human mind as had actuated the Hindus. He thus created the temptation which had impelled him, for others coming after him and history records that this mosque was probably plundered of its rich decorations by the idolators of Chin. Changiskhan whose desecration of the Jami Masjid of Bokhara is described at length in Jahan Kusha of Juwaini (Elliot II p. 388) and whose doings at Bokhara were described by a fugitive in one pithy sentence in Persian "The Moguls came, dug, burnt, slaughtered, plundered and departed," came to Ghazni on his return from the pursuit of Jelalluddin in 618 H (1226 A. D.), ordered all the inhabitants to be brought out of the city and counted, and after selecting artizans from among them, directed all the rest to be slain. He also destroyed the city and Ogtai returned towards Herat after burying the slain" (Elliot II p. 390). Another extract states that Ogtai took Ghazni by assault after a siege of four months; it was burnt and destroyed to the very foundations, after about two hundred thousand persons had been inhumanly massacred (Elliot II p. 569).

CHAPTER XVII

DEATH OF MAHMUD AND HIS CHARACTER

After the crowning exploit of his career viz. the plundering and destroying of Somnath, Mahmud did not undertake any important expedition; perhaps there were no more worlds to conquer. The fame of his last exploit reached Baghdad "which listened to the edifying tale of the destruction of Somnath with wonder and the Khalifa conferred upon him one more title 'guardian of the fortune and faith of Mahomet' (Gibbon) i. e. Kahaf-ud-daulat-wal-Islam" (Elliot II p. 474). The Khalifa also conferred titles upon his sons Mas'aud, Muhammad, and Yusuf. Thus honoured by the head of the Mahomedan faith and in the fullness of glory and without any reverse, Mahmud died about three years after his greatest exploit i. e. in 420 H. (A. D. 1029) at the advanced age of 61, leaving behind him grown-up sons and experienced ministers and generals.

Historians have recorded highly appreciative notices of the character of Mahmud, beginning with Gibbon. "Turning from accounts of bloodshed of which unfortunately history is too full" observes Gibbon "it is a pleasant task to stop for a while to appreciate the good qualities of Mahmud, undoubtedly one of the greatest kings of the world". "His name is still venerated in the East. His subjects enjoyed the blessings of prosperity and peace; and examples are recorded of his justice and magnanimity. Avarice was the only defect that tarnished the illustrious character of Mahmud and never has that passion been more richly satisfied". "In his last moment he viewed with tears in his eyes his whole wealth displayed before him, so laboriously won, so dangerously held, so inevitably lost", and he reviewed his army "which consisted of one hundred thousand foot, fifty-five thousand horse and thirteen hundred war elephants".

Mahmud's greatness as a general and commander has been acknowledged by all. Lane-Poole describes him as "a great soldier and a man of infinite courage and indefatigable energy of mind and body." Lane-Poole also extols his good government and justice and quotes the opinion of the great vazier of Seljuk that "Mahmud was a just sovereign, a lover of learning, of generous nature and of pure faith" (p. 35). That he was a patron of learned men is proved by the fact that great luminaries like Al-Beruni the astronomer, Al-Faribi the philosopher, Al-Utbi the chronicler, Al-Baihaki the gosipper, (Arabic writers) and Ansuri, Farukhi and Asjudi (Persian poets) and above all Firdusi the Homer of Persian literature resided at his court and obtained support from him. While thus duly appreciating the greatness of Mahmud, Lane-Poole thinks that "Mahmud was not a statesman; no new institutions or methods of government were initiated by him, and he did not attempt to organise and consolidate what he had acquired; for as soon as he passed, his ill-knitted dominions fell asunder."

Before we proceed to discuss the adverse remarks of Gibbon and Lane-Poole, we will add our meed of praise of Mahmud as a great soldier, a consummate commander and a just ruler and administrator. We indeed think that Mahmud was one of those great men whom nature produces at intervals, men of exceptional qualities and unparalleled capacities, men who like Akbar or Shivaji, Napoleon or Peter the Great create new epochs in the history of the world and change the destinies of nations. As a man Mahmud was a person of strict discipline and stern conduct. In all his expeditions we do not read, along with the plunder of towns and temples and even slaughter and enslavement of fighters, the slaying or ravishing of women. And he loved justice and hated oppression so thoroughly that he was ready to destroy his own son if caught in the act of adultery. He was a good ruler and administrator and laboured to promote the well-being of his people in every way, protected commerce by the suppression of robbery and kept the communications between distant provinces free of danger so that "caravans passed freely between Khorasan and Lahore" (Utbi). He appointed good governors to the provinces and exercised strict supervision over them so that they did not oppress the people. Utbi describes in detail how his brother Nasir, appointed governor of Khorasan in Nishapur, was also known for his excellent administration and "was so kind that he never uttered a harsh word or offered wrong or violence to any one" (Utbi p. 486). Utbi is not a flatterer when he praises Mahmud as "the glorious lord of the poor, who displayed the face of level equity between the widow and the wealthy so that the door of boasting and oppression was closed" "And he charged an examiner of weights and measures to go among the market people and guard the standard of weights and measures. He made each street a clear road for asses, camels, and stalls. Formerly the streets of the bazars were not covered and the market people were vexed by dust and rain and he ordered the roofs of the bazars to be connected and in two months the city was entirely covered with roofs, with light-affording devices interwoven, so that all may be gladdened by the penetrating of the rays of the sun" (p. 486). "He expended (yearly) nearly one hundred thousand dinars in promoting justice and gladness for the people and in honourable and pious liberalities" (ditto). This amply shows that Mahmud was fully alive to the duty of a sovereign to secure the happiness and promote the welfare of the common people in the cities and the provinces of his territory.

Mahmud was a zealous Mahomedan and had implicit faith in his own religion. He always prayed before he began his battles and often in the hour of trial he would place reliance on God's promise in the Koran to aid and give victory to the faithful. In this respect as in many others, he resembled Shivaji who also had firm faith in his own religion and his own mission and often in his hour of trial he too would appeal to his favourite deity for help and guidance. Such appeals were probably made from conviction, though in both cases they might have been made for the purpose of raising the spirits, and inspiring confidence into the hearts, of his followers. Mahmud's taking augury from the Koran at critical moments was like Shivaji's praying to Bhavānī and in a trance giving utterance to her words of encouragement and guidance. In both cases we believe these acts were not pretences but arose from an intense religious turn of mind and implicit faith in God.

It may also be added that Mahmud did not revel in cruelty as some conquerors did in history. He did not perpetrate those inhuman massacres of innocent and helpless human beings which Changis and Timur two and three centuries after him or even some Mahomedan kings of the Deccan later still, perpetrated in Asia and India. In inflicting punishment of death on heretics again, Mahmud always acted not on mere suspicion but after due examination and ascertainment of views of the learned orthodox Kadis. The descriptions of such religious assemblies or synods presided over by Mahmud himself, given by Utbi are interesting (p. 481) though they were in the nature of inquisition. And Mahmud's presence and power exercised a temperate influence on their proceedings. Even in his religious bigotry, therefore, we think that Mahmud was not inhuman or tyrannical.

NOTE:—TAHAKAT-I-NASIRI ON MAHMUD.

'This monarch by his manliness, his bravery and intrepidity, his wisdom and foresight, his prudent counsels and wise measures considerably extended the Mahomedan conquests in the east and greatly extended the dominion of Islam in that quarter. The whole of Khorasan and Khwarism·Tabaristan, Irak, the territory of Nimroj and Fars, the mountain district of Ghor, Tukharistan came under the control of his officers. The Maliks of Turkestan acknowledged his superiority. He threw a brigde over the Jihun (Oxus) and marched into Turan and the Khakans of Turkestan came and tendered him their allegiance. At their request the son of Seljuk was permitted to cross over the Jihun with all his kindred and dependents into Khorasan. The most sagacious men of the time considered this permission a grave error as they perceived the danger to his sons and descendants (p. 86 Raverty's tras.)

Turning now to the consideration of the blemishes in Mahmud's character, Mahmud's avarice, we think, has been greatly exaggerated. The very fact that he amassed riches as no man in history did, impels people to believe that he was avaricious. The story that he wept in the moment of death at the sight of those incalculable treasures he was going to part with, is probably an invention and a calumny. Mahmud was too religiously minded to weep at the inevitable lot of mankind, especially when we remember that he left behind him sons to whom man in his frailty is always willing and glad to resign his own acquisitions. He was no doubt not a spendthrift as princes who inherit vast riches usually are. But there is not the least doubt that he was generous as even the Vizier of Seljuk observed, a testimony more reliable than that of later writers. He spent every year vast sums on the encouragement of letters and had founded a well endowed college with salaried professors where students were fed at state expense near the Jami Masjid he had built, as already stated (Utbi p. 466). The story told about Firdusi that he was *promised* one thousand *gold* dirhams for every one thousand verses and offered *silver* dirhams when the work (Shahnāma) was completed with 60000 verses, has probably confirmed, if it has not actually originated this imputation of avarice to Mahmud. This story is also, we think, a later invention as "much of the traditional life of Firdusi is rejected by modern scholars". (Encyclopaedia Britannica). Indeed the current story would, in our view, rather prove the avarice and anger of Firdusi than the avarice and anger of Mahmud. In any case that same story shows the great encouragement which Mahmud gave to literature and the preservation of the ancient history of Persia. The fact that Firdusi, though a Shia and perhaps a heretic, was entrusted with this work of immortalising the history of *fire-worshipping* Persian kings brings out Mahmud's unalloyed love of letters. " Mahmud himself a Sunni and a fanatical Moslem still extended patronage to Persian literature and learning and developed it even at the expense of Arabic institutions ". (ditto). In this love of learning and knowledge for their own sake, Mahmud may be said to have even surpassed Akbar who encouraged the study of Sanskrit; for Akbar was not a rigid Mahomedan. Mahmud already had directed the completion of Persian legendary history commenced by the Samanides themselves but finally entrusted the work to Firdusi, a native of Tus in Khorasan the home of Persian poets, seeing that he was best fitted for it by his wonderful poetical talents and his intimate knowledge of the folklore of the ancient Persians. And Mahmud's patronage of Al-Beruni shows that he did not object even to the study of Sanskrit literature, philosophy and science. At any rate the galaxy of learned men, poets, and philosophers of unique ability, like Firdusi and Al-Beruni which illumined the court of Mahmud should make him as renowned as Akbar of modern and Vikramāditya of ancient fame. For these reasons we are disposed to attach not much value to the general imputation of avarice to Mahmud.

Nor do we think that Lane-Poole's remark that Mahmud was not a statesman can be justified. The reason why his empire fell as soon as he passed away was entirely different. In the first place we do not know for certain that Mahmud did not initiate any new methods of government or that he made no attempt to organise and consolidate his acquisitions. There are no records either to prove or disprove this statement. We have no author like Abul Fazal who wrote the Ain-i-Akbari and gave us full details about Akbar's administration, to tell us how Mahmud administered his empire. But that it was a well-organised and well conducted government we cannot doubt. We are told by Utbi that full records were kept at Ghazni even of his expeditions and that Mahmud himself, like Babar, wrote memoirs in the midst of his wars and sent them home. An extract is given by Utbi from his memoir written from Mathura in the very bustle and turmoil of fighting and plundering, admiring the beauties of the temples of Mathura. There were registers of the provinces and of their revenues and expenditures and provincial governors were strictly supervised by the minister who regularly attended the Diwan or office. The working of an ordered administration clearly appears from the gossipping tales of Baihaki also. Although, therefore, we do not know the exact nature of the system of Mahmud's administration, there is no doubt that it was a well-ordered system. Whether it was new or whether it was copied from the system of administration of the Samanide empire of which Ghazni was originally a subordinate member, we do not know. But even if Mahmud followed carefully and strictly an old system it would itself prove his statesmanship. Even Shivaji kept on, to a large extent, the old system of administration at Bijapur, while introducing many changes which were necessary for his Swaraj and the new spirit of a Hindu king. Akbar's administrative system was no doubt new and original but he had to rule an extensive empire inhabited by aliens in race and religion and comprising provinces differing in every detail such as land, climate, and people.

How Mahmud organised his army we have also no information as we have as to how Akbar or Shivaji organised their armies. But Mahmud's organisation must have been sound since we know that he had a perfect striking machine which was successful everywhere and he made marches to such distant lands as Kanauj or Somnath over broad rivers, high mountains and long deserts. The institution of his bodyguard was peculiar to himself and this bodyguard of 5000 men, the pick and flowers of the Turkish soldiers, was always used by Mahmud with effect at the opportune moment in the fight.

We have, therefore, no materials to say that Mahmud did not introduce or initiate new institutions of government or did not attempt the organisation of his provinces. On the contrary, we have every reason to believe that Mahmud's civil and military administration was well-ordered and strong. The reason why his empire fell as soon as he passed away was, according to our view, the fact that Mahmud's successors were incapable both as soldiers and administrators. This is the principal defect of all despotic system of government. It is only rarely that we meet with a line of successive kings possessing vigour of body and mind like the Mogul line wherein from Babar to Aurangzeb we have six successive emperors of remarkable ability and even power. Shivaji like Mahmud again was unfortunate in his successors and if the Maratha kingdom prospered in the eighteenth century, it was due to the vigour of the Peshwas whose four generations were men of great power as statesmen and generals. Even the British empire was and is strong not because of its good system of administration but because of its peculiar home constitution. The government in England is not despotic and is a government consisting of King, Lords and Commons which makes it impossible for voluptuous or despotic kings to come to the throne or incapable or ambitious governors or generals to come to India and its provinces. Laws may be imperfect or even bad. It is the strict observance of laws, good or bad as they may be, which ensures strength and prosperity to a kingdom. The system of government in England ensures the observance of laws and therefore the continuous succession of efficient administrators and commanders. Under despotic government, kings who enjoy absolute power by mere birth and not by fitness often turn out voluptuaries and becoming incapable are unable to restrain the ambition of generals of armies or governors of provinces and thus provinces fall away and even the ruling dynasty is eventually destroyed. Then again under a limited monarchy and under republics the people develop a feeling of nationality which further guarantees the strength of the kingdom or the empire. For even if there appear ambitious governors or generals now and then, a strong national sentiment prevents soldiers or peoples from assisting rebels and traitors, thus making them powerless to do mischief. In fine, it is not true that the empire of Mahmud fell to pieces after him because of its imperfect system of administration, but it fell because of the despotic nature of its government which could not secure a continuity of capable rulers and of able and loyal governors; and because of the absence of the feeling of nationality in the people making it impossible for traitorous governors to assume independence.

To sum up, we think that Gibbon is right when he says that Mahmud was one of the greatest kings of the world. He was an interpid soldier and a consummate commander, a lover of justice and a patron of learned men, a sovereign who laboured for the peace and prosperity of his people and strove to extend education and commerce. As a man, Mahmud was a person of strict discipline and was not by nature cruel or avaricious; but was temperate and generous. He was also highly religious and of pure rigid faith. The great and perhaps solitary blemish in his character was, according to our view, his bigotted intolerance. By this defect he was not only led to plunder temples and rifle idols but even to destroy them and forcibly convert people in the conquered territories. Firm faith in, and zeal for, one's own religion is not inconsistent with respect for the religious beliefs and sacred edifices of other peoples. For this reason Mahmud, in our view, ranks lower than Akbar in the list of great kings and can certainly not compare with Shivaji who was as zealous as Mahmud in his own faith yet was telerant enough to spare the sacred structures of Islam and to honour its holy men. This spot on Mahmud's character is indeed so great, that it does not disappear in the multitude of his good qualities like the spot on the moon in her rays (Kalidāsa), but like poverty mars his many merits (unnamed poet). The plundering of towns and temples may be excusable from the stand-point of international ethics, and may be forgotten but the forcible conversion of people can not be justified or excused from the higher view-point of humanity and can never be forgotten. The reasonable interpretation of the Koran does not countenance the forcible conversion of people, as even the learned in the Koran have lately declared. And Abu Bakr had declared that conquered people should be permitted to retain their religion on payment of a capital tax. Yet religious fanaticism impelled Mahmud not only to destroy temples and idols, but to forcibly convert hundreds and thousands of Hindus in the conquered territories. It can not be denied that man has the sacred and inviolable right to worship God in the manner he chooses and from this higher stand-point of humanity one can not too strongly condemn the *forcible* conversion of conquered people. In the present progress of civilization, one may even condemn peaceful but active propaganda for the spread of religion and time will soon arrive when nations will realise the utility and even the necessity of stopping all missionary or other efforts for the conversion of people by force, fraud or favour. But force especially, at all times, must be condemned as infringing the most precious right of man and we are constrained to look upon the bigotted intolerance of Mahmud which led him to forcibly convert thousands of Hindus as a great blemish on the otherwise high character of this great Mahomeden king.

NOTE:—WAS MAHMUD OR SHIVAJI A BANDIT?

The greatest condemnation of Mahmud is contained in the Oxford History of India by Sir Vincent Smith which states (p. 194) "So far as India was concerned, Mahmnd was simply a bandit, operating on a large scale. He did not attempt to effect any permanent conquest except in the Panjab and his raids had no lasting results beyond the destruction of property and priceless monuments." Mahmud's plundering-expeditions into India were so many and so successful like those of Shivaji, that one's attention is fixed on these plunders and one is led to look at Mahmud as at Shivaji as a great plunderer, a successful bandit. Many historians have written in the same strain and said in derogation of him that he merely plundered and did not annex, suggesting therein that annexation is less heinous than plundering. But is it really so? Is it not practically plundering other people of their immovable property, especially of their land which is the most valuable of all properties? And even if annexation mean stable government, it does always mean better government. Indeed Mahomedan government was not and could not have been better government than Hindu government. For that matter any foreign government is worse than native government, for it always leads to heavy taxation which is equivalent to continuous, systematic and legalised plundering of the people. That Mahmud did not annex but merely plundered Indian territories would be rather praiseworthy than otherwise. As a matter of fact, however, this statement itself is not correct as we proceed to show.

Let us see how like a consummate diplomat or statesman, Mahmud slowly extended his empire from Ghazni by gradual *annexations*, as the British did from their centres in Bombay, Madras, and Calcutta. Mahmud was originally king of Zabulistan or the territory round Ghazni which again formerly belonged to the Rajputs and he was also governor of Khorasan on behalf of the Samani emperors. When the Samani empire fell owing to the attacks of the Turkish hordes beyond the Oxus, he annexed Khorasan and allowed Ilek-khan, the Turk, to annex the northern portion of the Sāmāni kingdom beyond the Oxus, or Mawarannahar. Thus these two powerful kings accommodated each other. From Zabulistan, Mahmud extended his dominion eastward and from Khorasan westward by the gradual absorption of the adjoining kingdoms. Even this was not done all at once. Mahmud or his father first acquired Kabulistan, then he annexed the lower part of the present N. W. Frontier Province viz. Bannu and the adjoining territory and subsequently the northern portion viz. Peshawar and Wahind. These three provinces belonged, as we have seen, to Jaipal, the Brahmin Shahi king of Kabul who was also the ruler of the whole of the Panjab. We see how adroitly Mahmud deprived Jaipal of his provinces one by one without driving him to sudden despair like the British who from Bombay gradually acquired one district after another of the Brahmin ruler of the Deccan. Ānandpāla, like Bajirao, was for a time left in the possession of the Panjab, after the loss of his provinces to the west of the Indus, subject to a tribute. But the final collision came as it was bound to come and both Ānandapāla and Bajirao lost their kingdoms which were finally annexed by the conquering power. When Sir Vincent Smith makes an exception of the Panjab, the largest part of Mahmud's dominions in the east, he practically admits that Mahmud as a result of his various raids up to the twelfth expedition did annex vast territories and effected permanent occupation. Nay more, Mahmud attempted to consolidate his dominions by the forcible conversion to Islam of the people of the annexed provinces. He probably realised the necessity of unity of religious belief in the people as an important factor in the consolidation of kingdoms, and systematically carried out the forcible conversion of the people, for Example of Ghor on the west and Swat and Bajaur in the north-eastern corner of Afganistan on the west side of the Indus. On the east side, that is in the Panjab, it appears that the rigour of the policy of conversion was not continued though even in the Panjab he converted forcibly many peoples especially in the western part contiguous to the river Indus. Mahmud's statesmanship as a Mahomedan king in forcibly converting the people of the annexed territories immediately in the vicinity of his kingdom cannot be denied and Mahmud thus not only annexed but consolidated territories.

But it may be objected that Mahmud's later expeditions to Mathura and Kanauj and to Somnath were mere plundering expeditions undertaken with no desire of annexation or permanent occupation. Even this is not correct. Distant provinces like Antarbed or Oudh or Gujarat could not be at once occupied. It was necessary to gradually absorb them by the usual method of absorption viz. first exaction of tribute and then final overthrow, when the intervening territory was fully absorbed. Thus the British first absorbed Bengal, then Bihar, then Oudh, and then the Panjab. It must be remembered that when Rājyapāla first merely escaped, Mahmud reinvaded Oudh, conquered Bāri and finally subjected him to a tribute. It appears that this tribute was long paid by the Kanauj kingdom to Ghazni, for we have epigraphic evidence which shows that the charge of this tribute was distributed over the whole kingdom of Kanauj as a permanent tax in excess of the usual land tax. It is strange that scholars have not understood the real nature of the tax called "Turushkadanda" mentioned in the grants of this period coming from the territory of Kanauj only. The Jhusi grant of Trilochanapāla dated 1026 A. D. does not mention this Turushkadanda; but all later grants, even those of the Gāhadavālas, mention it, who though independent of Ghazni continued to exact this tax, as despotic kings rarely give up an impost which has become usual and of long standing, though the necessity of it no longer exists. In this Turushkadanda, we are reminded of the *chauth* of the Marathas, for the realisation of which they regularly maintained officers in the provinces of the Mogul empire. It is likely that Turkish soldiers and officers also remained in the country of Kanauj to collect this tribute and it is these Turks whom Bhoja or Karṇa drove away as we shall relate in their history. We have actually ascertained the fact that Turushkadanda is mentioned only in grants found in the Kanauj kingdom and not in any grants found in the Chedi or Bengal territory and certainly not in Paramāra or Solankhi territory viz. Malwa and Gujarat. We are, therefore, assured that Mahmud did subject Kanauj to a permanent tribute * which would naturally have led, in future years, to the annexation of that kingdom had the succeeding kings at Ghazni possessed his vigour and continued his policy in the manner in which British policy consistently worked throughout the nineteenth century. With regard to the raid on Somnath, even therein Mahmud had apparently an intention of permanent occupation in the distant future. Such raids, even if for plunder only, undermine the power of the plundered kingdom and make way for future annexation. We, therefore, think that it is unhistorical to look upon Mahmud as a mere plunderer without any design of permanent occupation. It is not only against human nature, but also against history, when we see that he annexed and permanently occupied the whole of the extensive territory of the Shahis from Kabul to Lahore in the east and extensive provinces of the Samanis in the west.

But granting that Mahmud led merely plundering expeditions into India without any intention of permanent conquest, would it be proper to describe him as a bandit as many historians have done? Such wrong descriptions have actually led to wrong theories and to baneful results as is well-known and historians should use such terms with care and depict persons in their proper light. Two persons in history have suffered much in this way. Mahmud and Shivaji have usually been called bandits and plunderers, in consequence of, the large number of their plundering expeditions and of their uniform success resulting in fabulous accumulation of riches. But we forget that correctly speaking neither Mahmud nor Shivaji can be called a bandit or a robber and if we do use the terms, we do so without attributing to them the moral degradation connoted by them. It must always be remembered that murder or dacoity is not only legally but morally reprehensible. The story of Alexander and the robber may be a very witty one but it inculcates a wrong theory. A robber when he robs a fellow citizen acts against the tacit agreement which he has entered into in acknowledging allegiance to a government that he would not deprive a fellow citizen of his property except in due course of law or of his life except in self-defence exercised within legal limits. The relations of nations or peoples are subject to no such tacit agreement. Indeed international law or custom has always recognized, from the most ancient times down to the present, the right of the stronger nation to attack the weaker and deprive it even of its independence. The law of the brute, to speak plainly, or of the fish as it is actually called in an inscription of Pāla kings of Bengal, has always been followed by nations. The Digvijayas in ancient Indian history can only be justified on this admitted right of the strong to humble the weak. There are no doubt instances in history, of noble sovereigns who refused to benefit by this law and who rose superior to the temptations of power, a Maria Theressa who refused to attack Poland because it was weak or an Aśoka who

* Turushkadanda is explained by some as a tax on Turkish settlers but it was not a tax on Turks but on all cultivators in the village, as appears clear from the grants of Inam villages of the time in Kanauj territory.

after slaughtering a lakh of people in conquering Kalinga was so seized by the feeling of remorse that he gave up war for all time to come. But these rare instances only prove the rule. It is only after the last European War that nations have become alive to the necessity and the propriety of conceding the right of the weak to live undisturbed. But throughout past history, we see that nations and kings have generally followed the law of brute force by which the strong can at any time and for any reason pounce upon the weak and deprive him of his land, property and even independence. While, therefore, the robber is legally or morally reprehensible, Alexander and many of his compeer conquerors cannot be considered morally depraved, when they deprived other nations of their liberty or property. And when Shivaji or Mahmud are described in historical writings as bandits or plunderers, it must always be understood that these terms do not convey the ordinary sense of condemnation connoted by them.

It must further be remembered that Shivaji never committed murder,* even in his high mission of establishing Swaraj. And he plundered rich cities in the Mogul or Bijapur territory only when he was at war with them, and only after setting himself up as a *de facto* independent sovereign. The right of belligerents to plunder the enemy has been recognised even in the west. Indeed plundering weakens the weaker nation's power of defence and increases the stronger's power of offence. England herself has plundered enemies many a time. Drake and Hawkins plundered the ships of Spain carrying gold from America to Spain when England was at war with the latter country. Drake even plundered the cities of Chili and Peru without the excuse of war and he has not been described by English historians as a bandit. The British have plundered the French at Pondichery in Indian history and have massacred and plundered the townspeople of Jhansi when that city fought and stood a siege in the mutiny of 1857. And yet these acts cannot, legally and even morally, be described or denounced as murders or dacoities. Mahmud or Shivaji never plundered their own subjects, and they both punished robbers in their territories severely. Shivaji so far recognised his duty as a king that he recompensed his subjects whenever his own soldiers or even the soldiers of an enemy plundered them.

It is, in fine, wrong both historically and philosophically to describe Mahmud or Shivaji as a bandit in the ordinary sense of the term. Their acts were committed as sovereigns and when there was an actual state of war and they, therefore, do not come under the code of ordinary law or morality. The law of nations as understood hitherto in the east and even in the west has always conceded the right of the strong to attack the weak

---

* The true account of Afzalkhan's death shows that Shivaji killed him in selfdefence. Shivaji did not instigate the murder of Chandrarao More as he is believed by many including Jadunath Sarkar to have done. A historical document recently found shows that the Chandrarao More supposed to have been murdered was an adopted minor at that time and he escaped to Rairi when Jawali was attacked. For further details we may refer the curious reader to our Marathi paper on Chandrarao More and Shivaji.

for any ostensible reason and the victor has always exercised the right to plunder the vanquished. The destruction of Hindu temples and idols may no doubt be condemned from the higher stand-point of humanity as acts of bigotted intolerance. But the plundering of cities and temples being an act of war committed by one sovereign against another cannot be described or denounced as dacoity even though it led to 'the destruction of priceless monuments' and we are constrained to record our view that even Mahmud, much more Shivaji cannot be properly described as a bandit.

CHAPTER XVIII

DOWNFALL OF THE PANJAB AND KABUL —APPARENT CAUSES

Sind fell before the Arabs under Muhammad Kasim in 712; the Panjab fell before the Turks under Mahmud in 1009, and Northern India fell before the Afghans under Ghori from 1193 to 1200 A. D. The causes of the downfall in each of these three cases were not the same; were in fact extremely different. We have discussed the causes of the downfall of Sind in Volume I and shown that Sind fell chiefly owing to the treachery of some feudatories of Chach and the pusillanimity of the Buddhists. Sind was then ruled by a Brahmin and Panjab also was ruled by a Brahmin king; but both Dāhar and Ānandapāla fought with the bravery of Rajputs. These ruling Brahmin dynasties were practically Kshatriyas. And from the most ancient times when Drona fought in the Mahābhārata war down to the time of the Peshwas, Brahmin kings and chiefs fought as bravely as the Kshatriyas. Indeed Brahmin soldiers also such as the Pandes of Northern India in the days of the mutiny fought as valiantly as other soldiers in the British army. Curiously enough the same accident befell Dāhar as befell Ānandapāla in their final hard contested battles and the elephant of Dāhar left the battle-field as that of the latter did and would not stop until it had thrown itself into a lake and allayed its fever. But accidents befall every man in his life and are not the real causes of downfalls; as stated before fate is an over-riding and common factor in all the concerns of this world and in a historical survey of causes it may be excluded from consideration. Though these two facts in the case of Sind and the Panjab are almost identical yet the real causes of the fall of the Panjab are different from the causes of the fall of Sind. In the case of the former we read of treachery or defection of no Indian king or feudatory. Perhaps the Mahomedan historian Utbi, the Secretary of Mahmud, who must have known all secrets omitted purposely the mention of such cases. But as in even Mahomedan histories of Sind we have such a mention, we may safely say that in the case of the Panjab treachery was not one of the causes of its downfall. Nor was there any great difference of religion in the Panjab causing pusillanimity of the people. As explained in the last chapter of Volume II, India at this time was under one and the same religion viz. Hinduism, without the feuds between 'Vaishnavism' and 'Śaivism' which later distracted that religion. As stated therein, India at this time was in the happiest condition of having one religion, Buddhism being dead and Mahomedanism being yet far off. India was also blessed in other respects in the tenth century A. D. and was at the height of its strength and prosperity from which as from a summit there was found to be a descent by the laws of nature. The historian has to find how this descent came on.

Various causes are assigned by historians or are usually imagined by people in this connection; but most of these in our view were non-existent or are not the real causes. Thus Lane-Poole remarks "To the contrast of union and disunion, north and south, race and climate was added the zeal of the Moslem and the greed of the robber". Sachau thinks that the princes of Northern India were too narrowminded to see the danger and to unite (preface to Al-Beruni). Sardesai states that Mahmud knew that there were small kingdoms in India which were constantly fighting with one another and that he had a large army which he had to feed and employ somehow. How these various views are, in our opinion, not well-founded, we proceed to discuss at length.

That the Hindu kingdoms in India were not alive to the danger and did not unite is not a fact, as we actually see in the history recorded by Mahomedans themselves. A new and dangerous religion had come to the frontiers of India long ago viz. in Sind in 712 and the Hindus then, under the first Rajput warriors of Mewad and Sambhar, as shown in Vol. II pp. 5 and 91, offered a most stubborn resistance to the Arabs and stayed their onward march for ever. Three hundered years later came the Turks fired with the fanaticism of new proselytes and establishing themselves at Ghazni began to harass the Hindus and destroy their temples. Nay the Hindus had an experience of what was coming on, 60 years before, when Zabulistan was first taken by Yakub-i-Lais and his governor destroyed a famous Hindu temple at Sakhāwand and Rai Kamlu of Kabul was staggered at the sacrilege (E. II p. 172). The Hindu kings were, therefore, alive to the danger from long experience and did thrice combine, brought large armies larger than those which Mahmud could oppose to them, yet failed. The idea, therefore, that the Hindu kings were oblivious of the peril and did not unite is entirely against the facts.

Nor was there any real need for this union. The idea that Hindu kingdoms of this time were small is not correct. The Shahi kingdom of Kabul and the Panjab was far more extensive than the small kingdom of Ghazni which was ruled by Sabuktagin or in his early days by Mahmud himself. That kingdom should alone have been able to destroy Ghazni if it had been well prepared. The kingdom of Kanauj was more extensive and more powerful still. Indeed that kingdom, as Arab travellers relate, kept four armies constantly in the field which were so powerful that they could have taken even Multan and driven the Arabs out of Sind. The kingdom of the Chandel king Dhanga was not insignificant and though Rājyapāla of Kanauj had fallen from the example of his great ancestor Bhoja, Dhanga the king of Kalanjar and Gwalior was powerful enough to be able himself alone to destroy Mahmud. It is generally not known that Mahmud's kingdom at this time was small and his army also was comparatively inconsiderable. It was also not drawn from one nation, the soldiers being Turks, Afghans, Kurds and Persians who were often at war with one another. Mahmud indeed did not come with an overpowering force of barbarians like Zangis or Timur who with Mogul horsemen of one race numbering seven or four lakhs swept like tornadoes over Asia from the Caspian to the Indus and wrought destruction in five years which five hundred years were unable to repair (Gibbon). Mahmud's army was undoubtedly small compared with the army of Jaipal, as even Mahomedan historians relate, in the first great battle and even in the second with Ānadapāla. Nor was it more united than the Hindu army so as to oppose union to disunion. The contrast of north and south also did not exist for Ghazni was opposed to Kabul; and the soldiers of Jaipal of Kabul were unquestionably Afghans yet unconverted and unconverted Afghans could not have been less valiant than Moslem Afghans. Even a difference of race between Turk and Aryan did not, in our view, make any difference in the fighting qualities of the two armies. It is indeed a common fallacy by which barbarians from the north, Turks and Afghans, are believed to be more hardy and valiant than the Aryans of the Panjab and Rajputana. This difference of race may have been one of the causes of the defeat of the Marathas at the battle of Panipat at the hands of the Afghans of Abdali, for as a matter of fact the inferiority of the Maratha compared with the Afghan in physique, ferocity and valour may be admitted. But no such difference existed or exists between the Turks and Afghans beyond the Indus and the Aryans of the Panjab and Rajputana so far as history or even present facts tell us. The Jats and Rajputs of the Panjab, whether Sikh, Mahomedan or Hindu are even now among the finest soldiers not only in India but in the whole world; and they were all Hindus in the days of Mahmud. Even now the Panjab is the chief recruiting ground for British Indian Army. The Amritsar Gazetteer states (p. 33) that the Sikh Jats of the Manjha territory can show men who in any country in the world could be deemed fine specimens of the human race. And as for the Rajputs of Rajputana, they have signalised themselves against Turks and Afghans and Moguls and Persians in many battles. The Rathods of Jaswantsing had even held Afghanistan under their sway for several years, in the days of Aurangjeb. We may believe, therefore, that so far as physical strength and valour were concerned the soldiers of Jaipal or Ānandapāla were not at all inferior to the Turks and Afghans of Mahmud.

Sir Vincent Smith, without actually discussing the causes of the fall of the Panjab, suggests them in the remark 'a new power, novel in religion, in social customs, ideas and methods of warfare appeared on the scene.' Superiority of arms and of discipline is one of the most potent causes of the prevalence of one nation over another, and it may be mentioned here that India was bound to be conquered by the British owing to their superiority in arms and discipline, their artillery and their battalions. But this factor did not exist in favour of the Mahomedans at this time. Firishta is guilty of anachronism when he mentions 'tops' (cannon) as being used by Mahmud, in the same way as he mentions Delhi and Ajmer as opposing Mahmud, since cannon had no existence in the days of Mahmud as much as Delhi or Ajmer. From the article "Gunpowder" in the Encyclopædia Britannica, the following facts appear: 1. Gunpowder is believed to have been invented either by a German about 1345 or by Roger Bacon about 1225 A. D. 2. Gunpowder was not known to the ancient Greeks, Hindus or Arabs. They no doubt knew some incendiary process which they used in war but they did not know explosives and had neither guns nor cannon. 3. History does not record the use of firearms in India except at the battle of Panipat by Babar. We are thus assured that Mahmud had no firearms and relied on the same weapons of war, swords, scimitars and lances, as the Hindus; and Mahomedan poet historians expatiate on the merits of these only (Elliot

Vol. II) as may be seen in Utbi or Baihaki. Indeed if there was superiority in weapons it was on the side of the Hindus. They knew, it is clear, how to make good steel. The iron pillar at Delhi is a wonder even to the moderns (who are surprised at its manufacture in a way that it does not rust); and Indian swords were prized by the soldiers of Mahmud. Utbi poetically makes the sword of a Turkish soldier exclaim "I am a Hindu of a good family" (p. 216) thereby referring to the better steel of that weapon made in India, and we find that in the plunder of battle-fields swords and arms of the slain Hindu soldiers were objects of special attention.* We do not think there was any superiority of discipline on the side of the Mahomedans or that the Mahomedan army had been disciplined in the modern sense. Their horses might have been better as Afghanistan and Persia produce better horses as even Rājaśekhara notes. But Rajputana horses were not bad and imported Arabian and Persian horses could be had in plenty. In fact the Pratihāra emperors of Kanauj, coming from Rajputana as they did, were well-known for their cavalry and they were for that reason called Hayapatis. And the Hindus had one powerful arm in addition viz. the elephant which the Mahomedans did not possess. Even the Turks subsequently coveted this arm and developed it; for we see Sabuktagin and Mahmud using elephants against the Turks of Kashgar and using them with effect (Utbi). It is curious to note that while the Hindus could not use the elephants against the Turks of Mahmud, Mahmud could use the same elephants against the Turks of Ilek-khan with great effect. This is sufficient to prove the great generalship of Mahmud and the incompetence of India's commanders. How Mahmud made the Hindu elephant arm ineffectual we are not told by Mahomedan writers though we are told by Greek historians how Alexander discomfited the same arm of Porus. It may be noted that even after Sabuktagin and Mahmud had begun to use elephants in their armies their drivers remained Hindus. In fact during a succeeding reign at Ghazni the Hindu drivers of elephants were remiss in their duty and were severly punished (Baihaki). Strangely enough at the present day this art is wholly lost by the Hindus and elephant-drivers are all Mahomedans now (E. II 143).

---

* Panjab produces iron at Kalabagh and Bhera and Nizamabad are well-known for the excellent swords which are manufactured there even now as may be known from specimens placed in the Lahore museum.

It is therefore, difficult to conceive how the method of warfare of the Turks was different from that of the Hindus unless we take into account the extreme cruelty with which the Turks treated the vanquished. It is undeniable that of all nations the Hindus in their history behaved with the greatest humanity towards their conquered foes. They never massacred even the fighting population as the Turks under Mahmud did. When we say that Mahmud was not cruel. we compare him with other Mahomedan conquerors, especially the Mogul Zangis or Timur. Compared with the conduct of Hindus when conquering, his method must indeed have struck terror into the hearts of the less cruel people of India. Fighting men were usually massacred and innocent people were enslaved and carried into captivity and towns and villages were often destroyed. Even in European history we find war conducted with far more cruelty both in ancient and modern times. Even the Greeks and the Romans were very cruel in the treatment of conquered foes and massacre and enslavement were the constant concomitants of conquest in war. In this sense Mahmud's method of warfare was novel; but this cannot be treated as one of the causes of the downfall of the Panjab. We are trying to find out why the Hindu armies were defeated; though no doubt the terrible consequences of one defeat might impair the morale of Hindu soldiers in subsequent encounters.

The political ideas of the Turks and the Hindus were almost exactly the same. Both had no idea of representative government, though the Hindus may have had them in pre-Gupta days of rights of people or of responsibilities of kings. They knew only one form of government viz. the despotic and had no idea of a nation in the modern sense. There was no feeling of nationality or of patriotism. The kings became kings by heirship or by the favour of God manifested by giving success in battle. Neither the Turks of Mahmud nor the Hindus of Jaipal fought as the Germans and the French fought in the last European War under the high impulse of nationality and patriotism. It cannot, therefore, be supposed that a feeling of strong nationality which always prompts stubborn fighting gave the Turks the success which they invariably achieved; for such feeling never existed among the Turks who only fought for Mahmud. They were fighting not for a nation but for a king. No doubt the zeal of Mahomadanism supplied the place of patriotism and the religious fervour of the newly converted Turks and Afghans was a great factor in the success of Mahmud. But this does not constitute a novelty of ideas nor would it have been a cause of the downfall of the Panjab had it been opposed by an equally strong religious zeal of the Hindus. Lastly we do not see any novelty in the social manners of the Turks that contributed to the downfall of the Hindus. Even in manners as in ideas the Turks were practically like the Hindus who opposed them. The Hindus of the Panjab and Kabul then were flesh-eaters and not vegetarians and even at this day Panjab is less vegetarian than the other provinces of India. The Hindus were not beaf-eaters no doubt, but that cannot, in our view, have contributed to any extent to the fall of Kabul and the Panjab.

CHAPTER XIX

DOWNFALL OF THE PANJAB-PROBABLE CAUSES

The causes of the downfall of nations, peoples, or kingdoms, have always been a subject of deep interest to historians both in ancient and modern times; and historians have formulated different theories in different cases which cannot have universal application. The fall of Greece before Rome, of Rome before the Goths and of Constantinople before the Turks present different aspects and must necessarily be assigned to different causes. Even in India, as said before, the causes of the fall of Sind in 712, of the Panjab in 1009, of Northern India in about 1200, and of Southern India about 1300 A. D., are different and Indian historians have the difficult task of explaining in each case the probable causes of the downfall of each. Yet the general observations of the great historian of the downfall of the Roman Empire have a perennial interest and supply maxims which are of universal application. Although the causes of the fall of the Roman Empire in the West are actually different from the causes which can properly be assigned for the fall of the Panjab, the observations of Gibbon well help us in our present inquiry to a great extent.

The natural impulse to " assign fortune of Rome as the cause of the misfortune of Greece" had to be first overcome in the manner in which Polybius a great historian of the Greeks did it by showing the deep foundations of the greatness of Rome. " The unique constitution of Rome which united freedom of popular assemblies with the wisdom of a senate and the executive powers of a regal magistrate, the oath of military service of ten years imposed on every citizen in the cause of the country which continually poured into the field young freemen and soldiers, the military system of Rome with its remarkable legion superior in active strength to the Macedonian phalanx, these institutions of peace and war explain according to Polybius the success of a people incapable of fear and impatient of repose. The ambitious design of conquering the world was attempted and achieved and the perpetual violation of justice was maintained by the political virtues of prudence and courage". But even this great world empire declined and fell. " It was the natural and inevitable effect of immoderate greatness. Prosperity ripened the principle of decay. The causes of destruction multiplied with the extent of conquest. The victorious legions in distant wars acquired the vices of mercenaries and first oppressed the republic and then violated the purple. The emperors were reduced to the expedient of corrupting the discipline which rendered the legions formidable alike to the enemy and the sovereign, the vigour of the military government was relaxed and the Roman world was overwhelmed by a deluge of barbarians ".

"The introduction or at least the abuse of Christianity had some influence on the fall of the Roman Empire. The clergy successfully preached the doctrines of patience and pusillanimity and the active virtues of society were discouraged; the last remnants of the military spirit were buried in the cloister; a large portion of public and private wealth was consecrated to the specious demands of charity and devotion; the soldiers' pay was lavished on the useless multitudes of both sexes who could only plead the merit of abstinence and chastity. The Church and even the State were distracted by religious factions, the attention of emperors was diverted from camps to synods. The Roman world was oppressed by a new species of tyranny and the persecuted sects became the secret enemies of the country." (Gibbon by Bury IV p. 172-5). This extract is rather long but these observations and some others in this chapter are of everlasting interest and validity; and although the causes of the fall of the Panjab with which we are immediately concerned are entirely different from the causes which led to the fall of the Western Roman Empire, they afford indications which are valuable not only in the inquiry before us but in the more important question of the causes of the fall of India in the days of Prithviraj with which we shall have to deal at the end of this volume.

If we take into view the condition of the Hindus of the Panjab and the Moslems of Ghazni and see how far the former were inferior or superior to the latter in those respects which contribute to the strength or weakness of kingdoms, we shall be able to arrive at a correct idea of the probable causes of the downfall of the Panjab. We have seen that the Turks were not more united than the Hindus; indeed disunion was as much a bane of the Turks as of the Hindus and Utbi, describing the disunion among the Turks beyond the Oxus, quotes the verses of the Koran "Their power is very great between them if they are united but their hearts are diverse. We have sent enmity between them and hatred for ever." The Turks were again as civilized or rather uncivilized as the Hindus using the same weapons, having no popular assemblies and no national spirit and without legions or phalanxes. The Hindu kingdom of the Panjab was not again so large, like the Roman Empire, as to fall by its own weight. The Turks did not attack India in overwhelming swarms like the Goths and the Vandals. Moreover the Turks were not more warlike or of stronger physique or more inured to toil and exertion than the Afghans of Kabul and the Rajputs of the Panjab who opposed them in the beginning. Indeed the Hindus of the Panjab were used as soldiers by Mahmud himself and his successors in their battles and in the battle fought by Mahmud against Ilek-khan king of the Turks beyond the Oxus Hindus fought bravely on the side of Mahmud. The Hindu kingdom of the Panjab was not further ill-governed and there were no traitors who assisted the Moslems. And finally Mahmud's kingdom of Ghazni in the beginning was small compared with the kingdom of Kabul and the Panjab ruled by Jaipal and his army must have been also comparatively smaller than that of the latter. There even do not appear to be any factions, religious or political, to distract the attention of Jaipal. These apparent causes of superiority in the one and decay in the other being absent may be kept out of mind and we will see in what respect the Turks were superior to the Hindus or the latter inferior to the former.

The foremost superiority of the Turks was in the personality of their general Mahmud. We do not generally realise the value and power of personalities. As stated before, nature produces from time to time men who by their mental and physical power change the destinies of kingdoms or the face of the human world. One Buddha or one Jesus was powerful enough to turn half the world towards peace, one Mahomet could turn the other half towards the principle of force in the propagation of truth. In the field of politics we see the immense influence of one Shivaji who secured independence to the Maratha people for two centuries and established their reputation for ever. It is our firm conviction that without the personal factor of Shivaji the Marathas could not have achieved what they achieved and it is our firm opinion that without Mahmud the Turks could not have overthrown the Hindus of the Panjab. The case of Mahmud is exactly similar to that of Shivaji. Endowed with indomitable courage and indefatigable energy they both formed great designs and had the necessary resourcefulness and resolution to put their conceptions into execution. Nobody at the time of Shahaji could have thought it possible to free Mahārāshtra from the yoke of Mahomedan rule by destroying the Bijapur power in its immediate vicinity and defeating the immense imperial Mogul armies of distant Delhi. And yet Shivaji formed that seemingly impossible plan and carried it out in his own life-time by his unique powers of organization and his immense moral force. Nobody similarly could then have thought that the small kingdom of Ghazni could destroy the powerful kingdom of Kabul in its vicinity or defeat the imperial armies of distant Kanauj. Yet Mahmud in his high ambition conceived that bold design and by his energies and personal influence put it into execution. Shivaji stands no doubt on a higher moral pedestal than Mahmud as he devoted his energies to the noble task of freeing his people from the thraldom of a foreign power and religion, while Mahmud conceived and carried out the project of enslaving other people, of conquering other kingdoms and imposing upon them a foreign religion. All the same, almost impossible purposes were formed by both and achieved by both by unique qualities. Both had in the beginning only a small army and a nucleus kingdom; but both increased them by their resourcefulness and their power of organization. Shivaji indeed had a very small army inherited from his father; yet he eventually organised a striking force that could defeat even the imperial Mogul armies and plunder rich Mogul cities. Mahmud did the same and created an army which at the close of his life amounted to a lakh of foot, half a lakh of horse and 1300 elephants as stated before. Mr. Sardesai thinks that Mahmud had already a large force which he had perforce to feed and employ in conquering India. But this does not seem to be true though probably he had at the beginning a larger force than Shivaji had. But even if he had a large force, if he had been incapable, what was there to prevent him from disbanding it gradually? And whence was the money to come, even if Turk or Afghan turbulent spirits were available in numbers? The plunder of Temples and idols came in later. And whence did Shivaji get his resources? Even the men whom he had at hand for turning into soldiers were peaceful Māvalas. The greatness of great men lies indeed in their power to find men and money and to train them and use them in the proper way. The greatness lies in the unshaking resolve and the burning desire. "Get up" says Vidulā, in the famous Mahābhārata episode, to her whining son defeated and dispossessed of his kingdom. "Get up with the firm resolve of fighting and getting your kingdom back and you will find the men and the money you want." The organizing power and the moral ascendancy of both Shivaji and Mahmud are apparent in their training up their people so as to fit them for tough fighting and make them ready to die for them and further in keeping the trenchant weapon they had forged under due control. For, as Gibbon has said, legions become dangerous not only to the enemy but also to their master. Where national feeling does not exist to restrain or defeat the ambition of traitorous governors and generals, they can only be kept in their proper sphere by the overpowering personality of the master. When the dominating personality is removed, the formidable army becomes the destroyer of its own master as we actually find happening later on in the case of the incapable successors of Mahmud himself. Many feudatories became independent and a king of Ghazni was seized and blinded by his own generals. The very formidable nature of the striking machine forged by Mahmud or Shivaji and the successful use of it by them for their own purposes, prove the immense power which they wielded over the hearts of their soldiers and captains.

Looking to the opponents of Mahmud, we do not find any men of great a capacities as a general or organiser. Jaipal no doubt acquitted himself honourably and valiantly in the task before him. But what was there to prevent him from organising a strong army when he became aware of the danger? Indeed what was there to prevent him from the beginning from maintaining a powerful army against all eventualities? It is the first duty of every king or state to maintain a strong army capable of defending the people against internal foes or external enemies. And Jaipal had ample materials at hand in men and money. Indeed Harsha who began with a moderately sized kingdom and who eventually conquered the whole of Northern India maintained an army, only one arm of which consisted of 60000 elephants. And he maintained this vast army without plundering any towns or temples. And yet he had immense riches to bestow in charity on Brahmins and Śramaṇas at his five-yearly almsgiving festivals at Prayāga. The great defect of the Hindu kings opposed to Mahmud both in Kabul and Kanauj was that they appear to have neglected their armies unlike their predecessors Bhima and Bhoja. The soldiers' pay, in the immortal words of Gibbon, was perhaps lavished on the endowment or temples and the decoration of idols; for we read of no large standing armies at both places. The Arab travellers of the tenth century A. D. recorded that India was famous for its armies. That fame was belied by the Indian kingdoms in the eleventh century. The kingdom of Fabul and the Panjab was extensive enough to support a strong army and Jaipal need not have sought the aid of neighbouring kings and collected a confederate force. Even this confederate force failed because it had not a great general to lead it; a Duke of Wellington to match Napoleon.* It is sometimes thought that a confederate army cannot fight with the strength of a single army. This is not true, as we actually find that confederate armies won on the plains of France both in the past and in the present century. There must be no doubt one controlling mind and we have stated that the confederate armies of India were under the single leadership of Jaipal or Ānandpāla. But they failed because they were no match for Mahmud and they failed for other reasons also which we proceed to notice.

I. The weakness of the religious feeling of the Hindus had a great deal to do with their defeat in the Panjab. The dominant binding sentiment on either side was not national but religious, as has already been stated. But while the religious zeal of the Mahomedans was stubborn and overpowering, the religious sentiment of the Hindus was weak and almost apathetic. It was to be expected that the zeal of the Moslem and the greed of the robber would be equally met by the fervour of the Hindu and the indignation of the robbed. Not only were temples plundered and idols rifled of their jewels but hundreds and thousands of Hindus were forcibly converted. It is, therefore, natural to expect that the Hindus would have fought with all the exasperation and the courage of the defiled and the despoiled. And equally matched as they were in number and civilization, perhaps even superior, they should not have accepted defeat. But the zeal of the Hindus has always been mild for various reasons. For one, he is usually tolerant. It is a common experience that while a Mahomedan's exasperation is most acute at the least insult offered

---

* The Oxford history of India by Smith states that the confederate army was led in 1008 by Vīsaladeva of Ajmer. Unfortunately we find no authority for this. And this Vīsala even if he led is not known as a great conqueror.

to the Koran or to the great Prophet, a Hindu quietly listens to any abuse of the Veda or of Rāma and Krishna. A Hindu is again by habit inaggressive. The Hindu religion has always preached Ahinsā and the Hindu is accustomed to pacific modes of life. Thirdly, the Hindus had wrong notions about their idols; and probably still have. As stated before, images have no miraculous powers and when the idols themselves were found to be powerless, it would be superstitiously thought useless for man to resist where even the deity has thought fit to submit. But it must be remembered that an image after all is an emblem and if the emblem is insulted it is not the metal or the stone that is insulted nor the deity which it represents, for it is above all insult. It is they who are really insulted, who believe in that emblem. When the face of the statue of Queen Victoria was tarred in Bombay, it was not the marble that was insulted nor the good Queen Victoria but it was the British nation which was, and which was intended to be, insulted which had set up the statue But by a wrong philosophy or rather by superstition the Hindus thought the deities powerless against Mahmud who was bound to succeed as it was destined that the Sanātana Dharma was to suffer in the Kali age. Such reasoning naturally acted upon the minds of the Hindus more forcibly when accidents actually happened which worked against them and they did not fight with that resentment and exasperation which should have animated those whose temples had been desecrated and whose houses had been dishonoured.

II. Secondly, the fall of the Panjab may also be attributed to the political apathy of its people. Unfortunately for twelve centuries before this, Panjab had been ruled by foreign kings. It may be said that for twenty centuries from the time of Porus down to the time of Ranjitsingh, Panjab had no kings of its own. It was ruled by foreign Hindu or Mlechchha rulers from the time of Alexander to that of Mahmud, by Macedonians, by Mauryas, by Śakas, by Bactrian Greeks, by Kushans, by Huns, by Kashmirians, by Sindhis and lastly by the Shahi kings of Kabul and after Mahmud by Mahomedan kings of Ghazni and Delhi for eight centuries more, till the Sikhs gave to the Panjab native kings, after a foreign rule extending over two thousand years. When Mahmud conquered the Panjab, there was no political consciousness awake in the minds of its people. Though Aryans the people had lost all desire, even if they had the ability, to enjoy self-rule or independence a people did not demur to be ruled by a Moslem Turk from Ghazni instead of a Brahmin Afghan from Kabul. They were apathetic to the change of rule that was coming upon them and they did not resist with that stubbornness which belongs to a people fighting to preserve independence. Panjab was thus lost to Mahomedans in one battle. Kingdoms have no doubt been lost in one battle in western history also. England indeed was acquired by William the Conqueror in one battle. But while the people of England made the Norman kings their own, the people of the Panjab were made their own by the Mahomedan kings of Ghazni and the Panjab was practically sliced off from India in 1009 as Sind was in 712 A. D.

It may here be objected that these two causes can be assigned as the causes of the downfall, not only of the Panjab, but of all Indian kingdoms; indeed of most Asiatic people. This is no doubt true and we shall have to mention these causes also when discussing the causes of the downfall of Northern India at the end of Book VII in this very volume. The weakness of the religious feeling of the Hindus and their political apathy are their dominant characteristics over the whole of India. But what we wish to emphasize here is that while those other causes which chiefly led to the downfall of the Rajput kingdoms of Northern India about 1200 A. D. as we shall show later on, did not exist in the Panjab viz. internecine fighting and rigidity of caste, these two causes which alone existed in the Panjab operated with greater force there than elsewhere and are thus the only causes which can be assigned to its downfall. How this is so we proceed to explain at length. The religious or political tendencies of peoples are the results of historical development and are capable of examination and explanation.

The Panjab had no doubt been the home of Vedic Aryans from the most ancient days; the place where the Vedic hymns were mostly composed and sung at sacrifices, the place where even later Vedic civilisation developed. Gāndhāra and Madra are the lands of Pāṇini and Aśvapati the teachers of grammar and philosophy. The Upanishads contain many references to the Brahmins and Kshatriyas of these famous lands on the west and east of the Indus. But the "land of the five rivers and the sixth Indus" subsequently became a home of Buddism, next only to Magadha. Buddha himself preached successfully in Afghanistan and the Panjab and later on Mahāyāna Buddhism was evolved under Kanishka in this ' ' Purushapura and Takshaśilā two places of Vedic fame became centres of Buddhist learning. The Pañjab, therefore, though originally the home of Indo-Aryans (and even now it is pre-eminently Indo-Aryan as Sir H. Risley found from facial measurements taken at the census of 1901), was less strong in the Hindu sentiment than the rest of India even in the days of the present Mahābhārata of 250 B. C. (see note). It continued to be so in the days of Hiuen Tsang who in 630 A. D. recorded that Kapiśa or Kabul with Nagar (Jalalabad). and Udyāna (Swat) with Taxila were entirely Buddhist, while Peshawar and the Panjab were half Buddhist (see Vol. I p. 48). Caste which was weak even in Vedic times became still weaker in Buddhist days. Brahmanism developed in the land of the Sarasvatī and caste gathered strength in Upper India, while it remained fluid in the Panjab "where a Brahmin would become a barber one day and a Brahmin again on the next" (See note). When, after Harsha, Buddhism was overthrown in India by the efforts of Kumārila and Śankara and modern Hinduism was evolved, Buddhism no doubt disappeared even from the Panjab, but the Hindu influence from the south was too distant to correct the laxity of caste and food prevailing there. And we can thus see why at the time when Mahmud conquered the Panjab, the Hindu sentiment among the people was particularly weak. The people lacked that intensity of faith in the Varṇāśrama Dharma which characterised the people of the Gangetic valley and they consequently did not resist forcible conversion with stubborness and ceased to worship the idols which Mahmud had broken with more ease than could have been expected of a Hindu population possessing all the physical superiority of the Aryan race.

As regards political apathy the Panjab at this time was also in a worse condition than the rest of India. No doubt political consciousness had been dormant not only in the Panjab but all over India from the most ancient times. The political ideas indeed of all the Eastern peoples are even now yet undeveloped. The idea that the country belongs to the people and not to the king is only slowly developing in recent years. The usual political conception under despotic rule is that the country belongs to the king and not that the king belongs to the country. The king, therefore, need not be from among the people. The Vedic Aryans had more advanced political ideas, it must be admitted, for the people then in reality formed the nation. In Vedic times the country and the king were both named after the people, the 'peoples' named in the singular denoting the king and in the plural the country ; e. g. Madra, Sālva, Kuru, Pānchāla etc. Even down to the days of Alexander there were nations or peoples in the Panjab among whom there were no kings. The Mālavas, the Yaudheyas, the Śālvas, and others according to Arrian were without kings; and had the republican form of government. These peoples are called gaṇas in the Mahābhārata. Whatever may be the case in Vedic or epic days, in later times, however, the kingly form of government became the rule throughout India and the country with its people came to be looked upon as the king's property. Nationality could not develop under such a form of government. But while in Northern India there were native kings and there was some national feeling alive, in the Panjab owing to long continuous foreign rule even this modicum of national feeling did not exist and the people were entirely apathetic as to who ruled them. This is the reason why the people generally offered no resistance when Ānandpāla lost his battle and they quietly acknowledged Mahmud as ruler.

For these reasons viz: weakness of Hindu religious feeling and political apathy, the Panjab thus fell easily before the onslaught of Mahmud. Political consciousness is awakening under the British rule and the changed aspect of the whole civilised world. But if the Hindus of the Panjab wish to maintain their position in the struggle of faiths in that province, they ought to strengthen their religious sentiment, abiding as it is even now, and develop it into a force equal to that of Śikhism or Mahomedanism.

It may perhaps be asked, were there no Kshatriyas in the Panjab at that or any previous time and if there were, why did they not attempt to establish their own kingdoms? That the Panjab is predominantly Aryan is, as stated before undoubted and there were then as now, thousands of Kshatriyas and Vaiśyas of Aryan blood in the Panjab. But the massacres of fighting populations which Alexander and later conquerors systematically perpetrated deprived the Panjab of almost the whole of the ruling class. The representatives of those valiant clans of Kshatriyas who opposed Alexander, of the Śibis, the Mālavas, the Madras, the Yaudheyas and others then survived (and still survive) in the Panjab. But they had become agriculturists and often heads of villages according to the Āpaddharma rule for the Kshatriyas prescribed in the Smṛitis and specially in the

Parāśara Smṛiti (See Vol. II page 183). The Kshatriyas of the Panjab, valiant and able-bodied as they were had thus long lost their ancient special characteristic viz: the desire and the determination to rule others and not to be ruled by others, the 'Īsvarabhava' noted in the Bhagavadgita as belonging to Kshatriyas and they ceased to care who ruled, so long as they preserved a sort of semi-independence in their village life. Such zamindars were not disturbed by any ruling power, whether Greek, Kushan, Hun, or Turk nor by Kashmir or Sind which ruled from a distance. This, however, led to a gradual distinction betweeen the ruling Kshatriyas and the agricultural Kshatriyas which is still recognised in the Panjab. The former in fact are the Rajputs, i. e. sons and descendants of ruling families who never cultivated land and who always ruled even if it be in one village if not more. This ruling passion of the Rajputs immortalized in the minimum demand of Yudhishthira from Duryodhana "Give us five villages one for each brother and you may keep the rest of our kingdom," this ruling passion of the Rajputs to rule and never to be ruled led the surviving Rajputs of the Panjab to emigrate to the submontane hills on the eastern border of the Panjab or to the deserts of Rajputana and to countries still southward and eastward. As shown in Volume II, the Rajput ruling families of Rajputana came originally from the Panjab from whence they had to retire in consequence of the inroads of Greeks, Kushans, Huns, and Turks. Notably the Chauhans, the Paramāras, the Bhātis and even the Rathors came from the Panjab, and at the present day the Hindu and even the Mahomedan Rajputs in the Panjab still declare that they belong to these clans. The Bhātis dispossessed of Zabulistan by the Turks spread over the Panjab and founded a kingdom finally in Jaisalmere in Rajputana. The fine Janjuas of the Salt Range (now Mahomedans) are believed to be Anavaes or descendants of Anu and are the most valiant Kshatriyas in the Panjab. These and other warlike modern clans are the ancient Kshatriyas who preserved their independence by becoming headmen of villages and even agriculturists.

But these also in ancient times did not care to establish kingly ruling families because the alien Mlechha rulers always accepted the religion of the conquered and in effect became native kings. Just as the Normans coming as conquerors became one with the conquered being already of the same religion as the Saxons and Britons, so the Greeks, the Kushans, the Śakas and the Huns became in India Buddhists or Vaishṇavas and latterly Mihirakula was a staunch Śaiva and their rule was never felt as a foreign rule. The kings of Kashmir, of Sind, and of Kabul who later on ruled the Panjab were Hindus and one with the people in manners and civilization and were never felt as foreign rulers. When the Turks conquered the Panjab the difference of religion indeed made the foreign rule intolerable by the destruction of temples and idols, and Mahomedan rule was also generally more oppressive, as we shall show later on, than Hindu rule. Yet the land-owning valorous Kashatriya tribes of the Panjab made no effort to establish a kingdom of their own for another reason and that was the forcible conversion of many of these tribes. The conversion of almost the whole fighting population of western Panjab has introduced a factor of cleavage in the people of this province,—the most warlike in the whole of India—which has unfortunately made it the most unfitted to attain self-rule. Why these tribes did not strenuously resist forcible conversion may be explained by their human desire to escape massacre and by their natural affection for their land and hereditary headship of villages as also by their weak Hindu feeling. The superstition of the Hindus that persons once defiled by eating beef and other heinous offences cannot be taken back into Hinduism made the cleavage permanent. The sympathies of these Mahomedan population, though originally Kshatriya by race and still observing certain Hindu customs, naturally went with the Mahomedan rulers; and the Panjab was again incapable of establishing a kingly line of its own, until we come to the Sikh rulers of the eighteenth century. Śikhism indeed resisted and eventually conquered Mahomedan oppression by organizing itself by a system akin to the conscription of ancient Greece and Rome or modern Germany and France. Guru Govindasing saw the necessity of transforming every Śikh into a soldier and the martial qualities of the people of the Panjab naturally aided him and enabled him to transform Śikhism into a militant religion like the Mahomedan religion itself. We have traced the history of the Panjab down to the present day to show why its people were and are politically apathetic. How modern enviroments will act upon the political consciousness of the people, now triply divided into Mahomedans, Hindus and Śikhs is outside the scope of our work and must be left to the political thinkers of the present and the future.

The reasons why Hindu kings of Northern India did not attempt to establish *their* rule over the Panjab may be briefly noticed. We have already seen that half the population of the Panjab was Mahomedan now and did not encourage such attempt. Kashmir was then not strong enough nor Kanauj, to make the attempt. The Chauhans of Sambhar were at a distance and finally no great hero arose among them who could attempt this difficult task though Visala III, had he lived long enough, might have made this effort which he expressly said he had left to his descendents (See his inscription noted in Chauhan chapter).

NOTE—MAHĀBHĀRATA ON THE LAXITY OF RELIGIOUS FEELING IN THE PANJAB.

In the Karṇa Parva chapters 40 to 45 we have a spirited dialogue between Karṇa and Salya, the former depicting the bad manners and the religious laxity of the people of the Panjab and the latter offering no defence practically. This shows that the people of Āryāvarta or modern U. P. and Delhi looked down upon the Hindus of the Panjab in the time of Alexander and succeeding centuries. "In their houses people laugh and dance eating beef and drinking wine eating also Saktu and fish. From the Madra country and in Gāndhāru (beyond the Indus) purity has disappeared. In the Mantra or charm against scorpion-bite they say 'I will not associate with a man from Madra country; this poison of thine is destroyed" (chap. 43). In chapter 44 we have "One should not go to the Vahika country in which the five rivers and the sixth Indus flow as it is unpurified by the Himalayas, by the Ganges, by the Jumna and the Sarasvati and as it is void of true religion and cleanliness. The eaters of beef with garlic and the drinkers of liquor prepared from rice jaugry are indeed void of good breeding. That country is called Aratta and is void of religion; one should not go there; it is the country of those who are Vrātya (without religious ceremonies and without the sacrifices). If you drink water in Yugandhara town or stay in Achyutasthala or bathe in the pond of Bhūtalavya, how will you go to heaven? An Arya should not reside for two days in the Āratta Vāhika country where a Brahmin becomes a Kshatriya and then a Vaiśya and then a Śudra and finally a barber and a Brahmin again." Śalya only replied that there were good and bad men in every country.

CHAPTER XX.

THE SUCCESSORS OF MAHMUD.

Although the Panjab with Kabul did not form part of Hindu India henceforward, we must give a short account of the kingdom of Ghazni during the reigns of Mahmud's successors, with such references to Hindu India as are found therein in detail. The history of the Ghaznavide kings is given in short by the Tabakat-i-Nasiri written by Minhaj-us-siraj a learned man who was Kazi of Delhi and its empire under several kings and lastly under Nasiruddin and Ghiyasuddin Balban (Elliot II p. 260), and who wrote this history and dedicated it to Nasiruddin about 1250 A. D. A detailed gossipping account of the reign of Masa'ud written by Baihaki who was almost an eye-witness of the events he describes and who wrote about 1050 A. D. is also available and is very informing. From these two we give below a short history of the Ghaznavide kings, who followed Mahmud, with such references in detail to Hindu India as are found therein.

Mahmud's two sons Masa'ud and Muhammad were born on the same day from different mothers. Masa'ud was so strong physically that his mace could not be wielded even by Mahmud but he was unruly and turbulent. Muhammad was, on the other hand, gentle and promising and therefore in the good graces of his father. Believing Masa'ud would oppress the people and the army, Mahmud had named Muhammad as his successor and the permission of the Khalifa to add his name in the Khutba had been obtained. When some officer expressed his condolence to Masa'ud privately, he in the usual Mahomedan spirit observed "The sword is a better guarantee of the throne than documents." And events actually happened as had been anticipated. Masa'ud was governor in Khorasan, like Mahmud himself, at the time of their father's death, and marched against his brother Muhammad who had meanwhile ascended the throne of Ghazni, in the same way as Mahmud had marched against his brother Ismail. But unlike Mahmud, Masa'ud blinded his defeated brother and always kept him a close prisoner. And when he became the master of the extensive empire of Mahmud he recovered all the sums Muhammad had distributed among his officers, even by torture. If Mahmud resembles Shivaji, his son Masa'ud resembles Sambhāji almost in every respect. The latter was as powerful physically as Masa'ud and he too after his father's death defeated Rajaram and killed his mother. He ruled vigorously for about ten years and was eventually seized by Aurangzeb and cruelly put to death. Masa'ud met a similar tragic end after reigning vigorously for about ten years. Both Sambhāji and Masa'ud were strong in their religious beliefs. Masa'ud persecuted heretics as Mahmud had done and also led some religious expeditions into Hindustan.

The ordered nature of government inherited from Mahmud appears from the interesting details given by Baihaki as to how ministers were appointed with the most elaborate ceremonies, how the Sultan consulted the minister in every matter and how correspondence passed between them through the private secretary and how regularly written orders were passed. The Indian province was administered through a Kazi and a commander-in-chief both of whom resided at Lahore. "The Kazi was the head of the civil administration and collected taxes and dispensed justice while the commander-in-chief made war, took tribute, seized upon elephants and chastised refractory Hindu chiefs" (Elliot II p. 118). When Ahmad Nialtagin was appointed commander-in-chief of Hindustan, he received a royal Khillat, "royal verbal orders and a written out diploma. Then an oath was given to him and he put his signature to his bond that he would serve faithfully and these papers after being shown to the king were given into the charge of the record keeper" (Elliot II p. 119). It is interesting to note that some refractory troops and slaves, liberated with leteers of freedom, were handed over to Nialtagin for safe keeping and employment, but they were not to be sent beyond the Chandrabhāgā river or mix with the Lahore army. Probably if they went to Lahore they would create mischief in that capital and perhaps going beyond it into Hindu independent territory they would create more trouble.

One of the duties of the commander was to make raids into Hindustan and to collect tribute from Thakurs, the refractory turbulent zemindars already described who belonged to the Kshatriya caste. And Nialtagin made a raid into Hindustan going as far as Benares where Baihaki states that even Mahmud had not gone. This makes it certain that Mahmud went as far as Bari only when he conquered Rājyapāla on the Rahib which must be some river in Oudh (Ghaggar or Gomati). There was a quarrel between Nialtagin and the Kazi (the civil and the military powers in India under the British too sometimes were at variance and caused loss and finally the constitution of India placed the military authority under the Governor-general). The minister had told Nialtagin that "he was the generalissimo of Hindustan and the Kazi had no control over him" (Elliot II p. 128). And Nialtagin quarrelled with the Kazi and led an expedition into Hindustan with the consent of Másа'ud who had sided with Ahmad in his quarrel.

The expedition is thus described by Baihaki: " He crossed the Ganges and marched by the left bank. He suddenly appeared before Benares which belonged to the territory of Ganga. The city was two parsangs square and contained plenty of water. The army could only remain there from morning till midday because of the peril. The markets of the drapers, perfumers and jewellers were plundered. The people of the army became very rich and carried off gold, silver, perfumes and jewels and got back in safety." This evidence coming from almost an eye-witness and unquestionably a contemporary, places the raid in 1033 A. D. It shows that the city was in the possession of Gāngeyadeva Kalachūri of Tripura a powerful king whose army was probably near and who was much feared as he was known to be a powerful king. The bazar contained shops of drapers, perfumers, and jewellers which trades are still thriving in Benares. And the statement that Benares had plenty of water means that well-water and pond-water was plentiful in the city which is situated on a high bank of the Ganges or in the country round Benares away from the river.

This successful raid of Nialtagin turned his head and he began to form schemes of founding an independent kingdom and to engage Turkaman soldiers direct from Turkey. The Kazi, however, reported the matter to Masa'ud, who dismissed Nialtagin and sent a Hindu commander to arrest him alive if possible. Eventually Nialtagin was defeated and pursued by some Jats on the Indus and killed. This and other events show how powerful generals and slaves become as dangerous to the master as to the enemy.

The employment of Hindu soldiers and generals, even on occasions of trust, shows that Hindus had already risen to posts of responsibility under the Moslem rulers of Ghazni. Their great bravery is extolled even by Moslem writers. This employment of Hindu soldiers began in the days of Mahmud himself. Indeed Jaipal maintained a force of 2000 Hindus at Ghazni for some years and Elliot himself thought it curious that Hindu soldiers should serve as mercenaries under their bitterest persecutors (E. II. p. 448). But considering the religious and political apathy of the Hindus described before, one need not wonder that Hindus have always accepted service under foreign governments and have always sought and obtained distinction by loyalty and efficiency. This early credit gained by the Hindus is noted by Elliot who mentions several instances of their employment by their bitterest persecutors such as that of Sāwandrai employed by Masa'ud against the nobles who opposed his accession (Sawand with his soldiers was killed in the battle) or Bijai Rai, a general employed even by Mahmud and called again by Masa'ud's successors (Elliot II. p. 60). This instance of Jats killing Nialtagin shows the loyal service performed by Jat subjects for their king.

The successful raid of Nialtagin shows the weak state to which the kingdom of Kanauj, no longer an empire, had been reduced. Rājyapāla was already dead and was succeeded by Trilochanapāla who made a grant at Prayāga in 1026 as already stated. But Prayāga must have, like Benares, gone subsequently into the possession of Gāngeya, who, as will be stated in the history of the Kalachūri kings, died at Prayāga. We do not know how long Trilochanapāla ruled and who succeeded him. A king Yaśahpāla is mentioned in a broken inscription published by Colebrooke in his essays (II. p. 278) wherein he is described as Mahārājādhirāja, but not Parameśvara. He made a grant in the Kauśambi Mandala south of the Jumna and southwest of Prayāga. Kanauj held undoubted sway in Oudh but the Turks of Ghazni emboldened by the raid of Nialtagin made further raids into Oudh. The improbable story of Salar Masa'ud, Mahmud's sister's son, may at least suggest the certainty of many raids by the Turks especially in Oudh where the scene of Salar's story is laid. It is believed that Salar Masa'ud, had his head-quarters at Saraikh in the present Bara-Banki District of Oudh and from there made raids in several directions. Many districts in Oudh contain sacred places supposed to belong to that saint. These raids took place probably from 1038 to 1050. The story of Sālār is not wholly a fiction, as we find from a Rathod inscription found at Badaun (Ep. Ind. II. pp. 64) that one of the kings Madanapāla made the raids of any Amir impossible. We will comment upon this inscription at great length elsewhere in another connection. The date of this inscription is not given and that of Madanapāla cannot, therefore, be fixed but we think this is a reference to the raids of Nialtagin or Sālār Masa'ud, who must have passed into Oudh via Badaun. The Hindu Rajput kings of India resented these raids on their sacred places particularly and, as we shall show later on, Bhoja of Malwa (1040 A. D.), Karṇa Kalachūri of Tripur and lastly Chandra Gāhadavāla drove out these Turks and others mentioned before from Upper India and "freed the country of its oppressors." The last king took Kanauj and established a powerful Hindu kingdom there, the effete Pratihāra line thus ending about 1080 A. D. These later Pratihāra kings, as shown already, were tributaries of Ghazni and levied an impost named Turushkadanda on the villages in their kingdom which under the Gāhadvālas continued to be realised though not paid to the Turks.

This is a digression, though a necessary one, and we may resume our narrative of the Ghaznavide kings. Baihaki relates that one year a sudden flood of the Ghazni river did great havoc in the city and bodily carried away the bridge on it. The fort of Ghazni built by Yakub-i-lais and his brother, however, stood firm. Masa'ud, who was a mathematician himself built a new bridge over the river of one stupendous span. He also built several new palaces and splendid gardens.

But inspite of the good qualities he was endowed with, viz. personal strength and valour, learning and care for his people, Masa'ud was unfortunate and was destined to loose the greater part of his kingdom. "In what was Amir Masa'ud destitute?" asks Baihaki. "Servants, officers of State, lords of the sword and pen, an overwhelming treasury were all his, but destiny decided that he should live a reign of pain and vexation and that Khorasan, Khwarisan, Ré, and the Jabbāl should depart from his hands." "The prince made exceeding exertions and collected large armies. He passed sleepless nights in contemplation of his schemes, yet his affairs were ruined" (Elliot II). Probably the cause may be found in his excessive independence of opinion and his refusing to accept advice. The trouble began in Khorasan where Mahmud himself had allowed some Turks to settle. Prince Mahmud, Masa'ud's eldest son, was as usual appointed governor of Khorosan and Balkh, and in his time Seljukian Turks rebelled. The Ghazni army was defeated. The province was also invaded from the north and the minister and other officers advised Masa'ud to advance personally against the Turks. He, contrary to their advice, insisted on leading a holy expedition into Hindustan and went and invested the fort of Hānsī which lay to the south of the Sutlej and in the present district of Hissar. Masa'ud thus tried to extend his dominions beyond the Panjab. This invasion took place in 1037 A. D. It cannot be determined who was in possession of this fort and the district. The Hissar Gazetteer (p. 19) states that this fort of Hānsī, which is a very old place, was in possession of Anuraj son of Vīsaldeo Chāhamāna and Teshtapāla the son of Anuraj was driven out and he then founded the Hādā dynasty of Boondi.* But as we shall see in the history of the Chāhamānas later, their king at this time was Vākpati and Gaurishankar Ojha states that the Boondi Chauhan dynasty was descended from Āsarāja, twelfth king of the Chauhan line of Nadul. Whatever the name of the person who held the fort, he was a Chāhamāna no doubt and he fought valiantly. Baihaki describes the siege as follows:—" Fights were constantly taking place in a manner that could not be exceeded in severity. The garrison made desperate defence. In the victorious (Moslem) army, the slaves of the household behaved very gallantly. At last mines were sprung in five places and the walls brought down and the fort was stormed on Monday ten days before the close of Rabiul-avval. The Brahmins and other high men were slain and their women and children carried into captivity. All the treasure that was found was divided amongst the army. This fort is known in Hindustan as the virgin fort " (E. II. 140).

The above description brings out two new facts. First the mining of the walls; when we hold that gunpowder was not known in those days, it could only have been carried out with some other explosive; but what that was it is difficult to say. Secondly the slaughter of Brahmins was an advance on the severity of Mahomedan fighting in the days of Mahmud (Utbi never mentions it in his detailed account, possibly by oversight). The Rajputs of Northern India were men of a different spirit than the Kshatriyas of the Panjab. They were accustomed to rule and never to be ruled. It appears that the fort and the district was retaken by the Tomars of Delhi, who were then rising to power under the Chauhans, in 1043 A. D. as Firishta has related (Hissar Gazetteer p. 20).

Masa'ud on returning to Ghazni, found that he had committed a mistake. While trying to extend his dominions south-east,

*It is difficult to know whence this statement is taken.

he had lost the most important province of Khorasan in the north-west. It was Mahmud alone who could vigilantly watch both east and west. The Seljukian Turks taking advantage of Masa'ud's forces being engaged in the distant Hindustan attacked and seized Khorasan. They were even preparing now to advance on Ghazni and Mass'ud was perturbed. He resolved upon retiring into Hindustan with all his family and treasure and gave orders accordingly. Frantic remonstrances were addressed to him by his nobles, generals and officers and even by his mother. But Masa'ud as usual was inexhorable and unamenable to advice. It is strange to find that this decision of the brave king was based on astrology. Curiously enough the Turks and even the Arabs were strong believers in astrology* like the Hindus, though Mahomet had strictly forbidden consulting the stars. "The prime minister wisely remonstrated that if his lord went into Hindustan with his ladies and his treasure when the news would be known among friends and enemies, everybody being desirous of increasing his power, calamity would befall him." But the ill-fated Masa'ud exclaimed "This dotard does not know what he says. That is right which I have determined. I am ready to acknowledge that you have written through affection for me. You must wait for further orders; *for that which I see you cannot see. He handed over the city and the fort of Ghazni to the Kotval* Bu-Ali and remarked "My son Maudud, the minister and a large army will be away. Whatever may happen, in the spring I will settle the matter in another way. *The astrologers have declared that my star is not propitious during winter.*" The Kotwal urged that the ladies and the treasure should be secured in strong forts, but the Sultan replied that he had determined that they would remain with him and prayed to God to grant him peace and welfare in his journey to Hindustan (Baihaki E. II. p. 52).

The Sultan wished to avoid the evil influence of his star by going into Hindustan, which then still included, as it includes even now the warmer country to the west of the Indus with the cities of Wahind, Mārminārā (?) Bershaur and Kiril (?) (E. II. p. 150); but the evil star destroyed Masa'ud even in Hindustan. The Tabakat-i-Nasiri relates that Masa'ud was seized by his own rebellious Moslem and Hindu slaves as he was going through the Margilan pass (in the hills between Rawalpindi and Attock,

* Al-Beruni himself was an astrologer as well as astronomer.

a few miles to the west of Hasan Abdal) and imprisoned. They liberated the blind Muhammad who was in custody and placed him on the throne. Masa'ud was taken to the fortress of Gur and there murdered. This tragic end of Masa'ud reminds us of the tragic end of Sambhaji who too like Masa'ud lost the large Mahārāshtra territory acquired by his father and had left to him a distant province Karnatic for refuge as Hindustan was left to the kings of Ghazni. Both though endowed with great courage and learning and strong in religious zeal came to grief by their obstinacy and unamenability to good advice. The unfortunate end of both shows how immense resources are of no avail without the capacity to use them; and the greatness of Mahmud, as that of Shivaji, appears in the fact that he achieved greatness even without any great resources in the beginning.

We have given the history of Masa'ud at some length because it brings out the greatness of Mahmud by relief and because the two important expeditions* into Hindustan took place in his time, one to Benares and the other to Hansi resulting in further acquisition of territory for some time. We will now go on to the history of the remaining kings of Ghazni which we give in the briefest manner, with such references in detail to India as occur therein.

Muhammud was king only for six months; for Maudud, son of Masa'ud flew from Balkh, where he was governor, to avenge his father's death. Taking possession of Afghanistan he went on to Hiudustan, defeated his uncle and took him and all his children prisoner. They were all killed as also the Turkish and Hindu slaves who had seized his father. He returned to Ghaznī and ruled for nine years. His sons were incapable and the officers and nobles raised one of them Mahmud and his uncle Ali together to the throne. But both being incapable, complete disorder prevailed. After two months they were sent to a fortress and Abdul Rashid, a son of Mahmud, was raised to the throne in 444 H. (1050 A. D.). Alp-Arslan, the Seljuk king of Iran and Khorasan advanced against Ghazni but was defeated by Tugril, a fearless slave disciplined under Mahmud, who was placed at the head of the Ghazni forces. When he returned

---

* A third is mentioned in which Masa'ud is said to have taken a fort on the Sarasvati in Kashmir. But Baihaki does not mention it and we do not think there is any Sarasvati river in Kashmir nor does the Taragini mention this invasion.

victorious, he killed the Sultan Abdul Rashid and ascended the throne himself. He killed eleven other princes and ruled tyrannically. After forty days of misrule, he was killed by a Turkish silahdar or arm-bearer (a term of general use in later Indian history) on the throne itself.

Only two princes remained imprisoned in a fort and Tugril had sent a messenger ordering their dispatch also. The seneschal at the fort cautiously delayed the execution of the order for one day only and a pigeon-carrier brought the news of Tugril's murder. The lives of these princes were thus fortunately saved and both became Sultans in succession viz. Farukhjad and Ibrahim. Both ruled justly and kindly. Ibrahim was a very religious man and translated the Koran into Persian. He had forty daughters and thirty six sons: so that the royal family was again full. These daughters were given in marriage to learned persons by the Sultan and one of them was married to the grandfather of the author of Nasiri. Ibrahim was like Shahu and ruled long (42 years) dying in 492 H. (1100) after a peaceful and prosperous reign. His son Masa'ud reigned even more justly and liberally. He abolished exhorbitant taxes throughout Mahmudi dominions and Zabulistan and remitted all tolls and imposts throughout the empire. In his reign a religious expedition into Hindustan was led by his Hajib who crossed the Ganges and "penetrated to a place where none except Mahmud had gone". The year and the place are not mentioned. But this makes the raid of Sālār Masa'ud improbable for Mahmud did not go beyond Bari in Oudh. This king died after 17 years of reign in 509 H. (1118). This makes the raid into Oudh the last under an Amir and probably this is the raid referred to in the Badaun inscription.

Arslan his elder son succeeded him but was driven away by his younger brother Behram by the aid of Sultan Sanjar who was his maternal uncle. But his reign though long (41 years) was unhappy. The governor of Hindustan twice rebelled and he had twice to attack him, once near Multan and another time in the Siwalic hills. The rebel was, however, eventually destroyed. The Ghori chiefs in his absence became powerful and took Ghazni which they destroyed by fire as will be related later in Ghori history. Bahram retired into Hindustan but when the Ghoris departed from Ghazni he returned. His son Khusru succeeded him in 552 H. (1159 A. D.). As the Ghori chiefs had shaken the Ghazni kingdom to the foundation and as Khusru was a weak king, a horde of Gozz Turks attacked and captured Ghazni and retained it for twelve years, when they were driven out by Ghiasuddin Ghori. Khusru as usual retired to Lahore and ruled there for seven years. His son Khusru the mild ruled in Lahore for some time but he was taken prisonor by Mahammud Ghori in 587 H. (1191) and eventually put to death with his son by order of Ghiasuddin Ghori in 598 (1206 A. D.), when the line of Mahmud ended.

The history of the Ghaznavide kings forcibly exhibits the great evils to which despotic systems of government are exposed where there is no national sentiment to check them. There is always a rule of succession recognised in every country and in the west there are formal acts of succession. But when ambitious and unscrupulous persons are not prevented by the strong national sentiment of the people from doing mischief, murders of kings and sometimes of possible claimants to the throne are often committed in such frightful manner and number that birth in a royal family becomes indeed a calamity. In the history of Hindu kingdoms such scenes are rarely met with though national sentiment was absent in them also because probably the Hindu nature is, for well known reasons, less cruel and more law-observing.

We here close this book and will give a detailed account of the Ghori kings who supplanted the Ghaznavi line, when we come to the history of Prithvīrāja in the last book as they overthrew him and finally conquered India. It is further necessary to add that there must have been many raids by Turkish adventurers into Hindustan, besides the one described above, as will appear from the history of the several Rajput kingdoms given in the following book though they are not mentioned by Mahomedan historians.

NOTE 1:—COINS OF THE GHAZNAVI KINGS.

We find the following intersesting information from a paper by Mr. Thomas in J. R. A. S. IX p. 67 and XVII p. 157. It may be stated that every king in Ghazni, and generally in India, struck coins in his name commemorating his coming to the throne. We, therefore, find coins of Alptagin, Sabuktagin, Ismail and Mahmud showing that they became kings in Ghazni in this order. But in all these coins the name of the Sāmāni emperor, Mansur of Nuh, is also inscribed showing that they were subordinate kings of the Sāmāni empire. Mahmud first assumed independence as his coin dated 389 H. (1000 A. D.) first omits the mention of a Sāmāni king. The first coins of Mahmud describe him as Saif-ud-dowla a title given him by Nuh in 389 H. (995 A. D.) then as Al-Amir-Yamin-ud-dowlat-va-Amin-ul-millit, a title given him by the Khalifa, later as Malik-ul-mamālik, and finally simply as Mahmud without any title when he had really become so great as to require no titles. He never calls himself, strangely enough, Sultan or Ghāzi. The title Sultan first appears in the coins of Ibrahim (coins 4652 H. or 1061 A. D.).

Mahmud's coins are found in bilingual form also, for the use of his Indian subjects. The legend in Devnāgari is interesting and shows that Indian Pandits were at the court of Mahmud. It is as follows.—"अव्यक्तमेक मुहम्मद-अवतार नृपति महमूद." They had made Mahmud an incarnation of Mahcmet and indentified the prophet again with the Avyakta, though sometimes the simple words अयं टक महमूद संवत् ४१२ are found. These coins were struck at Lahore. There were mints at Lahore, Ghazni, Nishapur, and three or four more places in the west. There was no mint at Kabul.

The Ghaznavi kings copied the Kabul Shāhi coins struck in the name of Sāmantadeva with recumbent bull (Nandi) on the obverse and horseman with the name of Mahmud or Masaud on the reverse. The Hindu bull was copied on Mandud's coins and also later on in Ibrahim's coins dated 432 H. (1041 A. D.) The coins of Sabuktagin and Mahmud approximate to the coins of the Hindu kings of Kabul in weight. It seems that Shahi Brahmin kings' coins were of silver (called dirhams) and Ghazni and Nishapur mint coins were of gold (called dinar); and copper and small silver coins belong both to Hindu and Mahcmedan kings.

NOTE 2:—SPELLING AND MEANING OF SOME MAHOMEDAN NAMES.

	Name		Spelling adopted	Meaning
1	Alptagin or Alptagin	(Turki)	Alptagin	Alp (strong) and Tagin or Tigin (wrestler)
2	Sabuktagin	"	Sabuktagin	Sabuk (active, expeditious)
3	Mahmud	(Arabic)	Mahmud	The praised
4	Muhammad	"	Muhummad	The praiser. (The name of the prophet is given as Mahomet)
5	Shihabuddin	"	Shihabuddin	The shooting-star of religion
6	Kutubuddin	"	Kutubuddin	The pole-star of religion
7	Ghiyasuddin	"	Ghiyasuddin	Supporter of religion
8	Iyaltimish	(Turki)	Altamas	The lion (?)
9	Al-Beruni	(Arabic)	Al-Beruni	The outsider (?)

We may add that the names of certain towns and provinces are spelt as follows in this book viz:—Khorasan, Sistan, Balkh, Baghdad (garden of justice), Nishapur (this appears to be a Sanskrit name) and Bokhara.

BOOK VII.

THE THIRD SET OF HINDU KINGDOMS.

CHAPTER I.

THE CHĀHAMĀNAS OF SĀMBHAR AND AJMER.

One of the famous Rajput clans of the preceding sub-period which still flourished in this sub-period and indeed attained to greater glory was the Chāhamānas of Sāmbhar. We have given the history of their rise in our second volume chapter III Book IV (pp. 90-97) and shown that the first king who established a kingdom in Sāmbhar, otherwise called the Sapādalaksha territory (of 1¼ lakh villages), was Sāmanta and he became famous by his vigorous opposition to the invading Arabs from Sind about 750 or 778 A. D. His successors down to the last Pṛithvīrāja had constant fights with Mahomedans and maintained the struggle with great vigour and obstinacy. We have also given in Volume II the genealogy of the Chāhamānas of Sāmbhar from Gūvaka I, the next important king, to Durlabha whose Harsha stone inscription dated V. E. 1030 (A. D. 973) has been found. In this volume we will give the genealogy of the Chāhamānas from Durlabha onwards to Pṛithvīrāja their last king and emperor of India. The whole genealogy is given in the Bijolia inscription published by Kavirāja Shyāmaldas in J. R. A. S. Bengal LV and the same is examined by Kielhorn in Ep. Ind. Vol. VIII and also discussed by Rai Bahadur Gaurishankar Ojha in his Hindi edition of Tod's Rājastan (p. 394). The value of Pṛithvīrāja Rāsā as history is almost nil according to most scholars, as has been proved by many inscriptions found since Tod wrote his great history. The Chāhamāna genealogy, therefore, and also the dates given by Tod mainly from Pṛithvīrāja Rāsā are naturally incorrect and we have to rely for correct genealogy and dates on inscriptions and such dates as can be guessed for particular kings by calculation. The Rajputana Gazetteer Vol. III B (page 65) gives a genealogy of the Chāhamānas based on the Bijolia inscription but there appear to be a few inaccuracies therein which according to your view require to be corrected.

We will here give the genealogy of the Chāhamānas of Sāmbha from Durlabha onwards down to Pṛithvīrāja as we conceive it t be, with probable dates, side by side with the genealogy give in the Rajputana Gazetteer for comparison.

Bijolia Insc. St. 1226

1 Durlabha A. D. 973
2 Govinda (c. 988)
3 Vākpati (c. 1003)
4 Vīryarāma
5 Srīchandra (c. 1033)
6 Sinhata Dūsala (c. 1048)
7 Vīsala alias Vigraharāja III (c. 1063) m. Rājadevī
8 Pṛithvīrāja I (c. 1078) m. Rāsalyadevī
9 Ajayadeva (c. 1093) m. Saumalyadevī
10 Arṇorāja or Āṇā (c. 1108)
Jagadeva
12 Pṛithvībhata II
11 Vigrahapāla IV alias Visala Ins. 1163 A. D.
13 Someśvara Ins. 1169 A. D.
14 Pṛithvīrāja III Ac. c. 1175 died 1193 A. D. in battle with Shihabuddin

Rajputana Gazetteer

1 Durlabha
2 Govinda
3 Vākpati
4 Son Vijayarāma
5 Durlabha
6 Vigraha
7 Pṛithvīrāja
8 Ajaipāla
9 Arṇorāja son or grandson
10 Vīsala or Vigraha
11 Pṛithvirāja
12 Someśvara
13 Pṛithvīrāja

Of Pṛithvīrāja III or the last we will speak in a separate chapter; for his conflict with Shihabuddin Ghori must be treated in great detail as it ended in the final overthrow of Northern India and in effect of the whole of this country. His dates of accession may be, as we shall show later on, taken to be about 1175 A. D. From Durlabha whose reign may be taken to begin in A. D. 973 down to Prithvīrāja III whose reign began in 1175 A. D. we have thirteen kings and a period of about 202 years giving an average 15½ years per king. In the previous section of the genealogy, as the reader may remember, we took, for fixing dates, an average of 15 years.

The first king Durlabha is said in the Harsha stone inscription to be a brother of the preceding king Vigraharāja who certainly was a great king. If we identify him with the Dhundā

Dānava Visala of the Prithvirāja Rāsā wherein the absurd legend is given of his becoming a demon and devastating Ajmer, we shall not be far wrong. But as said before, it is not possible to take the Rāsā for history, at least for the ancestors of Prithvirāja III; and we have to abandon the task of identifying Rāsā kings with kings mentioned in inscriptions. For, further, we find that this demon is said to have lived for 300 years before Prithvirāja and yet his son is said to be Sārangadeva a name not to be found in the inscription genealogies and his son was Arṇorāja. But Arṇorāja from inscriptions appears to be a great-grandson of the next Visāla or Vigraha III whose probable date of accession is 1063 A. D. and who thus preceded Prithvirāja III by about a hundred years only. Giving up the Rāsā, therefore, we may note that Vākpati was the king of Sāmbhar from A. D. 1003 and hence a contemporary of Mahmud of Ghazni.* But the Chāhamānas do not appear to have had any conflict with the Turks of Ghazni during Mahmud's time as Mahmud did not come to Ajmer. And Ajmer was not the capital of the Chāhamānas in 1000 A. D. When Firishta mentions Ajmer kings taking part in the confederacy of Rajput kings against Sabuktagin or Mahmud, he merely makes a surmise by ante-dating Ajmer owning to its fame in the days of Shehabuddin Ghori. Going further on, we find that instead of Śrichandra of the Bijolia inscription, R. B. Gaurishankar gives the name Chāmuṇḍa and mentions that he built a Vishṇu temple (as stated in Hammira-Kāvya) in a town in Marwar; while Kielhorn gives Simhata and Dūsala as separate kings (See Ep. In. VIII Appendix). Prithvirāja I is said to have given a golden kalaśa (pinnacle-pot) usually covered with gold to a Jain temple in Raṇathambhor. His son Ajayadeva is said to have built the fort of Ajmer and founded the modern town, towards the end of the 11th century A. D. and to have removed his capital from Sāmbhar to Ajmer. He must have been a powerful king as coins struck in his name and in the name of his queen Somalādevi have been found (Ind. Ant. 1912). His son Arṇorāja or Ānā was a more powerful king. He built the Ānāsāgar tank and bund and "thus purified the place defiled as it has been by the invasion of Mahomedans". (This is perhaps a poetic fancy of the Prithvirāja-Vijaya poem).

---

* It is difficult to state on what authority Sir V. Smth states in his Oxford History of India that Visaldeo of Ajmer led the confederate army against Mahmud in 1008 A. D.

His reign is assigned by Mr. Harbilas Sarda to 1125 to 1150 A. D.* which does not much differ from the computed date given in our genealogy. Pandit Gaurishankar mentions that Kumārapāla of Gujarat invaded Ajmer in the time of Arṇorāja in St.1207 or 1150 A. D. and Mr. Harbilas Sarda has in a paper in Ind. Ant. 1912 shown that Ānā twice warred with Kumārapāla of Gujarat, first in St. 1202 and again in St. 1207 when the latter invaded Ajmer to avenge an insult offered to his sister who was married to him. Arṇo's second son Vīsaladeva or Vigraharāja IV ascended the throne of Ajmer, setting aside his elder brother Jagadeva who had murdered Ānā and who probably did not at all rule. Vīsaladeva was a greater monarch than Ānā himself. He has recorded inscription on the Iron pillar of Delhi in which his exploits are extolled to the highest. "From Vindhya to the Himalayas, he, moving for pilgrimage, conquered all those kings who opposed him and favoured those who bent their necks to him and he made Āryāvarta again a real Āryāvarta or abode of Āryas by slaughters inflicted on Mahomedans." And he exhorts his descendants in this way. "We have made the portion of the earth between the Vindhya and the Himalayas tributory to us. May your minds be not devoid of exertion for the conquest of the rest."† This indeed shows the vigorous character of his rule and his high ambition. We have already shown that after their conquest and annexation of the Punjab the Mahomedans had sent several expeditions into mid-India and made settlements in many places. Vīsaladeva drove these Mahomedans back into the Punjab and clearing Āryāvarta made it so in reality. This further would confirm the statement in the Bijolia inscription that he conquered Delhi, a fact on which doubt

---

* It is inexplicable how Mr. Sarda assigns for Ajayapāla's reign the period 1165-1175 A. D. (Ajmer p. 33). Probably these figures are given there by mistake or misprint.

† आविन्ध्यादाहिमाद्रेर्विरचितविजयस्तीर्थयात्राप्रसङ्गात् ।
उद्ग्रीवेषु प्रहर्ता नृपतिषु विनमत्कन्धरेषु प्रसन्नः ॥
आर्यावर्तं यथार्थं पुनरपि कृतवान् म्लेच्छविच्छेदनाभि- ।
र्देवः शाकम्भरीन्द्रो जगति विजयते वीसलो क्षोणिपालः ॥
ब्रूते सम्प्रति चाहमानतिलको शाकंभरी-भूपतिः ।
श्रीमद्विग्रहराज एष विजयी सन्तानजानात्मजान् ॥
अस्माभिः करदं व्यधायि हिमवद्विन्ध्यान्तरालं भुवः ।
शेषस्वीकरणाय मास्तु भवतामुद्योगशून्यं मनः ॥

(I. A. xix p. 218)

has been expressed. The verse " प्रतोल्यां च वलभ्यांच येन विश्रामितं यशः । ढिल्लिकाग्रहणश्रान्तमाशिकालाभलंभितम् ॥ " of the Bijolia inscription is difficult to understand. The words Pratoli and Valabhī are indeed double-meaning as also Dhillikā and Māṣikā (which indicate probably towns of these names as also parts of a house). But it clearly indicates that he had to make great efforts to conquer Delhi. The Bijolia inscription as well as the inscription on the Iron pillar at Delhi are given in an Appendix for the curious reader.

Visaladeva was not only a great warrior, conqueror of Vaikunta, Jābālipura Palli and even Delhi (Bijolia inscription) but he was a poet and a patron of poets like Bhoja of Dhar of immortal fame. Two slabs of stone inscribed with two Sanskrit dramas one composed by Visaladeva himself and the other composed by his court-poet have recently been found at Ajmer. The Harakeli Nātaka is composed by Visaladeva himself and is based on the well-known Kirātārjunīya epic poem. The king represents himself as eventually having had *darśana* of Śiva like Arjuna. The drama is said to be composed in St. 1210 (A. D. 1153). The second drama is entitled Lalita-Vigraharāja and is composed by the court-poet Somadeva. Vigraharāja is shown to have fallen in love with the daughter of king Vasantapāla (probably an imaginary king) who requited his love and he sends a messenger to her informing her of his resolve to come to her after his fight with the Amir. This seems to be historically true and the Turks under their Hammīra (Amir) are said to be innumerable. Each party has sent spies into the other's camp. Eventually formal messengers are sent and a truce or peace is concluded.

Visaladeva has left his name in Ajmer in the Visaladeva or tank, constructed by him, in imitation of his father Ānā who is named as Avelladeva in his iron pillar inscription and who built the Ānā-sāgar tank on the bank of which Shahjahan later built a marble Bārādari or open pavilion. Visaladeva also built a college for Sanskrit students which was converted by Shihabuddin Ghori into a mosque which is now known as Adhai-Dinki-Zhopadi (a hut of two days and a half).

Visaladeva's last record found (Iron pillar of Delhi) is dated St. 1220 (A. D. 1163). He left a minor son named Aparagāngeya who is not mentioned in the Bijolia inscription. He must have been set aside by Visaladeva's nephew Pṛithvibhata or Prithvirāja II, a son of the parricide Jagadeva. He ruled for a few years only and was succeeded by Someśvara, Visala's younger brother. He also ruled for a short time and was succeeded by his son Prithvīrāja III the last king of the Chāhamānas. The dates of the succession of Someśvara and of Prithvīrāja III we will discuss in our chapter on the latter. But it seems necessarv to state here that Someśvara must actually have ruled for some time as the Bijolia Inscription records the grant of the village Rewanā by Someśvara and ends with this mention so that Someśvara was still ruling when the inscription was recorded in St. 1226, Phālguna Vadya 3 (about March 1170 A.D.).

The Chāhamānas are solar race Rajputs as shown in Volume II (p. 14) and as even the Prithirāja-Vijaya and Hammīra Kāvyas declare. The idea that they are Agnikulas is a later fiction which has been exploided from stone records, as even Pandit Gaurishankar believes. But it is strange that he looks upon the Chāhamānas as lunar race Kshatriyas (See his edition of Tod's Rājastan in Hindi). This is probably a misprint.

CHAPTER II.

THE GUHILOTS OF MEWAD

The kingdom founded by Bappā Rāwal remained intact in this sub-period and the Guhilot kings of Mewad were as valorous and independence-loving in this sub-period as in the preceding. They probably loved independence so truly that they never sought to extend their kingdom by depriving other peoples or clans of their territory and independence. For they never aspired to attain to the position of emperors of India (Samrāt or Chakravartin) as other kingly families did during this sub-period as in the preceding, such as Chāhamānas, Kalachūris and Gāhadavālas. In fact this aspiration was the bane of India from the most ancient days of the Pāndavas and Kauravas down to the days of Prithvīrāja viz. the desire to establish an empire in India without its advantages. For, this empire like the German empire, did not mean the welding together of the whole of Northern or Southern India into one kingdom; but it merely meant the humbling of other kingdoms without extinguishing them. The evil results of this idea of imperial sovereignty we will discuss in another place. It is sufficient to state here that the kings of Mewad never succumbed to the vanity of acquiring Imperial honour but held firmly to their own. This is perhaps the true reason why the kingdom of Mewad still subsists throughout the troubles and vicissitudes of twelve hundred years. The kings were content with their own territory and dignity and therefore they still rule in the territory where Bappā Rāwal first founded his kingdom.

During this sub-period (1000–1200 A. D.) the kings of Mewad were also generally free from aggression from without especially from the inroads of Mahomedans. Even Mahmud's Turks did not come to Mewad probably for this very reason viz. that the kings of Mewad were not kings of Hind as the Mahomedans styled the Imperial rulers of Kabul or Kanauj. Perhaps the kingdom was not rich and there were no famous temples or shrines in Mewad where riches had accumulated. The kings of Mewad, therefore, remained unmolested and the vigorous line of its kings continued to rule without exhibiting any signs of decay ending in death.

In our second volume we gave the line of Mewad kings from Bappā to Śaktikumāra from the Ātpura inscription dated

V. E. 1034 or A. D. 977. We will give in this volume the continuation of that line upto 1200 A. D. The mistake of the Pṛithvīrāja Rāsā in making Samarasinha a contemporary of Pṛithvīrāja III of Ajmer and Delhi has now been admitted on all hands; for Samarasinha's inscriptions plainly show him to belong to the end of the thirteenth century A. D. Unfortunately the Rāsā story has been accepted by bards in all Rajput states and has, therefore, vitiated their genealogies. We can in fact almost determine when this Rāsā vertion arose by comparing the various inscriptions relating to the Guhilots of Mewad themselves and the genealogies given therein. We have several such inscriptions (See Bhāvnagar Insc.). The first of them is the Abu Achaleśvara inscription dated St. 1342 (1285 A. D.) and it gives a great many details. Then comes the Rāṇapurā (Bāṇapurā) inscription in Jodhpur territory dated 1496 (A. D. 1439) which tersely gives the whole genealogy from Bappā. Lastly comes the Rayasāgara inscription dated St. 1732 (A. D. 1675) which first gives the Rāsā story that Samarasinha was married to Pṛitha sister of Pṛithvīrāja and died along with him in his last battle with Shihabuddin Ghori. The inscription distinctly refers to the Rāsā itself and has necessarily to distort the genealogy given in the preceding two inscriptions wherein Samarasinha is given as a son of Tejahsiṁha who was a son of Jaitrasiṁha in whose time the first conflict of Mewad with the Turks took place in about 1216 A. D. as distinctly mentioned in the Abu inscription, Jaitrasiṁha being described as a very Agastya to the ocean of the army of the Turks.* Of this conflict we will speak later on; but this suffices to show that even Jaitrasiṁha, grand-father of Samarasiṁha, was not a contemporary of Pṛithvirāja. We will, therefore, ignore the Prithvīrāja Rāsā account which obviously arose after the Rāṇapurā inscription dated 1439 A. D. and before the Rāyasāgar inscription dated 1675 A. D. and will give the genealogy of the Guhilots of Mewad in this sub-period from Abu and Bānapurā inscriptions and as accepted by Pandit Gaurishankar in his Hindi edition of Tod's Rajāstan. We have got a short inscription of Vijayasinha, one of these kings, dated St. 1164 (A. D. 1107) and later, of Jaitrasinha dated St. 1270 (A. D. 1213). Starting from Śaktikumāra, the last king mentioned in the Ātpurā inscription dated A. D. 977, we have, upto

---

* तुरुष्कसैन्यार्णवकुम्भयोनिः ।

Vijayasinha, 10 kings and the average comes to $\frac{1107-977}{10}=\frac{130}{10}=13$ years and from Śaktikumāra to Jaitrasinha we have 19 kings giving an average of $\frac{1213-977}{19}=\frac{236}{19}=12\frac{8}{19}$ years. This shows that the average for the Guhilot kings is still shorter than that for other families. We will use 13 and 12 years as average for this portion of the Guhilot genealogy and assign probable dates, with remarks for individual kings from Gaurishankar and other sources.

GUHILOT GENEALOGY

1 Śaktikumāra (Ins. 977 A. D.)

2 Ambāprasāda (c. 990 A. D.)

3 Suchivarman (c. 1003 A. D.)

4 Naravarman (c. 1016 A. D.)

5 Kīrtivarman (c. 1029 A. D.)

6 Yogarāja (c. 1042 A. D.)

7 Vairaṭa (c. 1055)

8 Hansapāla (c. 1068)

9 Vairisinha (c. 1081 A. D.)

10 Vijayasinha (c. 1094 A. D.) Insc. 1107 A. D.

*11 Arisinha (c. 1118)

12 Chonḍa (c. 1129)

13 Vijayasinha (c. 1140)

†14 Raṇasinha (c. 1151)

15 Bhīmasinha (c. 1162)

16 Sāmantasinha (c. 1173)

17 Kumārasinha (c. 1184 A. D.)

18 Mathanasinha (c. 1195)

19 Padmasinha (c. 1206)

20 Jaitrasinha (c. 1213) Insc. 1213 and 1222 A. D.

21 Tejasinha (c. 1238) Insc. 1267 A. D.

22 Samarasinha (c. 1267) Insc. 1278, 83, 87 A. D.

---

* From 11 we take 11 years' average to suit the date known from inscriptions for Jaitrasinha. † From 14 two branches started of which we take the elder Rāwal branch.

Proceeding to the case of individual kings we have first to observe that the Abu inscription differs a little from its compeer the Chitorgadh inscription drawn up by the same writer Vedaśarman in that the latter gives the two kings Ambāprasāda and Suchivarman after Śaktikumāra and before Naravarman. Further it records of Śaktikumāra that he destroyed the enemies of religion, terrible like Daityas. There is here plainly a reference to the Mahomedans. We have taken the date of this king from the Ātpurā inscription as ruling from 977 A. D. in which year Sabuktagin came to the throne of Ghazni and then that danger to India began which finally engulfed it. It is possible to believe that Śaktikumāra may have taken part in the first confederacy of Hindu kings convened by Jaipāla of Kabul against Sabuktagin in 989 A. D. (Smith's Oxford H. I.)

The Chitorgadh inscription stops with Naravarman and gives the subsequent genealogy in the Abu inscription and we have, therefore, not included it in our authorities; but even though the Abu inscription does not mention Ambāprasāda and Suchivarman we have to take them in the list of kings from the Chitorgadh inscription of the same author. This also proves that the Abu inscription list may make some further omissions as we actually see. Ambāprasāda is a strange name in this list of Guhilot kings and one might have omitted it but for its mention in the Chitorgadh inscription. Yogarāja (no. 6) and Hanspāla (no. 8) are also strange names in this line and they are not given in the Abu inscription but they are given in the Ranapurā inscription (the latter name being given as Yaśapāla). These three names, however, are confirmed by their mention in a Haihaya stone inscription to be noticed in their history. There is a copper-plate inscription of Vijayasinha as has been already noticed dated St. 1164. Then Vijayasinha (no. 13) is given as Vikramasinha in Abu and Bāṇapurā inscriptions. Raṇasinha or Karṇasinha is not mentioned in the Abu inscription but he is mentioned in the Bānapurā inscription. It is probable that this inscription mentions names which were subsequently invented by bards and one may suspect if these names are real kings. The Abu inscription again does not record the tradition that from Raṇasinha two branches sprang, the elder called Rāwal and the younger called Rāṇā and established at Śisoda. But his tradition cannot be doubted as we have to explain how former kings of Chitor were called Rāwals and later kings from Hammīra were called Rāṇās. The latest Rāyasāgar inscription embodies this tradition by stating that there were 26 Rāwals in all from Bappā Rāwal.*

From Raṇasinha we come at names which are the same in all inscriptions except the first Bhimasinha who is given as Khemsing in Abu and Raṇapurā inscriptions. These kings were nearly contemporary with or immediately preceded the Abu inscription and there could have been no mistake about them. The probable date of Sāmantasinha is 1179 A. D. and he may have been a contemporary of Prithvirāja III. Pandit Gaurishankar thinks that the amplifier or forger of the Rāsā mistook Sāmanta for Samara and thus committed the blunder of making Samarasinha of A. D. 1282, a contemporary of Prithvirāja.

---

* The name Rāwal was adopted from Bappā who was a Rāwal or small king. The later kings were called Rāṇās as they came from a minor branch, Rāṇā meaning a subordinate king as in Himalayan states. But the name Rāṇā being taken by the illustrious kings of Udepur, now bears a higher meaning in Rajputana.

CHAPTER III

THE PARAMĀRAS OF DHAR— BHOJA.

The Paramāras of Malwa were already a great power at the beginning of this sub-period, Munja and Sindhurāj having already established its independence and glory. But Malwa rose to still greater glory and renown, in fact its greatest, during the reign of Bhoja. When Munja died poets were in despair for the goddess of Sarasvatī though not for Lakshmī or Indrāṇī. The goddesses of wealth and valour might find their favourites but the goddess of learning was now, they thought, without support.* But Bhoja falsified their misgivings and in him the goddesses of wealth, valour and wisdom were equally well-seated. Bhoja in real history typified the best Kshatriya of Bhāratavarsha who cultivated both Śāstra and Śastra like Rāma and Yudhishthira of legendary days or Vikrama and Hāla of later legends. Bhoja not only patronised literary men but was a great author himself and he was master of many and diversified subjects. He studied Astronomy, Alaṅkāra (poetics), Architecture, Asceticism (Yoga) and Grammar and on each of these subjects he has left works which are still treated as authoritative. His Sarasvati-Kanthābharaṇa on poetics, Rāja Martanda on asceticism and Rāja Mṛigāṇka Karaṇa on astronomy are well known and speak of his high proficiency in these sciences. As a learned man, therefore, his fame has been established in history on a permanent foundation. He built a college for Sanskrit studies at Dhar in which Sanskrit aphorisms on various subjects were inscribed on stone. The college was converted into a mosque by Mahomedans; and it still subsists at Dhar being known as the Kamāl Maula mosque. The slabs of stone which were inscribed with Sanskrit works were used for flooring and are now so rubbed over that nothing inscribed thereon is now legible. But close to this Sarasvatīsadana or Bhāratībhuvana there is an old well which is still called Akkal-kuvī or well of wisdom; and it reminds us of the time when the learned men who studied in that college and held disputations in that hall, drank water from this well and advanced in wisdom and knowledge. These and other details about Bhoja's literary greatness given by Col. Luard and Mr. Lele in their book on the Paramāras of Dhar and Malwa

---

* लक्ष्मीर्यास्यति गोविंदे वीरश्रीर्वीरवेश्मनि । गते मुञ्जे यशःपुंजे निरालंबा सरस्वती ॥

are indeed interesting and we make no apology for giving such other facts here as are necessary to be given in this history from this work as every available source of information has been utilized by the learned authors of this book to give a connected and detailed history of the Paramāras of Dhar.

Bhoja is mentioned by several well-known writers as an author on Hindu Law also though no work of his on that subject is now available. He is so mentioned by Śūlanath in the Prāyaśchittaviveka, by Raghunandana and even by Vijñāneśvara in his famous Mitākshara. This not only shows the versatility of Bhoja's genius but also points to his being a great ruler. He could not have been an author on Hindu Law without being thoroughly acquainted with civil administration as with religion since Dharma or law with the Hindus includes both. We know that he had done much to educate his subjects and to promote their secular welfare. He built a great tank known as Bhoja-Sara by damming the spaces between hills encircling a vast area and used it probably for irrigation. His two grants found show the terse nature of his government records which we will notice further on; but it is pertinent to remark here that his system of government and administration was typical.

His political greatness is not, however, equally well-known and has not as yet been ascertained with exactitude. He came to the throne about 1010 A. D. (Col. Luard and Mr. Lele think that he may have come to the throne even earlier) and he ruled for about forty years at least. Sir Vincent Smith places his death in about 1060 A. D. while Pandit Gaurishankar places it sometime before 1055 A. D. (St. 1112). He had fights with many Indian kings, notably with the king of Chedi Indranātha, Joggala I and Bhīma of Gujarat and with kings of Karanāta and Lāta, and Gurjaras and Turushkas,as stated in the Udepur inscription (Ep. II p. 222). We will first speak of his fight with the Turks. As this inscription states immediately before that Munja had conquered a Hūna king, it seems clear that the record distinguishes between Hūnas and Turks and does not confound them. The Huna king, therefore, must have been a Hindu king as there were no Huns in India at that time and as Hūṇa is the name of a Rajput clan also. Munja, therefore, does not seem to have taken part in the Rajput confederacy against Amir Sabuktagin, as one is likely to think from the period of his reign viz. 997 to 1010 A.D. In what campaign of Mahmud of Ghazni Bhoja fought against the Turks it is difficult to determine. He certainly was not one of those who fought with Mahmud at Somnath for he is here said to have defeated the Turks. Perhaps as suggested by Col. Luard and Mr. Lele on the strength of a statement in Tabkat-i-Akabari, that Mahmud after conquering the Hindus at Somnath went with his plunder through the western part of the desert of Multan as he learnt "that Paramāradeva one of the greatest kings of Hindustan was preparing to intercept him," this may be construed into a defeat of the Turks by Bhoja. Of course the Paramāradeva described as one of the great kings of Hindustan by Tabkat-i-Akabari must refer to Bhoja and none else. And inscription-writers are usually panegyrists and Mahmud's avoiding Bhoja may well be construed by them into a defeat. It is further likely that this event is referred to by the Udepur Praṣasti as Bhoja is said therein to have also built the temple of Somnath. Probably Mahmud had not only broken the image but also demolished the temple of Somnath and it is certainly to the credit of Bhoja's greatness as a warrior and a devotee of Śiva that he should prepare to intercept the defiler of the temple which probably had just been built by him (See p. 91).

If we take the date of accession of Bhoja to be earlier than 1010 A. D. it is possible that he may have sent a contingent to the forces of Hindu kings collected by Ānandapāla in 1008 and the inscription speaks of Turks and others being defeated by contingents or general of Bhoja not by Bhoja himself. But in no other contest with Mahmud of Ānandapāla the Turks were defeated and hence the words of the Udepur inscription cannot be taken to refer to their earlier conflicts.

Bhoja's political relations and conflicts with surrounding Hindu kingdoms have been well described by Col. Luard and Mr. Lele in their book using all the available authorities. The kingdom of Malwa on the east was conterminous with the kingdom of Chedi, on the north with that of Chitod, on the west with that of the Chālukyas of Anhilwad and on the south with the kingdom of the Chālukyas of Kalyan and as neighbours are alternately friends and foes, Bhoja had often to fight with these kingdoms except the Guhilot kingdom or Chitod. The Guhilots never aspired to imperial power as stated before and never tried to extend their territory. Hence we have no mention of Bhoja's wars with Chitod. But with Chedi, Anahilwad and Karṇāṭa he had constant fights with intervening periods of peace and these wars were alternately successful and disastrous, the enemy usually coming as far as and even occupying Dhar. In Gujarat his foe was Bhīma who ruled from 1021-1063. While Kulchandra, a Jain general of Bhoja, once invaded Gujarat when Bhīma was absent and occupied his capital Anhilwad (Patan), he plundered it so completely that the sack of Kulachandra has become preverbial. Bhīma in return took Dhar by a sudden raid with his cavalry and plundered it. But Bhīma and Bhoja were not foes long and they had even vakils of each in the other's court, Damodara an envoy of Anhilwad "being well-known as a witty and clever diplomat."

The enmity with the Chedi kingdom on the east and with Karṇāṭa on the south was almost hereditary and more disastrous, the Chedi Haihayas and the Karṇāṭa Chalukyas being usually related by marriage. A sister of Yuvarāja of Chedi was the mother of Tailapa of Karṇāṭa and we have seen already (Vol. II) that Muñja constantly fought with Tailapa and was eventually taken prisoner and even put to death by him. Gāngeyadeva was Yuvarāja's successor and ruled from 1038 to 1042 and his successor was Karṇadeva who was the most powerful of the Haihaya line and had a long reign from 1042 to 1072. Bhoja's contemporaries at Kalyan in the south were Jayasinha (1018 to 1040) and Someśwar (1040 to 1069). It seems that Jayasinha once advanced on Dhar and defeated Bhoja an event mentioned in the inscription of Jayasinha * (I. A. Vol. V p. 15). Bhoja must have defeated this king in turn as also Gāngeya sometimes about 1040 which event might have given rise to the saying now current in Malwa "Kahān Rājā Bhoja, dur Kahān Gangā Teli" (originally it must have been Gangeya of Telangaṇa, as ingeniously suggested by Mr. Lele, Telangana being a subordinate of Chedi). † Whatever this may be Someśvara Jayasinha's successor again invaded Malwa and signally defeated Bhoja. This event is related in the Vikramānkadevacharita by Bilhaṇa (I. 91). Later Bhoja may have attacked Someśvara and defeated him. This or the earlier defeat may have been referred to in the Udepur Praśasti noted before.

These wars it may be noted did not diminish to any extent the power of Malwa or the kingdoms contending with it; for

---

* The date of this inscription is by misprint given as 900 Saka in Mr. Lele's work. It must be 941 Śaka or 1019 A. D. as the former date is inconsistent with Bhoja's period of rule.

† Karṇa is distantly called lord of Trikaliṅga in one of his inscriptions (Ep. Ind. II).

they were not waged with any desire of aggression; and the four states Malwā, Chedi, Karnāta and Gujarat were equally powerful and their rulers also equally able. They on the contrary kept up the material qualities of these rulers and their soldiers. But it seems that about the time of Bhoja's death (probably after, not a little before, as the wording of the Udepur Praśasti is quite clear *), the combined invasion of Malwa by Bhīma of Gujarat and Karṇa of Chedi created disorder and diminished the power of the kingdom of Malwa. The successor of Bhoja, Jayasinha went to the court of Āhavamalla Someśvara of Kalyan for refuge and he forgetting the hereditary feud between Malwa and Karṇāṭa lent him aid and enabled him to reign the throne of his ancestors at Dhār as stated in Vik. by Bilhaṇa (III 67). This shows that in those days Indian states did not fight with each other for extension of territory. This event further shows that people in every country wished to be ruled by some one of its hereditary ruling family. As stated in Volume II, p. 221, even Arab writers have recorded that when a king conquers another kingdom he always places on the throne some one belonging to the family of the fallen king. "The inhabitants could not suffer it otherwise." Even this little feeling of nationality gradually disappeared in this sub-period (we see in this instance Jayasinha being to be placed on the throne of Malwā by a third king), for reasons we shall explain later on. Bhoja's death must have occurred before 1055 A. D. as Jayasinha's grant issued from Dhārā in that year has been found (Ep. Ind. III P. 46) wherein he declares himself to be a son of Bhoja. It is inexplicable how even in his third edition of E. H. I. (1914) Sir Vincent Smith gives 1060 A. D. as the date of Bhoja's death; as no authority is quoted here we are unable to discuss this date further.† Bhoja conquered Konkan in St. 1076 or 1019 or the year before as appears plainly from his grant of that year (Ep. In. XI.). Why Bhoja fought with Konkan in his early age does not appear (he must have been about 20 at that time) and how he went so far from his kingdom remains to be solved though the fact of the conquest cannot be denied. Proba-

---

* तत्रादित्यप्रतापे गतवति सदनं स्वर्गिणां भर्गभक्ते ।
व्याप्ता धारेव धात्री रिपुतिमिरभरैर्मौललोकस्तदाभूत् ॥

† The probable authorities viz: Taranginī and Vikramānkacharita have been duly noticed and explained by Col. Luard and Lele in their book on Paramaras (pp. 22-23).

bly this was an offshoot of his first war with Vikramāditya V (1009-1018) whom he is said to have taken prisoner and put to death as stated by Col. Luard and Lele. But if this event is true, Bhoja might have made more of this affair in his inscription than his conquest of Konkan the king of which was less important than the king of Karṇāta, this war being dated, if true, about the same time. But these wars are practically of no interest to the general reader of Indian history and need not, therefore be investigated further.

The war with Karṇadeva and Bhīma which immediately preceded or followed Bhoja's death is, however, of great importance and we will examine the authorities mentioned carefully. It seems to us that a misconception has arisen here from the story given by Merutuṅga that Bhīma and Karṇa conjointly attacked Dhārā, conquered it and put to flight Bhoja who eventually died. It is notorious that these Prabandhas give fanciful tales of famous kings which require to be carefully sifted. Keilhorn first thought that the story given by Merutuṅga is supported by a verse in the Udepur praśasti (E. II). He subsequently however in giving a similar verse from the Nagpur Praṣasti (Ep. Ind. II) expressed the caution that the story was not likely and that various arguments could be adduced against the truth of the version. We think it quite unbelievable that such a powerful king as Bhoja could have been attacked and defeated in this way and that his end was miserable. On verse 9 of the Udepur praśasti, Kielhorn wrongly remarked that it virtually admits that Bhoja finally succumbed to his foreign foes, as the verse simply says that Dhārā was enveloped in darkness *after* Bhoja had left this world (when he whose valour was as great as that of the sun, the devotee of Śiva, had gone to heaven*). Similarly in editing the Nagpur Praśasti Kielhorn observed "Bhojadeva's end was unfortunate but thought it necessary now to state that the story of Merutuṅga was not quite reliable. Now even here the wording of the Nagpur Praśasti does not indicate that Bhoja's end was unfortunate: "When Bhoja became a brother of Indra (died) and when the kingdom was beset with trouble"‡ shows that Bhoja died peacefully and trouble arose afterwards. Neither record expresses any tinge of sorrow about the end of Bhoja. It seems, therefore, clear that it was

* तत्रादित्यप्रतापे गतवति सदनं स्वर्गिणां भर्गभक्ते ।

‡ तास्मिन्वासवबन्धुतामुपगते राज्ये च कुल्याकुले ॥

only after Bhoja's death that his foes thought it a proper opportunity to advance against Malwa. Bhoja's son and successor Jayasinha was the king whose end seems to have been unfortunate as we shall see further on. In short the Nagpur and Udepur praśastis do not lend any support to the story of Merutuṅga that Bhoja's end was unfortunate. Unfortunately the story is still retained in the 3rd Ed. of Sir Vincent Smith's history and has, therefore, to be refuted. There are further arguments to show why the story of Merutuṅga is concocted. Not only do the records of Chedi Haihayas not speak of this supposed successful attack on such a famous king as Bhoja but the records of Gujarat Chālukyas also do not mention this exploit of Bhīma. In fact in their many records Bhīma's name goes without any epithet while the name of Jayasinha Siddharāja is always extolled with the expression 'the conqueror of Avantinātha.' Had Bhīma conquered Bhoja, that exploit, the summit of his glorious career, would certainly have been considered higher than that of Jayasinha, in conquering a minor king of Awanti. But further the Nagpur Praśasti does not mention Bhīma at all when it mentions that Dhārā was attacked immediately after Bhoja's death. It mentions Karṇa of Chedi and Karṇāta who were either leagued together or were contending with each other for the overlordship of Malwa. This point we will discuss later on but this statement in the Nagpur Praśasti which makes no mention of Bhīma is sufficient to discredit Merutuṅga who probably wrote to please the Gujarat kings and concocted stories of their exploits. In conclusion, therefore, we believe that Bhoja's end was peaceful and that foes attacked Dhārā after his death.

Another misconception associated with this event is that the Gāhadavāla king Chandradeva assisted in—indeed effected— "the quelling of the anarchy which resulted in the defeat and death of Bhoja." This misconception has arisen on a misconstruction of the verses in praise of the Gāhadavāla king Chandradeva in two Gāhadavāla grants. The allusion to Bhoja in the grant of Madanapāla (Ind. Ant. XIV p. 103) is explicit but the verse cannot be construed in the sense that the Gāhadavāla king Chandra had anything to do with the death, or the anarchy which followed the death, of Bhoja nor can the verse in the other record (Ind. Ant. XVIII p. 11) be so construed. (Their correct construction we will discuss presently). Moreover the date of the rise of Chandradeva Gāhadavāla does not coincide with the date of Bhoja's death about 1055 A. D.

His rise must be and has been dated much later that is about 1080 A. D. And lastly there could have been no necessity for his interference, since while Karṇadeva of Chedi was the aggressor and the creator of anarchy, Someśvara of Karṇātaka was the friend of the Paramāra king as stated further on by Luard and Lele at p. 15 (though at page 27 we have the contradictory remark that Jayasinha, Bhoja's successor, was installed king at Dhar by Karṇa and Bhīma themselves). The Prabandhakāras have made many imaginary statements but even they do not appear to have brought in the Gāhadavāla (or Rathod) king Chandradeva and we may safely say that this idea has been suggested by a misconstruction of the two verses above referred to.

Bhoja was one of the great monarchs of India whose fame has been established in the annals of Indian history for all time to come. He was not only an independent king in his own country Malwa but his power was acknowledged throughout India. This has not been sufficiently realised. In the Udepur Praśasti he is said to rule the whole of India from the Himalayas to Rāma's bridge. This is no doubt untrue literally; but in ancient times imperial power did not mean in India actual rule but indicated overlordship only. Such praise when recorded in the inscriptions of the family itself would be treated merely as a hyperbole of the family bards; but when the praise is bestowed in the records of other kingly families the praise must be admitted to be based on truth.. And we have such confirmation of this praise in the inscriptions of the imperial Gāhadavālas themselves. The two verses in the grants of Madanapāla and Govindachandra which have been, as above stated, misunderstood contain clear proof that Bhoja was for a time acknowledged as supreme king of India. The verse in the second grant (Ind. Ant. XIV p. 103) states,* "When Śri Bhoja bhūpa became a guest of the eyes of the women of the gods and when Karṇa remained only in his renown and the earth was troubled, the husband whom the earth chose from love and the protector in whom she placed confidence was king Chandradeva." This clearly means that the two great wielders of imperial power on earth (the

---

* याते श्रीभोजभूपे विबुधवरवधूनेत्रसीमातिथित्वं ।
श्रीकर्णे कीर्तिशेषं गतवति च नृपे क्ष्मात्यये जायमाने ॥
भर्तारं यं धरित्री त्रिदिवविभुनिभं प्रीतियोगादुपेता ।
त्राता विश्वासपूर्वं समभवदिह स क्ष्मापतिश्चन्द्रदेवः ॥

Indian land) who immediately preceded Chandradeva were Bhoja and Karṇa. This Bhoja could not be Bhoja of Pratīhāra Imperial line of kings as he had long passed away (A. D. 840-890 vide Vol. II p. 113) and must be Bhoja of Malwa (who passed away in 1055 A. D.). The Karṇa referred to may be taken to be the Karṇadeva of the Chālukyas of Anhilwād who reigned from 1063 to 1093 A. D. or Karna son of Gāngeyadeva king of Chedi. The former seems somewhat doubtful for the sovereignty of India is said to have passed to Chandradeva after Karṇa's death. The Karṇa of Gujarat seems to have passed away in the nineties of the 11th century; and he is not extolled so much as his successor Jayasinha Siddharāja; while Karṇa of Chedi though the most powerful monarch of his line and is said to have conquered Malwa after Bhoja's death, yet he reigned long and seems to have been alive when Chandradeva rose to power about 1080 A. D. This verse says that Chandradeva attained imperial power when Karṇa passed away. Whatever may be the explanation of this difficulty, this verse does not speak of the land of Malwa for Malwa never acknowledged Chandradeva as king. It speaks plainly of imperial power in the whole of India, for the three kings Bhoja, Karṇa and Chandra were actual kings in three separate kingdoms viz: Malwa, Chedi and Kanauj. The trouble referred to in the word Kshmātyaya is the same as that referred to in the more general wording of the verse in the first record of the Gāhadavālas (Ind. Ant. XVIII p. 11) which may be translated as follows* "King Chandradeva who destroyed the darkness of violent and bold warriors and who allayed the troubles of all peoples by his greater valour." This refers plainly to the trouble caused to the whole people of India by the raids of the ferocious Turks. In fact it seems that Bhoja had also contributed his quota to the allaying of this trouble and hence it is that he is remembered as the first king to whom India looked to for redress and afterwards to Karṇa the king of Chedi, Bhoja ruled upto 1055 and Karṇa later and the mantle of removing the oppression of the foreigners fell in the third instance on Chandradeva who as shown later on in Kanauj history, for this purpose, removed the incapable Pra-

* तस्यासीत्तनयो नयैकरसिकः क्रान्तद्विषन्मण्डलो ।
विध्वस्तोद्धतधीरयोधतिमिरः श्रीचन्द्रदेवो नृपः ॥
येनोदारतरप्रतापशमिताशेषप्रजोपद्रवं ।
श्रीमद्गाधिपुराधिराज्यमसमं दोर्विक्रमेणार्जितम् ॥

tīhāra king on the imperial throne of Kanauj and established his dynasty there. Viewed in this light the praise bestowed upon Bhoja by the Udepur Praśasti that he was lord of the whole of India does not seem hyperbolical, supported as it is by this outside testimony of a Gāhadavāla inscription. Indeed the next verse in the Udepur Praśasti appears in another light from this standpoint and when it says that Bhoja conquered the king of Gurjaras, it refers not to Bhīma the king of what is now Gujarat, but to one of the Pratīhāra kings of Kanauj who are styled in records of other states of that period as kings of Gurjaras (See Vol. II p. 98, 163). In fact modern Gujarat came to be called so probably at the end of the next century as we shall ourselves show later on and Gurjaras in this verse means very probably Pratīhāra kings of Kanauj who had become effete and even dependents and allies of the Turks. It seems, therefore, probable that Bhoja had not only defeated Gāngeyadeva in the east but also the weak Pratīhāra king and successor of Rājyapāl of Kanauj and also the Turks who assisted him. He thus freed the land of Northern India from the troubles of the foreign and irreligious rule of the Turks. The verse declares that mere contingents or generals sent by Bhoja defeated these kings and it seems very probable that Bhoja had sent forces as far north as the Panjab and Delhi. Although, therefore, Bhoja did not, like Samudragupta to whom Sir Vincent Smith compares him, take a world-conquering expedition through India, his power was felt and acknowledged all over the country and it is this which must have enabled him to build Śiva temples in such distant places as Somnāth, Rameśvara, Sundīra (east coast?) and Kedāra, in the four quarters of India as he is described to have done.* That he built a temple of Mahākāla in his own kingdom needs no mention but that he was allowed to build temples to god Śiva whose devout devotee he was, in such foreign lands and at so great a distance, testifies both to his political power and his prosperity as also his organising capacity. One is reminded here of the same power, prosperity and capacity of a later sovereign of Malwa, Devi Ahalyābai of sacred memory, who similarly built temples and ghats in sacred places throughout India. Ahalyābai built these holy

---

* केदार-रामेश्वर-सोमनाथ-सुंडीर-कालानल-रुद्रसत्कैः ।
सुराश्रयैः व्याप्य च यः समन्तात् यथार्थसंज्ञां जगतीं चकार ॥

(Udepur Praśasti Ep. Ind. I.)

structures from the immense legacy left her by Malharrao Holkar from his plunder in other kingdoms. Possibly Bhoja also did the same and expended the plunder obtained from Anhilwad and other kingdoms by his generals in this charitable work throughout India. Bhoja did not, like his contemporary Mahmud, amass wealth from plunder for the pleasure of mere possession or for aggrandizement but spent his treasures in constructing such holy temples as would make him known throughout India. Even in distant Kashmir which could not have acknowledged him as suzerain, he had a tank built at his expense to commemorate his name in that country. This was probably allowed by Kashmir entirely through respect for Bhoja's great fame and virtues.* But history does not record that Bhoja plundered *many* countries as Mahmud did and we may surmise that Bhoja's resources were mostly derived from his own country. Malwa seems to have been extremely prosperous during his reign and his government was so good that it brought him large revenues without being oppressive. In this affluenc therefore, we have the evidence of both the prosperity of his country and the orderliness and benignity of his administration.

Bhoja was not only a great author but a great patron of learned men. Unlike again Mahmud, his contemporary, Bhoja was extremely generous to learned men and stories are related of his generosity to poets by story-tellers in which a lakh of rupees is said to have been the usual reward of poets who brought a single new and good śloka. This is exactly the reverse of Mahmud's reputation. Although we regard these tales as story-tellers' exaggertions, there is no doubt of Bhoja's extreme liberality to learned men and this has certainly been the greatest preserver of his glory and renown than his political successes or his great structures none of which is now remembered or left. We do not believe there was any Kālidāsa, new, or old, at his court and this name is a fiction of story-tellers or Padmagupta author of Navasāhasānkacharita and court-poet of his father also,

* Kalhaṇa gives the interesting story in the Rājataranginī and states that Bhoja of Malwa had taken the vow of washing his face every morning with water of this Pāpasūdana Tirtha in Kashmir and one Padmarāja a favourite attendant of the Kashmir king of the time enabled Bhoja to observe this vow by constantly sending him glass vessels filled with water from the tank. Of this incident we shall have to speak again in our general survey chapter.

was given the title of Kālidāsa. Dhanapāla another poet is properly associated with Bhoja and Ūvata a native of Vadnagar wrote his commentary on the Vājasaneyī Samhitā at Ujjain during Bhoja's rule (Luard & Lele p. 21). Many other learned men must have attended Bhoja's court but their names are not yet known.

Summing up one may bestow the highest praise one can on Bhoja and look upon him as one of the greatest monarchs of India. He is probably called Kavirāja and Mâlavachakravartin by the inscription writers of the time even in other countries, being king emperor of Malwa (the meaning of the eptithet chakravartin we will explain later on). The happiest way of expressing his greatness is by repeating what the Udepur Praśasti says of him "He accomplished, he ordered, he gave, and he knew in a way none else did." This pithily refers to his great undertakings in building throughout India, to his supreme political power, and to his extreme liberality to poets and learned men‡ and finally to his extensive studies and knowledge.

---

* क्षिप्रं मालवचक्रवर्तिनगरी धारेति को विस्मयः (Ep. Ind. I. p. 297 Vadnagar Praśasti of the Châlukyas of Gujarat).

‡ शासितं विहितं दत्तं ज्ञातं यद्यन्न केनचित्। किमन्यत्कविराजस्य श्रीभोजस्य प्रशस्यते (Ep. Ind. I. p. 222).

CHAPTER IV

PARAMĀRAS OF DHAR—LATER KINGS

We have devoted so much space to the reign of Bhoja as he was not only the greatest kings of the Paramāras of Malwa but undoubtedly one of the greatest kings of Hindu India. The Paramāra line of Malwa having attained its pinnacle of glory under Bhoja naturally came on the incline of deterioration after him. His son Jayasinha had a troubled and probably a short reign. His inscription dated 1055 A. D. was issued from Dhār and he appears to have been reinstated on the ancestral throne by Vikramāditya by order of his father Āhavamalla Someśvara to whom he fled for refuge when Karṇa of Chedi had driven him out of Malwa, probably soon after Bhoja's death. He made a grant to the Brahmins of Amareśvara of Māndhātā on the Nerbudda, of a village in the Pūrṇaka (Punāsā) Pattaka. As his reign was short and troubled and as he was restored by the aid of others and probably driven away again, his name is not mentioned in the two great stone records of the Paramāras viz. Udepur and Nagpur Praśastis. The kingdom was rescued from this troubled condition by the valour of one Udayāditya* who is said to be a relation of Bhoja. What relation he bore to him is not stated and has not yet been ascertained. From Udayāditya's time the kingdom of Malwa appears to have started on a second period of successful career, though not as brilliant as that of Munja and Bhoja, for about two hundred years, before it was finally subjected to the rule of the Mahomedans.

---

* Col. Luard and Lele are, we think, mistaken when they state about this king that "In this deliverance of Dhār this king was assisted by Chālukya Vikramāditya VI of Kalyan from a verse in Bilhaṇa's poem (Vik. III 67)." Curiously enough this aid is referred to by them in another connection also at p. 15. It seems clear from the reference to Udayāditya in the Nagpur and an Udepur Praśastis that he delivered Malwa by his own prowess and not by the aid of any foreign king. In fact the former document refers to the Karṇāṭa king not as a friend and supporter but as one of the troublers of Malwa. The translation of the verse

तस्मिन्वासवबन्धुतामुपगते राज्ये च कुल्याकुले ।
मग्नस्वामिनि तस्य बन्धुरुदयादित्योऽभवद् भूपतिः ॥
येनोद्धृत्य महार्णवोपममिलत्कर्णाटकर्णप्रभृ- ।
त्युर्वीपालकदर्थितां भुवमिमां श्रीमद्वराहायितम् ॥

Udayāditya was a powerful king and had also the literary taste of his ancestors. He was also a great builder like his predecessor. The lofty Śiva temple at Udepur, a town founded by him and bearing his name, still attests the greatness of his glory and art. For the temple has the highest pinnacle in ancient India and the stones are placed one upon another without any mortar. They are held together by being correctly worked and fitted. There are many Paramāra inscriptions in this temple which seems to have become the hereditary repository of their fame, the earliest being two of Udayāditya himself. These show that its construction was begun in 1059 A. D. and finished in 1080 A. D. (Luard and Lele p. 29). This king appears to

---

(we have read here प्रभृत्युर्वी and not प्रभुपुर्वी as read by Kielhorn in the lacuna after प्र of the original, as प्रभुर्वी gives no meaning and is also incorrect,) may run as follows :—

"When he (Bhoja) became a brother of Indra (died) and the kingdom was troubled and its lord was submerged, his relative Udayāditya became king who acted like Varāha (boar-incarnation) in lifting up this earth, troubled as it was by kings such as Karṇa and Karṇāṭa mingling like great oceans." Here clearly the Karṇāṭa king is not referred to as a friend. This incident has not been properly understood from the beginning. Kielhorn starting the theory that it was Bhoja himself who was troubled in his last days by Karṇa. It clearly appears from the words "*when Bhoja died*" use here as also from the wording in the Udepur Praśasti that the trouble arose *after* the death of Bhoja. The trouble probably arose by an invasion by Karṇa of Chedi, son of Gāṅgeya who probably took advantage of Bhoja's death to retrieve the glory of Chedi sullied by Gāṅgeya's defeat. Jayasinha son of Bhoja a weak prince fled to Kalyāṇa to seek help from Someśwara and he forgetting his hereditary enmity and perhaps to oppose the growing power of Chedi lent him assistance and replaced him on the throne of Malwa. It is to this installation of Jayasinha son of Bhoja that the verse in Vikramānkacharita III refers. Unfortunately the name of the Malwa king is not given in this verse स मालवेन्दुं शरणप्रविष्टमकन्टके स्थापयति स्वराज्ये ॥ Vik. III which mentions merely a Malwa king (Malavendu). But he could neither have been, Bhoja himself nor Udayāditya. Karṇa must have come again and driven the weak Jayasinha again and the unfortunate king is no more heard of. (This is suggested by the word 'Magnasvāmini' of the Nagpur record). It was from this trouble of the two great armies of the north and the south which like oceans meeting in Malwa sub-merged the kingdom that Udayāditya by *his valour alone* rescued the country (See also Ep. Ind. XIX p. 108 महाकलहकल्पान्ते यस्योद्दामभिराशुगैः । कनि नोन्मूलितास्तुङ्गा भूभृतः कटकोल्बणाः ॥). Merutuṅga has commenced this mischief but the inscriptions of the time and Vikramānkacharita of Bilhaṇa when properly construed clearly prove his version to be untrue and imaginary.

have had a long rule from about 1056 A. D. to about 1081 or later. He was succeded by his son Lakshmaṇadeva who was a great warrior and scholar also. In the Nagpur Praṣasti the greatest praise is bestowed upon him,occupying many verses. They contain a description of his Digvigaya, commencing from Gauda and including Chedi, Chola, Pāndya, Ceylon and many other kingdoms and ending with the Turushkas on the Vankshu (Oxus) and the Kīra king in the Himalayas (the usual pun on this word being made and the king of Kīra being represented as a parrot confined in a cage and singing the praises of Lakshmaṇadeva). This is certainly a hyperbole of the inscription-writer who is none else than his successor and younger brother Naravarman. This king was a great poet and has plainly copied Kālidāsa from his reference to the river Oxus (Vankshu) mentioned by Kālidāsa also in the Digvijaya of the mythical Raghu. We merely give this exaggeration as an illustration of such hyperboles even in inscriptions which are expected to give historical facts. Even inscriptions though contemporary and reliable records have, therefore, to be put into the crucible of credibility and examined carefully. Though there is nothing to show why the statements are false, they cannot be accepted unless we have corroborative evidence from records of other kingly families and, if possible, of foreign writers also.

Lakshmaṇadeva died childless and he was succeeded by his younger poet-brother Naravarmadeva sometime before his composition of the Nagpur praśasti dated 1104 A. D. A fragment of an unpublished praṣasti found in the Mahākāla temple at Ujjain was also his composition (Luard and Lele p. 29). In the Bhoja-Śālā at Dhār and in Umā and Mahākāla temples at Ujjain inscriptions have been found in serpentine form giving the Sanskrit noun and verb terminations of Pāṇini accompanied by verses containing the names of Udayāditya and Naravarman and making punning allusions to their valour and learning.* It appears that these were used in teaching in the schools at Dhār and Ujjain.

Udāyaditya's youngest son, Jagadeva, was a most chivalrous young prince and stories of his exploits in Gujarat in the service of Chālukya kings and in other places including his own native

* उदयादित्यनामांकवर्णनागकृपाणिका । ....मणिश्रेणी सृष्टा सुकविबन्धुना ॥ .... कवीनां च नृपाणां च हृदयेषु निवेशिता ॥ (Luard and Lele p. 30)

land are told by Prabandhakāras which may or may not be true. But history cannot proceed without recording his name and his legendary career of adventure.

Naravarman like his father Udayāditya and like Bhoja himself was a devotee of Śiva but they were all tolerant of other religions, especially Jainism which was then spreading in Gujarat and Malwa and whose teachers were indeed powerful disputants. Disputations were often held before Naravarman between Jain Pandits and Hindu orthodox Pandits. One such disputation is described as held at Mahākāla temple itself between Jain muni Ratnasūri and a Śaivite teacher named Vidyāśivavādin. In such disputations it appears that the Jain Pandits usually got the upperhand which led to their influencing the kings themselves before whom they were held. The Paramāra kings, however, remained devotees of Śiva throughout and Naravarman, though an admirer of Jain scholars and respectfully referred to by Jain writers, was never converted to Jainism (Luard and Lele p. 31).

Naravarman reigned till 1133 A. D. and he was succeeded by his son Yaśovarmadeva who has left a grant dated V. S. 1190 made on the first anniversary Śrāddha of his father. Malwa and Gujarat were enemies since long and fights had been going on between them since the days of Naravarman but in the reign of Jayasinha Siddharāja the power of Gujarat increased and Yaśovarman was towards the end of his reign vanquished in batttle by him and taken prisoner with his family. He is said to have been kept in a wooden cage in Anahilwād. This fact stated at length by many Prabandhakāras seems to be true as it is mentioned in an inscription of Jayasinha himself (Ind Ant. X p. 159). He annexed Malwa to his dominion and sent a Jain minister to govern the country. He is usually also called Avantīnātha in Chālukya inscriptions which proves that a large part of Malwa with Ujjain and Dhār was in possession of the Chālukyas for some time. At length Yaśovarman contrived to escape from his prison and with the aid of a Chauhān king of Ajmer regained a part of his dominions. And he succeeded in making his peace with Jayasinha. The latter died in 1142 A. D. and Yaśovarman also died soon after. Yaśovarman thus ruled from about 1133 to 1143 A. D. and in this time the power of Malwa finally declined. His mother was Māmalādevi a Chedi princes in memory of whom Yaśovarman made a grant in 1134 A. D.

which has been found. It grants the village of Reghva a few miles east of Tikari in Dhar State (Luard and Lele p. 34).

Yaśovarmadeva was succeeded by Jayavarman and in his reign Malwa was again conquered by Gujarat, when the famous Kumārapāla had established his power there after conquering his foes. A king Ballāladeva of Malwa is mentioned by Prabandhkāras as assisting these foes and Kumārapāla had his head cut off and suspended at the gate of his palace. The Vadnagar Praśasti of Kumārapāla mentions this fact but does not give the name Ballāladeva. Who this king was has not been ascertained, but he is believed not to be a Paramāra of Bhoja's family. Keilhorn suggests that during the time of Yaśovarman's captivity some portions of Malwa might have been taken possession of by adventures. But we can give another explanation and it is this viz: that Ballāladeva must be another name of Jayavarman himself. For we do not think it possible that the kings of Gujarat or other countries would recognise an usurper who did not belong to the family of Bhoja as king of Malwa or would take credit for destroying an usurper, as they distinctly do.* It seems, therefore, probable that Jayavarman was himself captured in the battle with Kumārapāla. At this time of trouble and defeat Jayasinha's youngest brother Lakshmīvarman set up his authority in the hilly parts of Eastern Malwa from Bhopal to Hoshangabad by his own prowess and called himself Mahākumāra. The epithet Samadhigata-pañchamahāśabda used by him no doubt shows that he did not pretend to be an independent king but that he was a Sāmanta of Malwa. Yet he had obtained his power not by gift but by the sword as expressly stated in inscriptions of this branch (Ind. Ant. XIX). For this reason we do not think that the words, interregnum and dual rule, used by Col. Luard and Mr. Lele in their account of this period properly apply to the situation of Malwa at this time. In Jayavarman's time much of Malwa went into the possession of Gujarat and after his death or his ceasing to rule a portion of the dominion of Malwa was appropriated by Lakshmīvarman. When Jayavarman ceased to rule and how is not clear. Kielhorn surmises that he was deposed by his younger brother Ajayavarman. But as suggested above, it is probable that he was taken prisoner in

* The wording in the Vadnagar Praśasti is द्वारालंबितमालवेशशिरः । and in Abu record यश्चौलुक्यकुमारपालनृपतिप्रत्यर्थितामागतं गत्वा सत्वरमेव मालवपतिं बल्लालमालब्धवान् (Ep. Ind. VIII p. 211).

his conflict with Kumārapāla and eventually beheaded by Yaśodhavala of Chandrāvatī. In view of the sadness of his death the expression "*Rājye vyatīte*" is probably knowingly used by inscription writers. It is at least certain that the cessation of his rule was strange. He appears to have ceased to rule sometime before 1063 A. D., the date of Lakshmīvarman's grant (Ind. Ant. XVIII p. 254 and XIX) and probably soon after 1043 A. D.

It seems also probable that Yaśovarman had three sons Jayavarman, Ajayavarman and Lakshmīvarman. When Jayavarman ceased to rule, Ajayavarman normally became the ruler of Malwa and his titles are the usual P. B., Mahārājādhirāja Parmeśvara and Lakshmīvarman who set up for himself a principality by his own valour about Bhopal and Hoshangabad took the titles of a Sāmanta as stated above. These two lines continued for about three generations and they eventually united under Devapāladeva as we shall presently see. We do not think however, that this was a dual rule as the latter family, though nominally, acknowledged the supermacy of the family of Ajayavarman by contenting itself with the titles of a Sāmanta.

Ajayavarman, the lineal representative of the kings of Malwa and ruling in the country round Dhār, the capital of Malwa since the time of Bhoja, is known only from the records left by his successors. We know nothing about him, but we may be certain that these records establish his identity as a different king from Jayavarman which is sometimes doubted. In Sanskrit especially where sandhis declare correctly the words employed, while in Lakshmīvarman's documents we distinctly read the name Jayavarman, in Vindhyavarman's record we distinctly read the name Ajayavarman. Why the former does not mention Ajayavarman is to be explained by the fact that Lakshmīvarman seems to have set up his principality in the days of Jayavarman and perhaps by his acquiescence. Ajayavarman continued the main line for some time and he was followed by his son Vindhyavarman who seems to have recovered much of the ancestral territory. From an inscription in the famous Udepur Śiva temple we know that part of the country was in the possession of Kumārapāla of Gujarat on 12th December 1163 on which day on the occasion of a lunar eclipse he made a grant (Ind. Ant. XVIII p. 343). His representative or viceroy was Mahā Rājaputra Śri Vasantapāla. There is another grant recorded by Chāhada, probably his successor in office, in 1166 A. D. and a third grant still by Ajayapāladeva of Gujarat in 1173 A. D. of a village in Bhaillaswami (Bhelsa) district. Vindhyavarman appears to have regained possession after Ajayapāla of Gujarat whose reign ended in 1176, as Ajayapāla's inscription at Udepur dated 1173 (Ind. Ant. XVIII) shows that he still had power in Eastern Malwa. Ajayapāla's successor was a minor and in his reign Malwa probably fully reverted to the Paramāras. Vindhyavarman is described as a great warrior in a grant of Arjunavarman, his grandson, dated 1215. He certainly had possession of Mandugadh the fortress of Dhar (Maṇḍapadurga), where an unpublished inscription shows that he had a minister named Bilhaṇa (Luard and Lele p. 37) who was a poet. * This shows that this king was a patron of poets. This hereditary tendency of this king is also referred to by the Jain writer Āśādhara of whom we shall presently give further particulars. Vindhyavarman ruled from about 1160 to about 1180 (Luard and Lele p. 58) and he was succeeded by his son Subhatavarman. He also was a powerful king and further restored the power of Malwa. He seems to have not only recovered his possessions but even led an expedition against Gujarat. ‡ A Yādava king of Devagiri is said to have conquered Malwa but probably this was an unimportant victory. Subhatavarman's reign is given by Col. Luard and Mr. Lele as extending from 1180 to 1210 A. D. He was succeeded by Arjunavarmadeva whose grants issued from Mandapadurga (Mandu), Bhrigukachchha (Broach) and Amareśvara (Māndhātā) on the Nerbudda have been found, dated respectively 1211, 1213 and 1215 A. D. He is said to have defeated Jayasinha II king of Gujarat and a drama composed by a court-poet on this victory and inscribed on slabs has been found at Dhār by Mr. Lele, used in the Kamāla Maula mosque. The drama has been deciphered and edited in Ep. Ind. VIII. It was composed by Madana a Gauda Brahmin who was a pupil of Āśādhara the Jain pandit and was *guru* of the king. The drama was acted in the Sarasvatibhuvana on the occasion of a spring festival. This drama describes Arjunavarman as an incarnation of Bhoja himself which prays appears to be well-deserved as Arjunadeva was not only a patron of poets but was himself a poet and an author. † Rasikasañjīvanī, a commentary

* विन्ध्यवर्मनृपतेः प्रसादभूः । सान्धिविग्रहिकबिल्हणः कविः ॥

‡ See Ep. Ind. IX p. 108 गर्जद्गुर्ज्जरपट्टण &c.

† काव्यगान्धर्वसर्वस्वनिधिना येन सांप्रतम् । भारावतारणं देव्याश्चक्रे पुस्तकवीणयोः

Ep. Ind. IX p. 108.

on the Amaruśataka is one of his known works. He is said to have also written commentaries on the works of Bhoja. He thus seems to have been brave, learned and liberal like his ancestor Bhoja and like him he seems to have been fortunate also; for the glory of Malwa departed after his death, which must have occurred about 1216 A. D. as his successor's record dated 1218 A. D. has been found.

This successor was Devapālavarman, a grandson of Lakshmivarman of the collateral line, Arjunavarman probably dying childless. The Jain Pandit Āśādhara lived during his reign also, as he says he finished his Triśashṭismṛiti in 1235 A. D. in the reign of this king and he lived on during the reign of the next king Jayatuṅgadeva also as he says he composed his commentary on Dharmāmṛita, a work of his own, in 1244 A. D. during his reign. Devapāladeva, therefore, may safely be taken to have ruled from 1216 to 1240 A. D. (Col. Luard and Lele).

It is thus during this reign that Altamash raided Malwa and destroyed the temple of Mahākāla at Ujjain in 1235 A. D. Malwa was not finally subjected to Mahomedan rule till many years after this event and descendants of Devapāla ruled in Malwa viz.: 1 Jayatungadeva (1240–1256), 2 Jayavarman (1256–1261), 3 Jayasinha (1261–1280), 4 Bhoja II (1280–1301) and 5 Jayasinha whose inscription dated 1309 A. D. has been found at Udepur. Malwa was finally reduced about this time by Ain-ul-mulk a governor from Delhi who reduced Chanderi, Ujjain, Dhar and Mandu (Luard and Lele). Thus ended the great Paramāra line of Malwa after a brilliant career of four centuries. The present representative of the Paramāras are in Malwa the princes of Rajgadh and Narasinggadh of Umatwada Bhopal Agency) and the chief of Bijolia in Mewad (Gourishankar Ojha in Tod's Rajastan).

It remains to shortly notice the branch line started by Lakshmīvarman in about 1144, at the time of Jayavarman's death or ceasing to rule. His son Mahākumāra Hariśchandra has left a grant dated 1178 A. D. and a grant of Udayavarman his son dated 1200 A. D. has been found. His son Devapāladeva became king of Malwa as stated above. The grants of this line were issued from near Bhopal and Hoshangabad in which parts of Malwa it appears to have ruled. Malwa usually comprised all the territory from the Nerbudda northwards, the Vindhya range and the plateau beyond as far north as Mandsaur and from Bhopal in the east to about Dohad in the west. Sometimes there was a diminution of this territory and sometimes an extension southwards as far as the Tapti; Berar and part of C. P. including Nagpur was also sometimes possessed by the Paramāras.

The genealogy of the family from Bhoja is as follows with known dates (Kielhorn's genealogies in Ep. Ind. VIII).

1 Bhoja 1021 (c. 1010 to 1055)
2 Jayasinha 1055 (c. 1056 to 1059)
3 Udayāditya a relative (c. 1059 to 1080)
4 Lakshmadeva (c. 1081 to 1104)
5 Naravarman brother, m. Momalādevi, 1104 and 1107 (c. 1104 to 1133)
6 Yaśovarman 1134,1135 (c. 1133 to 1142)

- 7 Jayavarman 1143 (c. 1142-1144)
- 8 Ajayavarman (c. 1144-1160)
    - 9 Vindhyavarman (c. 1160-1180)
    - 10 Subhaṭavarman (c. 1180-1210)
    - 11 Arjunavarman 1211,1212,1215 (c. 1210-1216)
- Lakshmīvarman
    - Hariśchandra (1178-1179)
    - Udayavaraman 1200
    - 12 Devapāla 1218,1229,1232 (c. 1216-1240)

Thus 12 kings ruled from about 1010 A. D. to 1240 A. D. giving an average for each reign of nearly ($\frac{230}{12}$) 20 years the usual rate for Indian kingly families.

It may lastly be noted that among these kings Jayasinha son of Bhoja was unfortunate and had only a short reign, being tossed between Karṇa and Karṇāta; while more unfortunate was Yaśovarman who was defeated, imprisoned and kept in a cage by Jayasinha Sidhharāja of Gujarat and Jayavarman was the most unfortunate as he was not only defeated and taken prisoner by Kumārapāla but his head was cut off and suspended at the gate of his palace. This treatment of Malwa kings by Gujarat no doubt struck terror in other kings' hearts* as stated in Vadna-

* See [illegible] ।

Ep. Ind. I p. [illegible].

gar Praśasti of Kumārapāla; but it was certainly unlike, and unworthy of, Indian kings as we shall show later on and was probably borrowed from Mahomedan methods of treating captive monarchs.

CHAPTER V.

THE CHANDELLAS OF BUNDELKHAND.

The Chandrātreya or Chandella Kshatriya family of Bundelkhand continued to flourish in this sub-period also (1000–1200 A. D.), though not with greater glory than before yet with the same vigour as in the preceding century (See Vol. II). The name of the family was a gotra name which was the ancient rule among Brahmins and probably among Kshatriyas also, the name being derived from the gotra ancestor Chandrātreya as Pārāśara is the name of a Brahmin family descended from Parāșara, much like Peterson and Johnson among the English people. This kingdom is well described by Al-Beruni who mentions the two most important fortresses in it, Kālañjara and Gwalior and also gives its capital, Khajuraho; and other Arab writers call its king Chandrarai which plainly is their Hindi name Chandra used even by Chanda Bardai.

The greatest king in this family was Dhanga the ruler in Bundelkhand at the end of the preceding sub-period. Indeed he was so powerful and well-known that his aid was sought by Jaipal of Lahore against Sabuktagin and inscriptions of the Chandella family declare that he was equal of Hammīra (Amir). It may be noted that inscription-writers, though they may exaggerate, rarely descend to falsehood and, as we have shown elsewhere, in the battle fought beyond the Indus by the combined Hindu forces against Sabuktagin, the result was victory for neither side and when Dhanga is described as equal to Amir, there is no falsehood in the declaration. Dhanga in extreme old age (about 100 years) burnt himself on a pyre of cow-dung cakes at the holy confluence of the Ganges and the Jumna at Prayāga.

Dhanga was succeeded by his son Ganda who was an equally powerful king also. He is said to have again given aid to Ānandapāla son of Jaipal in his fight with Mahmud. In this battle the Hindus were undoubtedly worsted. The course of events in this struggle of the Chandella family with Mahmud we have described elsewhere. Ganda may be said to have come to the throne in 1000 A. D. and to have ruled till about 1023 as two inscriptions of his dated 1002 and 1022 A. D. have been found. We have a detailed account about the kings of this family in Sir Vincent Smith's article on the Chandellas in Ind.

Ant. XXXVII and we take dates and facts from it with such additions here and there as we think necessary from the original records of the Chandellas and of others. The capital of the kingdom appears to be Mahoba henceforward.

Ganda was succeeded by his son Vidyādhara who ruled for a short time only (1025–1030). As crown prince he is recorded to have invaded Kanauj and defeated in battle Rāyapāla who had disgraced the Rajput name by submitting to Mahmud and accepting his overlordship. A Kachchapaghāta record shows that in this war he was assisted by his vassal king Arjunadeva of Dubhkund (in Gwalior) who is credited with having cut Rājyapāla's throat with arrows*. This established the fame of Vidyādhara as a warrior and a mutilated record of his states that he was served even by Bhoja (of Malwa) and the Kalachūri king as he lay in bed. Probably Bhoja and Gāngeya, both powerful kings of the time, were leagued with him in the task of opposing the Turks and driving them out of middle India, where they must have remained to assist and overawe Rājyapāla king-emperor of Kanauj. § It appears very probable that noted Hindu kings of the time led by the Chandella king Vidyādhara attacked the Kanauj king who had humbled himself before the Turks who kept a contingent of theirs to protect him. The Chandella country was contiguous to that of Kanauj and Vidyādhara properly enough was the leader of the confederacy. The epithet Talpabhāja shows that he lay on his couch and sent his general and feudatory the Kachchapaghāta king of Gwalior. Probably both Bhoja and Gāngeya merely sent contingents in this war which acted under the orders of Vidyādhara.

Vidyādhara was followed by Vijayapāla who also had a short reign from 1030 to about 1040 (Smith) and he was followed by his elder son Devavarman. He reigned long from 1040 to 1060

---

* श्रीविद्याधरदेवकार्यनिरतः श्रीराज्यपालं हठात् ।
कण्ठास्थिच्छिदनेकबाणनिवहैर्हत्वा महत्याहवे ॥

(Ep. Ind. IIp. 237).

§ The wording in this inscription (Ep. Ind. I. p. 222) is very important though somewhat obscure... विहितकन्याकुब्ज भूपालभङ्गम् । समरगुरुमुपास्त प्रौढभीस्तल्पभाजम् । सहकलचुरिचन्द्रः शिष्यवद्भोजदेवः ॥ There is possibly a mistake in reading प्रौढभीः. It ought to be प्रौढधीः (of finished intellect). The word Praudha can scarcely mean anything with the word Bhī. The writer seems to suggest that even such a learned king as Bhoja acted as a pupil to this teacher in battle, together with Gāngeya the famous Kalachūri king of Tripura.

and an inscription of his dated 1051 A. D. has been found (Ind. Ant. XVI p. 205). In this record Devavarman calls himself Lord of Kālanjara, taking the usual epithets of an independent king Paramabhattāraka etc. and makes a grant in a Sāmvatsarika (yearly śrāddha) of his mother Bhuvanadevī from his camp at Saharvāsa.

Devavarman was succeeded by his brother Kīrtivarman who had a longer reign and a greater fame. He reigned for forty years from 1060 to 1100, two inscriptions of his having been found one dated 1098 and the other an undated one which mentions Ganda, Vidyādhara contemporary of Bhoja, Vijayapāla contemporary of Gāngeya, and Devavarman contemporary of Karṇa. Karṇa of Tripur was the most powerful king of the Chedi line and had defeated and driven Kīrtivarman from his kingdom. But eventually the latter with the help of a Brahmin general named Gopāla defeated Karṇa "who had destroyed many princes" and regained his kingdom. This great victory is immortalised by the Prabodhachandrodaya drama composed by Kṛishṇamiśra and acted before the king about 1065. It is a drama based on Vedānta philosophy, all the *Dramatis Personæ* therein being allegorical representations of knowledge, devotion etc. Kīrtivarman also signalised his reign by striking the first Chandella coins. The form was copied from the coins of Gāngeya, the image of Hanūmān being substituted for that of Lakshmī. Hanūmān is not the tutelary deity of the Chandellas but was apparently their favourite deity; for we find an inscription of the Chandellas on the pedestal of a Hanūmān idol at Khajuraho. An inscription at Devagadh dated 1098 A. D. has been found (Ind. Ant. XVIII p. 238) which was recorded by his minister Vatsaraja who took the commanding fort of Devagadh from the Chedis, situated in a picturesque range of hills to the east of the present Lalitpur district (Smith). This inscription shows that Kīrtivarman's reign must have extended beyond 1098 A. D.

Kīrtivarman was succeeded by his son Sallakshaṇa who had a short reign from 1100 to 1110; it is recorded of him that he plundered the wealth of Mālwa and Chedi (Ep. I, 327); and he was followed by his son Jayavarman who had also a short and uneventful reign from 1110 to 1120. An inscription dated 1117 is mentioned against him by Kielhorn in his genealogies (Ep. Ind. VIII). But this is a mere re-recording of a Praśasti of his famous ancestor Dhanga by his Gaud Kāyastha writer (Ep. Ind. I p. 147). Jayavarman had no son and he was succeeded by his uncle Prithvīvarman younger son of Kīrtivarman and he naturally had a short reign from 1120 to 1125. All these three kings issued gold and silver coins which have been found, a copper coin of the last being also found.

We now come to the reign of the next illustrious king of the Chandella family namely Madanavarman son of Prithvīvarman. He reigned long and vigorously from 1125 to 1165 A. D. Eight inscriptions dating from 1129 to 1162 are mentioned against his name by Kielhorn (Ep. Ind. VIII). According to Chand Bârdai he defeated Siddharāja Jayasinha a famous king of Gujarat, while Gujarat chroniclers declare that he gave tribute to the latter. But they add the interesting story that even when Jayasinha arrived at his capital, Madanavarman remained so unconcerned that he did not stir from his pleasure garden. When informers told him of the arrival of Siddharāja, he merely said "the money-grabbing man wants some money; give him something". Siddharāja was struck with the character of Madanavarman and personally visited him in his pleasure garden where Madanavarman entertained him at a banquet. An inscription of Madana at Kālanjara, however, suggests that he defeated the Gujarat king. He is also said to have defeated Malwa and Chedi kings and to be in friendly relations with the king of Benares, the Gahadavala of Kanauj. Madanavarman built a tank at Mahoba with temples on its bank now known as Madanasāgara. In fact most Chandella kings built stupendous and splendid tanks and temples which we will notice in a note. Madanavarman also struck gold and silver coins which have been found in plenty.

As usual with kings reigning long, his elder son Pratāpavarman died before him and even his younger son Yaśovarman died and did not reign and Madana was succeeded by his grandson (Yaśovarman's son) Paramardideva or Paramala as he is commonly known who was the last famous king of the Chandella line. He reigned long from 1165 to 1203. His name is a household name in Bundelkhand together with the names of his warrior Sardars, Alha and Udalha of the Banāphara clan of Rajaputs, who sacrificed their lives for him in his war with Prithvīrāja Chauhan. The valorous and patriotic deeds of Alha and Udhala are sung by Chand Bardai in the Mahoba Khanda of Prithvīrāja Rāsā. They were killed fighting and Paramala was defeated by Prthvīrāja in the battle fought at Sisrāgadh on the Pahuj which is a tributary of the Kālīsindh. Prithvīrāja occupied

Mahoba and left his sardar Pajjun in charge of it. This event is confirmed by an inscription of Prithvirāja recorded at Madanapura a town founded by Madanavarman. But Chanda's account of Samarajit a son of Paramardin driving out Pajjun seems to be a fiction, since inscriptions show that Paramardin was succeeded by his son Trailokyavarman. (Perhaps Samarajit was another son of Paramardin probably younger).

Paramardin's defeat by Prithvirāja must not have been serious according to Smith as he was able to oppose Kutubuddin when the latter invaded his kingdom in 1203 A. D. But Prithvirāja's fight with Paramardin was in 1182 and Paramardin must have recovered himself during the period of 20 years which intervened. Paramardin's power was, however, in our view, greatly crippled by this attack of Prithvirāja which may be looked upon as a blunder and which caused the national disaster, as we shall elsewhere show, the Chandellas being one of the foremost Kshatriya clans in India. Paramardin opposed Kutubuddin and retired into the fortress of Kalanjar. Mahomedan historians relate that he eventually submitted and offered certain terms of submission such as payment of tribute and surrender of forts and elephants. But he died before these terms were put into execution and his general Ajapāla thought that he was strong enough to continue resistance and that Paramardin had unnecessarily submitted. The siege of Kalanjar, therefore, went on. Ajapāla had eventually to surrender in consequence of a draught. The tanks on the fort were all dry and the garrison unconditionally surrendered and walked out in enfeebled condition. Kutubuddin annexed the kingdom and returned to Delhi after appointing a govenor for the province. Thus closed the glorious career of the Chandella line of which Parmardin was the last and not the least king.

So many as seven inscriptions are mentioned against the name of Paramardin by Kielhorn (Ep. Ind. VIII) dating from 1167 to 1201. One more grant of Paramardin dated 1173 is since available (Ep. Ind. XVI) which mentions only two kings before him Prithvivarman and Madanavarman. On referring to these records we find that he was not only a great donor giving many villages to numerous Brahmins (Ep. Ind. IV p. 170) but was also a patron of learned men. In the inscription edited at p. 209 Ep. Ind. I, the praise bestowed upon him is worthnoticing. "There was no trace of any quarrel under his rule for he brought about friendship even between the goddess of learning and the goddess of wealth.* The prosperity of the country is also well described, a fact to which rarely a reference is made in inscriptions.§ This inscription is dated 1195, thirteen years after Paramardin's defeat by Prithvīrāja.

Although the glory of the Chandella line ended with Paramardin, it continued to rule in Bundelkhand for a long time after him. His successor Trailokyavarman is described in an inscription of his son Vīravarman as the "uplifter of the land from the ocean of distress caused by the Turks." There is no doubt that he drove out the Turks from the fort of Kālanjar and regained possession of it together with a large portion of the former territory of the Chandellas (Ep. Ind. I p. 327). ‡ The recapture of the fort is also attested by inscriptions on the fort (Smith). Trailokyavarman seems to have reigned long from 1203 to 1245. He was succeeded by his son Vīravarman many of whose inscriptions have been found (Kielhorn gives five dating from 1251 to 1286). In the inscription noted above (Ep. Ind. I p. 327) dated 1261 he is said to have married a princess named Kalyāṇadevi of Dadhīcha family of Rajputs (who are called Dahimas a gotra name again) and she built a well where the inscription was recorded. We do not know the extent of the territory which this king ruled though it seems that in Madanavarman's time it extended south as far as Bhaillasvāmin or Bhelsa (Ind. Ant. XVI p. 208). Vīravarman was succeeded by Bhojavarman two of whose inscriptions have been found, one dated 1288 A. D. We get no glimpse of the Chandellas hereafter till we come to Kiratasena who opposed Shershah and finally to the valorous queen Durgāvatī who opposed Akbar's generals and died on the field of battle as noticed in Vol. II (p. 133). The present representatives of the Chandellas of Bundelkhand are the well-known Mahārājas of Gidhaur in Bengal.

---

* परस्परविरोधस्य तस्य राज्ये कथैव का । संगतं श्रीसरस्वत्योरपि येन प्रवर्तितम् ।

§ उद्वभूवुराधिकं मणिश्यामल-कोमल तृणानि सर्वशः ।

‡ त्रैलोक्यमल्लश्च शशास राज्यम् । प्रसिद्धदुर्गप्रविधानवेधाः ।
तुरुष्ककुल्याम्बुधिमग्नधात्रीं—समुद्धृतिं विष्णुरिव प्रतन्वन् ॥

GENEALOGY OF THE CHANDELLAS OF MAHOBA.

I Gaṇḍa (c. 1000–1020) Ins. 1002, 19, 20

II Vidyādhara (c. 1020–1030)

III Vijayapāla (c. 1030–1040)
m. Bhuvanadevī

IV Devavarman Ins. 1051 (c. 1040–1060)

V Kīrtivarman Ins. 1098 (c. 1060–1100)

VI Sallakshaṇa (c 1100–1110)

VII Jayavarman Ins. 1117 (c. 1110–1120)

VIII Prithvīvarman (c. 1120–1125)

IX Madanavarman Ins. 1129, 30, 31, 39, 51, 55, 62, 68 (c. 1125–1165)

Pratāpavarman

Yaśovarman

X Paramardideva Ins. 1167, 68, 71, 82, 84, 95 and 120[illegible] (c. 1165–1203)

XI Trailokyavarman Ins. 1212 (1203–1245)

XII Vīravarman m. Kalyāṇadevi (c. 1245–1287)
Ins. 1261, 62, 62, 68, 81, 86

XIII Bhojavarman Ins. 1288

NOTE:—KHAJURAHO AND MAHOBA.

(From Sir V. Smith's article in I. A. XXXVII)

Khajuraho the former capital of the Chandellas is an insignificant village now to the south of Mahoba in Chhatarpur State. The still more ancient capital of Bundelkhand or Jajhoti (Jijāka-Bhukti) mentioned by Hiuen Tsang was Eran in Saugar District.* The boundaries of Jajhoti can be defined even now by the habitat of Jajhotia Brahmins. (As will be stated later on, Brahmins, from about the twelfth century, came to be divided into sections called after the land in which they resided; and Brahmins residing in Jajhoti were called Jajhotia as those residing in the Chedi country were called Tiwari from Tiwar its capital and those residing in Kanauj were called Kanojia). Khajuraho capital of Bundelkhand in the 11th century was out of the way of Mahomedan invasions, Mahoba being the capital in the 11th and 12th centuries; and hence fortunately, so to speak, its superb and stupendous temples still stand intact, exhibiting the wonderful art of that period and the prosperity and religious zeal of the Chandella kings. The largest temple in Khajuraho is the Kandaria Mahādeva temple built by Dhanga and next to it come the Viśvanātha and Lalji temples built by the same king and the Ramchandra temple built by his father Yaśovarman. Two Jain temples also built in the same period are noteworthy. Devi Jagadāmbi and Kunvar Math are among the best. These temples of Khajuraho "the finest in Northern India" are worthy of admiration for their harmonious design, massive dimensions and rich decoration. They are all remarkable for their curvilinear steeple which is raised without support of pillars.

At Mahobā also which became the capital of the Chandellas in this sub-period there are many remarkable structures. Especially Mahoba is distinguished for its many lakes built by many Chandella kings even in the second sub-period. Rāhilyasāgar was built by Rāhila in the former, and Kīratsāgar was built by Kīrtivarman in this sub-period. The great lake called Madanasāgar with the two fine granite temples on its bank and Kankaria Math were built by Madanavarman. Mahoba is a Tahsil town in the Banda district and can be reached from a station on the Jhansi-Manikpur line.

There were many notable forts in the Chandella territory and Al-Beruni has mentioned the two most important, Gwalior and Kalanjar. Kalanjar is an ancient fort and holy place noted as a sacred sthāna of Śiva from the days of the Mahābhārata. The wall surmounting the steep sides of the hill and the many strong gates placed at different places in the ascent are very ancient. Ajayagadh is another fortified place to which Trailokyavarman retired when Kalanjar was for a time taken by the Mahomedans. There are many inscriptions both at Kalanjar and at Ajayagadh.

---

* This is doubted by Hiralal in his paper at the Madras Oriental Conference (1924).

CHAPTER VI

THE KALACHŪRI HAIHAYAS OF CHEDI.

The third important Rajput family which flourished in the previous sub-period and rose to greater power and renown in this sub-period (1000–1200) was the Kalachūri Haihaya family of Chedī. This family as stated in Vol. II p. 137 was a pure well-known Kshatriya family and not a newly created Kshatriya family as some suppose. It belonged to the lunar race and was believed to be descended from Sahasrārjuna of Māhishmatī, well-known in Purāṇas for conquering even Rāvaṇa, as is distinctly mentioned in Chedi inscriptions even of this period. Indeed in one inscription (Ind. Ant. XVIII p. 216) their gotra Ātreya is given which is an unusual thing for inscriptions of this period. This shows that this family was very orthodox and religious as indeed its history also shows. Its tutelary god, as usual with Rajputs, was Siva. Its capital was Tripura near Jubbulpur and Tripura or Tiwari Brahmins are a distinct well-known sub-caste of the Brahmins of Northern India.

Gāṅgeya was the king of this family ruling in Tripura about the beginning of this sub-period. His date of accession is given as 1020 A. D, in Vol. II computed from the average of 20 years of each king but he may have come to the throne much earlier. He was the most illustrious ruler of this line. He struck numerous coins of gold, silver and copper which are still found in numbers. Curiously enough his coins alone are found and none of his successors. Their style was copied by neighbouring kings and even by Muhammad Ghori (Gaurishankar's Tod). He made extensive conquests, taking advantage of the fallen condition of the Pratihāra emperors of Kanauj. The eastern dominions of Kanauj must thus have fallen away and been taken possession of by Gāṅgeya and Benares was in his possession (Elliot II Baihaki p. 129) as stated before when Nialtagin raided it. Probably he even conquered Telangaṇa (Trikalinga) of the Eastern Chālukyas who had now been supplanted by the Cholas He had a fight with Bhoja of Malwa in which he was apparently worsted though neither Paramāra nor Chedi inscriptions mention this event. He does not appear to have been molested by Mahmud of Ghazni whose raids extended as far as Kālangar of the Chaṇdellas and did not probably go beyond ; though Gāṅgeya's fame was so great that his name is mentioned by Al-Beruni. In chedi inscriptions nothing particular is recorded about him but he is usually styled Vikramāditya (Ep. Ind. II p. 3). His one inscription found is dated 1037 A. D. (Keilhorn Ep. Ind. VIII) and he must have died about 1038 A. D. Inscriptions state that he retired in old age, resided at Prayāga and died there, one hundred queens burning themselves on his pyre as *satis*. This is probably an exaggeration but the fact is mentioned in a Chedi inscription (Ep. Ind. II p. 3.).

He was succeeded by his son Karṇa who was a still greater king than he. His conquests were more extensive and his dominion extended into Bihar beyond Benares in which city he built a temple named Karṇameru. He is often styled Lord of Trikaliṅga (Ep. Ind. II p. 305) in inscriptions of the Chedi family and he appears to have conquered large portions of Telaṅgaṇa from the Cholas. He founded the town named Karṇāvati (now the village Karṇabel close to Tewar) and gave it to Brahmins, learned in the Vedas (Ep. Ind. II p. 3). He conquered many kings and the list as usual includes Chola, Pāṇḍya, Murala, Aṅga, Vaṅga, Kaliṅga etc. and he is said to have devastated Champāraṇya (Ep. Ind. II p. 10). Keilhorn thought that Champāraṇya was some minor place in C. P. but Mr. Jayaswal has rightly shown that it is the ordinary Champāraṇya of Bihar and Karṇa's conquest extended as far as that place (Journal Bihar and Orissa 1924). He was waited upon by 136 princes (Gauriśhanker's Tod). His overrunning Malwa after the death of Bhoja and driving away his son has already been mentioned. This fact is noted in the Paramāra Nagpur Praśasti but strangely enough is not mentioned in any Chedi inscription. Probably Malwa was not long retained by him, being regained by Udayāditya and there is thus no mention of this victory in Chedi records.

Another inscription (Ind. Ant. XVIII p. 216) a hundred years after him gives the names of his opponents conquered in the south as Chola and Koṅga, in the east Hūṇa and Gauḍa and in the north Gurjara and Kīra carrying his conquests as far north as the Himalayas. It seems, however, really probable that Karṇa in the north defeated the Gurjara or Pratihāra emperor who was an ally of the Turks and drove the Turks out of the country. This fact appears clearly from the way in which Karṇa's name is mentioned in an inscription of the Gāhadavālas already noted (Ind. Ant. XIV p. 103). This evidence coming from the records of a foreign state is very valuable. "When

Bhoja went to heaven and when Karṇa remained only in renown and when the earth was being troubled, she found a refuge and protection in Chandradeva Gāhadavāla." We have already said that Bhoja here is Bhoja of Malwa and Karṇa is this Karṇa of the Chedis; they had successsively fought against the Turks and freed the middle land from their oppression, Bhoja from 1020 to 1040 A. D. and Karṇa probably from 1040 to 1080 A. D. Chandradeva conquered Kanauj and supplanted the effete Prâtihāras about that time. The words 'when the earth was troubled' must be referred to the trouble caused by constant raids of the Turks who having established their rule over the Panjab, from their capital Lahore, sent frequent incursions into middle India. A serious raid of this kind is recorded by Baihaki (who wrote in 1050 A. D.). He states that Ahmad Nailtagin, governor of Lahore, made a raid on Benares, a city to which even Mahmud had not gone and plundered the bazar in 1033 A.D. (Elliot Vol. II.). The city was under Gaṅga i. e. Gāṅgeya; but probably not completely. Karṇa finally took Benares into his possession and made incursions as far north as the Kīra country on the slopes of the Himalayas and removed the oppression of the Turks. He also conquered Champāraṇya and Bihar as stated before.

Like Bhoja whose illustrious example great kings tried to emulate, Karṇa was a patron of learned men also, a fact mentioned incidentally in an inscription. "His fame was greatly increased by poets who also enlightened his mind" (Ind. Ant. XVIII p. 216).* The names of these poets have not yet been known. Perhaps this fact has not attracted the attention of researchers.

Karṇa is said to have reigned long and his reign is supposed to have lasted into the 12th century; but from the verse above quoted in a Gāhadavāla grant, Karṇa was dead when Chandradeva conquered Kanauj about 1090 A. D. We, therefore, take his reign to extend from 1040 to 1080 A. D. He raised the Kalachūrī line to the pinnacle of its glory and fortunately his son was worthy enough to carry the glory on.

This son and successor Yaśahkarṇa, born of Karṇa's queen Avellādevī a Hūṇa princess, ruled long from 1080 to at least 1124, two inscriptions of his found being dated 1120 and 1122

---

* अनीयन्त परां वृद्धिं यशः संवेदनैः श्रियः । मनोविनोदनैर्यस्य कवीन्द्रैरिन्द्रियैरिव ॥

A. D. He also ruled vigorously, for he is said to have defeated Āndhra again which probably now means the Chola kings of the south, or the Gangas of Kalinganagara. He is even said to have worshipped the Bhīmeśvara Śiva temple in Āndhra country on the mouth of the Godāvari (E. I. II. p. 3), a fact stated in his own inscription also dated 1122 A. D. As the Gāhadavālas had taken possession of Kanauj, his dominion and influence in the north must have diminished. Govindachandra in an inscription confirms a grant made by him in 1120, showing that a portion of his northern territory was then in the possession of Kanauj. Kashi or Benares was certainly in the possession of Chandradeva as stated in his inscription. Lakshmadeva of Malwa is also said to have fought with him and defeated him.

Yeśahkarṇa was succeeded by his son Gayakarṇadeva who also appears to have ruled long and vigorously as inscriptions show. He married Ālhaṇadevī a princess of the Guhilot family of Mewad. An inscription recorded by her gives her pedigree as follows (Bheraghat inscription Ep. Ind. II. p. 10): "In the Gobhilagotra was Hansapāla whose son was Vairisinha, whose son was Vijayasinha. He married Śyāmalādevī daughter of Udayāditya king of Dhārā and their daughter was Ālhaṇadevī." This description is important in many respects. First, the Rajputs had begun to look upon their family or clan as gotra, Gobhila being of course Gohila. They probably began to count their Rishi gotra as of no importance, the theory being propounded that their Rishi gotra was the gotra of their Purohitas. The family name gotra is found in many inscriptions of this period. Secondly, the line of the Guhilot kings is correctly given as Hansapāla, Vairisinha and Vijayasinha in Mewad chronicles and inscriptions, of which we had some doubt (see Ind. Ant. XVIII p. 216). Thirdly, instead of Mewad, the word Prāgvāta is here used. It is difficult to determine what Prāgvāta meant though unquestionably it included Malwa. Fourthly, Udayāditya Paramāra was king of Malwa. He is said to be king of Dhārā which thus clearly appears to be in his possession. It is lastly important to note that this Haihaya family of Chedi was considered of the best Rajput blood as it had marriage relations with the Guhilots of Mewad and the Paramāras of Malwa two best Rajput families and with Prithvīrāja Chauhan whose mother the queen of Someśvara was a Kalachūri princess, as will be noted later on, probably a daughter of Ālhaṇadevī herself or her son Narasinhavarman.

This inscription is dated 1155 A. D. and probably Ālhanadevī was regent for her son Narasinhavarman. Yaśahkarṇa's rule ended about 1024 A. D. and Gayakarṇa's rule ended about 1054 A.D., his inscription found being dated 1151 (Ind. Ant. XVIII p. 210). He was succeeded by his son Narasinhavarman, three inscriptions of whom have been found, dated 1155, 1158 and 1169. He seems to have died young though his reign does not seem to have been without importance. For from the time of his inscriptions, the form of the title of Chedi kings appears to have changed. He and his successors called themselves "lords of three kings Narapati, Aśvapati and Gajapati by the power of their own arm."* They also call themselves Vāmadevapādānudyāta which is wholly inexplicable as their ancestors are mentioned same Gāngeya, Karṇa, Yeśahkarṇa and Gayakarṇa. It seems that the Chedi kings took the first title from Gāhadavāla kings of Kanauj who also use the same title in their inscriptions from about this time onward (See Govindachandra's grant Ind. Ant. XV p. 7 dated 1168). Now it will be remembered that the Pratihāra emperors of Kanauj were called Hayapatis, lords of horses and the kings of Bengal Gajapatis, lords of elephants (See Vol. II App. VI p. 349, 350). Prabably the kings of Āndhra were called Narapatis or kings of men and whoever conquered these countries may claim the title, conque. of three kings Aśvapati, Gajapati and Narapati. The Gahadavālas had conquered Kanauj, Bengal and even Āndhra and so had the Chedis. They, therefore, both appear to have taken this title, bombastic though it clearly was. Narasinhavarman appears to have been brave and probably fought with Āndhras only, though his ancestor Karṇa had undoubtedly conquered all the three Kanauj, Bengal and Āndhra. Curiously enough this title does not appear in Karṇa's inscriptions, but first appears in that of his great-grandson Narasinha.

Narasinha is called in his inscription dated 1159 (Ind. Ant. XVIII. p. 214) Dāhālīya Mahārāja which seems to suggest he was king of Bundelkhand or part of it at least. In his time a temple was constructed at a ghat near Kauśāmbi on the Jumna upto which river his dominion may have extended.

Narasinha may be taken to have ruled from 1152 to 1160 and he was succeeded by his brother Jayasinha who takes the same title in his two inscriptions found dated 1175 and 77 A. D.

* स्वभुजसमार्दित-नरपति-गजपति-अश्वपतिराज्यत्रय ।

Jayasihna ruled probably from 1160 to 1178 A. D.; for in 1180 we get an inscription of his son Vijayasinhavarman. Another inscription of his dated 1196 has been found (Ind. Ant. XVII p. 228, the exact date herein given is 27 Oct. 1195). Gaurishankar gives two more kings viz. Ajayasinha, a son of the last, mentioned indeed in Vijayapāla's inscription dated 1180 A. D., and Trailokyavarman whose inscription dated 1241 has been found. How this line ended does not appear. Probably it fell before Mahomedans in the days of Altamash or his successor. The seal of the family exhibits two elephants with the goddess Lakshmī between them and their banner ensign was a bull.

GENEALOGY OF THE HAIHAYAS OF TRIPURA.

1 Gāṅgeya (c. 1010–1038) Ins. 1037
|
2 Karṇa (c. 1038–1080) Ins. 1042
m. Āvelladevī Huṇa princess
|
3 Yaśahkarṇa (c. 1080–1124) Ins. 1120, 1122
|
4 Gayakarṇa (c. 1124–1152) Ins. 1151
m. Ālhaṇadevī Guhilot princess
|
5 Narasinha (c. 1152–1160) Ins. 1155, 1158, 1159
6 Jayasinha (c. 1160–1180) Ins. 1175, 1177
|
7 Vijayasinha Ins. 1180, 1196 (c. 1180–1198 A. D.)
|
8 Ajayasinha (Gaurishankar's Tod).

NOTE—TEWAR OR TRIPURA, CAPITAL OF THE KALACHURIS.

(Jubbulpore Gazetteer 1908).

Tripur, capital of the Kalachūris, was a well-known town in ancient India, but is now in ruins and it is represented by the modern village of Tewar about 10 miles from Jubbulpore near the marble rocks. Inscriptions from the 3rd century A. D. are found in and near Tewar. The town Karṇāvati founded by Karṇa near Tripura is also now in ruins and is the modern village called Karṇabel composed of Karṇa and bel, the latter being the name of the Bilva tree which abounds here. (Perhaps the Brahmins settled by Karṇa in this town were all Śaivas and planted many Bel trees the leaves of which are required for the worship of Śiva). Very little remains even of the ruins except beautifully carved images; for bricks and stones have all been removed and used in the construction of ghats and temples and railway bridges and even culverts in modern time. An ancient step-well has been discovered, however, under brushwood and it now supplies drinking water to the villagers and there is also an old extensive tank near the ruins.

CHAPTER VII.

CHAULUKYAS OF ANHILWAD.

The history of the Chaulukya (Solankhi) kings of Gujarat has been well told and in detail in Bombay Gazetteer Vol. I part II, from Jain records as also inscriptions found till then. The chief authorities are of course the former viz. Hemachandra's Dvyāśraya and the Vichāraśreṇi of Merutuṅga (which gives specific dates for the reigns of kings). But these and other Prabandhas contain fanciful accounts, often fictitious, intended to impress the marvellous (Adbhutarasa) and sober history has to reject many of their tales which further are not important from the point of view of the general history of Hindu India. We will, therefore, confine our attention to important and well-authenticated events and also incorporate information derivable from epigraphic records discovered since the date of the Gazetteer.

The first thing which requires to be pointed out is that this Chaulukya family and the Chaulukya family of the Deccan are not one and the same family, though the name is the same and though they are treated as the same by even ancient poets and story-tellers. As stated in Vol. II we attach great value to the recorded gotras of these several Rajput families and though names may be the same as among Brahmins, so even among Kshatriyas whose gotras are their family gotras and not the gotras of their Purohitas as propounded in later times by Vijnāneśvara and others, a difference of gotra indicates a difference of family. The Chaulukyas of the Deccan gave their gotra as Mānavya even in records as early as the sixth century A. D. and the later Chaulukyas Tailapa and others were of this family though they do not usually give their gotra in their records. The Chaulukyas of Gujarat unfortunately do not also give there gotra in their records. Yet we may be certain that their gotra was Bhāradvāja as given in a Chedi record (Ep. Ind. I. 253) of the 10th century and the same gotra is given by Chand in the Prithvīrāja Rāsā. Even now the Solankhis of Rewa and of Gujarat profess the same gotra and we may be sure that Bhāradvāja has been their gotra all along. The Chaulukyas of Gujarat are, therefore, a distinct family from the Chaulukyas of the Deccan of the 6th and 10th centuries, though it must be admitted, like the Gazetteer the opposite opinion is entertained by Pandit Guarishankar Ojha.

Secondly, the reader must note that the part of the country where the Chaulukyas founded their rule was not called Gujarat yet. Anahilwād Pāṭan was situate in what was then called Sārasvata Mandala, and we, therefore, still continue in the title of this chapter the mention of Anahilwād and do not use the name Gujarat though it is used by the Gazetteer. A record of Mūlarāja himself, the founder of the dynasty states that he acquired (I. A. VI. p. 1) Sārasvata Mandala and it was only towards the middle of the twelfth century that Chaulukya records begin to speak of this land as Gurjarabhūmi (See Ind. Ant. VI No. 4 dated 1280 St. or 1823 A. D). This is a view which Mr. Divatia also maintains. Gujarat was the name of the territory about Jaipur still in 1030 A. D., when Al-Beruni wrote his India. Why the name Gurjarabhūmi descended from that region southwards and began to be applied first to northern Gujarat and later on southern Gujarat which was called Lâta has yet to be explained. But it is certain that the name was not given to this country because the rulers of it the Chaulukyas were Gurjaras or Gujars. We still adhere to the view expressed in Vol. II (page 32); for we find that the Chaulukyas or Solankhis do not call themselves Gurjaras in any of their records. They are called Gurjara kings no doubt in the records of other kingdoms and they call themselves kings of the Gurjarabhūmi or land from the middle of the 12th century onwards, but they do not style themselves as Gurjaras by caste or race in any of their records and hence we may be certain that this country came to be called Gujarat for other reasons.

The third thing which requires to be pointed out is that these kings were Śaivites or devotees of Śiva and were never converted to Jainism as is often supposed. They were no doubt tolerant kings as Hindus generally are. They even went beyond tolerance and admired and venerated Jain Sadhus and learned men, yet they, like other Kshatriyas of Hindu period, remained Hindus and were devotees of Śiva. They never call themselves Jain in their records and these never begin with the praise of Jina but always begin with the praise of Śiva. Even Kumārpāla who was a devoted disciple of Hemachandra, the great Jain pandit of this period, styles himself devotee of Śiva, is desrcibed as having obtained power by the favour of Siva and builds temples to that god; in fact the deity of the family was Somnath whose famous shrine was situated in their country and was under their rule. Jain writers have no doubt tried to prove that Kumārapāla was a convert to Jainism. Indeed they represent even the Chāvadās as also Solankhis as Jains; but the inscriptions drawn up under the government of the Solankhis do not support their statements and we may believe that they continued to be Śaivites though they favoured Jainism which, no doubt, prospered under their rule as we shall show later on.

Having noted these three important points of difference, we will give in substance the history of the Chaulukya kings of Anahilwad, chiefly from the Bombay Gazetteer Vol. I part II. Mūlarāja was the founder of this family and he was sister's son of the last Chāpotkaṭa king of Pātan. Probably there was misrule in the country and Mūlarāja acquired the kingdom by force as the inscriptions generally represent and restored order, though chroniclers give the story of his seizing the kingdom wrongfully by putting his uncle to death. He ruled from 961–996 A. D. justly and vigorously as founders of kingdoms usually do. He had wars with the neighbouring kings such as those of Cutch and Sind. He had seized a kingdom which was already large and had necessarily to make good his claim to it by his prowess. He is said to have defeated one Gṛiharipu assisted by the Khengâr king of Cutch and also by Arabs from Sind and obtained possession of Somnath. The word Gṛiharipu probably shows that he was a rebel, being a subordinate of the previous Châvadâ kings. Mūlarāja had also to fight with kings of north and south, viz. Vigraharāja of Saṃbhar and Bārappa of Lāṭa. The latter probably was a general of king Tailapa of Karṇāṭa, as Karṇāṭa and Lāṭa even in Paramāra records are usually leagued together, Lâṭa being a dependency of Karṇāṭa ruled by a governor usually a scion of the reigning family. Bārappa is said to have been killed in battle and Mūlarāja fought battles separately with these invading forces and secured his dominions. Mūlarāja devoted himself in old age to a holy life. He built a Śiva temple at Pātan. He invited learned Brahmins from different parts of India and settled them at Sidhpur and elsewhere. Many Brahmins of Gujarat such as Audīchyas and Gaudas believe that they came to Gujarat in his reign.

Mūlarāja was succeeded by his son Chāmunda who reigned from 997 to 1010 A. D., according to the chronicles. Sindhurāja of Malwa was killed in a battle with this king as is stated in the Vadnagar Praśasti of Kumārapāla and this event is placed by Pandit Gaurishankar in 1010 A. D. (See Vol. II. p. 122). It cannot be later than this year but may have happened earlier. For, as stated already, Bhoja of Malwa might have begun to rule before 1010 A. D. The story that Munja insulted Mūlarāja when he was going on a pilgrimage to Benares via Dhar and Chāmunda revenged the insult is probably a fiction.

Châmunda had three sons Vallabha, Durlabha and Nāgarāja and the eldest succeeded and reigned for a short time only and his name is consequently often omitted in inscriptions. His brother Durlabha succeeded him and ruled for twelve years from 1010 A. D. to 1022 A. D. Nothing particular is recorded of him by chroniclers or in inscriptions. He was succeeded by his nephew Bhīma I, son of Nāgarāja. Bhīma certainly was a powerful king and ruled long (43 years) from 1022 A. D. to 1064 A. D. He was contemporary with king Bhoja of Malwa and king Karṇa of the Chedis both of whom were also powerful and able. His wars with Malwa have already been described. It is said that Karṇa of Chedi had a golden palanquin presented to him by Bhoja who was defeated by him and Bhīma defeated both Bhoja and Karṇa and took from the latter the golden palanquin and presented the same to his tutelary god, Somnath of Prabhāsa Patan. Whether these stories are true or not, it is true that all the three kings were equally powerful and had consequently constant fights, relieved by periods of friendship and amity. We have already said that Bhīma did not invade Malwa along with Karṇa and avail himself of the opportunity of crushing Malwa after Bhoja's death. Malwa records distinctly show that Karṇa of Chedi alone invaded Malwa and the version of the Gujarat chronicles in this respect is not true.

It was during this king's reign that Mahmud of Ghazni made his famous raid on Somnath. Whether such an event did take place or not we have discussed elsewhere. But an inscription at Somnath records that Bhīma built a stone-temple for Somnath in place of the wooden one which existed before. We have seen that the Udepur Praśasti states that Bhoja built the Somnath god's temple. No reference is given by the Gazetteer for the inscription and hence we have not been able to estimate its value. We may suppose that the work was the joint work of Bhoja and Bhīma. Indeed Bhoja could not have done the work without Bhīma's consent and collaboration.

Bhīma was succeeded by his second son Karṇa, the eldest Mūlarāja having died in his father's life-time. He had a peaceful reign from 1064 to 1094. He built a large tank called Karṇasara and he also founded a city, named it Karṇāvatī and made it his second capital. This city is modern Ahmedabad. As usual with Hindu powerful kings, he built many temples to Śiva and Durgā. He had very few conflicts with neighbouring kings, but the Hammīra-Charita states that he died in a battle with Dussala of Śākambhari.

Kielhorn in his genealogies (Ep. Ind. VIII) gives only one inscription each against Bhīma and Karṇa. The first dated 1029 A. D. does not give much information about Bhīma (I. A. VI p. 193) and the second dated 1091 A. D. also gives no information about Karṇa (Ep. Ind. I. p. 317). The Vadnagar Praśasti of Kumārapāla also does not furnish much information about either. Bhīma is said to have conquered Dhārā, the capital of the Mālava-*Chakravartin* (Bhoja) by means of his efficient cavalry versed in five modes of moving (Dhārā) or versed in the use of five-weapons (Dhārā); and of Karṇa it gives the usual praise. The inscription of Karṇa dated 1091 A. D., however, shows that the Gujarat chroniclers are not wrong when they assign him a reign from 1064 to 1094 or 1093 A. D.

Karṇa was succeeded by his son Jayasinha born of a Karnāṭa Kadamba princess married when he was old. Jayasinha was a minor when Karṇa died and the government was carried on by his mother with the aid of capable and devoted ministers. Jayasinha surnamed Siddharāja proved to be the most powerful king of Gujarat in the Chaulukya line. He was a great builder and every ancient structure in Gujarat is popularly attributed to him. He built the famous Rudramāl (Rudra-mahālaya) temple of Śiva at Siddhapura parts of which only remain; yet they attest the stupendous dimensions and the fine workmanship of the temple. He built the Sahasralinga lake at Pâtan. His wars were also great. He had a long war with Malwa lasting for twelve years beginning with an invasion of Malwa in the reign of Naravarman and ending with the defeat and imprisonment of Yaśovarman as related before. He is said to have attacked Dhârâ and from thence to have gone against Madanpāla Chandella and exacted tribute from him though a Chandella Kalanjar record states that Jayasinha was defeated (J. B. A. S. 1848 p. 319). Certain it is that he conquered Malwa and a large part of the country remained under the rule of Gujarat for a long time. He is usually called in inscriptions Avantīnātha. From an inscription it appears that he also conquered Cutch and annexed that kindom ruling it through a governor. In inscriptions he is said to have conquered Barbaraka, a word which has given rise to various legends and various surmises. The legends declare that Barbaraka was the king of demons or devils. And Jayasinha Siddharāja is said to have acquired such power over devils and goblins that he could accomplish anything. Such tales being absurd, antiquarians have attempted to explain the word by supposing that Barbaraka meant some aboriginal or even Mlechha people. Bühler thought that they were Bhils now known as Bābaras settled in south Kathiawar (Gazetteer). It is also suggested that they may have been the Berbers of the Hindu Purāṇas to be identified with Vara or the Berbers of Africa. The last suggestion seems acceptable with this difference that Berbers are to be identified with Arabs (See Vol. II p. 354). It is quite possible that Jayasinha defeated a formidable Arab invasion from Sind.

Jayasinha was, like Bhoja whose example was catching, a patron of learned men and many great pandits, Jain and Hindu, were patronised by him. The greatest of them was, of course Hemachandra the Jain Pandit whose grammar of Sanskrit is called Sidhdha Hema because it was dedicated to this king and whose poem Dvyāśraya gives a history of the Chaulukyas and also contains illustrations of grammatical rules. The king was also fond of disputations being held between pandits in his presence and in one such dispute a Digambara Jain pandit is said to have been defeated by a noted Śvetāmbara Sūri from Cambay as the former propounded that women could not obtain salvation, nor clothed ascetics. This story may perhaps emanate from a Śvetāmbara source, Śvetāmbaras being predominant in Gujarat.

Not only poets but warriors flocked to the court of Sidharāja for patronage and the most famous of them was Jagadeva Paramār, youngest son of Udayāditya. Marvellous stories are told of him by chroniclers but his bravery need not be doubted.

Jayasinha Sidhharāja has, therefore, been properly described by the Gazetteer as most powerful, most religious and most generous. At the intercession of his mother who was grieved to see the despair of devout pilgrims unable to proceed to Somnath on account of the heavy tax on them, he remitted the tax altogether, though its income was about 1 Lakh of rupees. Even in the Vadnagar Praśasti it is declared that he paid off the debts of all debtors in his kingdom and thus deserved the title of Chakravartin and Śakakartā or founder of an era. It is indeed a common belief in India that the founder of an era must pay off the debts of all debtors in his kingdom and it seems from the Vadnagar Praśasti that Jayasinha actually accomplished this great feat of generosity. That he founded an era cannot be doubted for inscriptions in Kathiawar and Gujarat have been found dated in that era. The last mention is probably in the Verawal inscription (Bhav. Ins. p. 214) which gives its date in four eras viz. Vikrama 1320, Valabhi 945, Sinha 151 and Hijri 642.* In short Jayasinha amply deserves the titles Siddharāja and Chakravartin bestowed upon him even in inscriptions.

Kielhorn in his genealogies mentions two inscriptions of Jayasinha dated 1138 and 1139 A. D.; the latter is not a Chaulukya inscription but one of their subordinate kings and in its first verse it simply states that king Jayasinha imprisoned the kings of Saurāshtra and Malwa. In the various inscriptions of his successors he is usually described as Avantīnātha, Tribhuvanaganda, Barbarakajishṇu and Siddha-Chakravartin (See I. A. VI. No. 6 &c.). Jayasinha ruled long from 1093 to 1143 as stated by chroniclers which is not improbable, as he came to the throne a minor and as the inscription noted above is dated 1139 A. D. proving a long reign. In spite of his supposed magical powers and Siddha-rasa or powerful medicines or of his highly meritorious works and actions, Jayasinha had no son and the succession went to Kumārapāla, son of Tribhuvanapāla who was a grandson of the third son of Bhīma I named Krishnarāja. The succession was naturally contested and foreign kings intervened in the quarrel. But Kumārapāla by his energies and the assistance of Jain ministers succeeded in defeating Arnoraj of Ajmer and Ballāla of Malwa as stated in the inscriptions. And Kumārapāla like his predecessors ruled justly and wisely for a long time i. e. thirty years from 1143 to 1173 according to the chroniclers. It is indeed rare to find four capable vigorous and justice-loving kings reigning successively as Bhīma, Karṇa, Jayasinha Siddharāja, and Kumārapāla undoubtedly did. Stories of Jayasinha and Kumārapāla of Naharwala are told even by

* This shows that four eras were current in Gujarat indicating four prominent rules in succession. Mahomedan rule was just commencing at the time of that inscription though it mentions Arjundeva Vaghela as ruling in Gujarat.

Arab writers as early as 1225 A. D. and we have no hesitation in identifying Jayasinha of Jamiyat-ul-Hikayat of Ufi who even mentions his power over spirits, with Jayasinha Siddharāja and Gurpāl with Kumārapāla whose just rule is attributed to the fact that this king, before he came to the throne, had travelled much and passed through adversity. Gujarat chroniclers also state that Kumārapāla, as a possible successor, came under the disfavour of Jayasinha and departing from Gujarat travelled in southern and eastern countries by the advice of Hemachandra who is said to have foretold his greatness. This explains his extreme reverence for that famous Jain pandit and also his regard for the Jain religion. His self-restraint and high moral character may be attributed indeed to the influence of Jain philosophy. Further, Kumārapāla was also fifty years old when he came to the throne and therefore past the age when kings are often led to become addicted to vice and oppression.

His first war was with Arṇorāja of Ajmer to whom his sister was married. Perhaps he moved against him, he being in favour of his brother. Absurd tales are told of this war but from inscriptions it seems clear that in this battle Kumārapāla exhibited personal bravery and drew blood from Arṇorāja's chest with an arrow.* His usual title in inscriptions is "the conqueror of the king of Śākambhari in battle by the strength of his own arms". Probably the king of Malwa named Ballāla in Vadnagar Praśasti was an ally of Arṇorāja and was killed in battle. He sent his general twice against Mallikārjuna king of Konkan and in the second battle Ambada his general climbed his elephant and cut off his head. A king of Chedi was proceeding against him when by accident the king was strangled by his own necklace being caught in a branch as he was riding an elephant. His inscriptions are found in the temple of Udepur in eastern Malwa showing that Gujarat still ruled a large part of Malwa. His inscriptions are also found at Balmer in Western Rajputana and at Chitod itself in Mewad. This is a little inexplicable as it is not possible that he conquered Chitod and the Guhilot king there. The inscription seems to mention that he went there to see the famous fort when returning from an expedition against Karna. The king of Chitod probably treated him as an honoured guest. Perhaps the legend that

* अर्णोराजनराधिराजहृदयक्षिप्तैकबाणव्रणात् त्यानल्लोहिततर्पणाद्मदयच्चण्डीं भुजस्याविर्मम् ॥

Vadnagar Praśasti Ep. Ind. I

one of Kumārapāla's queens was a Guhilot princess may also explain his friendly reception at Chitod as also the recording of an inscription on the capital fort of the Guhilots. Kumārapāla had extensive dominion no doubt but the Jain chroniclers exaggerate his power, probably because he was the most ardent admirer of their religion and represent him as ruling a territory the northern boundary of which was conterminous with the dominions of the Turks.

Kumārapāla like his predecessor was a great builder and many Jain vihāras are said to have been built by him or his ministers. He is certainly described by Jain chroniclers as building the temple of Somnath and it is said that Hemachandra himself, when asked by the king what was the most meritorious thing for him to do, replied that he should rebuild the temple of Somnath and the king built the temple of stones. We have already seen that Bhoja is credited with building the temple of Somnath as also Bhīma. Jayasinha is distinctly recorded to have done the same. Probably the temple was so contiguous to the sea that sea-waves dashed against the base of the temple and former builders only put up wooden pillars into the basin of the sea. The building of a stone-temple by Kumārapāla cannot be doubted; for an inscription in the Bhadrakāli temple without the precincts of Somnath dated 1169 A. D. mentions this fact in detail. A Kānyakubja Brahmin ascetic from Benares moved about in India, making Sthānoddhāra and came to Somnath via Malwa. He requested Jayasinha to build the Somnath temple and the latter began the construction. The work was, however, finished by Kumārapāla. This inscription gives the credit of inducing the kings of Gujarat to build the temple to the Brahmin ascetic Bhāva Brihaspati, a saint of the Lakulīśa sect. But the Jain chroniclers take the credit to themselves and attribute Kumārapāla's action to the advice of Hemachandra. We may give credit to both, for indeed Kumārapāla appears to have honoured both Hindu and Jain ascetics and learned men. On this inscription we have commented elsewhere.

It remains to consider how far we may believe that Kumārapāla actually became a Jain towards the close of his career. When the temple of Somnath was being built, he is said to have made a vow, at Hemachandra's suggestion, to abstain from flesh, wine and woman. And for two years he observed the vow and when the temple was finished he went there and worshipped the god and even Hemachandra bowed to the idol. That vow is not a

Jain vow only, being prescribed even by Manu.* But perhaps the king was equally divided between his devotion to his tutelary deity and his devotion to his preceptor Hemachandra. The Hindus are in this respect most tolerant and even now devout Hindus are known to be followers of Mahomedan fakirs. It is, therefore, not at all strange that Kumārapāla worshipped Jain ascetics or built Jain vihāras. Even Hemachandra like his tolerant disciple bowed to the Somnath idol, declaring that it may represent even Jain. It does not seem probable, however that Kumārapāla at last gave up his tutelary deity and turned a Jain since in inscriptions of his time and those of his successors, he is always described 'as prospering through the favour of Śiva' (Umāpati) and is nowhere described as a Jain, as Harsha is described in his inscriptions as a worshipper of Sugata (Parama Saugata) while his father is described as worshipper of Śiva (Parama Māheśvara).

There is, however, reason to believe that Kumārapāla was so far impressed latterly with the doctrine of Ahimsā specially preached by Jainism that he, like Harsha, used his political power to suppress slaughter of animals, though not wholly, yet on certain days at least. Jain chronicles relate that he prohibited killing of animals altogether and even gave strained water to his horses and elephants like Śilāditya of Molapo (See Vo. I. p. 23). But even if we do not believe this, inscriptions record that slaughter was prohibited by subordinate kings on certain days. There are two inscriptions of this kind, at Ratanpur and Harsoda, both in Marwad (Bhav. Ins. p. 206) which were recorded in the time of Kumārapāla by subordinate kings prohibiting slaughter on Ashtami, Ekadaśi, Chaturdaśi and Amāvāsyā days and prescribing a penalty of five drammas as fine. If subordinate princes prohibited slaughter, it must have been done with the consent of the suzerain, probably a similar order must have been promulgated by the suzerain himself though this does not necessarily follow. But even this Ratanpur inscription describes Kumārapāla as prospering through the favour of Pārvatīpati (Śiva). And the Vadnagar Praśasti relates that Kumārapāla built the wall round Vadnager the home of Nāgar Brahmins who are well-known worshippers

---

* न मांसभक्षणे दोषो न मद्ये न च मैथुने । प्रवृत्तिरेषा भूतानां निवृत्तिस्तु महाफला ॥

The abstention from the three M's is described as leading to great fruit.

of Śiva. The conclusion appears to be that while Kumārapāla still remained a staunch worshipper of Śiva as his forefathers had been, he admired Jainism so far and was so far under the influence of Hemachandra that he prohibited killing of animals on certain days sacred to the Jains. Such prohibitary orders were issued by Akbar also in response to Jain feeling, in certain towns, as sanads prove, during Pachosan fast days of the Jains.

Kielhorn gives seven inscriptions against Kumārapāla (genealogies E. I. VIII) ranging from 1145 to 1160 A. D. and this supports the length of his reign (30 years) given by the chronicles from 1143 to 1173 A. D. Kumārapāla had no son and he was succeeded by his nephew Ajayapāla who had a short reign as he was of a violent temper and vigorously persecuted Jains and oppressed even Hindu ministers. He was slain by his own door-keeper in 1176 A. D. He is credited in inscriptions with having brought under tribute the king of Sākambharī which does not seem likely.

He was followed by his son Mūlarāja who was then a minor and who is, therefore, often called Bāla Mūlarāja. His mother Naikidevi was the daughter of a Permāḍi Kadamba king in Karnāṭaka and acted as regent. It was during the reign of this king that Mahammad Ghori invaded Gujarat and was defeated. This defeat was certainly creditable to the Hindus and it is but natural that many Chaulukya inscriptions should describe Mūlarāja as "the conqueror of the difficult to be conquered king of Gurjan (Ghazni)."* The credit belongs to the king no doubt but in one inscription the credit is given to his mother. Rajput ladies are certainly famous throughout history for their contempt of death and for their high regard for their honour and religion. It is a matter of pride further that this queen was a Rajput lady from the Karnāṭaka. She must have been present at the battle and led the forces of Gujarat against the Ghazni king.‡ The battle is not described anywhere but seems to have been won by the valour of the Gujarat army composed, as it was, of cavalry and elephants, the latter being properly handled by Gujarat generals. It is said by Gujarat chroniclers that rain came to the help of the conquerors; but why rain should have helped them only is not obvious. It must also be conceded

---

* म्लेच्छतमोनिचयछन्नप्रद्योतनबालार्कआहवपराभूतदुर्जयगुर्जनाधिराज (I. A. VI p. 194).

‡ चौलुक्यराज्ञान्वयपूजितस्य । यस्यास्तुभावादबलापि संख्ये । हम्मीरराजं तरसा जिगाय etc. Veraval Inscription (Bhav. Inscrip. p. 24).

that Ghori must have had an insufficient force in comparison with the large army of Gujarat, as he is said to have come via Multan and across the desert. Whatever the reason of it, this defeat saved Gujarat from Mahomedan conquest for a hundred years more and established the reputation of the kingdom of Naharwala for valour. The battle was fought in 1178 A. D. and at Gadarar Ghatta (B. Gazetteer p. 195). Mahomedan writers do not generally mention this battle, but they mention one with the successor of Mūlarāja named Bhīma which is probably a mistake (Gaurishankar's Tod). Perhaps it may have been another attempt to retrieve his honour by Muhammed Ghori who tried to imitate Mahmud of Ghazni with less success in the beginning yet more complete success in the end.

Mūlarāja also ruled for a short time only and he was succeeded by his brother Bhīma who was also a minor then, his mother carrying on the regency. Bhima II called Bholā ruled long, like Jayasinha, from 1178 to 1241 A. D. a period of 63 years which is not unbelieveable, if we remember that he came to the throne when a boy. Like Jayasinha also he called himself Siddharāja or rather new (Abhinava) Siddharāja, though his attainments were not as great. There are many inscriptions of his time found dating from 1199 to 1238 A. D. It cannot, therefore, be doubted that he reigned till 1242 A. D. as stated by chroniclers. His power was, however, usurped by his nobles and feudatories, though they always acknowledged him as king of Anhilwad. Thus an inscription of one Jayantasinha, to be noticed further on, states that Bhīma ruled in Anhilwad. Subsequently the Vaghela chieftain Lavaṇaprasād and his son Vīradhavala became powerful and Bhīma II is said even to have declared that Vīradhavala was his successor. The Vaghela chieftains were a scion of the Chaulukya family itself and Arṇorāja the founder was a son of Kumārapāla's mother's sister. He assisted Kumārapāla in obtaining the throne and the latter gave him the village of Vyāghrapalli near Anhilwad, whence the family obtained the surname Vaghela. Lavaṇaprasāda, son of Arṇorāja was a great general under Bhīma II and eventually Vīradhavala, his son, established himself at Anhilwad in place of Bhīma's effete successor Tribhuvanapāla, who seems to have ruled for about four years after Bhīma (Gaurishankar's Tod). A copper-plate of Tribhuvanapāla dated 1299 St. or 1242 A. D. has been found and it seems that this king did for a time rule. But Vīradhavala who was virtual master must have soon set him aside and founded the

Vaghela kingly family at Anhilwad which lasted for four generations after him viz: Vīsaladeva, Arjunadeva, Sārangadeva and Karṇa (1286–1304) in whose time Gujarat was finally conquered by the Mahomedans. The Vaghela kings were a powerful family and their two great Jain ministers Vastupāla and Tejapāla built the famous Jain temples at Abu and Girnar. The modern representative of the Vaghela family is the family ruling at Rewa; while the Chaulukya family of Mūlarāja is represented by the chiefs of Rūpanagar in Mewad and of Kot in Marwad (Gaurishankar's Tod). There are some Maratha families such as Dubals of Karhad in Satara district who represent themselves as descendants of the Chaulukyas of Gujarat, their gotra being Bhāradvāja.

It remains to consider who Jayantasinha was whose inscription dated 1260 St. or 1202 A. D. has been found (I. A. VI No. 4 p. 197). In this inscription he is described as a Chaulukya, but what relation he bore to Bhīma is not stated; it, however, makes it clear that this king ruled in place of Bhīma while he was away, (tadnantaram sthāne). It further praises Jayantasinha as the extricator, like Varāha, of the Gurjara land sunk in the waters of the ocean of evil times and the nourisher, like rain, of the seed of Gurjara land burnt in the forest fire of calamities. He also takes to himself all the epithets taken by Gujarat kings and describes himself as established in Anhilwad. This contains, most probably, a reference to the invasion of Gujarat by Kutubuddin Aibak in 1197 A. D. (B. Gazetteer p. 195–7). It seems probable that like his former namesake Bhīma I when invaded by Mahmud of Ghazni, Bhīma II at the time of the invasion by Kutubuddin forsook Anhilwad and retired to some distant fortress. Kutubuddin who had come to Ajmer advanced on Anhilwad and defeated the force which opposed him at the frontier under the mount of Abu, Dhārāvarsha Parmāra and other generals of Gujarat being defeated (Gaurishankar), Gujarat lay prostrate and was plundered. Perhaps this valiant Chaulukya prince Jayantasinha remained in the city and eventually cleared the country of any forces that may have been left in the country by Kutubdudin. The eloquent description of these services given in the inscription* are not a mere

* भीमदेवः तदनन्तरं स्थाने परमभट्टारक महाराजाधिराज परमेश्वर चौलुक्यकुलकल्पवल्लीविस्तारणदिव दुःसमयजलधिजलमग्नमेदिनीमंडलोद्धरणमहावराह दुर्दैवदावानलदग्धगुर्जरधराबीजप्ररोहैकपर्जन्य एकांगवीर

(I. A. VI. p. 197).

hyperbole and Jayantasinha appears to have ruled vigorously in Anhilwad for at least three years, his inscription being dated 1202 A. D. Bhīma's grant dated 1199 A. D. (Bhādrapada or September) was issued from Anhilwad (Ind. Ant. XI p. 71) and discovers the fact that he was still there though the Mahomedan forces were in the country troubling the people. He must have left the capital of sheer necessity hereafter. Bhīma must have returned when the country was clear and ruled again in Patan for long time till 1242, his last inscription found being dated 1239 A. D. The titles which Bhīma II takes are indeed grandiloquent as he calls himself not only Abhinava Siddharāja but also Saptama Chakravartin. Why he calls himself the seventh Gujarat emperor of India cannot be explained unless we confine the enumeration to the Chaulukya kings of Anhilwad and begin it with Bhīma I. Unquestionably the kings of this line were almost all able and valorous kings with the exception of this last king who was indeed properly called Bholā or guileless as he did not sufficiently realise the absurdity of the praise bestowed upon him by inscription-writers. We give the genealogy of the Chaulukya kingly family of Anahilwad below with probable dates of accession and definite dates of their inscriptions. Jayantasinha may be omitted as he clearly ruled in place of Bhīma II during his absence (though Kielhorn gives his name in the genealogy of the Chaulukyas), following Gaurishankar Ojha in his note in Tod and the Bombay Gazetteer Vol. I. part I.

GENEALOGY OF THE CHĀLUKYAS OF ANHILWAD.

(Bombay Gazetteer Vol. I part II and Kielhorn's genealogies E. I. VIII)

- I Mūlarāja son of Rāji (c. 961-996 A. D.).
  - II Chāmunda (c. 997-1009).
    - III Vallabha (c. 1009)
    - IV Durlabha (c. 1009-1021)
    - Nāgarāja.
      - V Bhīma I (c. 1021-1063) Insc. 1029
        - VI Karṇa (c. 1063-1093) Insc. 1091
          - VII Jayasinha Siddharāja (c. 1093-1143) Insc. 1131-1139
        - Khemaraja
          - Haripāla
            - Tribhuvanapāla
              - Mahipāla
                - IX Ajayapāla (c. 1173-1176) Insc. 1173-1175
                  - X Mūlarāja II (c. 1176-1178)
                  - XI Bhīma II (c. 1178-1241) Insc. 1199, 1207-09-16-18-26-30-31-38
                    - XII Tribhuvanapāla Insc. 1242.
              - VIII Kumārapāla (c. 1143-1173) Insc. 1145-53-57-63-69

CHAPTER VIII

THE GĀHADAVĀLAS OF KANAUJ.

Of the new Rajput clans which came to the front in the third sub-period of Hindu history (1000–1200), the most noted as well as the most powerful was the Gāhadavāla family of Kanauj. The Gāhadvālas are considered to be a branch of the Rathods or Rāshtrakūtas but this fact is often disputed and we will examine this subject later on; it is also uncertain whence the Gāhadavālas came and we will give our view on this point also later. From inscriptions of this family found in scores, however, it appears certain that Chandradeva son of Mahīyala Gāhadavāla, 'by the prowess of his arms obtained the sovereignty of Kānyakubja and freed the country from trouble'. This praise is bestowed on Chandra in almost every Gāhadavāla grant. In what year this exploit is to be placed is not quite clear. Fortunately we have since Kielhorn gave genealogies of Northern Kings in 1908 (E. I. in VIII), found three inscriptions of Chandradeva himself and the eulogy of him in the two later records is more detailed; but unfortunately the epithets in them cannot be well understood. It seems that Chandra conquered Narapati, Gajapati, Triśankupati and a king of Pānchāla which must be indentified with the kingdom of Kanauj (E. I. XIV p. 192). These inscriptions are dated from 1093 to 1099 A. D. and there is another inscription of him dated 1091 with the usual epithets (E. I. IX p. 302). It seems thus certain that Chandradeva conquered Kanauj before 1091 A. D. In an inscription of a later king (I. A. XIV p. 103) it is stated that Chandradeva freed the earth from trouble which had come upon it after the death of Karṇa of Chedi. This king we have taken to have ruled up to 1080 A. D. It hence follows that Chandradeva conquered Kanauj some time after 1080 A. D. In this inscription it is also stated that Chandradeva defeated many enemy kings and then made Kānyakubja his capital. Kanauj was the Rome or Constantinople of India from the days of Harsha and whoever took it was considered as the emperor of Hind. Chandra must, therefore, have found many opponents to his occupation of Kanauj as his capital; though he must have defeated the last effete representative of the fallen Pratihāra line easily. The word 'chapala' or mobile applied to Pānchāla king in these two Chandra records (E. I. XIV) probably shows that he had to pursue the fugitive Pratihāra last king from place to place.

Having conquered the kingdom of Kanauj, Chandra freed the country from the Turks whose officers must have been present in the country in several places to collect the tribute paid to Ghazni by Kanauj as stated before, and as immortalized in the Gāhadavāla records by the word 'Turushkadanda.' Chandra further obtained possession of the chief sacred places in Northern India viz. Kāśī, Kuśika (Kanauj), Uttara Kośala (Ayodhya) and Indrasthāna (perhaps Indraprastha or Delhi) and as a Hindu king protected these sacred places from the incursions of the Turks (I. A. XIV); a praise bestowed upon Chandra in almost all Gāhadavāla records. He also made Tulādānas or gifts of gold of his own weight by scores to learned Brahmins. In short Chandra was not only a powerful king but also a most orthodox Hindu and his conquest of Kanauj may be looked upon as a strong religious effort by the Hindus to free Āryāvarta from the troubles of Mlechchha inroads and Mlechchha domination. Bhoja had rendered the same service (1040) and Karṇa later (1060) but Chandra (1080) established firmly Hindu India by conquering and consolidating the kingdom of Kanauj and thus ensured the life of Hindu India for a century more.

He was succeeded by his son Madanapāla who is also praised in his documents and in those of his successors but the praise is apparently conventional and we do not get any historical details from the praise. He was succeeded by his son Govindachandra who is undoubtedly the most famous and powerful king of this line, as usual the third from the founder. He is often described as 'strengthening the newly founded kingdom by his arms as with ropes and creepers'. His war elephants are described as moving in three directions without rest. Probably like Harsha, Govindchandra kept this arm at great strength constantly used it east, south and west. (In the north was the Himalaya mountain, the safe boundary of his kingdom which perhaps did not require much attention). He first takes the new epithet 'conqueror of the three kingdoms of Aśvapati, Narapati and Gajapati.' To what kings or kingdoms these terms refer it is difficult to state and has not been discussed. Probably the kingdom of Hayapati meant the kingdom of Kanauj, of Gajapati the kingdom of Bengal and of Narapati the kingdom of Chedi. The first two terms have already been used elsewhere and explained by us as above in Vol. II (p. 350) and Narapati may refer to the Chedi or Telingaṇa kingdom whose king is said to have kissed his feet i. e. entered into subordinate alliance with him. The Giripati mentioned in two Chandradeva's inscriptions may refer to the Āndhra kingdom or the Chedi, as both are full of mountains and the former is actually so described in the verse noted in Vol. II (p. 350). In any case it may be taken that Govindachandra extended his domination in all directions and thereby reduced the extent of the territories of the kings of Bengal, Āndhra and Chedi. He held Benares undoubtedly and much of the territory to the east of it, as he has made many grants of villages in the country round Benares, from Benares itself, which appears to have usually been a second capital with the kings of Kanauj. Indeed Jayachandra and others are often described by Mahomedan writers as kings of Benares and hence supposed by some as coming originally from that city itself.

In the same way as he had to fight with the Gauda kings in the east (and Chedi in the south), Govindachandra had necessarily to fight with the Mahomedans of Lahore in the west and we actually find these fights referred to, correctly and without boast, in an inscription of his which was recorded * while he was yet a Yuvarāj or heir apparent. The verse is very important and may be translated as follows:—(he was at the time on the Jumna at Āsaṭikā a place not identified but probably in the North-west and he makes the grant while Madanapāla was still ruling). "Terrible by breaking open the temples of the war-elephants of Gauda difficult to be opposed and compelling the Hammīra to cease hostilities by his game of unequal fighting, he accepted the kingship of the earth stamped, as it were, with seals in the form of the imprints of the hoofs of his horses constantly moving about." This shows the nature of his fights with the Turks of the Panjab who had constant tussels with Govindachandra and who, it appears, had eventually to make truce with him. This verse also shows that, like Bhoja Pratihāra of Kanauj, Govindachandra also kept a very large force of efficient cavalry which was always on the alert and constantly moving about.

Govindachandra was not only a powerful king but following the example set by Bhoja of Malwa and being himself a learned man, patronised learned men at his court. His epithet in most Gāhadavāla records is 'Vividha-Vichāra-Vidyā-Vācha-

---

* दुर्वारस्मारगौडद्विरदवरघटाकुम्भनिर्भेदभीमो । हम्मीरं न्यस्तवैरं मुहुरसमरणक्रीडया यो विधत्ते ॥ अश्रान्तस्फारवल्गत्तुरगखुरपुटोल्लेखमुद्रासनाथक्षोणीस्वीकारदक्षः स इह विजयते पार्थिवः कल्पवृक्षः

spati' a very Brihaspati (teacher of gods) in different sciences and philosophies. It is also stated that his Sāndhivigrahika (minister for war and peace), Lakshmīdhara by name, composed Vyavahāra-Kalpataru a treatise on law and procedure. Govindachandra thus can be placed in the same category of great kings as Samudragupta, Harsha, Bhoja, Mahmud, Akbar or Shivaji who were both great conquerors and patrons of learned men.

Govindachandra ruled long from about 1114 to 1155 A. D. Sir Vincent Smith, it appears, inadvertently includes the years 1104 to 1114 in the reign of Govindachandra (E. H. I. p. 384, 3rd Edn.). And Gaurishankar Ojha has rightly given the date of Govindachandra's accession as 1114 A. D. This discrepancy of dates was striking and we specially looked into the inscriptions concerned and it appears that these grants from 1104 to 1109 A. D., Govindachandra signs or makes as heir apparent, while Madanapāla was still ruling and hence these years must be included in the reign of Madanapāla. Kielhorn has also given the inscriptions of 1104, 1105, 1107 and 1109 as belonging to the reign of Madanapāla. The first insc. of 1104 is published in I. A. XIV (p. 103) and is the well-known Basāhi grant of that village in the Etawah District. Govindachandra is described therein as Mahārājaputra, meaning literally son of the Mahārāja, and in the last sentence the writing is said to be done with the consent of Purohita Jāgūka, Mahattaka (minister) Vālhaṇa and Pratihāri (chamberlain) Gautama. The inscription of 1105 is published in Ep. Ind. II (p. 358) and is similar in form to the above on which we will comment at length later on. It grants a village in the Pānchāla country while the donor was encamped on the Ganges and in the end the writing is said to be made with the consent of the above officers as also of the queen-mother Rālhadevi. The third insc. dated 1107 is published in short in J. R. A. S. 1895 (p. 786). It was made in Benares by queen Prithvīśrikā for Madanapāla. And the fourth insc. dated 1109 is published in I. A. XVIII (p. 15). The grant was made on the Jumna at Āsaṭikā mentioned above, on account of a solar eclipse, by Govindachandra Mahāraja-putra 'while Madanpāla was ruling' and it does not contain at the end mention of any consent by any state officers. We have detailed these facts purposely as some points of importance appear clearly therefrom. Madanapāla, it must first be stated, did not come to the throne in 1097 as is sometime supposed, for we have now an inscription of Chandra himself dated 1099. The insc. of St. 1154 or 1097 A. D. is given even by Kielhorn as belonging to Chandra. That insc. (I. A. XVIII p. 11) was recorded by Madanapāla to certify a grant made by Chandra in 1097 (St. 1154); when this certification or the inscription itself was recorded is not mentioned but it must have taken place after 1099 A. D., when Chandra was still ruling. We may take, therefore, the date of the rule of Chandra as circa 1080 to 1100; in which year Madanapāla may be taken to commence his rule. Strangely enough, the above noted four grants in the year 1104, 1105, 1107 and 1109 are made during his rule by his son Govindachandra and one by his mother queen Rālhadevī and one grant is consented to by his own queen Prithviśrīkā when the grantor was in Pānchāla country. It may be inferred that Madanapāla by reason of illness or for some other cause did not rule personally during these years and authorised his son and queen to make grants and do other acts which are solely the function of royalty. It further appears that Rajput queens were often invested with power to act for the king as regents. In the last grant of 1109, Govindachandra was so far advanced in age and also in power that his act did not require the consent of the queen mother. Govindachandra's first grant found in his own behalf is dated 1114 (Kielhorn and Gaurishankar) and we may take it that he came to the throne in 1110 A. D.

Govindachandra coming to the throne when young naturally ruled long. About 21 copper plates were found in one place near Benares out of which 14 belong to Govindachandra dating from 1114 to 1154 A. D. and are published by Kielhorn in E. I. IV. In all about forty grants of Govindachandra have been found; but the latest date yet found is the one above given, viz: 1154 A. D. Though Vijayachandra the next king is mentioned first in a grant of his dated 1161, we must take Govindachandra to have ruled from 1110 to 1155 and not later for reasons which will presently appear. Govindachandra had two queens named Nayanakelidevi and Gosalādevi and from the former he had a son Rājyapāla who as Yuvarāja made a grant dated 1142 A. D. He, however, seems to have died before his father.

Vijayachandra who succeeded Govindachandra was also a powerful and able monarch. He is described as having made a Digvijaya in inscriptions of his son. His name appears as Bijepal in the Prithvirāj Rāsā and he is therein also said to have conquered the world. His fight with Hammīra is described in his grant dated 1168 A. D. as more effective than that of his father; for it is said that he quenched the burning heat of the people's grief by the tear-flow drawn from the eyes of the women of Hammīra who had wantonly harrowed the world*, a strange method usual with Sanskrit poets of describing a victory over the enemy. At this time Khushru the Hamir was settled in Lahore (1152), abandoning Ghazni for fear of the Ghori and the Ghazni kingly line, in its decline, was nearing extinction. His defeat, therefore, need not excite surprise. Vijayachandra's son Jayachandra was already in 1168 A. D. a grown up man and Yuvarāja as appears from this very record (I. A. XV p. 7). The date of the coronation of Jayachandra is actually given in an inscription of his as 31st of June 1170; and we may, therefore, take Vijayachandra as ruling from 1155 to 1170 A. D.

Jaychandra was also a powerful monarch; but it seems that the Chāhamānas of Ajmer had wrested the vaunted overlordship of India from the Gāhadavālas of Kanauj, even in the days of Vijayachandra, as we find that Vigrahapāla of Ajmer had already conquered Delhi and recorded an inscription there dated 1163, boasting that he had conquered the land between the Himalayas and Vindhyas and cleared Āryāvarta of Mlechchhas. The Digvijaya of Vijayachandra must, therefore, be placed long before 1162 and hence his reign must be taken to have commenced in 1155 A. D. and his extensive victories placed between 1155 and 1160 A. D.

The epic poem Naishadha, one of the five great epic poems in Sanskrit, is the work of Śrīharsha who was a poet at the court of Jaichand, who was also a great king and, as related in a subsequent chapter, died an honourable death, drowning himself in the Ganges when wounded in fighting with the Mahomedans. The valiant Rathods of Jodhpur claim descent from the Gāhadavāla family of Kanauj, as the Guhilots of Mewad claim descent from the Maitrakas of Valabhī and the Bhonsles of Satara claim descent from the Guhilots of Mewad. Whether this claim of the Rathods is well founded or not, we proceed to examine in the following separate note.

---

* भुवनदलनहेलाहर्म्यहम्मीरनारीनयनजलदधाराधौतभूतोपतापः ॥

GENEALOGY OF THE GĀHADVĀLAS.

Yaśovigraha
|
Mahīyala (Mahīchandra)
|
I Chandra (c. 1080–1100 A. D.)
Insc. 1091, 93, 97, 99.
|
II Madanapāla (c. 1100-1114)
|
III Govindchandra (c. 1114 to 1155)
40 Inscriptions found.
|
IV Vijayachandra (c. 1155–1170)
Insc. 1168
|
V Jayachandra* (Jaichand)
(1170–1193 A. D.) Insc. 1175, 76 &c.

---

* This name is usually spelt as Jayachandra in inscriptions apparently a miswriting of engravers of inscriptions.

NOTE 1—RATHODS AND GAHARWARS.

The tradition of the Rathods of Jodhpur is that their ancestor Sihaji who first came to Marwad was a grand-nephew (some say a great-grandson) of Jayachand and the Gaharwars of U. P. whose chief representative at present is the Raja of Kantit in Mirzapur District consider themselves the direct descendants of Jaichand. Now when the family name Gāhadavāla was actually found mentioned in some of the grants of the kings of Kanauj, the question was discussed whether the Rathods of Jodhpur and the Gaharwars of U. P. are really one clan and were descended from the Gāhadavāla kings of Kanauj. Dr. Hoernle in I. A. XIV discussed this subject and expressed a doubt for two or three reasons. The first is that the gotra of the Gaharwars is Kāśyapa and that of the Rathods is Gautama. Secondly, these two clans intermarry. And thirdly, Gaharwars are despised as not of good family by other Rajputs. Although these facts may or may not be true, they do not go to prove that the Rathods of Jodhpur are not descended from the Gāhadavālas of Kanauj as tradition asserts for the following reasons.

In the first place, in the oldest inscription found of Chandradeva himself, the race of the family is given as the solar race (Asīdasītadyutivanśajatas &c.) and Chandradeva gives his name as Chadrāditya in his next two inscriptions. The Rathods of Jodhpur consider themselves all along as solar race Rajputs. (Strangely enough the Gaharwars look upon themselves as lunar race Rajputs though descended from Jaichand). They are, therefore, distinct from the Rāshṭrakūta kings of Malkhed described in Volume II who plainly were lunar race Rajputs. We have already noted that their name Rāshṭrakūta is an official position name meaning head of the country and is used as such in Eastern Chālukya inscriptions (See Vol. II p. 144) and the name may be borne by different clans and even castes like the modern names Deshpande or Joshi. This Rāshṭrakūta clan which ruled in the north is, therefore, distinct from that which ruled in the south, though the former may have originally belonged to the Deccan as Jodhpur tradition asserts and Gāhaḍa may have been a town in the Deccan somewhere. Secondly, let us see what the name of Gāhadavāla means and how it is mentioned in the documents of these kings of Kanauj. The modern name Gaharwar of which the original form Gāhadavāla is known only recently has been fancifully explained as meaning gharbāhar (out of home) or grahavara (subduer of the planet Saturn, Mirzapur Gazetteer p. 204); but now that we have to explain the original form Gāhadavāla, taking a hint from the similar name Jammuwāl among Kshatriyas and Agarwal among Vaiśyas we think that Gāhadavāla means belonging to the town of Gāhaḍa. It seems thus to be not a clan name but a family name based on town of residence. Probably the name was given to distinguish this family of Rathods from other families and the name was a popular one. In most of the inscriptions of the Gāhadavālas of Kanauj it is not given but simply the vamśa viz. the solar, is mentioned, as noted before even in the oldest inscription of Chandradeva. The name Gāhadavāla is found in the inscriptions which were written when Govindachandra was a young man acting as Yuvarāja under Madanapāla. It is curious to note that these inscriptions depart from the settled form of the inscriptions of these Kanauj kings. Instead of beginning with invoking blessings of Śrī, they begin with a salutation to Dāmodara and say that in the Gāhadavāla vamśa was born king Mahīyala (I. A. XIV p. 103 and E. I. II. p. 358) or Mahītala (I. A. XVIII p. 15. Probably here also the reading should have been Mahīyal which is the more populăr form of the name). These inscriptions were drawn up in the Pānchāla country and use the poular name of the family Gāhadavāla. Apparently it was not the clan name of the family and it has not been used in records drawn up in the usual style adopted by the court.

But the strongest reason which appears to prove to our mind conclusively, that Gāhadavāla was not the clan name of the family, is that this name does not appear in the list of the 36 royal clans of India accepted throughout the Rajput world. When this list was made and the number 36 fixed can be surmised with tolerable certainty. We have already shown in Volume II (p. 22) that Kalhaṇa who wrote his Rājataranginī in 1154 A. D. mentions the number 36 of the royal clans of Rajputs. The list must have been made before this date. Secondly as the list contains the name of the Kachhawāhas who came to the front about the end of the 10th century, it is clear that the enumeration was made in the 11th century A. D. Why such an enumeration was made we shall have to discuss later on when describing the social condition of India in this sub-period; but we may state here that while in the preceding sub-period (800–1000) caste was fluid and intermarriages between the Indian castes on Anuloma basis took place (Vol. II. p. 179), such intermarriages ceased in the third sub-period (1000–1200) and every caste began to consolidate itself and introduced rigid rules of marriage. It was natural that the Rajputs also should consolidate their sub-caste at this time and we are, therefore, doubly sure that this enumeration of 36 clans was made during the 11th century. Nay we even surmise from the very interesting verse noted later on in one of these inscriptions of Govindachandra (I. A. XVII p. 15 made as Yuvaraja, which contains more popular ideas than any other inscription quoted in the appendix), that the consolidation of the solar and lunar race Kshatriya clans must have taken place in the orthodox revival under Chandra the first Gāhadavāla king. Now as the enumeration of 36 families was made at this time, if Gāhadavāla had been a clan name, it would most assuredly have been enumerated in the list separately. The supposition may be made that the enumeration was made before the rise of the Gāhadavālas of Kanauj, say, in the first half of the 11th century and it is hence that the name Gāhadavāla does not appear in the list. But surely Chanda Bardai recited the names of the 36 royal families at the time of Prithvīrāja and Jaichand when the Gāhadavālas were in their glory, and most assuredly the name could not have been omitted from this list of Chand. It was impossible that such a powerful Rajput family as that of Jaichand should have been omitted by Chand when even minor families found mention in the list. We hold this list in the Rāsā to be the oldest we have (Vol. II p. 22); but supposing that the Rāsā is a fabrication throughout of the sixteenth century A.D. (we think it is an amplification of an original nucleus made about that time) and that Gaharwars being not considered good Rajputs were omitted in the list of the 36, we have still two other lists viz. the Jain list and the Kumārapāla-charita lists given by Tod which are very old but later than the rise of the Gāhadavālas, as the date of Kumārapāla, we have seen, is 1143–1173 and Kumārapāla-charita must be necessarily later. But these lists also do not mention the Gaharwars as a separate clan. In the days of Jaichand and at least a century or two later the Gāhadavālas must have been famous in India and their name could not have been omitted from the lists, which again had ample opportunity to mention their name as the names enumerated therein fall short of 36, the accepted number. Indeed in the Rambhā-manjarī drama by Nayachandra dated about 1400 A. D. in which Jaichand is the hero, in the very first epithet applied to him by the Sūtradhāra we have a reference to this list. Jaichand is said to be the forehead ornament of the 36 royal clans* of Ikshvākuvamśa. It is, therefore, certain that Gāhadavāla was not the name of a clan but of a family based on the town of residence. To what principal clan did these Gāhadavāla kings belong? Very probably to the Rathod clan whose name is included in the list of 36. There is, in our view, a strong indication of this in the Badaun Rāshṭrakūta inscription the date of which has not been ascertained but which certainly is anterior to the fall of Jaichand; as it mentions that one king of the line, Madanpāla, made incursions of Hamīra impossible (See E. I. I. p. 64). Now this inscription opens with† the expression "protected by the arms of the kings belonging to the famous and *Akhila* (all-pervading) Rāshṭrakūta clan." This suggests that the Rāshṭrakūta kula consisted of many branches and they protected or reigned over the whole of Pānchāla which included Kanauj. Indeed the kingdom of Kanauj was always known as the kingdom of Pānchāla (Al-Beruni states that Kanauj was famous for Pāṇḍavas meaning the Pānchālas who were their foremost supporters and Draupadi belonged to their country). The word Akhila in this verse would be meaningless if it did not refer to the other Rāshṭrakūta branches ruling in Pānchāla itself. This is a very old authority dating from before the last days of Jaichand to hold that Jaichand was also a Rathod as he is everywhere represented to be in later history. And there is no other family among the 36 clans to which the Gāhadavālas have been assigned as a branch in any tradition or record and we may conclude that the Gaharwars of U. P. and the Rathods of Jodhpur are one clan viz. Rāshṭakūṭa.

The reasons which are alleged as going against this conclusion are according to our view, of no great validity. The gotra of Gaharwars is now no doubt Kāśyapa, but it is likely that the Gāhadavāla direct descendants being deprived of their greatness could not maintain regular Purohits as kings do and can, and gradually lost memory of their gotra. When on rare occasions the gotrotchāra becomes necessary, to those who do not recollect their gotra, the Kāśyapa gotra is usually assigned. Or more probably the Gaharwars took other Purohitas in their days of adversity and following the dictum of Vijnāneśvara that Kshatriyas have no gotras of their own but have to take the gotras of their Purohitas adopted a new gotra, viz. Kāśyapa. Perhaps the descendants of Sihaji in

---

* षट्त्रिंशद्राजन्यवंशभालस्थलललायमानश्रीक्ष्वाकुवंशाविभूषणस्य

† प्रख्याताखिलराष्ट्रकूटकुलजक्ष्मापालदोः पालिता । पांचालाभिधदेशभूषणकरी वोदामयूता पुरी ॥

Jodhpur may have adopted a new gotra (Gautama) similarly, the original gotra of the Gāhadavālas being Kāśyapa; but the probability is otherwise for in the Rambhā-manjarī drama of Nayachandra king Jaichand addresses his queen as 'ornament of the Kāśyapa gotra.' (Among Rajput kings it is usual to address queens by their paternal gotra or kula as Chauhāni &c.). The inscriptions of the Gāhadavālas do not unfortunately mention their gotra; indeed inscriptions of the Rajput families of the time do not usually mention their gotras. We personally made careful enquiries at Kanauj to find out, from some Brahmin family, this gotra or to discover some old paper relating to the much-talked-of Rājasūya sacrifice performed by Jaichand at which the ancestors of noted Kanaujia Brahmin families acted as priests but no clue could be got to the gotra of Jaichand. The difference of gotra for the above reasons does not, in our view, invalidate the conclusion we have arrived at.

Nor does the fact that Rathods and Gaharwars intermarry. The fact is disputed by many; but even if it is admitted, we cannot thereby suppose that they were not one clan before. Indeed some Kshatriya clans have begun to marry within the clan itself especially in the Panjab and we were told at Jammu that even in the same gotra, after 25 generations, a Smṛiti text allowed inter-marriage. Though this is incorrect, it is undeniable that inter-marriages have begun to take place in the same clan. And as Gaharwar has later become practically a separate clan being mentioned in the fourth list of Tod, such rare intermarriages might take place now and then. It may, however, be noted that the rule of exogamy is strictly observed by the Rajputs of Rajputana based on the enumeration of 36 clans though perhaps the gotra rule is not observed. Thus, for instance, the Jadejas and the Chūdāsamas intermarry though of the same gotra and both are outside the older three lists of 36 clans, being mentioned in the fourth as separate clans.

Lastly, the suggestion that Gaharwars are looked down upon by other Rajputs is not correct. And if they are, there must be other reasons which apply to the Gaharwars of the present day. The fact now known that the ruling family of Kanauj was Gāhadavāla must finally set at rest such an idea, for Jaichand and Govindachandra and Chandra were considered best Rajputs of their days. It is suggested by Sir Vincent Smith that the Gāhadavālas were originally Bhars. There is no proof whatever of this supposition. There is an important verse* in the interesting inscription of Madanapāla-Govindchandra already noticed (I. A. XVIII p. 15) which may be quoted in this connection. The verse may be translated thus: "When the two famous races of Kshatriyas born of the Sun and the Moon were desolate, the creator thinking that the whole world is nearly void of the sound of Veda recitation inclined his mind to incarnate himself to re-establish the ways of religion as also to rehabilitate the two famous races of Kshatriyas." "Then there was born in the above family king Śri-Chandradeva crest-jewel of kings and he dispelled the darkness caused by

---

* प्रध्वस्ते सूर्यसोमोद्भवविदितमहाक्षत्रवंशद्वयेऽस्मिन् । उत्सन्नप्रायवेदध्वनिजगदखिलं मन्यमानः स्वयंभूः ॥
कृत्वा देहग्रहाय प्रवणमिह मनः क्षत्रबुद्धिर्धरित्र्याम् । उद्धर्तुं धर्ममार्गान् प्रथितमिह तथा क्षत्रवंशद्वयं च ॥
वंशे तत्र ततः स एष समभूद्भूपालचूडामणिः । प्रध्वस्तोद्धतवैरिवीरतिमिरः श्रीचन्द्रदेवो नृपः ॥

the insolent soldiers of the enemy." This shows that Chandra, the founder of the Gāhadavāla family, was then popularly considered as having rehabilitated the solar and lunar race Kshatriyas and the Vedic religion. It seems clear that he was looked upon as an orthodox Kshatriya who was well-versed, like Rāma, in both Veda and the Dhanurveda-vidyā. This also shows that there was a great slaughter before that time of Kshatriyas by the forces of Mahmud and his successor Masa'ud and also a great relaxation in the observance of the Vedic religion in the conduct of the remnant. Chandradeva Gāhadavāla, was, therefore, properly enough looked upon as an incarnation of Brahmā himself, the first reciter of the Veda and the creator of Brahmins and Kshatriyas. It cannot, therefore, be supposed that the Gāhadavāla family of Kanauj could in those days have been looked down upon as lower grade Kshatriya; and it ought to have been enumerated among the 36 royal clans; and was in fact included under the chief clan name Rathod.

Before closing we may mention two other inferences which arise from the above verses, viz. that in the first half of the 12th century the Kshatriya races were looked upon as only two and not three including the Agni-vamśa. The word vamśa again is used in two senses, viz. race and clan as it is used in these two senses in the above verses as also in the verses from the Rāsā quoted in Vol. II p. 22, enumerating the 36 vamśas. And thirdly at this period the theory that there are no Kshatriyas in the Kali age had not come into existence or into currency in northern India at least where this inscription was recorded wherein Brahmā is described as actually rehabilitating the solar and lunar races of Kshatriyas by incarnating himself as Chandradeva. This corroborates the view we have maintained in Volume II Appendix IV p. 312-317.

NOTE 2—DO THE RATHODS OR GĀHADAVĀLAS BELONG TO THE DECCAN?

The Rathods of Jodhpur and Bikaner are, according to our view, distinct from the Rāshṭrakūtas of Malkhed described in Volume II, as they in their inscriptions describe themselves as Chandravaṁśī, being descended from Sātyaki. But the Rathods of Jodhpur-Bikaner and also the Gāhadavālas of Kanauj are Suryavaṁśī from their records and inscriptions. If they, therefore, came from the Deccan, they must have belonged to a separate clan bearing the same official name Rāshṭrakūta. Did they, however, come from the Deccan as is generally believed? We will discuss this question in this note from bardic records as also from the Rambhā-manjarī Nāṭikā in which Jaichand is the hero.

The Gāhadavālas in their inscriptions do not say that they came from the Deccan as the Senas of Bengal in their inscriptions distinctly say that they came from Karṇāṭa and call themselves Karṇāṭa-Kshatriyas. But non-mention is not conclusive unless the mention is necessary. The official bardic record book in the Bikaner State Library states that the Rathods originally belonged to Ayodhyā and a king thence went direct to Kanauj and took possession of it. This is, however, not quite reliable, as Kanauj is known, in historic times from about 400 A. D. to the 11th century A. D., to have been in the possession of the Maukharis, the Vardhanas, the Varmās and the Pratihāras (see Vol. I and II). Moreover, this record mentions Jaichand and his father Bijepāl, but not Govindachandra and his ancestors. The bardic record at Jodhpur does not also give Govindachandra and his predecessors. In one bardic book at Jodhpur, no reference is made to the Deccan as at Bikaner, but in another it is stated that a king named Nandapāla son of Vipula became king of Karṇāṭaka and his descendants came to Kanauj and Jaichand son of Bijepāl is given as the last. Bijepāl's father's name is given as Abhaichand (which may be another name of Govindachandra). His father's name is given as Brahma and Chandra is stated in inscriptions to be an incarnation of Brahmā. This tradition, therefore, may be taken to indicate that the Gāhadavālas came from the Deccan Karṇāṭaka. But the name of Kalyan city is not mentioned even in this record.

In the corresponding record with the Rājāpurohita, the heading of the whole record is given as "Ayodhyā, then Konkana Deśa, Gada Kalyāṇa Karṇāṭaka deśa, then Kanauj." This is again ambiguous; for there is a Kalyan both in the Konkan as also in Karṇāṭaka. The latter Kalyan was, however, founded by Someśvara Chālukya abaut the latter half of the 11th century and the Gāhadavālas could not have come from there. It may, however, be that they first went to Konkan, and thence to Karṇāṭaka, and finally thence to Kanauj.

Notwithstanding this ambiguity, there are indications that the Rathods alias Gāhadavālas came from the Deccan. In the first place, the word Rāshṭrakūta as the name of an officer is found in southern inscriptions only. In fact the word Rāshṭra as denoting a kingdom or province is found in the Deccan only (see the Malla Rāshṭra, Gopa Rāshṭra and Pandu Rāshṭra of the Mahābhārata and Rashṭrika of Aśoka inscriptions).

Secondly, the tradition at Jodhpur is that the family goddess idol was brought from the Deccan by a Rathod prince named Khes (ancestor of the Jodhpur family) and is called by the Deccani name Nāganechi. Thirdly it is strange to discover a Marathi passage in the Rambhā-manjarī Nātikā of Nayachandra Sūri who wrote this drama about 200 years after Jaichand who is the hero. The customary eulogy of Vaitālikas in the beginning of the first act in which the praises of Jaichand are sung is, strangely enough, in Marathi, though nearly the whole of the drama is in the courtly Mahārāshtri or Sauraseni Prakrit. This passage is worth quoting and we do it below.* It may indicate that Nayachandra was a Jain pandit from the Deccan; but it is more indicative of the probability that the family bards of Jaichand must have belonged to the Deccan and that it was customary to sing these praises in Marathi. The Gāhadavāla family thus seems to have come from the Deccan and the tradition was still current in Nayachandra Suri's time. In the tenth and eleventh centuries, the Kshatriyas of the south and north were not differentiated and the Deccan Gāhadavālas were indeed looked upon as best Rajputs, as the very first epithet of Jaichand in this drama proves. This Deccan Rāshṭrakūta clan seems to have spread over the whole of Northern India from Badaun to Mithila as inscriptions of the 11th century A. D. prove, and one branch of it which conquered Kanauj was called Gāhadavāla. We must indeed state here that these Rāshṭrakūtas of the Deccan must have come there from the north originally, as all Kshatriyas or Aryans came to the Deccan from the north-west. We even find the name Rāshṭrika in the north in an edict of Aśoka, and the Rāshṭrakūtas must have come to the Deccan from the Panjab originally.

Before concluding we may draw the attention of the reader to two important facts which appear from this drama though we have noticed them elsewhere. The very first epithet is that the Gāhadavālas were considered the forehead-ornament of the 36 royal clans, thus showing that the Gāhadavālas, if they had been a separate clan, ought to have found a mention in the old lists of the 36 royal families. Secondly, Jaichand addresses his chief queen as Kāśyapa-kula-nandinī in this drama. As among the Rajputs queens are distinguished by their parent's family names, such as Chauhani, etc., even in modern times, this indicates that the queen's father belonged to the Kāśyapa gotra and that, therefore, the gotra of the Gāhadavālas could not have been Kāśyapa or Śāndilya.

---

* जारि पेखिला मस्तकावरि केशकलापु । तरि परिस्खलता मयूराचे पिच्छप्रतापू ॥
जरी नयनाविषयु केला वेणीदण्डु । तरी साक्षाज्जाला भ्रमरश्रेणीदण्डु ॥
जरी दृग्गोचरी आला विशाल भालु । तरी अर्द्धचन्द्रमण्डल भइल ऊर्णायुजालु ॥
भ्रूयुगल जाण्यूं द्वैधीकृत कन्दर्पचापु । नयनानिर्जित सुजला खंजन निःप्रतापु ॥
मुखमण्डलु जाण्यू शशांकदेवताचे मण्डलु । सर्वांगसुन्दर मूर्तिमंत कामु । कल्पद्रुम जैसे सर्वलोक आशा विश्रामु ॥

CHAPTER IX.

THE PĀLAS OF BENGAL.

We gave the history of the Pālas of Bengal during the second sub-period of our history in Vol. II Chap. IX ending with Mahīpāla I. The Pāla dynasty continued to rule throughout the third sub-period (1000–1200) also, a remarkable case of long-lived kingly line as Sir Vincent Smith rightly remarks. We may, however, divide it into two portions which curiously enough fall at Mahīpāla I about the beginning of this sub-period. It is a fact mentioned in most Pāla records that Mahīpāla or his father lost the kingdom about this time. It is usually stated that Mahīpāla won back the paternal kingdom which had been taken possession of by persons who were not entitled to it.* (See Sarnath inscription dated 1026 A. D. I. A. XIV p. 136). Sir Vincent Smith has given in I. A. 1906 a list of Pāla kings with detailed information of all their records found till then and has also given their genealogy as also probable dates of accession of the Pāla kings. We give at the end this genealogy from Mahīpāla I onwards with the dates of each king. Now the accession of Mahīpāla is placed by Smith in 980 A. D. as Mahīpāla is said to have reigned long and in Insc. No 17 the regnal year of this king is given as 48. If then we take Mahīpāla's accession as 980 A. D. we must also hold that his kingdom must have been seized by outsiders or false claimants about this time and not earlier. Unfortunately, no Pāla inscription mentions the nature of the usurpation or the name of the usurper. We made a surmise in the last volume (p. 141) that the shock given by Mahmud's invasions may have reached Bengal. Of course it is not possible that Mahomedan Turks came in those days so far east, but it is possible that dispossessed Rajputs of the Panjab or the North-western province may have sought for some territory to rule so far east, as dispossessed Rajput kings always did in Indian history (witness the Sisodias going to Nepal after being driven by Allauddin out of Chitor or the Rathods going to Marwad from Kanauj after Jaichand's defeat). Now the Dinajpur inscription published in J. R. A. S. Bengal 1911 mentions a Kāmboja, king of

---

* अनधिकृतविलुप्तं राज्यमासाद्य पित्र्यम् ।

Gauda building a temple of Śiva* in Dinajpur and it is suggested that its date Śaka 888 or 966 A. D. brings it near this event and that a Kamboja king (Kamboja is western Tibet) might have invaded Gauda and founded his power there. From this king or his successor Mahīpāla must have recovered the kingdom of Gauda belonging to his father. This, however, is too early; for this dispossesion is not mentioned as taking place in the time of Vigrahapāla who ruled probably from 960 to 980. This inscription does not state that the Kamboja took possession of the kingdom of the Pālas, nor do the Pāla inscriptions mention that their kingdom was seized by a Kamboja king. It is further possible that some Gauda feudatory may have caused this trouble and he may eventually have been ousted by Mahīpāla.

* काम्बोजान्वयजेन गौडपतिना तेनेन्दुमौलेरयं । प्रासादो निरमायि कुञ्जरघटावर्षे जगद्भूषणः ॥

Whatever the true account of this dispossession, Mahīpāla I began a new life of the Pāla dynasty and ruled justly and vigorously for 48 years and more. Of all the Pāla kings he is the best remembered and "songs in his honour are still to be heard in remote corners of Orissa and Kuch Bihar." His kingdom extended to the west over Magadha and Bihar and included northern and eastern Bengal and even Orissa and Assam. His reign was marked by the rivival of Buddhism and Dharmapāla and other holy men from Magadha went to Tibet in 1013 and did much to restore the religion of Goutama to honour in that country (Smith p. 400). Atiśa, another missionary from Vikramaśīla went to Tibet in the reign of Nayapāla the successor of Mahīpāla in 1042 A. D. Mahīpāla I reigned according to Smith from 980 to 1038 when his son Nayapāla succeeded him and he was succeeded by his son Vigrahapāla III in 1059 and he is credited with having defeated Karṇa of Chedi who was extending his power during the decline of the Pratihāra emperors to the east of Benares and particularly in Champāraṇya. His Āmagāchhi inscription has been noticed in Vol. II and has been thrice edited once by Keilhorn (I. A. XXI p. 97) correcting Dr. Hornle's edition (I. A. XIV p. 164) and lastly by R. D. Bannerji. In 1080 Vigrahapāla died and he was succeeded by his eldest son Mahīpāla II. The Pāla line in its second life had flourished for a hundred years and its power began to decline. Mahīpāla II imprisoned his brothers and began to rule oppressively. This led to a rebellion of the Kaivartas headed by one Divyoka. Mahīpāla was killed in this rebellion and he was succeeded for a short time by his younger brother Śurapāla. But the power of the Kaivartas in Varendra (North Bengal) was unbroken and Divyoka was succeeded there by his son Bhīma. But Rāmapāla who was the youngest son of Vigrahapāla III was a vigorous and capable king and succeeding Śurapāla made preparations to conquer Varendra (his seat of government was still probably Monghyr in Gauda or western Bengal). And assisted by his maternal uncle Mahana, feudatory king of Mithila, a Rāshṭrakūta by clan and other feudatories and some allies one of whom was Devarakshita king of Pīthī, Rāmapāla conquered Bhīma who was eventually killed and established his power in Varendra. These details are found from a poem every verse of which is double-meaning composed by Sandhyākara Nandi son of the minister for peace and war of Rāmapāla himself and thus almost a contemporary record. It is written from Paundravardhana capital of Varendra and it relates the story of Rāmapāla by one meaning and of Rāma the demigod and ruler of Ayodhyā by another meaning. There is a commentary on the poem which enables one to understand the first canto only. The other three cantos remain unexplored and Tārāprasād Shāstri who gives these details in his paper published in Proceedings R. A. S. Bengal 1900, on this Rāmacharita, is right when he observes that much historical information remains buried in these cantos of double-meaning verses (p. 73).

But fortunately for us, these facts are confirmed by the very important Sarnāth inscription of Kumāradevi queen of Govindchandra published in E. I. IX (p. 319). This inscription is extremely important as it furnishes valuable information about three Rajput families, the Pālas, the Rāshṭrakūtas and the Gāhadavālas. We will give it in detail in respect of these kingly families beginning with the Pālas. It is stated that Rāmapāla's prosperity was secured by his maternal uncle Mathana, king (feudatory lord) of Anga, by conquering Devarakshita king of Pīthī who had troubled him.* Where this Pīthī was cannot be decided though Stein Konow who publishes this inscription thinks it is Pīthāpura in Vengi country. Mahana is

* गौडेऽद्वैतभटः सकाण्डपटिकः क्षैत्रैकचूडामणिः ।
प्रख्यातो महणोऽङ्गपः क्षितिभुजांमान्यो ऽभवन्मातुलः ॥
तं जित्वा युधि देवरक्षितमधात् श्रीरामपालस्य यो ।
लक्ष्मीं निर्जितषैरिरोधतनया देदीप्यमानोदयाम् ॥ ७ ॥

described as a fearless warrior in Gauda and therefore was a feudatory of Rāmapāla, king of Gauda and is also called Angapa or ruler of Anga or Mithila. Now he had a daughter named Śankaradevi whom he gave to Devarakshita after defeating him in the usual Rajput manner. From them was born the famous queen Kumāradevī who founded the Bauddha Vihāra commemorated by the inscription. It seems, therefore, that Devarakshita was a Buddhist and his daughter Kumāradevī was also Baudha. She was married to Govindachandra, though a staunch Hindu, whose family is described as Gāhadavāla family and whose father was Madanachandra and grand-father Chandra.* The word Kshatravamśa applied to the Gāhadavālas shows that they were then considered as good Kshatriyas. Similarly Mahana is also described as crest-jewel of kshatriyas and hence was also a Rajput. In the Rāmacharita above noted he is stated to be a Rāshṭrakūta or Rathod. His sister was Rāmapāla's mother which shows that Rāmapāla was also a Kshatriya. Devarakshita to whom Mahana's daughter was married must also have been a Rajput. It will be noted that this relation does not contradict the theory propounded by us that Rāshṭrakūtas and Gāhadavālas were one clan; for here Devarakshita's daughter by a Rāshṭrakūta-born princess married a Gāhadavāla *i. e.* the daughter's daughter of a Réshtrakūta married a Ghāhadavāla and thus there was no inter-marriage between Rāshṭrakūtas and Gāhadavālas. An important fact, though not connected with the Pālas, may be noted here about Govindachandra who was in possession of Benares as we already know. In this inscription it is stated that he was an incarnation of Hari who was asked by Hara to protect Vārānasi defiled from Turushka soldiers.† Stein Konow thinks that this indicates that there were raids on Benares in the days of Govindachandra. But the sense of the above line may be taken as protecting Benares polluted (already) from Turkish soldiers. It would not be proper to connect "from Turkish soldiers" with the word protect; for the word polluted as applied to Benares would be unmeaning unless we take the above expression with the word 'polluted' and say that the pollution came from Turkish soldiers. This inscription no doubt confirms the fact that Benares was raided once by

* जगति गहडवाले क्षत्रवंशे प्रसिद्धे । ऽजनि नरपतिचन्द्रश्चन्द्रनाम। नरेन्द्रः ॥

† वाराणसीं भुवनरक्षणदक्ष एको । दुष्टां तुरुष्कसुभटादवितुं हरेण ॥
उक्तो हरः स पुनरत्र बभूव तस्मात् । गोविंदचन्द्र इति सुप्रथिताभिधानः

Turkish soldiers but it refers to past pollution and we may well take this as a reference to the raid by Ahmed Nialtagin. In the translation given by Konow the word 'dushtām' or polluted seems to have been omitted by oversight (verse 16 p. 327).

Although this inscription is not dated, the relations mentioned viz. that Rāmapāla was Mahana's sister's son and Kumāradevī queen of Govindachandra was his daughter's daughter make it clear that Rāmapāla preceded Govindachandra. His accession is placed by Smith in 1080 A. D. properly and he ruled vigorously over the whole of Bengal for a long time. His conquest of Mithila as also his fight with Bhīma are mentioned in the Kamauli inscription of Vaidyadeva (E. I. II, p. 350) wherein his son Kumārapāla is mentioned as the overlord of Kāmarūpa in a double-meaning verse stating that he like Râma killed Rāvaṇa in the form of Bhīma and had also obtained the land (daughter) of Mithila.* This shows that the rebellious Bhīma was a very powerful chieftain and fighting him was as difficult as the crossing of the ocean by Rāma. This rebellion is also referred to in J. R. S. Bengal LXIX p. 68 to be noted further on in speaking of Kumārapāla.

Rāmapāla was succeeded in 1130 by his son Kumārapāla referred to above in E. I. II and he was succeeded by his son Gopāla III in 1136 A. D. Nothing particular is found recorded of them and the name of the last has only been known recently from a record of Madanapāla (his uncle) who succeeded him in about 1140 A. D. A copperplate grant of his has been found and published in J. R. A. S. Bengal IXIX part I (p. 66) which makes the interesting statement that the village was granted as Dakshinā to a Brahmin for reading the whole Mahābhārata to his queen Chitramaṭikā; which shows that the king though a Buddhist was favourably inclined towards Brahmins and that his queen was a Hindu who heard the whole Mahābhārata recited to her by a Brahmin. We find that these Pāla grants are usually made in the Paundravardhana Bhukti or Varendra i. e. North Bengal where Sena grants are also made. The Sena kings enjoyed power chiefly in Eastern Bengal and probably divided power in Northern Bengal, West Bengal and Magadha with Behar being probably under the Pālas. We do not know much of the

* तेने येन जगत्त्रये जनकभुलाभाद्यथा तद्यशो ।
क्षोणीनायकभीमरावणवधाद्युद्धार्णवोल्लंघनात् ॥

political events in Madanapāla's days, but it is probable that the power of the Pālas must have declined in his time. Madanapāla was succeeded by his son Govindapāla in 1161 A. D. definitely, as an inscription in V. S. 1232 in the 14th year of his reign has been found (Smith's list J. A. 1909 No. 30). He was succeeded by a king named Mahīndrapāla mentioned in inscriptions, the last one found being dated 1193 A. D. He is identified with the king Indradyumna of local tradition who is said to have been destroyed by the Mahomedan invader Mahammad Bakhtyar Khilji.

It is a pity that Bengal was in the 12th century divided into two strong kingdoms opposing each other, that of Monghyr or West Bengal ruled by the Pālas and that of Gaur or Eastern Bengal ruled by the Senas. The division of authority in the same province, practically self-contained and united by race and language, led to the weakening of both and the difference of religion must have contributed to the same effect. That effect was the almost easy and bloodless conquest of both by a foreign power of a different faith as we shall have to show later on.

The chronology of the Pālas fortunately is not much in dispute and we give the genealogy of this second section of the Pāla line with dates of inscriptions found and probable dates of accession of each king suggested by Sir Vincent Smith (I. A. 1909). These dates will help us to tolerably settle the vexed chronology of the Sena kings of Eastern Bengal.

GENEALOGY OF THE PĀLA KINGS OF BENGAL.

(Sir V. Smith. I. A. 1909 p. 244).

I Mahīpāla I ac. 980 Ins. 1026
|
II Nayapāla ac. 1038 Ins. 1042
|
III Vigrahapāla III. ac. 1059
|
IV Mahīpāla II ac. 1080 — V Śūrapāla ac. 1082 — VI Rāmpāla Yakśapāla ac. 1084

(sons of VI Rāmpāla:)
VII Kumārapāla ac. 1130 — IX Madanapāla ac. 1146 m. Chitramatikā
|
VIII Gopāla III ac. 1136 (son of VII)

X Govindapāla ac. 1161 Ins. 1175, 1178 (son of IX)
|
XI Mahendrapāla ac. 1186 Insc. 1193 identified with Indradyumna of tradition.

CHAPTER X

THE SENAS OF LAKHNAUTI (BENGAL)

The Sena kings of Bengal, though only principally three, have been the subjects of much controversy; not only are the facts meagre and ambiguous, but historians and antequarians have also unfortunately looked at them with one bias or another. The Mahomedan historians have written with great exaggeration, perhaps in this case only, heightening the audacity of Mahammad Bakhtyar and the pusillanimity of Lakshmaṇasena of Bengal; while Hindu researchers have written about the Senas with a bias naturally in favour of this last Hindu king of Bengal. Dr. D. R. Bhandarkar again with his usual bias in favour of the non-Aryan origin of Rajputs, looks upon these Senas as foreign Brahmins or priests turned into Kshatriyas, while the modern Senas of Bengal who are Vaidyas by caste (a sub-caste born of the mixture of Brahmins and Vaiśyas) look upon these Senas as Vaidyas. It is, therefore, necessary to discuss these points in detail giving first the history of the Sena family so far as is practicable in this state of divergence of views.

The initial history of the Senas is given clearly in the Deopara stone inscription published in E. I. I (p. 300). The inscription states that a chief from the Deccan (a Dākshiṇātya) named Sâmantasena who was a feudatory under a Karṇāta king and who had fought with and killed there those who had come to plunder Karṇāta territory retired in old age to the banks of the Ganges and founded a small kingdom at Kāshipur in Eastern Bengal.* His son Hemantasena was a powerful king and from him and queen Yaśodevī was born Vijayasena the first powerful king of the dynasty. He is said in the inscription to have conquered the king of Gauda who had troubled the king of Kāmarūpa and also conquered the king of Kalinga. Gauda king here means the Pāla king of Monghyr in western Bengal and he and the king of Kalinga or Orissa were the really powerful kings opposed to the Senas. Vijayasena was an orthodox Hindu, while the Pāla kings were Buddhists and this establishment of Sena power may be looked upon as an assertion of Hinduism, a

---

* Kāsiari in Mayurbhanj territory. (Smith). M. M. Harprashad Sastri believes that the Senas were settled in Birbhum and Guswa and from these they spread (Law).

revival of Hindu orthodoxy in Bengal. Indeed the Deopara inscription relates that Vijayasena performed many sacrifices. Sir Vincent Smith rightly observes that Vijayasena was the first independent king of this line and that he wrested much territory from Pāla kings. But it may be said that Sir V. Smith may not be right in assigning 1119 A. D. as the date of his independence. It may have been earlier than this. 1119 A. D. is the initial date of the Lakshmaṇasena era, as Kielhorn has proved from several inscription dates given in that era and the Śaka era; and as Abul Fazal gives the starting year of the Sena era as 1041 Śaka. Kielhorn believes that the people of Tirhut are wrong in treating the Sena era as starting from 1028 Śaka (I. A. XIX p. 7). But though this point may be taken as settled, the question who started this era and when is one on which a great divergence of opinion prevails. Smith proposed the following dates for the commencement of the reigns of the three kings, Sāmanta 1080, Hemanta 1100 and Vijaya 1119 (E. H. I. 3rd Edn. p. 419) which means that he looks upon the Lakshmaṇasena era as founded by him commencing from Vijayasena his grand-father's reign. Gaurishànker Ojha, however, states that the era was founded by his son Ballālasena on hearing of the birth of his son Lakshmaṇa when he had just conquered the Mithila country (Prachīna lipimālā p. 42–45 and Hindi Tod p. 536). Mr. D. R. Bannerji in pubishing in E. I. XIV (p. 159) a new grant found of Ballāllasena thinks that the era was founded to commemorate the beginning of the reign of Lakshmaṇasena. The last opinion would seem to be the natural and proper interpretation of the starting of the era, and indeed Mahomedan evidence, almost contemporaneous, states (Tabakat-i-Nasiri) that Ballālasena died leaving his queen pregnant and Lakshmaṇasena was crowned even in the womb of his mother. This may be an absurdity like the other absurdities recorded by the Tabakat; but it is at least historically correct to say that Lakshmaṇasena was born in 1119 A. D. after the death of his father. And it is natural that he should have dated the era founded by him from his birth which was also the date of his coming to the throne. But a doubt arises when one takes into consideration the fact that Lakshmaṇasena makes a grant in the 7th year of his reign in which he calls himself Parama Vaishṇava (J. R. A. S. Bengal XLIV part. 1 p. 7). It may easily be supposed that as he reigned from birth, he might make a grant when a child of seven through his regent.

But it cannot be explained how he could then be a Parama Vaishṇava as his father and grandfather appear to be Śaivas. The whole question must, we fear, remain unsolved owing to the absence of any Vikrama or Śaka date in the grants of almost all the Sena kings, as indeed of the Pāla kings, and the grants only give regnal year figures for the donor kings. The chronology of these kings can, therefore, be given only conjecturally in a double set and we give two series of dates as proposed by Sir V. Smith and by Mr. R. D. Bannerji. Some also have suggested that there were two Lakshmaṇasenas. But following the Mahomedan tradition we will take it that there was only one Lakshmaṇasena and that he died in 1199 A. D. when he was 80 years old.

Barring dates which we give in the genealogy, the history of the Sena kings so far as it is undisputed may be given in brief as follows. Vijayasena was the first independent king who ruled over a large portion of Eastern Bengal, the Pālas ruling over Western Bengal. His son Ballālasena was a still more powerful king. He conquered Mithila and further reduced the power of Pāla kings of Bengal by conquering the Kaivartas who had rebelled against them and had imprisoned the Pāla king Mahīpala II or Rāmapāla. He was an orthodox Hindu king and like other Rajput kings of his time he was a learned man himself and a patron of learned men. He wrote the work named Dāṇasāgara and commenced another work which his son Lakshmaṇasena finished. In old age he retired with his queen to Prayāga and there drowned himself in the sacred confluence of the two rivers (Gaurishanker).

He was succeeded by Lakshmaṇasena who was as great a king as his father. The capital of the Senas was Gaura a town in the present Malda district in Bengal (which is indeed an ancient town). But Lakshmaṇasena built another town outside its wall and named it Lakshmaṇāvati in the same way as other great kings in this sub-period founded towns after their names viz: Karṇa of Chedi founded Karṇāvatī and Vikramāṅka of Kalyāṇa founded Vikramapura, both near their former capitals Tripura and Kalyāṇa. Lakshmaṇasena was powerful enough to found an era of his own like Vikrama of Kalyan or Jaisimha of Anhilwad. The starting year of this era is 1119 A. D. as settled by Kielhorn and the era, unlike the other two eras, is still prevalent in Tirhut.

Like his father, Lakshmaṇasena was himself a learned man and a patron of learned men. Noted Sanskrit pandits whose works still survive, floating on the surface of the ocean of time, sat in his court such as Halāyudha, Umāpatidhara, Śaraṇa Govardhanāchārya, Dhoyī, Jayadeva (author of Gītagovinda) and Srīdharadāsa. The king was a Vaishṇava as he distinctly calls himself so in his records while his ancestors were Śaivas and the modern poets who sing the praises of Hari in Bengal perhaps go back to his time. He was the pioneer of the worship of Hari in Bengal as his father was the rehabilitator of the Varṇāśrama Dharma as also the founder of the curious system of Kulīna marriages, both of which facts we shall have to notice in our general survey of the country in this sub-period. "Lakshmaṇasena was a Monarch of exceptional personal qualities. Trustworthy persons affirm that no one, great or small, suffered injustice at his hands and his generosity was proverbial" (E. H. I. p. 400, Smith.)

About the end of this king we will speak in another chapter; but the Sena power as the overlords of the whole of Bengal came to an end with him, the country being mostly conquered by the Mahomedans. But Sena kings continued to rule in further Bengal till about the end of the thirteenth century. Mādhavasena, Keśavasena and Viśvarūpa Sena, three sons of Lakshmaṇasena ruled in Vikramapura and grants of Keśava and Visvarūpa have been found. It appears from the Tabakat that when Nasiruddin invaded Lakhnauti, the Khilji rebellious governor had gone estwards against the Rajas of Bang or Eastern Bengal (who could have been none but Sena kings). Pandit Gaurishanker states (Hindi Tod p. 438) that Danujamādhava who perhaps for the above cause had left Vikramapura and settled in Chandradvīpa assisted Balban to punish the rebellious governor of Lakhnauti by preventing his escape by water, and that four kings ruled in succession after Danujamādhava in Chandrapur, the last being Jayadeva with whom the Sena dynasty ended.

Having given this short sketch of the Sena kings so far as their history has been made out, we will conclude with noticing the disputed question as to who these kings were by caste. The other disputed question as to how Lakhnauti fell we will, as stated before, discuss in our last chapter. It is maintained by Dr. D. R. Bhandarkar that these Sena kings belonged to the Brahmakshatra caste which is even now found all over India.

But it is clear that these Sena kings were Aryan Kshatriyas or Rajputs belonging to the lunar race. They were niether Brahmakshatra by caste as Dr. Bhandarkar maintains nor Vaidya as the modern Vaidyas of Bengal believe. For the Deopara inscriptions noted above distinctly begins with the statement that Sāmantasena was born in the lunar vaṁśa. Now this statement can only be made about a Rajput, for neither Brahmakshatras nor Vaidyas have any solar race or lunar race distinction. Dr. D. R. Bhandarkar, obsessed with the bias noted in the beginning, directs his attention only to the word 'Brahmakshatriyāṇam' in the verse about Sāmantasena and omits to notice that in the very preceding verse, these kings are said to be born in the lunar race. The word Brahmakshatriyāṇam requires to be construed consistent with the above statement so as only to apply to Rajputs. We have already noted in Vol. II that the word is often used in connection with Rajputs of the orthodox faith and mode of living. It is true that the translation given by Kielhorn is wrong as Brahmins cannot be brought into this epithet which really means "the head garland of the families (not of Brahmins and Kshatriyas but of Kshatriyas alone) who are endowed with Brahma or Vedic greatness (Brahmopeta-Kshatriyāṇām). In fact the epithet 'Brahmavādin' in the preceding line applied to Sāmantasena leads to the same meaning. The orthodox Kshatriyas, as opposed to the Buddhists or other Kshatriyas, often prided themselves upon being called Brahma-Kshatriya. There is no reference to any caste in this epithet as the caste is settled by the preceding verse which states that they were born in the lunar race and therefore could be none else but Rajputs.

But even granting that this epithet indicates the particular caste Brahmakshatra, as Dr. D. R. Bhandarkar believes, what ground is there for the further observation which he makes and which is quoted by Sir Vincent Smith with approval (E. A. I. 3rd Edn. p. 420) viz: "In my opinion, as stated elsewhere, these were Brahmins of new tribes afterwards turned Kshatriyas before their final mergence into the Hindu society"? The suggestion is wholly gratuitious and has no basis. It is impossible to argue that because they were called Brahma-Kshatriya and were a separate caste, therefore, they belonged to new and foreign tribes and were originally Brahmins who subsequently became Kshatriyas and this change took place before they were recognised finally as Brahmakshatras. We have already discussed this question at length in Vol. II and can only say that this inference arises from bias and Sir Vincent Smith has also accepted it from the same bias in favour of the theory of the foreign origin of many Rajput families.

The matter is not left to mere inference from the lunar vamśa mentioned of these Senas, but is settled by the express word Kshatriya used in the Mādharinagar grant of Lakshmaṇsena published in the Proceedings of Bengal R. A. S. Vol. V. p. 467 where the birth of Sāmantasena is stated to be in the Karṇātakshatriya family of Vīrasena. Whether Vīrasena the founder of the family was a Dākshiṇātya or Karṇāta is not of much moment. Dākshiṇātya, the word used in the earlier Vijayasena record of Deopārā, means usually a Maratha-country Brahmin or Kshatriya. But the distinction between a Maratha and a Karṇāta Kshatriya is illusory. And in those days even the distinction between a northern and southern Kshatriya had not become acute as intermarriages continued to take place between these Kshatriyas. And when these Kshatriyas went to Bengal, they became for all practical purposes Bengali; for they not only married with northern Kshatriyas but their servants and officers were entirely drawn from Bengal. A Karṇātaka or Maratha Kshatriya founding a kingdom in Bengal in those days was vastly different from a Maratha chief like Scindia in modern days founding a kingdom in northern India which is principally governed by men from the Deccan with which their marriage relations still continue. The Sena kings, therefore, were completely Bengalis though they preserved the memory of their having come from the Deccan. Curiously enough, two noted northern Kshatriya families preserved the tradition of their having come from the Deccan-Karnāṭaka especially from Kalyāṇa. This is, however, of no moment as Kshatriyas then all over India were one and we may conclude by reiterating that the Sena kings of Lakhnauti were Rajputs and Kshatriyas* by caste and not of the modern Brahmakshatra nor of the Vaidya caste. The word Brahmakshatra applied to them indicates their orthodoxy. Indeed Sir Vincent Smith himself states that "his (Lakshmaṇasena's) family, we are told, was respected by all the chiefs of Hindustan and he was considered to hold the rank of hereditary Khalif or spiritual head of the country."

*The Senas are thought to be Dravidians and probably Cholas, but Dravidas are entirely distinct from Karṇāṭakas and they cannot have been descended from the Cholas.

NOTE:—CHRONOLOGY OF THE SENAS.

The question of the dates of the Sena kings, three only in importance, bristles with so many difficulties that one almost despairs at arriving at truth in connection with the dates of kings who ruled only eight hundred years ago. We have, therefore, decided to give the chronology of these kings in a double set of dates as follows.

GENEALOGY OF SENA KINGS.

		According to Sir V. Smith.	According to Mr. R. D. Bannerji.
	Sāmantasena		
	Hemantasena		
1	Vijayasena	Ac. 1119 A. D.	Ac. 1080 A. D.
2	Ballālasena	„ 1159 „	„ 1100 „
3	Lakshmaṇasena	„ 1170 „	„ 1119 „

4 Mādhavasena Ac. 1205 (?)
5 Keśavasena Ac. 1205.
6 Viśvarūpasena Ac. 1220.
7 Śuddhasena (son of Keśavasena) ac. 1225.
8 Lakshmaṇasena (son of Śuddhasena) ac. 1243.

The name of the last king we take from Aîn-i-Akbari which gives the traditional catalogue of Sena kings as it was accepted in the days of Akbar (1556–1605) i. e, about three hundred years after the last king. It gives the years of the rule of each king and to Suddhasena it assigns 18 years and to Lakshmaṇiyā the last three years. Now the Tabakat was written about 1250 A. D. i. e. some years after the death of this Second Lakshmaṇasena. It is, therefore, possible that there were two Lakshmaṇasenas and in the oral exaggerated account which the author of the Tabakat heard from two illiterate Afghan soldiers in the army of Mahammad Bakhtyar, the two Lakshmaṇasenas were jumbled. The existence of two Lakshmaṇasenas has been questioned and we incline to the belief that there was only one king of that name; especially as Pandit Gaurishankar does not give this name but gives the name Danujamādhava. But if we believe that there was another Lakshmaṇasena, a great-grandson of the first and that he started the era known as Lakshmaṇasena era, many of the difficulties which otherwise appear are removed. Of course we must grant that he started the era not from his own coronation but from the establishment of the Sena power by Vijayasena as taken by Sir Vincent Smith. This is not a new suggestion and it solves, according to our view, many problems connected with the disputed chronology of Sena kings.

The era was started by the last king or by Danuja-Mādhava and named after the greatest king of the Sena line.

This explains why no Sena grant uses this era. We find that even Lakshmaṇasena's grants do not use this era but that they use regnal years. Nay even the Bakerganj grant of Keśavasena does not use this era. Secondly, Lakshmaṇasena died in the 80th year of this era and was, therefore, supposed by Mahomedan informers that he was 80 years old when he died and that he was crowned even when he was in the womb. Thirdly, the expression श्रीमल्लक्ष्मणसेनदेवपादानामतीतराज्ये सं. ७४ occurring in a Buddha Gayā inscription noted by Kielhorn in I. A. XIX (p. 2) is well explained. Kielhorn treats this date as given in Lakshmaṇasena era. We may note here that this is the earliest date supposed to be given in this era. But what seems to us proper is that the word atīta would not have been used in this sense. The wording would have been merely लक्ष्मणसेन संवत् if it referred to an established era (the words श्रीमत् and देवपादानाम् need not have been used). If the figure was intended to refer to regnal years, the words 'Rajyavarsha' or 'Vardhamana Rajya' would have been used. The expression means, as some have well-contended, that 74 years had elapsed since the death of the illustrious or revered, prosperous Lakshmaṇasena. Lakshmaṇasena's rule was, as we have already said, prosperous and blessed and he was remembered throughout Bengal. Hence it was natural for people to assign dates from *the end* of his rule as that was the end of Swarājya in Bengal. The date would thus be in our view 1273 A. D. This of course does not take cognisance of the Lakshmaṇa era started by his descendant and counted from 1119. A. D. . is probable that this document in Gayā takes no cognisance of an era started in a distant part of eastern Bengal. Fourthly and lastly, we have no record to show specifically that Lakshmaṇasena the elder started this era; and if so in what year of his reign. Jayasinha of Gujarat started an era after himself and it was called Sinha Samvat. Lakshmaṇasena's grant published in Ep. Ind. XII (p. 8) mentions at the end only Sam. 3. and not Lakshmaṇa Sam. 3.

Even if, however, it is supposed that the second and insignificant Lakshmaṇasena started the era from a previous king's reign, the question still remains whether the initial year of the era was taken from the date of Vijayasena's accession or that of the illustrious Lakshmaṇasena. There is unfortunately no definite data to settle the dispute. The Sena records give no Śaka or vikrama date; and only contain regnal years as do Pāla records. The Śaka year given in Dānasāgara, a work written by Ballālasena is given by some as 1019 and by others as 1091 (शशिनवदशमिते शाके); i. e. some take it as 1091 A. D. while others take it as 1168 A. D. Sir Vincent Smith thinks that Ballāla was alive on this date and hence takes Lakshmaṇsena as commencing to rule in 1170 A. D. Mr R. D. Bannerji believes that Ballāla ruled from 1100 unto 1119; and Lakshmaṇsena ruling from 1119 A. D. from whence his era, counted, probably finished the Dānasāgara in 1168 A. D. How Dr. Smith takes 1159 as the initial year of Ballāla's reign is not quite clear. There is, however, one argument which favours the chronology adopted by Smith viz. that the victories of Ballāla and even of Vijayasena in Mithila could not have taken place in the days of Rāmapāla, a victorious and powerful king of the Pāla line of Bengal who began his rule in 1084 (see p. 228). Secondly, it appears from Kumār's paper on Lakshmaṇasena era (I. A. 1913 p. 187) that Lakshmaṇsena must have come to the throne at about the age of 22, as he is said to have fought as Yuvarāja with Kalinga in the Mādharinagar copperplate (J. A. S. B. 1910). If Lakshmaṇasena's accession in 1119 is accepted his death in 1199 being certain, he must have come to the throne when quite a child. Indeed his inscription of Sam. 3 or 7 would have to be assigned to his childhood and as said before, he could not have been described as Parama Vaishṅava. As learned Bengali researchers are still not unanimous on this point we leave this subject as yet undecided.

We may take this occasion to mention a few more facts which may perhaps help us in fixing the dates of these kings. In Bengal J. R. A. S. XXXIV (p. 134) we find Halāyudha, a descendant of Bhatta Nārāyaṇa author of the well-known drama Veṇīsamhāra was the Dharmādhikārī of Lakshmaṇsena. He was a son of Dhananjaya of the Vatsa gotra. His brother Paśupati wrote a treatise on Śrāddhas and also Ānhikapaddhati or the daily duties of Brahmins. In the Brāhmaṇasarvasva are mentioned kings Vijaya, Ballāla, Lakshmaṇa, Mādhava, Keśava and Lakshmaṇeya.

From Proceedings Bengal V (p. 467) we find that Ballāla conquered Benares as also Kāmarūpa which is also mentioned in Madanapārā inscription of Viśvarūpasena. Ballāla appears to be alive in 1169 A. D. or Śaka 1091 which is the date of Dānasāgara and in the end of this treatise Ballāla is said to have conquered Kāmarūpa by his powess (विक्रमवशीकृतकामरूपावनीमण्डल).

It may finally be added that the Deopārā inscription found in Varendra (Rājashāhi District) is undated but it is believed to be recorded from its appearance about the end of the 11th century A. D. Vijayasena is therein said to have conquered a king of Gauda who had troubled a king of Kāmarūpa (the epithet अपाकृतकामरूपभूपम् should be taken with Gaudendra and can not be applied to Vijayasena himself). This would suggest that Vīrasena defeated a Pāla king before the end of the 11th century.

The reader will have a sufficient idea of the difficulties in settling decisively Sena chronology from the above facts.

CHAPTER XI

THE ŚILĀHĀRAS OF THANA

Of the kingdoms of Southern India we will first speak about the kingdoms of the Śilāhāras of Thana which in this sub-period of Hindu Indian history (1000–1200 A. D.) rose to greater importance and enjoyed practical independence. Theirs was an ancient country known as "Aparānta" in Mahābhārata days and Soparā (Śurpāraka), its capital, was a well-known place to which Buddha had sent his disciple Pūrṇa to preach his religion of peace and where in pre-Christian days Arab and Greek ships came to export and import goods and ideas. The kingly line of the Śilāhāras was also very old, the stone records of which begin with a king Kapardin who was a feudatory of Amoghavarsha Rāshṭrakūṭa and who made donations to Buddhist monks and recorded them (Śāka 765 or 843 A. D.) in the famous Kanheri (Krishṇagiri) caves of the Thana District, wherein Buddhist records are to be found from the days of the Śātavāhanas and Buddhist monks lived from about 100 B. C. down to about 1500 A. D., the days of the Portugese. This Śilāhāra line ruled for about five hundred years from roughly 800 to 1300 A. D., first as feudatories of the Rāshṭrakūṭas and then as independent kings from the time of Aparājita whose inscription dated 997 A. D. has been found and published (Bhadan charter E. I. III p. 257). In this document Aparājita still calls himself Mahāmandaleśvara and gives the whole of the Rāshṭrakūṭa lingly kine, his overlords, and states that the last king Kakkala was destroyed by Chālukya Tailapa. We quoted in Vol. II from an unpublished grant of the same king dated four years before (993 A. D.), a passage wherein the Rāshṭrakūṭa line is given with the same fullness and with an expression of sorrow over the fall of the Rāshṭrakūṭa kings. Probably Aparājita assumed independence hereafter though he used the title Mahāmandaleśvara from habit and from respect for the past, much as the Vaziers of Oudh or the Nizams of Hyderabad or the Peshwas of Poona continued their old titles indicative of subordination even after they became independent. Aparājita is given other titles in later records of the family such as Mṛigānka and Birudankarāma and he is said to have sumptuously received king Goma (?), fought with Aiyapadeva (?) and assisted Bhillama (of Sèundeśa). It thus appears that he ruled like an independent king. The country was called Konkaṇa with fourteen hundred (villages), capital Purī. The old extent and the old capital are here mentioned though a larger country including both the present Thana and Kolaba districts and even a part of the Ratnagiri district including Chiplun and the hilly territory above the ghats called Mawal appears to be under his sway from the yet unpublished grant referred to above. This territory at present contains certainly more villages than 1400 and we believe that the number 1400 was an old traditional number attached to the name Purī which was the former capital of Konkan and the extent of territory under the later Śilāhāras was much greater, using the same name Konkaṇa but with capital at Thana or Sthānaka. Under these Śilāhāras the country was also very prosperous as an Arab writer (976 A. D.) had recorded that in " the country from Cambaya to Saimur, the villages lie close to one another and there is much land under cultivation " (Vol. II. p. 166).

Commencing from Aparājita, therefore, the Śilāhāras became independant and more prosperous and began to be counted among the important ruling families of India. The family grew to greater renown still during the reign of succeeding kings ending with Aparāditya II, two inscriptions of whom dated 1185 and 1187 are found (J. R. A. S. Bombay XII p. 333). The latter calls himself, as others before him, Konkaṇa Chakravartin, a high sounding title indicative of independence and power. There were 11 kings from Aparājita to Aparāditya as shown in their genealogy and a period of about two hundred and ten years (990 to 1200 A. D.) roughly which gives the usual average of twenty years per king. Using this average generally, but keeping in view the dates of the known inscriptions of particular kings, we will assign probable dates for the reign of each (see the genealogy given at the end.). The first king Aparājita thus we take to have ruled from 990 to 1010 A. D. He was succeeded by his elder son Vajjada and the latter was succeeded by his brother Arikesarin whose inscription (Thana plates A. R. I. p. 357 and Kielhorn's genealogies) has been found and is dated 1017 A. D. We may therefore, assign a short reign to Vajjada from 1010 to 1015. We have also to assign a short reign to Arikesarin in whose reign we may place the defeat of Konkan by Bhoja Paramāra mentioned in a grant of his dated 1020 A. D. (Vol. II. p. 123

and E. I. XI. p. 81), as his successor Chhittarāja, son of Vajjada, has left an inscription dated 1028 A. D., the well-known Bhandup inscription (I. A. V. p. 277). We, therefore, assign to Arikesarin a reign of ten years from 1015 to 1025 and to Chhittarāja a reign of twenty years from 1025 to 1045. The Bhandup grant of Chhittarāja is important in many respects which we will notice later on. His brother Nāgārjuna reigned after him and we assign a reign of ten years to him and to his successor his younger brother named Māmvānī a reign of 30 years from 1055 A. D. to 1085 A. D. An inscription of his time dated 1060 A. D. has been found in the well-known temple of Āmranātha (now pronounced Ambernath) near the G. I. P. station of that name about 6 miles from Kalyan. The king's name is given as Mahāmvāni (sometimes given as Mamvani or Mammuni) and the record states that the temple was built of stone, in place of an old temple, by the Rājaguru or royal preceptor (Bombay J. R. A. S. IX p. 219). And there is another inscription found near the temple which records the erection of a building near it by a local officer (J. R. A. S. Bombay XII p. 329). This inscription is also of the same date viz. 1060 A. D.

Māmvānirāja was succeeded by his nephew Anantadeva (son of Nāgārjuna) who appears to have been a great king as we find him first calling himself Konkan Chakravartin in his inscription dated 1094 A. D. This grant (Kharepātan plates I. A. IX p. 33) was published by the well-known Sanskrit scholar K. T. Telang, who has given the genealogy of these Silāhāra kings with further remarks from records found till then. This grant remits customs duty on ships of a certain minister Śreshṭi (merchant) coming into the ports of Konkan. This king who is sometimes called Anantapāla may be taken to have reigned long from 1085 A. D. to 1125 A. D. His son Aparāditya I was the well-known king who sent an ambassador to a congress of pandits held in Kashmir as mentioned by Mankha in his Śrīkaṇṭhābharaṇa to be shortly noticed. He may be taken to have ruled from 1125 A. D. to 1145 A. D. His son Harapāla has left inscriptions so late as 1149 A. D., 1150 A. D. and 1153 A. D. We, therefore, allot forty years to Anantapāla, twenty years to Aparāditya and ten years to Harapāla.

Harapāla ruled from 1145 to 1155. The dates for Harapāla are found in stone records which are not now available to us for inspection but they are referred to in the history of Konkan given in Bombay Gazetteer Vol. I part I which first gives the available information about the Śilāhāras in a connected form. This account mentions that there were many civil strifes in the country in the reign of Anantapāla which harassed gods and Brahmins. It is difficult to understand what these disputes were and whether they proceeded from Mahomedans who were apparently settled in large numbers in this part of the country, the Rāshṭrakūṭas being friendly to the Arabs and not at all intolerant like the northern kings (see Vol. II. 166). There were Arab settlements in almost every sea-coast town from Somnath-Patan and Kambāya down to Cheul (Saimur) and they had even built mosques in each town. We have indeed mentioned of a dispute between fire-worshippers viz. Parsis and Moslems whose prayer time was loudly announced from a mosque at Cambay. The dispute was taken to king Jayasinha in Anhilwad and he is said to have personally gone to Cambay to inspect the demolished mosque and to have built it at his own expense (E. II p. 163). This dispute, however, appears to have been between the king and some of his relatives as appears from the inscriptions (I. A. IX p. 17) and Mahomedans allying themselves with the latter must have oppressed gods and Brahmins as they were then doing in the north. But the king Anantapāla was successful and suppressed the rebellion, sternly punishing his opposing relatives and the oppressors of gods and Brahmins. Konkan remained Hindu for two centuries more.

We have not much information about Harapāla but we may take him to have ruled from 1145 A. D. to 1155 A. D. so as to include his last known record dated 1153 A. D. in his reign. His son Mallikārjuna must have ruled long. He assumed the title Rājapitāmaha or grandfather of kings and this offended the Gujarat Chālukya king Kumārapāla who hence sent his general Ambada to conquer Konkan. A battle was fought near Balsad wherein Ambada was defeated; but Ambada returned again and Mallikārjuna was not only defeated but killed in battle by Jagadeva Paramâra as has already been told in Gujarat history. Mallikārjuna may be taken to have ruled from 1155 A. D. to 1175 A. D. He has left two grants dated 1156 and 1160 A. D. (Chiplun and Bassein) of which mention has been made by the Gazetteer but without reference as to where they are published.

His son Aparāditya II is the last king of this line in this sub-period; he is also the greatest in this line. He does not call himself Mahāmandaleśvara, but Mahārājadhirāja and also

Konkan Chakravartin. He undoubtedly ruled independently and over a large tract in the Konkan which retained its independence long after him. Marco Polo who visited Konkan nearly a century later also states that the king in his days was independent. Aparāditya like all great Hindu kings was also a great scholar and the well-known commentary on Yājnavalkya Smṛiti known as Aparārka, a work of recognised authority on Hindu law, was written by him. It is strange that this work is considered authoritative in such a distant country as Kashmir showing the great intercourse that went on in the different kingdoms of India even in those days. Pandits and classical works especially travelled far and wide. As already noted, we are told in the Śrikaṇṭhacharita of Mankha, a Kashmiri poet (1135–1155 A. D.), that a congress of learned men held in Kashmir was attended by Aparāditya's ambassador a Konkan pandit named Tejahkantha. This may also have made it possible that the second Aparāditya's work on Hindu law was soon known in Kashmir. Aparāditya's record dated 1184 has been found and published (Bombay J. R. A. S. XII p. 333), and his reign may be placed between the years 1175 and 1200 A. D.

We are not concerned with, nor do we know much of, the later kings of the Śilāhāra kingly line of Thana. Only one name Someśvara is mentioned by Kielhorn in his genealogies (E. I. VIII) whose inscription dated 1259 A. D. has been found and one more name Keśideva is given in the Gazetteer. But the line must have continued long after Someśvara till in the 14th century Thana was conquered by the generals of Mubārak after Malik Kafur had conquered the Deccan about 1328 A. D. The legend of a king named Bimba coming from Pātan (Somnath or Anhilwad) and some Kshatriyas from Paithan referred to in the Bombay Gazetteer Vol. I part II and described in detail by Mr. V. K. Rajwade, the well-known historical researcher of Mahārāshtra, is also outside the scope of this work; but it may be stated that their coming to Konkan must be placed after the fall of the Śilāhāras, at least after 1260 A. D.

There are some very important general remarks which we have to make regarding these Śilāhāra kings and their inscriptions. The first thing to point out is that these kings do not assign themselves in their inscriptions to the solar or lunar vaṁśas to which all Kshatriyas assigned themselves in those days. They derive their descent from Jīmūtavāhana, a Vidyādhara or heavenly being who in ancient legend is said to have offered his own body for being devoured by Garuda in order to liberate a Nāga or serpent. It is, therefore, natural to suppose that these Śilāhāras were not Kshatriyas. But that these Śilāhāras were Kshatriyas and were looked upon as Kshatriyas there is not the least doubt as their name is included in the list of the 36 royal clans. As related before, this enumeration appears tō have been made about the end of the 11th or the beginning of the 12th century A. D. during the reign of the orthodox emperor Chandra Gāhadavāla of Kanauj, "the rehabilitator of the solar and lunar races of Kshatriyas" or in the days of Govindachandra at the latest and this inference about its date is strengthened by the inclusion of the Śilāhāras among the 36. The Vidyādhara vamśa itself suggests to our mind, that they were Kshatriyas; for a Kshatriya alone could sacrifice himself in this manner and cut off flesh from his body (one is reminded here of Karṇa's legend in the Mahābhārata and possibly the Kshatriya Śilāhāras had assisted the Nāga race people of Southern India). The Śilāhāras always declare in their descriptions that they came from Tagarapura, a town mentioned by Pliny in Southern India on the Godavari east of Paithaṇ. Thus the Śilāhāras were Kshatriyas from the very centre of the Maratha country. They became famous throughout India as independent powerful kings under Anantadeva or Anantapāla who ruled from 1085 A. D. to 1125 A. D. and the list of 36 royal families which appears to have been made from Kshatriya ruling clans (Rajputs) at the time, properly included the Śilāhāras of Thana. They were Kshatriyas and Rajputs though they called themselves Vidyādhara-vamśa-born, and their fame had gone as far north as Kashmir where at the congress of pandits called by Mankha the ambassadors of two kings in India are mentioned as attending, Tejahkantha, ambassador of Aparāditya I of Konkan and Subala of Govindachandra of Kanauj. Kanauj, Konkan and Kashmir thus came together in about 1085 A. D. (B. B. R. A. S. XII extra number p. 51) and we need not wonder that we have a clear reference to the 36 Royal clans of India, in which number Śilāharas have a place, in Kalhaṇa's Rājataranginī of 1148 A. D. The Śilāhāras are the only people in this list who do not figure in Northern India and who have a kingdom in the south only. Rathods and Chālukyas are both northern Rajputs and southern Rajputs but Śilāhāras are only southern Rajputs or Marathas.

That these Silāhāras though Marathas have always been considered best Rajputs appears also from a grant of Bhoja Śilāhāra dated Śaka 1113 (1191 A. D.) quoted in extenso at p. 105 in Siddhānta-Vijaya recently published at Kolhapur in which the Silāhāra king styles himself Kshatriya-Śikhā-Chudāmani (crest-jewel of the Kshatriyas). 4. The Śilāhāras are now Śelars counted among the 96 kulis of Marathas and are looked upon as born in the Yādava or lunar vamśa.

The second peculiar thing in these inscriptions is that in every one of them along with the name of the grantor king his five ministers are always mentioned by name. That ministers should be considered to be of so much importance in this Konkan kingdom alone is really strange. It is possible that the modern maxim that kings are not responsible but ministers was known and acted upon in this kingdom The prime minister's name is always prefixed by the epithet Sarvādhikāri 'having all authority' (I. A. V. p. 227) or Rajyachintābhāra-samudvāhana Mahāmātya the great minister who bears the burden of the care of the kingdom'. There are sometimes two ministers for war and peace and a minister for land register Śrikarana, and always two treasurers (Bhāndāgarikas) possibly one for the public treasury and another for the private one or one for land-tax in kind and the other for cash. The collections in kind must always have been difficult for accounting, being kept in each division or even village. The ministers are usually stated to be five; when Sivaji introduced the Ashtapradhāna system, he was in 1660 in fact resuscitating a practice in the country which was as old as 1000 A. D. and even the word Pradhāna which is constantly used in these inscriptions.

The third peculiar thing is that the names of these ministers always end in the termination Aiya which has led scholars to believe that these Silāhāras, come from Tagara, were people from the Āndhra country and brought with the kings or that they always employed ministers from the Āndhra country where names usually end in Aiya. Now we do not believe that Tagara was in the Āndhra country, on the coutrary, we have already said that it was in the heart of Mahārāshtra. But even if it were so, the Silāhāras had been settled for so many centuries in Mahārāshtra, particularly in Konkan, that they were every inch Marathas, by relationship, by sympathies and by language. It is, therefore, unbelievable that their sympathies in 1000-1200 A. D. could have lain with the people of Āndhra who were entirely different in manners, in marriage relations and in language. We do not therefore, think that the ministers could have been people from Āndhra. Nor can it be believed that officers from Karnāta must have been employed as the Silāhāras were subordinate to the Rāshtrakūtas of Malkhed who were practically kings of Karanātaka though they were Marathas. For we think that the termination "Aiya" is peculiar to Āndhra only, not Karnātaka. We do not find in Rāshṭrakūṭa or later Chālukya records names of donees or others ending in Aiya. The riddle, to our mind, is however thus solved. In this tract of the country on the westcoast, as in Āndhra on the east coast, it was usual to designate higher people as Ārya of which "Aiya" is plainly the Prakṛit. The Konkan is generally inhabited by non-Aryan Koli population and these lower people always addressed the superior people of Āryan descent who came to the country later and who both subjected and civilized it, as 'Āryas.' In Ptolemy's geography this part of the country is particularly called Ariake; the cultivating population, being non-Aryan. In the conntry above the ghats it is mixed with Aryan or Maratha and hence there did not arise the practice of addressing the higher caste people as "Aiya," as we see in Āndhra where the cultivating population was and is non-Aryan still. We may give our own evidence on this point and state that we have heard even in these days a Konkan Koli villager addressed a clerk of higher caste as "Ajjā." This word of address was simply astonishing as it revealed the old practice still alive of addressing higher caste people as Ārya. The names which end in Aiya are not always of Brahmins; for in the Kharepatan grant we have Mahādevaiya Prabhu and Śri Somanaiya Prabhu. The Prabhus are apparently the ancestors of the modern Kāyastha Prabhus of Konkan as also Ananta Pai Prabhu mentioned in Aparāditya's grant dated 1187 (B. B. R. A. S. XII p. 333). Brahmin names sometimes also end in Bhatta while Kshatriya names are sometimes distinguished by the epithet Bhatta and Rāula.

Lastly we have to explain the inexplicable expression 'Hanjamana Nagara-paura Trivarga prabhṛitin' occurring in more than one record of these Śilāhāras. Hanjamana or Hanyaman is no doubt a town and may be identified with Sanjan of modern days and of the Arab writers of the 10th and 11th centuries. But why should the grant orders be addressed to the eople of the town of Hanjamana only and why are the people three-fold? Along with the usual officers of towns and talukas and provinces these orders are addressed to these particular people only. It is suggested that Hanjamana was the old capital town; but it does not appear so and the capital was either Puri or Thana and the inhabitants of neither are specially addressed. The expression can be explained only on the supposition that the three kinds of people there were very important. It appears probable that this particular part of the country was specially popular with foreigners for settlement. It is unfortunate that unlike China and Japan, India did not keep strict watch over the ingress of foreigners and allowed any people of any religion to enter the country and settle and even to enjoy jurisdiction of their own magistrates. These settlements were three and very important. There must have been Parsis, Arabs and Jews or perhaps Negroes. As important trading communities trading with the whole country and perhaps as very troublesome communities, they had special jurisdictions of their own as related by an Arab writer. The three classes of citizens of the town of Hanjamana had thus a special importance which required these orders to be addressed to them and brought to their notice also.

There are some other points of interest in these inscriptions relating to the general condition of the country which we will notice in our general survey. The country contained many towns to which foreign trade came such as Sanjan, Sopara, Bassein, Thana, Kalyan, Cheul and Chiplun and the customs revenue of the country must have always been very great. It appears that the fort of Thana was built by these Śilāhāras as in digging a foundation therein the copper plate of Anantarāja dated 1017 was found. The notable beautiful cave temples of Elephanta we will describe in a note.

GENEALOGY OF THE SILAHARAS OF THANA.

(Bombay Gazetteer Vol. I, Part II, Kielhorn's Genealogies E. I. VIII and Gaurishankar's Tod.)

I Aparajita Insc. 997 A. D. (c. 990—1010)

- II Vajjada (c. 1010–1015)
- III Arikesarin Insc. 1017 (c. 1015-1025).
  - IV Chhittaraja Insc. 1026 (c. 1025-1045).
  - V Nagaraja (c. 1045–1055).
  - VI Mamvaniraja Insc. 1060 (c. 1055-1085).

VII Anantadeva Konkana Chakravartin Insc. 1094 (c. 1085-1125).

VIII Aparaditya I Insc. 1138 (c. 1125-1145)

IX Harapala Insc. 1149, 1150, 1153 (c. 1145-1155).

X Mallikarjuna Insc. 1156 (c. 1155-1175).

XI Aparaditya II Konkana Chakravartin Insc. 1184, 1187 (c. 1175-1200).

Kesideva Insc. 1203, 1238.

Somesvara Insc. 1259.

NOTE 1—HANJAMANA NAGARA.

The identification of Hanjamana with Sanjan proposed by many has been accepted above. But this is doubted by Dr. Fleet who has republished the Bhandup grant of Chhittarāja in E. I. XII p. 275. Sanjan is the place where the Parsis allege that they came in 766 A. D. from Div in Kathiawar, in their migration from Persia. And they say that the name Sanjan is the name they gave to their setttlement. Dr. Fleet thinks that Hanjamana original cannot be changed into Sanjamana and further that Sanjan mentioned by the Arab travellers is Sindan on the coast of Cutch near Cambay and not this Sanjan. These are not unsurmountable difficulties and Dr. Fleet has not suggested any other town as the Hanjamana of the inscriptions. He suggests that it was some administrative head-quarters town of the Silāhāras beside their capital (p, 59). But this does not fit in with the description Hanjamana *Nagara*. Nor can Trivarga mean the three higher castes, for donations must be known by all classes. Our interpretation is that there were three classes of foreigners at Sanjan who had their own jurisdiction and who had dealings with the people of the land and who, therefore, were required to know of the grant of inam villages which enjoyed many rights. The name Hanjamana is no doubt a difficulty. It seems to us that Sanjan was a new settlement made by the Parsis near a village which must have existed at the place. The position of Sanjan is very favourable as a safe though small harbour just contiguous to the sea, and at present we are told there are remains of a fort near the harbour and also of a wall round the town of Sanjan. The remains are worth exploring. The Parsis appear to have come during the overlordship of the Chālukyas of Badāmi and in the Konkan there were many feudatories one of whom may be the Jādhava who gave permission to the Parsis to settle near the harbour. The place became probably a place for foreigners to settle and they managed their own affairs and had their own magistrates. The name Sanjan was probably given by the Parsis and the country people of the Konkan pronounced it Hanjamana or Haiyamana which appears to have been used in the inscriptions. Whether Sanjan is the Sindan of the Arab writers or not does not matter at all. It is almost certain that Sanjan is a Persian town name and it was given to their new settlement by the Parsis and not Hanjamana. This was the local pronunciation and it was naturally used in Konkan inscriptions.

It is not necessary to look upon Hanjamana as a separate name given to the town as J. J. Mody tries to do. The difficulty no doubt is to explain how m-got into the name Sanjan which was really the name given by the Parsis. Secondly, Trivarga may mean Parsi, Mahomedan and Hindu inhabitants also. The Parsis do not consist of three grades. Lastly, from Al-Beruni's description given with distances Sindan is identifiable with Sanjan and is to be placed north of Sopara immediately and it may be suggested that the word Hanjamana-Nagara may be interpreted to mean the city of i. e. belonging to (not named) Hanjamana or the Anjuman (community) of the Parsis.

NOTE 2—THE ELEPHANTA CAVES OF GHĀRĀPURI.

A few miles from Bombay by sea, in an island in the wide creek of Thana and Panwel are these caves with many beautiful carvings in stone and also statues. There were two stone elephants at the entrance of the principal cave which were visible from the sea and this fact gave rise to the name Elephanta caves given by the Portugese who first saw them. The town of Purī is now in ruins, but that there was once a great town which was then capital of Konkan, was in fact, the Bombay of the 6th to 10th century A. D. is proved by the inscriptions of the Śilāhāras which always mention "Purī Konkan, 14 hundred" as the name of the country. The island of Purī must have attracted attention in ancient days as a suitable site for a capital, being at the entrance of a large creek which is the natural harbouring place for ships trading along the coast as well as with distant Arabia. There are some Budhist remains also in this island but most of the structures are Brahmanical, and these appear to belong to the days of the Śilāhāra rule which began probably about the 8th century A. D. The style of the architecture and the beautiful figures carved, according to Bhāgavanlal Indraji, belongs to the period of the Elora carvings and therefore may be dated from the 8th to the 9th century A. D. The Rāshṭrakūta king Krishṇa excavated the Elora temple and it is probable that the Śilāhāras excavated these figures in imitation of their overlords the Rāshtrakūtas. And Puri was the capital of these earlier Śilāhāras from the 8th to the 10th centuries. It is possible that the Āryā Dvaipāyanī (island goddess) mentioned in the Bhāgavata as visited by Balarāma in his pilgrimage refers to the statue of the goddess of Pārvatī in one of the caves in this island, and the Bhāgavata Purāṇa may be held from this reference to belong to the 10th century. The most impressive Traimurti statue carved in the principal cave is, however the most important work of art in the Elephanta caves and it is not known to which Śilāhāra king the credit of it belongs. Purī fell into ruin in consequence of the capital being removed to Thana which is a more inland and safe harbour. An account of the Silāhāras of Thana would not be complete without this short description of Purī and the Elephanta caves and we have consequently given this short note on them.

CHAPTER XII

I. LATER CHĀLUKYAS OF KALYAN

In the Deccan ruled in this sub-period the later Chālukyas who became as powerful as the earlier Chālukyas of Badāmi in the first sub-period described in our first volume or the Rāshṭrakūṭas of Malkhed in the second. Both Rāshṭrakūṭas and Chālukyas were Maratha Kshatriyas. The former were the most ancient inhabitants of the Aryan race in the Deccan They were supplanted by the early Chālukyas and these in their turn were conquered by the Rāshṭrakūṭas. These Rāshṭrakūṭas were again conquered and supplanted by the later Chālukyas who in their Yevur inscription (I. A. VIII p. 19) have given the whole genealogy from the earlier Chālukyas down to Tailapa the conqueror of the last Rāshṭrakūṭa king, Kakkala. It is sometime doubted if the later Chālukyas were really descendants of the earlier Chālukyas; but there is no sufficient reason to deny this claim which they lay forth in their inscriptions, copying as they do the same titles and taking the same Māṇavya gotra (E. I. IX p. 206). The tradition that they were lunar race Kshatriyas and ruled for 59 generations in Ayodhya, they appear to have taken from the eastern Chālukyas of Vengi; as stated in Vol. I the earlier Chālukya records do not mention these facts. However we may believe that these statements are also true and that the Chālukyas came to the Deccan sometime about 400 A. D. Their descendant Tailapa was the son of Vikramâditya and Bonthādevi daughter of Lakshmaṇa, king of Chedi. (The Tripura Haihayas seem to have usually given their daughters to the Chālukya and Rāshṭrakūṭa Maratha Kshatriya kings of the Deccan). Tailapa was probably originally a powerful feudatory under Kakkala. It is not clear where he had his sway. Possibly it might have been in Badāmi itself. But Chālukya inscriptions do not mention his original capital. Seizing the opportunity of the decline of Rāshṭrakūṭa power, Tailapa defeated Kakkala and established once again the Chālukya line of Kings in the Deccan. He is said to have destroyed two great warriors or generals of Kakkala on the battle-field on whom he relied and who were his associates in oppressing the people. (Yevur grant I. A. VIII p. 17.) He is also said to have conquered Cholas, Āndhras, Utkalas as also the Maratha feudatory chiefs of the Deccan and ruled justly and vigorously in the country of Kuntala as is expressly stated in an inscription of the family (I. A. VIII p. 18) thus "securing happiness to the people" who were probably oppressed during the misrule which usually characterises the days of the decay of a dynasty. The Chālukya country is called Kuntala in most inscriptions and Kuntala is identical with what is now called the Southern Maratha country though the present language of the people is Kanarese. Indeed the three Mahārāshṭras of Pulakeśin (Vol. II p. 275) have already been noticed as Vidarbha, Mahārāshṭra proper and Kuntala; and these, forming together the greater Mahārāshṭra, may again be described as Northern Maratha country the basin of the Tāpti and the Wardhā, the Central Maratha country the basin of the Godāvari and the Southern Maratha country the basin of the Krishṇā river which distinguishes Kuntala (I. A. VIII p. 18). and here Mahārāshṭra and Karnātaka meet, the Karnātaka proper lying beyond the Tungabhadrā and being then under the Gangas and later under the Hoyasalas.

Tailapa ruled for 24 years from 973 to 997 A. D. His wars with Munja have been related in Volume II and he is said to have finally killed Munja ignominiously. We have already expressed a doubt about this story of Gujarat story-tellers; and Munja probably died on the battle-field. But the Yevur inscription and the Miraj plates refer, in our view, to the imprisoning of a great poet-king. As the Miraj record is dated 1024 A. D. and is very near the event, it may be believed that Munja was imprisoned after being made captive in war, though we may still disbelieve his being kept in a cage or made to beg from door to door and finally beheaded. This is too cruel for any Indian king and there is no hint of this in this record. (We understand the verses here differently from the way in which they are taken in the translation in I. A. XIII p. 17). When it is further stated that he conquered a king of Huṇas and kings of Marwad, Chedi and Utkala, it is probably an exaggeration. But there is nothing improbable in it if we remember that Tailapa was now the master of the whole power of the Rāshṭrakūṭas who in their palmy days had carried their arms as far north as Kanauj. There is not the least doubt that his general Bhārapa held Lāta and opposed and fought with Mūlarāja Solankhi who about the same time founded the northern Chālukya kingly power at Patan.

Tailapa had by his queen Jākabbā, a Rāshṭrakūṭa princess, two sons Satyāśraya and Daśavarman, the former of whom succeeded him. There is nothing particular recorded of him in the Miraj and Yevur records; but the Kharepatan grant (published in B. B. R. A. S. I.) was made during his reign by a Śilāhāra prince in Southern Konkan. Now this grant discloses two or three facts which are worthy of notice here. In this grant the Śilāhāra prince Rattarāja distinctly mentions the name of Satyāśraya his overlord. But in the grant of the Śilāhāra kings of Northern Konkan no overlord is mentioned though in their earlier grants they mention the then ruling Rāshṭrakūṭa king. It seems, therefore, that Northern Konkan was not under the later Chālukyas. Secondly, the names of ministers are not mentioned in the grant as they are mentioned in the grants of the Northern Śilāhāras. Thirdly, we find the name of the grantee Brahmin with the termination Ārya but not 'Aiya' as in the others. It is inferable that in Karnāṭaka, people used the termination Ārya at least in Sanskrit.

Satyāśraya ruled from 997 to 1008 A. D. and dying childless he was succeeded by Vikramāditya, son of his brother Daśavarman or Yaśovarman and Bhagavatī. He has left an inscription dated the year of his succession (J. B. R. A. S. IV p. 4). He ruled for a short time only and he was succeeded by his brother Jayasinha whose inscription dated 1019 A. D. has been found (I. A. V. p. 17). It mentions that he was a very sun to Bhoja lotus and that he defeated the Malwa confederacy. It may be taken for truth that Bhoja of Malwa was defeated by this king and Bhoja's efforts to wreak vengeance on the Chālukyas of the Deccan for killing Munja were frustrated. But the story told by Gujarat chroniclers that Bhoja took drastic vengeance on Tailapa himself and killed him is absurd (as the Bombay Gazetteer itself points out), as Bhoja came to the throne after Tailapa's death. Nor is it possible, as suggested by the Gazetteer, that the story relates to the successor of Tailapa, Vikramāditya who ruled from 1008 to 1018. His reign no doubt falls in the early years of Bhoja's rule but this fact is not mentioned in any record of these Chālukyas of the Deccan nor of the Paramāras of Malwa. We, therefore, think that it is the usual vengeance story, as imaginary as the vengeance story of Prithvirāja killing Shihabuddin concocted in the Rāsā. Bhoja may have gained some success over these Chālukyas but in the end he was defeated by Jayasinha.

But Vikramāditya must have suffered extremely from the invasion of the rising Chola king Rājarāja who is said to have devastated the whole country by his vast army consisting of nine lakhs of men and spared not even women and children. But this seems also to be a hyperbole of poets though Vikramāditya's defeat may be accepted as a fact. This hereditary fight between the Chālukyas and Cholas or rather between the Deccan and Madras continued long and Jayasinha is said to have defeated the Chola king Rājendra son of Rājarāja who had defeated Satyāśraya or his successor Vikramāditya. The Miraj grant distinctly states that after conquering the Cholas in the south and the seven Konkanas in the west, the king was encamped at Kolhapur in his march for conquering the north when the grant was made. The seven Konkanas have already been enumerated. They are not seven kings and probably they did not include Northern Konkan. This grant is dated in 1024 A. D. (946 Ś) and after this Jayasinha alias Jagadekamalla seems to have ruled long and defeated even Bhoja of Malwa. Gaurishankar surmises that he was finally killed in battle with Bhoja but this surmise may be true of the earlier king Vikramāditya (if the story of revenge is to be taken as true) and not Jayasinha. The Yevur record which was drawn up in the days of Vikramāditya makes no mention of any such sad end of Jayasinha.

Jayasinha is believed to have died about 1040 and he was succeeded by his son Someśvara who was certainly a far greater monarch than any of his predecessors. His power is thus described in the Yevur grant. "The king of Malwa is anxious to find out a Mandala (territory) for refuge. The king of the Cholas betakes himself to the forest of palm trees on the sea-coast. The king of Kānyakubja hides himself in a valley of the mountain (Himalaya) his mind being restless from fear of Someśvara's power." The king of Malwa may be Bhoja himself as his successor was assisted by Someśvara and the Kānyakubja king must be the effete representative of the Pratihāras vanquished by Mahmud while the Chola king may be Rājendra himself. We have got a graphic account of these events in the Vikramānkadevacharita of Bilhana, court-poet of his son Vikramāditya, which may be treated almost as a contemporary record though poetical. Therein Someśvara is represented as defeating Bhoja and occupying Dhārā, Bhoja wandering to find a place for refuge. He is also shown to have defeated Karṇa of Chedi and even killed him in battle (Vik. I verse 102–103). But this does not seem to be true. He may have extended his conquering expedition in to the north as far as Kanauj and the Kanauj Pratihāra king, as in the days of Mahmud, may have fled from his capital and taken refuge in the Himalayas. Though the Yevur plate does not refer to the death of the Chola king it is said that in the battle of Koppam fought with Rājendra Chola in 1054 A. D. the latter was killed. The Yevur plate should have referred to this event but it merely states that the Chola king fled to the sea-coast. As this record was made in the days of Vikramānka, it seems strange that it does not refer to the important battle at Koppam on the Tungabhadrā wherein Rājendra was killed.

Someśvara is said to have founded Kalyān and made it his capital. Where the later Chālukyas had their capital till then does not seem clear; probably they held their court in Malkhed the capital of the previous rulers or in Badāmi their own ancient capital. Blihaṇa distinctly mentions the founding of Kalyan, a town near modern Bidar, being perhaps nearer to the Cholas, the hereditary enemy. Someśvara, like most great Indian kings of this time, was a patron of poets and learned men (Yevur grant and also Bilhaṇa, I and IV). In 1068, like other great Hindu kings of the time such as the noted Dhanga, when he fell ill with fever, he put an end to his life by drowning himself in the Tungabhadrā, reciting praises of Śiva, on Chaitra vadya 8th Sunday (Gaurishankar Ojha).

While Someśvara was alive his second son Vikramāditya had distinguished himself by his wisdom and his valour; probably Someśvara's wars were waged by Vikramāditya. When Bilhaṇa describes Someśvara as taking Kanchī he is only stating that Vikramāditya his son had really seized and plundered Kanchī. It is not possible that Kanchī was twice taken, once by the father and again by the son. Bilhaṇa describes Vikramāditya as conquering the four directions while his father was yet alive. Bhilhana relates that he conquered Chera, Ceylon, Gangai Konda Chola, Vengi, Gauda and even Assam. It is likely that this is an exaggeration of the court-poet, though it may be granted that Vikramāditya conquered the whole of southern India. His father died while he was making these conquests and he returned, when he heard of his death, to the capital where his elder brother Someśvara had ascended the throne. The hero made due obeisance to his elder brother and king. The relations between the two were for some time very friendly. But eventually a quarrel arose as it was bound to arise and Vikramāditya left the capital and went towards Kanchī. Someśvara sent his forces after him but they were defeated. Vikramāditya went to Banavāsi and rested there for a while; he then turned towards Goa the king of which Jayakeśin, a Maratha Kadamba, submitted to him and gave him large presents. Vikramāditya in later life gave his daughter in marriage to Jayakeśin II grandson of this Goa king (B. B. J. R. A. S. IX pp. 242, 268, 579). He then subdued the Alūpas and the Cheras and turned towards the Cholas. The Chola king made peace with him and gave him his daughter. Vikrama thus strengthened returned to the Tungabhadrā.

Events, however, soon happened which eventually placed the crown of Kuntala on Vikrama's head. The Chola king died and his son Vikrama's brother-in-law was opposed by certain opponents. Vikrama marched to Kanchi, placed his new brother-in-law on the Chola throne and returned. But Rājiga a powerful feudatory again deposed him and with other refractory nobles marched against Vikrama, at the same time inciting his brother Someśvara to assail Vikrama in the rear. Vikrama thus caught between two armies successively fought with both on different dates and defeated Someśvara so completely that he was taken prisoner. He immediately marched on Kalyan and deposing Someśvara placed the crown on his own head. This event happened in 998 Ś. or 1076 A. D.; Someśvara thus reigned from 1069 to 1076.

Vikramāditya was the greatest king of the later Chālukyas and he also ruled long from 1076 to 1126 A. D. He assumed the title of Tribhuvana-Malla. (As the earlier Chālukyas called themselves by some name ending in Vallabha and the Rāshṭrakūṭas by names ending in Varsha, the later Chālukyas called themselves by names ending in Malla. The first king Tailapa assumed the name Āhavamalla, a name again taken by Someśvara I, Vikrama's father). Vikramāditya started an era of his own like his contemporary Gujarat Chālukya king Jayasinha. It is a strange coincidence that these contemporary kings were equally great and founded eras of their own which lasted for a time only and finally died (Fleet in I. A. XIII p. 189).

Vikramāditya is said to have married Chandralekhā daughter of a Śilāhāra prince of Karanātaka and Bilhaṇa describes the *svayamvara* of the princess. It is probably an unhistorical description; for svayamvaras or self-choice marriages were a dead institution at this time. And where Vikrama the imperial lord of the Deccan becomes a suitor it is impossible for the bride to marry any other prince for the other princes must all be feudatories. The princess was a lady of extraordinary beauty as it is recorded by Kalhaṇa that Harsha king of Kashmir intended to invade Karnāṭaka for the possession of that princess; * this is also, we think, another poetical but unreal fancy. Vikrama as usual with kings of those days had many wives and these queens had separate villages assigned to them.

Jayasinha younger brother of Vikrama who had been appointed ruler of Banavāsi rebelled and advanced against him with a large force. He was, however, defeated and eventually taken prisoner. Bilhaṇa represents Vikrama as pardoning him. Vikrama's long rule was practically undisturbed but a confederacy of kings of the south led by the Hoyasala king Vishṇu-Vardhana assisted by Goa Kadambas and others invaded his kingdom and devastated it upto the Krishṇā (I. A. II p. 300 and B. B. R. A. S. XI p. 244). A chieftain Āchagi of the Sinda family was sent against it and it was signally defeated. The king himself had to fight with Chola and there also he gained success. Āchagi is said to have conquered many kings including those of Gujarat and Malwa but these may be taken to be unimportant operations.

Generally speaking the reign of Vikrama was a happy period for the Deccan. He founded a new town named Vikramapura. That literature flourished under him and that his government was law-regulated may be known from the single fact that his minister Vijnānesvara wrote his famous commentary, the Mitāksharā, on the Yājnavalkya Smṛiti which is recognised as the leading Hindu law treatise all over India except Bengal and which is respected even by the lawyers and law-courts of British India. It seems that law was studied in India in all the great Hindu states of this time; for besides the Mitākshara, we find that Aparāditya Śilāhāra king of Thana himself wrote a learned commentary on Yājnavalkya Smriti a little after this and at Kanauj Lakshmidhara wrote Vyavahārakalpataru under the patronage of Govindachandra. The three

* कर्णाटभर्तुः पर्माडिः सुन्दरीं चन्दलाभिधाम् । अलिख्यलिखितां वीक्ष्य सोऽभूत्पुष्पायुधाहतः ॥
स विंटोद्रेचितो वीतत्रपश्चक्रे सभान्तरे । प्रतिज्ञां चन्दलावाप्त्यै पर्माडेश्च विलोडने ॥

राजत. ७-११२४ :

verses at the end of each section of the Mitāksharā praise to the skies the rare combination of the three great items the most beautiful city Kalyan, the most learned pandit viz. Vijnāneśvara and the most powerful monarch Vikrama "ruling from the Himalayas to Rameshwar and from the eastern to the western ocean."

Vikramānka was succeeded in A. D. 1126 (25 or 27) by his son Someśvara III who was as great a monarch as his father but who was greater than he in one respect, being a learned man himself. His work Mānasollāsa or Abhilashitārtha-Chintāmaṇi is a compendium of many sciences, politics, military art, horse and elephant rearing, poetry, dialectics, music, astronomy; in short all sciences which lead to the happiness of man. In astronomy he gave Dhruvānkas (constants to be added) for calculations of planets for Friday the first of Chaitra Śaka 1051, which shows that the work was composed in the fifth year of his reign. Coming after a long reign he must be taken to have been a grown-up man when he came to the throne and he naturally ruled for 11 years only.

Someśvara was succeeded by his son Jagadekamalla in 1138 and he was succeeded by his brother Tailapa II in 1150 A.D. The power of the Chālukya line now declined and Tailapa's commander-in-chief Vijjala, a Kalachūri rebelled against him. Vijjala was assisted by a feudatory king af Kolhapur named Vijayārka and also a Kākatiya king of independent Telingaṇa. Tailapa was taken prisoner but liberated. After a few years during which he was almost held a prisoner in Kalyan, he left the capital and retired to Annigeri in Dharwad district where he ruled for a time over a limited extent of territory, while Vijjala usurped the Chālukya power and ruled at Kalyan. In 1162 A. D. he again attacked Tailapa II driving him southwards to Banavāsi, and declared his independence. Of this Kalachūri usurpation we will speak separately.

When the Kalachūri power declined, Vijjala being assassinated, the Lingāyat sect rising in rebellion against him, Someśvara, a son of Tailapa II, regained the Chālukya kingdom and established himself at Annigeri in 1182 A. D. with the assistance of a loyal feudatory named Brahmā (I. A. II). The Yādavas of Devagiri and the Yādavas of Dvāra-Samudra were, however, rising to power and they attacked Brahmā. Vira-Ballāla of the Hoyasla line defeated Brahmā and the Western

Chālukya power was finally supplanted by the Yādavas. No. thing is heard about Someśvara after Śaka 1111 or 1189 A.D.

Minor branches of the Chālukyas must have ruled in several places in Mahārāshtra and one such ruled in the Konkan, where a grant has been found of a Chālukya king come from Kalyan And Maratha families of the name of Chālke are still found in the Ratnagiri district. The Dubal family of Karhad, however, though Chālukya, belongs to the Northern Chālukya clan with the Bhāradvāja gotra as stated already in Vol. II.

The later Chālukyas have left so many inscriptions and these have been known from so early a date (Walter Elliot of Madras Civil Service presented to the Royal Asiatic Society of London copies of 595 inscriptions of the kings of Southern India in 1835, J. R. A. S. IV), that their history has been well told by many an able scholar since long; notably by Sir Dr. R. G. Bhandarkar and Dr. Fleet. And in the above summary we have closely followed the account given by the former in his Early History of the Deccan; we have added only a few remarks of our own and some interesting new facts. It is really impossible to study all the inscriptions which Kielhorn has given in his Southern Inscriptions list under the later Chālukyas of Kalyan as even these are so many as 175 from No. 140 to No. 315. But we think that the history of the later Chālukyas has long been well traced out by scholars and there are vary few points in dispute regarding them except perhaps the question whether they were Maratha or Karnātak kings, a distinction without a difference.

GENEALOGY OF THE LATER CHĀLUKYAS OF KALYAN.

(Bhandarkar in Bombay Gazetteer Vol. I Part II and Kielhorn's genealogies E. I. VIII)

I Tailapa Nūrmadi Āhavamalla Raṇarāga (973–997 A. D.)
Insc. S 892, 905, 4, 11, 19

II Satyāśraya (997–1008 A. D.)
Insc. 924, 30.

Dasavarman (Yaśovarman)

III Vikramāditya I Tribhuvanamalla
(1009–1018 A. D.) Insc. Ś 930

IV Jayasinha Jagadekmalla
(1018–1040 A. D.) Insc. Ś 940, 41, 44, 46, 50, 55, 57 & 62

V Somesvara I Āhavamalla (1040–1068 A. D.)

VI Somesvara II Bhuvanaikamalla
(1068–1076 A. D.) Insc. Ś 993, 96, 77.

VII Vikramāditya II Tribhuvanamalla (1076–1125 A. D.) Insc. Ś 999, 1001, 4, 6, 8, 9, 13, 15, 17, 18, 20 &c.

VIII Somesvera III (1126–1138 A. D.)*
Insc. S 1051, 52

IX Jagadekamalla Pratāpachandra
(1138–1150 A. D.) Insc. Ś 1061, 64, 66, 69, 73.

X Tailapa II Nurmadi*
Trailokyamalla
(1150–1182 A. D.) Insc. S 1076, 77.

XI Somesvara IV Tribhuvanamalla
(1182–1187 A. D.) Insc. Ś 1106, 1111.

* Kielhorn mentions here the brother of Vikramaditya Jayasinha and his son Vishṇuvardhana Vijayaditya and also a son of his own Jayakarṇa who ruled subordinately from 1037 to 1137 A. D. and died before his father.

II. KALACHŪRIS OF KALYAN

The history of these kings may be given in brief as they did not rule long and were practically usurpers. Vijjana (Bijjala) was a Kalachūri feudatory. The Kalachūris of Tripura usually gave their daughters to the Deccan kings and he must have been a descendant of a minor chief who had some Jagbir granted to him as a relation of some Chālukya queen. in a grant published in A. S. Western India No. 10, he is described as a Mahāmandaleśvara under Jagadeka-Malla. Becoming powerful as commander-in-chief, he set aside his master and declared himself king of Kalyan in about 1162 A. D. (or 1159). He was, however, murdered in a religious feud. He had a Brahmin minister named Basava who founded a new sect called Lingayat, more in opposition to Jains than to the Brahmins. The details of this schism we will give in our religious survey chapter later. Vijjana was a Jain and persecuted the Jangamas (religious recluses of the Lingayats). The actual circumstances of this quarrel cannot be given as diametrically opposite accounts are given by Jains and Lingayats. It is difficult to determine the truth; nor is it necessary for purposes of general history. It is certain that Vijjana was murdered in 1167 A. D. He was succeeded by his son Soma (Someśvara or Sovideva). His queen made a grant to Brahmins which he confirmed (I. A. X. p. 183). He ruled till 1178 A. D., when he was succeeded by his son Sankama. He has left some inscriptions. In 1183 power was wrested from him by the dispossessed Chālukya king Someśvara as related before. The Kalachūri kings thus ruled from about 1160 to 1184 or about 24 years only. But their reign is signalised by the rise of the Lingayat sect and in their time Jainism declined among the Vaiśyas of the Deccan and Buddhism entirely disappeared; the Vaiśyas now in the S. M. country being generally Lingayats (Bombay Gazetteer Vol. I part II p. 288).

Of the social and religious transformation of Hindu society which began under these and previous kings in the Deccan as also in the whole of India and of the progress and then decline of Jainism in the south, we will speak at length in the last book in which a general survey of the condition of the country will, as usual, be taken.

J. R. A. S. IV (1837) states (p. 19) that the Kalachūris derived their descent from one Santarasa who according to the Jain guru of Malkhed was the Mahāmandaleśvara of Kalyan itself, born in the family of the Kalachūris of Kālanjarapura (described in chapter 6). It gives the genealogy from Vijjana eighth descendant of Santarasa as follows:—

Vijjana Tribhuvana-Malla

Someśvara Deva or Rao Morāri. — Sankamadeva Āhava-Malla.

CHAPTER XIII

THE EASTERN GANGAS OF TRIKALINGA AND ORISSA

During this sub-period of Hindu Indian history, a new kingly line came to power in the Kalinga country. The Eastern Gangas of Trikalinga are treated by Kelhorn as a Northern India line properly enough, though Kalinga (modern districts of Vizagapattam and Ganjām) is by race and language a southern country. But from the most ancient times, Anga, Vanga and Kalinga are always leagued together, as Bihar and Bengal or Orissa are leagued together in modern history. Kalinga was, however, in very ancient days taken possession of by Aryan invaders and though in prehistoric times it was considered a sin for Aryans to visit much more to reside in the country, from before the days of Aśoka and even in the days of the Brāhmaṇas, Aryans came in number to settle therein. Aśoka conquered the country with great effort, killing a lakh of people and the country became Buddhist. The country consisted of three parts even in the days of Pliny and hence probably arose the name Trikalinga (Vizagapattam Gazetteer p. 26). This fashion of prefixing a number to names of southern countries may be seen in the mention of three Māhārāshtras, seven Konkaṇas and Trairājya Pallavas (Vol. I p. 286). What these three parts were it is difficult to state. They probably meant 1 Kalinga proper, consisting of the East Coast Districts of Ganjām, Vizagapattam and Godāvari, 2 Āndhra the territory above the Eastern Ghats and 3 perhaps Odra or Orissa to the north of the Mahānadi, Vengi being considered distinct from Trikalinga (Vol. I p. 304). Till about the end of the ninth century Kalinga was certainly under the Eastern Chālukyas of Vengi whose capital lay to the south of the Godāvari. The common people of the country were Dravidians and these and even the incoming Aryans then spoke and now speak the non-Aryan language called Āndhra or Telugu.

The Eastern Gangas who rose to power in the beginning of the 11th century, A. D., in their inscriptions, state that they originally came from the south (Kolāhala town in Gangavādi J. Bengal LXV part I p. 237) and were long established in the country. Taking advantage of the downfall of the Vengi Chālukyas about this time before the rising Chola power, the Eastern Gangas became independent under Vajrahasta. His son

Rājarāja was married to Rūpasundarī daughter of Rājendra, a most powerful Chola king who practically destroyed Vengi power. Their son was Anantavarman Chodå-Ganga, probably called so because he was decended from Gangas and Cholas. He was the most powerful king of this family, as usual the third and also as usual he reigned long. Inscriptions of these kings have been found and as the Gangas in a sense inherited the power and the system of government of the Eastern Chālukyas of Vengi, their inscriptions are very definite and always give the Śaka era of the inscription as also the exact periods of rule of the several kings. Nay they even give the exact date, day, month and year of the coronation of the last or most important king. And even the gotra of the family with detailed descent from the moon is given in their inscriptions. There is thus no indefiniteness about these kings or their dates and we proceed to give their history as deduced from their inscriptions. Unfortunately the praises of kings are as usual fulsome and without much historical detail. But there are a few references to contemporaneous kings and from these some light is thrown on the general history of Hindu India.

The first important king who rose to power as stated above in Trikalinga was Vajrahasta II. His grant dated 1058 A. D. published in E. I. IV p. 175-189 gives full details about this family. It belonged to the lunar race and had the Ātreya gotra. The original ancestor who gave his name to the family was Gāngeya (not Bhīsma). It obtained power in Kalinga through the favour of Śiva named Gokarṇa whose temple was on the Mahendra mountain. The family was first feudatory, endowed with the five sounding instruments. It was divided into five branches which united sometime about the ninth century A. D. Vajrahasta who was crowned in 1038 A. D. is first styled Paramabhattāraka etc. showing that he was the first independent king. He was a Parama Māheśvara or devout devotee of Śiva, as was usual with the kingly families of the time. It seems that he defeated both Vengi and Orissa kings. He ruled for 30 years. He has left some inscriptions two of which have been mentioned against his name by Kielhorn. His inscription dated 1058 is chiefly in prose and very terse and gives the exact time with not only the year, month &c. but the exact *lagna* and the position of the moon and other planets at the auspicious moment of coronation. He issues the grant from Kalinga-nagara which has beeen identified with the place now named Mukhalingam in the Pārlākimedi Taluka of the Ganjam District some miles distant from the sea.

Vajrahasta was succeeded by his son Rājarāja in 1068 A. D. He ruled for eight years. In an inscription of his son Avantivarman (I. A. XVIII p. 166) we are told that he assisted Vijayāditya of Vengi against the Chola king as also Utkala (against probably the Sena king). Eastern Chālukya history given in Vol. I. (p. 310) shows Vijayāditya ruling from 1043 to 1078. Before him there is shown an interregnum of 27 years which probably gave the opportunity to these Gangas of Kalinga to assume independence. In an inscription of the Brahmin feudatory Vanarāja of Rājarāja (E. I. IV p. 314) it is stated that Vanarāja first fought with Chola (probably in assisting Vijayāditya) and then conquered Vengi and plundered it, killing one Dānārṇava. This inscription is dated 1075 A. D. and Rājarāja appears to have ruled till 1076.

Rājarāja was married to Rūpasundarī a daughter of the great Chola king Rājendra, but this did not prevent his fighting with Cholas for protecting Vengi. Anantavarman son of Rājarāja and Rūpasundarī succeeding Rājarāja became, as said above, the greatest king of this line. He has left many inscriptions (Kielhorn mentions four against his name, Genealogies E. I. VIII). The inscription dated 1080 noted above (I. A. XVIII p. 166) is most detailed. It mentions that Rājarāja fought against Dramila (Chola) and protected Vijayāditya. Anantavarman also himself set up Vengi in the east and Utkala in the west and thus set up two pillars of victory in two directions. Cholas allege that they conquered Kalinga at this time but it does not appear to be likely. Anantavarman is better known as Chodaganga a name which we have explained above. His coronation year is given as 1076 A. D. with axact details about the auspicious moment, and he made a grant on that account (I. A. XVIII p. 163) and there are three more grants of his dated 1081, 1118 and 1135 published in the same I. A. XVIII in one of which he makes a grant to a Śiva temple built by his father and hence named Rājarājeśvara.

In the long detailed copperplate inscription published in Bengal J. R. A. S. LXV part I p. 240, it is stated that Chodaganga eventually conquered and annexed Utkala or Orissa and thereby got land, treasures, 1000 elephants, 10,000 horses etc.

as from the churning of the ocean of Utkala.* This seems to show that at this time the Kesari dynasty ended in Orissa. It is further stated that Chodaganga built the present great temple of the god Jagannātha "who created and is coextensive with the whole world, a temple where even Lakshmī was glad to reside leaving her father's home " (V. 28). Chodaganga in his inscription calls himself Parama Vaishṇava. This change of worship shows that the Vishṇu cult was now becoming supreme not only in Kalinga but also in Orissa and a little later in Bengal where Lakshmaṇasena also became a Parama Vaishṇava. Of this rise and spread of Vaishṇavism we will speak in detail in in our religious survey chapter.

In this long inscription of 105 long-metred verses besides the last prose portion, Chodaganga is praised the highest. He is further said to have defeated a Mandāra king whose capital was destroyed and who fled beyond the Ganges. Who this king was cannot be determined. Chodaganga reigned as long as 70 years according to this inscription; but the coronation year of his son Kāmārṇava is given in this inscription as 1064 Ś. or 1142 A. D. showing that Chodaganga ruled sixty-six years (1076–1142). His son's rule extended over 10 years only. Coming after a long reign his reign was naturally short as he must have been quite an elderly person when he came to the throne. In 1152 A. D. he was succeeded by his half-brother Rāghava who also ruled for a short time i. e. 15 years. He was succeeded by a third son of Chodaganga named Rājarāja in 1167; he probably came to the throne young and ruled 25 years when he was succeeded in 1192 by a fourth son of Chodaganga named Aniyanka Bhīma. Customary praise is bestowed on all these kings in this long inscription (Bengal LXV part II) and they are generally said to have defeated their enemies. Their coronation dates with auspicious conjunctions are, however, not given and this probably shows that their reigns were not very important. Aniyanka Bhīma or Ananga Bhīma naturally reigned only 10 years. Orissa seems to be now completely under the Gangas as a Gautama-gotra lunar-race Kshatriya feudatory of Orissa named Svapneśvara fought many battles for Aniyanka Bhīma and built the Svapneśvara-Meghavāhana (Śiva) temple in Orissa during

* निर्मथ्योत्कलासिन्धुराजमपरं गङ्गेश्वरः प्राप्तवानेकः कीर्तिसुधाकरं...लक्ष्मीं धरण्या समम् ॥
मायद्दान्तिसहस्रमश्वनियुतं रत्नान्यसंख्यानि वै तं सिंधोः किमियं प्रकर्षमथवा भूयस्तदुन्माथिना ।

his reign and recorded a Praśasti there (Bengal J. R. A. S. LXVI p. 18).

Aniyanka Bhīma was succeeded in 1202 by his son Rājarāja who ruled for 17 years. Rājarāja is the last king we will notice in this chapter, though many kings ruled after him for about two centuries more and the last inscription we have of this line is one of Narasinha dated 1384 A. D. referred to above as the long inscription in LXV Bengal (page 260). When and how this dynasty fell does not clearly appear but the country was probably seized by another family in the days of the Bahamani kings as will be stated later on.

We may add a few general remarks about this dynasty. It was a lunar race dynasty and in its inscriptions following the Eastern Chālukyas, a detailed genealogy from the moon is given wherein Gāngeya is said to be a son of Turvasu, second son of Yayāti. The Turvasus along with the Yadus are mentioned in the Rigveda (Vol. II p. 288), but they are said therein to have finally become extinct or merged with the Pānchālas. In the Ganga inscriptions it is said that Turvasu was childless and obtained a son by propitiating the Ganges. The southern families Chola, Pāndya, Kerala and Kola are stated, in the Hari-vanśa also, to be descendants of Turvasu to whom in the division of earth, Yayāti assigned the south-east. Chola, Pāndya and other southern kingdoms are of ancient date; but that they do not claim descent from Yādavas shows that they are distinct from the Mahārāstra Aryans. The Gangas also in their inscriptions claim descent from Turvasu and belong to the southern mixed Aryan group.

These Gangas were, however, thoroughly orthodox and of the Vedic religion. They were previously worshippers of Śiva. They patronised Śiva worship in Āndhra which is even now predominantly Śaivite. The later kings were, however, Vaishṇavas probably from inspiration from Orissa which was also previously Śaivite but in this period became the home of Vaishṇavism.

These kings were as learned and patrons of learned men as kings in other countries at this time in India. Though the names of noted Sanskrit authors in their court are not yet known, we may accept the praise bestowed on these kings notably on Rājarāja and on Anantavarman Chodaganga in this respect viz. that Śri and Sarasvati both resided amicably in

Rājarāja's mouth and that Chodaganga was learned in the Vedas and the Śāstras and even in architecture and other fine arts as if Sarasvatī herself was his nurse.* His taste for architecture is immortalised in the Jagannath temple in Puri. He was in this way a true follower of Bhoja of Malwa. The Telugu language developed under the Gangas also and we actually find Telugu in an inscription of Rājarāja (E. I. IV p. 314). The Lānchhana or crest of these kings was a bull.

ORISSA

We will conclude this chapter with a brief reference to Orissa which practically formed part of Trikalinga in this sub-period. Odra along with Paundra was Dravida or non-Āryan in ancient times and the home still of Śabaras, as also of Khonds, and Bhuryas and Imayas, of Utkalas and Mekalas (Cuttuck Gazetteer p. 17). It was, however, early settled by Aryans but these Brahmins and Kshatriyas in Buddhist times became degraded and new Brahmins and Kshatriyas came in the days of the Kesari kings and established Śiva worship in place of Buddhist worship introduced by Aśoka. The history of these Kesari kings is given in Vol. I chapter 12. They ruled from the 8th to 12th century. The Cuttuck Gazetteer states that some persons doubt the existence of these Kesari kings as no epigraphic evidence is found about them. But the Gazetteer adds that this doubt no longer can be entertained as two inscriptions of Udyota Kesari have been found, one in a cave in the Khandagiri hill and the other in the Brahmeśvan temple at Bhuvaneśvara. M. Sylvan Levi has also pointed out that in a Japanese version of a Buddhist Sūtra sent by a Buddhist monk in 796-798 as from a king of Utkala to a Japanese Emperor the king's name is given as Parama Māheśvara Mahāraja Śubhakara Kesari (Cuttuck Gazetteer p. 22). These are new facts which are found in this Gazetteer and though relating to history given in Vol. I we record them here for the sake of completing that history. The Gazetteer gives further details about the temples built at Bhuvaneśvar by these Kesari kings. These stately temples exhibit the fine architecture of the time and the ample resources of these kings.

---

* धात्री तस्य सरस्वती समभवन्नूनं न चेत्पीतवान् तत्सारस्वतसार्थबालकतमः श्रीचोडगङ्गेश्वरः ॥ तादृग्वेदमतिः कथं निपुणता शास्त्रेषु तादृक्कथं तादृक् काव्यकृतिः कथं परिणतिः शिल्पेषु तादृक् कथम् ॥ (J. R. A. S. Bengal LXV p. 331).

From Chola records we learn that Orissa was conquered by Rājendra in 1021 but the conquest was not permanent. The Eastern Gangas who became powerful hereafter, however, conquered and permanently annexed Orissa and an inscription of Chodaganga dated 1118 A. D. states that he was complete master of Orissa. The famous temple of Jagannāth, as already stated, was built by him (probably about 1150) as also a temple named Gangeśvara after him at Jaipur. Rāghava son of Chodaganga was defeated by Vijayasena of Bengal (Gazetteer p. 24) but it is doubted if this is the Rāghava defeated by him, as this Rāghava's rule extended from 1156 to 1170 and Vijayasena could not have reigned so late. We have already noticed the building of the grand temple of Megheśvara at Bhuvaneśvara by a brother-in-law of the next king (Aniyanka Bhīma 1193–1198 ditto).

Orissa was invaded by armies of the Sultans of Bengal (Lakhnauti) and in an inscription in a Jagannāth temple in Chateśvara in Cuttuck District, Vishṇu a Brahmin minister of Bhīma is said to have fought and defeated Yavanas. The Tabakat and other Mahomedan histories mention many raids by Bengal Mahomedan Sultans into Orissa and even Firoz Tughlaq of Delhi attacked it. The kings of Vijayānagar as also the Bahamani kings attacked Orissa and its Gajapati kings. At last in 1435 on the death of the last Ganga king, his minister Kapilendradeva with the aid of the Bahamani king Adilshah II seized the kingdom and founded a new solar dynasty (Cuttuck Gazetteer p.25).

GENEALOGY OF THE EASTERN GANGAS OF TRIKLINGA.

Vajrahasta I r. 35 years (984–1019)
|
Madhukāmārṇava r. 19 years (1019–1038)
|
I Vajrahasta II r. 30 years (1038-1068) Insc. 1058
|
II Rājārājā r. 8 yeass (1068–1076) Insc. 1075
m. Rajasundri d. of Rajendrachola
|
III Anantavarman Chodaganga r. 70 years (1076–1142)
built the famous Jagannath temple.

IV Kāmārṇava r. 10 years (1142–1152)

V Raghava r. 15 y. (1152–1167)

VI Rājarāja r. 25 y. (1167–1192)
|
VII Aniyanka Bhīma r. 10 years (1192–1202)

VIII Rājarāja r. 17 years (1202–1219)

CHAPTER XIV

THE CHOLAS OF TANJORE

It is a phenomenon worthy of historical note that in the several divisions of India, forceful persons appeared at about the same time and established new kingdoms or raised the old to glory at the beginning of this sub-period of Mediæval Hindu Indian history (except unfortunately in the Madhyadeśa or Kanauj). Thus Mūlarāja founded the Chālukya kingdom in Gujarat in 961 A. D. and Munja established the glory of the Paramāras in Malwa in 974 A. D. Tailapa founded the later Chālukya kingdom in the Deccan in the same year and the Chola king Rājarāja I raised the Chola kingdom of South India to power and fame in 985 A. D. While Mahīpāla again raised the tottering Pāla power in Bengal in 980 A. D., Dhanga established the Bundelkhand renown for valour in the battle of 980 fought with Sabuktagin who founded the young Ghazni kingdom itself in 977 A. D. The appearance of powerful men of energy and ambition in the last quarter of the tenth century A. D. and at about the same time, is striking and leads to inferences which are outside the history.

Of such forceful men, Rājarāja Chola was not the least. He was the successor of Āditya Chola who had already done much to raise the Chola power by freeing it from Pallava dominion. Rājarāja I by his energy and valour raised the Tamil land or South India as we may call it, to the position of a South Indian empire and the Cholas enjoyed this position for nearly a century not only in South India but over a large portion of the adjoining territory. The history of this Chola kingdom (which properly falls within the period treated of in this volume) is well told by Mr. K. V. Subrahmanya Aiyar as also by Dr. Smith in his Early History of India and we give here a short summary of it from these authors, with a few remarks of our own, especially because the records of these Chola kings, numerous as they are solely in Tamil and Kanarese and thus are beyond our personal study of them.

The Tamil country or South India is a distinct part of the Indian continent, in climate, soil, produces, population and language. It is called Dravida in ancient Sanskrit literature, Dramila being another form often used in inscriptions. The people are Dravidian par excellence by race as the people of the Panjab are Aryans by race par excellence. Yet Tamil civilization was high in most ancient times and the Aryan immigrants being few were converted into Dravidians by language and even by race. The three kingly families Chola, Pāndya and Kerala are noted even in the Mahābhārata and the Harivamśa and are said to be descended from Turvasu son of Yayāti. The country is fertile but hot, plain in the east and mountainous in the west and produced even then certain articles which were its own viz. pearls, pepper and beryl prized in the western world which brought Roman gold to the land in abundance (Smith). We may add a fourth article viz. cotton and the Tamil country produced fine cotton cloth even in the days of the Mahābhārata; for Chola and Pāndya kings are said therein to have brought presents of extremely fine cotton cloth to Yudhishṭhira at the time of his Rājasūya or Imperial coronation. The Tamil country was thus prosperous and known from of old and Aryan, Buddhist and Jain religions strove for mastery here and the same intensity of religious animosity prevailed in this sub-period (as we shall show in our chapter on religious survey) as prevailed in ancient time and as even continues to this day.

In this old Dravida country and in the old Chola family, Rājarāja I came to the throne in 985 A. D. Like all ambitious kings he first paid attention to the raising and maintaining of an efficient army and then expanding his territory by the aid of that force. He trained up the Vellakurais or local bowmen as Shivaji trained up the Mawlas and he had several regiments of these named after his own titles (Aiyar's Historical Sketch of Ancient Deccan p. 245). He also had an elephant corps and infantry (in which Telugu people were chiefly enrolled). He kept also select body-guards like Mahmud. He ruled in Tanjore and from thence extended his dominion south, west and north, by conquering Pāṇdya, Kerala and Pallava kings. He even destroyed the Chera fleet on the west coast. From these conquests he got immense booty in gold, silver and pearls which is not incredible. He also conquered Gangavādi, Kudamalai (Coorg), Nolambavādi (Bellary) and Vengi of the Eastern Chālukyas and even Kalinga. These conquests meant, in our view, not annexation but mere subjugation of the territories. For in Vengi he established Śaktivarman an Eastern Chālukya king as his feudatory. He gave his daughter to the next successor Vimalāditya (See Vol. I p. 310); and this relationship was continued as Vimala's son and also grandson married Chola princesses. This sort of marriage is peculiar to the southerners who like to marry a daughter of the maternal uncle (a marriage prohibited by the Smṛitis) even from the days of Śrikṛishna and Rukmiṇī, of Arjuna and Subhadrā. Rājarāja also conquered Ceylon and assigned a part of its revenues to the maintenance of the Rājarājeśvara (Śiva) temple he hereafter built at Tanjore, a temple which has perpetuated his name in South India (Aiyar p. 248). He finally attacked Satyāśraya, Western Chālukya king and defeated him signally with a force the number of which is exaggerated to 9 lakhs of men and a cruelty which extended to the slaughtering of women, children and Brahmins, a thing unheard of in Hindu conflicts. This conquest certainly added to his renown, power and wealth and enabled him to build the superb and stupendous Rājarājeśvara temple at Tanjore and also other structures elsewhere which testify to the high skill in sculpture and architecture of South Indian workmen and builders.

But Rājarāja I was not only a great conqueror and a great builder but also a great administrator. South India is known from ancient times for its irrigation works but the great works of irrigation from the Kauveri were built by Rājarāja I. He also surveyed and settled the country in 1011 A. D. The survey and settlement was so minute that "even $\frac{1}{52\,428,800,000}$ of a Veli was measured and assessed for revenue" (Aiyar p. 249). This establishes the reputation of the revenue administrators and mathematicians of those days in South India a reputation still possessed by its administrators and mathematicians. Dr. Smith mentions a revenue survey under-taken by a successor of Rājarāja in 1086 A. D., the date of the Doomsday register in England (E. H. I. p. 486 3rd Edn.).

As a devotee of Śiva Rājarāja loved the stirring hymns composed in Tamil by Śaiva saints like Appar and others (63 in number) and he set up their images and made provision for the recitation of their hymns in the Rājarājeśvara temple. It may be further stated that he set up the images of his father and his mother (who burnt herself with her husband's dead body as Sati) both of whom were revered as pious persons throughout the Tamil land.

Lastly Rājarāja was a patron of music and dancing and he invited and settled in Tanjore female dancers as also singers, and drummers. Nātyaśāstra was specially studied and practised music-halls built for the purposes. Colleges were also built and learned teachers were appointed to them and they taught literature and Śāstra to students in these and in temples (Aiyar p. 251).

Rājarāja was extremely religious, it need not be told, and he made many gifts to Brahmins and temples and his queens and officers also made such gifts. But the gift ceremony of Tulādāna made by him deserves a sepcial mention viz. the weighing of the king in gold and its gift to Brahmins, a mode of gift which appears to have become very popular in this sub-period as it is frequently mentioned even in inscriptions of Kanauj and Trikalinga kings. It is further related that Rājarāja's chief queen passed through a golden cow on that occasion which thus multiplied the gift of gold to Brahmins (a manner of gift rarely heard or thought of). Of course Brahmins who are real Brahmins and who pass a religious life in teaching or worshipping deserve to be cared for by the state and such gifts served the purpose of modern educational and ecclesiastical endowments.

The administration of the country under Rājarāja was detailed and civilized and registers were duly kept and supervisors appointed for all state-business. Aiyar has not noticed, however, the elaborate village system of panchāyat administration which obtained in South India particularly and which is noticed by Dr. Smith who admires it and observes that it is a pity that it is no longer in existence. The details of this system we will try to notice in our chapter on the general survey of civil administration later on.

Rājarāja was succeeded by his son Rājendra in 1014 and he was a greater king, if possible, than his father and ruled long till 1044 A. D. He made more extensive conquests; he not only reconquered the rebellious Pāndya and Kerala kings, but annexing their dominions appointed viceroys called Chola-Pāndya or Chola-Kerala (terms which show that the viceroys still ruled for the rightful Pāndya or Kerala). He also again defeated the Western Chālukyas (under Jayasinha III) and also the Ceylon king. Emboldened by these successes it is said that he led his conquering expedition right up to the Ganges subjugating Kalinga, Bengal (Mahīpāla I), Indraratha (?), Kośala and even Kanauj. He took the name of Gangai-Kond to signalise this extensive conquest and founded a city near Trichonopoly by name Gangai-Konda Cholapuram, the ruins of which in the

Trichonopoly District are still admired, together with a vast artificial lake built by him with an embankment 16 miles long and with sluices at convenient places for irrigation (Smith E. H. I. p. 466). He even had a strong navy built and crossing the bay of Bengal conquered a part of Burma. Although these feats may have been exaggerated in his inscriptions, it cannot be doubted that he held extensive sway in the south-east. For even Al-Beruni mentions that south-east of Prayag almost the whole country (the present Madras Presidency and eastern parts of the C. P. and the Nizam's dominions) was under the Cholas. Such extensive sway could not have lasted long and we actually find Trikalinga and Chedi establishing their power about 1040 A. D. in the territory to the north of the Krishna.

Rājendra was a warrior and also a learned man as the title pundit is found prefixed to his name in inscriptions. He is said to have sent an embassy to China and he certainly had a large fleet. Rājendra is said to have brought Northern India Brahmins and settled them in South India, measure adopted by all religiously inclined kings in eastern and southern India of this time such as Ballālasena and others. The Chola empire attained its highest glory under Rājendra who was as usual, the third great king in this line.

Rājendra was succeeded by his son Rājādhirāja who was a powerful king no doubt but rather cruel in his treatment of rebellious feudatories. He killed a Ceylon king and had a Chera king trampled under the feet of an elephant. It is not necessary to give details, but this shows that decline had set in. He defeated Āhavamalla (Someśvara) once but in the next battle of Koppan in 1052 A. D. he was killed on the battle-field. He was immediately succeeded by his younger brother Rājendradeva who was present and who was crowned on the battle-field itself. This is the only battle we know of in Hindu history wherein the death of the commanding king did not lead to defeat. The younger brother Rājendradeva by his bravery retrieved the fortune of the day and eventually conquered Āhavamalla who is said to have fled across the Tungabhadrā. It may be stated that the Cholas and the later Chālukyas of this period and the Pallavas and Early Chālukyas of the first sub-period (600–800), like France and Germany, were neighbours who took delight in constant fighting with each other and who by their bravery never gained advantage, one over the other, for any long time.

Rājendradeva ruled for about 10 years from 1052 to 1062 and he was succeeded by his brother Vīra Rājendra who was also a capable ruler. Besides wars with the Pāndyas and Keralas, he had three successive fights with the Westesn Chālukyas, who divided empire over India, south of the Nerbudda with the Cholas. The Deccan and South India kings usually attacked each other, though the Tungabhadrā was their natural boundary and though they had no cause for quarrel except ambition. Vīra Rajendra was successful for a time but in 1070 A. D. lost his life in a battle, being cursed, it is said, by the Jains of Belgola whom he had oppressed (Aiyar p. 262).

Mr. Aiyar 's account ends with the reign of this king but we have to continue the account until the end of the 12th century. It is strange that Aiyar does not mention the fact recorded by Bilhaṇa that Vīrarājendra gave his daughter to Vikramānka Chālukya. It seems certain that after Vīrarājendra's death in 1070, the succession was disputed and Vikramānka went and placed on the throne of Kanchī (not Tanjore ?) his wife's brother named Adhirājendra. He was, however, after Vikrama's departure soon murdered and eventually the succession went to Rājendra Chola II, a son of a daughter of Rājendra I married to an Eastern Chālukya prince. This Rājendra had lived from his childhood at the Chola court and had even given up his paternal kingdom of Vengi on the death of his father in 1026 to his uncle. He, it is alleged, was adopted by Rājendra Gangai-Konda, (adoption among Kshatriyas of a daughter's son could not be valid). Whatever his claim, he may be said to have duly come to the throne and started a new Chola line called Chālukya-Chola by Smith. He came to the throne in 1074 A. D. (Smith assigns the four years from 1070 to 1074 to Adhirājendra the brother-in-law of Vikrama murdered); and he ruled vigorously for 48 years counting his reign from 1070, and his capital was Gangai-Konda-Cholapura. He is said to have defeated Anantavarman Chodaganga ; but this defeat must have been an insignificant one, as we have seen that Chodaganga of Kalinga was a powerful king. This war is described in a Tamil poem Kalingatupparani (Gaurishankar's Tod p. 428 and I. A. XIX). The revenue settlement of Tamil country mentioned by Smith was carried out in his reign. His reign is also important for the fact that Rāmānuja the founder of the Śrivaishṇava philosophy flourished during his time. Of this and the death of Adhirājendra his predecessor which is attributed to a course of this great saint we will speak at length in the chapter on religious survey. Here it will suffice to remark that here began the great feud between Śaivism and Vaishṇavism which has distracted Hinduism since that time and which forever destroyed the unity of the Hindu religion which fortunately had subsisted through three centuries.

Rajendra II who took a new title Kulottunga was succeeded in 1118 by his son Vikrama Chola who was also a powerful king. He had his hereditary fights with the Chālukyas, the Pāndyas and the Kalingas and others and his exploits are celebrated in a special poem (J. A. XXII p. 142). He was succeeded in 1135 A. D. by Kulottunga II who reigned for 11 years and who was followed in 1145 by his son Rājarāja II who ruled 19 years. From 1165 to 1267 A. D. four more kings ruled viz: Rājādhirāja 1172, Kullottunga III 1178, Rājarāja III and Rajendra Choda III 1216 and the kingdom of the Cholas was subverted by the Pāndya king Jatāvarman Sundara Pāndya. The final subjugation of South India or at least its dissolution by the Mahomedans happened later during the raids of Malik Kafur a general of Allauddin Khilji about 1310–11.

There are a few general observations to make on this Chola dynasty. The Cholas represent themselves in their inscriptions as solar-race Kshatriyas born in the line from Śibi. But as stated before, the Harivaṁśa represents Chola, Pāndya, and Kerala as born from Turvasu in the lunar line. These kings were Śaivites and it is to be regretted that about the time of the fall of the first Chola portion, the kings became bigotted and departing from the usual tolerant attitude of Hindu kings used their political power to suppress Jainism and Vaishṇavism which was indeed a great blunder. The subject will be discussed fully later on. The ensign of the Cholas was a tiger. The Cholas struck many gold and silver coins which have been found.

GENEALOGY OF THE CHOLAS OF TANJORE.

(Gauriśankar's Tod pp. 425 and 426)

Parāntaka

- Aditya
- I Rājarāja I (1985-1014)
  - d. Kamaradevi m. Vimalādity E. Chālukya
    - Rājarāja E. m. d. Ammagā.
      - VII Rājendra Kulottunge (1070-1118)
        - VIII Vikrama Choda (1018-1135)
          - IX Kulottunaga II (1135-1146)
            - X Rājarāja II (1146-1165)
              - Interregnum
                - XI Rājādhirāja II (1165-1178)
                  - XII Kulottunga III (1178-1216)
  - II Rājenpra (1014-1044)
    - III Rājādhīrāja (1044-1052)
    - IV Rājendradeva (1052-1062)
      - V Virarājendra (1062-1070)
        - VI Adhirājendra murdered in 1072

CHAPTER XV

IMPORTANT FEUDATORY KINGDOMS OF SOUTHERN INDIA PART I

The two great kingdoms to the south of the Nerbudda which were almost empires, viz. the Deccan kingdom of western Chālukyas and the south Indian kingdom of the Cholas have been described as also the independent Śilāhāra kingdom in Konkan on the west coast and the independent Eastern Ganga kingdom of Trikalinga on the east coast. Besides these important kingdoms which flourished in the third sub-period of Hindu history (1000–1200) there were some important feudatory kingdoms which rose to greater power in the 12th century A. D. than before recording inscriptions and which became independent and powerful in the 13th century, which require to be noticed, though their history in the 13th century is outside the scope of, and will not be dealt with in this volume. The fall of southern India in the beginning of the 14th century under Allauddin Khilji and his general Malik Kafur is so important as to require a separate volume for its treatment. The history of these kingdoms in the 12th century though they were then feudatories must, however, be given in this volume and we proceed to give a short sketch of that history in this chapter and the following.

1 YĀDAVAS OF DEVAGIRI.

The first kingdom deserving notice is the Yādava kingdom of Devagiri (Daulatabad). Its founder is said by Hemādri to be Dridhaprahāra who founded a small kingdom at Chandrapuri or Chandor in the Nasik District in about 843 A. D. (Gaurishankr's Tod and Bombay Gazetteer Vol. I part I). One of his descendants named Bhillama II was a powerful feudatory of Tailapa Chālukya of Kalyan. He fought bravely in the battle of Tailapa with Munja of Malwa in which Munja was taken prisoner. An inscription of his dated 1000 A. D. has been found. His son named Vesugi ruled after him and Vesugi was followed by Bhillama III who was married to a daughter of Jayasiñha III Chālukya and fought in several battles of his as his feudatory. After three intervening kings we come to Seuṇachandra who according to Hemādri's Praśasti assisted the famous king Parmādi Vikramāditya Chālukya in obtaining the throne of Kalyan. An inscription of his (dated 1069 A. D.) has been found. After seven successors one Bhillama IV son of Apara Gāngeya assumed independence when Someśvara Chālukya after the rise of the Kalachūri intervening kings at Kalyan practically became powerless and Bhillama founded an independent kingdom in the north part of the Deccan and founding Devagiri made it his capital in 1187. A. D. Bhillama's dominion eventually extended from the Nerbudda to the Krishna and he fought with many neighbouring kings especially with the Hoyasala Yādavas of the south whom we will presently describe. He died about 1191 probably in a battle with the Hoyasalas. His son was Jaitugi or Jaitrapāla and he had a great fight with the Kākatīya Āndhra king Rudra who was killed in battle and whose son Gaṇapati was taken prisoner. But he liberated the latter and placed him on the throne of the Āndhras. Jaitugi was a learned man himself and a patron of learned men. The famous Deccan astronomer Bhāskarāchārya lived a little before his time as his son Lakshmīdhara was the chief court-pandit of Jaitugi. He died about 1210 A. D. and he was succeeded by Singhaṇa another powerful king of this line. We stop our account of the Yādavas of Devagiri with Singhaṇa and leave their later history for later treatment, and also because that history is well-known. Eventually the kingdom was subverted by Mahomedans under Allauddin.

2 KĀKATĪYAS OF WARANGAL.

The next kingdom to be noticed is the Āndhra Kākatīya kingdom to the east of Devagiri. The Kākatīyas claim to be solar-race Kshatriyas and they had a kingdom in Āndhra (above the Eastern Ghats) and their chief town was Annamakonda subsequently called Orungallu (Warangal). They were in the beginning, like the Yādavas of Chandod, feudatories of the Western Chālukyas. Their first independent king was Prola (son of Bela) and he began to reign about 1117 A. D. of which year an inscription of his has been found (Aiyyar p. 277). It is also dated 42 of the Chālukya Vikrama year which proves that this part of the country was till then subject to the Chālukyas. Prola ruled long till about 1160 and he is said to have defeated Taila III. He was succeeded by his son Rudra who certainly was a great king. He is said to have destroyed many hostile towns and settled the people therein at Orungallu. He built many temples and he patronised learned men. "His power was so great that all kings between Kānchi and the Vindhyas sought his protection" (Aiyyar-do). He was succeeded by his younger brother Mahādeva in about 1191 A. D. It is surmised by Aiyyar that Mahādeva was killed in the battle with Jaitugi Yādava mentioned before. Certain it is that Gaṇapati son of Mahādeva began to rule in 1198 and he ruled brilliantly for so many as 62 years and many inscriptions of his time have been found including one in the 62nd year of his rule. He is said to have successfully fought with Chola, Kalinga, Seuṇa, Karṇāta, Lāta and Velanādu. Of course his war with Seuṇa, or Devagiri Yadavas was a natural and hereditary one, being between neighbours and was waged with alternate success. His latest inscription found is dated 1250 A. D. He left no son and his daughter Rudrammā ruled after him for 30 years. The last king was Pratāparudra (1316) the famous patron of poets in whose reign, Pratāparudriya a well-known work on poetics was written by Vaidyanātha and was dedicated to and named after him. The kingdom was eventually conquered by Mahomedans. The present state of Bastar in C. P. is ruled by chiefs who are said to be descendants of Kākatīyas (Gaurishankar p. 550).

3 HOYASALAS OF HALEBID.

The third imporant kingdom was that of the Hoyasala Yādavas of Halebid or Dvārasamudra, in the present Mysore State. It was also in the beginning a feudatory of the Western Chālukyas of Kalyan (perhaps of the Rāshṭrakūṭas also). The first important king was Vinayāditya whose inscription dated 1040 A. D. has been found (Gaurishankar's Tod p. 333). His son Erayanga had three sons, the eldest of whom Ballāla was a noted feudatory of Jayasinha III, Chālukya king. The chief town of these Yādavas was Belāpur (modern Belur) upto this time; but his successor Bettiga alias Vishṇuvardhana who was the first powerful and independent king of this line made Dvārasumudra his capital. He acquired independence from such a powerful overlord as the famous Vikramānka of Kalyan, though he did not actually succeed in defeating the latter. But he defeated other neighbouring kings, the Gangas, the Kadambas, the Tuluvas and the Pāndvas. Many inscriptions of his time have been found dating from 1115 to 1138 A. D. (Gaurishankar). His reign is more famous for the support he gave to Rāmānuja and the spread of Vaishṇavism. He was converted to that faith by that saint and he built the famous Vishṇu temple at Dvārasamudra which excites admiration even now, and another magnificent temple at Belur also.

He was succeeded by his son Narasiñha who ruled up to 1173 and he was succeeded by his son Vīra Ballāla. This was the greatest king of the line. He defeated Brahma general of the last Chālukya king Someśvara and he also defeated the Yādava king of Devagiri in 1191 A. D. and in effect annexing Kuntala divided the imperial sovereignty of Southern India with those Yādavas. He first assumed the title Mahārājādhirāja of an independent king. He died about 1220 after a long reign and he was succeeded by his son Narasinha. The Hoyasala power declined from his time, though the kingdom remained powerful for about a century more when it was conquered and devastated by Mahomedans under Malik Kafur about 1310 A. D.

4 PĀNDYAS OF MADURA.

The fourth kingdom which must be noticed though it remained feudatory throughout this sub-period is that of the Pāndyas famous from ancient times. The Pāndyas are mentioned with Cholas in the Mahābhārata and are also mentioned singly in the Rāmāyaṇa. Kālidāsa mentions a Pāndya king alone and not Chola as competing in the svayamvara of Indumatīī in his Raghuvamśa and mentions Uragapura as his capital. This capital together with Pāndya power was destroyed by Karikāla Chola from whose time (about 100 A. D.) the Pāndyas became subordinate to the Chola or other powers through many centuries. Their next capital was Madura, mentioned by Pliny. This fact establishes that Kālidāsa flourished before Pliny i. e. in the first century B. C. as he mentions Uragapura and not Madura as the capital of the Pāndyas. This is, however, an incidental observation. The Pāndyas remained subordinate even in the present sub-period (1000–1200) the Chola king Rājarāja having established Chola empire in the south in the beginning of the 11th century. It is only in the 13th century that Jatāvarman Sundara Pāndya became independent and established an extensive power (1251–1271). Kielhorn has given a connected genealogy of the Pāndyas from 1100 A. D. to 1567 A. D. but we think it unncessary to give it here as the Pāndyas rose to power and assumed independence after 1200 A. D. Though Malik Kafur's invasion about 1300 shook Pāndya power, they continued to rule in the south of India (Madura and Tinnevelly Districts) for a long time. They always derived a large revenue from the pearl fisheries in the mouth of the Tāmraparṇī river. With this short notice of the Pāndyas we turn to the Cheras or Keralas.

5 KERALAS OF TRAVANCORE.

The history of Kerala or Malabar and Travancore during this sub-period has been patiently found out and laid before the reader by P. Sunder Pillai, M. A. in I. A. XXIV (pp. 249-257) and we make no apology for giving from it select facts here. Kerala or Cherala means hilly country and included Malabar in the north and Travancore in the south, on the west coast of Southern India. The Kongu land is sometimes included in it viz. the present districts of Salem and Tinnevelly but not naturally. In this corner of the south, as in the Himalayas in the north, the oldest Dravidian and Aryan races with their institutions and manners and religion are yet preserved as in a fossil form, from the Kanikar or hillman to the Nambudri the highest type of Aryan Brahmin (to which clan the famous Śankarāchārya belonged). Language, ethnology, social condition and marriage customs or this part are, therefore, worth studying, being untampered by any revolutions within or invasions without. (But this land of Nambudri Brahmins and Nair (Nāgara) Kshatriyas sent out a religious invasion under Śankara which subjugated the whole of India). The history of Kerala goes back to the days of the Mahābhārata and the Rāmāyana like that of the Eastern coast belonging to the Pāndyas with whom they are always allied in ancient Sanskrit works.

The present Travancore ruling dynasty is very old and official records give 35 generations to the present ruler from 1335 A. D. We have, therefore, to find the history of this dynasty before this period from inscriptions and Mr. Pillai has succeeded in evolving a tolerably clear account. It may be stated first that the alphabet in Travancore is different from the Sanskrit alphabet and is called Vattelatte or Chera-Pāndya and even the era of Travancore is distinct being called Kollam era, the first year of which corresponds to 825 A. D. The first king of Travancore whose name is mentioned in a stone record is Vīra Keralvarman. His date is 1135 A. D. He was a feudatory of Rājendra Chola in whose name and honour a Mahādeva temple was built. Venad or Travancore appears at this time to be a well-governed country paying taxes in kind and money. Vīra Keralav seems to be the first important king who secured power from Chola and Chālukya supremacy. He is mentioned in another inscription dated 1144 A. D. The government of the country included village organisations and temple authorities which shared power in the civil government.

Stone inscriptions dated 1161, 1173 and 1180 A. D. mention the next kings Ravivarman, who ruled over Travancore including the southernmost districts independently, the Cholas having declined in power after Rājendra, Vīra Udayamārtandvarman and Āditayarāma. Mr. Pillai thinks that the last king extended his sway northward by absorbing Kūpadeśam or country of Kūpakas, also a part of Malabār. Keralavarman II (Trivedi) is mentioned in a book and in a stone record dated 1193 A. D. and Vīrarāmavarman Tiravadi in a datailed inscription dated May 1196 A. D., which speaks of a body of six hundred who supervised the working of the temples and of chieftainships into which the kingdom was divided. This interesting detail shows that the administration of the state was chiefly in the hands of the peoples' representatives, a curious relic of ancient Vedic times. Next come Vīrarāmakeralvarman and Vīra Ravivarman whose long document dated 1235 shows the nature of the land revenue system in their days. The capital was Trivendram even in those days.

CHAPTER XVI

IMP. FEU. KINGDOMS OF SOUTHERN INDIA-P. II

1 ŚINDAS OF YELBURG.

To the north of the Tungabhadrā, in Kuntala or Southern Maratha country, we have four important feudatory kingly families who require to be noticed in this volume, as they belong to this sub-period and as they were powerful though not independent. The first of them is the family of the Śindas of Yelburg in modern Nizam's territory. They have recorded inscriptions in Kanarese which have been found. Their history is given in the Bombay Gazetteer Vol. I part II (p. 572-575) and we give here a summary of it with observations of our own. The part of the country ruled by these Śindas is collectively called Śindevādi Nād in inscriptions. This clearly shows that these Śindas were Marathas, though they ruled over a Kanarese-speaking territory. (As stated in Vol. II, however, the distinction between Marathas and Karṇātakas is illusory and not of race but of language). This territory extended from about Badâmi in the Bijapur District and included Bāgalkot and Naregal in the Dharwar District. There is another Śinda family mentioned in Ep. Ind. VII p. 306. The king Munja here is described as Bhogāvatīpuravarādhiśvara and Nāgavaṁśatilaka ruling in Pratyaṇḍaka four thousand.* In our view this Śindha family was the same family as the one appearing under the name of Sendraka in the first sub-period; a Sendraka chief Senānandarāja, maternal uncle of Pulakeṣin Chālukya, is mentioned as requesting a grant of land in Karnāṭaka between the Krishna and the Tungabhadrā (Vol. I; p. 270). The Sendrakas belonged to the Nāgavaṁśa and the Śindas of Yelburg also belonged to the same vaṁśa; and even the Scindia family of the present day who are very probably their modern representatives are also of the Nāgavaṁśa. These Śindas of Yelburg were very powerful feudatory chiefs under the later Chālukyas. The first noted prince was Āchugi who had two sons Bamma and Sūrya who are mentioned in an inscription dated 1079. Bamma's son was Ācha or Āchugi II who was

---

* Indeed there were several Sinda families, including one in Karahad territory (See Ep. Ind. Vol. XIV).

a noted general of Vikramāditya and who defeated a Hoyasala prince. He is mentioned in an inscription dated 1122 A. D. Āchugi's two sons Permadi and Chavunda II are mentioned in wo inscriptions dated 1144 and 1163 respectively. Chavunda sad four sons Āchugi III and Permadi by one wife and Bijjala and Vikrama by another wife. All these four are mentioned on inscription from 1168 to 1190 A. D. Probably after the fall of the later Chālukyas of Kalyan and the increase of the power of the Hoyasalas this Śinda family lost its power and was not able to establish an independent kingdom. Their country vas eventually absorbed by the Yādavas of Devagiri whose lominion now extended to the Tungabhadrā.

2 RAṬṬAS OF SAUNDATTI.

The next feudatory family which deserves a mention is hat of the Raṭṭas of Saundatti. Their history is given by Dr. Fleet in Bombay Gazetteer Vol. I part II. p. 549–55 and we give here a summary of it. They were clearly descendants of a Rāshṭrakūṭa Imperial king of the Deccan and they ruled in he Kundi territory comprising 3000 villages which corresponds o a portion of the present Belgaum and Dharwar Districts. Their capital was Saundatti (Sugandhāvatī) and latterly Belgaum itself (Veṇugrama). The Gazetteer doubts if these Raṭṭas were really descended from the Rāshṭrakūṭas, but the short iame Raṭṭa for the Rāshṭrakūṭas is as old as the 9th century and even the modern Reddis may be Raṭṭas or Rāshṭrakūṭas and they also called themselves original lords of Laṭṭalūrapura. There crest was a Sindūra (elephant) and their dhvaja (banner) carried a golden garuda which is shown in their seal. These chiefs were first subordinate to the Western Chālukyas and when the Kalachūri rebellion occurred they asserted independence. But being not very powerful they appear like the Śindas, no have been conquered by the Hoyasalas; their territory, however, was eventually absorbed in the kingdom of the Yādavas of Devagiri.

The first prince was Kārtavīrya I or Katta I who is mentioned in a stone record of 980 A. D. He was a feudatory of Taila II Āhavamalla) and fixed the boundary of his principality of Kundi. His sons were Dāvari and Kanna Kaira whose son Eraga has recorded a Sanskrit inscription dated 1040 A. D., oublished in I. A. XIX p. 161 in which he declares himself to be a sāmanta of Jayasinha Jagadekamalla. In his birudas, he calls himself Raṭṭavaṁśodbhava, Lattalūrapuravarādhīśvara, Garuda-dhvaja &c. In one epithet he is described as a Vidyādhara in singing. He is mentioned in a Jain grant inscription published by Prof. Pathak in I. A. XIV (p. 23). His brother was Anka (mentioned in an inscription at Saundatti dated 1048 A. D.) and his son was Sena I. His son Kannakaira II has left many inscriptions dating from 1069–1087 A. D. He appears to have ruled long with his brother Kārtavīrya II and they are described as sāmantas of Vikramāditya VI. His son was Sena II mentioned in records from 1096 to 1121 and his son was Kārtavīrya III mentioned in records dated 1143 and 1165 : he is also called Katta or Kattama. Taking advantage of the rebellion of the Kalachūris at Kalyan, he appears after 1165 to have declared independence and in one record he calls himself Chakravartin (Bombay J. B. B. R. A. S. X p. 181). This position the Raṭṭas retained though first disputed by Someśvara Chālukya for three generations viz. his son Lakshmīdhara I, his son Kārtavīrya IV and his son Lakshmīdhara II. He was conquered by Vichana viceroy of Singhaṇa, Yādava king of Devagiri about 1228 A. D.

These Raṭṭas were worshippers of Śiva but they also favoured the Jains and made grants to Jain temples.

3 KADAMBAS OF HANGAL.

The third feudatory family which we have to notice is that of the Kadambas of Hangal. They were an old Maratha family, as old as the Raṭṭas or Rāshṭrikas of Aśoka, being descended from the Kadambas, the contemporaries of the early Chālukyas whose Mānavya gotra and Haritīputravaṅśa they always copied or used in their inscriptions, being of the same stock probably and ruled in Banavāsī. The present Kadambas (the form Kādamba is also often used) called themselves lords of the town of Banavāsī and sometimes ruled over that part also ; but their present position was in Hangal 500 (Hannugal of inscriptions) a Taluka of the Dharwar District. Their Lānchhana or crest was a lion and on their banner was Hanūmān, king of monkeys. They were worshippers of Vishṇu Mādhukeśava of Jayanti or Banavāsī town. We give a summary of the account of these Kadambas given by Dr. Fleet in Bombay Gazetteer Vol. I part II (p. 559 to 563).

The first record (I. A. X. p. 249) which gives a detailed genealogy of these Kadambas is dated 1108 A. D. and the first king, we may notice in this period, is Kīrtivarman II who ruled in 1058 A. D. (980 Saka). He was a feudatory of Someśvara Chālukya and also of Vikramāditya VI (I. A. IV p. 206). His uncle Śāntivarman II ruled in Hangal 500 as also in Banavāsī twelve thousand under Vikramāditya VI in 1089 A. D. Of his son Taila we have many inscriptions from 1099 to 1128 A. D. including the Kargudari inscription of 1108 mentioned above. All these inscriptions are found in the Hangal Taulka. His capital Hangal is also called Pānthīpura and also Virāṭanagar. He died about 1135 A. D. This capital was besieged and taken by the Hoyasala Vishṇuvardhana. His two sons Mayūravarman and Mallikārjuna ruled conjointly with him. It must be noted of all these southern kings that Yuvarājas (brothers or sons) usually ruled conjointly. His third son Tailama is mentioned as ruling in Hangal alone in 1147 A. D. His son Kāmadeva is mentioned in 1189 as ruling in Banavāsī, Hangal and Puligeri under the last Chālukya king Someśvara IV. He was finally vanquished by the Hoyasala king Vīra Ballāla. There were other Kadamaba chiefs also of minor importance, but we need not notice them and we go on to describe the Kadambas of Goa who were an important allied branch of this family.

4 KADAMBAS OF GOA.

These Kadambas of Goa or Gopakapaṭṭaṇa were a branch of the same Kadamba family.though their origin in the records is given differently from that given in the records of the Kadambas of Hangal. They seem to have wrested Goa from the Śilāhāras of Southern Konkan (Konkan 900) and they also had territory above the Ghauts in the present Khanapur Taluka of the Belgaum District, then called Palasige. They were devotees of Śiva named Sapta Kotīśvara and not Vishṇu and they used the Kaliyuga era and not the Śaka era in their records, and their records are in Sanskrit they being residents of Goa in Konkan where Kanarese is not spoken. In other respects they were one with the other Kadambas being originally lords of Banavāsī, having the Sinha Lānchhana and Vānara Dhvaja. They even mention their old Mānavya gotra, Hāritīputra vamśa and Māhaseṇa Mātrigaṇa favour (Bombay J. IX p. 235) even mentioned in the old Kadamba records (Vol. I. p.

266). They do not give fictitious names of ancient kings but begin with Gūhalla whose son Śashthadeva or Chhatta has left a record dated 1007 A. D. He may possibly be the same as the Chhatta the first king in the line of the Kadambas of Hangal whose approximate date is 1000 A. D. and the line may have bifurcated from him. Chhatta's son Jayakeśin was a very powerful prince and he is spoken of highly in the Gudikatti inscription (Bombay J. R. A. S. IX p. 272). He is said to have killed a king of Kapardidvīpa (which is identified by the Gazetteer with the island of Salsette) probably Māvani. There is, however, in our view, no connection of the troubles of Anantadeva, king of Thana, with the invasion of this king. He is further said to have established friendship between the king of Chola and Chālukya Vikramāditya VI, at Kānchī* and he is said to have made Goa his capital. His certain date is 1052-3 A. D. The queen of Karṇa of Gujarat (1063–1093) Mayanalladevī said to be a Kadamba princess is thought by the Gazetteer to be a daughter of this king. Of his successor Vijayāditya we do not know much. His son was Jayakeśin II and we know that Vikramānka Chālukya gave his daughter, sister of Soma, to this prince ‡ (I. A. XIV 288); probably this was a child marriage. His certain dates are 1119 and 1125 A. D. in an inscription which gives Vikrama Chālukya year 50. He then ruled the Palasige 1200 and Konkan 900, but he also had other territories assigned to him, being a son-in-law of Vikrama. He even assumed the title of Konkan Chakravartin and aspired to independence. This led to his being attacked and defeated by Āchugi I his feudatory who in his inscription is said to have taken Goa and Konkan. The Lakshmaṇa inscription dated 1147 mentions that presents were given to him at the time of making grants to the god Somnath (Gazetteer page 569).

The two sons of Jayakeśin were Parmadi and Vijayāditya who were respectively devotees of Śiva and Vishṇu. They are also styled Malavara Māra an epithet applied to Hoyasalas. Vijayāditya was a very learned prince and earned the title Vāṇibhūshaṇa, and the praise bestowed on him in an inscription

---

* चालुक्यचोलभूपालौ काञ्च्यां मित्रे विधाय यः ।
पेर्माडिर्तुयनिर्घोषोऽप्यासीद्रायपितामहः ॥ १ ॥ Bom. J. R. IX p. 242.

‡ See also
श्रीपेर्माडिनृपा पयोनिधिनिभः सोमानुजां कन्यकां यस्मै विस्मयकारिभूरिविभवैर्दत्वभकोशादिभिः ।
....ख्यातः श्रीपतये स मेललमहादेवीं कुनार्योभवत ॥

is well worth quoting* below. Kamalādevī queen of Parmadi belonging to the Somavaṅśa built two finely carved temples one to Nārāyaṇa and the other to Lakshmī, which still exist in the Sampagaon Taluka, Dharwar and they contain inscriptions which give for Parmadi a date in 1147 A. D. It appears that Vijayāditya was shortly afterwards associated with him in rule, and is mentioned in an inscription dated 1158 A. D. (I. A. XI p. 273) as also in the Halśi inscription dated 1171 Kaliyuga era 4272. The Karad prince Vijayāditya is said in Śilāhāra records to have re-established the prince of Goa who thus must have been dislodged by some one. These princes were, however, powerful enough to have issued coins of their own and a golden coin struck by Parmadi has been found dated 1182 A. D.

Vijayāditya's son Jayakeśin appears to have come to the throne in 1187, as two inscriptions of his 13th and 15th year dated 1199 and 1201 have been found. Gold coins of his have been found dated 1200 and 1210. His son was Tribhuvanmalla and his son was Chhatta or Shashṭhadeva II. He came to the throne in 1246, from a record at Goa dated in his fifth year 1250 A. D. and another record dated 1257 found in the Hubli Taluka shows that he was an independent king. When and how this kingly line came to an end cannot be stated as no further records have yet been found. Probably they were conquered by the Yādavas of Devagiri (J. B. R. A. S. IX p. 247).

The first ancestors Harivarman and others declare themselves as Mānavya-sagotra &c. even in Jain records many of which are found in Palasige (Belgaum Dt.). See Bombay J. R A. S. IX p. 235-241.

5 ŚILĀHĀRAS OF KARHAD.

The last feudatory kingly family which must be mentioned is the Śilāhāra family of Karhad or Kolhapur. It was a purely Maratha Kshatriya family and its inscriptions are recorded in Sanskrit. The Śilāhāras were originally divided into three branches, those of Thana, those of Rajapur (Kharepatan) and those of Kolhapur. They were all feudatories of the Rāshṭrakūṭas. When they fell, the Śilāhāras of Thana, as stated already, assumed independence; while the Śilāhāras of Karhad

---

* भृगौ कुन्ते प्रासे धनुषि विषमे चासिफलके वरे वाद्ये गीते सरसकविताशास्त्रविसरे ॥
तुरंगाद्यारोहे स्मृतिषु च पुराणेषु पुरुजित् परिज्ञानाद्योऽभूत् जगति बहुविद्याधर इति ॥

though still remaining Mahāmandaleśvaras, being nearer the centre of Chālukya power, became powerful and annexed Konkan territory to their rule. The southern Konkan branch founded by Sanaphulla thus disappeared in this sub-period and we have two Śilāhāras to describe in this volume.

These Śilāhāras ruled in the Karnatak 4000, Miraj 3000 and Kundi 4000 as also in southern Konkan. Their capital was Karahāṭaka and their chief fort was Panala (Parṇālaka) thus bringing us in contact with later Maratha history. They were descended from a heavenly Vidyādhara and originally ruled in Tagara. Their crest was a golden Garuda or eagle and they called themselves Mahākshatriyas* (E. I. III p. 209). They were worshippers of Mahālakhsmī of Kolhapur from whose favour they believed they had obtained power† (ditto). The Śilāhāras of Thana were worshippers of Śiva; but it is probable that their tutelary goddess was Pārvatī or Āryā Dvaipāyani (i. e. island goddess) mentioned in the Bhāgavata. These facts establish the affinity of the two Śilāhāra families beyond any doubt.

The history of the Śilāhāras of Karhad is given in the Bombay Gazetteer Vol. I Part II by Dr. Fleet (p. 544) and by Dr. R. G. Bhandarkar in his history of the Deccan (p. 92) from many inscriptions and we will begin with Jatiga II who ruled probably in the beginning of our sub-period (1000–1200). He had four sons Gonka and others and Gonka's son was Mārasinha whose inscription dated 1058 A. D. has been found. He was a powerful king and built many temples. Gonka had probably annexed south Konkan before him and he is said to have ruled from the fort of Khiligili. This is not identified (Fleet); but it must be distinct from Panālā, though Dr. Bhandarkar suggests its identification with that fort. Dr. Fleet thinks that Chandralekhā, the famous queen of Vikramānka was a daughter of this king. She was undoubtedly a Śilāhāra princess. As the date of Vikramānka's accession at Kalyan is 1076 A. D., this is not improbable. Mārasinha must have ruled long.

Mārasinha had five sons and each of them appears to have ruled. The eldest was Gūvala and his younger brother Bhoja

* श्रीशिलाहारमहाक्षत्रियान्वय.

† माहालक्ष्मीदेविवरप्रसाद.

I has left an inscription. His younger brother Ballāla is mentioned in a Kanarese inscription (I. A. XII). But the last son Gandarāditya has left many inscriptions and he is said to have fed one lakh of Brahmins at Prayāga. He also built a large tank in the Miraj country and built temples of Śiva, Buddha and Jina on its bank. His government was good and just (Bhandarkar).

He was succeeded by his son Vijayāditya, two records of whom, dated 1148 and 1153, have been found. One of them (Ep. Ind. III p. 207) is the record of a grant to Jain temple and begins with adoration of the Jina. It tersely gives the genealogy of Vijayāditya without praise: but praises the donor most. The birudas or epithets of Vijayāditya are many, some of which are Kanarese, one of them Śanivāra-Siddhi being strange and inexplicable. As the king is described even in this Jain record as prospering through favour of Mahā-Lakshmī, it is certain that these Śilāhāras were Hindus though, as usual with tolerant Hindu kings, they patronised Jain saints and Jainism spread during their rule in southern Maratha country as it did in Gujarat in the days of Kumārapāla. From a grant of his son Bhoja II, it appears that Vijayāditya was a powerful king who assisted the Thana Śilāhāra king (Mallikārjuna probably) to regain his throne when dispossessed. He also assisted the Kadamba king of Goa and he also added Vijjana Kalachuri to supplant the Chālukya power at Kalyan about 1157 A. D. Naturally the power of Vijayāditya must have greatly increased and it is not strange that his son Bhoja II assumed independence; a Jain work which was written in his days calls him Mahārāja and Paśchima Chakravartin, as the northern Śilāhāras began to call themselves Konkana Chakravartin.

Many inscriptions of Bhoja II have been found dating from 1179 to 1205 A. D. He gave grants in Konkan to Brahmins for feeding Brahmins and also to Jain temples. The grant published in Ep. Ind. III (p. 214) mentions Karahāṭaka and Ghaisasa Brahmins, the importance of which we will show later on; but this is the oldest record we have wherein Brahmins are mentioned not by their gotra but by their new sub-castes or surnames. This record also shows that Maratha chiefs began to be called Nāyakas at this time. Bhoja though powerful could not succeed apparently in maintaining his independence and finally the line was subjugated by the **Yādavas** who came to power in the Deccan after the western **Chālukyas.** We do not get any further information about this after 1205 and it is nearly certain that it did not continue as a ruling family.

GENEALOGY OF THE KADAMBAS OF GOA

(Bombay Gazetteer Vol. X & XI p. 565).

- Gūhalla
  - Chhatta or Shashthadeva (1007-1008)
    - Jayakeśin I (1052-53)
      - Vijayāditya
        - Jayakeśin II (1119-1125) m. Mallaladevī d. of Vikramāditya VI
          - Śivachitta Parmādi (1147-8, 1187-8)
          - Vishṇuchitta Vijayāditya II (1158 & 1172)
            - Jayakeśin III (1187, 1210-11)
              - Tribhuvanmalla
                - Chattaya or Śivachitta Shashthadeva II (1246-7 and 1257 A. D)

GENEAIOGY OF THE KADAMBAS OF HANGAL

(Bombay Gazetteer Vol, I part II page 559)

- Chatta (c. 1000)
  - Jayasinha (1020 c.)
    - Taila (c. 1040)
      - Kirtivarman II (1068)
    - Śantivarman (1089 A. D.)
      - Taila II (1099-1129)
        - Mayūravarman II (1131 A. D.)
        - Mallikārjura (1132-1145)
        - Tailama (1149)
          - Kīrtideva II
          - Kāmadeva (1181-1203)

GENEALOGY OF THE RATTAS SAUNDATTI

(Bom. Gaz. Vol. I, part 2 p. 551 with dates of inscriptions).

Davari | Kannakaira I

Kannakaira I → Eraga (1040 A. D.) | Anka (1048 A. D.)

Eraga → S n I

S n I → Kannakaira II (1068, 1076 & 1082, 1037) | Kār avīrva II (0 9. 1076, 1086 & 1087)

Kār avīrva II → Sen II (1096, 1102, 1123)

Sen II → Kārtavīrya III (1143, 1165)

Kārtavīrya III → Lakshmīdeva I

Lakshmīdeva I → Kārtavīrya IV (119 , 121) | Mallikārjuna (1204,1208)

Kārtavīrya IV → Lakshmīdeva II (1228) conquered by Singhan Yādava ı 1203.

GENEALOGY OF THE ŚILĀHĀRAS OF KARHAD

Jatiga II

Jatiga II → Gonka | Three brothers

Gonka → Mārasinha 1058

Mārasinha → Gūvala | Bhoja | Bal...a | Gandarāditya | Vijayāditya

Vijayāditya → Bhoja II (1179–1205)

CHAPTER XVII.

IMPORTANT FEUDATORY KINGLY FAMILIES OF NORTHERN INDIA.

In this chapter we propose to notice those feudatory princely families whose inscriptions have been found, who ruled in Northern India during this sub-period. To begin with the north-east corner; we must first notice Assam which, throughout Indian history down to the present day, has been sometimes an independent kingdom, and sometimes a dependency of Bengal. We have a Brahmin general Vaidyadeva ruling there and making a grant in behalf of and under Kumārapāla of Gauda (E. I. II p. 351) which we have already noticed. Then there was a Rāshtrakūṭa subordinate prince (Mahaṇa) in Bihar or Anga who was a maternal uncle of Rāmapāla of Gauda as also stated already. There may have been many such feudatories in Bengal and Bihar, but these appear to be the important ones.

In the tract south of the Gauda kingdom of the Pālas we have the Haihaya Kalachūri feudatory kingly family of Ratnapura in what is called Dakshiṇa Kosala. Kielhorn has given their line as follows (E. I. VIII). Kalingarāja, descendant of a younger son of Kokalla who had 18 sons, first conquered this country. He was followed by his son Kamalarāja and he by his son Ratnarāja who is said to have founded Ratnapura and built a Śiva temple there, "thus making the city a rival to the city of Kubera where Śiva always resided." His son was Prithviśa and his son was Jājalla I. His inscription dated 1114 (E. I. I. p. 34) has been found. In this inscription he gives a village to a Śiva temple for his Guru Rudraśiva. He also is said to have founded Jajallapura. His son Ratnadeva II defeated Chodaganga of Eastern Gangas of Trikalinga. His son Prithvīdeva II has left an inscription dated 1141 (I. A. X. p.84). His son Jājalla II made a grant in 1167 (E. I. I. p. 40) and his son Ratnadeva III a grant dated 1181 (I. A. XXII p. 82). His son Prithvīdeva III has left an inscription dated 1190 (E. I. I p. 47). We have no further clue to this dynasty. It was practically an independent ruling line, though it might have been subject nominally to the Haihaya kings of Tripura The country is also called Tummāna in their records (See E. J. I 4047). They were worshippers of Śiva and Brahmanical orthodox Kshatriyas as their gotra Krishnātreya is given even with its pravaras in their records (E. I. I p. 40).

Going on next to what is modern U. P. there must have been many feudatory princes in Oudh, Antarbed and Bundelkhand. But we have to mention two important Rajput families only which subsist to this day. The Gautamas are a well-known Rajput clan in U. P. From the Fatehpur Gazetteer we learn that they are an ancient clan with the Bhāradvāja gotra and a former Rāja of Argal had married a sister of Jaichand. Probably the fort of Asni where Jaichand's treasure was kept was in their possession. The second Rajput clan of which we have even an inscription is the Sengar family. This clan is mentioned among the 36 royal clans. Its present chief principality is that of Jagmanpur in the Jalaun district and there is also a small principality in the Etawa district viz., that of Bhareh. The Sengars claim Rishyaśṛinga a Rishi and Śāntā daughter of Daśaratha and sister of Rāma as their ancestors. The tradition among them is that they originally ruled in Anga or Bihar where was born Chaturanga, the first Sengar, from Daśaratha's daughter Śāntā. When the kingdom of Anga was given to Karṇa by Duryodhana they went to Dāhāla which comprises Central Provinces west and Central India east where they ruled for a long time and where their principalities still survive. They also claim to have ruled in the Deccan and in Gujarat and they state that some Sengars went eastwards also and founded a kingdom in Bardwan in Rādha country and it is believed that a prince from Bardwan went to Ceylon and founded a kingdom there. The name Sinhala is derived, it is believed, from Sinha-Bāhu the name of the father of this prince, as is evidenced by the Mahāvanśo. A Sengar king Karṇa-Deva is said to have founded Karnāvati or Kanār on the southern bank of the Jumna. This was the original seat of power of the Sengars of Jagamanpur and there are still ruins of an old fort there which is visited on the Dasera day by the Maharajas of Jagamanpur. They are also said to have ruled in Sironj in Malwa (where they came from Gujarat) so far late as the days of the Moguls.

The inscription of this family which has been found however, was issued from Benares where perhaps the donor prince may have gone for pilgrimage. The prince Vatsarāja of the Singāra-Anvaya gave a village to a Brahmin in 1134 A. D. (St. 1191), while Govindachandra was ruling. The inscription is drawn up in the usual Gāhadavāla style, and the first chief is said to have come from Śingarota and acquired Rājapaṭṭi or royal tiara. The names of the ancestors of Vatsarāja given are 1 Kamalapāla, 2 Stralhana, 3 Kumāra, 4 Lohaḍadeva; and Vatsarāja the fifth is the grantor. This would take the founder Kamalpāla to about 1050 A. D. i. e. to a time before the rise of the Gāhadavālas. Tradition states that Viśokadeva of Kanār married a daughter of Jaichand. The family appears to be an orthodox Vaidic Rajput family as its gotra Śāndilya is particularly mentioned in this record (E. I. IV p. 131), which is an unusual thing for this period. This incidently proves that Jaichand's gotra could not have been Kāśyapa.

It deserves to be mentioned that under king Bhagavantadeva of Bhareh, the eldest offshoot from the ruling house of Kanār who was, like Bhoja and other great Hindu kings, a patron of pandits, was composed the well-known treatise on Hindu Dharma named after him Bhagavanta-Bhāskara by Nilakantha Bhaṭṭa. The Vyavahāra Mayūkha, a part of this treatise, is recognised as authority on Hindu law in Konkan, Gujarat and some other parts of the Bombay Presidency.

Westward there were Yādavas at Mathura and Mahāban still ruling in about 1150 A. D. A branch of this line is said to have been found at Biana in 993 A. D. And a stone record of Vijaya has been found at Biana dated 1143 A. D. We know from Mahomedan chronicles that Shihabuddin attacked this place in 1196 and drove Kunvarapāla westward. From him the present rulers of Karowli are descended (Gaurishankar's Tod).

We may mention next the princes of Meerut and Badaun. The first were Dora Rajputs mentioned in the history of Mahmud. Hastinapur is a village in the Meerut district on the Ganges and perhaps the Doras were Kshatriyas of the race of the Pāndavas. The Tuars however, are supposed to be the direct representatives of the Pāndavas. In Badaun ruled a branch of the Rāshṭrakūṭas as stated in an inscription (E. I. I p. 64) found in the old fort there. The date of the inscription is not given. We have already commented on it at length. It mentions 1 Chandra, 2 Vigrahapāla, 3 Bhuvanapāla, 4 Gopāla, 5 Tribhuvanapāla, 6 Madanapāla his son (it is recorded of him that through his valour the Hammir could not come to the Ganges), 7 Devapāla, brother, 8 Bhīmapāla, 9 Śūrapāla, 10 Amṛitapāla, and 11 Lakshmaṇapāla his brother. As Badaun was taken by

Kutubuddin in the beginning of the 13th century, we may place these 11 kings between 1000 and 1200 A. D. But if we take an average of 12 years per king we have for Chandra a date somewhere about (1200–132) 1068 A. D. and this would make this Chandra identical with Chandra Gāhadavāla who seized Kanauj and founded his empire there. R. B. Gauri-shankar Ojha does not think that Chandra of the Badaun inscription is the same as the Chandra of the Gāhadavāla line of Kanauj; but Pandit Rāmakaran of Jodhpur in his history of the Rathods expresses the opinion that they are identical (p. 260–61 ditto).

These Rathods and the Gāhadavālas according to our view as already propounded, as also the Rāshṭrakūṭas of Aṅga (Bihar) belonged to the same clan which was solar by race and were different from the Rāshṭrakūṭas of Malkhed in the Deccan who belonged to the lunar race though both Pandits Rāmkaran and Gaurishankar look upon them as one family. The Rathods of Central India and of Gujarat probably belonged to the southern clan though not the Rāshṭrakūṭas of Hathondi in Rajputana as Gaurishankar also thinks (Tod p. 364). The Rathods of Jodhpur and Bikaner who now represent the northern Rathod clan are like the Gāhadavālas solar in race though they may have the tradition that they came from Kalyan in the south. Rāshṭrakūṭa is an official name as explained elsewhere and the name may be borne by different clans.

In Kathiawar Chūdāsamas who are Yādavas and in Cutch the Jādejas who are also Yādavas ruled during this sub-period and the latter are said to have come from Ghazni before Mahmud's time probably. We have no inscription, howeer, to rely upon. The most important Guhila clan of Kathiawar to which the rulers of Bhavnagar belong, is however, mentioned in an inscription which is dated St. 1202 or 1145 A. D. which shows that they were an important feudatory family ruling under the Chālukyas of Anhilwād and in which a king Sahajiga is mentioned as ruling in Mangrol. These Guhilas are distinct from the Guhilots of Mewad having a different gotra and are separately enumerated in the list of 36 royal families by Chand in the Rāsā.

The next important family was that of the Paramāras of Abu. The Paramāras originally must have belonged to Abu; for the legend of their origin states that their first ancestor was created by Vaśishṭha on Mount Abu from his sacrificial fire. The first known king of Abu was Dhūmarāja, but the prince in the beginning of our period was Dhandhuka whose minister Vimala-shah built a beautiful temple to Ādinātha on Mt. Abu in 1031 A. D. His son Pūrṇapāla was a sāmanta of Bhīma of Gujarat in 1045 A. D. (1102 St.). His son was Dhruvabhaṭa and his son Rāmadeva is mentioned in the Praśasti of Tejapāla-Vastupāla on Abu. His successor was Vikramasinha. In the fight of Kumārapāla with Arṇorāja, Vikramasinha suddenly went over to Arṇorāja whereupon Kumārapāla gave the principality of Abu to his nephew Yaśodhavala. His son was the well-known warrior Dhārāvarsha who was the general of the Gujarat army which defeated Ghori, as stated by Mahomedan writers, in the battle fought in 1178 A. D. during the minority of Mūlarāja as already stated in Chālukya chapter. Dhārāvarsha again was one of the commanders in the Gujarat army when it fought with Kutubuddin in 1197 and was defeated. Many inscriptions of his time have been found dating from 1163 to 1208 A. D. (Gaurishankar's Tod p. 384). The princes of Abu named Jetā and Salakh given in the Rāsā, Gaurishankar thinks, are imaginary persons. But it is possible to suppose that they were brothers of Dhārāvarsha and went consequently to Prithvirāja to seek their fortune and became his sardars.

The Chauhans of Nadul were a valorous line of feudatory kings which deserves to be mentioned. It was a branch form the Chauhans of Sambhar, the first king Lakshmaṇa being a younger son of Vākpatirāja as already stated (Vol. II p. 96). His descendants ruled in Nadul and were usually feudatories of the Chālukya king of Gujarat in whose behalf they usually fought. Thus one of these Āsarāja fought with Malwa as a general of Kumārapāla. He was a great prince, built many tanks and temples and patronised learned men. The present Bundi and Kota ruling families are descended from Māṇikarai younger son of this prince (Gaurishankar's Tod p. 408). Two inscriptions of his son Alhaṇa and of his grandson Kelhaṇa have been found dated 1209 and 1224 St. (1152 and 1167 A. D.). Kelhaṇa's younger brother Kīrtipāla was a famous chief. He was in the Hindu army which defeated Shihabuddin Ghori below Abu. He possessed Jalor and other forts. But Kutubuddin attacked Jalor and Altamash attacked Mandawar and in both places he must have opposed the Mahomedans. In the days of the last prince Kanhada-deva, Jalor was attacked by Allauddin (Gaurishankar's Tod p. 40).

There are other Rajput kingly families which flourished in this sub-period and which require to be mentioned such as the Bhattis of Jaisalmere. The Bhattis, when Bhatia was destroyed, went into the desert and founded a kingdom in the present Jaisalmere territory and ruled there. The present ruling family of Patiala is believed to belong to this Bhatti line. For want of reliable evidence we can not give further details, and content ourselves with this bare mention.

The last two most important families of Northern India which require to be noticed are the Tomaras of Delhi and the Kachhapaghātas of Gwalior from whom are descended two of the most famous Rajput clans of modern India viz. the Tuars and the Kachhwahas. The name Tuar is easily derivable (like Kachhwāha from Kachhapaghāta) from Tomara mentioned in inscriptions. It is believed that Anangapāla Tomara some time in the ninth century founded Delhi. But Delhi was not an important town in the days of Al-Beruni; and this principality of Delhi under the Pratihāras must have been then insignificant. They were supposed to be the direct descendants of the Pāndavas who first founded Indraprastha or ancient Delhi. That there was a village of the name of Indrapat near Delhi in the days of Kutubuddin is clear from the Taj-ul-Ma'sir (E. II p. 210) a contemporary history. The Tomaras are also mentioned, as already noted, in the records of the Chauhans as their natural opponents, being neighbours. There are no Tomara records yet found but their rule in Delhi is mentioned in other records and we proceed to give a short account from these and from the Delhi Gazetteer.

The famous iron pillar of Delhi, a pillar unrusted for 1500 years, with letters still clearly readable, is said to have been brought from Mathurā and set up near his new Delhi by Anangapāla about 1052 A. D. There is a note of this on the pillar. This prince seems to have become powerful when the power of the Kanauj emperors was destroyed by Mahmud; and he founded a new town, called it Delhi and made it his capital as we will show presently. The family of Anangapāla ruled in Delhi and the surrounding country for about a century when it was conquered about 1152 A. D. by Vīsaladeva or Vigraharāja III, Chāhamāna, uncle of Prithvīrāja, from whose time the country passed under the rule of the Chauhans. The story of the Rāsā that Anangapāla, the last Tomara king, gave the kingdom to Prithvīrāja as he was his daughter's son and being himself childless retired to Badarikāśrama is not reliable as Prithvīrāja's mother was a Chedi princess, not a Tomara. In fact the whole story of the Rāsā proves to be imaginary and it is rather difficult to treat as historical many of the events and statements recorded therein. The Gazetteer states that the fort, called Lalkot and still visible, was built by the first Anangpāla (II); and Prithvīrāja built the outer wall of the old town which is still traceable. When Kutubuddin attacked and took the city, the wall and the fort were there and seemed to be invulnerable.

It is impossible to determine whether Govindarai, mentioned by Mahomedan historians as of Delhi and as wounding Shihabuddin in the first battle and as killed in the second, was a Tuar or a Chauhan. The Tuars dispersed over many provinces after their defeat but the bulk of them went to Gwalior territory and settled there in a district which is specially named Tawarghār after them. Tuars are found even in Mahārāshtra under the Maratha name of Māne and others.

A genealogy of the Tomaras of Delhi is given by General Cunningham from Abul Fazal and from bardic records and it is taken by Gaurishankar at page 348 (Tod); but no inscriptions can be quoted in support of it. Copper coins of Anangapāla II who built Delhi fort have been found (1051 A. D.). That Delhi was originally founded by the Tomaras and that the country about it called Hariyāna was ruled first by them and subsequently by the Chauhans is found recorded in an inscription in a well dated St. 1384 or 1327 A. D. and four generations of the Chauhans must have ruled there after the Tomaras viz., Vīsaladeva, Prithvibhata Someśvara and (Delhi Prithvīrāja Museum stone Insc. I. A. XIX p. 218).*

The Kachhapaghāta family has left many records especially the Sāsabahu temple record on the Gwalior fort and the Dubhkund Jain temple record in Gwalior territory seventy-six miles south-west of Gwalior. We give the following account of the Kachhapaghātas from these records as also from Gaurishankar's Tod and Kielhorn's genealogies in E. I. VIII.

The Kachhapaghātas originally ruled in Narwar (Gwalior territory) or the Nishadha country of Nala of Mahābhārata fame as also of the scene of Bhavabhūti's Mālatī-Mādhava. A

---

* देशोऽस्ति हरियानाख्यः पृथिव्यां स्वर्गसन्निभः । ढिल्लिकाख्या पुरी तत्र तोमरैरस्ति निर्मिता ॥
तोमरानन्तरं तस्यां राज्यं निहतकण्टकम् । चाहमाना नृपाश्चक्रुः प्रजापालनतत्पराः ॥

prince of this family named Vajradāman, son of Lakshmaṇa seized the fort of Gwalior during the declining days of the Pratihāra empire of Kanauj and established his power there about 977 A. D. (See his record in J. R. A S. Bengal XXXI p. 393). He is called therein Mahārājādhirāja and was probably independent. But he must have soon been compelled to acknowledge the nominal suzerainty of the Chandellas of Bundelkhand; and Al-Beruni properly says that the two great forts in Chandella territory were Gwalior and Kalanjar. Vajradāman's son was Mangalarāja and his son was Kirtirāja who is described as having defeated Malwa (probably king Bhoja is here meant). Mahmud of Ghazni invested Gwalior in the days of Kīrtirāja and he was discreet enough to save himself and his kingdom by presenting 30 elephants and accepting nominal subjection. His son was Mūladeva alias Trailokya-Malla and Bhuvanapāla. His son was Devapāla alias Aparājita and his son was Padmapāla whose nephew Mahīpāla or Bhuvanaika-Malla recorded the inscription above mentioned dated 1093 A. D. (I.A. XV p. 36) which gives these details. The inscription further mentions that Kīrtirāja built a temple to Pārvatīpati in the town of Sinhamana. Mahīpāla had come to the throne a little before the date of this inscription (St. 1150) in the Sāsabahu temple on the Gwalior fort. It is a Vishṇu temple and it was commenced by Padmapāla and consequently the deity was named Padmanātha. The Kachhwahas seem to be Vaishṇavas from this king, a peculiarity which still distinguishes them. There is some misconception about the origin of the above mentioned name Sāsabahu given to these two temples on the Gwalior fort. We think that the name merely means the larger and smaller temples. The Gwalior Gazetteer derives the name from Sahasrabāhu which is not tenable not being a usual name of Vishṇu or Śiva. The lesser Sāsabahu temple which is like the bigger one was built in 1108 A. D. (I. A. XVI p. 201).

Gaurishankar mentions the following kings after Mahīpāla with dates (Tod p. 373): son Tribhuvanapāla (named Madhusūdanapāla in the Gwalior Gazetteer) with date 1104 A. D., his son Vijayapāla date 1133, his son Śūrapāla date 1155 and his heir-apparent Anangapāla. His successor must have been Solankhapāla who was invested in the fort by Shihabuddin Ghori in 1196 A. D. But the Gwalior Gazetteer states that the Parihāras took the fort from the Kachhwahas in 1129. In this view, Solankhapāla must have been a Parihāra. It appears that the fort was surrendered formally to Kutubuddin. But the Gwaliornāma published by Prince Balwantrao Bhyyasaheb Scindia states that the Pariharas took possession of he fort again and they were dislodged by Altamash as will be related later on. The Kachhapaghātas must have left the place as too near Delhi and receded to a more distant place or gone back to Narwar.

A branch family of this line ruled at Dubhkund seventy-six miles south-west of Gwalior and two inscriptions of these have been found (I. A. XIV p. 10 and E. I. II p. 293). These inscriptions give very interesting information. The first king mentioned is Yuvarāja and his son was Arjuna who is said to have himself killed with an arrow, Rājyapāla Pratihāra king of Kanauj when attacked by a Rajput confederacy headed by the Chandella king Ganda assisted by the Gwalior Kachhapaghāta king. His son was Abhimanyu whose skill in horsemanship and archery was extolled even by Bhoja king of Malwa.* His son was Vijayapāla whose date is 1044 and his son was Vikramasinha dated 1088. This family must have been a feudatory of the Gwalior kings who were practically independent though acknowledging nominal suzerainty of the Chandellas.

The name of the family Kachhapaghāta is also given in inscriptions as Kachhapāri and is undoubtedly the original form of the modern name Kachhwaha which is clearly derivable from it according to the rules of Prakrit transformation. What the name means it is difficult to state and we have already said that names arise in various ways. Whatever the origin, the Kachhwaha clan was always acknowledged as among the best Rajput families, being the first named in the list of 36 royal clans enumerated by Chand and as their rise precedes the rise of the Gāhadavālas in whose time the list was first probably made, their mention first was natural especially as they were entrusted with the command of the army assembled to punish the apostate Pratihāra king of Kanauj, as stated above.

---

* यस्यात्यद्भुतवाहवाहनमहाशस्त्रप्रयोगादिषु ।
प्रावीण्यं प्रविकत्थिते पृथुमतिश्रीभोजपृथ्वीभुजा ॥ Dubhkund Insc. E. I. III.

NOTE—HARAPRASHAD SHASTRI'S WRONG VIEW ABOUT THE ORIGIN OF THE KACHHWAHAS.

It is indeed a pity that we have to write a special note in this volume also to refute the wrong view of a great *Indian* pandit as we had to write a note in the previous volume on Sir Vincent Smith's wrong view about the Chandellas. In his Report for Search of Bardic Chronicles (1913) M. M. Haraprashad Shastri writes "The Kachhwahas claim descent from Kuśa son of Rāma and say that they came from Narwar which is a country of hunters (Nishāda) and anciently there was a race called Kachhapaghāta, who are probably represented by the modern Kachhawas, who are an untouchable race; but their rulers seem to have become Kshatriyas at some period". This is the most lamentable instance we have of wrong previous bias having misled even our pandits into drawing the most amazingly illogical inferences. We have already said many times that the bias of most European and a few Indian scholars is to look upon Kshatriya clans as developed out of aborigines and even untouchables or foreigners. The above is a very striking instance of how most illogical and absurd inferences are drawn through this bias.

In the first place Narwar is not a country of Nishādas but Nishadhas and Nala the famous Naishadha king ruled here. Secondly, because there are untouchable people there, at present named Kachhawas, therefore it does not follow that they are the modern representatives of the Kachhwaha people named Kachhapaghātas. The Kachhawas are not the only people now in Narwar District, nor is Kachhawāha the same as Kachhwa. Further even if Kachhwas are the predominant people there, it does not follow, therefore, that their rulers must also be Kachhwas. This is the same fallacy as led Sir Vincent Smith to argue that because the Chandellas ruled among Gonds, therefore they also were Gonds. In fact, the trend of Indian history shows that Rajput adventurers going out of their original home, the middle land, founded kingdoms in distant countries inhabited by Bhils, Gonds &c. Because Bappā Rāwal ruled in a country full of Bhils, therefore it does not follow that he was also a Bhil. Because the British rule among Bengalis therefore it does not follow that the British are Bengalis. In short, the Kachhwāhas ruling in a country mostly inhabited by the modern untouchable Kachhwas does not make them originally Kachhwas.

Thirdly, even granting that the names are identical, we have still to pause before we put forward the inference that the two people are identical in race. Kachhwāhas may have taken this name from the country they ruled, just as we showed in our second volume that the Gurjara Pratihāras were so called, only because they ruled in the Gurjara country, and not because they were themselves Gurjaras. Then again the Kachhwas themselves may have taken their names from their rulers. Several instances may be cited to show such taking of a higher class name by some untouchable classes. The Chamars e. g., have such names as Chauhans among them. The Sondias of Malwa have Chauhans, Paramāras &c. among them. It is, therefore, necessary to pause before making such an inference from identity of names with respect to a clan of Kshatriyas which has always been considered one of the best among Rajput clans and whose name stands first in Chand's list of 36 royal clans And in caste-ridden India is it possible that chiefs of untouchable peoples could have risen to this high status, without any striking brilliant service in the cause of religion? Nothing is known about the supposed rulers among these untouchables, or of any great exploits which should raise them to such a high status. We cannot but conclude without expressing our surprize and sorrow at such gratuitous aspersions thrown on a well-known Rajput clan by such a learned Indian pandit.* Lastly it may be added that Kachhwāha is clearly distinct from Kachhwa, being the Prakrit form of Kachhapaghāta. This word or its equivalent Kachhapāri both used in inscriptions should suggest that the Kachhwāhas were the slayers, the enemies of Kachhwas, the aboriginal people or untouchables and not themselves Kachhwas The origin of the name Kachhapaghāta is unknown as stated already; but if there are Kachhwas about Narwar (of which on inquiry at Shivapuri there seems to be great doubt) who are untouchables, the origin of the name becomes clear as the Kachhwāhas originally ruled in this part of the country unquestionably and it is called even now Kachhwāhaghar?

---

* We are constrained to state that on inquiry from the Gwalior state Narwar Shivapur revenue officer Mr. Bhalerao we find that there are no untouchable people named Kachhawas in or about Narwar. The whole argument of M. M. Haraprashad Shastri would then fall to the ground. His source of information must be inquired into.

CHAPTER XVIII

THE HIMALAYAN KINGDOMS

It remains to give the history of the Himalayan kingdoms during this sub-period. These were the kingdoms of Kashmir, Champā, Nurpur, Kangra, Mandi and Suket and finally of Nepal; we have already given the history of each of these states down to the end of the Hindu period so far as it has been ascertained. We will, however, restate that portion of their history which falls in the sub-period treated of in this volume viz. 1000–1200 A. D. with such additions and emendations as are necessary from recent information available from research publications, especially the Journals of the Panjab Historical Society.

1. KASHMIR

The kingdom of Kashmir at the beginning of this sub-period came under the Lohara dynasty after the death of the notorious queen Diddā. She was the daughter of a king of Lohara and grand-daughter of Bhīma, Shahi king of Kabul and she died in 1003 A. D. after a long reign both as regent of her sons and grandsons and latterly in her own name. Sangrāmarāj, her brother's son, came to the throne of Kashmir by Diddā's selection after her and his descendants ruled over Kashmir throughout this sub-period. The rulers of this dynasty were all capable men and they were, therefore, able to save the kingdom of Kashmir from being swallowed up in that flood of Mahomedan conquest which submerged first the Panjab under Mahmud and later, Northern India under Shihabuddin Ghori. We have already given the history of this dynasty from the Rājataranginī down to 1148 A. D. wherewith ends the work of Kalhaṇa and we give here the subsequent history from the supplementary work of Jonarāja. We may first recapitulate the former portion given in Vol I pp. 227-232 with some further remarks.

Sangrāmarāja, as usual with founders of dynasties, was a wise and able ruler. He ruled from 1003 to 1029. As we have already shown in this volume, Mahmud made two attempts to take the frontier stronghold of Kashmir but failed. Kashmir was a sealed country and Mahmud could not break the seal.

When Sir V. Smith says that Kashmir was protected by its inaccessible mountains, he is right; though it does not appear, as Smith thinks, that Kashmir was defeated. We must, however, vary our statement made in Vol. I. p. 228 that Kashmir was not invaded at all in the days of Sangrāma and state that though attempt was twice made to invade Kashmir, it could not be entered. We have already described the defeat of the Hindus in the battle fought by Trilochanapala, Shahi king, in 1021 A. D. with the aid of Kashmir troops sent by Sangrāma both in this volume and in Vol. I. p. 227. Trilochanapāla fled from place to place and probably his son Bhīma also whose end is recorded in 1027. But his other sons or cousins Rudrapāla and others remained in Kashmir under the protection of Sangrāma who was probably their relative.

These Shahi princes gave valuable aid to Anantarāja the son and successor of Sangrāma who ruled from 1029 to 1039 A. D. In his reign a treacherous Kashmir Sardar brought into Kashmir an invasion by the Turks assisted by Daradas. By the valour of the Shahi princes and of Anantarāja himself this formidable force was utterly defeated and Kashmir was saved from being subjected to Moslem rule for 300 years. We have already described this battle in Vol. I (p. 228).

Anantarāja and his queen Sūryamatī daughter of a Trigarta king were a very religious pair who ruled justly and ably for a long time. In their old age they retired and placed their son Kalaśa on the throne of Kashmir. They were ill-treated by this son and Ananta died in grief and his queen died a sati on his funeral pyre. Kalaśa in other respects was a good ruler. His son Harsha rebelled against him but was defeated and imprisoned. When Kalaśa died in 1073 A. D., he was succeeded by his second son Utkarsha. Harsha was, however, liked by the people. He was the most accomplished prince of his time, learned, fond of music and a patron of learned men. He may be compared to his namesake Harsha of Kanauj or to Bhoja; but unlike both his end was miserable. His second brother Vijayamalla raised a rebellion in his favour against Utkarsha who was defeated and killed in battle in 1089. Harsha being liberated and placed on the throne by Vijayamalla ruled long from 1089 to 1101. In the latter part of his reign Vijayamalla by the instigation of unscrupulous courtiers rebelled against Harsha but was unsuccessful. Harsha thereafter relentlessly persecuted his partisans and misrule and oppression so far increased that Uchchala, a collateral cousin, successed in leading a rebellion, and defeating Harsha took possession of the capital. Harsha's queens burnt themselves in the palace while he himself took refuge in a Maṭha. His son Bhoja who had been expelled came into Kashmir to relieve him but was killed in a battle with Uchchala. Harsha, finding everything going adverse, rushed upon the soldiers who had surrounded the Maṭha and was killed. Thus ended the first branch of this Lohara dynasty which ruled Kashmir ably for about a hundred years (1003 to 1101). Uchchala ruled till 1111 and his brother Sussala ruled after him till 1128. Sussala's son Jayasinha was ruling in 1148 A. D. when Kalhaṇa finished his Rājataraṅgiṇi. These rulers were also able and good rulers, though various intrigues described by Kalhaṇa went on as usual.

The Lohara dynasty was a Rajput dynasty and thus in the 11th and 12th centuries, as elsewhere in India, there were Rajput kings in Kashmir also. The preceding dynasty of Parvagupta was a Vaiśya one while that which preceded it viz. that of Yaśaskara was a Brahmin dynasty. It may, however, be added that these two were also practically Kshatriya as they married into Kshatriya families and followed Kshatriya life. The Lohara ruling family is said to belong to the Bhatti clan of Rajputs and hence the Kashmir kings were probably Bhattis.

The Dāmaras in Kashmir were a turbulent local people who were always troublesome to the reigning king and helpful to rebels. "King Harsha ordered a slaughter of these Dāmaras; but they combined with two refugee princes and put an end to his life" (Panjab H. S. Vol. II p. 81). Thus it seems that Uchchala gained the throne with the usual help of powerful Dāmaras.

2. NEPAL.

Nepal is the next large kingdom in the Himalayan region whose history in the first sub-period (600 to 800), we have given in the first volume. In the second volume we stated that in the second sub-period (800–1000) reigned in Nepal a Rajput kingly family which founded the Nepal era (885 A. D.) which is still in use in Nepal. In the third sub-period (1000–1200) the same family appears to have ruled in Napal unmolested by either Hindu or Mahomedan kings and we have found nothing particular which may be recorded of these kings. We, therefore, proceed to the minor kingdoms intervening between Kashmir and Nepal of which many important particulars have come to light in recent research.

3. CHAMBĀ.

We have already given in Vol. I a short account of the Chambā state which comes before us proceeding south-east from Kashmir. It was subordinate generally to Kashmir. This kingly line was founded about 620 A. D. by Ādivarman of the solar race (Vol. I p. 378), as Cunningham calculated. But later information from inscriptions on stone and copper read by Dr. Vogel and published in Archaeological Survey Report, New Imp. Series Vol. XXXVI part I (1911) and summarised by Dr. Hutchinson in J. Panjab H S Vol. II (pp. 75–80) shows that the state was founded by one Meruvarman of the solar race from Kalāpa town in the Gangetic valley about 700 A. D. The territory of the state gradually extended in the Rāvi valley the capital being Brahmapura or Brahmor One of his descendants Sāhilavarman (a household name in the state) founded the present capital Champā. His son Yugākaravarman recorded two copper-plate grants which are the oldest yet found. There are no dates given in Champā records except regnal years before A. D. 1330 when first the Sāstra or Kaliyuga era or the Vikrama era figure is given and these are recorded in Gupta characters generally and later on in Śāradā and next Nāgari characters. On palæographic grounds these two records may be placed in the 10th century A. D. From Rājatarangini we know that Ananta (1028–1039) invaded Champā and conquered Salavarman. Āsaṭavarman visited Kashmir in the days of Kalaśa in 1087 A. D. his sister Bappikā being Kalaśa's queen. Their son was the unfortunate Harsha and Āsaṭa assisted him and his son Bhoja and Āsaṭa's son Jāsata assisted without avail Bhikshāchāra son of Bhoja in 1103 A. D. Jāsata's successor Udayavarman, however, assisted Sussala in 1121 A. D. as Sussala had married two Chambā princesses. The civil war in Kashmir probably made Chambā independent (p. 79).

We need not mention the names of the later kings of Chambā upto 1200 A. D. But it may be stated that this family still rules in Chambā. This hill state was not troubled by Mahomedan invaders whether in the days of the Ghaznavide family of Mahmud or of Muhammad Ghori or later Sultans down to the days of Akbar.

The kings are Kshatriyas of the solar race with Moshināśva (Yuvanāśva?) gotra and are called Rajas. There are local chiefs who came to the country earlier; they are called Rāṇās (Rajānakas of inscriptions) and earlier still came the Raṭhis or Thakurs who now are probably a mixed race lower in rank than the Rāṇās ('Chanāl Jetha Raṭhi Kanetha').

4. NURPUR.

The kingdom of Nurpur is not an old Himalayan state. According to Nurpur tradition it was founded by a Tomara prince from Delhi. He is said to have dispossessed a Pathan chief from Pathankot and from thence going into the hills he built a fort at Nurpur, the original name of which was Dhaner (Nurpur being a name given, it is said, by Nurjahan). The date of the founding of a kingdom at Pathankot is believed to be the middle of the 11th century. But the story seems improbable as Panjab was at this time under the strong rule of Ghazni and it is difficult to believe that any Rajput prince could have been allowed to dispossess a Pathan force from Pathankot and found a kingdom. The story is, on the face of it, a name-legend based upon the name Pathankot. But the name Pathan here is really the Prakrit form of Pratishṭhāna and it seems to us that there was some Tomara king in Pratishṭhāna in pre-Mahmud days and in consequence of Mahmud's raids he removed into the hills and founded the kingdom of Dhaner. He built the fort of Nurpur (which is now in a ruinous condition) in a convenient strong place by the side of a river. His family ruled in this part during the sub-period treated of in this volume and continues even to this day, the present chief being, however, not a ruling prince.

The gotra of these Pathania Rajputs is Atri which raises a doubt as to whether they are really Tomaras. They also call themselves Pandirs or descendants of the Pāndavas, but the gotra of the Pāndavas as also of the Tomaras who are their modern representatives is Vaiyāghrapadya. Perhaps the Paithanias changed their gotra when they came to Dhaner and adopted a new Purohita, according to the wrong dictum of Vijnāneśvara or they are really lunar race Kshatriyas but not Tomaras.

The Panjab Historical Society's Journal Vol. II (p. 17) states that the original town of Pathankot was on the high ground to the east of the old fort, the site of which is marked by high mounds where old coins have been found. This shows that Pathankot is an ancient town and its ancient name must have been Pratishṭhāna. Two genealogical lists of the ruling family at Nurpur have been available differing in many details. Cunningham gave 1095 A. D. as the date of the founding of the Nurpur family and Jyethpāla, the founder, is said to have been a younger brother of a king of Delhi. A remark in the genealogy against Jaspāla states that he was 15th from the founder and opposed Allauddin Khilji (1295-1315). This takes Jyethpāla to about 1000 A. D. by the average of 20 years and it is extremely probable that these Tomaras did not come from Delhi which was not in existence at that time but from the plains of the Panjab itself, through the stress of Mahmud's invasions and took possession first of Pratishṭhāna already existing and from thence moved into the hills to Nurpur alias Dhaner.

NOTE—THE FORT OF NURPUR AND ITS TEMPLES.

The ruined fort of Dhaner or Nurpur is a very interesting fort near the town of Nurpur and the present Tahsil and hospital are built inside the fort. There are many tanks in the fort which was thus well supplied with water. There is a small temple well-preserved of Mahādeva; but the most interesting structure in this fort is the basement of an old temple the upper part of which is gone, which has been recently excavated from debris. The basement is well-preserved and there can be seen very beautiful figures carved in stone, depicting scenes in the Purāṇas and also of men, elephants, horses, camels, cows as they moved in the actual social life of mediæval Hindu period. The figures are true to nature and prove the great art of the carvers. These carvings are as beautiful, if not more, as the carvings on the pillars used in the Kutub mosque at Delhi. This temple appears to have been a Vishṇu temple. The heads of the figures have all been chiselled off by Mahomedan idol-breakers.

At some distance from this old temple there is a new temple, probably built in Akbar's days, wherein is to be seen a fine black statue of Muralīdhara (Krishṇa sounding his pipe). The idol is placed in the upper storey which is quite unusual. In the hall underneath and also on the second storey there are paintings on the walls of scenes from Krishṇa's early life which are very creditable and which give an idea of the dress, the ornaments and the social life of the people in Akbar's days at Nurpur.

5. MANDI AND SUKET.

We have already given a short history of this hill state in our first volume (pp. 379 and 380) and we give further particulars here from an article by Hutchinson and Vogel (J. Panjab VII pp. 1-4) with a few remarks of our own. This part of the Himalayan country including Kulu seems to have been an ancient kingdom, the original people therein being Kunindas or Kenets who still are the chief cultivators there. The country is visited by Tibetan Buddhists annually as they believe that the great Buddhist saint Padmasambhavā resided at the Rawalsar lake in Mandi territory; the Hindus believe that Lomaśa Kishi resided at this place.

The ruling family of Mandi and Suket is a Chandravanśi Rajput family with Atri as its gotra. Their names end always in the suffix sena. This has given rise, as usual, to the wrong tradition that they came from Bengal where Lakshmaṇasena of Lakhnauti was their last great king (1169–1198). This tradition accepted by Sir L. Griffin in his book "the Rajas of the Panjab" was, however, disbelieved by Cunningham who placed the founding of the Suket family nearly five hundred years before 1200 A. D. and Hutchinson and Vogel accept his view in their article on several grounds. Further confirmation of this view may also be found in the fact that the epigraphic records of the Sena kings of Bengal clearly state that they were Kshatriyas come from Karnāṭaka; while the Suket-Mandi tradition is that their ancestors first ruled in Indraprastha and from there they went to Bengal and founded Lakhnauti. Local traditions founded on names are often unhistorical and have to be given up and in the same way as we gave up the tradition about Pathānias having driven Pathans from Pathankot, we have here to give up the tradition that the Mandi-Suket Rājas with names ending in Sena came from Lakhnauti in Bengal after the fall of Lakshmaṇasena in 1198 A. D.

We have, however, to accept Vaṁśāvalis as some evidence, though not as reliable as inscriptions, and some history may be deduced out of Mandi Vaṁśāvalis. As already stated in Volume I p. 380, according to Cunningham, the founder of the Suket-Mandi family, Vīrasena, founded the state about 765 A. D. Cunningham calculated this date from the fact that from Vīrasena to Sāhusena and Bāhusena under whom the state divided into two, Suket and Mandi, there were 10 generations and upto Samudrasena who recorded the Nirmand inscription there were 6 more. From Samudrasena to Ajbarsena whose date is fixed from a copper-plate inscription dated for the first time in Vikrama era viz. St. 1584 or A. D. 1527, there were 11 more kings. Thus there were 27 generations from Nīrasena to Ajbarsena of 1527 A. D. and taking 30 years for each generation we get for Vīrasena 1527 – 810 = 717 A. D. and for Bāhusena who founded the Mandi state 1017 or 987. "Roughly speaking we may take Bāhusena founding Mandi about 1000 A. D. and Samudrasena recording inscription at Nirmand about 1150 A. D." Hutchinson and Vogel think that even if we take 25 years, average we shall have to take into consideration that some names might have dropped out of the Vaṁśāvalis and hence we may accept the date assigned by Cunningham as fairly correct, especially as it tallies with the legend current in Chambā that the pregnant queen of a king of Chambā had taken refuge with a king in Suket and her son Moshanāśva was set up in Chambā by this king. If we take 25 years average, we get for Vīrasena (1527–675) 852, for Bāhusena (852 plus 250) 1102 and for Samudrasena (1102 plus 150) 1252 A. D. In any case, Suket may be taken as founded not later than 800 A. D. and Mandi than 1100 A. D. Dr. Fleet does not believe that the Nirmand inscription of Samudrasena is dated in St. 1227 or 1170 A. D. as Cunningham thought. The date given in that inscription is only 6 which may belong to the Śāstra era and on palæographic grounds the inscription cannot be later than the 7th century, A. D. This difficulty, however, need not disturb the dates above given for the founding of Mandi and Suket, as Samudrasena of the Nirmand inscription can be treated as a king different from the Samudrasena of the Vamśāvalis which really appears to be the case from the difference of the names of his immediate ancestors given in the inscription and in the Vamśāvalis.

If we take the date of the founding of Mandi as 1000 A. D. or even 1100 A. D. it is possible to explain that the kingdom was founded by Sena Rajputs during invasions of Mahomedans into the Panjab under Mahmud or later. The story that it was founded by Bāhusena, brother of Śāhusena with whom he disagreed is of the usual fashion wherein two brothers having names sounding like each other found two kingdoms and may be disbelieved. Suket is, however, an older kingdom and was founded about 800 A. D. (It is a strange revelation that while Kangra Katoch Rajputs marry with the Suket family they do not marry with the Mandi family though of the same clan, as the Maharaja of Guler informed us).

We are not concerned with the history of Mandi or of Suket later than 1200 A. D. It seems that this family of Rajput hill princes remained undisturbed by Mahomedan invasions for a long time. They appear to have been independent of Kashmir also during this and the preceding sub-periods (800 to 1200).

6. KASHTAWAR.

The small hill state of Kāshṭhavāta (modern Kashtawar was ruled during this period by a Rajput family which was a dependent of Kashmir, as the name of a king Uttamarāja of Kāshṭhavāta appears among the names of those eight feudatories who attended on Kalaśa king of Kashmir in 1087 A. D. (See Vol. I p. 236). It may be noted that Suket and Mandi kings are not mentioned therein. From the article of Hutchinson and Vogel in J. Panjab H. S. Vol. IV (p. 29-41) on the history of the Kashtawar state, the princes of Kashtawar appear to belong to the family of Suket and Mandi and also believe that they came from Gaur. Their names also end mostly in the suffix sena. This tradition, as stated already, is wrong being based on the name-ending sena only. The king Uttamarāja mentioned as ruling in 1080 A. D. however, did not belong to this family as his name does not appear in the Vamśāvali of Kashtawar supplied by the modern representative who is a Mahomedan convert Rajput. It seems to us that the first king Kahnapāla who was sprung from the Suket family came to this part later and conquered it about 1200 A. D. or thereafter. We are not concerned with the history of this family in later and Mogul times though it is given in detail by Hutchinson and Vogel in the article above referred to. This state is now a part of Kashmir, having been conquered by the Sikhs in the days of Ranjitsing. The family was a Chandravamśi family with Atri as its gotra, being of the same clan as the Suket family. To what clan Uttamarāja's family belonged which ruled during our sub-period, there is no material to determine.

7. VALLĀPUR (BALOR) OR BASOHLI

This was another hill state subordinate to Kashmir the Raja of which was among those who attended on king Kalaśa in 1089 A. D. as stated above. The history of this family down to the present day is given by Hutchinson and Vogel in J. Panjab H. S. Vol. II, (pp. 77-98) and we give the following few facts from this interesting article relating to our period. The family claimed to be descended from the Pāndavas and they believe that they came from Allahabad to Almora, from there to Hardwar and from there into the hills via Suket. This tradition may be accepted as descendants of the Pāndavas last ruled at Kauśāmbi and their greatest king in historic times was Udayana well-known from the Kathāsaritsāgara who with his minister Yaugandharāyaṇa ruled in Kauśāmbi. The Rajas are therefore Chandrabansi; their gotra has not been ascertained; though the main branch is now extinct, there are many collateral descendants known as Baloria Rajputs. The kingdom was founded by one Bhogapāla long before 900 A. D. and the ancient capital was Vallāpura or Balor. The names of the kings usually end in pāla. Trailokyapāla ruled in the first half of the 11th century and his son was Tunga and grandson Kalaśa. This king is mentioned in the Rājataranginī as visiting Kashmir to attend on Kalaśa the Kashmir king, Padmaka and his son Ānanda are other names of Vallāpur kings mentioned in the Taranginī but they are not found in the Vamśāvali of Baloria kings. They assisted Bikshāchāra, grandson of Harsha, to regain the throne of Kashmir seized by Uchchala and Sussala, being his relatives. But they failed and eventually went over to the latter. Jayasinha is said to have deposed another king of Balor; but apparently the later kings became independent. Their names down to 1200 A. D. need not be given as we know nothing about them beyond their names.

8. KOT KANGṚĀ.

The kingdom of Jālandara has been noticed already in Vol. I pp. 383-84, as subsisting from the most ancient times of Mahābhārata days when Suśarman the first known ancestor of the Katoch kings fought on the side of the Kauravas. His descendant in the direct line at present is the Maharaja Sir Jaichand of Lambagraon, Kangṛā District; a Rajput chief of great learning and influence among the Rajputs of Eastern Himalayas. Who the king of Trigarta which then included Jālandhara in the plains and Kangṛā in the hills was at the time of Mahmud has not yet been ascertained from him. We have already stated that the king must have been a dependent ally of Ānandapāla, king of Kabul and the Panjab, and must have fought in his last battle with Mahmud. The Hindus were defeated and probably Mahmud suddenly made a raid on Kot Kangṛā before the king could come back. The fort fell though defended for a time by the garrison and it was seized with all the immense treasure kept therein. As stated in the note on

Kot Kangṛā already given, the fort was impregnable and hence it was made the depository of treasure by Hindu kings. From the account given by Utbi, a contemporary historian of Mahmud, it appears that the garrison lost heart on seeing the immense force which invested the fort and capitulated soon without much resistance. They were, we think, a mercenary force and not a band of gallant defenders fighting for national independence. For Utbi states "They capitulated and consented to serve under the banners of the Sultan. Then they opened the gate and humbly offered their services" (Utbi p. 341). Thus the impregnable fort with its immense riches fell into the hands of Mahmud who permanently occupied it and kept trusty guards there, when he retired. It appears that the Trigarta kings lost their kingdom in the plains henceforward, and they must have further retired into the hills. They, however, took back the fort, it is said, in 1044 A. D. at the suggestion of the kings of Delhi after a seige of 4 months. Utbi does not relate the throwing down of any temple or the destruction of any idol at Kangṛā Kot as other historians do. But it is nowhere stated of what deity the idol was. From inquiries at Kangṛā it appears to us that there was a famous temple of Devi Ambikā there, distinct, of course, from the Devi of Jwālāmukhi which is about 20 miles distant from Kot Kangṛā. The Devi idol must have been, as already stated, destroyed by Mahmud and it was replaced by the Kangra king when he retook the fort.

The later history of Kangṛā kings upto 1200 A. D., the end of our period, is soon told. Kalhaṇa mentions king Indrachandra in 1040 A. D. and he must be the king who took the fort back. We do not find any mention of any later king in Kangra except for a reference to a king of Trigarta defeated by the Turks in Jonarāja's Rājataranginī. He fled to Kashmir and with the help of Jayasinha about 1150 A. D. retook his kingdom after defeating the Turkish invader It is not necessary to give mere names of kings from the Vaṁśāvali of Katoch kings which is undoubtedly one of the most reliable Vamaśāvalis in the Himalayan states down to the end of our period, as nothing particular can be related about these kings. We have already given a description of the fort of Kangṛā and its temples in chapter X Book VI.

CHAPTER XIX.

RAI PITHAURA, THE LAST HINDU HERO-EMPEROR.

The history of the life of this last Hindu chivalrous emperor of India has been given in great detail in the Rāsā supposed to be composed by Chand Bhāt, a contemporary of Prithvirāj. But as the present Rāsā has nearly wholly transformed the probable original nucleus and as many events and statements given therein have been proved untrue from trustworthy records, it is difficult to determine which part of its account is true. There are two historical poems, however, which will assist us, first, the Prithvīrāja-Vijaya-kāvya composed by a Kashmiri court-poet of Prithvirāj himself, first brought to notice by Būhler and later by Mr. Harbilas Sarda of Ajmer (J. R. A. S. 1913) and second, Hammīrkāvya published by J. S. Kirtane. The first is, however, incomplete and does not come down to the close of Prithvirāja's career; while the second devotes itself more to the glory of Hammīra a descendant of Prithvirāj. We will try to construct an account of the life of this hero from all these sources, using the Rāsā account so far as it is probable and uncontradicted.

In an inscription of Prithvirāj himself found at Madanapur and recorded by him in 1182 A. D. after defeating Paramardi-deva Chandella, we are told that Prithvirāj was son of Someśvara and grandson of Arṇorāja. Unfortunately, though the practice of inscriptions often is, the names of the mother of Prithirāj and Someśvara are not given. The Rāsā makes a daughter of Anangapāla of Delhi, mother of Prithvirāj; but the Hammīra kāvya and Prithvirāja-Vijaya state that he was born of a Chedi Haihaya princess named Karpūradevi, which of course is the more reliable statement. Prithvirāj according to the Rāsā was born in Ānanda St. 1115 or A. D. 1149 and when he died he was 43 years old, which gives correctly the years of his death viz. 1192 A. D. Tod gives the date of Prithvirāja's birth as St. 1215 or A. D. 1158 which makes his age at the time of his last battle, 34 years. Rai Bahadur Gaurishanker Ojha thinks that the date ought to be St. 1225 or A. D. 1168 which would make him 24 years old at the time of his death, which seems incredible.

From the Bijolia inscription (J. A. S. Bengal LV part 1 pp. 31-40) we are certain that Visaladeva or Vigraha III conquered

Delhi and this event from Vīsala's inscription on the Śiwalik pillar at Delhi the exact date of which is 9th April 1164 (Kielhorn I. A. XIX p. 218) must have happened sometime about December 1163. The Bijolia inscription mentions Prithvirāja II as ruling after Vīsala and making a grant to a Jain temple and after him Someśvara as ruling and also making another grant to another Jain temple. The date of this Bijolia inscription is 1170 A. D. We have two inscriptions of Prithvībhata or Prithvirāj II dated 1167 and 1169 (E I. VIII Kielhorn). Thus we are certain that he came to the throne some time between 1164 and 1167 and ruled till the end of 1169, when Someśvara succeeded him. How long he ruled after 1170 is not clear. Gaurishanker thinks that he ruled till St. 1236 or 1179 A. D.; and at that time Prithvirāj was a minor, the government being carried on by his mother during his minority according to the Prithvīrāja-Vijaya Kāvya. But in 1182 he was grown up and powerful enough to defeat Paramardideva. If we take him 21 years old at this time then his birth would be about 1161 A. D. and his age would be 18 at the time of Someśvara's death in 1179 which would not make him a Minor for a Hindu prince and this would contradict Prithvirāja-Vijaya. It is, therefore, probable that Someśvara did not rule so late as 1179 A. D. but ruled till about 1175 A. D. We thus have four uncertain dates for the birth of Prithvirāj viz. (1) 1149 A. D., Vaiśākha Badi 2 (May) according to the Rāsā (2) Prithvirāj. Vijaya gives the following date and positions of planets viz: Jyeṣtha Badi 12, being after the end of bright Vaiśākha and Mars in Capricorn, Saturn in Aquarius, Jupiter in Pisces, Sun in Aries, Moon in Taurus and Mercury in Jemini, (this gives no clue to the year of his birth)* (3) 1158 according to Tod and (4) 1168 according to Gaurishanker. Someśvara at the time of the birth of Prithvirāj was not king. It is related that during the rule of his brother Vigraha III he resided at the court of Jayasinha Sidharāja of

---

* For the curious we may state that the horoscope of Prithvīrāja according to the Rāsā is different from the one which results from the positions given above. But even these are imaginary as it is impossible that on Jyestha Badi 12 the sun can be in Aries and the moon in Taurus. The Rāsā date of birth is Śaka 1071 Vaishākha Vadya 2 (A. D. 1149); and the Vijaya date is Jyeshtha Vadya 12 (Purnimanta month); this *miti* may be believed though the year may be *uncertain* taken to be 1159 A. D. or Śaka 1081.

Anhilwad whose daughter Kānchanadevi was his mother. He came to Ajmer on the death of Prithvirāj II. And he ruled there for some years, as is also proved by his copper coins found. The place of Prithvirāja's birth is given by the Rāsā as Delhi; but it must have been Anhilwad or Tripur the capital of the Chedis, the former being mentioned by Prithvirāj-Vijaya (J. R. A. S. 9913 p. 276).

Having discussed the date as also the place of birth of Prithvirāj we will go on to speak of his marriages. He must have been certainly a precocious boy and according to the Rajput fashion of the day and indeed Hindu practice generally of the time, he must have married early. The Rāsā mentions many queens of his; but the first and notable of them was Inchhinī daughter of Jaita Paramāra of Abu. The Rāsā story of this marriage is however, absurd. An elder daughter of the Paramāra chief of Abu was married to Chaulukya king Bhīma; who, learning of the great beauty of her younger sister, insisted on marrying that princess also. Her father, however, gave her in marriage to Prithvirāj. The kingdom of Abu was invaded in consequence by Bhīma. Prithvirāj moved against Bhīma who, thereupon, incited Shihabuddin to attack Prithvirāja from the north while he himself attacked him from the south. Prithvirāj and his general Kaimāsa, however, defeated them severally; Shihabuddin being even captured. (The Rāsā, by an amazing exaggeration, makes Prithvirāj capture Shihabuddin several times releasing him each time through generosity). The story seems improbable, though we may believe that Prithvirāj was married to Inchhinī a Paramāra princess and that he had a fight with Bhola Bhīma of Gujarat for some reason in which the latter was defeated.

We need not describe the other queens of Prithvirāj mentioned by the Rāsā; but we must notice his last queen viz: Sanyogitā daughter of Jaichand Gāhadavāla king of Kanauj. The Rāsā makes a most poetical story of this marriage. It represents Jaichand holding a svayamvara of his daughter and Prithvirāj being his enemy was not only not invited, but in derision, an image of his in the dress of a Bhāldar or macebearer was placed at the entrance of the marriage hall. Sanyogitā who had already been married to Prithvirāj in a dream by the god Kali threw the garland of marriage round the neck of his image. The chivalrous Prithvirāj seized the princess and carried her off, fighting through the army of Jaichand. This story is too enchanting to be true; but it is difficult to reject it altogether as some do and we believe that Prithvirāj to whom Sanyogitā must have communicated her love like Juliet, by a sudden raid on Kanauj must have carried her off. Svayamvaras were obsolete at this time, though described by Chand in the Rāsā and by Bilhaṇa in Vikramānkacharitra, a little earlier (1125 A. D.). This love story has, however, immortalized the name of Prithvirāj as much as his defeat of Shihabuddin Ghori. Sir Vincent Smith places this marriage in 1175 A. D. following probably the Rāsā (E. H. I. p. 387 3rd Ed.); but if we believe that Prithvirāj was born in 1158 according to Tod, he would be only 17 years old in 1175 A. D.; (according to the Rāsā he would be 26 years old) and further the fall of Prithvirāj would come 17 years after this marriage. But the Rāsā represents the fall as coming soon after the marriage and it is probable, therefore, that this event happened at least 10 years later i. e. about 1185 A. D. which date indeed, we find, is given in the Rāsā and not 1175 A. D.

We need not mention the many incidents in the life of Prithvirāj described by the Rāsa such as the destruction of Kaimāsa, his most able minister and general. It is sufficient if we mention the probable wars which Prithvirāj must have waged beside his war with Mahomedans. The most important and powerful kingdoms in Northern India then were those of Gujarat, Bundelkhand and Pānchāla or Kanauj, ruled by Chālukyas, Chandellas and Gāhadavālas. And the kings in these at this time were also able and powerful viz. Bhīma, Paramardideva and Jaichand. With each one of them Prithviraj fought and established his superiority over them. Each of these wars is full of chivalrous incidents which it would be out of place here to detail, such as the story of Alha and Udhalha of the Banāphara clan, two heroes who had been driven away by Paramardideva but who by the entreaty of their mother and for the sake of their mother-land came back to Mahoba to fight with Prithvirāj when he attacked it and died fighting with him. The whole poem of Chand is full of such daring incidents, so dear to the chivalrous Rajputs and thus deserves the vast popularity it enjoys in Rajputana. The historian, however, is unable to accept these stories as historical in the absence of corroborating epigraphic or other reliable evidence. The war with Paramardideva was waged in 1182 A. D. and the latter was conquered; as appears from Prithvirāja's inscription recorded at Madanpura in Chandella territory already mentioned.

The summary of Prithvīrāja-Vijaya-Kāvya given by Mr. Harbilas Sarda in J. R. A. S. 1913 contains no details either about Prithvirāja's marriages or his wars. It mentions two ministers Kadambavāsa and Bhuvanika-Malla who were great warriors; but even their achievements are not mentioned. However it introduces at the end a messenger from Gujarat announcing its victory over Shihabuddin. This was after Prithvīrāja was major and himself ruling. The battle as stated in Gujarat history was fought in 1179 A. D. and Prithvirāja appears then to have been major at this date. His minority must have lasted for a short time only.

On the disastrous results of these wars with the neighbouring kingdoms we will speak later on; but they established the fame of Prithvīrāja and he has rightly been called emperor of Northern India. He was king of Ajmer and Delhi and emperor or Chakravartin of Northern India (like George V, king of England and Emperor of India). This position of a chakravartin was the bone of contention among Rajput kings: and each powerful king tried to assert it; even the kings of Konkan, as we have seen, called themselves Konkana-Chakravartin. The competitor of Prithvirāj to Imperial dignity was Jaichand of Kanauj whose grand-father Govindachandra was really emperor over the hole of Northern India; that position was wrested from his son by Vīsaladeva in about 1160 A. D. and the conquest and annexation of Delhi added to the power of the Chauhans. This contest between Prithvīrāja and Jaichand weakened their power to resist the Mahomedans under Ghorī. How it finally led to the conquest of both, we go on to describe.

NOTE:—1 RĀSĀ DATES IN PRITHVIRĀJA'S LIFE.

The Rāsā gives five dates of events in the life of Prithvirāj (Benares Edn. of the Rāsā p. 140). viz.

1	Birth	1115 Anand St.	=1149 A. D.	=1205 V. E.
2	Adoption at Delhi.	1122 „	=1156 „	=1213 „
3	Fight with Kaimāsa.	1140 „	=1174 „	=1231 „
4	Kanauj expedition	1157 „	=1185 „	=1242 „
5	Final fight and death.	1158 „	=1192 „	=1249 „

NOTE:—2 THE OLD DELHI OF PRITHVĪRĀJA.

From "the Seven Cities of Delhi" of Gordon and from ancient Mahomedan accounts and Indian records, as well as from a personal inspeoption of the locality, an idea may be formed and given of the old city of Delhi ruled by Prithvīrāja. Indraprastha appears, from Mahomedan records, to have existed separately in the time of Kutubuddin and at a distance from the Delhi of Prithvirāja. This is probably the same place which is now known as Indrapat. To the south-west of it, at a distance of about two miles, Anangapāla Tomara built a fort called even then Lalkot, and founded a city which may be the same as the modern small town of Mehrauli. This Lalkot is the same place as where now stands Kutubuddin's mosque; the ancient iron pillar, believed to have been brought from Mathura and set up by Anangapāla, being in the centre of the court-yard of this mosque. At present the western wall of the Kutub mosque is not standing. In Anangapāla's fort, there must have been many Jain and Hindu temples. These were thrown down by Kutubuddin and their beautifully carved pillars were utilized by him for building the four sides of the court-yard of the mosque. That Kutubuddin preserved the carvings of these pillars and allowed the iron pillar to stand where it was set up, shows the greatness of that first Mahomedan Indian emperor. "How the iron pillar (dating probably from the 5th century A. C.) so long remains without rusting is a thing which manufacturers of the present day long to explain. It is a single shaft about 17 tons in weight. It was originally raised to Vishṇu (by a king named Chandra as an insoription on it states) and probably had a Garuda upon it." "All honour is due to Kutubuddin for leaving it in front of the mosque (and taking it in the centre of its court-yard while the Moslem conquerors of Rhodes sold the Colossus there to a Jew for the brass," (Fergusson). "There are pillars of Jain temples of the same order as those on Mt. Abu"—(Fergusson) but "there are others of Hindu temples with carvings showing cow and calf and Krishṇa and his mother" (Fanshawe). There can be distinctly seen the head of Kīrtimukha with rows of teeth clearly markable, who is a well-known servant of Śiva. The fort of Anangapāla was extensive enough apparently to contain many palaces and temples.

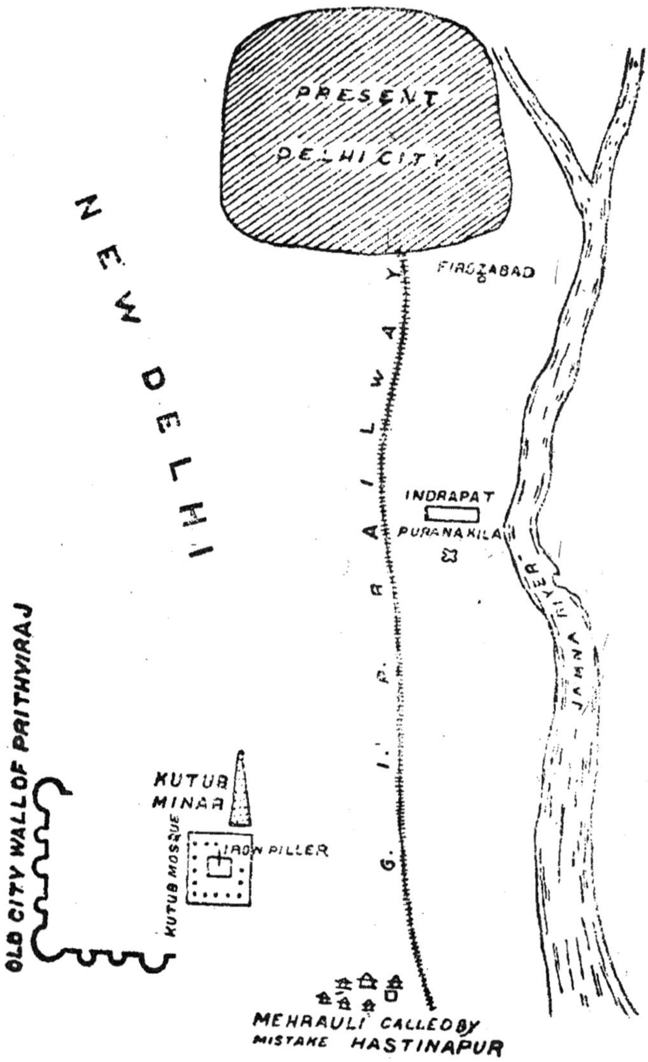

This fort and city of Delhi was founded by Anangapāla Tomara in about 1052 A. D. in which year the pillar was set up there according to an inscription on the pillar itself. A hundred years later the Chāhamānas conquered it and annexed the Tomara kingdom. Prithvirāja is said to have extended the city and built a wall round it. "The wall of Prithvīrāja can be traced round the Kutub mosque." There is still a portion of the wall standing, with bastion-towers, to the west of the mosque at a distance of some two furlongs, which may be the wall of a city or another circumvallating wall of the fort itself. We have to imagine a ground fort round about the present Kutub Minar "rising like a mountain" (Taj-ul-Ma'sir).

The name of the new city and the fort appears to be really Dhillikā, a new name given by the Tomaras so far as we can see. The name in this form is used in two inscriptions already quoted, viz., the Bijolia inscription dated St. 1226 or 1169 A. D. and the well inscription of 1336 A. D. which distinctly states that the city was founded by the Tomaras and subsequently ruled by the Chāhamānas. Thus the name Delhi goes back to about 1050 A. D. What the name means is not clear as the original form Dhillikā is difficult to be converted into its Sanskrit equivalent. It is a Prakrit word meaning loose as the modern vernacular word means, and there may be some truth in the legend usually mentioned about the city's name.

CHAPTER XX

SHIHABUDDIN GHORI AND HIS CONFLICT WITH PRITHVĪRĀJ.

Panjab fell before Mahmud, Turkish king of Ghazni; Northern India fell before Shihabuddin, Afghan king of Ghor. It is, therefore necessary to give a short account of this king before we proceed to narrate the history of the fall of the Rajput kingdoms of Northern India, in the same way as we gave an account of the rise of the Turkish kingdom of Ghazni, before we gave the history of the downfall of the Panjab.

Ghor is a mountainous territory to the northwest of Ghazni peopled by Afghans and the king and people of Ghor were originally Hindus, as elsewhere in Afghanistan. They were converted to Mahomedanism before and during the days of Mahmud of Ghazni. The kings of Ghor ruled in subordination to the Sultans of Ghazni for a long time, till in the time of Sultan Bahram a quarrel arose between them. Bahram unnecessarily first killed Kutubuddin Ghori and then his brother Saifuddin with the greatest possible indignity at Ghazni. Allauddin, their brother, vowed vengeance and marched on Ghazni, when Bahram marched out of Ghazni to oppose him with a formidable force, the chief arm of which was the elephant force. By the bravery of certain heroes, Allauddin was able to defeat the elephant force as also the army of Bahram who fled leaving Ghazni to the tender mercies of Allauddin. A most terrible vengeance was exacted by him from Ghazni which was plundered and burnt for seven days continuously. Every man that was found there was slain and the women and children were made slaves. He destroyed all the palaces of the Mahmudi kings "which had no equals in the world." After that he returned to Ghor with the remains of his brothers and he interred them in the tombs of their ancestors (Tabakat-i-Nasiri E. II p. 289). A terrible vengeance indeed on the people for the fault of their king! Bahram fled to India but died on the way. Allauddin Ghori for this act of cruelty is properly called Jahān-soz or burner of the world. After his death his son succeeded him and after the death of the latter within a short time Ghiyasuddin Muhammad bin Sam, his cousin, succeeded in Ferozkoh, the capital of Ghor. His brother Muez-ud-din Muhammad bin Sam became king of Ghazni in 1172 A. D. The Gozz Turks who held the possession of Ghazni for twelve years, the Mahmudi Sultan Khusru having fled to India, were driven away by him. He ruled in behalf of his brother Ghiyasuddin and was virtually the master. He was an ambitious energetic king and naturally formed the design of conquering all the Indian territory of the Mahmudi Sultans of Ghazni and of conquering Hindustan itself. Muhammad Ghori was also called Shihabuddin or 'flaming star of religion.'

He first conquered Multan and the adjoining territory in 1175; and in 1178 A. D. he led his army by way of Uchh and Multan against Naharwala. The Rai of Naharwala was a minor (the name Bhīma is wrongly given here by the Tabakat, it ought to have been Mūlarāja as we have already seen in Gujarat history; he was, however, elder brother of Bhīma) but the Rai had a large army and many elephants and the Sultan was defeated and compelled to retreat.

In 1179 A. D. he took Peshawar and two years later he advanced against Lahore which was the capital of the Mahmudi Sultan Khusru. The power of the Ghaznavides was on the decline and their glory was departing. Khursu Malek sent his son as hostage and an elephant as present and he was spared this time. Muhammad Ghori thereafter turned his attention towards Sind and conquered Debal and the surrounding country upto the sea. In 1184 he again marched towards Lahore, ravaged the country, founded the town and fort of Sialkot and finally took Lahore. Khusru Malek could offer no resistance; he came forth peacefully to meet the Sultan and was made a prisoner and he was subsequently sent to Ferozkoh the capital of Ghor and thence to a fort with his son in 1191 A. D. and there put to death about 1205 A. D. This conduct and fate of the last Ghaznavide Sultan reminds one of the similar conduct and fate of the Sultan of Bijapur before Aurangjeb. Muezuddin appointed a governor in Lahore, made the father of the author of the Tabakat Kazi of the army of Hindustan, and then returned to Ghazni (E. II p. 295). Thus was substituted in the Panjab a new dynasty of rulers in place of the effete old Mahmudi dynasty and a new ambitious powerful king came to the throne of Ghazni, who had the energy and ambition, though not the greatness of Mahmud and who fought with the Rajput kings of Northern India as neighbouring kings must always do.

HIS CONFLICT WITH PRITHVĪRAJ.

The important kingdom in his immediate neighbourhood was the kingdom of Ajmer and Delhi ruled by Prithvīrāj and the two emperors were equally matched in their personal capacities and the extent of their resources. The history of this conflict is differently told in the Rāsā of Chand and the Taj-ul-Ma'sir of Nizamuddin followed by the Tabakat-i-Nasiri. Both sides exaggerate the merits of their heroes; but historically considered, the account of the Taj and the Tabakat, written about 20 and 50 years respectively after the event, is more reliable than the almost fabulous account given in the Rāsā amplified to its present form nearly 300 years after Prithvīrāja. We will, therefore, mainly follow the account of these Mahomedan writers and try to test it historically; though it may be regretted that the Taj is not more detailed and less poetical, in fact it is not to be compared with the well-known chronicle of Mahmud by Utbi.

We may first notice the extract from the Tabakat given by Elliot II (p. 295). The first attack was made by Muhammad Ghori who invaded Hindu territory and seized the fort of Sirhind and placed it under a Mahomedan governor. "Rai Pithaura came up against the fort and the Sultan faced him at Narain. All the Rais of Hindustan were with the Rai Kola (a term of abuse)." Probably Prithvīrāja for this conflict, in order to nip this aggression by Mahomedans against Hindus, in the bud collected a confederate Hindu army and then advanced against the Sultan. But there is no corroborating evidence from epigraphic records to prove this confederacy. "In the fight, the Sultan seizing a lance attacked Govindrai of Delhi who was riding an elephant, the Sultan being on horseback. The Sultan drove his lance into the mouth of Govindrai and knocked down two of his teeth. The Rai, however, by his blow wounded severely one arm of his adversary. The Sultan reined back his horse and turned aside. As the Sultan began to totter on his horse, an intrepid young Afghan sprang upon the Sultan's horse and supported him and took the horse safely away. But the army thinking the Sultan killed, gave way and fled; and thus was inflicted a severe defeat upon the Mahomedans."

Whether this account is true and whether the defeat was not, in the usual fashion, due to superior numbers or superior tactics or superior heroism, we need not discuss. One thing may be said, however, that the Mahomedans, even according to their account, like the Hindus, fled unbeaten because of the report of the death of their king. This is not strange. Eastern armies fight not for nations but for kings. The Mahomedans were no more fired by a national sentiment than the Hindus: and the substitute of a religious for a national sentiment was equal on both the sides. Certain it is that in this battle, Shihabuddin Ghori was signally defeated (1191 A. D.).

The tradition among the Hindus is, as recorded in the Rāsā, that the Sultan was captured. The story of Dhīra Pundīra given in the Rāsā is clearly fictitious; but it is possible that when Govindrai (who is not mentioned in the Rāsā at all and who is represented as killed in the next conflict with Prithvīrāj) inflicted a severe wound on the Sultan and he began to totter on his horse, he may have been seized by Pundir and finally captured. The Sultan was allowed to return by Prithvirāj after a ransom of 30 elephants and five hundred horses was taken from him. This much may be historically true. The Taj does not mention this defeat at all but discreetly begins with the Sultan's next advance against Prithvīrāja. It is, of course, entirely unbelievable as alleged by the Rāsā that the Sultan was many times captured in battle and at each time released and sent back by Prithvīrāja. This is the usual reduplication of events noticeable from the story of Krishṇa in the Purānas down to the story of Munja by the chroniclers who is supposed to have six times defeated and captured Taila Chālukya of Kalyan (see Vol. II p. 120). But an exaggearation like this generally has some truth behind it and we may believe that Shihabuddin was captured in this battle and released on ransom just as Jaipal was released by Mahmud after his first defeat on a similar ransom.*

Whatever be the reality of this incident, the fact that the Sultan was defeated in this battle is accepted on both sides. The place of this battle is given as Narain which, in the original, must be Tarain. The scene is said to be on the Sarsuti but Cunningham thinks that the exact site was on the banks of the Raukshi river, four miles south of Tirauri and ten miles to the

*Rāsā mentions guns and even canon in this battle which plainly indicates that the Rāsā account was written after Babar who first used guns in India in the 16th century.

north of Karnal. "Tirauri is also called Azimābād" (note Elliot II p. 295). The Karnāl Gazetteer (1918) gives the latest information and states (p. 10) that the battle was fought at Nardina a village in the Nai Wafi in the Nardak, 12 miles south of Thanesar and 3 miles from Taraori.

The Tabakat proceeds to relate that when the Sultan retired, Prithvīrāja invested the fort of Sirhind for 13 months. If this is true it can not be believed that the Sultan was captured in battle and released. For one condition of such release would naturally have been the surrender of the fort which had been wrongly seized by the Sultan; and probably the fight would not have been continued or even renewed so soon. The Sultan according to the Tabakat made fresh preparations and returned to the fight with an overwhelming force.

The Taj-ul-Ma'sir suppresses all this and begins with the statement that the Sultan sent a venerable reliable man to Ajmer calling upon Prithvīrāja to accept Islam and subordination to the Sultan; thus giving the affair a wholly religious aspect. It does not seem to us that Muhammad Ghori's war upon India was from religious motives as that of Mahmud was, though Mahommedan writers naturally give it this form. The war was waged solely for aggression and extension of dominion as the more truly historical Tabakat describes.

The Taj gives no details about this final conflict but merely says that the army of Islam was victorious and a hundred thousand Hindus swiftly "departed to the fire of hell." The more truly historical Tabakat gives interesting details. Quoting an eye-witness who was in the army, it states that the army of Islam numbered a hundred and twenty thousand horsemen clad in armour. The numbers on the Hindu side are not given. "Before the Sultan arrived, the fort had capitulated and the Hindu army was encamped in the vicinity of Narain." It thus appears that the site of the second battle was nearly the same as before. The tactics adopted at this battle are described by the Tabakat as follows:—

"The Sultan drew up his battle array, leaving his main body in the rear with the banners, canopies and elephants. The light-armoured horsemen were made into four divisions of 10,000 each and were directed to advance and to harass the enemy, on the right, on the left, in the front and in the rear. When the enemy collected his forces to attack, they were to support each other and to charge at full speed. By these tactics the enemy was worsted, the Almighty gave us the victory over them and they fled." (p. 297).

The manner of fighting adopted by the Mahomedans at this momentous battle as described above appears similar to that adopted by Mahmud in his battles with Jaipal and Ānandapāla; frequent attacks by bodies of cavalry and a final attack by a reserve force, a measure also adopted by Ahmed Shah Abdali. How the Hindus fought cannot be stated as the descriptions in the Rāsā are imaginary and as the author copies the Mahābhārata in describing Vyūhas in the form of birds or animals, and the description is not from an eye-witness but from a poet who wrote centuries afterwards. But that the fighting was tough and the battle was severely contested appears clear from the single sentence of the Tabakat. "The Almighty gave us the victory". There being no superiority of arms as at Assaye or at Plassey, and there being no lack of heroism on the side of the Hindus, we may take it that the battle was not a walk over, as may perhaps be thought. It cannot be gainsaid that Prithvīrāja fought most bravely in this final fight and that fate was against him at this time. The story of the Rāsā that Prithvīrāja after his marriage with Sanyogitā gave himself up solely to pleasure and neglected the army is probably fictitious. And this is doubly true when we remember that Prithvīrāja was not in Delhi as the Rāsā represents but in Ajmer. The importance of Delhi commences from Kutubuddin. Those who wrote in later centuries, as even Firishta, could not resist the idea of bringing in Delhi, much less could the amplifier of the Rāsā and the whole story of the Rāsā including the names of the fighters on both sides, notably of Samarasinha of Chitod has to be given up as unhistorical.

But the story of the Rāsā as to how Prithvīrāj ended his life is the climax of its unhistorical nature. It is the usual story of vengeance, a story invented after the true account of the death of Muhammad Ghori at the hands of Gakkhar assassins on the south bank of the Indus had been forgotten. The real manner of Prithvīrāja's death, however, still remains a mystery like that of Bhaoosaheb or Jankoji Scindia at Panipat. The two accounts of the Taj and Tabakat differ. The latter merely records that "Pithaura alighted from his elephant, mounted a horse and gallopped off but he was captured near

Sarsuti and sent to hell". The Taj, however, records (p. 215) that the Rai of Ajmer was taken prisoner and his life was spared. At Ajmer where he was taken, he was detected in an intrigue (*which is only obscurely hinted*) and orders were, therefore, given for his being beheaded and a sword accordingly severed the head of that accursed wretch from his body." In this state of the evidence, it is difficult to decide how Prithvīrāj met his death; but we prefer to believe that Prithvīrāja was captured on the Sarsuti and immediately put to death as the Tabakat relates.

NOTE:—1 MUHAMMAD GHORI AND PRITHVĪRĀJ.

The translation of the Tabakat by Raverty gives a somewhat different wording from Elliot and states "When the ranks were duly martialled, the Sultan seized a lance and attacked the elephant on which Govindrai of Delhi was mounted and on which elephant he moved about in front of the battle. The Sultan struck Govindrai on the mouth and he launched a javelin at the Sultan and inflicted a very severe wound. The Sultan turned his charger's head round and receded and from the agony of the wound he was unable to continue on horseback any longer. Defeat befell the army of Islam and it was irretrievably routed. The Sultan was very nearly falling from his horse, seeing which a Khilji stripling recognised the Sultan and sprang up behind and supporting him in his arms urged the horse with his voice and brought him out of the field of battle. On the Muhamadan forces not seeing the Sultan, lamentations broke from them and they reached a place where the defeated army was safe from pursuit. Suddenly the Sultan arrived. (p. 431).

Raverty in his note gives here the different account given by later authors and the account of Firishta as also of modern English historians based on the last. Firishta gives the army of Pithora as amounting to two lakhs of men and 3,000 elephants. He also states that the right and left wings had already been defeated and had turned their faces; and that the Sultan in the centre not heeding this led a furious assault. One account lastly states that the Sultan fell from his horse and was not known till night when slaves came searching for him among the slain on the battlefield. All this gives plausibility to the Rāsā account that the Sultan was captured. From the Tabakat even, it is clear that the Sultan was far from his men when wounded and turning back went on somehow for some time. It is likely that Dhīra Pundīra, a young Rajput from the Hindu side, seeing his condition rushed on and seized him. That he was set free and asked to fight again is not inconsistent with the chivalrous character of Prithvīrāj who perhaps imitated the tradition of Munja releasing his enemy Taila six times. It may further be added that Mahmud had released Jaipāl on ransom though he knew he would have to fight with him again.

NOTE:—2 MAHOMEDAN TACTICS AT THE LAST BATTLE.

The translation of the Tabakat by Raverty gives the following somewhat different version of the fighting in the last battle with Prithvīrāja (p. 467). "The Sultan made the disposition of his forces. The centre division of the army, baggage, banners, canopy and elephants were left several miles behind. He marshalled his ranks and advanced leisurely. The light-armed and unencumbered horsemen he had divided into four divisions and had appointed them to act against the infidels on four sides saying "on the right and left, front and rear, 10,000 mounted archers should keep the infidel force in play and when their elephants, horsemen and foot advanced to the attack, you are to face about and keep the distance of a horse's course in front of them. The Mussalman force kept the instructions and having wearied the unbelievers' force, Almighty God gave the victory to Islam and the infidel host was overthrown."

Major Raverty, a military officer remarks on this that the tactics above described are not quite clear. It is impossible for us to make any comment from the military point. But it is necessary to remark that in all the three great battles which Mahomedans won (two by Mahmud and one by Shihabuddin) the Mahomedan cavalry did great execution. The Hindus usually relied on their elephant force. Indeed in inscriptions, the usual praise is that the warriors broke open the temples of elephants. But from the days of Alexander elephants in India could not withstand trained cavalry. Elephants were used no doubt by Mahmud against the Turks of Turkestan but their cavalry was unaccustomed to the sight of elephants. Secondly, harassing and attacking the enemy both in front and rear is a great factor in securing victory. Shihabuddin purposely advanced slowly so as to allow his cavalry divisions to reach the enemy's front and rear. The ancient Hindu mode of fighting including Vyūhas of the Mahābhārata has yet to be studied by modern experts but we may remark that the Hindus were straight fighters and did not adopt deceptions or even surprizes. Lastly a strong reserve and a final attack in the centre by such reserve is often effective. Elephants, moreover, when defeated are a source of terror and destruction to their own force. Shihabuddin in this battle kept his elephants several miles behind.

NOTE:—3 THE RĀSĀ ACCOUNT OF THE LAST BATTLE.

It would be interesting to give here a summary of the account given in the Prithvīrāj Rāsā of the final fatal fight of Prithvīrāja with Shihabuddin Ghori, almost wholly imaginary as it is. We have often said that the Rāsā is plainly modelled after the Mahābhārata. Following it, it first gives the numerous evil omens that preceded the fight; it tells even of a curse on Prithvīrāja. It speaks further of Prithvīrāja having entirely neglected state affairs in his infatuation over his new queen Sanyogitā. Also it states that Prithvīrāja had affronted his sardar Hāhulīrai who consequently left him, went to Kangra and induced Shihabuddin to attack Prithvīrāja. There is no corroboration of this in Mahomedan accounts. The whole description of this battle seems to indicate that the Rajputs were already overpowered with a sense of the impending doom like the Marathas at Panipat. This is not what Mahomedan accounts would lead us to believe. Prithvīrāja had conquered in the first battle and in overweening confidence had even released Ghori. The fort of Sirhind had also just fallen. But the Rāsā misrepresents the whole story and gives a different time and place to this conflict. We have seen that the battle was fought in the very next year while Prithvīrāj was still before Sirhind. The Rāsā makes the battle come after some years after the capture of Shihabuddin and while Prithvīrāj was whiling away his time with Sanyogitā in Delhi. The place is given as the plain of Panipat; the whole Kurukshetra may be called the plain of Panipat; but though near enough the battle cannot be called a battle of Panipat.

The forces of Shihabuddin are described as numbering one lakh horse, nine lakh foot and ten thousand elephants. This is plainly an exaggeration. The Hindu army is estimated once at 80 thousand and again at 70 thousand. This is probably a correct estimate. Prithvīrāja's force must have been reduced by fatalities in the previous fight and also in the investiture of the fort of Sirhind. It seems that in this fight the Mahomedan army given as 125 thousand horse by their own writers outnumbered the Hindu army.

The disposition of the Hindu army, imaginary as it is, is given as follows :— Samarasinha on the left with 33 thousand supported by many sardars; on the right was Jaitrao Paramāra with 21; in the van was Chāmundarai with 19, and in the centre was Prithvīrāja overlooking the battle, with 10 thousand. This is also a description in the Mahābhārata fashion; and many names of noted ancestors of modern Rajput families are given as being with one or other army, a detail which is of perennial interest to the Rajput clans of India.

The practice of sending proposals of peace at the final moment and making recriminations, old as the Mahābhārata and recent as the modern European war, has also not been neglected. But the unhistorical nature of the messages is apparent when Shihabuddin demands half the Panjab only and delivery of the heir-apparent as hostage. The whole of the Panjab was already in the possession of Ghori. Indeed that province with Lahore was in the possession of the Mahomedans for nearly two hundred years before this battle.

The actual fight goes on for three or four days and different Vyūhas described in the Mahābhārata are also mentioned. Usually the fight resolves itself into duels between the different chiefs on both sides. In detail of imaginary fighting the Rāsā equals the Mahābhārata. And it follows it even in making repetitions. Prithvirāja is four times described as captured. Prithvīrāja slays many with his arrows, his sword and finally his dagger before he is seized. He is taken to Ghazni and there kept in prison and blinded. The story of Prithvīrāja killing Shihabuddin even in his blindness by his unerring aim, hearing the mere voice of Shihabuddin is the final embellishment of the Rāsā story which we have already disbelieved as a vengeance story likely to be concocted.

It may be added that, as in the Mahābhārata fight, all the leading generals on the side of Prithvīrāja are shown as killed in battle after deeds of great heroism. The date of the fight is, however, given correctly as Ānanda Vikrama Samvat 1158 which is equivalent to 1192 A. D.

CHAPTER XXI.

FALL OF AJMER AND KANAUJ

(I) AJMER AND DELHI

When Prithvīrāja was defeated and killed in the second conflict, memorable as the first of the battles wherein Hindu independence was finally lost, Shihabuddin, like a consummate general, at once advanced upon Ajmer the chief capital of his enemy. It fell without resistance and so much booty was obtained that " you might have said that the secret depositories of seas and hills were revealed. While the Sultan remained at Ajmer, he destroyed the idol temples and built in their place mosques and colleges". We have already stated that the building now called Adhai Dinki Jhopdi was originally a Sanskrit college built by Vigraharāja III (Taj. p. 215). Having conquered and plundered Ajmer like a consummate general, Shihabuddin entrusted the government of Ajmer to Prithvīrāj's son, like a consummate politician : he did not at once annex the conquered kingdom but made Rainsi, son of Prithvīrāja, king of Ajmer, no doubt paying a yearly tribute as a dependent king. The Taj says that " in him were discovered indexes of wisdom and prognostications of goodness " which means that he was good and wise enough to see the situation and accept subjugation and tribute. This, to our mind, makes it further certain that Prithvīrāja was not beheaded in Ajmer but was killed in battle, as his son Rainsi would not, in the former case, have thought it fit to accept the kingdom.

Having secured Ajmer, the Sultan marched against Delhi, the second capital of the Chauhans, where " he saw a fortress which in height and strength had no equal in the whole of India, " (E. II 26). " The fortress resisted and torrents of blood flowed on both sides " ; but eventually the governor submitted, " placed his head upon the line of slavery and made firm the conditions of tribute, Malgujari and service. " " The Sultan then returned to Ghazni but the army remained outside Delhi at the Mouza of Inderpat. " It is always necessary to keep an army in a conquered country to enforce subjection and the payment of tribute.

The author of the Tabakat states that " the capital Ajmer and all the Siwalik hills and Hānsi, Sarsuti and other districts were the results of the victory which was gained in the year 588 H. (1192 A. D.)." Siwalik hills mean here, as stated before, hills on the border of the Sapādalaksha or Ajmer kingdom. Kutubuddin was appointed governor and was placed in the fort of Kohram (?). Who was in Delhi at this time who first resisted and then submitted, cannot be determined. The Tabakat states that the governor of Delhi was killed in the final battle with Prithvīrāj; possibly there was another governor in Delhi in behalf of the Chauhans and he submitted seeing that Rainsi the king of Ajmer had accepted service.

But this respite was for a short time only. The stage of partial subjection was certain to be followed by final extinction and this next stage came on almost immediately. A Chief named 'Jatwan' by the Taj (this is plainly a misreading or miswriting for Chauhan in Persian) attacked the fort of Hānsi and Kutubuddin at once marched to its relief. A fierce battle was fought "the armies attacked each other like two hills of steel and the battle-field became tulip-red with the blood of the warriors. Jatwan was killed and the Hindus were signally defeated. Hānsi fort being relieved and repaired, Kutubuddin turned towards Meerut and conquered that fort. He finally attacked Delhi and captured that fort also". He entered the city which was then freed from idols and idol-worship and in the place of temples, mosques were raised." What gave the occasion for attacking Delhi again is not mentioned by the Taj. The Tabakat also in brief states that from thence (Kohram) he took possession of Meerut in 1193 and in the same year from thence captured Delhi. But it may be imagined that Kutubuddin was in need of a strong and important place to reside in and Ajmer being given to a son of Prithvīrāja, Delhi was the next best place to make the seat of his power. No reason needed to be given or a plausible reason is always at hand and Delhi finally became annexed to the Mahomedan kingdom. It became the capital of India a few years later as we shall presently see.

The turn of Ajmer came next. The Taj first states that rebellion was raised by Hiraj brother of Prithvīrāj (this is plainly a mis-writing for Hari Rāja) against the dependent Chauhan king at Ranthambhor and Kutubuddin flew to its relief. Harirāj fled and the Taj records that the son of Pithaura was honoured with a robe and he in return sent abundant treasures and three golden melons which with extreme ingenuity had been cast in moulds." Thus supported by the Mahomedans, Rainsi ruled for a time in Ajmer. What became of him hereafter is not apparent. Probably he died soon and he was succeeded by Harirāj himself who is now called Rai of Ajmer by the Taj (E. 11 225). He of course did not brook subjection and raised the standard of revolt. "Jehtar (?) advanced even to the border of Delhi the people of which were suddenly caught in the darkness of oppression." Kutubuddin sent against him the largest portion of his forces and when Jitwan was defeated, he in hot season advanced against Ajmer itself. Jhitar (or Hariraj) retired within the fort which was invested. "Finally in despair he sacrificed himself in the flames of a pyre and the fort was then easily taken." The country of Ajmer was restored to the honours of ancient times and religion was re-established." The roads were freed from robbers and the oppressed subjects were delivered from their distresses." This clearly means that the country was annexed and ordered government was established. The subordinate Rais and Rāṇas (Zamindars) submitted and "the earth was rubbed by the foreheads of chiefs and celebrated men of Hind." After settling the affairs of Ajmer, Kutubuddin returned to Delhi. This event happened in 1194 A. D. and Ajmer henceforward always remained a province of the Mahomedan Empire.

These facts are corroborated by an inscription at Manglānā (Marwar) published in I. A. XLI (p. 87) dated Samvat 1272 or 1215 A. D., dedicating a step-well and imposing some cesses recorded by a feudatory Dāhimā prince. The inscription first records the name of the Mahomedan emperor then ruling as Shamsuddin Suratrāṇa (Sultān), Hamir (Amir), king of Gor-Garjana (Ghazni and Ghor) under whom ruled at Raṇthambhor Valaṇadeva. This shows that Raṇthambhor was now the capital of the Chauhans and their king was Valaṇadeva whom the editor of this inscription Pandit Ramākarṇa of Jodhpur identifies with Vallaṇa, grandson of Prithvīrāja through Govinda, from the Hammīra Kāvya. It seems probable that while Rainsi became king in Ajmer, he gave Raṇthambhor to Govinda a brother of his and Harirāj being opposed to the Mahomedan rule first attacked Raṇthambhor. He subsequently seized Ajmer itself on Rainsi's death and was eventually crushed by Kutubuddin.

(2) FALL OF KANAUJ AND BENARES.

Ajmer and Delhi having fallen and the Chauhans having accepted subjection, Shihabuddin next turned his attention to the subjugation of the next powerful kingdom in Northern India, viz. that of the Gāhadavālas of Kanauj and Benares. It is commonly believed that Jaichand had in fact incited Shihabuddin to attack Prithvīrāj as he was his enemy; and he thus fell eventually a prey to the enemy he had himself called in. But so far as we have ascertained, there is no evidence to hold that Jaichand had ever called in the foreign foe. It may be that he did not assist Prithvīrāja when he collected a confederate army to oppose Ghori; probably Prithvīrāja did not call for such aid. The collection of a confederate army by Prithvīrāja is spoken of by the Tabakat as stated already. Who were the kings that joined Prithvīrāja, we have no historical record to determine. The story of the Rāsā that Samarasinha fought on the side of Prithvīrāja is belied by inscriptions which show that Samarasinha lived a hundred years later and we may even doubt if a Guhilot king (who must be Sāmantasinha and not Samarasinha) was among the allies. Whatever this may be, we have no evidence to hold that Jaichand had incited the attack. No Mahomedan historian mentions it and the Rāsā has no value as history of Prithvīrāja. Jayachand's turn came not as a punishment but as a natural next step in the conquest of Hindustan aspired to by the ambitious Muhammad Ghori.

The rhapsodical Taj does not give any details of this conflict. It says simply that "the Sultan advanced from Ghazni with 50,000 horsemen clad in armour (E. II p. 222–23). The Rai of Benares, Jaichand, chief of idolatry, opposed him with an army countless as the particles of sand. The Rai who prided himself upon the number of his forces and war elephants, seated on a lofty howdah, received a deadly wound from an arrow and fell." "The impurities of idolatry were purged from that land and immense booty was obtained, such as the eye would be weary to look at." "The imperial army then took possession of the fort of Asni where the treasure of the Rai was deposited." The Tabakat dismisses this conflict with the short sentence (E. II. 297) that the Sultan came back from Ghazni in the year 590 H. (1193 A. D.) by way of Benares and Kanauj and defeated the Rai Jaichand in the neighbourhood of Chandanwah and captured over 300 elephants." It is a pity that the author of the Tabakat does not give a more detailed account of this conflict which he probably thought was of less importance than that with Prithvīrāj. But Jaichand was the most powerful monarch in India and he was a proud and brave Rathod who, unlike Rājyapāla, firmly opposed and bravely fought against the formidable foe of his religion and independance. It was, therefore, to be expected that greater details would be given of the memorable battle at Chandanwah which place is said to be somewhere between Kanauj and Etawa. Indian records do not also give us any details of this event; but tradition (Abul Fazal) tells us that Jaichand died by drowning in the Ganges while crossing the river on his elephant. Putting the contemporary Mahomedan evidence and this tradition together, we may believe that Jaichand was wounded in battle and in order to avoid being captured led his elephant into the Ganges and like a devout and dauntless Hindu sought death by Jalasamādhi and drowned himself in the Ganges. The Tabakat says that search was made on the battle-field for Jaichand's body but it was not found. It, however, adds that after a long search, a body was discovered which was believed to be Jaichand's from his old age. (This is from some later account given in the Tabakat by Raverty p. 470–Note.) But Jaichand could not have been an old man; he came to the throne in 1169 when young and died in 1193 after 24 years of reign. *

After plundering Kanauj and Asni, Shihabuddin naturally pressed on to conquer and plunder Benares which was the second capital of the Gāhadavālas. The Taj thus describes this event. "The royal army proceeded to Benares and there one thousand temples were destroyed and mosques were raised on their foundations and the face of the Dinar and Dirham was adorned with the blessed name and titles of the king." This means that the country was annexed, Hindu coins of gold and silver being restruck with the Name of Shihabuddin. "When the king had settled all the affairs of the city and its vicinity and the record of his celebrated holy war had been written in history and circulated throughout the world," he returned. He halted at Asni for some days "where the chiefs and elders all around hastened to offer submission and rarities as presents."

* We were told at Kanauj that there was a Persian Bakhar there giving details of the storming of the temple of Lakshmi called Sitā Rasoi temple (a place where Sitā had cooked food for Rāma) which has now been converted into a mosque, wherein the many pillars of the old temple are still retained. There was a most desperate fight at the storming of this temple in the fort and hundreds of Rajput and Mahomedan warriors were killed in the fight.

This shows that the country itself offered no resistance and the people accepted readily and quietly the change of government, a fact on which we will comment later on. Shihabuddin returned to Ghazni leaving Kutubuddin as his viceroy.

MINOR OPERATIONS.

Kutubuddin whose life we shall presently relate was a most capable governor and administered justice with such impartiality that " The wolf and the sheep drank water out of the same pond. " (Taj. E. II p. 225.) This certainly assisted the pacification of the country but he also severely punished rebellious persons. " There was a certain tribe in the neighbourhood of Kol which gave great trouble and they were so completely slaughtered that three bastions were raised with their heads. " The rebellion of Harirāj at Ajmer, as we have already noticed, was put down by Kutubuddin in 1195 A. D. In 1196 Shihabuddin again came to Hindustan and Kutubuddin joined him. They marched on Thanger which had a strong castle and the place was invested. Kunwar Pāla on finding it impossible to resist asked for pardon. "His life was spared but his kingdom was annexed." (Taj. E. II p. 227). This place cannot be identified; (Gaurishankar states that this Kunwar Pāla was a king of the Kerowli Yādava line and was driven out of Biyana at this time; Tod p. 346). It seems that the Sultan was bent on reducing the various strongholds of opposition in the conquered territory; and he next invested the fortress of Gwalior. The Taj states that Solankhapāla, its king, offered submission and tribute and was pardoned and even allowed to retain the fort. The Sultan then returned to Ghazni, leaving Kutubuddin again his viceroy, who continued the work of reducing refractory chieftains. He assisted Muhammad Ghori in reducing to subjection the troublesome Gakkhars. Muhammad Ghori was murdered, as stated before, by these Gakkhars on the left bank of the Indus in 1205 A. D.

Kutubuddin was elected Sultan and Emperor of India by the Turkish nobles and generals in Hindustan and this position was recognised by the king of Ghor, Shihabuddin's brother, who had probably no ambition to rule both Ghazni and India. Thus began the independent Slave Turkish dynasty in India with Delhi as capital which Kutubuddin made his chief place of residence.

NOTE—'KUTUB MINAR'.

Whether the Kutub Minar is by design and construction Mahomedan from the beginning or whether it is a conversion of a pre-existing Kīrtistambha into a Minar by Kutub-ud-din and Altamash is a question which has engaged the attention of researchers from General Cunningham down to R. B. Dayaram Sahani, Archaeological Superintendent, Panjab Circle. The theory that it was a pre-existing Kīrtistambha was ably put forward some years ago by Mr. Kanwar Sain, M. A. (then Principal, Law College, Lahore, now Chief Justice, Kashmir State) and is still maintained by him though he accepts the reading of Samvat 1704, instead of 1204, in a Sanskrit inscription on the Minar, now given by Mr. Sahani. It must be noted that besides Arabic texts from the Koran inscribed on the outer surface of the first story of the Minar, and certain Persian inscriptions mentioning the name of Shihab-ud-din, Ghiyas-ud-din, Qutub-ud-din and Altmash, there are strangely enough some Sanskrit inscriptions and Hindi too, in the several storeys of the Minar; but these are all of later date than 1193 A. D. and need not be much discussed as the only inscription supposed by Mr. Kanwar Sain to be Samvat 1204 old is also now accepted by him to be dated in Samvat 1704.

But the chief arguments advanced by Mr. Kanwar Sain still remain. That the Minar is not a Ma'azina or prayer-call tower is accepted by all and is clear as the Minar has no connection with the Kutub mosque. Secondly, there is no Persian or Arabic inscription on the Minar recording *its erection* by Kutub-ud-din or Altamash though their names merely appear. Thirdly, the Arabic texts appear to have been subsequently inscribed on the outer surface of the lower storey, if critically examined. The original stones appear to have been taken out and replaced as Mr. Beglar, Archaeological Assistant of General Cunningham actually found. There are other indications also that these bands of inscriptions were subsequently put up.

It is not possible to give in this note all the pros and cons of this theory or notice the several inscriptions in Arabic, Persian and Nāgari and explain them. Dr. Horovitz has puplished all the Arabic and Persian inscriptions and Gordon Sanderson avoided going into the controversy which he says " is still going on whether the Minar is of Hindu or Mahomedan origin ". He remarks, however, that the only claim, on the architectural ground, that the Minar has a Hindu origin viz: that its starlike plan resembles the form of certain old Hindu temples, is weakened by the existence of Minars on a similar plan *believed* to exist at Ghazni". ....The Sanskrit and Nāgarī inscriptions have not yet all been studied and examined and R. B. Dayaram Sahani is not yet positive about his view. Under the circumstances the question is still not settled. It is, however, necessary to point out that the architectural argument advanced by Mr. Kanwar Sain is based not only on the starlike plan, but on the position of the bands of Arabic letters as also on Mr. Beglar's statement that the stones appear to have been replaced.

We may lastly point out that the practice of raising Kīrtistambhas is very old in India (vide Raghu canto XII verse*) and we find in a Sena

* कीर्तिस्तम्भद्वयमिव तटे दक्षिणे चोत्तरे च ॥

inscription that Lakshmaṇa Sena of Lakhnauti raised (three) Kīrti-stambhas in Allahabad, Benares and Jagannāth. It is probable that this Kīrtistambha upto the first storey was built by Vīsaladeva Chauhan whose conquest of the whole of Northern India and whose driving out of Mlechhas from Āryāvarta and making it real Āryāvarta (verse already quoted) was memorable and is commemorated on the Siwalik Pillar of Delhi. It is possible that Vīsala after his arduous conquest of Delhi ("fatigued in the capture of Delhi"-Bijoliya insc.) raised a column of victory in the Lalkot of Anangapāla. Vīsala is nearly contemporaneous with Lakshmaṇsena and both were emperors, the first in the west and the second in the east of Northern India. The latter is recorded, as stated above, to have raised victory pillars and it is plausible to hold that Vīsala raised a column at Delhi.

We have already shown in Chauhan chapter that Vīsala built the college at Ajmer which was converted by order of Shihabuddin into the present mosque (called Adhai-Dinki-Jhopadi); Vīsala's inclination to build memorable structures is thus apparent. It is likely, however, that his Kīrtistambha remained at the finishing of the first storey as he died soon after his conquest. His successor Prithvīrāja II had also a short reign as also Someśvara. Perhaps they might have continued the building even in the days of Prithvīrāj III. After the conquest of Delhi by Kutubuddin he built a mosque by throwing down temples and utilizing their columns. It is natural that he should convert the Kīrtistambha of Vīsala into a Mahomedan Minar and Altamash built the third and forth storeys and completed it.

Whoever the original author was, there is no doubt, we think, on architectural grounds, that the present Minar is an old Kīrtistambha converted into a Mahomedan Minar.

CHAPTER XXII.

THE FALL OF OTHER RAJPUT KINGDOMS IN NORTHERN INDIA.

Ajmer and Delhi, Kanauj and Benares having fallen before Shihabuddin Ghori and the two most powerful Rajput kingdoms having been conquered and annexed, the other Rajput kingdoms of Northern India fell with ease and with almost amazing suddenness within a quarter of a century and the whole of Northern India was finally enslaved by the Mahomedans. The story of this fall, as given by Mahomedan historians, must necessarily be appalling; but exaggerated as the account may be, it is not incredible, as Northern India was ready to fall for reasons which we will discuss in a separate chapter. Although most of these events happened after 1200 A. D. they are so intimately connected with this history that we can not conclude this book without describing them. They form the closing chapter in the history of Mediaeval Hindu India, though Hindu kingdoms in the south continued to exist for a century more.

This work of conquering the other Hindu kingdoms of Northern India was carried out by the generals of Shihabuddin and chiefly by his slave Kutubuddin. It is extremely surprizing to read that in those times, among the Mahomedans, slaves especially those brought from Turkestan were treated in a manner diametrically the opposite of that in which Negro slaves were treated by Christians in America and elsewhere. The history of Kutubuddin is indeed marvellous; from an ordinary slave, he rose to be the first emperor of India. He was not even a handsome man and he was called Aibak because he had lost the little finger of his right hand. But he was powerful in body and valorous in battle. He had remarkable wisdom which enabled him to rise from place to place and his generosity was so great that Mahomedan historians delight in telling stories of his munificence, one of which is that as Emperor of India he never made gifts of less than a lakh of rupees. Kutubuddin, when a boy, was sold to the Kazi of Nishapur in Khorasan and at his house, along with his sons, he learned horsemanship and the use of arms, a treatment which indeed does immense credit to his Mahomedan master. From the Kazi he was taken by a merchant to Ghazni where he was purchased by Shihabuddin Ghori and employed in the army and in the civil administration of his empire. He rose from place to place till he was appointed governor of his Indian provinces beyond the Panjab at Kohram after the fall of Prithvirāja.

We give this short history of the rise of this great general because we believe in the influence of the personality of individuals, of great men who are born from time to time to mould the destinies of nations. The rise of the Mahomedan power in India and the fall of Hindu kingdoms may in part be attributed to the birth of such men as Mahmud, Shihabuddin and Kutubuddin. The author of the Tabakat-i-Nasiri, in beginning the history of this great man, observes properly "When the Almighty God wishes to exhibit to his people an example of greatness and majesty, he endows one of his slaves with the qualities of courage and generosity and then friends and enemies are influenced by his bounteous munificence and warlike prowess" (E. II p. 298). Such men, witness Shivaji or Bajirao, easily collect bands of brave warriors about them and eventually become the founders of kingdoms and kingly lines. The work of conquering Northern India was carried out by Kutubuddin and also by Altamash also a slave from Turkestan brave generous and fortunate like Kutubuddin himself who gave his daughter in marriage to him. It is also surprising to find that hese slaves continued to be slaves even when they rose to the highest position and letters of freedom were given them at a very late stage in their life. The history of their conquests we give from Taj-ul-Ma'sir the almost contemporary history already quoted and from Tabakat-i-Nasiri also a nearly contemporary account written in the days of Nasiruddin.

1 ANHILWAD.

The first kingdom to fall next was that of Anhilwad or Gujarat, an event which we have already described from Gujarat Chālukya records. But we must give also the account given by the contemporaneous Mahomedan history Taj-ul-Ma'sir. It relates that in 1195 when Kutubuddin was again at Ajmer he was informed that the Mers (who were then Hindus) had invited an army from Naharwala. He sent an army to oppose and forestall that movement, but that army was defeated and pursued to Ajmer, the fort of which appears to have been even invested by Naharwala forces. Kutubuddin requested reinforcements from Ghazni which were sent. The army of Gujarat appears to have then retired. The Mahomedans now took the offensive and advanced on Gujarat. "The lofty forts of Pali and Nadul were found abandoned, the Hindus had collected at the foot of Mount Abu under Rai Karan and Dārāburs in the mouth of a pass." As Muhammad Ghori had been defeated in that very pass before, the Mahomedans would not attack them there. They, therefore, made a feint as if they were terrified and retreated towards Ajmer. The Hindus leaving the pass came into the open to attack them. A severe action was fought and the Hindus were signally defeated, most of the Hindu leaders being killed or taken prisoners. Rai Karan escaped ; but twenty thousand slaves, twenty elephants and arms beyond computation fell into the hands of the victors. "You would have thought that the treasures of the kings of the inhabited world had come into their possession. The city of Naharwala and the kingdom of Gujarat came under the dominion of the Mussalmans. The standards of victorious Khusru returned to Ajmer and thence to Delhi. Kutubuddin sent to Ghazni various treasures and rarities" (E. II p. 280-1).

This account shows that Kutubuddin after his victory somewhere near Mount Abu must have proceeded to Naharwala (Patan) and occupied and plundered that city. This event is said to have happened in 1197 A. D. but as stated before, Bhīma issues a grant from Anhilwad Patan in 1199 A. D. It seems, therefore, that Anhilwad was occupied later in 1199. The fact that Gujarat was overrun and the capital occupied appears clear from the reference to the terrible condition of Gujarat described in the grant of Jayantasinha dated 1202 who, after Bhīma had fled, retrieved the fortunes of Chālukya arms and driving out the Mahomedans recovered Gujarat and its capital and ruled for a time in Anhilwad in place of Bhīma. The destruction of some of the temples built by Siddharāja Jayasinha may be dated at this time. Gujarat was sorely shaken, but was not finally subjugated by the Mahomedans till a century later.

2 KALANJAR

Having destroyed the power of Gujarat and secured Ajmer, Kutubuddin turned his attention towards the next powerful Hindu kindom on his border and attacked Kalanjar. We have already given the history of this attack in the chapter on the Chandellas and we will only give here a few particulars from the account given in the contemporaneous Taj-ul-Ma'sir. "In 599 H. or 1202 A. D., Kutubuddin accompanied by Altamash marched against Kalanjar. The accursed Parmar (Paramardideva) fled into the fort but after a desperate resistance submitted and accepted the same terms as had been imposed upon his ancestor by Mahmud. He, however, died and his Mehta Ajadeo was not disposed to surrender so easily and gave much trouble. He too was compelled to capitulate in consequence of a severe drought which dried up all the reservoirs of water in the fort. The fort of Kalanjar, celebrated throughout the world, was taken and the temples there were converted into mosques. Fifty thousand men were carried into slavery. Twenty elephants and countless arms were among the spoils. The reins of victory were then directed against Mahoba. The government of the country was conferred upon Hasan Amiral." This account as that about Gujarat is corroborated by Chandel inscriptions. The Chandellas obtained back the possession of Kalanjar and a large part of Chandel territory and like the Chālukyas of Gujarat lived as an independent ruling family for a century more as detailed in the chapter on the Chandellas.

3 LAKHNAUTI

The third kingdom on the borders of Mahomedan rule now firmly established in Delhi, Kanauj and Benares was the kingdom of Bengal under the Senas; and the history of the fall of Bengal is the most marvellous that has been recorded by historians. The conquest was made by Mahammad son of Bakhtyar Khilji and not by Kutubuddin and the account of it is to be found not in the contemporaneous Taj-ul-Ma'sir but is given by the author of the Tabakat-i-Nisiri from admittedly hearsay reports.

We give the account as given by the Tabakat with such comment as seems proper. Mahammad Bakhtyar was a Khilji (not Turk but Afghan) adventurer who sought employment and fortune under the expanding power of Shihabuddin Ghori. It is natural that when victorious people conquer countries far and wide, turbulent spirits from the home country come forward in numbers to advance their fortunes (as Maratha cavaliers did under Shivaji or Bajirao) and find employment as military administrators of newly conquered territories. Mahammad Bakhtyar Khilji was one such hair-brained adventurer who after some refusals obtained employment as governor of Mirzapur. Collecting an army of Turks and Afghans, he first attacked Bihar and conquered it, plundering town and country. He is said to have seized a Buddhist settlement described as a Vihāra (probably Vikramaśila) and massacred all the defenceless shaven-headed Brahmins (Buddhists) and thrown away their sacred books "which none was left to read or explain." This event probably happened in 1199 A. D. as Mahammad Bakhtyar is described by Taj-ul-Ma'sir as appearing before Kutubuddin with presents from the conquest of Oudh and Bihar (probably at Mahoba). He was honoured with a robe and again sent to Bihar.

"He then planned the conquest of Bengal and secretly prepared an army and suddenly made a raid on Nadia the capital of Bengal. In his impetuosity he reached the city with only eighteen horsemen with him and entering it in an inoffensive manner, looking as if he were a dealer in horses, reached the palace and at once drawing swords attacked the guards. The palace was in consternation and none opposed him. The aged king Lakshmaṇasena heard the uproar as he was about to sit to dinner and knowing the reality fled by the back door. He escaped and went to Jagannath. The palace and the city were taken possession of by the army which soon arrived. It is needless to say that there was no resistance and the city was plundered and even destroyed. Mahammad Bakhtyar made Gaur or Lakhanauti his captial which was the principal capital of the Sena kings."

Doubts have been expressed about the truth of this account. That the political government of Bengal should have been so lax and supine as not to know of the advance of an army over such a great distance (Vikramaśila to Nadia) or that there was no preparedness to resist the dangerous enemy, when the whole country has talking of the fall of Delhi and Kanauj or that there was actually not a single blow struck in defence of Nadia or the kingdom is indeed strange. This is, however, a sheer exaggeration of the Mahomedan informants of the author of the Tabakāt-i-Nasiri if not of the historian himself. The absurd story that the birth of king Lakhamaṇia was delayed for the arrival of the fortunate moment of birth by tying up the feet of the pregnant queen which is told in the Tabakat is proof enough of the absurd nature of the whole story. This event is placed by the Tabakat in 1199, the 80th year of the Lakshmaṇasena era, but it probably happened after his death and in about

1202 A. D. The account tries to explain the entire absence of defence by Lakshmaṇa by the supposed superstitions of the Brahmin counsellors of the old king who had told him long before that the kingdom was fated to be taken by a Turk according to the prognostications of astrology. It is even added that when the king enquired what the mark of the conqueror would be, it was stated by the learned astrologers that the conqueror would have long arms reaching below the knees. The king sent men to ascertain what Turk had that mark and Mahammad Bakhtyar was found to have such long arms. There may be some truth in the fact that the resistance of the Hindus was weakened to some extent by the foretelling of the Purāṇas that Bhāratavarsha was fated to be conquered by Mlechhas or the absurd and fearful prognostications of astrologers. But the above story is on the face of it too absurd to be true and we at once set down this account of the fall of Bengal as exaggerated and untrue and Bengal may be taken to have fallen after much resistance against Mahamad Bakhtyar and not all at once but gradually as in the case of Gujarat and Bundelkhand.

For, this account of the Tabakat written about 1250 A. D. distorted as it must be from the natural desire of the bragging adventurers who accompanied Mahmmad Bakhtyar to exaggerate the courage of the conquerors and the cowardice of the conquered, as also from the inaptitude of foreigners coming suddenly into the midst of a strange people to understand their feelings and their ideas, and thirdly probably from a wish to have a hit at the Hindu belief in astrology, this foreign account must be tested and equated with the evidence of a contemporaneous Indian record, viz. the Bakerganj inscription of Keśavasena (J. R. A. S. Bengal Vol. VII pp. 40–50). This inscription no doubt exaggerates the prowess both of Lakshmaṇasena and his son, the grantor Keśavasena, and thus errs on the other side. But it makes no mention whatever of this ignominious defeat of Lakshmaṇasena. It may be urged that its omission was natural as inscriptions rarely record the defeats of the inscriptor; though disastrous fights with Turushkas are mentioned even in inscriptions as in Gujarat and Bundelkhand; but we may at least take into account the fact that Lakshmaṇasena is herein rightly praised as a valiant king who had raised three victory columns at Allahabad, Benares and Jagannath. It is impossible to believe that the valiant Lakshmaṇasena fled without striking a blow. Secondly we must admit that Keśavasena was still a powerful king ruling in Eastern Bengal. It is, therefore, certain that the descendants of Lakshmaṇasena ruled in Eastern Bengal for a long time after this event. It is also possible that Nadia may have been attacked after the death of Lakshmaṇasena during Mādhavasena's reign whose name appears to have been *erased* from this Bakerganj cooper-plate (ditto p. 42). We, therefore, think that if we put the two opposite accounts together, we can only believe that Bengal fell after much resistance and not all at once, as already stated.

But even if it be conceded that the account given by the Tabakat represents facts, these are not as dishonourable as is usually supposed. In the first place it must be noted that Nadia was not the chief capital of the Senas. It was a Brahmin settlement newly made, which was almost a Brahmin vihāra, in an island of the Ganges and Lakshmaṇasena only occasionally resided there. The guards at the place must have been few and the army in the city only nominal. Secondly, a sudden raid on such a place is not impracticable.* Indeed such raids are recorded in history. Allauddin made such a sudden and willy raid on Devagiri in the Deccan a hundred years after this event. Nay only five years after this event, Shihabuddin Ghori the conqueror of Hindustan was surprised in his tent pitched on the eastern bank of the Indus by a few Gakkhars who eluding guards reached the place through water and murdered Shihabuddin. Thirdly, to escape from such an attack and start fresh resistance from a new capital was not at all dishonourable but on the contrary proper and creditable. This was what Rājyapāla of Kanauj or Bhīma of Gujarat did against Mahmmud or Rajaram did in Maratha history against Aurangjeb and this is what even modern governments do. They give up the capital attacked and making another town the capital, carry on resistance from there. This is exactly what Lakshmaṇasena and his descendants appear to have done. They established themselves at Vikrampur which was an important town to the East of Nadia (a grant issued from Vikrampur by Lakshamaṇasena has been found) and ruled for nearly a century more in Eastern Bengal, continuing their resistance

*The coming of Mahomedan dealers in horses was again a common thing at that time, at capitals of kings. Arab and Persian horses were prized by Hindu kings who paid high prices for them and Mahomedan dealers in horses constantly visited Hindu camps in those days and it was a common incident exciting no suspicion at all.

to the Mahomedans, as in Gujarat or in Bundelkhand. The Tabakat-i-Nasiri records that when Nasiruddin marched on Lakhnauti, the Khilji had marched his forces from Lakhnauti "with the intention of entering the territory of Bang," i. e. against the Sena king (Raverty p. 629). Why such resistance eventually failed to re-establish Hindu power not only in Bengal but in the other parts of Northern India also, is the real question and the cause of this failure we will discuss at length later on.

Kutubuddin conquered or humbled the strong kingdoms on the borders of his Mahomedan empire. The work of destroying kingdoms a little more remote was carried out by his successor Altamash who was an equally brave and fortunate Sultan. Altamash was like Kutubuddin a slave but his valour was noted by Shihabuddin and he was given his deed of freedom and preferred from place to place by him as also by Kutubuddin who gave his daughter in marriage to him, having originally purchased him at Delhi as the Sultan had forbidden his sale and purchase at Ghazni (Tabakat, E. II 322). When Kutubuddin died at Lohur (Lahore), the commander-in-chief of Delhi with the consent of nobles invited Shamsuddin Altamash from Badaun where he was governor and elected him Sultan. Some officers and governers like Kubacha opposed the election but they were defeated ; " by divine favour every one who opposed or rebelled was subdued and all territories belonging to Delhi Badaun, Oudh, Benares and the Siwalik hills came into his possession." Even Lahore was taken from Yildus and Sind and Bakkhar from Kubacha in 1217 A. D. (E. II 324). Altamash subdued Bengal under Ghiyasuddin Baktyar who acknowledged him suzerain and paid him tribute (1225).

4 RANTHAMBHOR AND MANDAWAR.

Thus the Mahomedan Empire of Delhi came into the possession of another capable sovereign and he naturally turned his attention towards first conquering refractory Hindu nobles in his own territory. "In 623 H. (1226) he marched against Ranthambhor before which seventy sovereigns had failed. The Sultan's servants by the favour of the Creator took it. In 624 H. (1227) he marched against Mandawar within the Siwalik (territory) and its capture likewise, the Almighty facilitated and the sultan returned with much booty " (Raverty's Tabakat p. 611). These two places were probably in the possession of Chauhan chiefs and they proving refractory were attacked and dispossessed.

We have seen that Ranthambhor had been attacked by Kutubuddin also but the chief had then submitted and been spared. Ranthambhor was again taken by the Chauhans and its last king was the valorous Hammir hero of the Hammira Mahākāvya. There is some dispute as to what Mandawar was and the mention of its location in Siwalik (not hills as in E. II but territory as in Raverty) leads to some doubt. Hānsi is similarly supposed to be in the Siwalik hills at the base of the Himalayas but it really is a place in Karnal District. But we have already shown that Siwalik meant Sapādalaksha territory of the Chauhans of Sambhar (Vol. II p. 36). Probably Mandawar which was originally the seat of Nāhararai Pratihāra conquered by Prithvīrāja, was now a part of the dominions of the Chauhans and a Chauhan chief was ruling there. Mandawar is now in ruins and is about 4 miles from the modern city of Jodhpur.

5 GWALIOR

The next place which Altamash attacked was the fort of Gwalior which had been spared by Kutubuddin on its submission. This was a strong place within the Mahomedan empire and required to be seized. This place was not now in the possession of the Kachhwahas who seem to have removed to Amber a more distant place. It was in possession of Parihāras who (according to Gwaliornāmā published by Prince Balawantrao Bhayyasaheb Scindia) had seized the place. The Gwaliar Gazetteer states that the Parihāras took the fort from Kachhawahas in 1129 A. D. Solankhapāla from whom Kutubiddin took it was a Parihāra. It was put in possession of Altamash in 1210 and was retaken by the Parihāras and hence this attack by him. "In 629 H. (1232 A. D.) Altmash marched against the fort and invested it. Malikdeo (Raverty reads Mangaldev) son of Basil (Raverty reads Maldev) began the fight. For 11 months the army sat before it. At last Malikdeo fled at night. About 500 men received punishment before the tent of the king. After appointing officers to Gwalior the Sultan returned to Delhi." (E. II p. 327). We think that the men punished were those of the Sultan's army itself who had been careless enough to allow Malik to escape and not men of Malikdeo; for none is stated here to have been captured nor could they be described as punished. And further an inscription on the Gwalior fort existing in Baber's time showed that Rajput ladies on the fort destroyed themselves in a pyre and the place is still called Johartal (Gwalior Gazetteer p. 125). The Rajput soldiers must have either died in the attack on the investing army or escaped. The subsequent history of the fort of Gwalior is given by Prince Balvantrao Bhayyasaheb which we need not give here in detail. The place changed hands often, the Tuars taking it in the days of Timur and holding it for a time when it was taken again by Babar. During Mogul days it was used as a prison for princes. It was again taken by Bhadaura kings from whom it was taken by Scindia. From them it was taken by the English twice but it is now with Scindia.

6 BHELSA AND UJJAIN.

"In 632 H. (1234 A. D.) Altamash sent an army against Malwa and took the city and fort of Bhelsa. There was a temple there which was three hundred years in building. It was 105 gaj high. It was demolished" (E. II p. 328). This was probably the famous Bhaillaswāmin (sun) temple mentioned by Al-Beruni. The Garudastambha inscription of the 1st century B. C. belonged probably to a vishṇu temple on the other side of the river Betwa which probably had already fallen.

Whatever this may be, the Udepur temple of Śiva some miles distant from Bhelsa is not the one referred to here. For this temple built by Udayāditya Paramāra which has also a very high pinnacle still survives to attest the glory of the Paramāra rule. This event happened during the reign of the last Paramāra king Devapāla who, as stated in the chapter on the later Parmāras, ruled from 1216 to 1240 A. D.

"From Bhelsa he (Altamash) proceeded to Ujjain where there was the temple of Mahākāla which he destroyed as well as an image of Vikramāditya who ruled Malwa 1346 years before this time. The Hindu era dates from his reign (as this figure leads to 1289 A. D. as the date of the capture of Ujjain which really is 1234 A. D. we may take 55 years as the length of Vikrama's rule). Some other images cast in copper were carried to Delhi with the stone image of Mahākāla" (E. II p. 328). There is no reason to doubt the truth of this concise unexaggerated statement, though we find no corroborating contemporaneous Hindu record. The temple of Mahākāla was then converted into a mosque which, history tells us, was again converted into a Hindu temple of Mahākāla in the days of

Ranoji Scindia whose descendants still rule in Ujjain and worship Mahākāla. It may be mentioned that the present high-pinnacled temple of Mahākāla was built by the Shenvi Diwan of Ranoji Scindia, Ramchandra Bābā, who was childless and who, therefore, used most of his wealth in this great work (1745 A. D.). Probably the present temple stands in the very place where the old temple stood. It may also be noted that later on the Mahomedan rulers of Malwa allowed the Hindus to have a Mahākāla idol set up at a short distance from the original temple (destroyed and converted into a mosque) and it is known now as the Vridhha or old Mahākāla.

This expedition into Malwa was apparently for the sole purpose of destroying famous Hindu idols, a religious expedition in the manner of the Somnath expedition of Mahmud. There was no attempt at conquest of Malwa and its reduction into a Mahomedan province. Probably the territory was too distant and not contiguous like Gwalior. We have already stated that the Paramāra rule endured for about a century more just as Gujarat remained under Chālukyas for about the same time. Malwa was finally conquered by Allauddin Khilji.

7 NAGDA, CAPITAL OF MEWAD.

We have sketched above the fall of almost all the leading Hindu kingdoms of Northern India, Chauhan, Rathod, Chandella Chālukya, Sena, Paribāra and Paramāra. The Guhilots of Mewad came in their turn to be attacked later. Though we have not many details, we find that Mewad was attacked in the days of Nasiruddin while Jaitrasinh was ruling (1253 A. D.) and that its capital Nagda was destroyed. The Mahomedans were, however, defeated by Jaitrasinh and its hill capital Chitod remained intact. It continued to rule with vigour till even Chitod was taken by Allauddin Khilji.

CHAPTER XXIII.

THE DOWNFALL OF NORTHERN INDIA —PRINCIPAL CAUSES.

The causes which led to the downfall of Northern India must be, and indeed are, different from those which led to the downfall of the Panjab. In the Panjab there were no Rajput kingdoms. Panjab, as stated before, was always ruled from outside, by Sind, by Kashmir, by Kabul. Northern India was always ruled by Hindu and local kings. Panjab was usually the land of foreign invasions and of foreign rule. Northern India had always defeated and driven out foreign invaders. Alexander did not cross the Sutlej at all. Menander came as far as Ayodhya but was eventually driven out by Pushpamitra. The Śakas came as far as Mathura but were driven away by Vikramāditya. The Kushans and the Huns indeed ruled rather long in the western part of Northern India but they were driven away by Skandagupta of Patna, by Vishnuvardhana of Mandsaur and finally by Pratāpavardhana of Thanesar. From 600 A. D. down to 1000 A. D. there were no foreign invasions. Mahmud indeed conquered Rājyapāl and imposed a tribute on Northern India but the Gāhadavālas soon drove out the foreign foe and stopped the tribute, while Rājyapāla had even been killed by the Chandellas and Kachhwahas for submitting to Mahomedan yoke. In short the Aryan kings of Northern India had always held their own against foreign invaders. The Rajput kingly families of the Hindu period were unquestionably most heroic and did not brook submisson. Why did they fall before Shihabuddin Ghori? There could be no lack of armies or of capable generals. Indeed Prithvīrāja was the greatest warrior put forward by the indomitable Chauhans to oppose the Mahomedan onslaught. He had actually defeated four kings successively. He held up the flood of Mahomedan conquest like a strong bund. Strangely enough as soon as the bund gave way, the flood rushed over the whole of Northern India and uprooted all the Rajput kingdoms within the course of twenty five years. Why did the heroic Rajput kingly families, like the Chauhans and the Rathods, the Chandellas and the Paramāras, the Solankhis and the Haihayas succumb and why did Northern India fall so completely as never to rise again?

There was no superiority of physique or valour in favour of the Mahomedan combatants. The Rajputs were as hardy, powerful or heroic as the Turks and Afghans who conquered them. There was no difference of weapons. Neither the Afghans nor the Rajputs had fire-Arms. Both fought with the same weapons, the sword, the lance and the arrow. Both had elephants in perhaps equal numbers. The Moguls indeed conquered the Rajputs by the use of cannon; and so did the Marathas under Scindia. As stated already, before the scientific weapons of destruction of the western nations, India was bound to fall. But in the days of Shihabuddin Ghori, neither side used fire-arms, though Firishta and Chand Bardai by anachronism mention their use.

It can not be alleged that the religious fervour actuating Shihabuddin and his Mahomedans was stronger than that actuating the Rajputs. Although Mahomedan historians describe the former as making a religious war, Shihabuddin was fighting for conquest of territory and not for extending religion. Indeed we find that conversion of the people to Mahomedanism was not his motive in conquering Northern India, and conversions did not take place on a large scale in Northern India for reasons which we will presently see. On the other hand the Rajputs and the Hindus of Northern India were actuated by a more fervent religious zeal than the inhabitants of the Panjab. As stated before, religious zeal in the Panjab has always been weak; but the land of the Sarasvati, the Jumna and the Ganges has always been the stronghold of Hinduism being its birthplace. We, therefore, think that the impelling force of religion was equally strong on either side.

The foremost cause which is usually and properly assigned to the fall of the Rajputs is their internecine fighting. The Rajput kingly families always fought amongst themselves not so much for extension of territory as for establishment of superiority. At this very time we find Prithvīrāj attacking his three great neighbouring kings of Gujarat, Bundelkhand and U. P. These fights were always tough fights as between European nations and doughty warriors on both sides always fell in great numbers. The fighting strength of all the four powerful kingdoms, i. e. of the Chauhans, the Rathods, the Chandellas and the Solankhis was thus reduced and each fell when fighting singly and separately against the strong common foe. Internecine warfare has always been the bane of the Rajputs. Though the Rajputs always neglected artillery and were, therefore, always weak in modern times, they could even then have driven out the Moguls, if only they had combined, as Manuchi distinctly states in his memoirs and they could have withstood even the Marathas, though not the English, for the Maratha artillery was in the hands of Europeans. Against Shihabuddin whose ambition was threatening India, of which the Rajputs must have had ample knowledge from informants, the Rajputs should have stayed their quarrels and combined. They did not stop their fights even against the common impending danger and they consequently were all destroyed.

The condition of India at this time resembled that of Germany at the end of the eighteenth century. Germany was divided at that time into several small but strong kingdoms the Ruler in each of which aspired to the imposing dignity of Emperor of the Holy Roman Empire and consequently tried to humble though not destroy the others. In the same way in India each Rajput king aspired to being called Chakravartin or emperor and for that end tried to conquer other kings without attempting to annex his kingdom. Thus while the power of both was lessened, the conqueror gained no strength from increase of resources or dominion. Bhoja of Malwa for example fought with and humbled other Rajput kings and was called Mālava Chakravartin. Karṇa of Chedi followed his example. And Kumārapāla attempted to obtain the same honour. The rivalry between the Gāhadavālas and the Chauhans lasted for nearly thirty years, between Vijayachandra and Vigrahapāla and Jaichand and Prithvirāj and weakened both. As the Rāsā relates, ninety out of a hundred of Prithvīrāja's sāmantas fell in his conflict with Jayachand in carrying off Sanyogitā. It is, therefore, no wonder that the Rajput kingly families fell before Shihabuddin as the Germanic states severally fell before Napoleon.

But while Germany was never finally conquered and subjected to foreign domination, Northern India was laid prostrate for all time. We have, therefore really to find out the reason why even after temporary conquest as the natural consequence of defeat in battle, Northern India could not regain its feet and make itself free. The cause of this, in our view, lay in the rigidification of caste which took place about this time. We will show in our General Survey Book how caste which was fluid in the beginning of this sub-period became rigid by the end of the 12th century and the modern rigid caste system of India with its intricacies and its numberless subsections inside the main castes was evolved. While Kshatriyas married in previous times Vaiśya wives and Brahmins married Kshatriya and Vaiśya wives and often vice-versa, each caste and subcaste now confined marriage and even food to itself. The social sympathy which existed previously among the various sections of the Hindu people was gone and it was replaced by a feeling of aloofness and even aversion.

But the most injurious result of this rigidification of caste was the vast dimunition in the fighting strength of kingdoms. Even now this evil of the caste system in India is not adequately realised. It is often wondered how a nation consisting of 33 crores of inhabitants can be ruled by a nation of four crores. But it must be remembered that the fighting people in India scarcely number four crores while the whole British nation of four crores is the fighting reserve of Britain. In India, excepting the Panjab, the people are divided firstly by race into Aryans and Dravidians and secondly by caste into fighters and non-fighters. The Dravidian section of the Indian population is nearly more than one half and chiefly consists of non-fighters. In the Aryan section of the population again, only the Kshatriyas are by heredity and present occupation inclined to fight. The result is that in India about 10 per cent of the population is fit and disposed to fight, while the remaining 90 per cent by nature and heredity is not fit to fight and is, therefore, ready to accept the rule of any strong nation which happens to be successful. As we will explain elsewhere, the idea of a nation did not develop in India and the people as a whole never thought of opposing foreign conquest. Especially at this time by the rigidification of caste the number of those who fought for independence was owing to internecine fighting limited and as soon as these viz. the Rajputs fell, the country as a whole submitted without demur to the foreign yoke.

This baneful effect of a rigid caste system, wherein the number of those who fight for the independence of the community becomes limited, was seen by the ancient law-givers and they attempted to remedy it by laying it down that though ordinarily it is the duty of the Kshatriyas to take up arms, it was yet the duty of all the three higher varnas to take up arms when religion was threatened and religion or Dharma, according to the Hindu notion, included politics and imposition ofthe yoke of a foreign people and religion was certainly a danger to religion. But where the people are, for generations, bred up in professions which are docile and in a spirit of submission, it is impossible to expect them to suddenly become fighters. Indeed, as stated before, when Shihabuddin conquered Kanauj, the rais and land-holders came forward and tendered submission. Moreover it must be noted that the population of Northern India is predominantly Dravidian, unlike the Panjab. It is even now so, the total number of Kshatriyas in U. P. is remarkably small. While, therefore, Shihabuddin Ghori could raise an army from the whole of the overflowing population of the Panjab, of Afghanistan and of Turkestan, the Rajputs could not raise large armies in India nor would the people offer resistance as a whole to foreign yoke. It may be noted that in western countries at the present day, the whole population of a country becomes the recruiting ground for an army fighting for the nation's existence. Germany in the recent war could place in the field nearly 70 lakhs of soldiers and so could France and England. And the national sentiment is so strong in the west that the whole country takes the greatest interest in the national struggle. The condition of Northern India at this time was exactly the opposite. The Kshatriya population alone was the recruiting ground; it is indeed true that some Brahmins and Vaiśyas did fight even at that time, but these exceptions prove the rule viz. that the Brahmins and the Vaiśyas then, as now, were as a rule unwilling and even unfitted to take up arms. The case was different during the days of the Guptas and the Vardhanas, of Dahir and Lalliya. Secondly, the people as a whole took no interest in the national struggle and without demur offered their submission to the foreign yoke, especially because, as we shall presently show, the Mahomedan rulers did not adopt any coercive measures for the spread of their religion.

Many of the remnants of the chivalrous, independence-loving Rajputs retired to the deserts and hills of Rajputana, or the ravines of the Chambal and the Jumna and other retired tracts and there preserved their independence, thus leaving Northern India in general and the Madhya-deśa in particular, all the more helpless. Northern India, therefore, fell prostrate never to rise, because there was no national resistance. This will explain how while in Europe even small nations have successfully resisted attempts to enslave them, in India large countries like the Kanauj kingdom fell *finally* before the Mahomedans. These countries or kingdoms were large enough even singly to oppose successfully any Mahomedan conqueror. But the reality is that there was no national resistance and the resistance offered by the Rajputs was unavailing owing to their being outnumbered by reason of rigidity of caste. It is not a mere matter of accident that Sobieski the greatest leader of the Poles was able to finally stop the onward rush of the Turks at Vienna. The Poles were more heroic than the Greeks, no doubt, but the Poles fought as a nation and hence succeeded. In Northern India unfortunately, both Prithvīrāj and Jaichand were defeated; but if the people had resisted as a whole, Northern India could not have been finally subdued by the Mahomedans.

The efficacy and the necessity of national resistance, was first realised in India, in our view, by Shivaji, under the inspiration of whose spirit Mahārāshtra resisted as a nation and fought against Aurangzeb. The Marathas, meaning thereby Kshatriyas, Brahmins, and the common people or Sudras combined and fought as a man in the days of Rajaram and rose superior even to the whole combined power of the Mogul empire with which Aurangzeb in vain strove to crush them. The Marathas of the days of Shivaji and Rajaram, alone in Indian history, offered national resistance and attained and preserved independence. They alone in Indian history verified the maxim laid down in western politics that no power however great can crush the independence of a people however small if they resist as a nation. India naturally could not realise the necessity of national unity when its kingdoms were ruled by Hindu kings of whatever clan. The Marathas first realised it after three centuries of Mahomedan rule. The Sikhs followed them with their religious conscription. The Indian people under English rule must realise the necessity of national effort if they are to attain Swaraj or political freedom.

The message of history for the future, therefore, is that not only the Rajputs should learn to confederate and unite, but the whole of the people of India and especially the Hindus whose caste system makes disunion their normal characteristic. It is not indeed possible to suggest that caste should be abolished. The evolution of the Hindu society for thousands of years has been developing caste and it would be impossible to induce the Hindus to give up caste. Moreover, the Rajputs have developed their highly chivalrous and heroic nature, through this very principle of heredity. Indeed the preservation of caste purity of which the Rajaputs take particular care has everything to recommend it. But the Rajputs not only of the east and the west but also of the north and the south, the Gurkhas, Dogras, the Bundelas and the Marathas must learn to unite on terms of absolute equality and more imperatively confederate for national uplift. But still, the Hindus, inspito of their caste distinctions must learn to confederate on terms of equality of status while preserving the independent growth of each main caste (though not of each subordinate subdivision which has come into being for fanciful reasons). The principle of confederation of independent units for political purposes was first thought out and practised by the American states and has now been followed by Germany. The confederation of Hindus, subdivided as they are, into independent castes, is the real problem of the future as previous history teaches us, and it must be practicable to achieve it, even if it be necessary to adopt for it, commensality of food and drink and of some religious worship. There is, and there should be, no idea in this confederation of the Hindus, of opposing or harassing the Mahomedans; for the confederation of Hindus and Mahomedans is also absolutely necessary for the political progress of the country. But it must be remembered that the Mahomedans are already a united and a strong community, and the confederation of Hindus and Mahomedans can only be achieved and made permanent if the Hindus also become a united and strong community.

To conclude the disunion among the Rajputs the fighting arm of India and the rigidity of caste by which 9/10 of the people were made incapable or unwilling to resist foreign domination were the two main causes which led to the permanent enslavement of Northern India.

CHAPTER XXIV.

DOWNFALL OF NORTHERN INDIA
SUBSIDIARY CAUSES.

In the last chapter we have given what appear to us to be the chief causes of the fall of the Rajput kingdoms of Northern India, viz : first, the constant fighting among the several Rajput states and their consequent weakening and second, the rigidification of caste which made the several important sections of the people in each state, except the Rajputs, incapacitated and unwilling to fight. In this chapter we notice some subsidiary causes which contributed to the fall of these kingdoms, though these individually could not have led to that result. Most of the facts given here will have to be noticed again in our survey of the general condition of the country ; but it is as well to mention them here separately.

1. One may first again mention the absence of the feeling of nationality in the people of all these states. We have already said that in India at this time, as elsewhere in Asia, there were kingdoms but no peopledoms. The people did not feel that the state was theirs and the king ought also to be theirs. The country belonged to the king and any one might be king whom God chose. Under this view of the state, the sentiment of nationality cannot arise, nor, as stated in Vol. II (p. 220) and Vol. I (p. 123), the virtue of patriotism. There was the sentiment of loyalty, no doubt, and you find in the Prithvīrāj Rāsā that sentiment appealed to everywhere. To die for the master was the highest dharma of the Rajput soldier. But when that master failed and another master was substituted by the will of God, the soldier was ready to die for him also. Thus we find even Kshatriya soldiers dying for Mahomedan kings and masters. This was doubly true of the common people who were not Rajputs i. e. of the caste whose duty it was to rule.

Though one essential of a state in its modern sense was indeed developing in India in the rise of separate modern languages and Gujarat, Rajputana, Antarbed, Bengal, Mahārāshtra, Telangana, Tamilnādu and Malyālam could now be considered as separate countries by reason of separate languages, viz., their modern vernaculars, this did not develop the feeling of nationality among the speakers of the same language for the above reason and in each of these countries or provinces, there were consequently several kingdoms which fought with one another. Why these did not coalesce, we shall discuss later on, but we may state here that the sameness of language did not develop the sentiment of nationality in these provinces in the absence of the other essential conditions which give rise to the feeling of nationality.

2. There being no sentiment of nationality, the ingress of foreigners was usually not objected to. Except in Kashmir and Tibet which had impregnable boundaries, the ingress of foreigners was not prohibited, was not even watched. Hence Mahomedans came into the several kingdoms freely and often settled therein. Thus we find them settled in Nāharwala, in Cambay, in Sopara, in Mahārāshtra and even in the Kanauj kingdom.* They even insisted on being governed by their own magistrates, as is evidenced by Mahomedan writers, as also by the expresssion Hanjamana-Nagara-Trivarga already noticed in Thana inscriptions. That the strength of states is impaired by the presence of foreigners is seen clearly by the modern states of the west which exercise strict watch over the ingress of foreigners. Indian states did not realise this or feel the necessity of strict watch over them owing to the absence of the feeling of nationality. Though there is no recorded evidence of it, one can imagine how the presence of Mahomedans in the several kingdoms must have contributed to their eventual subjugation.

3. Superstition sometimes contributes its quota to the fall of nations and superstition acted like a double-edged sword towards the fall of India. While the Mahomedans believed that victory was bound to come to them "for the judgment of God was upon those who were against him and could not be avoided," the Hindus thought that India was bound to be overrun by the Mlechchhas in the Kali age. Superstition has

* The Benares Gazetteer states that in the city of Benares there are Mahomedan Mchollas which are anterior in date to the final conquest of Benares by the Mahomedans according to tradition, though it is difficult to believe that Chandra or Govindachandra or even Jaichand could have allowed Mahomedans to settle in Benares. Perhaps they settled in the time of the subservient Pratihāra kings.

often acted thus upon the mind of peoples. The Aztecs of Mexico believed that they were destined to be conquered by men coming from the east. When the Goths and the Vandals overthrew the Roman Empire, the Christians thought that the end of the world was coming on as foretold in the Bible and made no opposition. In India too, though there is no recorded evidence of it, except in the case of Lakhnauti where the Tabakat records that king Lakshmaṇasena had been told that he would be conquered by a long-armed Turk, the Hindus generally must have submitted to the new state of things through the superstitious belief that it was inevitable.

4. The maintenance of a strong and sufficient army is the first duty of every state. The Hindu states had probably neglected this duty at this time. The great reputation of India in this respect noted before had been lost by it at this time. The probability is that Hindu states did not at this time maintain standing armies as in the days of Harsha or Bhoja. The army consisted chiefly of the quotas furnished by the Sāmantas. Though not exactly alike, these Sāmantas were like barons in England, who maintained for the use of the state certain quotas of fighters, the expenses of the same being borne by the barons or Sāmantas from their fiefs. This is the same system as existed under the Moguls viz., of Hazaris and Panch Hazaris. Prithvīrāj had probably no standing army of the state. He had probably only a small Huzur force. We know that the Peishwas, after the battle of Panipat, neglected to maintain a strong Huzur army, and the sagacious Ahalyābai expostulated often with Nana Fadnis for neglecting the Huzur pathak. The quota supplied by Sāmantas cannot always be relied upon, either in respect of number or of efficiency. The standing army of Mahmud or Shihabuddin Ghori must have been a more reliable force than the armies composed of the forces of Sāmantas called together hastily by the Hindu kings. Sāmantas or military sardars are again not disposed to fight stubbornly as there is a temptation to save themselves and their fiefs. We believe that the absence of sufficient standing armies in the Hindu states at this time strongly contributed to their eventual fall.

5. It may further be observed that Hindu intelligence neglected the study of the science of war as well as the science of the proper conception of the state. Brahmin and Kshatriya

intelligence revelled more in this subperiod in the study of poetics than in the necessary study of more useful sciences. The distinctions of heroines in love and despair, the essentials of poetry, poetical blemishes and embellishments, and the figures of speech engaged the highest intelligence of the land and even kings devoted their attention to writing elaborate treatises on poetics and dramaturgy. These works, no doubt, prove the fineness of Hindu intellect, but it should have devoted itself to more important studies. The attention and affluence of kings were bestowed more upon court-poets than upon generals ; the stage attracted them more than the camp. The minute study of poetics led to the deterioration of taste and morals and the increase of voluptuousness can be marked from the Karpūra-Manjari of Rājaśekhara to the Rambhā Manjarī of Nayachandra. The debasement of popular and kingly test will be apparent from the first verse of adoration adopted even in Kanauj for such ceremonious and meritorious documents as inscriptions of grants of villages to pious Brahmins. Indeed luxury and voluptuousness were bound to overtake the people in this sub-period, since the last sub-period was the most prosperous period of Hindu history as shown in the last chapter of Volume II (pp. 247-258). Height of prosperity leads to decadence of morals and voluptuousness which undermine the physical and moral capacities of the people, as we see in the case of the Romans, the Arabs, the Moguls and others and it need not be wondered that the Hindu kingdoms in the twelfth century became weak, by reason of the very prosperity and happiness they had enjoyed.

6. Lastly, we cannot conclude this short survey of the subsidiary causes of the downfall of Rajput kingdoms in Northern India without drawing the attention of the reader to the recrudescence during this sub-period of the Buddhistic sentiment of Ahimsā which, as we shall show in our chapter on religious survey, is evidenced by the rise of new Vaishṇavism and the great popularity, power, and progress of Jainism and of Lingayat and other sects during this period. Though the rise of Vaishṇavism or the spread of Jainism or other sects cannot be assigned as a direct cause of the downfall of Northern India, as Buddhism can be as a cause of the downfall of Sind, it cannot be denied that the dominance of the docile doctrine of Ahimsā throughout the Hindu society at this time made it inoffensive and weak. Most Brahmins whether Śaiva or Vaishṇava, and almost all Vaiśyas Śaiv, Vaishṇava and Jain accepted at this

time the non-slaughter of animals as a binding religious principle and gave up animal food altogether as we will show later on. The result was that with the exception of the Rajputs the whole Hindu mass became unfitted as well as unwilling to fight. This influence of food on the nature of people can not be denied. The masses of Indian people in the several states excepting the Rajputs, (the Śudras generally following the Brahmins and Vaiśyas through imitation as well as indigence) were like Indian elephants. Inspite of its enormous size and strength, the elephant is by nature timid and inoffensive. The elephant's arm of offense, its trunk, is delicate and is easily slashed. The elephant is usually afraid to endanger its life and shrinks at the least display of fire. No doubt, it can be trained to fight and to courageously withstand fire. So also the vegetarian Hindu can be trained to fight and perform deeds of valour. But where there is no such training, both by nature being inoppressive are easily subdued and made to obey the master. There are no doubt examples of Brahmins and even Jain brave generals and soldiers in this sub-period, but the generality of the people being unaccustomed to fight and becoming by their food inagressive and docile, when the Rajputs failed, all the Hindu kingdoms from the Sutlej to the Brahmaputra and from the Himalayas to the Vindhyas succumbed and almost willingly submitted to the Moslem yoke within the short period of a quarter of a century. As stated in the perface to Volume I, the message of history to Hindus, especially those who have conscientious objection to a meat diet, is so to strengthen themselves by physical training and mental alertness as to enable them to take their share honourably in the internecine physical struggles of the human race which will never cease but will ever go on.

BOOK VIII.

GENERAL SURVEY.

CHAPTER I.

RAMIFICATION OF CASTE.

As stated in the beginning of this volume, we have a very valuable guide for ascertaining the social condition of Hindu India at the outset of this sub-period, in Al-Beruni who wrote his book on India in 1030 A. D. Al-Beruni lived among the Hindus at Multan and elsewhere in the Panjab and was an accurate observer. But unfortunately he sometimes mixes what he read in Hindu religous books which he studied in the original, with what he saw and his observations, therefore, are not always as reliable as those of previous Arab writers quoted in our second volume. However, we begin the description of the social condition of India in this sub-period, with quqting what Al-Beruni says on subject of caste in his book on India. Fortunately he was acquainted with Persian and Greek history and gives us facts from the west for comparison with Indian condition.

Al- Beruni shows that caste had developed in ancient times among the Persians, not to speak, of the Greeks and Romans. "The ancient Chosroes had created great institutions of this kind (caste) which could not be broken through by the special merits of any individual nor by bribery. When Ardashir restored the Persian empire, he also restored the classes or castes in the following manner :—

1. Knights and princes.
2. Monks, fire-priests and lawyers,
3. Physicians and astronomers and other men of science.
4. Husbandmen and artisans.

" And within these classes there were subdivisions distinct from each other, like the species within a genius. The Hindus have also institutions of this kind. We, Moslems, consider all men equal except in piety and this is an obstacle which prevents understanding between us and the Hindus.

"The Hindus call their castes, varnas or colours and from the genealogical point of view they call them Jatah (Jati). They are four from the beginning. The highest are the Brahmins; next come Kshtariyas. Their degree is not much below that of the Brahmins. Then follow the Vaiśyas and the Śudras. Between the two latter classes there is no very great distance. Much as these differ, they live together in the same towns and villages, mixed together in the same houses and lodgings." (Sachau I pp. 99-101).

This long extract will show to us that this description of Hindu castes is not as accurate as that given in Volume II from previous Arab writers. The splitting of Kshatriyas into ruling Kshatriyas and cultivating Kshatriyas spoken of by Ibn Khordadba (Vol. II p. 179) is not even mentioned here. Probably in 1040 A. D. Rajputs had been so decimated and perhaps had fallen so low that they did not impress Al-Beruni separately. The statement in the Gāhadavāla inscription quoted before (p. 221) seems thus to be true of the condition of things at this time, that the Kshatriya ruling clans had almost been destroyed at least in the Panjab and U. P. and the recitation of the Veda had almost stopped when Chandra Gāhadavāla rehabilitated both. Secondly, Al-Beruni speaks somewhat from the books and not from actual observation and further says nothing about marriage. Ibn Khordadba stated that the Brahmins and Rajputs married from the lower caste of Kshatriyas and we have the historical mention of Rājaśekhara marrying a Chauhan lady. Probably in Al-Beruni's time (or later when castes were consolidated) such marriages had altogether stopped. Thirdly, Al-Beruni does not speak of intermediate castes which must have been many, nor of any subdivisions of the principal castes which probably had not yet arisen.

The castes among the Persians who were all Aryans were naturally different from those among the Hindus who were formed by a combination of Aryan and non-Aryan populations; and hence the class of Śudras did not exist among the Persians. Moreover we do not know if caste distinctions among the Persians were not matrimonial, but were purely occupational. Among the Hindus, Pratiloma marriage was stopped in pre-Buddhist days and Anuloma marriage ceased probably at this time. Lastly, Al-Beruni says that all castes lived mixed together in the same houses and lodgings. This is probably a correct observation so far as the Panjab is concerned; for there was not much difference of food or habits between the different classes. all being flesh-eaters. In the rest of the country, this could not have been so; even if it were so in 1040 A. D. things changed so completely during the next two centuries owing to the recrudescence of the doctrine of Ahimsā that many castes gave up animal food and vegetarians and non-vegtarians could not have lived together in the same houses. Hence, after Al-Beruni, caste developed in exclusiveness to such an extent that the original four castes of India gave place in this sub-period to hundreds and thousands of sub-castes as we proceed to show.

We stated in our first volume that Brahmins, Kshatriyas and Vaiśyas formed undivided castes during the first sub-period (600–800). They remained so during the second sub-period also (800–1000 A. D.). But during the third sub-period, each of these castes became split into hundreds of sub-castes as inscriptions prove. The reasons were apparently, as shown above, 1st, a difference of food ; 2nd, ideas of racial purity and 3rd, different social customs prevailing in different countries. We will take each of these castes separately and show how it became subdivided in this sub-period.

BRAHMINS.

In the beginning of this sub-period Brahmins all over India were one caste undoubtedly. In previous centuries Brahmins were distinguished by their gotras and their Śākhās only. Inscriptions of all countries, in previous sub-periods give only their gotras and Śākhās (or Vedic ritual) and never mention the names of any sub-section. Even in this sub-period for about fifty years we find the same practice prevailing. Thus a Chandella grant dated 1050 A. D. (I. A. XVI p. 206) describes the donee as a Bhāradvāja gotra, Tripravara Brahmin of Yajurveda Śākhā. In a Kalachuri inscription again (Kahla, Gorakhpur District U. P.) dated 1077 A. D. (E. I. VII p. 86), we have many Brahmin donees whose description consists of their gotras with pravara number of each and their Śākhās plus their place (village or town) of residence. So also a later Chālukya grant dated 1040 describes the donee as Kauśika gotra and Bahvricha (Ṛigvedi) Brahmin (B. B. R. A. S. XII p. 51). Later we begin to have the mention of the Brahmins' country of residence. Thus Kumārapāla's Praśasti at Vadnagar mentions the writer as a Nāgara Brahmin (St. 1208, 1151 A. D.). Some Chandella and Gāhadavāla inscriptions describe the Brahmin donees as Thakkura (E. I. IV p. 121) and in Gāhadavāla and Haihaya inscriptions they are described as Rāuta (E. I. XIV p. 274). In a feudatory southern Malwa inscription dated 1135 A. D. we find the Brahmin donee described as Karnāta (I. A. XIV) with the Brahmin's gotra and Pravara added and it was an important discovery to find a Śilāhāra of Karhad grant describing the Brahmin donees as Karhātaka and Ghaisāsa Brahmins, the importance of which we will shortly notice. Names of country became so important that latterly the mention of gotra and Śākhā was omitted for Brahmins, though in the previous sub-period it was considered necessary (Vol. II p. 276). Thus in the Sāsabahu temple inscription (I. A. XV p. 36) dated 1093 we find names of many Brahmin donees without the mention of gotra. In an inscription of Bholā Bhīma of Gujarat dated St. 1256 or 1200 A. D. (I. A. XI p. 72) the Brahmin donee is described without the mention of his gotra or Sākhā by his name only and by his Raikavāla Jāti or sub-section of Brahmin caste. In a Konkan inscription dated 1249 A. D. (J. R. A. S. Bombay IX p. 248) we have names of 32 Brahmin donees whose gotras are given but whose Śākhā is not stated and instead of it every Brahmin's surname is given. Surnames grew by this time, either from profession or from place of residence or other peculiarities and the importance of Śākhā was lost sight of. Surnames probably came into use among Brahmins in this sub-period such as Dīkshita, Raut, Thakur, Pāthaka, Upādhyāya, Pattavardhana * and so on. It is no doubt true that even so late as 1200 A. D. we find gotra and pravara of Brahmins mentioned; the continuance of their mention is not strange as Brahmins still keep up the memory of their gotra and pravara. But what is pertinent to remark is that along with gotras, family surnames begin to be mentioned and later on subcaste names based on country of residence. Thus in a Paramāra inscription dated 1226 A. D. (E. I. IX pp. 108 and 121) we have many names of Brahmin donees with gotra and pravara mentioned but in each case the surname is added, such as Pandit, Dīkshita, Dvivedi, Chaturvedi, Āvasthika and so on, and the places from which these Brahmins of the same surname came are different such as Mathura, Tripur, Akola, Dendavāna. So also in an inscription of Jayachchandra dated 1177 (E. I. IV

* The name Trivādi occurring in this inscription is inexplicable as also Kramita.

p. 129) the many Brahmin donees are thus described, 1 Deva Śri Lotārka (gotra not given), 2 Bandhula gotra Purohita Śri Paharajaya, 3 Sarkarākshya gotra Pandit Sri Rishikeya and so on; the word Pandit is abbreviated into Pam for four Brahmins and one is styled Dviveda. These epithets gradually grew into surnames of these Brahmins. In I. A. XIX (p. 353) we have the donee Brahmin described as Dākshiṇātya Karnāta Diveda Thakkura as also Āvasthika. The surname Avasthi has survived in Oudh among Brahmins but not among Deccani or Karnāṭaka Brahmins. The gotra thus retains for some time its importance among Brahmins at least and finds mention in inscriptions almost invariably. But as stated above, Pravara and Śākhā are usually omitted though all Brahmins have retained their memory down to this day.

Whatever this may be, we have not mentioned yet of the division of Brahmins into the modern two main sections viz. Pancha Gauda and Pancha Drāvida. It is not found even in the Skanda Purāṇa which we have placed in the ninth century A. D. (see Vol. II p. 39) properly enough. For the distinction arose even later than 1200 A. D. This main division is probably based on the flesh food of the former and the vegetarianism of the latter. But there is no doubt that Brahmins had sub-divided themselves into numerous sub-sections long before 1200 A. D., according to country of residence or its chief town, owing to peculiarities of customs, as also of ideas of purity of race. We find it recorded in the Nāgara Khanda of the Skanda Purāṇa where the whole history of Nāgara Brahmins and their special good Hāṭakeśvara Śiva is given that an unknown Brahmin came to their town and a Nāgara Brahmin gave him his daughter in marriage. He was subsequently found out to be a Chāndāla to the consternation of the community and the Nāgaras thereupon made it a rule not to give daughters in marriage to any but known Nāgara Brahmins and the Nāgara known Brahmin families were enumerated. This arrangement seems gradually to have been adopted by all castes and sub-castes came consequently to deserve the name jnāti or known section. In the Abu inscription we have the word Nāgara jnātibhājā (Vol. II p. 85) actually used by the writer to describe his caste or subsection (St. 1331 or 1274 A. D.). This story is apparently a later invention and probably an interpolation in the Skanda Purāṇa but it indicates the reason why marriage relations were gradually restricted to people of known pedigree residing in the same country. And thus began the subdivisions of Brahmins based on country of residence. Commencing from Kashmir we have thus Brahmins divided into 1. Kashmiri. 2. Nagarkotia (those who reside in Nagarkot the capital of Katoch kings in Kangra). 3. Muhyal in the Panjab (al is a termination which indicates subcaste). 4. Sārasvata. 5. Gauda (of Guda or Thanesar). 6. Narnol. 7. Kanojia and 8. Sarjupāria or residing beyond the Śarayu. 9. Jajhotia. 10. Tiwari. 11. Srimāli and 12. Pushkarnā or residing at Pushkar in Rājputana. 13. Sindhi. 14. Nāgara (of Ánandpura). 15. Dasor (of Daśapura). 16. Modha (of country formerly named Dharmāraṇya). 17. Gujarāti. 18. Malvi. 19. Bengali. 20. Ooriya. 21. Deshastha. 22. Konkanastha or Chitpāwan (belonging to Chittapolana a town in Ratnagiri District). 23. Karhade (living under the Śilaharas of Karhad). 24. Karnāṭa. 25. Āndhra or Telugu. 26. Tamil and 27. Malyali or Nambudri. These are the main subsections of Brahmins recognisable as named after country of residence; but there are many subdivisions of these again based on various other grounds such as Daśas and Viśas in the north and Aiyars and Ayyangars in the south. For Brahmins divided further from their acceptance of this or that philosophy. The Ayyars are Smārtas i. e. those who look upon Śiva and Vishṇu as equal, while Aiyyangars believe Nārāyaṇa to be the highest god and follow the philosophy of Rāmānuja. Later still the followers of Madhva and his Dvaita philosophy became a separate sub-section of Brahmins and were called Āchāryas. These gave up not only intermarriage but in many cases interdining also; though we have no direct mention of these restrictions in the Dharmaśāstras.

Strangely enough the northern Brahmins were looked upon in the beginning of this sub-period as purer in race as also in Āchāra or religious life and we have evidence traditional no doubt, of many southern kings inviting northern India Brahmin families to settle in their countries. Thus we find the Sena king Sāmanta or Ballāla inviting Kanaujia Brahmins to settle in Bengal though tradition speaks of these Brahmins as having come in the time of Ādisūra, a fictitious king of earlier date; and we have mention of Brahmins coming from the north and settling in Orissa also in the days of the Kesari kings. We have mention again of Northern Brahmins being invited to settle in Gujarat by Mūlarāja and even so far south as the Tamil land we have mention of a Chola king inviting and settling in his country Brahmins from Northern India. In all these cases, these Brahmins formed separate sub-castes owing to their unwillingness to mix with local Brahmins, considered to be of lower purity, either in food or marriage. The Nagarakotia Brahmins alone who believe that they were invited by a Katoch king say that they consist of 13 families, 3 of whom were Kashmiri, 3 Kanaujia and 3 Sārasvata, the remaining four being local Brahmins. (These probably were not agriculturalists). The number of sub-castes was thus further increased. Then again we may believe that certain sections of Brahmins migrated to safer lands from the Panjab and the U. P. owing to invasions first and then oppression of Mahomedan conquerors. The Gauda Sārasvata Brahmins of Goa territory thus appear to have come from the region of the Sarasvati about this time. It is an unhistorical idea that they came from Bengal, for Guda is a name which originally was applied to the country round Thanesar and the peculiarity of these Brahmins viz. that they eat fish is mentioned even in the Mahābhārata as arising among Brahmins residing on the banks of the Sarasvati during a long famine. The Bengali Brahmins were emigrants from the same ancient country of the Sārasvatas and are also hence called Gauda. We disbelieve the tradition of the Gauda Sārasvatas of Goa coming from Bengal because there is no historical reason why they should have left Bengal and further because their speech does not exhibit any linguistic and phonetic peculiarities of Bengal such as the change of s into sh and a into ō. The Chitpāvans are another section of Konkan Brahmins which has the tradition of coming there from outside. As stated in our Mahābhārata Mīmānsā they from their fair complexion appear to have come from the Panjab hilly districts into the hilly region of the Ratnagiri District after a short halt in the Thana District about Bassein where is the original first Konkan sanctuary of Paraśurāma. These instances will suffice to show that in this sub-period we have evidence of Brahmin families migrating to, or being invited to settle in, southern and eastern countries. The example again of Deccani Brahmins going to the Āndhra country in the wake of Chālukya conquest of Vengi and forming a separate sub-section of Brahmins called now Niyogi shows that there may be instances of Brahmin migrations after conquest, as happened in modern history after the conquests of the Marathas. The mode adopted by Nāgara Brahmins of defining their sub-castes by counting their families and their gotras was followed by all these various sub-sections and hence have arisen those hundreds of sub-castes into which Brahmins are now sub-divided and which restrict marriage and food to themselves. All these sub-sections acquired new names from country or town of their residence or from other causes, which became of paramount importance owing to restriction of marriage to each sub-section and gotra and Sākhā became consequently of minor importance. But it must be stated that all the sub-sections of Brahmins appear to have adhered loyally to their ancient Vedic religion. They not only preserved their Veda or Śākhā but also its special ritual and also the memory of their gotras and pravaras and still preserve the gotra and pravara law of marriage prohibition enjoined by the smritis, the gotras and pravaras being enumerated in the Śrauta Sūtras. And hence it is that gotra and pravara among Brahmins and even Kshatriyas remain the same throughout the whole of India though Brahmin and Kshatriya families everywhere acquired new names from curious causes. These names became no doubt predominant, but they never acquired so great an importance among Brahmins at least as to destroy the importance of gotra, and the gotra law of marriage is still the supreme law of marriage among Brahmins.

Many of these subcastes of Brahmins especially in Northern India were then non-vegetarian and they continue so down to this day. Al-Beruni describing the food of Hindus says "Christians are not allowed to kill, so also the Brahmins." The rules given hereafter apply to Brahmins (as Christian rules apply to bishops and monks), but not others. First, strangulation of certain animals only is allowed viz., sheep, goat, gazelle, rhinoceros (genda), water and land birds such as peacock etc.; second, forbidden animals are ox, camel, horse, elephant &c., tame poultry, fish and all kinds of eggs.

NOTE:—MARCO POLO ON LAD BRAHMINS.

The description given by Marco Polo of Brahmins of the country called Lar by him deserves to be quoted and discussed here. Marco Polo travelled in India about 1280 A. D. roughly and wrote about 1300 A. D. Though this account is thus a hundred years later than our period, it cannot be considered inapplicable, as the condition then of the country must have been the same as in 1200, Mahomedan conquest coming later. Speaking of the province of Lar, he says (Marco Polo by Miss Yule Vol. II. p. 360) "All Brahmins come from that country on the west. They are best merchants and most truthful. They eat no flesh and drink no wine and lead a life of chastity. They wear a thread of cotton on their shoulders which crosses the breast and the back. They have a rich and powerful king who sends Brahmins to purchase best diamonds in Soli (Chola) and best pearls. They believe in bad and auspicious hours for every week day and transact business only at auspicious times. They are long-lived as they are very abstemious and they have capital teeth owing to a certain herb they chew."

"There are other Brahmins called Chugi (Jogi) who are longer-lived, who are devoted to the idols. They live upto 150 or even 200 years. They eat rice and milk only. They drink a portion of sulphur and quicksilver twice a day which leads to longevity. Some of them are ascetics who go about stark naked. They have a small ox of pewter or gold tied over their forehead. They daub themselves with cowdung ashes. If any one does them good, they put the ashes in the middle of his forehead. They eat from dry leaves of the apple of paradise (plantain?). They would not kill any animal even a fly or a flea. They fast many days and drink nothing but water. They sleep on the ground and yet they live long. They burn their dead."

Miss Yule observes on this in a note that "Lardeśa included southern Gujarat, Thana and Chaul. Konkani Brahmins adopted trade only when they were expelled from Goa. This high praise of the truthfulness of Brahmins was just and as old as the Greeks. It is not only given by Greek writers but by Hiuen Tsang and also by Arab travellers."

It is somewhat difficult to determine to whom the above description applies. Lar no doubt according to Arab travellers included Thana and Kolaba districts and had a language of its own called Lari. But Marco Polo later describes the kingdom of Thana separately. We have seen that Śilāhāra kings ruled in Thana. Lārdeśa was again distinct from Gujarat which is also separately described by Marco Polo and which with its capital Patan was ruled by Vaghela kings in about 1300 A. D. The language of this part is described again as distinct and peculiar (p. 392). Thus upto 1300 A. D. modern southern Gujarat or Lārdeśa was distinct from Northern Gujarat politically as well as in language. The people apparently had a king of their own, though in previous centuries, they were under the Rāshatrakūṭas and later under Western Chālukyas of Kalyan. The Brahmins of Lārdeśa are not now, however, known as a separate sub-caste. But probably they were a distinct sub-caste then and went for trade to such distant countries as the countries of Chola and Pāndya which produced diamonds and pearls. The Konkan Brahmins are not much known as traders though their truthfulness as of other Brahmins must have been anciently well known. The surnames Pattavardhana, Ghalisa and Ghaisāsa now found among Konkan and Karhada Brahmins only and mentioned in a Goa Kadamba inscription dated Śaka 1171 or 1249 A. D. (J. R. A. S. Bombay IX p. 243) indicate, that these families were traders; what trade these surnames indicated, we are not able to determine. The four Brahmins mentioned in an inscription dated 1190 A. D., of Bhoja II Silāhāra king of Karhād are named: 1. Adityabhatta 2. Lakshmidhara-bhatta 3. Karhātaka Prabhākara Ghaisāsa and 4. Vāsiyana Ghaisāsa

(gotra nowhere mentioned). The word Karahātaka here plainly indicates a subcaste and Ghaisāsa plainly imports a profession which is not religious. But certainly these did not trade in diamonds and pearls as Marco Polo states. We must, therefore, believe that Lad Brahmins were a distinct sub-caste spread over the whole of southern India who traded in diamonds and pearls and who were known then for their great veracity. It appears that Marco Polo met them in the Pāndya country as he describes Lar Deśa just almost immediately after the Pāndya country. The country named by him as Maabar is certainly the Pāndya country which produced pearls. Of this country he says rightly that "there are no tailors here, All people, men and women, rich and poor, including even the king go about naked with a strip of cloth round their loins. Even the soldiers go to fight naked, with lance and shield." He describes the naked king as distinguished only by the fineness of the loin cloth and the necklace of precious stones, a description which reminds one of that by Kalidāsa in Raghu (पाण्ड्योयमंसार्पितलम्बहारः). The Brahmins of Dravida even now move about almost naked. Marco Polo next describes the kingdom of Mutfili, an inexplicable name; but it is certainly the Āndhra kingdom of Warangal as it is described as ruled then by a queen (daughter of Pratāparudra) and as diamonds are said to be found in its mountains referring probably to the mines of Golkonda. It is in these countries apparently that Marco Polo came across the Brahmins of the Lar country which is described next as lying in the west and which must mean the country of Lāta or modern southern Gujarat.

The ascetics described seem to be Saiva ascetics but those with a metal ox on their foreheads can not be Jangamas as these do not burn their dead but bury them. The Vīraśaiva schism (Lingāyat) had no doubt arisen already. But the Lingāyats had probably not yet gone to Konkan or Lāta where even now they are scarcely to be found. These ascetics, therefore, do not now survive as even Miss Yule thinks.

They again cannot be Jains, though their abstention from all animal slaughter, their injuring not even a fly or a flea and their long fasts may suggest their being Jains. But Jains do not use cowdung ashes nor apply them to the forehead of their disciples. They therefore, must be Śaiva ascetics of an order which is not now in existence. They perhaps were followers of Lakulīśa whose chief sacred place is near Broach, as already stated. The whole description, therefore, according to our view, does not apply to Konkan Brahmins though it is suggestive of them and applies to Lad Brahmins who are now found, not in South Gujarat, but all over the Deccan including Hyderabad territory and Berar. They are still a mercantile community but are very religious orthodox Brahmins.

THE RAJPUTS

Going on to consider the next chief caste of the Kshatriyas, we find that it also subdivided during this sub-period though not into numerous sub-sects. It could not, for obvious reasons, subdivide on the basis of town or country of residence. It had already divided itself into two main sections viz. those who cultivated and those who did not. The former were naturally considered lower in grade and the latter who were rulers of kingdoms, at least heads of villages or districts, were considered to be higher in grade. These latter were now called by distinction Rajputs a word used in inscriptions of this period to denote the ruling Kshatriyas generally (e. g. E. I. XIV p. 129 Ballālasena insc. जह्निरे राजपुत्रा:). They were first looked upon as even higher than Brahmins, as shown in Vol. II (p. 178). This higher status of the Rajputs described by Arab travellers of the preceding century is not mentioned by Al-Beruni who, as often stated before, speaks more from Hindu law books than from actual observation. Or it may be that during the period of Mahomedan invasions many of the Panjab Rajput ruling families were destroyed; and when the Gāhadavāla king Chandra drove the Mahomedan oppressors out of northern India and reconstituted the Kshatriya caste, it naturally assumed its position as defined in the Hindu Śāstras, viz. next to that of the Brahmins. Yet they were considered equal to the Brahmins in all respects as Al-Beruni himself admits that their degree is not much below that of the Brahmins. Thus they were allowed to study the Vedas and did study Veda and Śāstra and we have already seen how noted kings such as Bhoja and Govindachandra were as learned in the sacred and profane lore as the most learned Brahmins.

In the usual manner, the Rajput or ruling families of India constituted themselves into a sub-section about 1100 A.D. by the enumeration of the orthodox pure Kshatriya ruling families of the time. In this enumeration Panjab remained naturally excluded, being then entirely under Mahomedan rule; and there indeed were no ruling Kshatriya families then in the Panjab. The Himalayan ruling families also did not come in the enumeration for another reason which we will notice later on. The South Indian ruling families were also excluded as they were apparently not considered of pure Aryan race and of Kshatriya descent. The Kshatriya families ruling in Mahārāshtra were, however, included as they had continuous marriage relations with the ruling Kshatriya families of Northern India. The number of these Rajput families was found to be 36 and this number soon became traditional, as we find it mentioned in the Rājataranginī of Kalhaṇa of 1159 A. D. Which were these 36 families in the beginning it is difficult to determine, as no unquestionable list of that date has come down to us. We have treated the list in the Rāsā as contemporaneous with Prithvirāj though the Rāsā in its present form is undoubtedly to be placed in the 16th century A. D. (vide Vol. II p. 70) and we will examine in a note how far that list represents the correct political condition of the country about 1100 A. D. It may be noted that by this enumeration the surnames or family names of the several clans further acquired importance and the gotra of each family, although each had its separate gotra, gradually became of no value even in matters of marriage. Indeed inscriptions of this period often look upon the clan name as gotra itself e. g. Guhila gotra, Pratihāra gotra etc. (See also Vol. II p. 177).

In the Rāsā list firstly the Senas of Lakhnauti are conspicuous by their absence and this supports the view that their power in Bengal was established later than 1100 A. D. Next we note that all ruling families of South India viz. Gangas, Cholas Pāndyas and Keralas are also not in the list. The only explanation seems as stated above, to be that their claim to pure Kshatriya origin was not admitted as they had no marriage relations with the Kshatriyas of Northern India. The ruling Kshatriya families of Mahārāshtra occupying an intermediate position geographically, naturally came to occupy an intermediate position racially. We have already said that the Śilāhāras, are the only truly Maratha family which finds a mention in the list of the 36 royal clans (p. 247). As to the Chālukyas and the Rāshtrakūtas of the Deccan, though they are, according to our view, distinct from the families of the same name of Northern India, their inclusion in the 36 under the same names can not be denied. But it is remarkable that the Kadambas of Goa are not mentioned among the thirty-six. We have uncontested evidence that two princesses from this family were married into the Gujarat Chālukya family during this sub-period.* Probably the Rajputs of Northern India gradually confined their sub-caste to Northern India and refused to continue marriage relations with Kshatriya families of Mahārāshtra, ‡ as these families had marriage relations with Non-Aryan ruling families of South

* The Kumārapāla Charita mentions such a marriage in the verse कर्णोपि कर्णाटनृपाङ्गजायाश्चकार पाणिग्रहणं जयायाः। ; it also mentions Karṇa's marriage with a Kashmir princess कर्णाय काश्मीरपतिः स्वपुत्रीं प्रैषद्दिधो मैणळ्देविनाम्नीम् ॥

‡ Karṇa Vaghela declined for example to give his daughter to the Yādava king of Deogiri about 1300 A. D.

India also. The Maratha Kshatriyas, consequently, after this period, including the Śilāhāras, became a separate group or sub-caste and they too had their own enumeration of 96 Maratha families to which marriage was thenceforth confined.

The Rajputs from Western Himalayas formed a third group which became a distinct sub-section, not only on account of its isolation but also of certain marriage customs peculiar to them. In the Himalayas then survived and still survive marriage customs of ancient India by which the higher castes could take wives from lower castes, the caste of the progeny being unaffected viz. that of the father. We find thus, even now, three grades of Kshatriyas in the Himalayan region adjacent to the Punjab viz. Rajputs, Rāṇas or Thakurs and Rāṭhis. The Rajputs take girls from the Thakurs and these from the Rāṭhis but do not give them their girls. The Rajputs of the Himalayan region, however, though they have old mixed marriage customs still prevalent among them, are pure in race as the Rāṭhis are not Mongolians but Aryans, are in fact Kshatriyas lower in grade only because they follow agriculture. They further allow Karewa or widow remarriage which is prohibited to the Rajputs as to Brahmins and Vaiśyas. Full information is given in "Castes and Tribes of the Punjab" relating to minor sub-divisions of the Rajputs of the Himalayan region amongst whom the Katoch are the leading family with the Maharaja of Lambagram at their head. But the names of the several Sūryavanśi and Chandravanśi families of the highest,* middling and lowest grades with names based chiefly on place of residence such as Jammuwāl, Guleria, etc. it is not necessary to give here in detail.

In the Punjab itself the Kshatriyas of the western parts were mostly forcibly converted to Mahomedanism in the days of Mahmud and of Shihabuddin and these do not now use or even like the name Rajput, though they still preserve old Kshatriya clan names of Mahābhārata or Greek days such as Yaudheyas (Johiyas), Ānavas (Janjuas) etc. and still observe certain Hindu customs such as calling a Brahmin at the birth of a child or at marriage. In the eastern parts, Rajputs are still found but they are immigrants from lands further east and south in Mahomedan times, as they use the orthodox clan name.

---

* The Miyans are the highest, a name taken from the Mahomedans Miyan meaning the most respected.

from the list of the 36 royal clans such as Paramāra, Chauhan, Tuar, Rathod, Kachhwāha, &c.; and these have still marriage relations with the Rajputs of Delhi and Rajputana. The Panjab and the land of the Sarasvatī as also Pānchāla was the ancient land of Brahmins and Kshatriyas and all Brahmins and Kshatriyas in the east and south of India came originally from this region. It, therefore, follows that Parmāras and Chauhans, Rathods and Kachhwāhas are clan-names which originally must have come from the Punjab itself in ancient times. Or these names which do not find a mention in the Mahābhārata may have come into existence in the south and the east, in the middle land and in Rajputana, in the sixth century or later, among Kshatriya clans driven out of or leaving the Panjab under stress of Kushan and Hūṇa invasions. Certain it is that most of the names of clans in the list of 36 are not found in the Mahābhārata; and as they are found in the eastern parts of the Panjab at the present day, these Rajputs must have gone from the south. Local tradition also supports this inference as the Rajputs of Eastern Panjab believe that they came there from the Delhi region and from Rajputana in Mahomedan times. These Rajputs, therefore, cannot be treated as a separate group and must be included in the Rajputana group.

Thus we have three sub-sections of the Kshatriyas of India; sub-sections which probably came into existence between 1100 to 1200 or 1300 A. D. viz. 1st the Rajputs of the 36 clans inhabiting Rajputana, Gujrat, Kathiawar, Malwa, U. P. and Eastern Panjab; 2nd Rajputs of Western Himalayas and 3rd the Maratha Kshatriyas. These three groups do not intermarry and do not interdine and they may, therefore, be looked upon as real sub-castes with their usual restrictions. Though the sub-castes of pure Kshatriyas thus are only three, there are numerous other sub-castes who claim to be Kshatriyas and whose existence probably goes back to our sub-period. We may, of course, include those Kshatriyas who are considered lower in grade because they follow the occupation of agriculture, the Rāṭhis for example of the Himalayan region and the Marathas of the Deccan. The words Rāṭhi and Maratha probably have a common origin viz. Rāshtra* which shows that they form the

---

* The word Rāshṭrika in Aśoka inscriptions is explained by Smith as meaning inhabitants of Western Ghats but the word may indicate these Rāṭhis of the Himālayan region also.

country, being the common people or the settled agriculturists and must be distinguished from the Sudras or labourers. The description by Al-Beruni of the four castes, however, indicates that while the Rajputs or Kshatriyas were treated as equals of Brahmins, the agricultural Kshatriyas and Vaiśyas had come to be looked upon as not much superior to Śudras, being prohibited the study of the Veda. Besides these agricultural Kshatriyas, there were other sub-castes which also claimed the rank of Kshatriyas and which must have come into existence in this sub-period such as Bundellas, Raghuvanśis &c. though we have no positive written evidence about their claim. The tendency of Hindu society at all times in India is to establish various sub-castes which usually claim to be included in the higher varṇa nearest to them.

The Kshatriyas of South India claim to belong to solar and lunar races also. They form a saparate sub-caste which we have not taken into consideration in the above enumeration. So far as we have seen, we have not found in inscriptions an example of a South India Kshatriya marrying a northern Kshatriya princess. The Dravida warrior clans were no doubt treated as Vrātya Kshatriyas by the Manusmriti and the Purānas support their solar and lunar race origins. The Āndhra Kshatriyas are called Rāju—a Sanskrit word—and Vellala. It is unnecessary to go further into the status of the Kshatriyas of South India as we have not found the subject discussed at length anywhere.

NOTE :—THE 36 RULING FAMILIES OF KSHATRIYAS.

We have held that the list of 36 ruling families of Kshatriyas was made during the reign of Chandra Gāhadavāla who is said in inscriptions to have rehabilitated the Solar and Lunar Kshatriya races. This king ruled from 1080 to 1100 A. D. and the 36 families then enumerated must have been actually ruling at that time. We have not got the original list; but two ancient lists, incomplete and rather incorrect, are given by Tod viz. the Rāsā list and the Kumārapāla Charita Sanskrit list (the other two given by him seem to be later as they contain undoubtedly later names). If we compare these two lists they appear to be copies from the same original list. Let us see how they agree and differ.

Rāsa List	Kumārapāla-Charita Sans. List
Ravi	Ikshvaku
Śaśi	Soma
Yadu	Yadu
Kakustha	X
Paramāra	Paramāra
Sadāvara	X
Chauhan	Chauhan
Chālukka	Chālukka
Chhindaka	Chhindaka
Silāra	Silāra
Abhīra	X
Doyamata Makvāna	Makvāna
Chapotkaṭa	Chapotkaṭa
Parihāra	Parihāra
Dhānyapālaka	Dhānyapālaka
Rājyapālaka	Rājyapālaka
Nikumpa	Nikumpa
Hula	Hūṇa
Guhila, Guhilaputta	Ohila X

From the note of Gaurishankar on this list we find there are some eight or nine names which are found in the Kumārapāla-Charita list which were omitted by Tod and the three out of which found in the other list are,

Rathod	Rath
Kārattapāla	Kārattapala
Aniga	Anaga

There are many names in both lists which are now unidentifiable; and even Tod could not identify them. Moreover the identification by Tod of some is unquestionably mistaken, as it could not but be, in the absence of the epigraphic evidence which we now possess. We proceed to show how this list, especially that in the Rāsā, correctly depicts the political state of the country and its Rajput kingdoms about 1100 A. D. We take the identification of names made by us in Vol. II.

The first five namely Kakustha (Kachapaghāta), Paramāra Sadāvara (Tomara), Chāhamana, Chhandāka (Chandella) are the well-known kingdoms of Gwalior, Malwa, Delhi, Sambhar and Bundelkhand described in this volume. The Sixth Śilāra is the Śilāhāra kingdom of Thana. The seventh Abhiyara or Ahira kingdom has not been located by Tod but it must have been in southern India. Chapotkaṭa and Parihara were the kingdoms of Anhilwad and Kanauj which had just passed away but there still must have been small kingdoms remaining such as that of Mandawar of the Pratihāras. The Guhilot kingdom of Mewad was well known as also the small kingdom of the Guhilas in Mangrol (Kathiawar) already described (p.301). The Yadus under whom come now Yādavas, Bhatis and the Jādejas and Chūdāsamas of Kāthiawar were reperesented then by the Yādavas of Biana and Mathura or Mahāban. The Bhātis of Jaisalmere are not mentioned in this list because probably they were not then in Jaisalmere which according to tradition was founded in 1157 A. D. (Gaurishankar's Tod p. 224) and the latter two were not yet established in Kathiawar and Cutch which were then under the Chālukyas of Anhilwad. The Tānks had a kingdom at this time at Kāshtha on the Jumma as pointed out by Tod. They are not, according to our view, descendants of Takshaka Nāga as many imagine. The Hauṇas had a kingdom at Badoli on the east-coast of the Chambal opposite Bhalsroda "where in a beautifully carved temple there is a Huna Vivāha Mandapa." (Gaurishankar's Tod). The Gaudas or Gaurs have nothing to do with the Senas of Bengal whose power was established in Bengal itself later than 1100 and who are consequently not mentioned in this list. They came from Guda or the country about Thaṇesar and they had at this time an extensive kingdom about Ajmer which was taken from them by the Chauhans as tradition recorded by Tod states. (This tradition is not believed by some). The Badgujars also were a powerful ruling family then and were in possession of the country round Amber with Rajpur as their capital and from this they were dispossessed by the Kachhwāhas according to another tradition recorded by Tod. They are mentioned in the Rāsā list under the name or Garua which certainly is the Prakrit form of Gurjar. Nikumpa lastly had a kingdom at that time in Khandesh as an inscription noted by Gaurishankar dated 1153 A. D. proves. They had also a small kingdom in Jaipur territory. Nikumps, therefore, unlike the Silāhāras are both Northern India and Southern India Kshatriyas. Among the Marathas their name is now pronounced Nikam.

Besides these, we have of course the mention of Rathod or Rāṭh and Rājapala, the leading kingly families of Kanauj and Monghyr, while the Kalachūri Haihayas of Chedi are also included in the Rāsā list. What ruling families the other names indicate it is difficult to decide and neither Tod nor Gaurishankar or Mohanlal Pandya has been able to ascertain. The Dāhimas were well-known and as descendants of Dadicha Rishi are mentioned in inscriptions; but the name given in the Rāsā list is Dadhishat. This vamśa is detailed in an inscription dated 1000 A. D. in the Kansern temple in Parbatsar Dt. Jodhpur State (E. I. XII p. 61). They were feudatories of the Chāhamanas of Sāmbhar. They migrated from Thalner on the Godavari to Marwad, and held Parbratsar, Jalor and Sanchor up to 1300 A. D. "Chhacha (the inscriptor) was a ruling prince and not an Ādā Rajput (ditto)", Kārattapāla, however, are not Kathis and Kathis had no kingdom in Kathiawar about 1100 A. D. Nor can Jats be mentioned in the list as they never were looked upon as Kshatriyas, nor had they any kingdom at this time. In the absence of historical evidence we can only say that the remaining names of ruling families are not yet ascertainable.

KĀYASTHAS

The Kāyasthas who claim to be of Kshatriya origin find frequent mention in the inscriptions of this sub-period. They can be included in the Kshatriya varṇa though they form an intermediate caste according to the Smṛitis. The Kāyasthas were writers by profession and hence as writers of inscriptions they are constantly mentioned. They too seem to be divided at this time into sections according to their country of residence, like the Brahmins; for we have mention of a Gauda Kāyastha in an inscription dated 1000 A. D. (E. I. XII p. 6); the word Anvaya is not used here; but where it is used it indicates the family such as Naigamānvaya of Bijolia Insc. (Bengal J. R. A. S. LV p. 40) or Gaudānvaya of Siwalik pillar Insc. (I. A. XIX p. 218). It may be noted that we sometimes come across Kāyastha writers in inscriptions from southern India, as in the Konkan insc. of Aparāditya. The tradition among the Kāyastha Prabhus of Konkan that they came there from Northern India in later days be reconciled with this mention of Kāyasthas in about 1100 by holding that these are represented now by the Davane Kāyasthas.*

VAIŚYAS

The Vaiśyas also split into sub-divisions during this sub-period, following the example of Brahmins, on the basis of habitat. There is no mention, however, in the records of the period, of the names of the modern 84 sub-divisions of the Vaiśyas of Northern India. There are some family names such as Prāgvātānvaya or Kārāpaka Vamśa (Bijolia Insc.). There is also a mention of Poravāla and of Modha (I. A. XI p.72), Modhānvaya-Prasūta-Mahākshap; but the word anvaya added shows that they were family names and not names of sub-castes. These Vaiśyas were often Jains and hence perhaps the sub-sections were not endogamous. In the south and in the Himalayan region, there were Vaiśyas who were Saivas; the temple of Baijanāth in Kangra is stated in its inscription to have been built by two Vaiśya brothers; and the Lingāyat Vaiśyas in the south are well known as Vīraśaivas.

ŚUDRAS

It is needless to say that the Śudras must also have sub-divided at this time into innumerable sections not only on the basis of the province of residence, but also of their innumerable employments; each profession or employment consolidating itself into a sub-caste restricting marriage to itself. Indeed at this time the practice of Anuloma marriage entirely ceased, as we shall presently show, and every caste and sub-caste from the Brahmins downwards restricted marriage to itself. This

* The word Prabhu is added in this inscription to a minister's name and not to the name of the Kāyastha writer.

together with ideas of purity and peculiarities of food and customs was a great incentive to the formation of sub-castes all over the society. The formation of all the innumerable sub-castes in every varṅa or chief caste and intermediate caste into which Hindu society is divided at present took place, according to our view, during this sub-period (1000–1200), whereas in the preceding sub-periods the main castes and intermediate castes were one and undivided throughout India. Although, therefore, Al-Beruni mentions only four varṇas following the Smṛitis, the tendency to the development of sub-castes had arisen even in his time; but the actual division took place after him.

UNTOUCHABLES

From the most ancient times, the outcasts or untouchables were divided into many classes and they always lived outside of towns and villages. Those usually mentioned in inscriptions are Meda and Chāndāla, the scavenger and the executioner, who were the lowest among them. But Al-Beruni gives other names. He describes the outcasts as follws: "After the Śudra follow the people called Antyaja who render various kinds of services and who are not reckoned among any caste. There are eight classes of them, *who freely intermarry* with each other, except the fuller, the shoe-maker and the weaver. These eight guilds are fuller, shoe-maker, juggler, basket and shield maker, sailor, fisherman, hunter of wild animals and birds and weaver. These guilds live near the villages and towns of the four castes and outside them."

"The people called Hādi, Doma, Chāndāla and Badhatau, are not reckoned among any caste or guild. They are occupied with dirty work like the cleansing of the village. They are considered as one sole-class. In fact they are considered like illegitimate children and they descend from Śudra father and Brahman. mother as children of fornication. Therefore, they are outcasts." (Sachau Vol. I chap. X). The above extract shows that eves in Al-Beruni's time (1030 A. D.) there were two main divisions of the outcastes, the second one being the worse of the two. Indeed Khurdadba (900 A. D.) also mentions two untouchables' castes viz. the Chāndāla and the Lahuda. The latter viz. Lahuda were rope-dancers or naṭas. Thus this two-fold division is very old and the eight untouchables of the Lahuda class mentioned by Al-Beruni are exactly those enumerated in a Smṛiti text viz. the fuller, the shoe-maker, the weaver, the basket-maker, the rope-dancer, the fisherman, the hunter and the juggler. That they intermarried except the first three is a strange observation which perhaps may be a mistake. At any rate in modern times, they do not, following the usual tendency of all Hindu sub-castes to restrict marriage to their own self. It passes understanding why the fuller, the weaver and the basket-maker should have been treated as untouchable. They had no doubt been treated as such until recently. Being a sub-division with work not unclean and with marriage restricted to itself as mentioned by Al-Beruni, their untouchability was nominal. And since they have now become touchable, there is no reason why the other five classes of the same list should remain untouchable. The word Dom is not found in the Smritis nor Hādi and the word Badhatau is inexplicable. These four untouchable castes performed uncleanly work and must have, therefore, been treated as most untouchable.

Caste in India, as we have elsewhere explained, rests on racial as well as occupational difference and it is well-known that the first three varṇas are Aryans by race, as also the castes intermediate between them. The Śudras and the untouchables are Dravidian by race. The main profession of Brahmins is that of religious service and of Kshatriyas is that of arms. Vaiśyas were agriculturists in ancient times; but they gave up agriculture in the Buddhist period as it involved the killing of insects (see Vol. II p.182). In mediæval times the occupation of agriculture mainly belonged to Śudras; and Khurdadba in 900 A. D. properly says that Śudras were those who were husbandmen by profession (ditto p. 172). But while Vaiśyas gave up agriculture, some Brahmins and Kshatriyas took to agriculture in the mediæval period and the Parāśara Smṛiti by a special provision made it allowable (see Vol. II p. 183). But this led to the degradation of these to the status of Śudras as in the Deccan and even in the Himalayan region. The Nagarkotia Brahmins, we were informed in Kangra, did not intermarry or interdine with the local Brahmins who were agriculturists and who are now even labourers or coolies. The Rāṭhis who are Kshatriya agriculturists in the Himalayan region are admitted to be only third grade Kashatriyas who may give daughters to, but cannot take daughters from, higher grade Kshatriyas. We find local agriculturist Brahmins similarly treated as Śudras by new-coming Brahmins in Orissa (see Vol. II). In the Deccan there are some agriculturist Brahmins who are also looked upon as degraded, and the agriculturist Kshatriyas, Malis and others, are treated though improperly, as Śudras.

It is a thing worth noticing that the Rajputs in this sub-period, though their profession was that of arms, distinguished themselves not only by their valour but also by their learning. Indeed some of the most famous learned kings in this sub-period have made their names immortal, such as Bhoja, Govindachandra, Ballālasena and Lakshmaṇasena, Aparāditya, Someśvara Chalukyā, Rājendra Chola and others, by their treatises on different subjects which still survive and are read with benefit. The art of singing and dancing was also developed and patronised by these kings, notably by Harsha of Kashmir, Udayāditya of Malwa and others but most notably by Rājarāja of Tanjore. Tanjore is still famous for its singing and dancing. The Kshatriyas, therefore, were properly described as almost the equals of Brahmins by Al-Beruni. They were proficient both in Śastra and Śāstra and kept up their traditional love of independence and of knowledge characteristic of the Āryan race.

CHAPTER II.

CHANGE IN MARRIAGE AND OTHER CUSTOMS.

The marriage customs of the Hindus underwent a momentous change during this sub-period. In previous centuries Brahmins and Kshatriyas could marry and did marry women from castes lower than themselves. Even Khurdadba writing about 900 A. D. states that Brahmins could take wives from Kataria or Kshatriyas (though they did not give them their daughters) and we have the well-known instance of Rājaśekhara marrying a Chāhamāna lady about 900 A. D. Al-Beruni, however, writes that "formerly a Hindu could marry a woman of his caste or lower caste, but in our time a Brahmin never marries a woman except from his own caste". Naturally in all castes and even sub-castes marriage outside the caste ceased entirely. Why this restriction arose does not appear clear. Probably the lower position assigned by the new provisions of Smṛitis to children of lower caste wives, a fact corroborated even by Al-Beruni who states that the progeny of such former marriages was treated as of the caste of the mother, must have been found inconvenient. In the same house thus of a Brahmin father, there would be children who would be Brahmins, Kshatriyas and Vaiśyas. The Manu Smṛiti rule was, as shown in Vol. II, that all such children were Brahmins and in some cases, of an intermediate caste higher than that of the mother. The difference of food and drink between a Brahmin, a Kshatriya or a Vaiśya, the Brahmins and Vaiśyas in the middle land and southern India abstaining from flesh also, must have again caused great trouble in such a mixed family. The result naturally was that marriage was restricted to the same caste and even sub-section of a caste or sub-caste.

The other conspicuous change which came over Hindu society was the growth of the custom of child marriages. When such marriages began to take place can not be definitely determined. But certain it is that child marriage was a general custom in the days of Al-Beruni who observes (Sachau Vol. II chapter XIX p. 155), "The Hindus marry at an early age and hence parents arrange for the marriages of their children." This is in fact the rule that obtains at present. Al-Beruni's remark is certainly from observation and not from Smṛitis though we may believe that the Parāśara Smṛiti provision (अष्टवर्षामुद्वहेत) making marriage of a girl of 8 years as the normal marriage was already formulated. We have seen that Prithvīrāj's first marriage was a child marriage. Vikramānka Chālukya of Kalyan's daughter's marriage with the Kadamba of Goa heir-apparent was also a child marriage. Such examples among Rajput princes indicate that child marriage was the prevailing custom among all the Hindus of the period. Bāṇa describing the marriage of Rājyaśri in about 600 A. D. describes her as fully grown-up and his description of the marriage ceremony indicates that consummation of marriage took place on the day of marriage. Thus child marriages must have come into vogue between 600 and 1000 A. D. Why they did so, it is difficult to determine. As child marriages were already prevalent in 1030 A. D., it can not be argued, as is sometimes done, that they came into vogue owing to Mahomedan oppression. We have stated elsewhere that they came into vogue owing to people's desire to prevent women becoming Buddhist nuns. Buddhism allowed women of a grown up age to become nuns and hence the marriage of girls at an early age must have become popular as a precaution. Buddhism was suppressed towards the end of the 8th or 9th century A. D. and the custom of child marriage must have grown further into popular favour. Whatever the reason, certain it is that it was an established custom in the beginning of this sub-period and further grew during its course.

Among the Kshatriyas and the Vaiśyas, Śākhā and gotra lost their importance during this sub-period and the different sub-castes counted by names the families or nukhs which formed that sub-caste or sub-section and marriage outside the family or clan or nukh and inside the sub-section became the rule and continues to be so to this day. This example was followed by all the different sub-sections of Śudras and even the outcasts, and throughout the Hindu society marriage became restricted not only to the same caste but also to the same sub-caste, or sub-section of a sub-caste. Naturally the feeling of solidarity in the Hindu society decreased and the Hindus have always consequently remained weak as a people. As stated before, it is not possible to give up caste among the Hindus, the division being both racial and occupational; but it is possible and advisable to reduce the number of sub-castes, by amalgamating their sub-sections which have come into existence for fanciful ideas of purity of blood or other fastidious reasons.

The prohibition of widow remarriage among the Aryan castes is an ancient custom among the Hindus, as old as the Sūtras or perhaps the Vedas : and Al-Beruni says rightly of his time that widows could not re-marry; they might either burn themselves on the pyre of their dead husband or lead an ascetic life (Sachau Vol. I, p. 155). "The widows of kings" he adds "are usually burnt unless they are old or have sons alive." The new custom of child marriage combined with the ancient custom of the prohibition of widow-remarriage led, however, in due time to that miserable class of women among high caste Hindus called child-widows; and strangely enough the rule of Manu-smriti which provided for the remarriage of girls whose husbands died before consummation of marriage was also at this time put into abeyance by a Kalivarja provision. We will speak of these Kalivarjas later and show that these provisions came into being probably during this sub-period itself. It passes understanding why the remarriage of child-widows was also stopped.

Al-Beruni states that a Hindu cannot have more than four wives. This is indeed strange as we have come across no such limit to the number of wives in the law-books nor in tradition or history. Kings especially married as many wives as they liked and Śrīkrishna had 108. Prithvīrāj too had, according to the Rāsā, more than 8 queens. Al-Beruni, rightly however, states that the Hindus have no divorce among them which is perhaps a custom which characterizes Hindus only and continues to this day undoubtedly to their honour.

"The Hindus marry strangers and not relatives" (Sachau Vol. II, p. 155). This refers to their law of marrying outside the family but inside the sub-caste as already described.

Marriage outside and below the caste was, as said above, prohibited. But even in the same caste different sections arose based on purity of blood and Āchāra or religious conduct and this led during this sub-period to the rise of that strange usage called Kulinism in Bengal. The five Brahmin and the five Kāyastha families which were imported by Ballālasena who was himself a learned man in the Hindu Dharma Śāstra were directed by him not to mix their blood with the local castes believed to be inferior in purity of blood and Āchāra. By degrees, however, the inferior families were allowed to give their daughters to higher family men and these Kulinas married many wives for the sake of the dowry they brought. This was allowed in the days of Lakshmanasena according to a writer in J. B. XXXIV. It is believed by him that 28 generations have passed since these families were brought.

The strangest observation of Al-Beruni in this connection is that harlotry is allowed among the Hindus meaning (vide Vol. II, p. 185 statement of Khurdadba) probably that fornication is not punished. No doubt in all temples there were harlots dedicated to the worship of the idols by dancing, especially in Śiva temples. And kings derived large revenues from the temples. But Al-Beruni thought the presence of harlots drew people to the temples and thus increased their revenues. Al-Beruni is good enough, however, to remark that the Brahmins would not allow a single harlot to dance in temples but the kings allowed them for revenue to pay the soldiers, an observation which, however, is not probably very correct both as regards the Brahmins as well as the kings.

Going on to describe other customs of the Hindus at this time we have noticed already the prevalence of the practice of Sati, which was then a living institution. Then there was the custom of putting an end to one's life in old age by drowning in the river Ganges or other sacred river. We have instances of noted kings so destroying themselves, such as Someśvara of Kalyan and others. The tree at the confluence of the Ganges and the Jumna at Prayag, was still famous and is mentioned by Al-Beruni. But his statement that "burning oneself is forbidden to Brahmins and Kshatriyas by a special law; they, therefore, drown themselves in the Ganges" (chap. LXV p. 158 Sachau Vol. II) is remarkable. The special law probably refers to the Kalivarja provision on the subject viz. भृग्वग्निपतनैश्चैव वृद्धादिमरणं तथा ॥. This rule strictly interpreted would mean that the suicide of old men and others by falling into fire or from precipices was prohibited; and would leave the permission to drown oneself in a river intact. However, as the practice of committing suicide by drowning oneself still continued, such interpretation would be necessary. There is here clear reference in Al-Beruni to a Kalivarja provision.

With regard to dress and ornaments we have to record very little, as we have not come across any special remarks of Al-Beruni on the subject. As stated in Vol. III (p. 187) the dress of the people in Sind, the Punjab and the adjoining parts of the country must have been composite, with tunic and trouser added to the old dress of the Hindus viz. two dhoties. The rage of the Hindus for ornaments remained the same as before and the ornaments of idols mentioned in the Sāsabahu temple record (I. A. XVI) show what ornaments princes and rich men used. But there is an interesting description of the dress of the women of Kanauj in the following verse of Raja-śekhara in his Kāvyamīmānsā : "With ear-rings dancing on the cheeks and with the long necklace moving, down to the navel' the dress of the women of Kanauj deserves to be honoured, their upper cloth going completely round the west down to the anklet.* This shows that northern women wore two pieces of cloth the upper one covering not only the shoulders but also the lower person down to the feet. It left the head, however, uncovered as otherwise the ear-rings would not be visible and the necklace was put over the uttarīya. The women of the south, including Gujarat, at present have no upper cloth; but their one cloth is long enough to serve the purpose of the upper cloth also. The custom of covering the face in the north and in Gujarat seems to be a later custom arisen in Mahomedan times. We may infer that men too all over India wore two pieces of cloth.

Lastly the food of the people has already been described in detail. The Brahmins in the north ate the flesh of certain animals only and abstained from wine. In the south Brahmins abstained from both. The Vaiśyas followed the Brahmins. Indeed Jainism having prospered and Vaiśyas being generally Jains it may be said that Brahmins followed the Jains and disarmed their criticism by logically and correctly observing the doctrine of Ahimsā. The wave of Ahimsā was on the land in this sub-period and beside Jains, Vaishṇavas and Lingāyats became strict vegetarians. This led to the restriction of confining food also to each sub-caste. Whereas in former times Brahmins had no objection to dine with Kshatriyas, Vaiśyas and even some good Śudras, they now restricted themselves to their own caste, nay, even sub-caste, since some Brahmins still continued to eat flesh, as proved by a Kalivarja text. Thus not only intermarriage but even interdining ceased during this sub-period among the different sub-sections into which Hindu society was now split up.

---

* ताटंकवल्गनतरङ्गितगण्डलेखमानाभिलंबिदरदोलिततारहारम् ।
आश्रोणिगुल्फपरिमण्डलितोत्तरीयं वेषं नमस्यत महोदयसुन्दरीणाम् ॥

The Kshatriyas also were impressed and some of them also gave up flesh though at certain times only. There are a few Vaishṇava Kshatriyas also who do not eat flesh. Nor does it appear that they kept up their old reputation of being abstainers from wine, at least the reigning kings as Arab writers of the last sub-period testified. For Al-Beruni records: "They drink wine before having eaten anything; then they take their meals" (p. 180 Vol. I Sachau). This is observed of Hindus generally; but we must restrict it to Kshatriyas. The further remark that they "they do not eat their (cows') meat" (ditto) is, however, applicable to all Hindus. The Hindus had long ago given up beef and considered its eating one of the five most heinous sins. The slaughter of cows and bulls even for sacrifice had also long been given up and in the returning tide of Ahimsā at this time this prohibition must have formed one of their most absolute tenets as even now it is; and Hindus and Mahomedans then must have been as now at bitter feud on this most tender point.

The Hindus then as now burnt their dead. The Sūtaka was duly observed. Al-Beruni mentions even the Sūtaka for child birth, 8 days for a Brahmin, 12 for a Kshatriya, 15 for a Vaiśya and a month for a Śudra. This appears strange. The four unclean days of menstruation of women are also mentioned. The godāna or hair-cutting ceremony took place in the third year and the perforation of the ear in the 7th or 8th year. The last custom distinguished the Hindu from the Mahomedan in particular. Al-Beruni also mentions the garbhādhāna ceremony the importance of which must have increased when the custom of child marriage became predominant.

CHAPTER III.

RELIGIOUS DISUNION.

While in the preceding sub-period, India was in the happy condition of having one religion viz. Hinduism, except in Sind, in this sub-period India drifted back into the unhappy condition of professing three religions and having schisms within each, notably within Hinduism. In addition to Sind, Ghazni, Kabul and the Panjab, in this sub-period, came under the sway of mahomedanism and Gujarat and Rajputana came under the sway of Jainism, though Jainism declined in the south. And within Hinduism itself the dissensions among the different philosophies and worships became most acute. The result was that India became weak in one essential characteristic at least, of a strong nation viz. unity of religious belief among the people. We will in this chapter describe the spread of Mahomedanism in the north-west and the progress of Jainism in the west and will also describe the growth of antagonistic schisms within Hinduism itself.

MAHOMEDANISM

We have already described the founding of the Moslem Turkish kingdom at Ghazni and the conquest of Kabul and the Panjab by Sabuktagin and Mahmud. As a consequence not only 'White India' (to the west of the Indus consisting of Kabul and Zabul) and the Panjab lost their independence but most of their population was forcibly converted to Mahomedanism. This happened in the beginning of this sub-period (975—1025 A. D.). Both Sabuktagin and Mahmud adopted the policy of forcibly converting the people of the conquered country to Mahomedanism, from motives of political expediency as well as from religious fanaticism. The opposition of the people to such forcible conversion was weak owing to the weakness of their Hindu religious feeling, especially to the west of the Indus. These people have since then so completely become Mahomedan that they have even lost all memory of the fact that they were Hindus only 900 years back, even in the mountainous tract of Ghor. Afghans and Pathans have now even come to believe that they are the descendants of Semitic peoples, come from Assyria and Arabia. The people of the Panjab in its western portion where they have mostly been converted, however, still maintain their old clan names as Rajputs or Jats and continue to confine marriage relations to themselves and to observe certain ceremonials of the old Hindu days. Panjab became generally Mahomedan by the end of this sub-period (1200). Shihabuddin Ghori having further carried on the work of forcible conversion to Mahomedanism though not to a great extent. The hilly portion of the Panjab, however, and Kashmir which still retained its independence remained Hindu.

In eastern Panjab even Mahmud, as we have seen, did not rigorously carry out the policy of forcible conversion and Shihabuddin also did the same. In the region of the Sarasvati, the Jumna and the Ganges, it was practically abandoned and the United Pr. still remain mainly Hindu. The reasons of this changed attitude appear to be; first even Mahomedan fanatical conquerors get tired of forcibly converting people. Secondly, perhaps Mahmud saw the political utility of keeping the people divided in religion in provinces remote from the centre. Thirdly, Kutubuddin and Altamash were not fanatical Moslems and were wise rulers who, like the British, saw the justice and even the wisdom of not interferring with the religion of the people. Lastly, the people of this religion were far more staunch Hindus than the people of the Panjab and notably of the region beyond the Indus. This region is the birth-place of the Brahmanic faith, the home of the Āchāryas of Hindu philosophy, of Rāma and Krishna adored as Avatāras of God by the Hindus. For these various reasons we think the people of this part of the country remained unmolested in their religious belief and still continue to be the staunchest orthodox section of the Hindu population in the whole of India. The present Mahomedan population in these parts is not descended from converted Hindus, but from those outsider Mahomedans who came in as officers during Afghan or Mogul rule at Delhi. It is naturally in a minority and hence in the political map appended to this volume, this tract may be taken as Hindu. Lower down in Bengal the policy of forcible conversion was, it seems, later adopted by Khilji governors and succeeding Bengal kings to some extent and hence the Mahomedan population in Eastern Bengal predominates. But this happened later than our period and hence Bengal may also be taken as Hindu in the map above referred to. But though thus from the Sutlej to the Brahmaputra and from the Himalaya to the Vindhya, the country was wholly Hindu in the beginning of this period and only sparcely Mahomedan at the end of it, the unity of religious belief even in this region was marred during this sub-period by the progress of Jainism notably in Gujarat and Rajputana and of Vaishṇavism in Bengal. Curiously enough Jainism declined in the south in this sub-period. It would be interesting to note this progress of Jainism in one part and decline in another and try to explain it as far as can be done from the scanty historical evidence available on the subject. It will be necessary for this purpose to sketch briefly the rise and progress of Jainism up to the beginning of this sub-period.

JAINISM

Jainism is often confounded with Buddhism both by many western scholars as also by some Purāṇa writers for the simple reason that Ahimsā is a common tenet of both and that Jina is a name applied both to Mahāvīra and to Gautama. And even the name Buddha can be and is applied to both (e. g. बुद्धो जिन: पातु न:) meaning awakened. Jina means conqueror (of the mind) and the epithet was originally applied to both these teachers. Then again the name Jaina of the followers of Mahāvīra is only a later name, the former name applied to them being Niggrantha. Both Mahāvīra and Gautama were again contemporaries. But there is no doubt that Gautama is the later of the two. As a protestor against the Vedic religion, Gautama Buddha is the last and Mahāvīra preceded him in time as also in thought as we proceed to show. Let us see in what points they protested against the Vedic religion. The thinkers of the Upanishads had already begun to speculate on the highest metaphysical questions and had developed certain philosophic ideas, though they continued to stick to their old Vedic religion. That religion including the philosophic thoughts of the Upanishads taught the following namely :—

1st—The revelation of the Vedas.

2nd—The worship of the Vedic gods Indra, Varuṇa etc. and the post-Vedic developments of Vishṇu and Śiva.

3rd—Highest efficacy of animal-sacrifices to the Vedic gods.

4th—The Chāturvarṇya theory including the sacerdotal sanctity of Brahmins i. e. the priests at the sacrifices.

5th—The theory of Āśramas chiefly of the third for practising Tapa and the 4th for attaining Moksha by Sanyāsa or renunciation. The Brahmins began to teach that these two Āśramas were open to Brahmins only.*

6th—The theory of Ātman (soul) and the highest Brahman or impersonal God or Supreme Soul, and

7th—The Theory of Karman and transmigration of Ātman.

Already the teachers of the Upanishads had begun to preach that animal sacrifices did not lead to the highest goal but were lower in merit, though they did not condemn them, and preached that Moksha could be obtained by Sanyāsa only. The Bhagvadgītā countenanced both; indeed as an orthodox doctrine it did not condemn the views about sacrifices and Sanyāsa or the Chāturvarṇya or the Āśrama theory with the allied philosophies of Tapa and Sanyāsa (Yoga and Sāṅkhya). But it preached the new doctrine of Bhakti of Vishṇu which would take even *women and śūdras* (denied absolution by Brahmins) to the highest goal.

Such was in a nutshell the development of religious thought in India till about 1000 B. C. While the orthodox believed in all these tenets, different teachers denied some of them and accepted others. The many protestant thinkers who arose hereafter are, however, forgotten but the last two Mahāvīra and Gautama were more powerful than the rest and founded protestant religions which survive to this day. Both Gautama and Mahāvīra denied the first five items, and accepted the last viz. the law of Karman: but while Mahāvīra accepted also the two Āśramas of Tapas and Sanyāsa, Gautama went beyond him and denied Tapas and only stuck to Sanyāsa. Naturally he was heard with greater zest, especially as he admitted all people whether Aryans or non-Aryans (the Traivarnikas and Śūdras), whether male or female, to his order of Sanyāsa and did not recognise Tapas or self-mortification at all. There was no God nor Atman; at least, Buddha asked his followers not to think about them. He, however, laid the greatest stress on a moral life for a layman and on renunciation in addition for a monk. Mahāvīra was behind him, so to speak, in protest and believed in self-mortification such as fast etc, and insisted on

* Not only Sanyāsa but even Tapas was not allowed to the Śūdras, though it was for a long time allowed to Kshatriyas and Vaiśyas. The episode in the Rāmāyaṇa in which Rāma is told that a Brahmin child died owing to the sin of a Śūdra practising penance and Rāma goes to Daṇḍakāraṇya to kill that Śūdra and when he is killed the Brahmin child regains its life is illustrative of this belief that Śūdras are not allowed to perform Tapas much more Sanyāsa.

absolute renunciation including the abandoning of clothes for monks. He too laid the highest stress on a moral life for laymen. Both, of course, supported the Yoga and Sānkhya philosophies but absolutely denied the Vedas and the Brahmins.

Naturally Buddhism, as the latest and the greatest protest against Brahminism succeeded more than Jainism. Moreover, it seems to us that while Buddha preached to the common people in their language, Mahāvīra did not, and the Buddhist canon was soon evolved in Pali while the Jain canon remained unwritten for a long time. The Buddhist monk life again was easy, while Mahāvīra insisting on nudity and self-mortification, Jain asceticism was more difficult to practise. And finally, Buddhism received immense impetus from the two imperial followers, Aśoka and Kanishka. Buddhism, therefore, became the predominant religion, especially in Northern India, for many centuries while Jainism remained in a minority. In the religious map of India we have prepared from the detailed account of the travels of Hiuen Tsang and which we have appended to the first volume, it will be seen that in some parts such as Kapiśa, Sind, Magadha and Malwa, Buddhism was predominant while it shared the inhabitants equally throughout almost the whole of India. Jainism appears only in isolated places and in a minority i. e. in Bihar, in Orissa or Kalinga, in Chola and in Karnātak in the 7th century A. D. Later when Kumārila and Śankara made the final attack on Buddhism, Jainism, as an unimportant opponent, was not chiefly noticed and went on, while Buddhism was rigorously attacked and finally supplanted. It must be remembered, however, that in intellectuality Jainism was never inferior to Buddhism, for we find Jainism, as a separate philosophy, is tried to ber efuted in the Brahma-sūtras of Bādarāyaṇa. Indeed we think that the Jains from the very beginning were posted in all the necessary Śāstras, logic and grammar especially, and their proficiency in astrology and medicine always attracted the respect of the common people. It seems that intellectual Brahmins also joined the ranks of Jains as of Buddhists from time to time owing to conviction as well as for honour and contributed to the maintenance of the reputation of the Jains for learning.

Like Buddhism, in fact like every other religion, Jainism was early divided into two sects. While the Digambaras insisted on nudity for monks, the Śvetāmbaras allowed them white clothes (two in number). The Jains who went to and preached in the south were of the Digambara sect, the Svetāmbaras in southern India being mostly traders come in recent times from Gujarat or Rajputana. The first great teacher who went into the southern country was Bhadrabāhu who is said to have gone from Ujjain during a famine and went with many followers as far as Sravaṇa Belgola in Mysore territory. There must be others who went from Bihar via Kalinga along the eastern coast. It is thus we find the Jain religion established in Āndhra, in Tamil land and in Karnātaka, though not in Mahārāshtra, from early centuries of the Christian era down to the days of Hiuen Tsang and later. The Jain ascetics being learned men took up the three vernacular languages of the three countries and produced the first literature in them viz, in Tamil, Kanarese and Telugu, and for this reason they succeeded in impressing the common people in these lands. There were thus and there still are Jains among the common people in these provinces while there are very few in Northern India among the illiterate masses.

The Jain pandits first used Sanskrit words in their unchanged or Tatsama, forms in vernacular writing and thus embellished Tamil, Kanarese and Āndhra literatures. They did not use the modulated prakrit forms like the Buddhists; and thus added beauty to their vernacular writings. They also wrote the grammars of these local vernaculars in Sanskrit. They again appear to have started schools for children; as strangely enough we find in Āndhra, Tamil and Karnātaka and even in Mahārāshṭra that the first sentence taught to children in writing varṇamālā is still the Jain salutation "Om Namah Siddham". The Telugu people use the formula "Om Namah Śivāya, Siddham Namah" (Andhra-Karnatak Jainism p. 64 Studies in South Indian Jainism by Ramaswamy Ayyangar, M. A. The latter portion is said by him to be Buddhist; but it seems also to be Jain). "The first part has been added subsequently by Śaivas in the south to obliterate the influence of Jains, and when the Śaivas themselves started Matams and Pāthaśālas or primary schools in villages and towns." "In Kalinga or Ooriya the formula is "Siddhirastu" which is clearly Jain" (ditto). In Mahārāshṭra "Srī Ganeśāya Namah" is added to "Om Namah Siddham". These relics show that formerly Jain ascetics took a great share in teaching children in the southern countries.

The Jains also exerted their best to secure influence at the several Hindu courts in the south. In the Tamil land, the Pāndyas and Cholas made donations to Jain gurus, and Jain temples and monastaries were built near Mādura, the capital of the Pāndyas, even in the early centuries of the Christian era. In Gangavādi in Mysore territory, the Ganges appear to have specially patronised the Jains and probably they were themselves Jains. Samantabhadra was a great Digambara Jain teacher who according to Śravana Belgola Inscription No. 44 "beat the drum" (literally and invited opponents to refute him) at Pātaliputra, in Malwa, in Sind, in Thakka country (the Panjab) and then came to Kānchī in the south and thence came to Karnātaka. "He was followed by Sinhānandi who founded, it is believed, the Gangavadi state." Samantabhadra is the author of the important Jain work "Āpta Mimānsā" the most authoritative exposition of the Syādvāda doctrine. Pūjyapāda was another learned Jain who is the author of the Jain Sanskrit grammar "Jinendra Vyākaraṇa", Akalanka is said to have confuted the Buddhists at the court of Himaśītala in Kānchī and thereby procured the expulsion of Buddhists from South India" (p. 33 ditto). Thus the Jains both by their learning and asceticism secured favour in the court of the several kingdoms in the south and many kings gave them inam villages as also built temples and carved colossal images of Jina. It may be noted that both Buddhism and Jainism while they denied God and idol-worship eventually drifted into the worship of Buddha and Jina as God and built temples with their images (though it must be conceded that certain Jain sects do not believe in images or worship any forms). The Jains erected statues to their Tīrthankaras and worshipped them in large temples. "This method of worship was highly impressive and attractive and it was imitated by the Hindus" (p. 77 ditto). The result was that stupendous Hindu temples arose in the south under different kingly dynasties as has also been related in vols. I and II. In fact we have always held that idol-worship among the Hindus, though not originated by the Buddhists and the Jains, has been greatly fostered by their example.

Having so far cursorily described the progress of Jainism we will now go on to describe its decline and even fall in the south during the sub-period treated of in this volume, chiefly by the aid of the above mentioned treatise by Mr.

Ramaswamy Ayyangar. The opposition came from the revival of Śaivism and its powerful preachers. "If Sambandar (a Śaiva saint) brought about the downfall of Jainism in the Pāndya kingdom, Appar drove the Jains out from the Pallava country" (p. 66). This was in the beginning of the 8th century; but the Cholas who came to power at the end of the 10th century were devotees of Śiva and persecuted the Jains more cruelly than the previous rulers. We have already seen that one Chola king is said to have died because of the curse of the persecuted Jains. It need not, therefore, be doubted that the Cholas did use their political power for the suppression of Jainism. In the great temple built at Madurā by Rājarāja Chola, he placed the statues of the 63 Nāyanārs or Śaiva saints of the Tamil land for worship; but "in the frescoes on the walls of the Mantapam of the Golden Lily tank of the temple of Mīnākshī at Madura are paintings of the bloody episodes in the bitte struggles between Jainism and Hinduism." (p. 79).

Turning from Tamil land, to Karṇataka i. e. the Southern Maratha country and Mysore, we find that the early Chālukyas, in the former, though staunch Hindus themselves, patronised Jains and made grants to Jain temples and sadhus. Under the Rāshṭrakūṭas in the second sub-period of our history (800–1000) Jainism prospered and as stated in Vol. II (p. 203) even some Rāshṭrakūṭa kings became devotees of Jain saints and Jainism spread even among the cultivating population of the Southern Maratha country, the Vaiśyas being generally admirers of Ahimsā here as elsewhere and therefore usually Jains. The Ganga kings in Mysore were themselves Jains; and the last representative of the Rāshṭrakūṭa line Indra IV being a son of Krishṇa III by a Western Ganga princess was a devout Jain. When the later Chālukyas overthrew the last Rāshṭrakūṭa king Kakkala, Indra IV tried to set up the Rāshṭrakūṭa power but failed and as a devout Jain killed himself by Sallekhana, a Jain vow (Vol. II p. 151). In Malkhed, we found in the fort the remains of a Jain sanctuary (Vol. II p. 354) and in the town itself, there is a Jain Basti. It seems, therefore, clear that Jainism progressed in the Southern Maratha country at the end of the 10th century. But the later Western Chālukyas who came to power in this sub-period (1000–1200), Tailpa and others, were devout Śaivites and persecuted Jainism. "If the traditions of the country are to be believed, Jain statues and idols in the *Bastis* were thrown away and the Paurāṇic gods were substituted." (p. 112). Mr. Ramaswamy wrongly considers the rule of the later Chālukyas as short-lived. It was not overthrown by the Kalachūris in 1126 but in 1159 A. D., and Kalachūri rule was itself short-lived. It is, however, probable that the Kalachūri usurpation was a religious movement, Vijjana Kalachūri being a Jain. But Vijjana and the Kalachūri rule fell soon before the returning tide of Śaivism, as we will shortly describe, in a new form viz. the Lingayat schism.

In Karnāṭaka proper beyond the Tungabhadrā, the Gangas ruled for a long time and they were followers of Jain saints. The Gangas were overthrown by the Cholas of Tanjore in about 1004 A. D.; but gradually the Hoysalas established their power in Gangavādi. They were in the beginning followers of Jainism but the famous Vishṇuvardhana was converted to Vaishṇavism by Rāmānuja and Vaishṇavism has since then been firmly established in Mysore territory. "Loosing support of the kingly family in Mysore, persecuted by the Cholas in Tamil land and displaced by the Lingāyats in Southern Maratha country, Jainism naturally succumbed in southern India finally. Though a respectable number still followed the faith, they no longer obtained political influence from popularity either among the people or with the princes."

It remains to describe how Jainism declined in Āndhra where it had been established since the days of Khāravela when Digambara Jains came to it from Bihar directly. From the monogram by B. Seshagiri Rao attached to the above-mentioned treatise, it appears that local tradition and *Kaifiyats* show that Jainism was overthrown by the rising power of Śaivism there also. Āndhra Rajputs, Pūsapātis and others, stood for the Vaidic religion. The Eastern Chālukyas later patronised Śaiva poets one of whom Nannaya translated the Mahābhārata into Telugu and added support and strength to Śaivism. This Śaiva revival was further strengthened under the Eastern Ganges who were Śaivas in the beginning. The Kākatiyas of Warangal were also Śaivas and persecuted the Jains more rigorously. Lastly "the worsting of the Jains by Ganapatideva of Warangal when they were defeated in disputation with Tikkaṇa, author of the Telugu Mahābhārata (?) is more famous and is described in a poem in the Oriental Manuscripts Library in the Madras Museum" (p. 28 ditto).

Such is the history in substance of the decline and fall of Jainism in southern India during this period and the fall may be attributed chiefly to the revival of the popularity of Śiva worship. We need not recount the many stories of miracles wrought by Śaiva saints or of victories of Jain disputants and of the Yogic powers of both, Yoga being taken up and lauded to the skies by both religions; nor need we detail the stories of how the Jains were persecuted and even impaled by Chola intolerant kings who gave up the traditional toleration of Hindu monarchs. But we proceed to describe how Jainism while it decayed in the south prospered and progressed in the west in this very sub-period.

We have said in Vol. II that Jainism was not in ascendancy in Gujarat and Rajputana during the previous sub-period (800–1000) and we may place its progress there in this sub-period. Why this Ahimsā religion progressed at this time under the rule of Śaivite Rājput kings with all their pride of arms and their trade of killing is really a wonder. And yet in all Rajput states, in Sambhar and Mewad, in Malwa and Gujarat, Jainism made progress at this time, the rulers being all worshippers of Śiva, in fact as staunch Śaivites as the Kshatriya rulers of southern India. There was no doubt the returning tide of the Buddhistic or Jain feeling of respect for non-slaughter. From the Upanishadic times, the Hindus have alternately been swayed by this regard for Ahimsā and have alternately given up their adherence to Vedic animal sacrifice. The revival of Hinduism or rather Vedic-Āryanism under Kumārila and Śankara had subsided and the tide of Buddhist Ahimsā feeling was no doubt returning. But while it did not assist Jainism in the south for reasons which we will presently explain, it led on Jainism to popularity in Gujarat, Malwa and Rajputana. We believe in the powerful influence of personalities and we attribute the progress of Jainism in the western parts of the country in this sub-period to the influence of the great Jain pandit Hemachandra.

The story of the life of this great Jain teacher is not obscure as that of Kumārila or Śankara; for he is associated with the reigns of two great kings of Gujarat, Jayasinha Siddharāja and Kumārapāla. It does not, however, appear (as we once thought) that he was a southern Jain or he received his inspiration from the south. Indeed the Jain teachers of the south were all Digambaras, who, it may be admitted, carry the doctrine of renunciation to all its logical demands. The Jains of Gujarat and Rajputana were and are mostly Śvetāmbaras who allow two white clothes to their Munis; and Hemachandra was a Śvetāmbara both as student and teacher. He was born in a Jain Vaiśya family in Gujarat and was given in early life by his mother to her Jain teacher who saw his great intelligence and his future promise. He became an Āchārya and came to Anhilwād as the head of its Jain sanctuary. His birth is placed in 1084 A. D. and death in 1168 A. D. at the age of 84. He signalised himself by his great works viz. his Sanskrit and Prakrit grammar, his Kāvya Dvyāśraya wherein the history of the Chālukyas of Gujarat themselves is told and illustrations of his grammatical rules are also given and his Deśi Nāmamāla or dictionary of Deśi or local (not Sanskrit) words. It is said that he was once taunted by a Hindu pandit that after all he used the grammar of a Hindu (Pāṇini). He thereupon composed an exhaustive grammar of Sanskrit and Prakrit himself. The grammatical treatise was taken in a great procession laid on the temples of an elephant on which the author was himself seated and was deposited in the royal treasury. It was dedicated to Jayasinha Siddharāja and hence named Siddha Hema. Hemachandra does not appear to have travelled through India, but his influence on Kumārapāla was so preponderant that he procured several privileges for Jains from him and had animal slaughter prohibited on certain days sacred to the Jains.* The preponderance of Jainism in Gujarat may be dated from his time, at least, the great respect which is paid to the doctrine of Ahimsā in that land.

In the Chauhan country also and as far north as the Sutlej Jainism seems to have spread during this period, so much so that almost all Vaiśyas in Marwar may be said to have accepted Jainism. And these merchants of Marwar have carried Jainism to the farthest parts of India by their sojourn therein for trade. In Malwa and Mewad too, under later kings though they themselves remained staunch Śaivites. Jainism seems to have come into favour at this time. Examples of kings who favoured the Jains have been recorded in the several chapters of this history and it is not necessary to mention them here again.

NEW VAISHṆAVISM

In the rest of Northern India we do not find Jainism much in favour with the princes or the people though Jain Vaiśyas

* Jains represent that Kumārapāla was converted to Jainism in old age by Hemachandra and the date assigned is St. 1216 or 1159 A. D. But this does not appear probable for reasons given in chapter 7 Book VII.

were to be found all over the country. Neither under Gāhadavālas, nor under Pālas or Senas, do we find Jainism much in favour. But though Jainism did not prosper in the middle nor in the east of Northern India, the revival of the feeling of Ahimsā was not less strong there than in the west in this sub-period. We have seen that the religion of Buddha received fresh inspiration in Magadha from new teachers and some learned Buddhists went as usual on a preaching mission into Tibet and reformed that religion of peace in Tibet (p. 225). But more marked than this was the revival of Ahimsā doctrine in the appearance of new Vaishṇavism. This new Vaishṇavism appeared in Bengal at this time with the same intense regard for Ahimsā as was exhibited by Jainism and Buddhism. Indeed new Vaishṇavism may be looked upon as Jainism tacked on to the old worship of Śrīkrishṇa, as Christianity may be described as Buddhism tacked on to Judaism. Buddhism was dead in India at this time except in Magadha. Buddha had been changed into an Avatāra of Vishnu and Buddhists had generally turned into Vaishṇavas. Naturally the respect for Ahimsā came back with the force of a returning tide; and Vaishṇavism took up Ahimsā as it had never done before. The Bhagavadgitā, no doubt, preached Ahimsā long before the rise of Buddha himself but the Ahimsā of the Bhāgavatas was reconciled as evidenced by the Mahābhārata with Vedic religion of animal sacrifice by the doctrine that slaughter in Vedic sacrifices was no slaughter. But the slaughter of animals in propitiation of the Deity was plainly indefensible and was always the weak point of the Vedic religion as of Judaism and both Jaiṇs and Buddhists assailed it with success on this point and their preachers generally scored victory over Hindu or Vedic opponents. New Vaishṇavism, by taking up the doctrine of Ahimsā more rigidly than before, disarmed the Jains and thus succeeded in appealing to the common people by returning to their old god Vishṇu in the form of Śrīkrishṇa and by stopping Vedic sacrifices with animal slaughter. This new Vaishṇavism not only stopped animal sacrifices but further adopted the Jain doctrine of abstaining from meat diet. From the Indus to the Brahmaputra this new Vaishṇavism became predominant at this time (1000–1200) and animal slaughter and animal food was renounced by Vaishṇvas. Even now in the Panjab Vaishṇava food means meatless food.

It does not appear that this new Vaishṇavism came from the south or was due to the teaching of the Vaishṇava Bhāgavata Purāṇa. Nor was its rise due to the teaching of Śankara who was a thorough supporter of the Vedic ritual. Whatever the influencing cause in Northern India, it was certainly not the Bhāgavata Purāṇa, the date of which, we have elsewhere shown, could not be earliar than the tenth century A. D. And we find in Kashmir history king Avantivarman (855-884) a thorough Vaishṇava of the new type, prohibiting totally the slaughter of animals in the kingdom of Kashmir (see Vol. I p. 221) as in the old days of Meghavāhana. The Buddist love for Ahimsā returned again in the ninth century and Avantivarman used his political power for establishing Ahimsā, being himself a devout Vaishṇava. The imperial Pratīhāra Bhoja was a Parama Vaishṇava (Vol. II p. 109) as also his grandson, though we are not quite sure if they were of the type of Avantivarman i. e. total abstainer from animal food and prohibitors of animal slaughter. The Gāhadavālas were worshippers of Lakshmī or Śrī who is invoked in their inscriptions in the beginning and also of Dāmodara. They were practically Smārtas as they are described in inscriptions as Māheśvaras but they are also always described as worshipping Vāsudeva at the time of making land grants. In Magadha, the Pālas were Buddhists and therefore thorough supporters of the doctrine of Ahimsā; but even there we find a queen hearing the whole Mahābhārata recited to her. In Eastern Bengal the Senas were in the beginning devotees of Śiva but Lakshmaṇasena, their most noted king, became a Parama Vaishṇava and he must be taken to be a perfect supporter of the doctrine of Ahimsā. He himself must have abstained from flesh, though we have no evidence to hold that he prohibited animal slaughter in his kingdom. His Vaishṇavism appears to have come from Jagannātha in Orissa where the new Vaishṇavism became dominant at this time for reasons we shall sketch later on. Thus in Northern India at this time, Jainism in the west and Vaishṇavism in the north and east became predominant with their doctrine of Ahimsā as their prominent tenet.

But though this new Vaishṇavism and Jainism were at one on the doctrine of Ahimsā, they unfortunately differed most strongly on the question of asceticism. The Hindu world has also swung alternately between asceticism and epicurianism, the philosophy of self-mortification and that of self-indulgence. Śrīkrishna's life practically preached the doctrine of the enjoyment of world's blessings, though he always preached the value of the golden mean. His worship, however, soon drifted into what may be called for want of a better word, Epicurianism which appeared in Bengal and in Mid-India at this time and soon became popular. While therefore, the new Vaishṇavism taught Ahimsā like Jainism, unlike Jainism it taught the enjoyment of worldly blessings. The swing went naturally to the other extreme point of the swing like a pendulum and licentiousness became the leading feature of this new Vaishṇavism. The cult of Rādhā worship does not appear to have yet arisen; for Rādhā is not mentioned even in the Bhāgavata. But the amours of Krishṇa with the Gopīs had become the leading doctrine of the Vaishṇavas at this time; for even the Bhāgavata the chief new Purāṇa teaching the Vaishṇava cult, could not but depict these amours in their objectionable character, concealed in later times under the allegorical cloak of Vedānta. For in the Bhāgavata, a direct question is asked by Parīkshit as to whether these immoral deeds of the great are an example to be followed by ordinary beings. Śuka does not say in reply in the Bhāgavata that these were mere allegories embodying the yearning of the human soul for the Supreme Soul; but straightly answers that the teachings and not the actions of great men are to be followed. The Bhāgavata, therefore, plainly held these amours to be not only historical, but also unworthy of being imitated. The Rādhā cult was, however, a natural outcome of this belief in the amours of Śrikrishṇa, as the human mind can not be satisfied without assigning one woman as the object of greatest love and we find Gītagovinda of Jayadeva, a court-poet of Lakshmaṇasena, describing at this time in most enchanting tones the amours of Krishṇa and Rādhā who is still an adulteress.

We are not concerned here with the further development of the Rādhā cult wherein she becomes a wife of Krishṇa; as this belongs to a period later than 1200 A. D. In the days of Lakshmaṇasena this Rādhā cult was just rising and probably the Vaishṇavism which came to Bengal in his days from Orissa was without Rādhā. But that it was full of lascivious teaching can not be denied. As we have said above, the Hindu mind had swung at this time towards Epicurianism from asceticism and the extreme prosperity of the Hindu kingdoms at this time tended in the same directions and we have already adverted to the popularity of the Alamkāra Śāstra at this time. This is a question which has to be carefully sifted yet; but we have no doubt that the Vaishṇavism of Bengal and Orissa of this time fully countenanced the legends of the amours of Śrīkrishṇa and the Gopīs, and in general placed enjoyment above asceticism.* Though Vallabha and Chaitanya had still to come and to debase or refine this amorous aspect, the seed was sown at this time. This epicurian aspect of Vaishṇavism coupled with its Ahimsā must have appealed more to the people than Jainism and thus prevented the Spread of the latter in Northern India.

New Vaishṇavism also appeared in the South at this time; but it was devoid of this debased feature. It took up of course Ahimsā and disarmed Jain criticism. It, however, supported asceticism. It further accepted the revelation of the Vedas and the priesthood of the Brahmins and the Varṇāśramdharma and thus appealed to the orthodox sentiment of the people. It also opposed the philosophy of Śankara which left little room for the practice of devotion which was a dominant doctrine of Vaishṇavism from of old and for this purpose had to put a new interpretation on the Upanishads, the Bhagvadgītā and the Brahmasutras, the sacred philosophical books, so to speak, of the orthodox. A new powerful Vaishṇava teacher arose at this time in the South. The Tamil land always was, even according to the Bhāgavata Purāṇa, the stronghold of Vaishṇavism and Vaishṇava saints or Ālavārs sang the praises of Vishṇu there from of old as the Śaivite saints the Nāyanārs sang the praises of Śiva. But Vaishṇavism had to be supported by a new philosophy opposing that of Śankara and Rāmānuja came forward at this time to do that work. His life is well-known and is well-given in Dr. Bhandarkar's "Vaishṇavism". He was born in 1017 A. D. and he first studied under an Advaita (Śānkara) philosopher, Yādavaprakāsha, at Kānchī. Being dissatisfied with his teaching, he applied himself to the study of the Prabandhas of the Ālavārs and "drank in their spirit of devotion." He succeeded Yāmunāchārya as a Vaishṇava teacher at Śrīrangam near Trichinopoly and did his life's work there by writing his Bhāshyas on the three sacred books above mentioned. The Chola kings of his time were Śaivas and they wanted him to renounce Vaishṇavism. He thereupon took refuge with the Hoysala king Vishṇuvardhana in Mysore

* The obscene figures sculptured on the temple of Jagannath built by Chodganga at this time (1150 A. D.) can have no other explanation.

who was inclined towards Jainism (1096 A. D.) and converted him to his faith.

The teachings of Rāmānuja spread in the south and in later centuries were taken to the north by his future follower Rāmānanda. "His Vaishṇavism is that of the old Pāñcharātra system combined with the Nārāyaṇa and Vishṇu elements. The most prominent name of God with him is Nārāyaṇa and the name Gopāla Krishṇa is conspicuous by its absence (p. 57)." Rāmānuja's system is free from the debased cult of Rādhā. He takes up no doubt the Bhakti doctrine of the Bhagavadgītā but it is reduced to the form of a continuous meditation on the Supreme Soul. He has given a Brahmanical form to the traditional doctrine of devotion wherein Śūdras are not regarded as capable of attaining highest Moksha. But in the later school of Rāmānuja from Rāmānanda, the Śūdras asserted themselves (ditto). Thus though Rāmānuja stuck to the orthodox doctrine about the sanctity of the Brahmins, his northern school gave it up and removed its objectionableness on the ground of caste, though it did not give up Varṇa altogether.

NEW OR VĪRA ŚAIVISM.

While this new Vaishṇavism in different forms was thus developing in opposition to Śaivism in the east and the south i. e. in Āndhra and Tamil land, Śaivism was again asserting itself in Karnātaka in the rise of the Lingayat schism at this very time. It was in fact a strenuous re-assertion against Jainism which for a few years suddenly strove to obtain mastery over it in northern Karnātaka under the Kalachūri usurpation, a frantic effort so to speak by Śaivism to regain its lost ground. Before we give the history of this neo-Śaivism, we must give a short summary of the history of Śaivism itself from the beginning as we gave the summary of the history of Jainism which it supplanted, in order that the Lingayat schism may be properly understood.

Saivism is no doubt as old as the Vedas, Rudra being praised even by Ṛigvedic Ṛishis both in his terrible as well as his gracious form as Śiva. When the Vedic philosophers developed the idea of a supreme God of which all other gods were manifestations, and when the thinkers of Upanishad days evolved the Para Brahman doctrine, there was a division among the Vedic worshippers. Some raised Vaishṇu to this highest position while others adopted Śiva as the highest God, though the predominant opinion seems to be in favour of Vishṇu.

(See अग्निर्वैदेवानामवमो विष्णुः परमः Ait. Ār.). The identification of Śiva with the Para Brahman appears to be a later idea, as it is not to be found in the oldest ten Upanishads but is to be found distinctly first in the later Śvetāśvatara. This difference of opinion was bound to arise since, as stated before, every religion in its growth splits itself into two stems (like a tree), these again giving rise to several branches. Vedic Aryan religion thus in the post-Vedic period divided itself into Vaishṇavism and Śaivism. Śaivism appears to have, however, become the religion of the commonalty as the common people are more afraid of ghosts and demons, as also of the terrific aspects of nature; and Rudra Śiva was early considered to be the god of demons and of diseases. Moreover, the phallic worship of the aboriginal people, to which there are plain allusions in the Vedas, was identified with Rudra worship in the post-Vedic period at a very early date; much earlier than Dr. R. G. Bhandarkar is disposed to assign to it (p. 115). For non-mention, as we have often insisted, is not conclusive proof and because Patanjali refers to images of Śiva and not to the Linga form, or because the coins of Wema Kadphises give on the obverse the human figure of Śiva, it cannot follow that Linga worship was not known in their days. The plain reference to linga worship as the worship of Śiva in the Mahābhārata shows that it was already orthodox about 300 B. C. Of course, Śiva was then as now worshipped in both forms namely a human form with five heads and the Linga form. But the Linga worship became popular especially as it soon assumed a highly philosophical or esoteric meaning in which its original idea was entirely lost. Even now Linga worship is nowhere associated with any obscene idea. This esoteric blending of Aryan and Non-Aryan worship made it the worship of the common people at a very early period.

Śaivism like Vaishṇavism also early developed its own separate philosophy and the Pāśupata philosophy is referred to in the Mahābhārata along with Pāncharātra and Sānkhya, Yoga and Vedānta. (Indeed knowledge is therein said to be five-fold as above). The Vedānta Sūtras of Bādarāyaṇa (150 B. C.) also refute both the Pāncharātra and the Pāśupata tenets. What these doctrines were we are not able to find at first hand. They are quoted by Śankara in his Bhāshya or given by Mādhava in his Sarvadarshanasangraha. There are many Śaiva Āgamas but they are of *recent* date. All Śaiva sects believed strongly in asceticism and Hiuen Tsang speaks of Śaiva monks residing in

Śiva temples. These appear mostly to be followers of the Āgama of Lakulīśa, a famous Śaiva philosopher probably of the sixth century, who arose in Gujarat (at Kāyāvatāra Tīrtha in Broach District). They are described minutely even in inscriptions as well of this sub-period as of the previous sub-period. Their names end usually in Śiva or in Rāśi (e. g. Hārīta-rāśi, the guru of Bappā Rāwal). They had also an apostolic succession and in one inscription the saintly line is described with as great fulness as the kingly line. But the questions vital to our inquiry remain unsolved. We do not know whether these ascetics were Brahmins only or belonged to all castes, whether the Lakulīśa Āgama accepted the sanctity of Vedic sacrifices with animal slaughter and whether it prohibited animal food. The Śivatāntrika works have to be studied carefully for the elucidation of these points and with our limited knowledge of them it is difficult to express a definite opinion. No work of Lankulīśa himself has yet been found.* But it is very probable that the different Śaiva sects allowed all castes to become ascetics of their order and for them at least they prohibited animal food. But for lay devotees, it does not seem that Śaivism insisted on vegetable food as Vaishnavism did and it is for this reason that Śaivism was the general religion of the common people and especially of all heroic Rajput families which came to the front in the seventh and eighth centuries by opposing the onward rush of the Mahomedans. The great deeds of Bappā Rāwal in this connection were inspired by his saintly guru Hārītarāśi. The other Rajput kingly families also, as we have seen, were followers of Śaivism during the past sub-period and even in this sub-period with a few exceptions. Such was the religious condition of the country generally and of Kuntala especially under the later Chālukyas who were staunch Śaivites, when Jainism suddenly made headway under the Kalachūri usurpation.

Though the accounts of the Jains and of the Lingayats as given in their Basava Purāna differ, certain central facts are common to both. Basava the founder of the Lingayat sect was a Brahmin who was for some time even minister to Vijjana, the Kalachūri commander-in-chief of the Chālukyas who had just usurped their power. Basava appears to us to be himself a great reformer and thinker and we differ, with due deference, from the view of Dr. R. G. Bhandarkar that Basava was "merely

* The Panchādhyāyī of Lakrulīśa is not yet found though references to it are numerous.

a strenuous supporter of an existing sect" called Ārādhya. Basava's doctrines are so distinct and novel that he must be considered the founder of a new sect. The Basava Purāṇa in effect expresses this view when it represents that Basava was an Avatāra of Nandi sent by Śiva to establish Śiva worship which according to Nārada had disappeared from the land. He may have taken some tenets from an older sect called Ārādhya; but he certainly gave it a new and a distinct turn. His maternal uncle Baladeva was the minister of the king before him and he himself became minister after his uncle's death. It is said that his sister was married to the king while the Jains represent her to be a mistress of the king. It seems that the latter is a misrepresentation; and it is probable that Basava, not being a believer in the caste system, must have had no objection to this Pratiloma marriage. This itself shows that Basava made a most pronounced departure from old practice. Basava and the king who was a Jain must both have had a contempt for the caste system believed in by the orthodox; but their religions differed on other most vital points and naturally brought them into violent conflict. Basava spent large sums from the treasury on Jangamas or Lingayat religious men. The king thereon denounced Basava who fled. There are discrepant accounts as to what happened thereafter. But certain it is that Vijjana was assassinated by a Jangama (1167 A. D.). Thus began the feud between the Jains and the Lingayats. The Kalachūri usurpation was short-lived being supplanted by the Chālukya Someśvara, the rightful king in 1182 A. D. But the Lingayat sect spread in Kuntala or Southern Maratha country rapidly and finally almost drove Jainism out of the Karnātaka country.

We must advert here to the peculiar doctrines of this new Vīra Śaiva or valiant Śaivite sect which enabled it to drive out Jainism. In the first place Basava adopted Ahimsā as his main doctrine and thus satisfied the popular trend of opinion which was now entirely in favour of non-slaughter, and removed one vulnerable tenet of Hinduism which Jains successfully attacked. He also denied the Varṇāśrama Dharma, another vulnerable point of Hinduism. He denied that Brahmins had any special sanctity and affirmed that every one was entitled to attain the highest goal. The Vaishṇavas of the South could not give up the ancient varṇa system of the Hindus and stuck to it. But Basava boldly came forward to abandon caste and in his days intermixture between Brahmins and even Chāndālas took place.

He even denied Sanyāsa and Tapa and thus going beyond the Jains scored a point over them and every one, he preached, must live by his own toil and never beg, not even the Jangamas, their priests. Basava is thus almost the first Indian thinker who preached the dignity of labour and stopped all beggary. He alone preached that only Kāyaka (work) led to Kailāsa. He insisted on a strictly moral life for all men with perhaps greater success than Jainism and Buddhism; for the Lingayats as a community eschew all frivolity and generally lead a highly moral life. Lastly, he stuck to the old Linga worship of the common people and did not thus disturb their god. Of course Basava had to infuse a higher esoteric meaning into the symbol and to insist upon his followers wearing constantly upon their person the sacred Linga. He had done away with the Brahmanic thread and he substituted for the same a silver thread with Linga attached to it. Having denied the Brahmins and the caste system, Basava had naturally recourse to the language of the people in which to preach to them. Basava cared not to copy the Jains in carrying on disputations with orthodox pandits in the Sanskrit language; but spoke pithy words of advice and doctrine in the Kanarese which have become the scripture of the Lingayats. For this reason also, Basava's sect secured victory over the Jains and even over the orthodox in the view of the common people. To the present day, among the agriculturists and the trading population in Karnāṭaka, the Lingayats are in preponderance from his time.

It does not concern us to detail the various philosophical tenets of the Lingayats as compared with those of Rāmānuja or Śankara for which the reader may refer to the learned treatise of Dr. R. G. Bhandarkar on Śaivism. But we may mention that the Lingayats after denying caste, as usual with Hindus, developed a sort of caste system in which the Āchāryas and the Jangamas are Brahmins so to speak, the latter being married. The Panchamas also consist of other castes though they are few in number. The Lingayat sect as a social reform is very much in favour of women who have the same Upanayana ceremony as men in early age, who are not compelled to observe untouchability in their monthly sickness and who are believed to be as capable of attaining the highest goal (Sāmarasya) as the men. The sect have prescribed a Gayatrī of their own (Om Namaḥ Śivāya) and have also a gotra-pravara system of their own. They are total abstainers from flesh and wine.

NOTE—RICE ON VĪRAŚAIVAS AND THEIR APOSTLES.

We give the following extract from Rice's History of Kanarese Literature in connection with the Lingayat sect and its founder Basava and other apostles (pp. 49–55). The Vīraśaivas (stalwart) are distinguished from three other Śaivas viz : 1 the Sāmānya and 2 Miśra who worship Vishṇu as well as Śiva and 3 the Suddha Śaivas who worship Śiva only but do not wear linga. The distinctive peculiarity of Vīraśaivas is that they (both men and women) always wear on the person a small stone linga in a silver or wooden reliquary suspended from the neck. The Jangamas or Lingāyat "religious" wear it on their head. The investiture with the linga like Upanayana is the most sacred rite of childhood.

Basava taught that men of all castes and even outcastes were eligible to enter the Lingayat sect. Other peculiarities are that they do not cremate their dead but bury them ; and they permit the remarriage of widows. Their scriptures consist of 28 Śaivāgamas. Śivagītā is also highly placed. Their leading doctrines are ashṭāvaraṇam and shatsthala. Reverence is paid to 63 ancient saints (Tamil), only eight of whom are Vīraśaivas. Among the later saints are Basava and his chief disciples. Their principal Maṭha is at Chītaldrug in Mysore territory.

Basava the reputed founder of the sect was an Ārādhya Brahmin. In his childhood he resided at Kappadi at the junction of the Malaprabha and the Krishna where was a Śiva shrine named Sangameśvara. Here he became conscious of a call to revive the Vīraśaiva faith. When his father-in-law and maternal uncle who was a minister to Bijjala died he was called to succeed him. His sister Padmāvatī was married to the king. He had another sister whose son was Channa Basava his greatest disciple. In concert with him he began to propound his new doctrine and new mode of worshipping Śiva. Having charge of the king's treasury, he spent large sums in supporting the Jangamas. A Brahmin minister named Manchana accused him of embezzlement. The king tried to arrest him but he fled and being joined by his adherents defeated the king who was compelled to re-instate him.

Of what followed there are different accounts. The Lingayats say that the king wanted to put out the eyes of two Lingayat devotees when Basava cursed Kalyan, directed one of his disciples to kill the king and retired to Sangameśvara where he was absorbed into the Linga. The Jains say that Basava sent the king a poisoned fruit and fled to Ulavi at the foot of the Western Ghats where he was besieged by the king's son and in despair he threw himself into a well.

To Basava are attributed prose works (in Kanarese) expository of the Lingayat faith viz. Shatsthala-vachana, Rālajnāna-vachana, Shat ι chall-ravachana, Rājayoga-vachana and Mantra gopya.

His chief disciple was Channa Basava who is considered even higher than Basava, being looked upon as an avatāra of Śiva himself. As Basava was engrossed in state business, the religious movement was largely under his direction. It is said that after his uncle's death he was admitted to the royal favour. Other leading associates were Madivāla Māchayya, Prabhudeva and Siddharāma of whom wonderful stories are told in Channa Basava and other Purāṇas.

Thus during this sub-period, Jainism spread in the west and Śaivism in the south and Vaishṇavism in the east and even in the north as far as Kashmir. These two again were divided into several sects which developed different philosophical systems with their different concepts and different terminologies, so that the intellegentia of the country was torn by conflicting views on metaphysical questions. These schisms not only adopted different gods as the supreme deity but further represented other deities as subordinate to their highest God. Along with the two dominant schisms Śaivism and Vaishṇavism, the worship of Durgā and Gaṇapati also developed their philosophies and Āgamas and separate modes of worship in which these gods were represented as the highest. These schisms probably also belong to this sub-period though we have no definite grounds to hold this. The social changes effected by these different schisms were also various and the lay followers who could not fight on high philosophic questions fought on minor points such as the supremacy of this god or that god or such questions as the sacred character of Brahmins, the necessity of nudity for monks or the fitness of women to attain salvation. The Hindu world was thus divided into different and differing sections which often warred with one another; and thus lost national strength for which unity of religious beliefs is an essential qualification. And the one point on which these differing schisms were unanimous was the Ahimsā doctrine; they all discountenanced, if not actually prohibited, animal slaughter and animal food and thus added to the weakness of the Hindus for national defence. Even the new Śaivism of Kashmir propounded by Abhinavagupta and Kallata* appears to countenance Ahimsā for otherwise it could not have prospered in the reign of the thoroughly Vaishnava king Avantivarman mentioned in the beginning. It may, however, be admitted that the generality of people in Northern India and in Mahārāshtra were followers of the old Smārta religion in which all the five gods of Hinduism were treated as equally great. But in the south and the east Śaivism and Vaishṇavism which had together supplanted Jainism fought with each other with great animosity and kings used their political power for the

---

* In Vol. I (p. 221) we said that we did not know who this Srikallata (said by Kalhaṇa to be born in the days of Avantivarman for the salvation of the country) was and that we surmised that he was a Vāishṇava writer. It appears, however, from Dr. Bhandarkar's Śaivism that he was a Śaiva philosopher but he must have been as above stated an advocate of Ahimsā.

suppression of worships other than their own. We have seen how a Chola king called upon Rāmānuja to declare that Śiva was the highest God. Even to this day this animosity between even the lay followers of Śaivism and Vaishṇavism continues in Karnatak, Āndhra and the Tamil land, the religion and philosophy of Madhva—a religious philosopher of the 14th century—adding a third party to the contest.

We were surprised to come across an attempt to combine the two antagonistic worships of Śiva and Vishṇu made by Vijayasena of Bengal in his Deopārā inscription (E. I. p. 307). He was a Śaiva but the Vaishṇava cult was probably spreading in Bengal from Orissa and his grandson Lakshmaṇasena, as we have seen, became a Parama Vaishṇava. Vijayasena, therefore, may have thought of combining the two worships, by combining the two gods Śiva and Vishṇu in the same image and in the temple he built and properly called Pradyumneśvara, he placed an idol which was composed of Śiva and Vishṇu joined together. The description of the idol given in this inscription is as follows: "We bow to this image called Pradyumneśvara wherein both the husband of Lakshmī and the husband of the daughter of the mountain reside and play in unity in which the two goddesses standing between their lords have somehow caused an obstacle in the carving of one undifferentiated body. The decoration of the Destroyer of the world is formed by a spotted silken cloth serving as the elephant's skin and the big necklace on the chest as the big serpent, sandal-wood paste as ashes and the string of sapphires in the hand as the rosary of Rudrākshas the Garudamaṇi being the Gonasa and the string of pearls as the necklace of bones".* This description shows to our mind that the same idol looked as Śiva and Vishṇu.

Vijayasena was a Kshatriya from Deccan Karnātaka and curiously enough this unifying spirit was exhibited in Mahārāshtra itself in the new Vaishṇava cult which arose about the end of this period in the worship of Vithoba of Pandharpur. Dr. R. G. Bhandarkar thinks that this worship came from the south and that the word Vithoba is a Kanarese form of Vishṇu. But the Vithoba Vaishṇavism was entirely different from the

* लक्ष्मीवल्लभशैलजादयितयोरद्वैतलीलागृहं प्रद्युम्नेश्वरशब्दलांछनमधिष्ठानं नमस्कुर्महे ॥ यत्रालिङ्गनभङ्गकातरतया स्थित्वान्तरे कान्तयोः देवीभ्यां कथमप्यभिन्नतनुताशिल्पेऽन्तरायः कृता ॥ २ चित्रक्षौमेभचर्मा हृदयविनिहितस्थूलहारोरगेन्द्रः श्रीखण्डक्षोदभस्मा करनिहितमहानील रत्नाक्षमालः ॥ वेषस्तेनास्य तेने गरुडमणिलतागोनसः कान्तमुक्ता नेपथ्यास्थिमालांसमुचितरचनः कल्पकल्पालिकस्य ॥ ३ ॥

Vaishṇavism of Rāmānuja. And the Prakrit form of Vishṇu in Bengali and Ooriya is also Vishthu.* But the Vaishṇavism of Pandharpur is different from the Vaishṇavism of Bengal also. It has no lascivious aspect. It entirely eschews all reference to Gopīs. Even Rukmiṇī appears in Pandharpur at a later time. The Vishṇu idol at Pandharpur is unaccompanied by any female deity. Its form is also unique, having both hands akimbo and it has a linga on the crown of its head. Who put up this idol is yet undiscovered as Pundalika the first devotee of Vithoba is a mythical person. The historical references given by Dr. Bhandarkar show that originally the place was holy on account of Vishṇu idol only. The Bhimarathi is mentioned in an inscription of 1249 A. D. This leads us to believe that the Vithoba of Pandharpur must have been there about a hundred or at least fifty years before. In a stone-inscription in Pandharpur itself dated 1270 A. D., Bhānu, a son of Keshava is recorded to have performed an Aptoryāma sacrifice in which "crowds of people and Vithal and the gods were gratified." (Bhandarkar, Vaishṇavism p. 81–88). Pānduranga is a name of Śiva according to Hemachandra and there is a temple of Śiva at Pandharpur which pilgrims have to visit first before visiting Vithoba. The Vitthal worship at Pandharpur is again unconnected with any philosophy and is a purely devotional worship as developed by Nāmadeva (1270 A. D.) and Jnāneśvara, the oldest leading Vaishṇava saints of Mahārāshtra. The temple of Vithoba was built from subscription raised all over Mahārāshtra as appears from the Chauryaśi-stone-record in the temple itself of about 1300 A. D. Though the Vithoba cult developed in Mahārāshtra in the 13th century, it came into Pandharpur probably about the end or the middle of the 12th century § in the sub-period treated of in this volume. Strangely enough it was devoid of all animosity against Śaivism or against the Vedic religion of sacrifice and has no connection with any philosophy Dvaita or Advaita. It further does not renounce caste though people of all castes are admitted into this cult and are all equal before God and absolution through devotion is open to all, male or female, Brahmin or non-Brahmin.

---

* The Kanarese form is Bittideva.

§ The Mahānubhāva cult arose in śaka 1185 or 1263 A. D. after this sub-period in Mahārāshtra itself no doubt with asceticism and complete renunciation of caste added to Ahimsā and the Bhakti of Dattātreya added to that of Vishṇu. It has connection with the later history of the Deccan and its fall.

It truly carries on thus the pure Bhaktiyoga doctrine of the Bhagavadgītā.

It is unfortunate that these attempts at unifying Śaivism and Vaishṇavism did not catch and that Hinduism remained and remains split into two main schisms. It is not possible to ask Hinduism or Jainism to give up Ahimsā as it is but the logical outcome of their spiritual development. It is difficult also to decide whether monism is true or dualism and nothing is lost if people agree to differ on the question whether God and the world are one or are two. But surely, Hinduism can give up the controversy whether Śiva is greater or Vishṇu. Yet a Chola king persecuted people for believing that Vishṇu was greater and Adhirājendra called Krimikantha by the Vaishṇavas destroyed a Vaishṇava temple on the Chidambaram hill (I. A. 1912). Attempts were made by later thinkers like Tulasidas, in imitation of the plain attempt of the Mahābhārata, to reconcile the two worships, the animosity between which seems to be as old as the Mahābhārata, by showing that Śiva praises Vishṇu as the highest God and Vishṇu praises Śiva as the highest (see Upamanyu Ākhyāna in the Anuśāsana Parvan). But an attempt may also be made in the wake of Pradyumneśvara by combining the two gods in the same idol or like the idol of Vithoba in Pandharpur having a Śiva Linga on its head, a Śiva Linga may have an image of Vishṇu carved or fastened on its top. If such attempts at combining the two worships are systematically made, this split in Hinduism can be made up and one cause of weakness among the Hindus at least can be removed.

NOTE 1—DIFFERENT VIEWS ON MOKSHA OR ABSOLUTION.

There was a diversity of opinion among the Hindus and even the Jains as to who were fitted to attain Moksha or final deliverance from rebirth. Of course every religion has an idea of Moksha or absolution differing in its form; but in other religions there is no disqualification for any particular class of people. Al-Beruni says on this subject (Chap. IX Vol. I p. 104). "The Hindus differ as to who will attain Moksha. Some believe that only Brahmins and Kshatriyas will attain Moksha as they alone can study Veda. But others say that every one is entitled, as Vyāsa says, 'Learn the twenty-five and you will be liberated whatever your religion may be.' Again the Bhagavadgītā states that "even women, Vaiśyas and Śūdras will come to me if you follow me. What then Brahmins and Kshatriyas." Al-Beruni's knowledge of the subject is clearly accurate. Anciently it was believed that only through Veda Moksha could be achieved. This is not unnatural as Christians also believe that final beatitude can be attained only through the Bible and Mahomedans believe that it can be attained through the Koran only. The Upanishadic Aryans developed the further doctrine that Moksha could come only through Sanyāsa or renunciation and this idea was taken up by Buddhism and Jainism. (Christ seems to have taught the same doctrine). As women and Śūdras were debarred from both the study of the Veda and Sanyāsa, they were believed to be unfit for attaining Moksha. The liberal yet orthodox Bhagavadgītā preached the new doctrine of Bhakti or devotion and held that although women and Śūdras (Vaiśyas were also added to these) could not study Veda or do Sanyāsa like Brahmins and Kshatriyas according to the orthodox view, they could approach God through devotion and attain to final beatitude. Vyāsa laid stress on knowledge only as believed in Sānkhya and preached "Know God truly and we will be absolved." The liberal broad-minded view of the Bhagavadgītā is indeed creditable to the thinkers of the time of Śrī Krishṇa and Al-Beruni recognises it. But he attributes it to the circumstance that Śrī Krishṇa was himself a Śūdra. It is inexplicable how this wrong notion was entertained by Al-Beruni who had very accurate knowledge of the Hindu religious books. Shrīkrishna was thought to be a son of Nanda who really was a Vaiśya. But in Al-Beruni's days, a Vaiśya was little better than a Śūdra; especially cowherds were Śūdras and hence probably this mistaken idea of Al-Beruni about the caste of Śrī Krishṇa. In the present sub-period the Hindus appear to have still believed that Brahmins and Kshatriyas alone could attain Moksha. The Kshatriyas yet retained their right to the study of the Veda. But the theory grew later on that they were debarred from performing Sanyāsa and hence Brahmins alone could attain final beatitude.

The Vaishṇava idea of final beatitude was different from the Vedantic but Rāmānuja was a strict orthodox philosopher and it seems to us that he insisted on Sanyāsa as a *sine qua non* for the attainment of Moksha. The Vīraśaivas or Lingāyats had a different idea of Moksha their highest God being Śivā; but they believed that every one including women could attain to Moksha i. e. to the service of Śiva in Kailāsa. The Buddhistic idea of Moksha was again different and their word for it was Nirvāṇa; but they insisted on the necessity of Sanyāsa which was open to all including women. The Jains originally were a little less liberal, as already stated, than the Buddhists and the Digambaras preached that Sanyāsa in the highest sense was necessary for attaining Kaivalya. We have already mentioned the disputation which was held between a Digambara philosopher and a Śvetāmbara, on this very subject at Dhar before a Paramāra king, the former holding that clothed monks and women were not fit to attain final deliverance. The idea of final deliverance from re-birth was common to all these different sections; but they differed as to the nature of Moksha and as to the persons who were fit to attain it as above and thus added to the state of religious disunion in the country.

NOTE 2—RELIGIOUS TOLERATION IN SOME PARTS.

It may be noted that the kings of Northern India were tolerant and there are no instances of Śaiva kings persecuting Vaishṇavas and Hindu kings persecuting Buddhists or Jains or vice-versa. Indeed they were so tolerant that they also extended their liberality to the opposite faith. Thus Govindachandra Parama Śaiva made a grant of 6 villages to two Buddhist saints for the maintenance of Bhikshus in a Vihāra in Jetavana (E. I. XI p. 22). On the other hand, we find the Buddhist king Madanapāla granting a village to a Brahmin for reading the Mahābhārata to his queen who appears to have been a Hindu. Indeed it may be remarked that in Northern India Saivites married Vaishṇava ladies and Buddhists married Hindu ladies. One of the queens of Govindachandra, a Parama Maheśvara was a Buddhist princess. Jains and Hindus also intermarried and inter-marry even now in Northern India. The Gāhadavāla kings from their inscriptions appear to have been very tolerant; for in the religious ceremony performed by them at the time of making gifts of land they, though Māheśvaras, worshipped both Śiva and Vishṇu while other kings are described as worshipping either Śiva or Vishṇu only.

Again inspite of the destruction of Hindu temples by Mahomedans in Northern India in this sub-period, the Hindu kings of Gujarat and Mahārāshtra, as also the people, were tolerant enough to allow Mahomedans to build mosques in their towns especially on the sea coast. Nay we find in Somnath itself a Khoja merchant from Hormuz in Persian gulf building a 'Mijigiti' (Masjid) with the consent of Parama Pāśupatāchārya Mahā Pandita Mahattara Dharmamūrti and Abhaya of the Panch Kula while Malikdeva was the local officer in behalf of Arjunadeva Chālukya who ruled in Anhilwad. The Mijigiti was not only given land for its building but some bazars were assigned for its maintenance by the Hindus and this whole thing was recorded in a stone inscription drawn up in Sanskrit dated St. 1320, Valabhi 945, Sinha 151 and Hijri 662 with the usual imprecations against any one interfering with the Masjid and the gift (Bhav. Insc. p. 225). This speaks volumes of the tolerant spirit of the Hindus of Gujarat. We have already noted that Jayasiṁha Siddharāja personally inquired into the complaint of a Mahomedan about Parsis throwing down a

Masjid in Cambay and restoring it at his own cost (E. II.). The Rāshtrakūṭas again and even the Chālukyas before them, allowed Mahomedans to build Masjids in their territory, allowing Mahomedans to have even their own jurisdiction (Vol. II. p. 166). The Śilāhāras of Thana again addressed their grants to Parsis and Mahomedans who were settled in Sanjan and who appear to have enjoyed special rights. This attitude of the Hindus of Gujarat and Mahārāshtra and their kings is indeed fit to be extolled and specially noticed. There is no wonder, therefore, if the people and kings of these two regions were tolerant towards the Jain religion. We have already shown how the Chālukya kings of Gujarat in this sub-period and later the Veghela kings gave encouragement to Jainism, honoured Jain Pandits and gave donations to Jain temples. Though the Chalukyas of Kalyan were not tolerant towards the Jain faith, the Silahāra kings of Karhad, especially Vijayāditya, while they remained devotees of Mahalakshmī of Kolhapur, were very liberal to the Jains and gave their temples and ascetics many villages (E. I. III p. 207). Jainism probably spread both in Gujarat and the southern Maratha country during the reigns of these kings.

CHAPTER IV.

THE CHANGED ASPECT OF HINDUISM.

In the previous chapters we have spoken of the ramification of caste and the change in marriage and other customs which took place in this sub-period of Hindu history. We have also spoken of the rise of new sects of Śaivas and Vaishṇavas in this sub-period which caused religious disunion in the Hindu society. We will speak in this chapter of other aspects of Hinduism generally and show how Hinduism assumed its modern form at the close of the mediæval Hindu period and how essentially it differed from the Vedic form of Hinduism or what may be called Vedic Aryanism. It is impossible that Hinduism could have remained the same through the long period of 4000 years which elapsed from the recital of the Veda-sanhitās by Vyāsa down to the conquest of Northern India by Mahomedans. Yet it seems that the Hindu religion still kept itself in touch with the religion of the Vedic Ṛishis.

THE VEDAS.

We will commence with the Vedas which were always looked upon as the revelation of the Hindu religion. Vedas were still learnt by heart especially by the Brahmins whose prime duty it was to preserve them. The following observations of Al-Beruni are important in this connection: "The Brahmins recite the Veda without understanding its meaning and in the same way they learn it by heart. Only a few of them learn its explanation and fewer still master its contents" (Sachan Vol. I p. 128). This state continues to this day and there are very few Brahmins learned in the Vedas. The change from ancient or pre-Buddhistic times may be marked when almost every Brahmin and even Kshatriya and Vaiśya had necessarily to study the Veda. Al-Beruni proceeds to state that "the Brahmins teach the the Veda to Kshatriyas, but they are not allowed to teach it even to Brahmins. The Vaiśyas, and Śūdras are not allowed to learn it." The Vaiśyas, as said before, having turned Buddhists neglected the study of Veda and lost touch with it. The orthodox Kshatriyas still learnt the Veda and can learn it even now, though very few do it. But we have clear evidence here that the modern doctrine that there are no Kshatriyas in the Kali age had not yet arisen and Al-Beruni's statement not only proves the acceptance of the existence of Kshatriyas but also their right to study the Veda in the eleventh century. The dictum कलावाद्यन्तयोः स्थितिः arose in the fourteenth century, according to our view explained in Vol. II (Appendix) and this is a further confirmation of that view.

"The Veda mostly contains hymns of praise and treat of the various kinds of sacrifices to the fire which are so numerous and difficult that you can hardly count them." Even orthodox Brahmins at present do not know how many sacrifices these are, for, as we shall presently show, Vedic sacrifices became obsolete since Al-Beruni wrote his interesting account of India.

"They do not allow the Veda to be committed to writing, because it is recited according to certain modulations. They, therefore, avoid the use of pen as it is liable to cause error. The Veda is consequently often lost." There is no doubt that in consequence of this superstition a large part of Vedic literature had been lost already before the 10th century. But Al-Beruni gives the further information that not long before his time Vasukra a native of Kashmir, a famous Brahmin, undertook the task of explaining the Veda and committing it to writing, because he was afraid that the Veda might be forgotten. "He has taken upon himself a task from which all shrink." Thus Veda was first written about 1000 A. D. in Kashmir for the purpose of commenting upon it, by Vasukra. We do not know whether this first Bhāshya on the Veda survives. Of course it must have been utilized in the existing Bhāshya of Mādhava Vidyāraṇya composed in the south at Vijayanagar

VEDIC SACRIFICES.

The religion of the ancient Vedic Aryans consisted chiefly of keeping the sacrificial fire and performing daily and occasional Vedic sacrifices. King Aśvapati, in an Upanishad, speaking of the religiousness of his subjects said that "there was no householder in his kingdom who did *not* keep the sacrificial fire." Things had so changed by this time that it might have almost been said of the subjects of any Hindu king that there was no householder who kept the sacrificial fire. Even Brahmins have now given up keeping the sacrificial fire. However, there were a few Brahmins in Al-Beruni's days who did keep the Vedic sacrificial fire. He records "those Brahmins who kept one fire were called 'Ishtins' while those who kept three

were called Agnihotris" (ditto p. 102). "If he besides offers an offering to the fire (performs a sacrifice higher than the daily one) he is called Dikshita." We come across Dikshita and Āvasthika as honorable epithets of Brahmins in inscriptions of this period. In modern days these epithets have become mere surnames. A few higher sacrifices are no doubt now and then performed throughout the whole of India especially in the south. But it may be taken that this Vedic mode of worship viz. the daily sacrifice in the household fire is now generally in abeyance.

OCCASIONAL SACRIFICES.

But occasional sacrifices must then have been performed as now such as at the time of upanayana or of marriage. The ceremony of the gift of land appears in this sub-period to have always been performed accompanied by a sacrifice in fire. Indeed inscriptions of this sub-period recording grants of land always mention the elaborate religious ceremonies which were performed on such sacred and ceremonious occasions. The descriptions are indeed very interesting and show how all over India, Hinduism was practically a blend of Vedic and Purāṇic worships. The grantor king bathes in some sacred river at a well-known Ghatta or Ghat, offers Tarpaṇa water to gods, mortals and the manes (a ritual enjoined in Vedic Sūtras), praises the sun (also a Vedic worship), then worships Śiva and Vishṇu (Purāṇic deities) and finally offers oblations of ghee into the sacred fire (Vedic worship again) and then pours water on the hand of the donee consecrating the gift.* This ceremony shows that the Rājput kings were not only orthodox Hindus but attached importance to and actully exercised the right of, performing Vedic sacrifices. But these sacrifices were always performed with ghee offerings as is often specially mentioned. It is remarkable that even Jains accepted gifts after such Vedic sacrifices for the greater validity of these gifts by Hindu kings.

IDOL-WORSHIP.

Though thus Hinduism was in this period and is even now a blend of Vedic and Puranic worships, the Vedic ritual such as Tarpaṇa, Suryopasthāna and Havana gradually declined in

---

* यमुनायां स्नात्वा यथाविधि देवऋषिमनुष्यभूतपितृंश्च तर्पयित्वा सूर्यभट्टारकमुपस्थाय सर्वकर्तारं भगवन्तं शिवं विश्वधारं वासुदेवं समभ्यर्च्य हुतवहं हुत्वा (I. A. XIV p. 103). Sometimes the mention of the worship of Vāsudeva is omitted.

importance and the worship of the Puranic gods, Śiva, Vishṇu, Devi, and Gaṇeśa and even Sūrya became the normal and chief part of Hindu daily worship. Whether idol-worship is countenanced by the Vedas or not we will not stop here to enquire. But the Vedic Sūtras do not mention worship of idols in the daily service of God. After the suppression of Buddhism which began in the denial of God and ended in the universal worship of Buddha's images, Hinduism took up idol-worship with greater zest and it seems that the daily worship of small idols in every household came into vogue and was prescribed in the various nibandhas and works on religious practice. It is difficult to say whether the modern Panchāyatana worship came into vogue at this time or was prescribed by Sankara in order to avoid the constant fight between worships of different gods. But certain it is that there were small images of different deities in every household at that time as at present. For the ceremony of worshiping Śiva or Vishṇu or both by kings when making land grants mentioned in inscriptions can not refer to worship in temples. The images worshipped must have been the images in the royal household. They were either images of metal or small unfashioned stones of a particular appearance and with particular signs to be seen even now in Hindu households, which were considered to represent the different deities. This idol-worship in every household must have eventually thrown into the background the Vedic sacrificial fire therein.

Of course there were besides temples in every town and village dedicated to different deities in which idols of stone or metal were placed and worshipped. Kings, queens, ministers. rich merchants and even mendicant Brahmin ascetics who secured large donations made in reverence to their holy character, vied with one another in building superb and stupendous temples to their tutelary deities, chiefly Śiva and Vishṇu and India was in this period full of such temples throughout its length and breadth. The idols placed in these temples were usually of stone, but these were sometimes of silver and gold and even of precious stones; and bigotry came to the help of opulent kings and merchants by prescribing different merit and fruit to the construction of idols of different precious materials Al-Peruni, probably quoting from Varāhamihira, details this different merit as follows: "The benefit of a statue made of precious stone will be common to all men and women of the empire. A golden statue will bring power to him who erects it; a statue of silver will bring him renown and one of bronze will bring him increase of rule, while one of stone will bring acquisition of landed property " (ditto p. 121). Thus were rich kings and merchants prompted to make statues of gold and silver and even precious stone inviting marauders and conquerors to commit sacrilege. Al-Beruni, however, cleverly adds that the Hindus honour the idols on account of those who erected them and not on account of the material of which they are made. Thus a stone idol was as good as a golden one for the devotee and precious idols were useful only to the plunderer and the thief. In spite of the plundering of temples and the removal of golden idols by Mahmud, the Hindus, however, still continued to make golden idols and to decorate stone idols with precious ornaments during this sub-period as inscriptions already noticed prove. This rage of decorating idols still continues though perhaps the fashioning of golden idols is no longer in vogue.

We have already described in Chapter VI-16 how idolatry had drifted into bigotry at this time in India. The idolatry of the Hindus was a mystery to the philosophic mind of Al-Beruni, though even he notices how the whole human race in ancient times including even the Arabs was idolatrous. There were, however, sober men in India, candidly admits Al-Beruni, who did not worship idols. While commenting on the ludicrous views of the Hindus on the subject of idols, he states that these views were held by the common uneducated people. " Those who march on the path to liberation or who study philosophy and theology would never dream of worshipping an image manufactured to represent God. We may not give the stories of Ambarīsha and Nārada related by him to explain how Hindus took to making idols ; but it is necessary to detail the several famous idols in India described by him. First there was the idol of the sun at Multan " It was of wood covered with red Cordovan leather with two rubies for the eyes. It was said to have been made in the last Kritayuga (i. e. 43 lakhs of years before). Mahomed Kasim who conquered Multan spared it as it was a source of a great revenue. On the same place, however, he built a mosque. When Karmatians occupied Multan, Jālam Ibn Shaiban broke the idol and killed the priests. He shut the mosque built by the Caliphs and made the sun-god's mansion his (Karmatian) mosque. When the blessed king Mahmud swept away the Karmatian rule, he made again the old mosque the place of the Friday worship and left the Karmatian mosque to decay."

This is a very interesting account about the temple of the sun-god of Multan and the vissicitudes of its fortune.

The information given in the next para of Al-Beruni is still more important; indeed we must apologise to the reader for not having looked into this mine of information earlier. It is to be wondered how even Elliot did not come across this passage. It solves two difficulties which puzzled both Elliot and ourselves. Al-Beruni says (p. 117, Vol. I, Sachau) "At Thanesar there was an idol highly venerated by the Hindus, called Chakrasvāmin. It is of bronze and is nearly the size of a man. It is now lying in the hippodrome at Ghazna together with the Lord of Somnath which is a linga of Mahādeva. The Chakrasvāmin idol is said to have been made in the time of Bhārata as a memorial of the war of that name." Now this statement solves two mysteries. The name of the idol of Thanesar given as Jagasom by later Mahomed writers is a plain misreading in Persian of Chakrasvāmin which must be a Vishṇu idol and not a Śiva one. Secondly, although Utbi does not relate Mahmud's expedition to Somnath, this statement of Al-Beruni recorded in 1030 A. D. and therefore almost a contemporary statement, removes all doubts about the truth of the Somnath expedition.

These idols superstitiously believed to be fashioned thousands or even lakhs of years before must have been highly venerated and must have also been invested in the popular mind with miraculous powers. Riches consequently flowed into Multan and Thanesar which, therefore, eventually invited destruction on themselves.

Al-Beruni refers to one more famous idol viz. that of Śāradā in Kashmir visited even by Śankara. The other famous idols in India of which we have historical mention were the Śiva-idols in Kashi and Ujjain, the Bhailkasvāmin idol (Vishṇu) at Bhelsa, the Vishṇu idol at Jagannath (p. 268) and of Vithoba at Pandharpur and the Mahālakshmī idol at Kolhapur (p. 293), not to speak of the Śiva idols at Kānchī and Rameśvar referred to by Al-Beruni himself. We have already spoken of the Devī idol at Kotkangṛa and the idols at Mathura and Kanauj described vaguely by Utbi as destroyed by Mahmud.

Varāhamihira's Brihatsamhitā is by name quoted by Al-Beruni here with regard to how the idols of different gods were to be fashioned. Two or three interesting points may be first noted which appear from this quotation. First, it is doubted by many if there were temples of Rāma before Rāmānanda; but Varāhamihira refers to idols of Rāma, son of Daśaratha and as Al-Beruni quotes this statement, it shows that there were idols of Rāma certainly from the 6th to the 11th century A. D. Secondly, idols of Vishṇu are said to be with *eight*, four and *two* hands, and in these, different weapons or things are to be placed. The idol of Vishṇu with two hands has to be made with conch in one hand and as drawing water by the other; a description which is rather strange and which does not apply to the idol of Vithoba at Pandharpur. Thirdly, there were idols of Baladeva, of Pradyumna, of Sāmba, of Brahmā, of Indra, and Yama, of Revanta son of the sun, of the sun himself, of the seven mothers, of Bhagavatī and lastly of Vināyaka * with the elephant's head, or a human body." All these except the last two have latterly gone out of fashion. We, however, ourselves saw in the Baijanath temple in Kangra at the entrance an idol of Gaṇeśa with six hands with weapons in the several hands as described by Jnāneśvara in his famous Marathi commentary on the Bhagavadgītā. This Baijanath temple has images of different gods carved on the outside of its walls and its pinnacle which are so charming and so true in detail to the description of the different Āyudhas, Pārishadas and Vāhanas of the several gods that they are worth studying. This temple was built about 1200 A. D. as an inscription in its records.

"The worshippers of these idols kill sheep and buffaloes with axes (Kuthāra) that they may nourish themselves with their blood." This is a strange observation, perhaps taken from the Tāntric worship of Devī and not from actual observation. With regard to the pujaris of the different gods, Al-Beruni gives the following information: "To the idol of Vishṇu are devoted the Bhāgavatas, to the idol of the sun the Magas, to the idol of Mahādeva, "anchorites with long hair, who cover their skin with ashes, hang on their persons the bones of dead people and swim in the pools" (p. 120). This observation is supported by inscriptions of the period, especially with regard to the worshippers of Mahādeva. Thus in the Badaun inscription (E. I. I p. 64) there are two Śaiva ascetics described at length. The First named Varmaśiva was an inhabitant of Ana-

* Hanumān though not mentioned here must have been worshipped in this period as we find his figure stamped on coins of the Chandelias (p. 181).

hilpātana who in his boyhood, while in the Deccan country removed an idol put up by the Bauddhas and who in later age by his austerities and learning became famous. He came to Badaun in his wandering and was placed in charge of a Śive maṭha built by one Rulha, a Divira minister to the king on Badaun. The other ascetic was originally "a Brahmin in the Hariyāna country (round Delhi) who gave up wealth and the world for the worship of Śiva. His disciple a Gaudaja (of Gauda country) Brahmin with Vatsagotra having five pravaras and named Iśānaśiva, was placed on the throne of ascetics by his guru after due trial. He built a fine Śiva temple, with a high pinnacle in that city of Bharata with the help of the same minister Rulha to the king of Badaun and the temple was given in charge of the first ascetic." From this description Śaivite ascetics appear to be both Brahmins and non-Brahmins and they followed the same severe austerities and pious mode of life. The non-Brahmin ascetic was usually entrusted with the worship of the deity in Śiva temples, as is the practice even now. Many inscriptions speak similarly of Śaivite asectics being placed in charge of temples. Thus the Bheraghat inscription of Ālhaṇadevi speaks of a Lāta ascetic* being placed in charge of a Śiva temple built by her (E. I. I p. 52); and two Śiva temples built by a Brahmin ascetic of the Vātsava gotra and by Gangādhara a pious and learned Brahmin of Madhyadeśa are mentioned as placed in charge of Śaiva ascetics in E. I. II (p. 52 and 41).

MAṬHAS.

These anchorites whether Śaiva or Vaishṇava lived in Maṭhas which were usually built alongside of the temples Hiuen Tsang has recorded that Śaiva anchorites and Jain or Nigrantha ascetics lived in their respective Maṭhas and temples The institution of Maṭhas is thus as old as 600 A. D. undoubtedld and was probably copied from the Buddhist Vihāras. In this sub-period Buddhism disappeared except in Magadha and it is probable that Buddhist temples and Vihāras were converted into Śiva or Vaishṇu temples and Maṭhas. We have however, distinct mention of Maṭhas being built in inscriptions of this period, E. I. II (p. 310) mentions a Vyākhyānaśālā also, and an Udyānanśālā as built near the Śiva temple erected. Thus the temples

* लाटान्वयः पाशुपतस्तपस्वी श्रीरुद्रराशिर्विधिवद्व्यधत्ताम् ।
स्थानस्य रक्षाविधिमस्य तावद्यावन्निममीते भुवनानि शम्भुः ॥

provided halls for Vyākhyāna or preaching as well as Maṭhas for the residence of Tapasvīs. These Maṭhas have now disappeared in most places excepting South India. At present we ordinarily see neither Vihāras for Buddhist Sanyāsis nor Maṭhas for Paśupata Yogis or ascetics.

ĀGAMAS AND TANTRAS.

The different modes of worship of the different gods and the different modes of Tapas and Sanyāsa followed by the different sects of ascetics gave rise probably during this sub-period to new codes called Āgamas and Tantras which laid down provisions for such worship and asceticism. The Āgamas were many but related to the special worship of the five gods of modern Hinduism. There were sub-sects even under these five different systems and the forehead marks prescribed by them were also different, so as to distinguish one sect from another at first sight. The Vedas were called Nigama and this new scripture which was held more binding was called Āgama. The Tantras were again similar treatises giving different modes of worship with Mantras and practices of a secret character. It seems that in these methods, both Brahmins and non-Brahmins stood on an equal level. The Vedic Tapas and Sanyāsa was reserved for Brahmins only but the asceticism of the Āgamas was open to all Hindus apparently. It is necessary to study this Āgama and Tantra literature, varied and vast as it is, before one can treat it historically and in detail. But it is certain that such scripture had come into existence even before Śankara's time, as he seems to have had disputations with Pāśupatas and others. But they grew into greater importance in this sub-period and various ascetics are described in inscriptions of this time.

MULTIPLICATION OF CEREMONIES OR RITUAL.

The rise of this new sacred literature naturally led to the multiplication of ceremonies and ritual. Dharmaśāstra was studied in almost every kingdom and elaborate treatises on ceremonies and ritual were composed by learned Brahmins and even kings. Vijnāneśvara's Mitāksharā was the first detailed treatise of this period on Dharma based on Yājnavalkya Smriti; it was composed at Kalyan in the Deccan. King Aparāditya of Thana composed another treatise called Aparārka. In Bengal Ballālasena himself wrote Dānasāgara on various dānas or gifts and the learned men in the court of his son Lakshmanasena composed other treatises such as Brahmakarma-Samuchchaya. At Kanauj under Govindchandra also, Dharmaśāstra treatises were composed and lastly we may mention the voluminous work of Hemādri viz. Chaturvarga Chintāmaṇi composed about a hundred years after this period. These will give us an idea of how modern Hinduism has gradually evolved from Purāṇas and Āgamas and has changed the original simple aspect of Vedic Aryanism. For example we may refer to the simple ceremony at the obsequies of such a great king as Pratāpavardhana described by Bāṇa, noted at length in Vol. I (p. 98) and to the elaborate ceremony with many gifts and Śrāddhas described in the Garuḍa Purāṇa. In almost all matters, ceremonies were multiplied; while new rituals and vratas came into vogue in relation to the worship of the five Purānic deities which it is not necessary to detail. The daily religious duties of a Brahmin especially became so engrossing and detailed that very little time was left unoccupied. The occasional ceremonies were also multiplied. In place of the Vedic sacrifices,new sacrifices were prescribed with elaborate ceremonial, but without animal slaughter especially in connection with the worship of Vishṇu and Devī. Rathayātrās in connection with the Purāṇic gods came into vogue, perhaps in imitation of Jain Rathayātrās. In short the worship of Purāṇic gods in accordance with new Āgamas or the amplified Purāṇas threw into the back ground Vedic religious worship of the Vedic Sūtras, though among Brahmins and Kshatriyas, these continued to be performed with added Purāṇic ritual.

We give in a note the fast and festival days described in detail by Al-Beruni observed in the Panjab in his time. They are nearly the same as now, though some have fallen into abeyance. They relate to the worship of Śiva and Vishṇu chiefly and to the worship of Devī and Sūrya. There must have been added many new holy days as fasts or festivals after the time of Al-Beruni in accordance with the Āgamas and Purāṇas. Indeed Al-Beruni's list itself can not be considered as exhaustive; such specially holy days are sometimes mentioned even in inscriptions and we have the mention of Govindadvādaśi in a Kalinga grant (E. I. IV). The editor of the inscription has given the definition of this day* which contains certain astronomical

* फाल्गुनस्य च द्वादश्यां कुंभस्थितदिवाकरे। नक्रस्थिते सूर्यसुते जीवे कार्मुकसंस्थिते।
पुष्यर्क्षे बवसंयुक्ते शोभने भानुवासरे। गोविंदद्वादशी प्रोक्ता देवानामपि दुर्लभा॥

peculiar conjuctions. Particular positions of the sun and the moon and the several planets in different Nakshatras and constellations came in for special holiness also and added to the number of specially holy days. It is needless to add that the number of Śrāddhas also increased. We have the mention of the Kanyāgata Śrāddha in an inscription of Vīsaladeva of Gujarat dated 1254 (I. A. II p. 194).

EXTENSION OF PURĀṆA LITERATURE.

Besides the rise of these sectarian Āgamas and Tantras, the mediæval Hindu period was characterised by the amplification of the Purāṇa literature. The old eighteen Purāṇas were again amplified by the addition of sectarian matter relating to the worship of the above mentioned five deities which are properly called Purāṇic. The Purāṇa glorify Śiva and Vishṇu, Devī and Gaṇapati and prescribe various vratas in propitiation of them. The worship of Śiva was the most popular and ten Purāṇas are devoted to the glorification of Śiva, four being devoted to that of Vishṇu and two each of Devī and Gaṇapati.* Sun worship probably lagged behind; but the addition of the Bhāgavata Purāṇa in the 10th century A. D. gave great impetus to the worship of Vishṇu. Different rituals and modes of worship of these deities came into vogue. The several holy places in the whole of India in connection with famous idols of Siva, Vishṇu, Devī, and Gaṇapati are enumerated and extolled in these Purāṇas. The Skanda Purāṇa describes eighty-four Śiva lingas in India, with Puraṇic stories in connection with the greatness of each linga. The holy places belonging to Vishṇu, to Devī and to Gaṇapati are mentioned with appropriate stories in other Purāṇas. All this literature may be assigned to the first and second sub-periods till in the third sub-period we find the Purāṇas, as they are today.

RISE OF MINOR SMṚITIS AND PURĀṆAS.

The needs of these changed aspects of Hinduism and of the increase of ritual and ceremony could not be satisfied by the promulgation of Āgamas and the extension of the eighteen Purāṇas. Hence minor Smṛitis besides the old eighteen conventional Smṛitis and new minor Purāṇas besides the old eighteen were composed probably in this or preceding sub-period. We have shown elsewhere that the Bhāgavata must have been com-

* अष्टादशपुराणेषु दशभिर्गीयते शिवः ॥ चतुर्भिर्गीयते विष्णुर्द्वाभ्यां शक्तिश्च विघ्नपः ॥

posed in the tenth century. It would be an interesting study to see how the minor Smṛitis and Purāṇas introduce new practices which came into vogue in the Hindu period, to see in fact to what time and place they can be ascribed by a consideration of their contents. The literature is, however, extensive and its study is a matter of great labour; but it seems nearly certain that this literature arose about this sub-period, especially when we find the mention of Kalivarjas in some of the minor Purāṇas and notably in the Āditya Purāṇa. These Kalivarjas give us almost a complete idea as to how modern Hinduism has changed from Vedic religion of the Sūtra period. The practices said to be prohibited in the Kaliyuga, as enumerated in detail in these Purāṇas, are really practices which had gradually ceased during the long period which had elapsed from the Vedic Sūtras (circa 1000 B. C.) down to the end of the mediæval period (circa 1200 A. D.) and which could be easily found from a comparison of what modern Hinduism allows with what the Vedic Sūtras and even the Smṛitis sanction. This list gives us a complete idea of the changed aspect of modern Hinduism. Such transformation required some sanction; the Kalivarja provisions, therefore, were enunciated as given in these new minor Purāṇas and the Nibandhakāras or writers of modern treatises on Dharmaśāstra quote them as authorities from these Upapurāṇas.

THE KALIVARJAS.

A minute study of the Kalivarjas which we give in an Appendix will reveal to us the fact that some of these prohibitions came into vogue in this very sub-period, though some must have been introduced in older times. We have already shown that the prohibition of suicide by burning or leaping from a precipice referred to by Al-Beruni as a special provision must have come into vogue about 1000 A. D. For in the previous sub-period we have historical evidence of devout Hindus destroying themselves by burning on a pyre. Kumārila himself in this way is said to have put an end to his life by ascending a pyre (700 A. D.) and Kumāragupta is also described in an inscription (Vol. I p. 97) as burning himself to death in a pyre of cowdung cakes. So also the prohibition of marriage outside of caste or Anuloma Asavarṇa marriage clearly belongs to this sub-period, as we can be sure from the instance of Rājaśekhara marrying a Kshatriya wife (circa 940 A. D.). Again Sanyāsa seems to have been prohibited during the Buddhist period as also Agnihotra. Both appear to have been resuscitated after Kumārila and Śankara; and they are still practised though by a very few Brahmins only. They are thus contradictory provisions in the Kalivarjas on the subject. Secondly, while some of the Kalivarjas are reasonable and clearly prompted by a sentiment of humanity, or moral purity such as the prohibition of cow-sacrifice (go-medha), horse-sacrifice (aśva-medha) or human sacrifice (purusha-medha), there are many prohibitions which can only be attributed to the growth of bigotry. The ideas of purity of caste increased so far among all castes and especially among Brahmins that not only marriage but food and even water was prohibited with any person outside the caste. Nay in some sub-sections of Northern Brahmins such as the Kanojias, water and food from a stranger but of the same caste is prohibited. In South India even the shadow of an untouchable is looked upon as polluting. In the previous sub-periods Brahmins could take food from Kshatriyas and Vaiśyas and certain Śūdras (Vol. II p. 186). This was now prohibited by a Kalivarja text. But interdining among Brahmins and Kshatriyas or Vaiśyas does not seem to be prohibited by any text; but the practice gradually ceased, probably in this sub-period owing to bigotted notions of caste purity.

PROHIBITION OF RECONVERSION.

But the greatest harm caused by such bigotted notions of purity of caste was the prohibition of reconversion which came into practice even in Al-Beruni's days and without any provision in the Kalivarja texts. It seems that Al-Beruni had a talk with some learned Brahmin on the subject; for he clearly says that there is a penance prescribed for the purification of persons "carried away into a Moslem country as slaves and returning" and he actually describes the penance; but adds that the Brahmin remarked that such persons were never taken back into the caste (Sachau Vol. II p. 163). Such was the state of public opinion even in Al-Beruni's days; it is needless to state that in the course of this sub-period and later this bigotted sentiment of the Hindus must have gathered strength and persons forcibly converted had no help but to remain in the religion forced upon them. 'Once a convert always a convert' became the maxim of intolerant Hinduism and we know that thousands of Hindus have consequently, most often without their fault, become irretrievably Mahomedans and Christians.

NOTE :—AL-BERUNI'S ENUMERATION OF FASTS AND FESTIVALS.

FAST DAYS.

Al-Beruni describes Hindu fast days in detail. They belong to the Panjab and Kashmir. They are the same as now but there are important variations. He says (Vol. I p. 175 Sachau) "The 8th and 11th of the bright half are fast days, the 11th being specially sacred to Vāsudeva and they wake all night." The Ekādaśi fast as observed even now is here properly described. The fast on the 8th has practically disappeared. It was sacred to Devī; among Jains it is still observed. The Bhādrapada black Ashtami is described by Al-Beruni as Janmāshtami. This shows that his months are Pūrṇimānta. "The sixth day of Chaitra is holy to the sun" a fast day not now observed, as sun-worship has nearly disappeared now. "Ashādha day with moon in Anurādhā was observed as a fast day," is not well understood; but the Devaśayanī Ekādaśi is well described. It is a fast day all over India now. "The Śrāvaṇa full moon day was holy to Somnāth." It is not a fast day now, but in Somnāth on the sea-coast its importance must have been great as it is the Nārali Pūrṇimā day when the south-west monsoon gets spent and the sea becomes calm. "Aśvina 8th is holy to Bhagavatī, the fast is broken when the moon rises." This is observed even now especially by women. "The 5th Bhādrapada is holy to the sun. His rays admitted through windows are offered incense and flowers." This must have been a special day of Multan the famous sun temple of which has already been described. The wakening of Vāsudeva day in Kārtika (11th) is also mentioned; its special importance when the moon is in Revati is not now known. "It is also the first of the Bhīshma Pāncharātra days of fast. Brahmins break fast on the second day." This is also not generally known now. "The sixth day of Pausha is a fast day in honour of the sun." This is the day preceding Rathasaptamī but they do not fast now on this day. "The third day of Māgha is a fast day for women; it is called Gaurītritīyā." Al-Beruni mentions more Tritīyās than one and Akshattritīyā is one of these as will presently appear. It is remarkable that Rāmanavamī fast is not mentioned by him. Probably Rāma was not much worshipped in the Panjab and perhaps this is so even now.

FESTIVALS.

We go on to describe the festival days mentioned by Al-Beruni (chap. LXXVI). "The second of Chaitra is a great festival day in Kashmir in honour of victory of its king over the Turks." This probably refers to the victory of Lalitāditya the conqueror of Hindustan over the Turks described in Vol. I (p. 211) as a memorable one "since this was a singular exploit of Lalitāditya deserving a prominent record in this history of Mediæval India." "The 11th of Chaitra was the Hindola festival of Vāsudeva and 15th of Chaitra was festival for women called Vasanta festival. Both these are not known to us. The 3rd of Vaiśākha was Gaurī Tritīyā. "On the 10th of Vaiśakha Brahmins go out at the king's command and sacrifice for four days." This is a thing unknown to us and it is a festival which we have not been able to trace in Hindu treatises. The vernal equinox festival is peculiar to the Panjab and still observed there, being called Vaiśākhī. "Jyeshtha Śuddha 15 is a festival day for women." "All Ashādha days are festival days and on Śāvana 15 alms are given to Brahmins." "On Aśvina Mahānavamī sugarcane juice is poured for Bhavānī and kids are also killed." "The 15th of Aśvina is dedicated to animals and they wrestle with one another." The Bhādrapada Pitripaksha is also mentioned, especially the day when the moon is in Maghā.'. (This should have been called Aśvina Vadya according to Pūrṇimānta months). "The 3rd Bhādrapada is observed by women who grow seeds in baskets and worship Devī at night." "The 1st of Kārtika is Diwali day when Balirāja is liberated for one day by Lakshmī." "The 3rd of Mārga śīrsha is a festival day for women. The 3rd of Māgha is a sacred day to women and is a festival day for them; women bathe in cold water the whole month." "The full moon day of Fālgun is the Dolā feast for women; they make fires in villages." "The 16th of Fālgun they call Śivarātri day and worship Mahādeva and remain awake the whole night." This is a correct description of Śivarātri except for the number, which ought to be 14th. "In Multan there is a special festival of the sun and it is called Sāmbapariyātrā." We recognise in the above many festivals which are still observed which therefore are certainly as old as Al-Beruni (1030 A. D.).

CHAPTER V.

POLITICAL CONDITION.

As described in Vol. II (p. 228) at the end of the 10th century India was divided, from Kabul to Kamrup and from Kashmir to Kumārī, into several kingdoms, some large and some small which were ruled by despotic Hindu kings most of these being Rājputs. These kingdoms were so to speak, limited monarchies; for according to the modern theory of politics in the west, the sovereign has an unlimited power to legislate and a limited monarchy means a state where the monarch's power to promulgate laws is limited by the power of parliament or popular assembly to legislate. In India, as explained in Vol. II (p. 225), the kings or even the people had no right to promulgate new laws or to alter or abrograte existing ones, all the necessary laws having been in the beginning given by the creator to Manu the first king to guide him in the government of the people. This divine Smriti-made law was followed in the different kingdoms of India and this set a limit to the despotic power of kings by preventing despotic administration becoming doubly oppressive by the addition of despotic legislation. The several despotic kingdoms in India, thus, were really limited monarchies in this sub-period and were, therefore, generally well-governed and happy.

The difference again, as noted in Vol. II (p. 226), in soil climate, and nature of land and the language of the people and their provincial peculiarities made the existence of different kingdoms in the country, a normal and perhaps a necessary condition. And the kingdoms arising in this sub-period correspond almost exactly to the different divisions of India according to these circumstances. Thus Kashmir, U. P., Rajputana, Gujarat, Konkan, Malwa, Bundelkhand, C. P., Bengal, Telangaṇa, Dravida, Kerala, Karṇātak and Mahārāshtra were distinct kingdoms with territories naturally distinct throughout this sub-period. The only factor which was favourable for the evolving of an empire combining all these kingdoms was the unity of race, religion and ancient tradition. But as in Mediæval Europe under the Holy Roman Empire, so in Mediæval Hindu India, the kingdoms did not coalesce into one empire for exactly the same reasons as in Europe. The idea of an Indian empire was, however, constantly before Indian kings, an idea which did not involve the destruction of subordinate kingdoms but only their subjugation or nominal acknowledgment of the imperial master, the Samrāt or Chakravartin as he was called. And all the wars among Hindu kings were usually waged with the object of establishing the imperial status. For imperial status was not considered as descending hereditarily from father to son but was considered to depend on actual power; and every ambitious and resourceful monarch in the different kingdoms might aspire to imperial honour and attain it by Digvijaya. Rājaśekhara makes a curious distinction between a Samrāt and a Chakravartin and states that he who conquers Bhāratavarsha from the southern sea is called a Samrāt while he who conquers the country from Kumārīpura to Bindusara, beyond the Himalayas, a distance of one thousand yojanas is called a Chakravartin. The obvious difference is that Kashmir and Nepal are to be further conquered by a Chakravartin in the north and the Chola-Pandyas in the south. We, however, find in this sub-period several kings of much smaller importance calling themselves Chakravartin. Thus a Śilāhāra king of the 12th century called himself Konkana-Chakravartin or emperor of Konkan only; and Lakshmansena called himself कमरूपावनीमंडलचक्र: (Pro. Ben. V p. 467). It is not usual for high names coming down slowly in significance like the title Mahārājādhirāja taken in inscriptions by many minor kings. But the title Chakravartin was well deserved by Bhoja of Malwa (1000–1040) whose word was respected even in Kashmir. Aśoka and Samudragupta in ancient Indian history and Lalitāditya in mediæval history were indeed Chakravartins according to the definition of Rājaśekhara and in modern history Aurangjeb. However in this sub-period, Chola, Chālukya, Gāhadavāla and Pāla kingdoms were ordinary empires or Sāmrājyas, as there were many feudatory princes under subjection to each of them.

We have already commented (p. 325) on the baneful effects of this struggle of ambitious Hindu kings to attain imperial honour. Empire did not in Hindu political philosophy mean the annexation of minor kingdoms like the Mogul or British empire. Bhoja or Karṇa were Chakravartins without destroying conquered kingdoms and thus increasing their own territory or resources. This rivalry for imperial honour thus weakened the contending powers without strengthening the conqueror. Vigraharāja of Ajmer, however, seems to have annexed the conquered kingdom of Delhi, probably because Anangapāla had no son and consequently his power became equal to that of the Gāhaḍavālas of Kanauj and the rivalry between the Chauhans and Rathods went on to the days of Prithvīrāj and Jaichand whose deadly animosity weakened them both and consequently led to their destruction by a third power.

The different kingdoms subsisting at the end of the last sub-period continued to thrive during this sub-period, also with some notable exceptions. Most notable of these was the Panjab which fell at the beginning of this sub-period, as we have already seen, before Mahmud of Gazni and was lost to Hindu India. We have discussed the causes of the fall of the Panjab elsewhere; but we may note here again one important cause viz. the absence of a strong and sufficient standing army. This was a feature of almost all the mediæval Hindu kingdoms on which we have commented in Vol. II (p. 223). Hindu armies, as the Arab writer Sulaiman has testified, consisted chiefly of levies and auxiliary forces of the Sāmantas, paid by them from the revenues of the districts assigned to them. The Imperial Pratihāras of Kanauj in the last sub-period maintained a strong standing army but it appears that, like the Peshwas in later Indian history, the Pratihāras of Kanauj latterly neglected to maintain an efficient Huzur force and Rājyapāla consequently was compelled to submit to the Turks. U. P. was saved, however, from being finally subjugated by Ghazni for two reasons, 1st the incompetence of the successors of Mahmud and secondly, the conquest of the Kanauj kingdom by Gāhadavālas. Their kings down to Govindachandra appear to have maintained a strong standing army consisting of foot, horse and elephant and as stated in an inscription already noted (p. 212), Govindachandra compelled the Hammira to consent to a treaty recognising the inviolibility of his frontier. The Pratihāras hereafter disappeared as a ruling independent clan.

The other ruling clans which disappeared at the beginning of this sub-period were the Rāshtrakūtas of the Deccan and the Chāvadas of Gujarat. In both countries, new strong ruling clans were substituted which re-established the power of Mahārāshtra and Gujarat. In Bengal, the Pāla power declined in this sub-period and a new power arose viz. that of the Senas and divided rule in Bengal with the Pālas, while in Dravida, the Chola power became ascendant and attempted a Digvijaya extending as far as the Ganges and even the Himalayas. Soon however, the Eastern Gangas established again a separate kingdom in Kalinga or Telangaṇa and confined the Cholas to the Tamil or Dravida land. Thus practically the several divisions of India marked by distinct peculiarities of language, climate and soil were under distinct ruling families in this sub-period also and formed distinct kingdoms. Why these kingdoms large enough as they were compared with the small kingdoms of Mediæval or even modern Europe, did not develop into strong countries or nations is the problem which a historian of Mediæval Hindu India has to solve. Small Christian kingdoms of Europe could withstand the onslaught of Arabs and Turks and preserve their independence while Hindu kingdoms in India, large though they were, finally fell before the Turks and Afghans at the end of this sub-period.

The reason appears to be, as shown elsewhere, that these different Hindu kingdoms did not develop the sentiment of nationality under the influence of which even small states in Europe like Holland or Belgium, Hungary or Poland, have preserved their independence against the onslaught of Germany or Turkey for hundreds of years. There was a modicum of the sentiment of nationality no doubt in the Hindu states in the last sub-period, but even that disappeared in this sub-period "for reasons which we have to elucidate in this volume" (See Vol. II p. 227). The chief cause lies in our view in the solidification of cast which took place in this sub-period as already described.

Various causes such as the growing ideas of purity of race and the adoption of vegetarian food by many communities under the revived influence of the doctrine of Ahimsā in this sub-period led each caste and sub-section of caste to isolate itself in food and marriage. The Hindu society consequently split up into hundreds of self-contained communities and thus lost its solidarity. The feeling of self-interest in the independence of country as a whole was gone. Intermixture of blood by marriage in the previous sub-section kept up the idea of unity and interdining added its unifying quota of influence. Under the revived religious fervour of orthodox Hinduism again, it came to be considered that it was the duty and the privilege of the Kshatriya alone to rule. Indeed it is remarkable that all the different ruling families in India in this sub-period were Kshatriyas or claimed to be Kshatriyas. These ruling families, especially the Rajputs, formed themselves into a closed group under the same influence of caste solidification; and lost touch not only with the other varnas but also with the agricultural Kshatriyas. The political apathy of the people became, therefore, phenomenal. It was believed that the kingdoms belonged to the kings as their private property and if the Rajput kings lost their property, the people had only to transfer their allegiance to the next owner, whoever that may be. The rights of kings were to be defended by the ruling clan whose privilege it was to rule. The peoples' duty was to obey any king whom God chose by giving him success in battle. The feeling of nationality thus completely died; and even among Rajputs, neither patriotism nor nationality remained but only the sentiment of loyalty. The Rajputs forgot that it was their duty to preserve the independence of the people of the kingdom. The only sentiment that remained or was appealed to in the Rajput soldier, was that of loyalty or service of the master who paid him; and as shown elsewhere, the Rajput soldiers were ready to die even for their Mahomedan king and master when the rule of the Ghaznavide Mahomedan kings was substituted for that of the Shahi Hindu kings of Kabul. It is, therefore, no wonder that the Hindu kingdoms of this sub-period were weak and that no national resistance was offered when the Rujput armies of Prithvirāj and Jaichand were defeated in single battles and these two heroic kings were killed in the contest.

It is a pity that the keen intellect of the Hindus did not find out the true essentials of a state and did not evolve its true theory. But this is not to be wondered, as even in the west, the paternal theory of kingship was in the acendancy so late as the eighteenth century. In India the same theory is propounded in its law treatises. It must be said, however, to the credit of Hindu kings, generally as of this period, that they always carried this parental idea into real practice and rarely oppressed their subjects by acts of wanton cruelty. The legend of the herb of longevity given by Ufi in his Jamiyat-ul-Hikayat (E. II. p. 174) is interesting in this connection and shows how Indian kings, in comparison with Mahomedan kings, were less oppressive and believed that tyrannical kings had their lives shortened by the curses of their oppressed subjects. Whatever the value of this story, it may be believed that the inspiring example of Rāma, the ideal king of Ancient India was always before the Hindu kings and we rarely meet with mention of tyrannical kings in mediæval records except perhaps in the history of Kashmir. The expenses again of Hindu states were very limited. The absence of standing armies and of foreign bureaucracies explains the inexpensiveness of mediæval Hindu kingdoms and the generally less cruel Hindu temperament made even despotic kingdoms of mediæval Hindu India well-governed and happy. They in fact secured internal and external peace with the minimum of taxation. It may seem paradoxical but it is nevertheless true that a despotic Hindu king in mediæval times was less expensive than a modern foreign bureaucracy. As we shall presently see, civil and military rule in mediæval Hindu kingdoms was much less costly than modern British or Mogul rule. Lastly, the Hindu kings had no legislative power and could not enact new laws or amend old ones or impose new taxes. Their zulum where it did exist was always personal. The common people were content to live under such limited monarchies and never consequently worked to obtain political power through popular assemblies as in the west. Moreover, popular assemblies also, according to the religious belief of the Hindus, had no power to enact new laws or to alter or abrogate old ones. Even civil law and the law of offences and punishments together with even the nature and amount of taxation was laid down by the Smṛitis. Hence the need of peoples' assemblies was never felt in Hindu kingdoms. The absence, however, of such institutions, coupled with the wrong theory of state wherein the king was looked upon as the owner of the kingdom and not the people, led to one baneful result viz. weakness of the sentiment of nationality which, completely dying in this sub-period, the Hindu kingdoms of India were easily destroyed.

The king was thus not assisted in the administration of the country, by any popular assembly or constitutional ministers, but by ministers appointed by him and holding office during his pleasure. How many these were and what were their functions, it would be interesting to find out, not from Nītiśāstras (books on polity) whose dates of compositions are yet unsettled, but from inscriptions recorded in this sub-period. And curiously, inscriptions usually recording grants of inam villages do contain the names of all the ministers as well as local and provincial officers. This list is generally most detailed in Bengal inscriptions and we find the following ministers mentioned therein: 1 Rājāmātya, 2 Purohita, 3 Mahādharmādhyaksha, 4 Mahāsāndhivigrahika, 5 Mahāsenāpati, 6 Mahāmudrādhikrita (Great Keeper of the Seal), 7 Mahākshapaṭalika, 8 Mahāpratihāra, 9 Mahābhogika and 10 Mahāpīlupati (E. I. XIV p. 159).* The word Mahā attached to these names showed that there were officers subordinate to them while they personally waited upon the king and were the head of their departments. (This word Mahā was first added to these names by a Kashmir king Vol. I p. 209). Besides these there were the chief queen, the chief prince (heir apparent) and subordinate kings who are also mentioned in inscriptions; but these were probably not always consulted though the land grants required to be brought to their notice also. In Gāhadavāla grants we have mention of the following officers: 1 Mantrī, 2 Purohita, 3 Pratihāra, 4 Senādhipati, 5 Bhāṇḍāgārika and 6 Akshapaṭalika, besides 7 the Physician, 8 the Astrologer and 9 the Master of the Household (Antahpurika). The Dūta is mentioned also and the queen and the Yuvarāja or heir apparent (Govindachandra's inscriptions I. A. XVIII p. 15 and E. I. IV p. 101). In a Chedi inscription of Karṇa are mentioned: 1 The great queen, 2 The great prince, 3 Mahāmantrī, 4 Mahā-Sāndhivigrahika, 5 Mahāmātya, 6 Mahā-Dharmādhikaraṇika, 7 Mahāpratihārī, 8 Mahākshapaṭalika, 9 Mahābhāndāgārika, 10 Mahāsāmanta, 11 Mahāpramattkarī and 12 Mahāśvasādhanika (E. I. XI p. 41). Unfortunately we have no mention of court officers in grants of the Paramāra, Chandella and southern Chālukya kings. But as already stated (p. 247) Thana Śilāhāra grants not only contain the mention, but also the consent-signatures, of 1 Mahāmātya, 2 Mahāsāndhivigrahika, 3 Śrikaraṇa and two Bhāndhāgārikas. The Bhadan plates (E. I. XII p. 251) in addition to these, mention 1 Rājaputra. 2 Mantrī. 3 Purohita and 4 Amātya. The chief minister is further described as 'bearing the burden of the care of the whole state.' From these descriptions not differing much from one another in the several states, we will try to find out what and how many ministers assisted the kings in this sub-period of mediæval Hindu history.

The chief queen and the chief prince as also the physician, the astrologer and the Purohita or religious preceptor were persons of importance in every kingdom; but they were not ministers. The prime minister there was, but he was called Mantrin in some and Mahāmātya in others. The word Mantrin means counsellor and Amātya means a constant attendant.

* In Madanapāla's grant (J. B. LXIX p. 71) we have besides 1, 4, 5, 7, 8, Mahāsāmanta, and Mahākumārāmātya i. e. the great sardar and the great minister for princes.

The foreign minister or Mahāsāndhivigrika is there, as also the chief revenue minister called Mahākhapaṭalika, a word substituted in Thana by Śrikaraṇa or master of land register. The finances and treasury were under the Bhāndāgārika. The commander-in-chief was also there. In Bengal there was in addition the chief officer for elephants, the elephant arm in Bengal being maintained at great strength (in fact the kings of Bengal were called Gajapatis) and in other states there was the chief cavalry officer. It is curious to find no mention of the Chief Justice or chief judicial officer. Probably the king himself decided such cases as came to the highest court with the help of all these officers and assessors, as we will show later. The king was not bound to consult his ministers though he usually did so. In Thana, however, it seems that not only was he bound to consult them but that the signatures of consent of his five ministers were necessary for the validity of land grants and presumably of other state orders. This was a practice peculiar to the Śilāhāra kingdom of Thana. It shows the advanced nature of its administration, involving the doctrine of the responsibility of ministers. Or perhaps it may be that Thana being originally subordinate to the Rāshtrakūtas, important ministers were appointed from the imperial court and their consent was considered necessary to every important act and the practice continued even after the Śilāhāras became independent. This system, however, of mediæval ministry together with ministers' names entirely disappeared in Mahomedan times, so much so that when Hindu rule was revived under Śhivaji, we have different names and functions assigned to ministers as we proceed to show in a note.

NOTE—SHIVAJI'S ASHTAPRADHĀNA.

One would expect to find the names of ministers in Hindu kingdoms of the 12th century used in the constitution of ministry created by Shivaji when he resuscitated Hindu kingship in the 17th century. But it seems that the Mahomedans of both Northern and Southern India had so completely changed the whole system of administration that nothing remained of the mediæval system or nomenclature. This speaks highly of the independence and originality of the Mahomedan administrators. For even the British administration retains some names and features of the preceding Mahomedan or Maratha administration. How the names and functions of Shivaji's ministers differ from those of ministers in mediæval Hindu India will appear from the following. Shivaji's Ashṭapradhāna or eight ministers were: 1 the Peshwa or prime minister, head of both civil and military administration, 2 Senāpati, 3 Amātya, 4 Sachiva, 5 Mantrī, 6 Sumanta, 7 Panditrao, and 8 Nyāyādhīśa. Amātya was revenue minister and Sumanta was foreign minister while Sachiva was privy seal or record keeper and Mantrī was Private Secretary (Rānade's Rise of Maratha Power p. 126). The name of the chief minister Peshwa was taken from the Mahomedans as people had been so completely accustomed to it that even Shivaji could not change the name and thought it fit to retain it. But the Mahomedans who succeeded Mediæval Hindu kings never thought it necessary to retain any old names. Perhaps Shivaji considered it necessary to show to the people that he was as independent and powerful as the Bijapur Sultan and had his own Peshwa. The other names of ministers introduced by the Mahomedans such as Mujumdar, Surnis, Sabnis, Dabir &c. were changed and new Sanskrit names were assigned and associated with some different functions. Mr. Shejvalkar in his paper published in the Quarterly of Itihāsa Sanshodhaka Mandala, Poona (July-Oct. 1923) has the credit of pointing out that the names of the eight ministers were taken by Shivaji from Śukranītisāra with one or two exceptions,* viz: 1 Sumantra, 2 Pandita, 3 Mantrī, 4 Pradhāna, 5 Sachiva 6 Amātya, 7 Prādvivāka and 8 Pratinidhi. The Senāpati was properly put in place of Pratinidhi; but the functions of others were changed from those given by Śukranītisāra. Thus "Sumantra was finance minister, but with Shivaji he became foreign minister. Amātya was land minister but with Shivaji he became finance minister. Mantrī was foreign minister, but he became household officer. Sachiva was war minister but he became Privy Seal" (Shejvalkar). These details are perhaps not quite correct. It is clear that these names and offices are quite distinct from the names and offices mentioned in mediæval inscriptions. Even the Śukranītisāra does not give the names and functions which were in vogue in the 12th century A. D. and we are led to surmise that the Nītisāra is a work written in Mahomedan times. Pandita is a new name entirely though the function was the same as that of the old Darmādhyaksha of mediæval times. Prādvivāka is a name not retained by Shivaji but it was changed into Nyāyādhīśa a name not found in mediæval times or even in Smṛitis. The Akshapaṭalika, the Sāndhivigrahika and the Bhāndāgārika are names forgotten in the days of the Nītisāra. Amātya has a new meaning and function assigned, while Sachiva is entirely a new name and is assigned a function for which strangely enough there was no distinct provision in mediæval times. Thus the whole system of court administration was forgotten in later times. How local administration also underwent change of nomenclature will be seen from the next chapter.

---

* सुमंत्रः पण्डितो मंत्री प्रधानः सचिवस्तथा।
अमात्यः प्राड्विवाकश्च तथा प्रतिनिधिः स्मृतः॥ (p. 75)

CHAPTER VI.

ADMINISTRATION.

The nature of civil and military administration in all countries was practically the same, though slight variations existed. Its system has been well described in the Smṛitis as also in the different Nitiśāstras and since the discovery of the Arthaśāstra of Kauṭilya, we have got now a complete idea of how administration was carried on in so ancient a time as the days of Chandragupta Maurya (300 B. C.). The same system of administration with important changes continued through the mediæval Hindu period treated of in these volumes. We have already described the system in our first volume as it existed in the first sub-period (600–800 A. D.) and in the second volume as it obtained in the second sub-period (800–1000). We will here describe the system of administration which obtained in this sub-period (1000–1200 A. D.) and which, though practically the same as before, discovers several variations. Unfortunately Al-Beruni does not assist us on this subject as his treatise on India does not speak of the nature of civil and military administration in the Hindu kingdoms of his time. But the detailed deeds of grant of inam villages issued in this sub-period supply us as before with interesting information on the subject and we proceed to give the details of administration as they appear from these grants. It is strange to find, as we shall show later on, that this system of administration of mediæval Hindu kingdoms entirely disappeared in Mahomedan times; and we find no trace of it in the revival of Hindu rule under the Marathas.

THE EXECUTIVE.

India remained divided, as stated before, into several kingdoms large and small, their number being given as fifty-nine in the Yewur inscription of the Chālukyas of the Deccan (I. A. VIII p. 18); probably this number is preserved in the number fifty-six of the Marathi poets of later days. The larger kingdoms such as those of Gāhadavālas, Pālas, Chālukyas and Cholas included several minor kingdoms which were feudatory; but these practically wielded independent power and must have been counted in the traditional number 59. The head of the executive in each kingdom was of course the king who was always a Kshatriya or Rajput and kingship descended hereditarily. The most important branch of administration in a modern state viz:—legislature, was absent in mediæval Hindu kingdoms and the king was thus only the highest executive and judicial authority in the country as also the source of all honour and greatness.

The chief queen or Pattamahishi* and the chief prince or Yuvarāja were important personages next to the king and appear to have had some executive powers in the state. They of course acted for the king in his absence or during his illness as has been seen in some Gāhadavāla grants issued by them in Madanapāla's name (p. 214). From ancient times (vide Rāmāyaṇa) the Yuvarāja was appointed with great ceremony and a Gāhadavāla inscription mentions the appointment of Jaichand as Yuvarāja (E. I. IV p. 123). In some southern inscriptions, the name of the Yuvarāja, usually a brother, is joined in inscriptions. What the exact limit of his authority was cannot be determined. We have in the last chapter described the king's ministers with their duties and designations.

Proceeding to describe first the revenue administration of the Hindu kingdoms, we find each kingdom divided into what are now called Districts and Tahsils or Talukas. The Sanskrit words for these are sometimes different. In the north a district was called Bhukti while in Malwa and Deccan it was called Mandala and Rāshṭra respectively. But in the South we find no names used but the number of villages mentioned signified the district as well as the taluka. Even the Kokan kingdom is described as Puri-Kokan fourteen hundred. The districts or divisions were often very large and their limits sometimes changed. Thus the Karahātaka 12000 in Chālukya days included even Poona which is a very old town as a grant recently edited (E. I. XII) by Stein Konow shows. The mode of describing a portion of a taluka by the number of villages it contained is to be seen even in the north as shown later on. The Tahsil or Taluka was usually called Vishaya and its boundaries rarely varied. The word Pattalā a new word used in this period is, however, constantly found in U. P. (Gāhadavāla) grants. Its meaning or modern equivalent cannot be ascertained. These Gāhadavāla grants do not often mention the district but simply mention the Pattalā which was really quite sufficient. In Sena

* So called from Patta or golden band bound round the head of the queen who participated in the ceremony of coronation of the king.

grants in Bengal we have both Bhukti and Mandala mentioned, and in Pāla grants we have Bhukti, Vishaya and Mandala mentioned, Mandala being subordinate to Vishaya. In a Malwa record we have Mandala and Prati-Jāgaranaka (a new word) while within it a smaller division is mentioned as the 48 of Vodaśira (see Appendix). The town and the village was the last unit, except in Bengal, and there is no mention of a smaller division than these.

The authorities entrusted with the administration of these several denominations were the Rajasthāniya (viceroy) for the Bhukti or province, the Rāshṭrapati for the district mentioned only in southern India grants, the Vishayapati or Tahsildar mentioned in almost all provinces and the village officer called Pattakila in Malwa only. In grants from northern India the inhabitants generally of the village granted as also of the adjoining villages are addressed and they are always described as consisting of Brahmins and others, the latter described further in detail as Kuṭumbi (from which the Marathi word Kulambi is derived, meaning the settled family-man agriculturist), Kāyastha, Dūta, Vaidya and Mahattara (Patel probably) down to the "Meda and Chāndāla" vide an inscription of Paramardin (Appendix); often they are described simply as Jānapada. These named persons seem to have some duty, with some income assigned to them, in the village. There are besides many district officers mentioned such as Śaulkika, Gaulmika and Tarika i. e. officer for customs duty, officer of gulma which very probably was a Police Thana and officer for navigation. In U. P. and Bengal much traffic, both passenger and goods, was carried on by rivers and this was under a special officer. In Southern India, in places where rivers were crossed, there was a small tax to be paid to the state as also a fee to the nāvikas or boatsmen; these were also under an officer. There were separate Adhyakshas or superintendents as they were called for state forests, as also for royal gośālās or cattle-breeding operations. Finally operatives or servants in employ under all these civil officers were called Chāṭas, the employees in army being called Bhaṭas. All these persons or public servants required to know of inam grants of villages as they had their duties to perform in connection with them. For instance inam villages are in all grants declared as free of the entry of Chāṭras and Bhatas. No civil or military servant could enter them to purchase provisions or exact labour.

The head of the village was called Pattakila as stated above in Malwa records and Grāmapati in Gāhadavāla records and Grāmakūṭa or chief of the village in Gujarat and southern India records, the word Grāmakūṭa still surviving in the form of Gamot in Gujarat, Malwa, and Konkan. The village was self-contained. It had its guard, its messenger, its doctor and its astronomer, also its scavenger and executioner or Meda and Chāndāla.

The details of the rights given to donees in the villages are explicit and are very interesting, showing that in non-inam villages such rights belonged to the state or the villagers themselves. In U. P. grants under the Gāhadavālas, the right to the iron and salt found in the village was very important. Iron and steel were necessary for carpenters and soldiers while the sea being distant and means of conveyance difficult, salt was a precious thing in U. P. and the inamdar was entitled to all the salt that could be produced from saltish wells in the village. Very probably as stated in Vol. I, salt was taxed by the state and there was a special officer who superintended the income from salt-tax. The ditches and the unculturable land, garta and ushara, were also valuable and belonged to the donee in khalsa villages such land belonged to the state or the villagers conjointly. The details of things granted in inam villages are interesting and discover the nature of revenue administration in these mediæval kingdoms. Thus in Gāhadavāla grants the detailed list of items granted are water, land, waste-land, stones, hills, river, forest patches, mango and madhūka (Mahua), trees, iron, salt sources, "whatever is above and below." The mango and Mahua trees were important trees in U. P. and unless specially owned, they belonged to the state in khalsa villages. So also were stone quarries and iron mines and salt wells, hills and forest patches.* But with regard to the last we have further to remember that there were certain portions of state forests which were open to the villagers for cutting firewood (see Vol. I p. 135). The further description in almost all grant deeds that the village is granted upto (including) Tṛiṇayūti and Gochara which may be translated as grass meadow and cow-grazing-land, shows that every village had its pasture and cow-

---

* In plain Bengal there was not much forest and the small brushwood trees thus were important. These are specially mentioned in the word 'Zhāta and Vitapa included.' The word Zhāta is Zhāda of modern vernaculars.

grazing-land and hence the supply of cow's milk and of bullocks, for ploughs was always assured. Grass meadows and cow-grazing-lands to which the cattle of the village had free access are apparently not now reserved in villages. A grant of Paramardin dated 1166 (Appendix) mentions even sugarcane, cotton and saṇa (jute) plants along with mango and Madhūka trees Apparently these were important products in Bundelkhaṇd and are, therefore, specially mentioned. It does not, however, mean that in khalsa villages government had any rights in them.

Turning now to the taxes levied in villages we find these mentioned in detail also as they were to be paid to the inamdar of the village. It is curious to note that the word Udranga which was in common use in the first period (Vol. I p. 132) is nowhere used now (except in a grant in Thana E. I. III p. 267). The expression generally used is Bhāga-Bhoga-Kara-Hiraṇya which to our view refers to the usual portion of land produce in kind (1/6 of the land produce)† and to the tax in money on profits of trade and manufacture (1/50 of profits) mentioned from ancient times in the Mahābhārata and the Smṛitis. It, however, appears that in the kingdom of Kanauj under the later Pratihāras several minor taxes were imposed in addition, many of which it is difficult to make out. The list is as follows : 1 Kūtaka, 2 Daśabandha, 3 Vinśatyaprastha, 4 Akshapatalikaprastha, 5 Pratihāraprastha, 6 Ākara, 7 Turushkadaṇḍa and 8 Varavajjhe (Basahi grant I. A. XIV p. 103). There are other taxes mentioned in other Gāhadavāla inam grants such as Kumaragadiyānaka (I. A. XVIII p. 15) and Pravaṇikara (E. I. IV p. 109, 123). E. I. IX (p. 102) also adds the word " the permanent and temporary taxes such as Kumaragadiyānaka." This indicates that the revenue administration under the declining Pratihāras became somewhat oppressive and the system continued even under the Gāhadavālas. Turushkadaṇḍa, of course, as already explained, was imposed for paying tribute to the Turks; but perhaps this was taken as a precedent for imposing other minor taxes, a prastha or handful for the Akshapaṭalika or revenue minister, another for Pratihāra or chamberlain, and so on. The tenth and the twentieth imposed, for what persons or purposes is not clear, remind one of the chowth and the tenth part (Sardesh-

---

† This included no doubt other products besides corn such as flower, vegetable etc. detailed in Vol. I. p. 132.

mukhi) of the Marathas levied from Mogul dominions. All these were paid in kind.

The money tax on sale and purchase and on profits on manufactured goods was taken at the Mandapikā or toll house in every town and probably the bazar in every village. And here also besides the government tax of 1/50, minor taxes were imposed for charitable purposes, and possibly for the benefit of certain persons. An interesting description of these taxes is found in an inscription in Kathiawar, (Bhav. In. p. 157): "In the Mangalapura (Mangrol) Mandapikā, on every cart loaded with corn 4 Kārshāpaṇas and on every ass-load 1/2, on every camel-load of betel leaves 1, on a cartload of such leaves &c.* Some contribution was also made from the state daily income in the Mandapikā. Many of these details are not well understood now, but it is certain that the money tax was called Śulka and was levied at the toll house.

Passing on to describe the revenue officers, we have the old name Vishayapati for the Tahsil officer in almost all grants. The Rāshtrapati is mentioned as the District officer in Deccan grants while in Bengal grants he may be indicated by the Rājasthānīya. The Gāhadavāla grants strangely enough do not mention these officers though for the Pattalā there must have been a chief officer. In Malwa we have the name Mandaloi still surviving which is the Prākrit form of Mandalapati. Thus generally there was a revenue officer with name ending in pati. He was probably not hereditary but removable at the will of the king or the chief revenue minister. It is worthy of notice that the names Deshmukh and Deshpande which were in use in the Deccan even in Mahomedan times and are still in use there, are not found in inscriptions of this period. Though they are Sanskrit and not Mahomedan names, they from this appear to have come into use in Mahomedan times. Further there is no officer corresponding to Deshpande who kept the record of the District in the mediæval inscriptions. Record certainly was kept in the village as the village record keeper named Karanika is often mentioned in inscriptions. We have already shown in Vol. I (p. 130) that Akshapaṭala, according to Kautilya's Arathaśāstra was revenue record house and Akshapatalika was the head of the office in the village; a word which probably was shortened and changed into Pattakila of Malwa

* There [illegible] to be paid on every Dyūta or gambling.

inscriptions. It is the origin of the modern word Patel or Pātil. The head of the village is called in inscriptions of other kingdoms, grāmapati (J. B. LXIX p. 71) or grāmakūta or simply Mahattara (the modern form of which is Mhātre in Konkan). The Patel was assisted in the village administration by the Karaṇika (keeper of register of tenants), a word which survives to this day as Karṇika of Konkan, Kulkarṇī of the Deccan and Karaṇam of South India and called Kāyastha in Northern India, see Parmardideva's inscription (E. I. IV p.). The other village servants mentioned in it are 1 Dūta or messenger, 2 physician and 3 Mahattara (Patel) down to 4 Meda and 5 Chāndāla. Among villagers there were Brahmins also who are usually particularly mentioned as in Paramāra insc. (I. A. XVI p. 204) which simply addresses itself to 'Vaishayika or Tahsil officers, the Pattakila and the country people (Jānapada) Brahmins and other than Brahmins.' For towns or Paṭṭaṇa there were special officers (E. I. IV p. 101). These village and town officers must have been hereditary as at present.

Land was measured (Vol. I p. 133) and Nivartana (acre) is a word usually used. But sometimes the extent of the land granted free is given as cultivable with so many ploughs (I. A. XVIII p. 15). The Naihatti grant of Ballālasena (E. I. XIV p. 159) gives not only in very great detail and precision the boundaries of the village granted which are unintelligible but which detail the nature of land record) but gives the whole area of the village in number of Unmāna or measures (not properly understandable), as also total produce (again not understandable) and the income in money. This is strangely enough, very small being 500 old Kapardikas. If Kapardika means one fourth of an anna, this means an income of about eight rupees. But we must remember that money value then must have been much greater than now and again apparently this was only the cash income of the village, the greater income being in kind (1/6th of grain produced). The sale and purchase of land as also of inam villages appears to have been allowed, as we find the fact expressly stated in the Semra plates of Paramardideva (E. I. IV p. 153).* These transactions were probably registered as they could be verified from official records (see Vol. II p. 239).

It must be noted that documents, especially state documents, must have been drawn up with care and ceremony; for we find

* दानाधानविक्रयं कुर्वतां बाधा न केनचित् कर्तव्या ।

the land grants inscribed on copper signed and sealed. The grantor king usually signed the deed himself using the word Svahasta or 'my hand.' This signature must have been made originally on the Bhurja-leaf paper and then copied on the copper plate. Sometimes instead of signature, the grantor king wrote at the end the words 'Mangalam Mahāśrih' (auspicious and prosperous) and sometimes added his signature also as in I. A. XIV (p. 349). The land grant was proclaimed on the spot before inhabitants of the village granted and surrounding villages by special state officers; and their names are mentioned at the end in every copperplate grant. Some grants are terse as in Malwa while others are very detailed and write a great deal of the family history of the grantor as in Bengal, (there are instructions in Smṛitis as to giving this history).

Among other revenue departments, the Śulka or tax on merchandise and manufacture was the most important and there was a Śaulkika (modern Sayar officer) in every Vishaya. There was also a Tarika (officer for river crossings), also an officer for mines Ākara, for breeding operations of cows, buffaloes and sheep (J. B. LXIX p. 71). Bengal inscriptions usually contain a detailed list of officers which include a Kshetrapāla (officer for fields). Prāntapāla (protector of state boundaries), Kottapāla (officer for forts) besides the above (ditto). The list shows that the revenue administration in Bengal (and presumably in the other states) was as detailed and organised as in modern times.

It would be interesting to see what coin was in use and of what value. The drama and the Dīnāra are constantly mentioned, the former usally of silver and the latter of gold. Dramma is Dām of Mahomedan times now only remembered. * Its value was probably equal to four Rupees (Vol. II. p. 242). Rupee is a word which appears in an inscription in Kathiawar of the last period (ditto). In Thana we have mention of Drammas. In Konkan there is a mention of Malavara Nishka (Bombay J.R.A.S. IX p. 241). Malavara is Malbar and it appears that the Nishka varied in weight and value in different countries as rupee did in Mahomedan and Maratha times. Nishka is a golden coin mentioned even in the Mahābhārata. Of lesser coins we have the

* The Mogual Dām was a copper coin and not a silver one and 40 Dāms made one rupee.

mention of Kārshāpaṇa which is probably the equivalent of the modern anna, the very word anna being probably its abbreviation; and next of Kopardika which was $\frac{1}{4}$ of it probably. It would have been most instructing if we had anywhere the mention of the total revenue of any particular state in money value ; so that not only the value of mediæval money but also the income of mediæval kingdoms could have been determined by comparison with present figures ; but unfortunately we have not come across any such statements.

JUDICIAL.

The next, and according to Hindu ideas the most important, function of the state is the Judicial. The Hindu king from the most ancient times personally dispensed justice to his people and sat in court every morning to hear suits (Manu). In his absence the Prādvivāka (judge) acted for him. In mediæval times the same practice obtained as may be seen from the Rājataranginī (Vol. I. p. 206). There is no mention of the Prādvivāka, however, among officers of the court in inscriptions and as stated before the king probably always himself dispensed justice with the aid of his ministers and sabhyas or assessors, according to Smṛiti rules. The officer named Dandanāyaka mentioned in almost all inscriptions was the magistrate in the district. He awarded punishments when the accused was tried in his court before himself and a jury. According to Smṛitis there is no difference between civil and criminal proceedings. All civil and criminal cases came under certain heads and in each the losing party was punished with fine and in cases of heinous offences imprisonment, mutilation or death. The police and the jail were probably under the Dandanāyaka and there were co-ordinate officers with him, named Dāndika and Dandapāśika (Bengal. J. R. LXIX p. 71). There was also a special officer in each district for catching thieves and robbers called Chauroddharaṇika. Hindu law and Hindu states attached great importance to the ferretting out of thieves and robbers and these were mercilessly punished when caught red-handed, having always their left hands cut off.

Minor criminal cases were always disposed of by village Panchayats or village officers. The expression 'sadaśāparādha' used in every inām grant-deed shows, according to our view, that ten offences of a minor character were finally disposable by the village officers and hence in inam villages the inamdar had the right to try them and to have the fines levied in connection with them. With regard to other offences and higher civil disputes, the practice must have been for the complainant or suitor to appear either before the king or before his district representative the Rājasthānīya or Dandanāyaka who probably had the same power as the king to try cases with the help of assessors. And further Hindu judicial system knew no appeals; a person losing his case in the district court might take it before the king and the case was tried *de novo* if the king thought fit. Apparently this was the practice even down to the days of the Peshwas.

Finally, we may quote here what Al-Beruni records in this connection (chap. LXV p. 158): "The plaintiff has to file a statement and his document. If there is no written document witnesses are produced, at least four being required. Cross examination of witnesses is not allowed. Brahmins and Kshatriyas are not punished for murder; but they are expelled from the kingdom after confiscation of property. For theft a Brahmin is blinded and his left hand and right foot are cut off. A Kshatriya, however, is not blinded. Other castemen are killed." This evidence shows the severity of punishment inflicted even on a Brahmin for theft in this sub-period. There is no rule in Smṛitis as to the number of witnesses. As the parties were never represented by pleaders (entirely a British institution in India) cross-examination was perhaps never thought of. But the great formality in swearing of witnesses and the dread of punishment in the next world probably made witnesses more truthful than now. The august presence of the king must also have added its influence in compelling witnesses to tell the truth. This must also have reduced the number of cases, especially civil, to the minimum.

Al-Beruni describes the various kinds of ordeals which were resorted to in cases of extreme doubt. Perhaps he speaks from law books and not from observation. For it has always been a mystery as to how any party could consent to perform such ordeals as are described, since the man performing the ordeal is always sure to be defeated, as nature must have her course whether the party performing the ordeal was right or wrong, unless some trick was resorted to. Whatever the explanation, ordeals are prescribed in Hindu law books: and apparently they were resorted to in this sub-period also, as evidenced by Al-Beruni.

POPULAR ASSEMBLIES IN SOUTH INDIA.

In the peculiar condition of South India i.e. in Kerala and Tamil countries, unlike in the rest of India, popular assemblies existed and enjoyed executive and judicial powers. In these countries, the ancient Dravidian population was not only preponderant but probably more advanced than in the rest of India; while the superimposed Aryan people were in a great minority and they considered themselves so pure that they lived in almost repellant aloofness. Yet there were village Panchayats everywhere and district popular assemblies and assemblies for the whole state as is evidenced by inscriptions. These inscriptions being in Tamil and Malyalam, we are precluded from studying them in the original; but we take the following extract from a note on K. P. Menon's History of Malabar, in the Journal of Indian History (April 1925). We have already referred to the body of Six Hundred which supervised the working of temples (p. 204) mentioned in Mr. Pillay's article in I. A. XXIV.

"There were three kinds of assemblies or Kuṭṭams, those for the tara (village), for the nādu (district) and for the whole of Kerala country. The first was the meeting of the villagers as represented by the Kāraṇavars of the families, to discuss matters of local interest, while the assembly of the nādu discussed matters of wider interest; and was a representative body of immense power which set at naught, on occasions, the authority of the king".

"From the 'Keralotpatti', we learn that after the Perumāl, began to rule the country, the Brahmins with a view to impose some check on royal authority organised the country into eighteen divisions and supplied the kings with assemblies which were always to be consulted on all important occasions. Assemblies known as 'the Five Hundred', the 'Six Hundred' and the 'Six Thousand' are mentioned in the Syrian copper-plate described in Logan's collection (No. III), belonging to the 9th century. The Jews and the Christians also had certain privileges in their assemblies." (Christians and Mahomedans also early came to and settled in Malabar.)

"Mr. P. Menon refers to various inscriptions which mention village assemblies. This is a feature which bears close similarity to the well-known growth of local representative bodies in Tamil country as proved by later Pallava, Chola and Pāndya records. The village assembly of Kerala met under the presidency of the asan or headman, decided social disputes, settled petty cases and attended to the various requirements of temples. The early British administrators of Malabar ignored the tara organisation of the Nairs. The great assembly of the whole country was held once in twelve years. It was presided over by Valluvanad or Vallattiri Raja till the 13th century when the Zamorin assumed the presidency. The last assembly was held in 1743".

"The local administration seems to have been in the hands of hereditary chiefs. The country was divided into Nādus presided over by Nāduvālis and these into Deśams under Deśavālis. The Deśam was divided not into territorial groups but into caste or tribal groups such as the Grāmams of the Namburis, the tara of the Nairs and the cheri of the low castes. The Nādu and Deśams of this coast differed from similar divisions elsewhere in that they consisted not of so many towns and villages but of so many Nairs etc." (pp. 115-117).

MILITARY.

Lastly we have to speak of the military administration of Hindu kingdoms in this sub-period. We have described at length the system as it was in vogue in the preceding sub-period (Vol. II. pp. 242-246) and the same system continued in this sub-period. There were very few standing armies in the states, the state army consisting usually of levies of the sardars. Govindachandra, from an inscription already noticed, must, however. have kept a large standing army. Moreover the elephant force must everywhere have belonged to the state which alone could provide the heavy expenditure required for it. In Bengal the army consisted of mercenary soldiers from other countries also as appears from Madanapāla's inscription (Bengal LXIX p. 71) of this period, the same foreign soldiers being mentioned as in the Bhagalpore inscription of the previous period; viz. Gauda, Mālava, Khasa, Hūṇa, Kulika, Karnāṭa and Lāṭa with one addition viz. Choda. We have seen that in this sub-period the Cholas (also written Chodas) became powerful and it is no wonder that the Chodas having established their reputation as soldiers were employed in Bengal. It may be added that the reputation of Karnāṭa soldiers is attested to even by Al-Beruni and Karnāṭa or 'Kannara' soldiers were employed as far north as the Panjab. For Al-Beruni describes Karnātaka as the country "whence those troops come which in the armies are known as Kannara". (Vol. I Sachau p. 173). This condition is now reversed, a fact which further strengthens our view expressed in vol. II that peoples' nature is often changed; for the Kannad people, though still strong and martial, do not much seek military employment in distant lands.

The inscription of Madanapāla above noted mentions nearly the same military officers as the Bhāgalpore inscription of the preceding sub-period viz.: 1 Mahāsenāpati, 2 Dauhsādhyasādhanika, 3 officers for elephants, horse, camels and naval forces, besides 4 Preshaṇika (messengers or spies), 5 Gamāgamika and 6 Abhitvaramāṇa, two names which, we said in Vol. I, it was difficult to understand. The same officers existed in other states than Bengal also, except perhaps the naval officer. Sometimes there was a special chief for cavalry as in Bundelkhand. The ordinary soldier was called Bhaṭa mentioned along with Chāṭa or policeman in inscriptions, as "inam villages were not to be entered by Chāṭas and Bhaṭas." The police department was apparently kept separate from the army which was intended mainly for external enemies. The police had their thanas or gulmas which were under officers named Gaulmikas; and these were probably under the Dāndika of the district and he and others were under the Rājasthānīya. We make these surmises from the order in which these officers are mentioned in inscriptions (See Appendix).

We have no indication in records of this sub-period also as to how the soldiers and officers were paid. They probably got, as stated in Vol. II, cash payment as well as grain from the state granary. The civil officers, however may have been paid by assignments of lands and villages and in the case of highest officers, both civil and military, of towns.

The army on the battlefield was usually led by the king who always was in the van, riding an elephant. We have described, as far as we could, the fights between the Hindus and the Mahomedans who used the same weapons but different tactics. Both Hindu and Mahomedan armies, however, gave way when the king who led them was killed or lost sight of. As explained in vol. II. (p. 246) the cause of this behaviour was the absence of the feeling of self-interest in the Hindu or Mahomedan soldiers. They fought for the king and master and not for the nation.

SOURCE OF HONOUR.

The king granted titles. Even the title Śreshṭhin was granted to merchants by the king (E. I. II p. 237).

CHAPTER VII.

LANGUAGE AND LITERATURE.

We showed in Vol. II (p. 3) how the second sub-period of Hindu Mediæval History (800-1000 A.D.) was characterised by the rise of the modern vernaculars of India under the combined influence of political and religious causes. Buddhism being supplanted and Hinduism coming to be reconstructed, the study of Sanskrit was resorted to with greater energy and the new philosophy of Śankara especially had to be explained to the people in their own language. The Apabhranśa languages, therefore, throughout Aryan India underwent change by the use of Sanskrit loan-words in their original or Tatsama form and Sanskrit and new conjugational and inflexional forms also were introduced from Sanskrit. Even the Non-Aryan languages assumed new forms by the use of pure Sanskrit words and acquired new grace (Vol. II p. 168). Thus the modern Sanskrit-born vernaculars were evolved in the preceding sub-period, viz. Bengali, Hindi, Eastern and Western (Rajastāni), Panjabi, Gujarathi, and Marathi; as also the modern Non-Aryan vernaculars Kanarese, Telugu, Tamil and Malyalam. In the present sub-period we find all these languages so far developed as to give rise to literature as classical as that in Sanskrit. And it is curious to note that in each of the provinces of these languages different forms of the alphabet also grew out of the same old Sanskrit Devanāgarī alphabet as evidenced by Al-Beruni. He enumerates the different alphabets of India as follows (Vol. I p. 173): "The most generally known alphabet is called Siddha Mātṛikā used in Kashmir and Vārāṇaśhi. These are the high schools of Hindu sciences. The same writing is used in Madhyadeśa, the country round Kanauj also called Āryāvarta." This is the Eastern Hindi script. "In Mālwā there is another alphabet called Nāgar which differs from the above only in shape. Then comes the alphabet known as Ardhanāgarā as it is compounded of the above two. It is used in Bhatia and some parts of Sind. (This is a verification of our view in the geographical chapter that Bhatia town and province (173), was to the north of Sind, a part of the Panjab to the west of the Jhelum.) This is probably the modern Panjabi script. Other alphabets are Malaivari used in southern India on the seacoast; the Saindhava used in Almeansūra; the Karnāta used in Karnāṭadeśa 'whence those troops come which in the armies are known as Kannara,' the Āndhri used in Āndhradeśa; the Dirwari (Drāvidī) used in Dirwardeśa; the Lāri used in Lāradeśa; the Gaurī used in Pūrvadeśa by the Buddhists."

Now this is a complete survey of India so far as alphabet is concerned, and we may take it that it also represents the state of the country as regards language, a state which is practically the same as now. In Eastern Panjab and Kashmir, down to Benares we have the Eastern Hindi with its peculiar script, in Malwa and Rājputana western Hindi, in northern Sind and Western Panjab we have a language distinct from others; and Sindhī in Sind. On the sea-coast a still more distinct language and writing which is called Malawāri. Perhaps this was imported from Malabar by sea and the Saindhava at Almansura must be a mixed jargan of Arabic and Hindi. Both apparently do not survive now. Gujarati (alphabet and language) apparently had not a distinct existence in 1030 A. D. as even the name Gujarat for the province had not come into existence at that time. It will be seen that Al-Beruni does not mention the Marathi alphabet; probably the Lāri or the language of Lāta as spoken in North Konkan is another name for old Marathi which became uniform when the Yādavas became supreme in the 13th century even in Konkan. Marco Polo (1280) mentions that there were different languages in Gujarat and in Thana. Marathi is now a general language which has suppressed its different dialects viz the Lādi of north Konkan, the Konkani in south Konkan as far as Goa, and the speech of Mahārāstra proper, Vidarbha and Khandesh, owing to the supremacy of the Yādavas and the prevalence of the Bhāgavata worship of Vithoba of Pandharpur both of which things happened about the end of this sub-period viz. from 1170 to about 1200 A. D. That Marathi as a distinct language with minor dialectic differences had not only come into existence but had developed about the 12th century is clear from the literature now found of the Mahānubhāvas and even Dnyāneśvari of 1290 A. D. in its finished excellance presupposes the development of the language at least a century before it. We find a Marathi sentence in an inscription from Konkan recorded by the Śilāhāras of Thana. In Bengal also it may be taken that the modern vernacular of that province had come into literary existence at this time. Its different script, the Gaudi, is mentioned by Al-Beruni.

In South India already its different vernaculars, the Kanarese, the Telugu, the Tamil also called Drāvidī and Malyālam had come into literary existence. We have given in Vol. II. (pp. 173-4) extracts from Dr. Sir Grierson's Survey of Indian Languages showing how far Kanarese, Telugu, and Marathi literatures go back.

Besides we have many inscriptions in this sub-period written in Kanarese, Tamil, and Telugu. A Sanskrit inscription of the Eastern Gangas of 1075 A. D. gives its subsequent portion in Telugu (E. I. IV p. 314). We may, therefore, be certain that all the modern vernaculars of India, both Sanskrit-born and Tamil-born, were fully developed at this time as spoken and written languages with graceful literature in each. Mahānubhāva writings in Marathi with Dnyāneśvarī coming a hundred years later, Pampa's Ādipurāṇa in Kanarese, Nannaya's Mahābhārata in Telugu are works which still survive. Some works in Eastern Hindi and in Rājastānī (Dingal) still exist though they have not yet been studied. And Prithvīrāj Rāsā, though in its present form it is an extensive amplification, in its nucleus goes back, according to our view, to the end of our sub-period.

This vernacular literature is chiefly in verse and is generally a translation or imitation of Sanskrit poems or Purāṇas. But original works in Sanskrit on a vast range of subjects were written in this sub-period to which it would not be out of place to direct the attention of the reader. The great seats of learning were Kashmir and Benares, as even Al-Beruni records and Nadia in Bengal, Tanjore in South India and Kalyan in Mahārāshtra. Kanauj and Ujjain perhaps were also as famous as before; the learned men of the Madhyadeśa who were great Mīmānsakas in the time of Bāṇa and Kumārila were still famous, studied Vedas and performed Vedic sacrifices as zealously as before.* The list of subjects includes poetics (Alankāra), philosophy, law (Dharmaśāstra), Logic (Nyāya), grammar, astronomy, medicine and music. Mr. P. V. Kane has given a detailed history of the development of Alankāraśāstra and shown how Mammata (1100) and others evolved the theory of Dhvani in this period. Philosophy also had its contribution from Rāmānuja and others which swelled the already vast philosophi-

* अश्रान्तक्रतुकुण्डमण्डलचलद्धूमावलिश्यामल-व्योमाशावलयं विलोक्य विलसन्नीलाम्बुदालिभ्रमात् । विप्रालयेरितवेदराशिविततोद्घोषोद्धुरे यद्गृहे सत्पक्षप्रसरा रटन्ति पटवो हृष्टा मुहुः केकिनः ॥ (E. I. I p. 41).

cal literature of India including, as it did, Sānkhya and Yoga (common to all), Jain and Bauddha (unorthodox), and Kumārila and Śankara (orthodox) philosophies.* We have already noted how law was studied in all Hindu kingdoms at this period and how solid works like the Mitāksharā were written. In Logic again a new departure was made by Hindu logicians at Nadia. Hemachandra's grammar Siddha Hema has already been mentioned. In astronomy Someśvara son of Vikramānka of Kalyan was a royal author in this period and Bhāskara's Siddhānta-śiromaṇi (1150) the greatest Hindu work on the subject belongs to this time. In medicine Dalhaṇa of Bhadāvara near Mathura and Chakrapāṇi, court-physician of Nayapāla of Bengal, wrote detailed commentaries on Charaka about 1050 A. D. The great learning of king Bhoja of Malwa and his authoritative works on many subjects have already been noticed. The land of Kerala was famous for learned astrologers and physicians (Marco Polo p. 376). On the west coast and the east coast, under the Kadambas and the Cholas, music was greatly studied and dancing was specially developed. And in Kashmir Harsha acquired fame by his musical compositions and also his patronage of music. Thus Hindu intellect maintained its reputation for acuteness and brilliancy in this sub-period by the production of such works as Kāvya-Prakāsha and Siddhānta-śiromani, Naishadha Mahākāvya and Gītagovinda the most charming lyric in the world. Indeed this galaxy of eminent authors Bhoja and Mammata, Bhāskara and Rāmānuja, Jayadeva and Sriharsha and many others illumines to some extent this sombre period of Mediæval Hindu history of India.

---

* All these were zealously studied by learned men of this period as will appear from the following description of a great Pandit in E.I.I.p. 41
मीमांसाद्वयपारगो गुरुरसौ यः काश्यपीये नये सांख्ये चाप्रतिमल्लता नयनिधिस्त्र्यक्षोऽक्षपादोक्तिदृक् । यश्चार्वाक-
विद्याऽस्मानमलनो दुर्वारबौद्धाम्बुधेः पानानन्दितकुम्भसम्भवमुनिर्दिग्वाससामन्तकः ॥

APPENDIX.

I. SOME CRITICISMS ANSWERED.

(1) DR. KRISHNASWAMY AIYANGAR ON AGNIKULAS.

Dr. Krishnaswamy Aiyangar in his Journal of Indian history (April 1925 pp. 123-124) endorses our view about the Gotra and Pravara of Rajputs and agrees "that our position is sound." He, however, expresses his dissent from our view that the Agnikula tradition is a myth and says that it goes back to centuries earlier than even the Rāsā. We have maintained in Vol. II that the myth arose after the Rāsā, from a wrong construction of its story. The doctor refers to a mention, in a Tamil poem of Sangam date, of a chieftain born in Agnikula. But we have shown that the Paramāra tradition always was that their first hero was born from the sacrificial fire of Vasishtha. But even the Paramāra was known as a solar-race Kshatriya being born from Vasishtha's fire and inscriptions of this sub-period (1000-1200 A. D.) nowhere mention three Rajput vamśas solar, lunar and fire-born. We have already shown the importance of an inscription of the Gāhadavālas wherein Chandra is said to have resuscitated Rajput vamśas which are said to be solar and lunar only (p. 221). And Chandra probably enumerated the 36 Rajput royal families. It is, therefore, certain that in the Mediæval Hindu period only two vamśas of Rajputs solar and lunar were known.

Secondly, Dr. Krishnaswamy Aiyangar refers to the tradition of Pratihāras being born from Lakshmaṇa as known in the south and mentions that the Pallavas were also said to be born from Vishṇu's brother. But the Doctor forgets that he is arguing here against himself. If he believes that the tradition of Pratihāras being descended from Lakshmaṇa is well founded, then there is no *jumping to the conclusion* that the Agnikula tradition is a myth as the conclusion becomes irresistible and itself jumps on us; for the Pratihāras being really Sūryavamśi can not be looked upon as Agnivamśi. Indeed the Agnikula tradition has no basis in history, being unknown to inscription of this period, all the four Agnikula families Chauhan, Paramāra, Pratihāra, and Chālukya being described in inscriptions as solar or lunar. The Marathas in the Deccan have no Agnikuli among them, though they have Chauhan, Paramāra, Pallava and Chālukya among them.

(2) P. GAURISHANKAR ON GOTRAS OF RAJPUTS.

Rai Bahadur Gaurishankar Ojha of Ajmer, on the other hand, believes the Agnikula tradition to be baseless but holds that the gotras of the Rajputs are not indicative of their descent, but of their discipleship. In short he follows the dictum of Vijnāneśvara laid down in his Mitāksharā (c. 1100 A. D.) that Kshatriyas have no gotras of their own but have to take the gotras of their purohitas. In his paper in Nāgarī Prachāriṇī Journal Vol. V, No. 4 (p. 435-443) he holds that the gotras of the Rajputs were always taken from the purohitas upto the period they observed Vedic ritual; but "now even that is given up and now the gotra of the Rajput and his purohita are different". This itself is wrong for the Rajput still performs Vedic ritual and there is no reason why the gotra of the purohita should be different from that of the Rajput. We have given the arguments which show that Rajputs had always gotras of their own and that Vijnāneśvara's dictum is wrong, in Chapter V, Vol. II. The arguments advanced by P. Gaurishankar against our view are: 1st, that in the Saundarānanda Kāvya of Aśvaghosha, Krishṇa and Balarāma are shown as taking different gotras from their different gurus and the Śakyas similarly took Gautama gotra; 2ndly, that in inscriptions we have instances of Rajput families having changed their gotras. How both these arguments are ineffectual we proceed to show.

The fact that Kshatriyas have gotras of their own appears from the ancient Vedic Sūtras dating from before 200 B. C. as shown by us in Vol. II and this is our strongest argument. To quote against this Vedic authority a story given in a Buddhist poem of about 200 A. D. has not much value. Indeed this is a question of Dharamaśāstra and must be decided on Dharamaśāstra and particularly Vedic authority. As will appear from the Śāstric opinion obtained recently by us and attached hereto, the Vedic Sūtras distinctly hold that Kshatriyas have gotras of their own.

The Buddhist tradition that Krishṇa and Balarāma had different gotras because they had different purohitas is absurd and is not known to Hindu Purāṇas. The guru of both was Sāndīpani of Ujjain as stated in Harivamśa and Bhāgavata. Secondly, it is not true that Śrīkrishṇa's gotra was Gautama as stated in Saundarānanda (Patrikā p. 439) and that of Balarāma was Gārgya. Śrīkrishṇa's gotra must be Atri as his descendants the Chūdāsamas and others have that gotra still. The statements in the Saundarānanda are on their face absurd and may even be interpolations. We know that the Buddhists made many misrepresentations of Hindu traditions (e. g. they stated that Sītā was wife and sister of Rāma); and one cannot attach any value to this Buddhist poem in this connection.

Nor is the historical argument of Pandit Gaurishankar sound. The instances of change of gotra are all found in inscriptions later than the 12th century and were all influenced by Vijnāneśvara's dictum. Vijnāneśvara's authority being generally respected is still wrongly influencing the Rajput community. But we have quoted in Vol. II inscriptions dating from before the Christian era wherein Kshatriyas mention their gotras. And the Chālukyas of the Deccan and the Pallavas of South India never fail to mention their gotras, Mānavya and Bhāradvāja, in inscriptions which date as early as the sixth century. If these gotras were not their own but were those of their purohitas, they can never be expected to have been mentioned in inscriptions. And indeed inscriptions of later times distinctly mention that the gotra-rishi is the progenitor of the Kshatriya clan as we go on to show in detail.

Let us take the four supposed Agnikula clans first: 1. The Paramāras are distinctly said to belong to Vasishtha gotra because they were *born* from his fire and not because Vasishtha was their purohita. In the Udepur Praśasti we have वसिष्टगोत्रोद्भव एष लोके स्यातस्तदादी परमारवंशः. And this gotra still continues in this clan even among the Marathas. 2. The Chāhamānas are Vatsagotri. In one inscription the first Chāhamāna is said to be *born* from Vatsa Ṛishi's tear; and in the Bijolia inscription in the first Chāhamāna is said to be *born* from Brahmin of Vatsa gotra (or in the gotra of Vatsa Brahmin or Ṛishi.) Vatsa is not this purohita. 3. The Pratihāras are said to be *born* from a Pratihāra Brahmin and in another place from Lakshmaṇa brother of Rāma. (Their gotra has not been ascertained.) 4. The Chālukyas are said to be *born* from Droṇa's chuluka and hence of the Bhāradvāja gotra as stated distinctly in a Kalachūri inscription. In fine, these four Rājput clans are born in the gotras they invariably claim upto now; and the inscriptions referred to above are all of a date anterior to Vijnāneśvara. His dictum was clearly then unknown.

Turning to Rajput clans which are lunar, we find that their gotra is usually Atri and Atri is no doubt their progenitor being the father of the moon according to the Purāṇas. This fact is distinctly stated in the inscriptions of the Kalachūri Haihayas and of the Senas. The Yādavas the Chudāsamas and the Jādejas also give Atri as their gotra and this is true by the theory of descent and not discipleship.

The solar Rajputs no doubt present a difficulty. The Guhilots of Mewad, the Kachhwahas of Jaipur-Alwar and the Rathods of Jodhpur-Bikaner are solar race Rajputs and their gotras are respectively Baijavāpa, Mānava and Gautama. Now in the Vamśāvalis given from Manu the names of these Ṛishis do not come in. We have, however, shown in Vol. II that many Brahmin gotra Ṛishis are Kshatriyas such as Hārita, Gārgya, Mudgala and others. We have, however, no tradition in the Purāṇas to hold that Baijavāpa, Mānava and Gautama were solar or lunar Rājarshis. For all that we know, they may be. But the most plausible explanation seems to be that these clans, when they became distinct in most ancient days, attached themselves to these Pakshas for ritual practice and were in effect adopted into these families, and therefore they have these gotras and Pravaras. The expression in the Purāṇas that Hārita and Mudgala attached themselves to the Paksha of Angiras shows this clearly and in one place they are called even sons.* It was by adoption and not by discipleship that these gotras were taken in ancient times. For the theory as well as the fact is that if a different Purohita is taken, the gotra does not change but remains the same. Therefore, the theory of some is that the gotras of these Rājput clans were taken in very ancient times from their Purohitas; but these once taken cannot be changed at any subsequent time (see the opinion quoted below). This is in a sense adoption and this is the reason why the gotras of the Kshatriya clans have remained unchanged for centuries. Gotra and Pravara, like Veda and Śākhā which the clan took up in ancient times for the performance of ritual in accordance with it, cannot change at any subsequent change of purohita.

Gotra and Pravara amongst Brahmins cannot change and they indicate descent and not discipleship; why should they indicate a different thing among Kshatriyas? This difficulty, as also the fact that even in ancient

* हरितो युवनाश्वस्य हारिताः शूरयः स्मृताः । एतेऽह्याङ्गिरसः पुत्राः क्षत्रोपेता द्विजातयः ॥

inscriptions, Kshatriyas mention their gotras with pride and hence they could not have been borrowed from purohitas led us first to our view and we discussed it with two learned Pandits in Jaipur, Madhusūdana Śāstri (Maithila) and Vīreśvara Śāstri (Telanga), and on their agreement propounded it with confidence in our second Volume. As doubts have since been expressed in many quarters, we quote below their written opinion specially obtained for this volume.

१

श्री जयपुर चै० शु० ५ रवौ सं. १९८२

सान्ति ब्राह्मणानामिव क्षत्रियस्य वैश्यस्य च प्रातिस्विकानि गोत्राणि नवेति प्रश्ने उत्तरम्। दर्शपूर्णमासादियाग प्रकरणस्थे आर्षेयं वृणीते इति विधो कल्पसूत्रकाराणां सांप्रतिके ग्रन्थान्ते च प्रकरणे प्रवरनिर्णायकसूत्रेषु गोत्राणां वर्णनस्य क्षत्रियवैश्यसंबंधेन बहुशो विद्यमानत्वेन सन्ति तयोरपि प्रातिस्विकगोत्राणि। याज्ञवल्क्यस्मृति-व्याख्यायां मिताक्षरायां तदभावकथनं तु प्रबलहेत्वनिर्देशेन न विश्वासार्हमन्येषामपि तथोपवर्णनं तदनुयायित्वेनेति त्यक्तव्यमेवेति मन्यते द्राविडो।

वीरेश्वरशास्त्री

२

श्री

क्षत्रियोंका उत्पत्तिदृष्ट्या गोत्र मनु है और वैश्योंका भलन्दन है, क्षत्रियोंके जो भारद्वाजवत्सादि गोत्र प्रसिद्ध हैं वे पूर्वकालमें उनके प्राचिन पुरोहितोंसे प्राप्त हुवे है. वे अब बदल नहीं सकते. क्योंके नया पुरोहित करना मना है. हालमें पुरोहितोंका गोत्र इसी सबबसे भिन्न है. यह पुराणे पीडियोंसे चला हुवा गोत्र एक तऱ्हेसे प्रातिस्विक गोत्र होगया है क्योंके वुह बदल नहीं सकता.

सम्मतोयमर्थो जयपुरस्थस्य राजपण्डितस्य मधुसूदनशर्मणो जयपुरस्थानम् ३०।३।२५

विद्यावाचस्पतेः

These two opinions proceed on different grounds but come to the same conclusion. Vīreśvara Śāstri bases his opinion on the Sūtras and distinctly says that Vijnāneśvara's dictum is wrong. Madhusūdana Śāstri says that the gotras were taken from Purohitas in most ancient times and cannot now change and thus they may even be looked upon as Prātisvika (their own). He thus avoids the above mentioned difficulty, of explaining how the solar Kachwahas of Jaipur have Mānava gotra. The difference of gotra, therefore, indicates difference of clan. The Guhilas of Bhavanagar are different from the Guhilots of Mewad and the Rathods of Jodhpur-Bikaner are different from the Rathods of the Deccan.

II IMPORTANT EXTRACTS FROM ORIGINAL INSCRIPTIONS.

(1) Bijolia inscription A. S. J. Bengal Vol. LV pp. 41-43.

विप्रश्रीवत्सगोत्रेभूदहिच्छत्रपुरे पुरा । सामन्तोऽनन्त सामन्त पूर्णतल्लो नृपस्ततः ॥ १२ ॥ तस्माच्छ्रीजयराज विग्रहनृपौ श्रीचन्द्रगोपेन्द्रकौ तस्माद्दुर्लभगूर्वकौ शशिनृपो गूवाकसच्चन्दनौ । श्रीमद्वप्पयराजविंध्यनृपतिः श्रीसिंहराड्विग्रहौ श्रीमद्दुर्लभगुन्दुवाक्पतिनृपाः श्रीवीर्यरामोनुजः ॥ १३ ॥ श्रीचण्डोबनिपेतिराणकवरश्रीसिंहलो दूसलस्तद्भ्राताथ ततोपि वीसलनृपः श्रीराजदेवीप्रियः ॥ पृथ्वीराजनृपोथ तत्तनुभवो रासल्यदेवीविभुस्तत्पुत्रोऽजयदेव इत्यवनिपः सोमल्लदेवीपतिः ॥ १४ ॥ हत्वापाधिगमिंचलाभिधयशोराजादिवीरत्रयं क्षिप्रं क्रूरकृतान्तवक्त्रकुहरे श्रीमार्गदुर्गान्वितं । श्रीमत्सोल्लणदण्डनायकवरः संग्रामरंगांगणे जीवन्नेव नियन्त्रितः करभके येनेष्ठानि...सात् ॥ १५ ॥ अर्णोराजोऽस्य सूनुर्हृतहृदयहरिः सत्ववाशिष्टसीमो गाम्भीर्यौदार्यवर्यः समभवदपराल्लभ्रमध्यानदीप्तः ॥ तच्चित्रं जंतुजातस्थितिरनृतमहापंकहेतुर्नमथ्यो न श्रीमुक्तो न दोषाकररचितरतिर्नैद्विजिह्वाधिसेव्यः ॥ १६ ॥ ...कृतान्तपथसज्जोभूत्सज्जनो सज्जनो भुवः । वैकुन्तं कुन्तपालोगाद्यतो वैकुन्तपालकः ॥ २० ॥ जाबालिपुरं ज्वालापुरं कृता पल्लिका पल्ली । वाततूलतुल्यं रोषात्तद्दलं च सौर्येण ॥ २१ ॥ प्रतोल्यां च वलभ्यां च येन विश्रामितं यशः । ढिल्लिकाग्रहण-श्रान्तमाशिकालाभलम्भितः ॥ २२ ॥ तज्ज्येष्ठभ्रातृपुत्रोभूत्पृथ्वीराजः प्रभूपमः ॥ तस्मादर्जितश्येनागोहेमपर्वतदानतः ॥ २३ ॥ अतिधर्मरते—पि पार्श्वनाथस्वयम्भुवे । दत्तं मोराकरीग्रामं भुक्तिमुक्तिश्चहेतुना ॥२४॥ स्वर्णादिदाननिवहैर्दशभिर्महद्भिस्तौलानरैर्नगरदा नचयैश्च विप्राः । येनार्जिताश्चतुरभूपतिवस्तुपालमाक्रम्य चारुमनसिद्धिकरी गृहीतः ॥ २५ ॥ सोमेश्वराल्लब्धराज्यस्ततः सोमेश्वरो नृपः । सोमेश्वरनतो यस्माज्जनसोमेश्वरोऽभवत् ॥ २६ ॥ प्रतापलंकेश्वर इत्यभिख्यां यः प्राप्तवान् प्रौढपृथुप्रतापः । यस्याभिमुख्ये वरवैरिमुख्याः केचिन्मृताः केचिद्विद्रुताश्च ॥ २७ ॥ येन श्रीपार्श्वनाथाय रेवातीरेस्वयंभुवे । शासने रेवणाग्रामो दत्तः स्वर्गाय-कांक्षिणा ॥ २८ ॥......(संवत् १२२६ फाल्गुनविद ३)...षड्विंशे द्वादशगते गुरौवारे च हस्तके । वृद्धिनामनि योगे च करणे तैत्तिले तथा । गुहिलपुत्र सदाम्बर महंघणसीहाभ्यां दत्त...नैगमान्वयकायस्थछोतिगुसूनुकेशवेन लिखितं । नानिगगोविंदसूनपाल्हणपुत्रदेल्हणेनोत्कीर्णम् ॥

(2) Govindchandra's inscription (1109) I. A. XVIII p. 15.

ओम् परमात्मने नमः । अकुंठोत्कंठवैकुंठकंठपीठलुठत्करः । संरंभः सुरतारंभे स श्रियः श्रेयसेस्तु वः । अभून्नृपो गाहड्वालवंशे महीतलो नाम जितारिचक्रः । शेते धराभारमशेष एव शेषः सुखी यस्य भुजे निधाय ॥ प्रध्वस्ते सोमसूर्योद्भवविदितमहाक्षत्रवंशद्वयेस्मिन् । उत्सन्नप्रायवेदध्वनिजगदखिलं मन्यमानः स्वयंभूः ॥ कृत्वा देहग्रहाय प्रवणमिह मनः शुद्धबुद्धिर्धरि-

त्याम् उद्धर्तु धर्ममार्गान् प्रथितमिह तथा क्षत्रवंशद्वयं च ॥ वंशे तत्र ततः स एष समभूत् भूपालचूडामणिः प्रध्वस्तोद्धतवैरिवीरतिमिरः श्रीचंद्रदेवो नृपः ॥ येनोदारतरप्रतापशमिताशेषप्रजोपद्रवं श्रीमद्गाधिपुराधिराज्यमसमं दोर्विक्रमेणार्जितम् ॥ तीर्थानि काशिकुशिकोत्तरकोशलेंद्रस्थानीयकानि परिपालयिताभिगम्य ॥ हेमात्मतुल्यमनिशं ददता द्विजेभ्यो येनांकिता वसुमती शतशस्तुलाभिः ॥ तस्यात्मजो मदनपाल इति क्षितींद्रचूडामणिर्विजयते निजगोत्रचंद्रः । यस्याभिषेककलशोल्लसितैः पयोभिः प्रक्षालितः कलिरजः पटलं पृथिव्याम् ॥ तस्मात्ततो रजनिजानिरिवांबुराशेः गोविंदचंद्र इति कांतिभराभिरामः । राजात्मजेन भवता समुपार्जितानि रामेण दाशरथिनेव यशांसि येन ॥ दुर्वारस्फारगौडद्विरदवरघटाकुंभनिर्भेदभीमो हम्मीरं न्यस्तवैरं मुहुरसमरणक्रीडया यो विधत्ते ॥ शश्वत् संचारिवल्गत् तुरगखुरपुटोल्लेखमुद्रासनाथ क्षोणीस्वीकारदक्षः स इह विजयते प्रार्थनाकल्पवृक्षः ॥...परमभट्टारकमहाराजाधिराजपरमेश्वरपरममाहेश्वरनिजभुजोपार्जितकान्यकुब्जाधिपत्यश्रीचंद्रदेवपादानुदध्यात परमभट्टारकमहाराजाधिराजपरमेश्वरपरममाहेश्वरश्रीमन्मदनपालदेवविजयराज्ये ॥ अस्यैवात्मजो महाराजपुत्रगोविंदचंद्रदेवः ॥ सिंधुरोढपत्तलायां रामैठग्रामे समस्तमहत्तमजनपदानिवासिलोकान् प्रतिवासिलोकांश्च ॥ राजराज्ञीमातृपुरोहितामात्याक्षपटलिकभांडागारिकभिषक्नैमित्तिकसेनापत्यन्तःपुरिकसमस्ताधिकारिपुरुषादीन् समाज्ञापयति संबोधयति च यथा । अस्तु वो विदितं अनित्यायुर्गता युष्माभिः वातातपवशात् तृणाग्रलग्नाश्यायबिंदुरिव न स्थिरपदम् बध्नाति जीवितम् मत्वा ॥...अस्मिन् ग्रामे हलानां चतुर्भिप्रमाणुः । सजलस्थलः सोषरपाषाणगिरिनदीवनवाटिकाम्रमधूकलोहलवणाकरऊर्ध्वाधः सिद्धियुतः सदशापराधदण्डःतृणपर्णाद्याकरआदायसहितः संवत् ११६६ पौष वद्य १५ रवौ अद्येह आसटिकायां देवतामुरैठघट्टे यमुनायां यथाविधिना स्नात्वा देवमनुष्यपितृतर्पणाद्यनंतरं भगवंतं सूर्यमुपस्थाय तदनु चाभीष्टदेवतामहेश्वरं पंचभिरुपचारैः समभ्यर्च्य भगवते जातवेदसे पूर्णाहुतिं दत्वा राहुग्रस्ते सवितरि मातापित्रोरात्मनश्च पुण्ययशोभिवृद्धये भट्टब्राह्मणाय गूगापौत्राय रिल्हेपुत्राय भट्टकवडग्रामविनिर्गताय सांख्यायनशाखिने गौतमऐतिथ्य आंगिरसत्रिप्रवराय श्रुताध्ययनसंपन्नब्राह्मणगुणचंद्राय विशुद्धेन मनसा कुशपूतहस्तोदकेन क्षित्यब्धिपवर्ताबरं यावत् । राणकश्रीलवणप्रवाहेन चासनत्वेव प्रदत्तो इति मत्वा यथादीयमानं भागभोगकूटकविंशतिच्छवथा तुरुष्कदंडं अक्षपटलादाय वलदीकुमरगद्दियानकआकराहिरण्यबाह्याभ्यंतरासिद्धि एतत् सर्वं अन्यदपि भूम्यावारणउत्पत्स्यमानं मदाज्ञापालनप्रवणैर्भूत्वा एतत् सर्वं अस्मै उपनेतव्यम् । एतत् संतत्यैअपि ॥ न केनाप्यत्र बाधाकार्या श्रुत्वा मुनीतां वचः.................लिखितोयं महत्तकश्रीगांगेयानुज्ञया त्रिभुवनपालेन ठक्कुरश्रीदेवांगसुतेन सुनरकुडनेन सातेहरसुतेन

(3) Extract from another Gāhadvāla grant.

अकुंठोत्कंठ० ॥ १ ॥...चतुष्पंचादशाधिकशतैकादशसंवत्सरे माघे मासि शुक्लपक्षे तृतीयायां सोमदिने वाराणस्यामुत्तरायणसंक्रान्तौ अंकतः संवत् ११५४ माघसुदि ३ सोमे वाराणस्यां देवश्रीत्रिलोचनघट्टे गंगायां स्नात्वा श्रीमद्राजाधिराज श्रीचन्द्रदेवेन... प्रचुरपायसेन हविषा हविर्भुजं हुत्वा...कौशिकगोत्राय विश्वामित्रौदलदेवरातत्रिप्रवराय छंदोगशाखिने...गोकर्णकुशलतापूतकरतलोदकपूर्वमापद्म पद्मनो हूहूकान्तं यावत् शासनीकृत्य प्रदत्त इति ज्ञात्वाऽस्माभिः पितृदानशासनप्रकाशनार्थं निजनामाङ्कितमुद्रया ताम्रपट्टके निधाय

प्रदत्ते...श्रीमन्मदनदेवेन पितृशानप्रकाशकः । शाश्वतस्य निबन्धोयं कारितः स्वीयमुरूप ॥ १० ॥ लिखितं करणिक ठक्कुर श्रीसहदेवेन शिवमस्तु मङ्गलं महाश्रीः श्रीमदनपालदेवेन ॥

(4) **Extracts from Gāhadavāls grants E. I. IV.**

(p.101.) हल्दीयप्रत्ययां महाशोणसौग्रामनिवासिनो निखिलजनपदानुपगतानपि च राजराज्ञीयुवराजमंत्रीपुरोहितप्रतिहारसेनापतिभाण्डागारिकाक्षपटलिकाभिषड्नैमित्तिकान्त : पुरि-कदूतकरितुरगपत्तनाकरस्थानगोकुलाधिकारिपुरुषांश्चाज्ञापयति बोधयत्यादिशति च...स ग्रामः सजलस्थलः सलोहलवणाकरः समत्स्याकरः सपर्णाकरः सगर्तोषरः समधूकचूतवनवाटिकावि-टपतृणयूतिगोचरपर्यन्तः सोर्ध्वाधः श्चतुराघाटविशुद्धः...श्रीवास्तव्यकुलोद्भूत कायस्थोल्हणसू-नुना । लिखितस्ताम्रपत्रोयं कीठनेन नृपाज्ञया ॥

(p. 109) ...यथा दीयमानभागभोगकरप्रवणिकरतुरुष्कदण्डकुमरगादियानकप्रभृति समस्तदायान् दास्यतेति ।

(p. 120) वैष्णवपूजाविधिगुरवे

(p. 121) प्रचुरपायसेन हविर्भुजं हुत्वा

(p. 123) प्रवणीकरहिरण्यनियतानियतान् दायान्

(5) Extract from Basahi grant Inscription of Govindchandra I. A. xiv p. 103.

नमो वासुदेवाय ...संवत् ११६१...यमुनायां स्नात्वा यथाविधानं मन्त्रदेवऋषिम-नुष्यभूतपितृंश्च तर्पयित्वा सूर्यं भट्टारकं सर्वकर्तारं भगवन्तं शिवं विश्वाधारं वासुदेवं समभ्यर्च्य हुतवहं हुत्वा जीवन्तीपत्तलायां वसभीग्रामे समस्तजनपदान् संबोधयति यथा । ग्रामोयं मया क्षेत्रवनमधूकाम्राकाशपातालसहितः सदशापराधदण्डः भागकूटकदशबन्धविंशत्युक्तयप्रस्थाक्ष-पटलप्रस्थप्रतिहारप्रस्थआकरतुरुष्कदण्डवरवज्ञोहिरण्यसर्वादायसंयुक्त...चतुराघाटविशुद्धः...... गौतमगोत्राय....मेमे पौत्राय...ज्योतिर्विद्ब्राह्मण अल्हेकाय प्रदत्तः...लिखितंच पुरोहित-जागूकमहत्तकश्रीवाल्हणप्रतिहारश्रीगौतम एषां सम्मत्या

6) Naihatti grant Ballālasena E. I. XIV p. 159.

ॐ नमः शिवाय...स श्रीकंठशिरोमणिर्विजयते देवस्तमीवल्लभः ॥ वंशे तस्याभ्युद-यिनि सदाचारचर्यानिरूढी प्रौढां राढामकलितचरैः भूषयन्तोनुभावैः । शश्वद्विश्वाभयवितरण-स्थूललक्ष्यावलक्ष्यैः कीर्त्युल्लोलैः स्नपितवियतो जज्ञिरे राजपुत्राः । तेषां वंशे महोजाः प्रतिभट-पृतनाम्भोधिकल्पान्तसूरः...सत्यशीलो...निरुपधिकरुणाधामसामन्तसेनः । तस्मादजनि वृष-ध्वजचरणाम्बुजषट्पदो गुणाभरणः । हेमन्तसेनदेवो वैरिस्मरः प्रलय हेमन्तः । ...तस्मादभूद-खिल पार्थिवचक्रवर्ति निर्व्याजविक्रमातिरस्कृतसाहसाङ्कः । दिक्पालचक्र पुटभेदनगीतकीर्तिः पृथ्वीपतिर्विजयसेनपदप्रकाशः...अस्य प्रधानमहिषी जगदीश्वरस्य शुद्धान्तमौलिमणिरास विला-सदेवी । देवी सुतं सुतपसं सुकृतैरसूत वल्लालसेनमतुलं गुणगौरवेन...स खलु श्रीविक्रमपुरस-

मावासितश्रीमज्जयस्कंधावारात्। महाराजाधिराज श्रीविजयसेन देवपादानुध्यात परमेश्वर–परममाहेश्वर–परमभट्टारकमहाराजाधिराज श्रीमद्बल्लालसेनदेवः कुशली समुपजातअशेषराजराजन्यराज्ञीराणकराजपुत्रराजामात्यपुरोहितमहाधर्माध्यक्षमहासांधिविग्रहिक महासेनापतिमहामुद्राधिकृतअंतरंगबृहदुपरिक महाक्षपटलिक महाप्रतिहारमहाभोगिकमहापीलुपति महागणस्थ दौस्साधनिकचौरोद्धरणिकनौबलहस्त्यश्वगोमहिषाजाविकादिव्यापृतक गौल्मिकदण्डपाशिकदण्डनायकविषयपत्यादीन् अन्यांश्च सकलराजपादोपजीविनो अध्यक्षप्रचारोक्तांश्च इह अकीर्तितान् चट्टभट्टजातीयान् जनपदान् क्षेत्रकरांश्च ब्राह्मणान् ब्राह्मणोत्तरान् यथार्हं मानयति बोधयति समादिशति च। मतमस्तु भवतां यथाश्रीवर्धमान भुक्त्यन्तःपाति उत्तरराढामण्डले स्वल्पदक्षिणवीथ्यां खाण्डयिल्लशासनशासनोत्तरस्थितः संघटियानद्युत्तरः नारीचाशासनोत्तरस्थसिंघटियानदीपश्चिमोत्तरः...एवं चतुःसीमावच्छिन्नवाल्लहिट्ठग्रामः श्रीवृषभशंकरनलेन सवास्तुनालखिलादिभिः तालत्रयाधिकचत्वारिंशत्उन्मानसमेत आढकनवद्रोणोत्तरसप्तभूपाटकात्मकः प्रत्यब्दं कपर्दक पुराणपञ्चशतोत्पत्तिकः सझाटविटपः सगर्तोषरः सजलस्थलः सगुवाकनारिकेरः सह्यदशापराधः परिहृतसर्वपीडः तृणयूतिगोचरपर्यन्तः अचाटभटप्रवेशः अकिंचित्प्रग्राह्यः समस्तराजभोगकरहिरण्यप्रत्यायसहितः। वराहदेवशर्मणः प्रपौत्राय भट्टेश्वरदेवशर्मणः पौत्राय लक्ष्मीधरदेवशर्मणः पुत्राय भारद्वाजसगोत्राय भारद्वाजाङ्गिरसबार्हस्पत्यप्रवराय सामवेदकौथुमशाखाचरणाध्यायिने आचार्यश्रीओवासुदेवशर्मणे अस्मन्मातृश्रीविलासदेवीभिः सुरसरिते सूर्योपरागे दत्तहेमाश्वमहादानदक्षिणात्वेन उत्सृष्टः मातापित्रोरात्मनश्च पुण्ययशोऽभिवृद्धये आचंद्रार्कक्षितिसमकालं यावद्भूमिच्छिद्रन्यायेन ताम्रशासनीकृत्य प्रदत्तोस्माभिः अतःभवद्भिः सर्वैरनुमन्तव्यं भाविभिरपि भूपतिभिरपहरणे नरकपातभयात् पालने धर्मगौरवात् पालनीयम्। भवन्ति चात्र धर्मानुशंसिनः श्लोकाः.................जितनिखिल क्षितिपालः श्रीमद् बल्लालसेनभूपालः ओबासुशासने कृतदूतं हरिघोषसान्धिविग्रहिकं संवत् ११ वैशाखदिने १६ श्रीः

(7) Extract from Madanapāla's Insc. LXIX J. B. (p. 11).

...रमावतीनगरपरिसरसमावासितश्रीमज्जयस्कन्दावारात्। परमसौगता महाराजाधिराजश्रीरामपतिदेवपादानुध्यातः परमेश्वरः परमभट्टारकः महाराजाधिराज श्रीमन्मदनपालदेवः कुशली ? श्रीपौण्ड्रवर्धनभुक्तौ कोटीश्वरविषये हलावर्तमण्डले काष्ठागिरिसंबिंशायाबाधिकोपेतसकैवदार्वचट्टरदके त्रिंशतिकायां भूमौ समुपागताशेषराजपुरुषान् राजराजन्यकराजपुत्रराजामात्यमहासान्धिविग्राहिकमहाक्षपटलिकमहासामन्तमहासेनापति महाप्रतिहारदौःसाध्यसाधनिकमहाकुमारामात्यराजस्थानीयोपरिक चौरोद्धरणिकदाण्डिकदण्डपाशिकशौल्किकक्षेत्रपप्रान्तपालकोट्टपालाङ्गरक्षकतदायुक्तविनियुक्तक हस्त्यश्वोष्ट्रनौबलव्यापृतक किशोरबडवागोमहिषाजाविकाध्यक्ष दूतप्रेषणिकगमागमिक अभित्वरमाण विषयपतिग्रामपतितरिक शौल्किकगौल्मिकगौडमालवचोडखसहूणकुलिककर्णाटलाटचाटभटसेवकादीन्। अन्यांश्चाकीर्तितान् राजपादोपजीविनः प्रतिवासिनो ब्राह्मणोत्तरान् महत्तमोत्तमकुटुंबिपुरोग चण्डालपर्यन्तान् यथार्हं मानयति बोधयति समादिशति च। विदितमस्तु भवताम्। यथोपरिलिखितोयं ग्रामः स्वसीमातृणपूलूतिगोचरपर्यन्तः सतलः सोद्देशः साम्रमधूकः सजलस्थलः सगर्तोषरः सझाटविटपः सदशापराधः सचौरोद्धरणिकः परिहृतसर्वपीडः अचाटभटप्रवेशः अकिंचित्करग्राह्यः समस्तभागभोगहिरण्यादिप्रत्याय-

समेतः रत्नत्रयराजसंभोगवर्जितः। भूमिच्छिद्रन्यायेन आचन्द्रार्कक्षितिसमकालं पित्रोरात्मनश्च पुण्ययशोभिवृद्धये कौत्ससगोत्राय शांडिल्यासितदेवलप्रवराय पंडितश्रीभूषणसब्रह्मचारिणे सामवेदान्तर्गतकौथुमशाखाध्यायिने चम्पाहिट्टीयाय चम्पाहिट्टिवास्तव्यायवत्सस्वामिप्रजापतिस्वामिपौत्राय शौनकस्वामिपुत्राय पंडितश्रपुत्रश्रीनरेश्वरस्वामिशर्मणे पट्टमहादेवीश्रीचित्रमटिकायाः वेदव्यासप्रोक्तप्रवाचित महाभारतसमुत्सर्जितदक्षिणात्वेन भगवन्तं बुद्धभट्टारकमुद्दिश्य शासनीकृत्य प्रदत्तोस्माभिः श्रुतो भवद्भिः सर्वैरेवानुमन्तव्यः भाविरपिभूमिपतिभिर्भूमेर्दानफलगौरवात् अपहरणमहानरकपातभयाच्च दानमिदमनुमोदानुमोघपालनीयम्। प्रतिवासिभिश्च क्षेत्रकरैराज्ञाश्रवणविधेयी भूय यथाकालं समुचितभागभोगकरहिरण्यादिप्रत्यादेयोपनयःकार्यः इति संवत् ८ चंद्रगत्याचैत्रकर्मदिने ५। ...कृत सकलनीतिज्ञो...श्वैर्यमहोदधिः। सान्धिविग्रहिकः श्रीमान् भीमदेवोत्र दूतकः॥ राज्ये मदनपालस्य अष्टमे परिवत्सरे। ताम्रपट्टमिमं शिल्पी तथारीतसरोखनत्॥

(8) Extract from Semra plates of Paramadidéva (Chandella) St. 1223 (1166 A. D.) E. I. IV. p. 153.

ओम्। स्वस्ति। जयत्याल्हादयन् विश्वं विश्वेश्वरशिरोधृतः। चन्द्रात्रेय नरेन्द्राणां वंशश्चन्द्र इवोज्वलः। तत्र प्रवर्द्धमाने विरोधिविजयभ्राजिष्णुजयशक्तिविजयशक्तिवीराविर्भावभास्वरे परमभ. म० प० पृथ्वीदेवपानुध्यात...मदनवर्म...पर० परममाहेश्वरकालंजराधिपति श्रीमत्परमर्दिदेवो विजयी॥ ... विकौरविषये सहौडा द्वादशक तथा राष्ट्रसत्क टांटद्वादशक... ग्रामाणामुपगतान् ब्राह्मणानन्यांश्च मान्यानधिकृतान् कुटुम्बिकायस्थदूतवैद्यमहत्तरान् मेदचण्डाः लपर्यन्तान् सर्वान् संबोधयति समाज्ञापयति चास्तु वः संविदितं यथोपरिलिखिताः ग्रामाः सजलस्थलाः सस्थावरजङ्गमाः स्वसीमावच्छिन्नाः साधऊर्द्ध्वाः भूतभविष्यद्वर्तमाननिःशेषादायसहिताः प्रतिषिद्धचाटादिप्रवेशाः...अजयसागरसंबद्धलटिआनां हलचतुष्टयावच्छिना मदनपुरे भूमिः संवत् १२२३ वैशाखसुदि ७ गुरुवासरे...विधिवत्स्नात्वा देवमनुष्यपितृन् संतर्प्य भास्करपूजापुरःसरचराचरगुरुं भगवन्तं भवानीपतिमभ्यर्च्य हुतभुजि हुत्वा कुशलतापूतेन हस्तोदकेन नानागोत्रेभ्यो नानाप्रवरेभ्यो नानाशाखाध्यायिभ्यो नानानामभ्यो ब्राह्मणेभ्यो प्रदत्ताः ...पराशरगोत्रजयशर्मपुत्रहरिशर्मा एषां पदमेकं...इति मत्वा भवद्भिः भागभोगादिकं सर्वमेभ्यः समुपनेतव्यम्। अमीषां समन्दिरप्राकारान् सनिर्गमप्रवेशान्ससर्वांशनेक्षुकपीससणाम्रमधूकादिभूरुहान् सवनस्वभ्रनिधानान् सलोहाद्याकरान् सगोकुलान् अपरैरपि सीमान्तर्गतवस्तुभिः सहितान् सबाह्याभ्यंतरदायान् भुज्जानानां कर्षतां कर्षयतां दानाधानविक्रयं वा कुर्वतां न केनचित् काचिद्बाधा कर्तव्या स्वहस्तोयं राजश्रीपरमर्दिदेवस्य मतं मम॥ लिखितं वास्तव्यवंश्येन प्रभीधरेण। उत्कीर्णं च पित्तलहारपाल्हणेन। मंगल महाश्रीः॥

(9) Bhopal plates of Udayavarman Paramāra I.A. XIV p. 254-5.

ॐ स्वस्ति जयोऽभ्युदयश्च। जयति व्योमकेशोऽसौ यः सर्गाय बिभर्ति तम्। ऐन्दवं शिरसा लेखं जगद्बीजाङ्कुराकृतिम्॥ तन्वन्तु वः स्मरारातेः कल्याणमनिशं जटाः। कल्पान्तसमयोद्दामतडिद्वलयपिङ्गलाः॥ परमभ० महारा० परमे० श्रीमद्यशोवर्मदेवपादानुध्यात प. भ. म० प० श्रीमज्जयवर्मदेवराज्ये व्यतीते निजकरकृतकरवालप्रसादावाप्तनिजाधि-

पत्यसमस्तप्रशस्तोपेतसमधिगतपञ्चमहाशब्दालंकार विराजमान महाकुमार श्रीमल्लक्ष्मीवर्मदेवपादानुध्यात समस्तप्रशस्तोपेत समधिगतपञ्चमहाशब्दालङ्कार विराजमान महाकुमार श्री हरिश्चंद्रदेवसुत श्रीमत् उदयवर्मदेवो विजयोदयी ॥ विन्ध्यमण्डले नर्मदापुर प्रतिजागरणक बोढशिरासत्कअष्टाचत्वारिंशन्मध्ये गुणौराग्रामनिवासिनः प्रतिग्रामनिवासिनश्च समस्तराजपुरुष वैषयिक पट्टकिल जनपदादीन् ब्राह्मणोत्तरान्बोधयत्यस्तु वः संविदितम् यथा ॥ अस्माभिः श्रीविक्रमकालातीत षट्पञ्चाशदधिकद्वादशशत संवत्सरान्तःपाति अङ्के १२५६ वैशाख शुदि १५ पौर्णमास्यां तिथौ विशाखा नक्षत्रे परिघयोगे रविदिने महावैशाख्यां पर्वणि गुवाडा घट्टे रेवायां स्नात्वा स्निनपवित्रवाससी परिधाय देवऋषिमनुष्यान्संतर्प्य चराचरगुरुं भगवन्तं भवानीपतिं समभ्यर्च्य समित्कुशतिलाभाज्याभूतिभिः हिरण्यरेतसं हुत्वा भानवे अर्घं विधाय कपिलां त्रिः प्रदक्षिणीकृत्य उपस्पृश्य च संसारस्यासारतां दृष्ट्वा नलिनीदलगत जललवतरलतरं यौवनं धनं जीवितं चावेक्ष्य...गर्गगोत्राय गर्गशैन्याङ्गिरस इति त्रिप्रवराय वाजसनेयशाखिने अग्निहोत्रि यज्ञधरसुत द्विवेद पुरोधास माल्हुशर्मणे ब्राह्मणाय उपरिलिखित गुणोराग्रामो निधिनिक्षेप कल्याण धनसहितः सवृक्षमालाकुलः । चतुष्कंटकविशुद्धो वापीकूपतडागारामनदीश्रोतवाडवाटिकाद्युपयुक्तः सर्वाभ्यंतरसिद्धया सह यावच्चंद्रदिवाकरसमुद्रसरिच्छासनीकृत्य प्रदत्तः तदत्र ग्रामनिवासि पट्टकिलादि लोकैः तथा कर्षकैश्च यथोत्पद्यमानभागभोगकरहिरण्यादिकमाज्ञाश्रवणविधेयैर्भूत्वा अत्र ग्रामीयं सर्वं अस्मैः प्रदातव्यम् सामान्यैतद् पुण्यफलं बुद्ध्वा अस्मद्वंशैरन्यैरपि भाविभोक्तृभिरस्मत् प्रदत्तधर्मादायोयमनुमन्तव्यः पालनीयश्च...स्वहस्तोयं महाकुमार श्री उदयवर्मदेवस्य दूतकः श्रीमण्डलिक क्षेमवराजः श्रीः

(10) Extract from Goharwa plates of Karṇadeva E. I. XI p.141.

(शिवस्तुतिः...चन्द्रवंशः...भरतः...हैहय...) स एष परम वामदेवपादानुध्यात प०–परममाहेश्वरत्रिकलिंगाधिपतिश्रीमत्कर्णदेवः निजभुजोपार्जिताश्वपतिगजपतिनरपतिराजत्रयाधिपतिः कुशली।...महादेवी महाराजपुत्रो महामंत्री महासान्धिविग्रहिको महामात्यो महाधर्माधिकरणिको महाप्रतीहारो महाक्षपटलिको महाभाण्डगारिको महासामन्तो महाप्रमत्तवारो महाश्वसाधनिको एतानन्यांश्चाकीर्तितान् यथास्थाननियुक्तराजपुरुषान् कोशाम्बपत्तलायां चन्द्रपहाग्रामनिवासिनो निखिलजनपदान्यथार्हं मानयति बोधयति समाज्ञापयति विदितमस्तु भवतां यथा ग्रामोयं सजलस्थलः साम्रमधूकः सगर्तोषरः सलोहलवणाकरः स्वसीमापर्यंतः सवनतृणयूतिगोचरपर्यन्तः । विदर्भीकौण्डिनगोत्रायाङ्गिरसाम्बरीषयौवनाश्वत्रिप्रवराय वाजसनेयशाखिने उपाध्याय सीलुपौत्राय अवसथिक मालुपुत्राय पण्डितश्रीशान्तिशर्मणे...गंगायां स्नात्वा भगवन्तं शिवभट्टारकं समभ्यर्च्य—प्रदत्तः इति मत्वा यथादीयमानभोगभागहिरण्यादिसमस्तराजप्रत्यादायाः एतस्याज्ञाश्रवणविधेयैर्दातव्या...लिखितं करणिकश्रीसर्वानन्देन । उत्कीर्णं च विद्यानन्देन । मंगलं

(11) Extract from Miraj plates of Jayasinha Western Chlālukya of Kalyan A. D. 1024 (I. A. VIII, p. 18).

...स तु श्रीपृथ्वीवल्लभमहाराजाधिराजपरमेश्वरपरमभट्टारकसत्याश्रयकुलतिलकसमस्तभुवनाश्रयचालुक्याभरणश्रीमज्जगदेकमल्लदेवः श्रीमद्वल्लभनरेंद्रदेवः कुशली। सर्वानेव यथासंबध्यमान-

कान् राष्ट्रपतिविषयपतिग्रामकूटकआयुक्तकनियुक्तकाधिकारिकमहत्तरादीन् समादिशत्यस्तु वः संविदितम् यथा अस्माभिः शकनृपकालातीतसंवत्सरशतेषु नवसु षट्चत्वारिंशदधिकेषु अंकतः संवत ९४६ राक्षसी संवत्सरान्तर्गतवैशाखपौर्णमास्यामादित्यवारे यं च द्रमिलाधिपतिं बलवन्तं चोलं निर्घाट्य सप्तकोंकणाधीश्वराणां सर्वस्वं गृहीत्वा उत्तरदिग्विजयार्थं कोल्हापुरसमीपसमावासितनिजविजयस्कंधावारात्...विषयान्तःपाति मुहुनीरग्रामजाताय कौशिकगोत्राय बह्वृचशाखिने ब्रह्मचारिणे श्रीधरभट्टपौत्राय रेवणार्यभट्टपुत्राय वासुदेवार्यशर्मणे यजनयाजनादिषट्कर्मनिरताय वेदवेदांगपारगाय पड्डेरेट्टि सहस्रान्तःपातिकरटिकन्नविंशतमध्ये मडभूरुग्रामः सधान्यहिरण्यादेयः निधिनिधानसमेतः राजकीयानामनङ्गुलिप्रक्षेपणीयः सशुल्कः सर्वकरबाधापहृतः सर्वनमस्योऽग्रहारो दत्तः...शासनाधिकारिमहाप्रचण्डदण्डनायकश्रीमत्प्रोणार्यप्रतिबद्धलेखक माइय्येण लिखितम् । मंगलं महाश्रीः श्रीः श्रीः ॥

(12) Extract from Bhadan grant of Aparājita Silāhāra E. I. III, p. 267.

ओं...(समग्रराष्ट्रकूटवंशो वर्णितः)...श्रीमत्कक्कलदेवसंजातव्यपायनष्टभ्रष्टरट्टराज्ये स्वतेजोनुभावात्समधिगतपंचमहाशब्दो तगरपुरे...मलगलगण्ड...नन्निसमुद्रप्रतापमार्तंड शनिवारविजयादिसमस्तराजावलिसमलंकृत...अपराजितदेवराजः सर्वानेव यथासंबध्यमानकान् आगामिग्रामप्रभक्तृसामान्तराजपुत्रपुरपतित्रिवर्गस्थानप्रभृतिप्रधानाप्रधानान्जनान् प्रणतिपूजासमादेशैः समनुबोधयति...संवत् ९१९ आषाढवदि ४ श्रीस्थानके समवस्थितस्य राज्ञो दक्षिणायनकर्कसंक्रान्ति ... चतुर्दशग्रामशतोपलक्षितकोंकणान्तःपातिमहिरिहारविषयान्तर्गतभादानग्रामो...आघारपडिगह...(दोषसमन्वित ?) सोद्रंगसपरिकरः अचाटभटप्रवेशः...श्रीलोणादित्यदेवाय...आम्रश्रेष्ठिवापैयाधेष्ठिमणिकचेलापैयभोजकविप्रगोवर्णैयादिगुणपौरनगराधिष्ठितहस्तोदकं विधाय हरिहरहिरण्यगर्भदहनादिदेवान् श्रद्धया संपूज्य पुत्रपौत्राद्युपभोगवृत्तित्वेन ग्रामः प्रदत्तः । भुंजतो भोजयतो वा कृषतः कर्षयतो वा न केनचित् परिपन्था कर्तव्या । ...महामण्डलेश्वरश्रीमदपराजितदेवो लेखकहस्तेनारोपयति स्वमतम् मतं मम श्रीमदपराजितदेवस्य विरुदंकराजानियमान् महामात्य श्रीसंगलैयेमहासान्धिविग्रहिकसीहपैयेच सति जसंगवैद्यसुनुना सजाताभ्यनुज्ञेन प्रतिहस्तकअन्नपैयेन शासनमिदं लिखितं तच्च स्थानके ध्रुवम् । ...तथा भूयोपि व्यवस्था चात्र नन्वव्यावशप्रतिविर्षनगरेण राजकुलस्य अर्हणाभाव्यार्थं द्रमणौ २६० अंकतः दातव्यम् । मङ्गलं महाश्रीः

(13) Extract from Bhandup plates of Chhittarāja E. I. XII. Silāhāra seal has a raised Garuda and a golden Garuda banner.

...तथैतद्राज्यचिन्ताभारसमुद्वहत्सु सर्वाधिकारिश्रीनारायणैय्य सांधिविग्रहिकश्रीसीहपैय्यकर्णाटसांधिविग्रहिकश्रीकपर्दि श्रीकरणादिपंचप्रधानेषु सत्सु समागामिराजपुत्रमंत्रिपुरोहित अमात्यप्रधानाप्रधाननैयोगिकांस्तथाराष्ट्रपतिविषयपतिनगरपतिग्रामपतिनियुक्तानियुक्तराज-पुरुषजनपदांस्तथा हैयमननगर पौरत्रिवर्गप्रभृतींश्च प्रणतिपूजासत्कार समादेशैः समादिशति शक नृप... ...९४८ कार्तिकशुद्ध १५ आदित्यग्रहणपर्वणि स्नात्वा सवित्रे अर्घं दत्वा...उमापतिमभ्य-

च्यें...पाराशरगोत्राय छन्देागशाखिने आमदेवाय...बलिचरुवैश्वदेवअग्निहोत्रक्रतुक्रियात्त्रयारे-ग्रहपोषणार्थं १ स्थानकान्तर्गतषट्षष्टिविषयान्तः पातिगैाराग्रामान्तर्वर्तिक्षेत्रं ।.........

(14) Extract from Bhavnagar Insc. p. 157.

ॐ...राज्येऽमुष्यमहीभुजोभवदिहश्रीगूहिलाख्यान्वये श्रीसीहार इति प्रभूतगरिमाधारी धरामडनम् । चौलुक्यांगनिगूहकः सहजिगः ख्यातस्तनूजस्ततस्तत्पुत्रा बलिनोबभुवुरवनौ सौराष्ट्रक्षाक्षमाः ॥ ओ० श्रीसहजिगपुत्रठ० श्रीमुलुकेनश्रीसहजिगेश्वरदेवस्यानवरतपञ्चोपचारपुजाहेतोःश्रीमन्मंगलपुरमंडपिकायां का० १ दिनंप्रति । तथा बलीवर्दछाटमाणकामध्ये छाटं प्रतिका० १ कणभृतगडकं प्र० का० ४ तथारासभछाटाप्र०. ॥ ०तथा समस्तलोकेन निःशेषवल्लिकारैः पञ्चहराबेरीवाटयाप्र० ॥ तथापत्रभरकडंटभरंप्रातिका। ० २ तयापत्रंभरगंत्री प्रतिद्र. १ क्षेत्रं प्रतिउच्चाराभाध्येका. १ आगरमध्ये खुंटितखरालिहासाका । ...तथालाटिवद्रावपथकेबहन्तशुल्कमंडपिकायामध्याव दिनंप्रतिठ श्रीमुलकेन रूपकेकः प्रदत्तः ॥ ...? द्यूतमध्येदिनंप्रातिका १...तयावीडहराकेरीप्रभृतीनां प्रत्येक पत्र ५०...मडावापूग १... विक्रमसं १२०२ सिंहसं० ३२ अश्विनवदि १३ ॥ कृतिरियं परम पाशुपताचार्यमहापंडितश्रीसर्वज्ञस्य

III निर्णयसिन्धौ कलिवर्ज्यानि ।

बृहन्नारदीये–समुद्रयातुः स्वीकारः कमण्डलुविधारणम् । द्विजानामसवर्णासु कन्यासूपयमस्तथा ॥ देवराश्चसुतोत्पत्तिर्मधुपर्के पशोर्वधः । मांसदानं तथा श्राद्धे वानप्रस्थाश्रमस्तथा ॥ दत्ताक्षतायाः कन्यायाः पुनर्दानं परस्य च ॥ दीर्घकालं ब्रह्मचर्यं नरमेधाश्वमेधकौ ॥ महाप्रस्थानगमनं गोमेधश्च तथा मखः । इमान्धर्मान्कलियुगे वर्ज्यानाहुर्मनीषिणः ॥

हेमा. आदित्यपु.–विधवायां प्रजोत्पत्तौ देवरस्य नियोजनम् । बालिकाक्षतयोन्याश्च वरेणान्येन संस्कृतिः ॥ कन्यानामसवर्णानां विवाहश्च द्विजातिभिः ॥ आततायिद्विजाग्र्याणां धर्मयुद्धेन हिंसनम् । द्विजस्याब्धौ तु नौयातुःशोधितस्यापि संग्रहः ॥ सत्रदीक्षाच सर्वेषां कमण्डलुविधारणम्। महाप्रस्थानगमनं गोसंज्ञप्तिश्चगोसवे । सौत्रामण्यामपि सुराग्रहणस्य च संग्रहः ॥ अग्निहोत्रहवन्याश्च लेहो लीढापरिग्रहः ॥ वृत्तस्वाध्यायसापेक्षमघसंकोचनं तथा । प्रायश्चित्तविधानं च विप्राणां मरणान्तिकम् । संसर्गदोषस्तेयान्यमहापातकनिष्कृतिः ॥ वरातिथिपितृभ्यश्च पशूपाकरणक्रिया । दत्तौरसेतराणां च पुत्रत्वेन परिग्रहः ॥ सवर्णान्याङ्गनादुष्टैः संसर्गः शोधितैरपि । अयोनौ संग्रहे वृत्ते परित्यागो गुरुस्त्रियः ॥ परोद्देशात्मसंत्याग उद्दिष्टस्यापि वर्जनम् । प्रतिमाभ्यर्चनार्थाय संकल्पश्च सधर्मकः ॥ अस्थिसंचयनादूर्ध्वमङ्गस्पर्शनमेवच । शामित्रं चैव विप्राणां सोमविक्रयणं तथा ॥ षड्भक्तानशने चान्नहरणं हीनकर्मणः ॥

माधवीये पृथ्वीचन्द्रोदयेच—शूद्रेषु दासगोपालकुलमित्रार्द्धसीरिणाम् । भोज्यान्नता गृहस्थस्य तीर्थसेवातिदूरतः ॥ शिष्यस्य गुरुदारेषु गुरुवद्वृत्तिशीलता ॥ आपद्वृत्तिर्द्विजाग्र्याणामश्वस्तनिकता तथा । प्रजार्थं तु द्विजाग्र्याणां प्रजारणिपरिग्रहः ॥ ब्राह्मणानां प्रवासित्वं मुखाग्निधमनक्रिया । बलात्कारादिदुष्टस्त्रीसंग्रहो विधिचोदितः ॥ यतेश्च सर्ववर्णेषु भिक्षाचर्या विधानतः । नवोदके दशाहं च दक्षिणा गुरुचोदिता ॥ ब्राह्मणादिषु शूद्रस्य पचनादि क्रियापि च । भृग्वग्निपतनैश्चैव वृद्धादिमरणं तथा ॥ गोतृप्तिशिष्टे पयसि शिष्टैराचमनक्रिया । पितापुत्रविरोधे तु साक्षिणां दण्डकल्पनम् ॥ यतेः सायंगृहत्वं च सूरिभिस्तत्वदर्शिभिः । एतानि लोकगुप्त्यर्थं कलेरादौ महात्मभिः ॥ निवर्तितानि विद्वद्भिर्व्यवस्थापूर्वकं बुधैः ।

निगमः—अग्निहोत्रं गवालम्भं संन्यासं पलपैत्रिकम् । देवराच्चसुतोत्पत्तिं कलौ पञ्च विवर्जयेत् ॥ एतत्सर्वाधानपरम् । स्मृतिचन्द्रिकायाम् । चत्वार्यब्दसहस्राणि चत्वार्यब्दशतानिच । कलेर्यदा गमिष्यन्ति तदा त्रेतापरिग्रहः ॥ संन्यासश्च न कर्तव्यो ब्राह्मणेन विजानतेति व्यासवचनं व्याख्यानम् ॥ सर्वाधानेपि विशेषमाह देवलः । यावद्वर्णविभागोस्ति यावद्वेदः प्रवर्तते । संन्यासं चाग्निहोत्रं च तावत्कुर्यात्कलौ युगे ॥

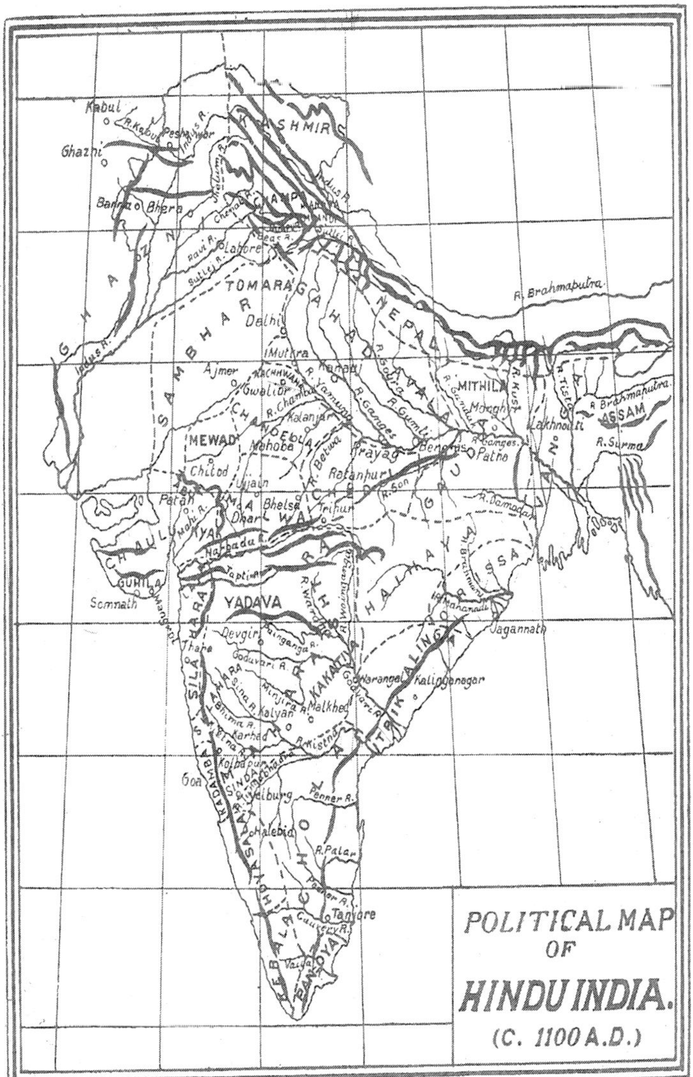

Poona Litho Works.

INDEX.

CHRONOLOGICAL TABLE

A. D.	
766	Parsis come to Sanjan.
855	Beginning of Kollam Era.
885	„ „ Nepal Era.
903	Ismail Samani of Bokhara.
903–1015	Duration of Samani Empire.
912	Yakub-i-lais first invades India (Ghazni).
942	Nuh Samani, Turks enter service.
995	Mansur Samani.
961–996	Mūlarāja first king of Anhilwad.
967 Sept. 30 or 971 Oct. 2	Birth of Mahmud.
973–977	Tailapa II founder of later Chālukya power.
997	Sabuktagin ascends Ghazni throne.
977	Śaktikumāra (Guhilot).
977	Vajradāman founds Kachhapaghāta power at Gwalior.
980	Sabuktagin advances against Jaipal of Kabul.
980–1038	Mahīpāla re-establishes Pāla power in Bengal.
984	Vajrahasta I founds Eastern Ganga power.
985–1012	Rājarāga I founds Chola power.
986–1006	Nuh II Samani. Fight with Turks of Kāshgar and Mahmud's first lesson in fighting.
988	Govinda (Chāhamāna).
989	Sabuktagin's first fight with confederate Hindu kings.
990	Ambāprasāda (Guhilot).
990–1010	Aparājita (Śilāhāra, Thana)
997–1008	Satyāśraya, Later Chālukya king of Kalyan.
997–1010	Munja (Paramāra).
997	Chāmunda (Anhilwad).
1000–1022	Ganda (Chandella).
1001	Mahmud's first fight with Jaipal.
1003	Vākpati (Chāhamāna).
1003	Śuchivarman (Guhilot)
1003	Death of Queen Diddā (Kashmir).
1008–1029	Sangrāmarāja, king of Kashmir.
1004	Mahmud invades Bhatia.
1008	Mahmud's fight with combined Hindu forces.
1008	Mahmud's invasion of Nagarkot.
1009	Vikramāditya V of Kalyan.
1010–1055	Bhoja (Paramāra).
1010	Vajjada (Śilāhāra, Thana).
1010	Durlabha (Anhilwad)
1010–1038	Gāngeya (Chedi).
1011	Rājarāja (Chola); makes survey settlement of land.
1013	Mahmud's first fight with Trilochanapāla.
1014	Mahmud's expedition against Thanesar.

1014-1014	Rajendra (Chola).
1015	Arikesarin (Śilāhāra, Thana).
1016	Naravarman (Guhilot).
1017	Birth of Rāmānuja.
1017	Mahmud invades Mathura and Kanauj.
1011-1040	Jayasinha (Kalyan).
1019	Mahmud again invades Kanauj and imposes tribute
1019	Madhukāmārṇava, Esteren Ganga.
1021	Rājyapāla killed by Rajput confederacy
1021	Mahmud's invasion and fight on the Rāhib.
1021	Mahmud's second fight with Trilochanapāla.
1021-1063	Bhima I (Anhilwad).
1022	Mahmud conquers Swat.
1023	Mahmud's expedition against Gwalior and Kalanjar
1025	" " " Somnath.
1025-1045	Chhitta (Śilāhāra, Thana).
1027	Death of Bhima Shāhi. End of Shāhi dynasty.
1028	Vidyādhara (Chandella).
1028-1063	Anantarāja (Lohara king of Kashmir).
1029	Death of Mahmud.
1030	Al-Beruni's treatise on India.
1030	Vijayapāla (Chandella).
1032	Nayapāla (Pāla).
1033	Srichandra (Chāhamāna).
1033	Nialtagin raids Benares.
1038-1068	Vajrahasta II Eastern Ganga.
1038-1080	Karṇa (Chedi).
1040	Bhoja defeats Jayasinha.
1040	Devavarman (Chandella).
1040-1068	Someśvara I (Later Chālukya of Kalyan).
1042	Yogarāja (Guhilot).
1044	Vijayapāla Kachhapaghāta.
1044	Rājādhirāja (Chola).
1045	Nāgārjuna (Śilāhāra of Thana)
1052	Anangapāla II founds Delhi and sets up Iron pillar.
1052	The battle of Koppam.
1052	Rājendra Chola.
1055	Vajraṭa (Guhilot).
1055	Death of Bhoja Paramāra.
1055	Jayasinha Paramāra.
1059-1080	Building of Udepur Śiva temple.
1059	Udayāditya Paramāra.
1059	Vigrahapāla III (Pāla).
1060	Kirtiwarman (Chandella).
1062	Vira Rājendra (Chola).
1063	Visala III (Chāhamāna).
1064-1093	Karṇa (Anhilwād Chālukya).
1065	Acting of Prabodhachandra drama.
1065-1076	Rājarāja Eastern Ganga.
1069	Hansapāla (Guhilot).

1069–1076 Someśvara II (Later Chālukya of Kalyan).
1070–1118 Rājendra Kulottunga Chola.
1073 Utkarsha (Kāshmir).
1076–1126 Vikramānka Later Chālukya.
1076–1142 Anantavarman Eastern Ganga.
1078 Prithvirāja I (Chāhamāna).
1080–1100 Chandra Gāhadavāla.
1080 Mahīpāla II (Pāla).
1080 Sāmantasena (Bengal).
1080–1124 Yaśahkarṇa (Chedi).
1081 Vairisinkka (Guhilot).
1081–1104 Lakshmadeva (Paramāra).
1082 Śurapāla (Pāla).
1084–1130 Rāmapāla (Pāla).
1084–1168 Hemachandra Jain Pandit.
1084–1115 Anantapāla (Śilāhāra, Thana).
1089 Harsha (Kashmir).
1093 Ajayadeva (Chāhamāna).
1093–1143 Jayasinha (Anhilwad).
1094 Vijayasinha (Guhilot).
1100 Hemantasena (Bengal.)
1100 Probable date of founding of Mandi state.
1100 Sallakshaṇa (Chandella).
1101 Uchchala (Kashmir).
1101–1133 Naravarman (Paramāra).
1110 Javavarman (Chandella).
1110–1155 Govindachandra (Gāhadavāla).
1111–1128 Sussala (Kashmir).
1117–1160 Prola (Āndhra).
1118 Arisinha (Guhilot).
1118 Vikrama (Chola).
1119–1199 Lakshmaṇasena (Bengal).
1120 Prithvirivarman (Chandella).
1125 Arṇorāja (Chahamāna).
1125 Apārāditya (Śilāhāra, Thana).
1125 Gayakarṇa (Chedi).
1125–1165 Madanavarman (Chandella).
1126 Someśvara III (Later Chālukya).
1129 Chanda (Guhilot).
1129 Pārihāras take Gwalior fort Kachhwahas.
1130 Kumārapāla (Pāla).
1133 Naravarman (Paramāra).
1133 Yaśovarman (Paramāra).
1135 Kulottunga (Chola).
1136 Gopāla (Pāla).
1138 Jagadekamalla (Later Chalukya).
1140 Vijayasinha (Guhilot).
1140 Madanapāla (Pāla).
1142 Jayavarman (Paramāra).
1142 Kāmārṇava Eastern Ganga.

1143-1173 Kumārapāla (Anhilwad).

1144-1160 Ajayavarman (Paramāra).

1144-1155 Harapāla (Śilāhāra, Thana).

1146-1165 Rājarāja III (Chola).

1148 Rājataranginī finished.

1149 Birth of Prithvirāj III.

1150 Building of Jagannath temple by Chodaganga.

1150 Kumārapāla invades Ajmer.

1150-1182 Taila II (Later Chālukya).

1152 Vīsala Chāhamāna takes Delhi.

1152 Narsinha Chedi.

1153 Harakeli drama composed by Vīsala Chāhadhmāna.

1155 Raṇasinha (Guhilot).

1155-1170 Vijayapāla (Gāhaḍavāla).

1155 Mallikārjuna (Śilāhāra, Thana).

1157 Founding of Ajmer.

1160 Vindhyavarman (Paramāra).

1160 Jayasinha (Chedi).

1161 Govindapāla (Pāla).

1161-1191 Rudra (Āndhra).

1162 Bhimasinha (Guhilot).

1162 Rebellion of Vijjana (Kalachūri).

1165 Usurpation by Vijjana „

1167 Soyideva Kalachūri (Kalyan).

1167 Rājarāja II Eastern Ganga.

1168-1203 Paramardideva (Chandella).

1170 Jayachandra (Gāhadavālla).

1172 Rājādhirāja (Chola).

1172 Muezzuddin Ghori takes Ghazni.

1173 Sāmantasinha (Guhilct).

1173 Ajayapāla (Anhilwad).

1173-1220 Vira Ballāla (Hoyazala).

1174 Pr.thv rāja's fight with Kaimāsa.

1175 Mahammad Ghori seizes Multan.

1178 Hariśchandra (Pāramāra).

1178 Defeat of Ghori by Gujarat army.

1178 Kulottunga III (Chola).

1178-1231 Bhima II (Bhola) Anhilwad.

1179 First defeat of Ghori by Prithviraj.

1179 Ghori takes Peshawar.

1180 Mahendrapāla (Pāla)

1180-1198 Vijayasinha (Chedi).

1180-1210 Subhaṭavarman (Paramāra).

1181 Mahammad Ghori invades Lāhore.

1182 Prithvirāja defeats Paramardin.

1182 End of Kalachūri usurpation in Kalyan.

1182-1189 Someśvara IV (Later Chalukya).

1184 Kumārasinha (Guhilot).

1184 Mahammad Ghori invades Lahore again.

1185 Prithviraj marries Sanyogita.

1187	Bhillama founds independent rule at Deogiri
1190	Rājarāja III (Chola).
1191	Prithviraj defeats Ghori a second time.
1191	Mahādeva (Āndhra)
1192	Defeat and death of Prithvirāja.
1192	Aniyanka Bhima Eastern Ganga.
1193	Kutubuddin takes Merut and Delhi.
1193	Defeat and death of Jaichand.
1195	Mathanasinha (Guhilot).
1195	Kutubuddin suppresses rebellion of Harirāja at Ajmer.
1196	Shihabuddin Ghori takes the fort of Gwalior.
1197	Kutubuddin invades Gujarat.
1198–1260	Gaṇapati (Āndhra).
1199	Kutubuddin takes Anhilwad.
1199	Mahammad Bhaktyar plunders Bihar (Vikramaśila).
1202	„ „ seizes Nadia (Bengal).
1202	Kutubuddin invades and takes Kālanjar.
1203-1245	Trailokyavarman (Chandella).
1205	Assassination of Shihabuddin Ghori.
1208	Kutubuddin takes Badaun.
1210	Arjunavarman (Paramāra).
1216	Turks invade Mewad and destroy Nāgdā.
1216	Devapāla (Paramāra).
1227	Altamash takes Ranathambhor.
„	„ „ Gwalior fort.
1234	Invades Malwa (Bhelsa and Ujjain).
1235	Destruction of Mahākāla temple.